BUREAU OF INTERNATIONAL RESEARCH

HARVARD UNIVERSITY AND RADCLIFFE COLLEGE

THE DIPLOMACY
OF IMPERIALISM

THE DIPLOMACY

of

IMPERIALISM

1890-1902

VOLUME II

WILLIAM L. LANGER

HARVARD UNIVERSITY

New York & London

ALFRED · A · KNOPF

1935

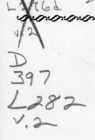
Contents of Volume II

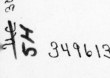

v

of Bluff — The Franchise Issue — Chamberlain goes over to the Milner Policy — Preparations of the Boers — The British Government decides to send Reinforcements — The Last Negotiations and the Boer Ultimatum — Some Other Aspects of the Situation — England and Germany Once More — The Samoan Embroglio — Obduracy of Salisbury — Rhodes' Visit to Berlin — Anglo-German Recriminations — England's Need of German Good Will — Chamberlain arranges a Settlement with Eckardstein and Emperor William agrees to Visit England — The Foreign Office evens the Score — The so-called Windsor Treaty

List of Maps in Volume II

THE DIPLOMACY
OF IMPERIALISM

XIII

The New Navalism

 ᕗ

THE PROCESS OF " PEACEFUL PENETRATION " THROUGH THE EXTORTION OF concessions, as carried out by Russia and France in China during the years 1895–1897, was abruptly disturbed when the Germans occupied the harbor of Kiao-chow in November 1897 and thereby gave the evolution of the Far Eastern situation an entirely new turn.

The German action cannot be studied as an isolated episode. It must be viewed rather in the general setting of the German " Weltpolitik " which was the counterpart to the concurrent outburst of " Imperialism " in England. In France and Russia the movement for expansion was essentially an artificial one, resting upon considerations of national prestige, drawing its support from a group of statesmen who looked to the future, from a relatively small number of explorers and colonial enthusiasts, and from a syndicate of bankers and speculators who saw in the movement unusually good " diggings." With Britain and Germany the situation was quite different. England was the industrial and trading nation *par excellence,* dependent for her food supply upon importation and literally living upon her foreign trade. Her position in the world was, in the nineties, seriously threatened by the economic rise of Germany, a country rapidly becoming industrially top heavy and feeling ever more sharply the need for markets. Summed up in a few words, the story of European international relations in the 1890's is the story of the assault of Russia and France upon the territorial position of Britain in Asia and Africa, and the story of the great economic duel between England and her all-too-efficient German rival.

It has been argued, and with some brilliance, that it is incorrect to speak of Bismarck's policy as a " continental " policy, and to describe the policy of his successors as a " new world policy." Bismarck, it has been said, pursued a " world policy " in the sense that he took advantage of world events to gain his immediate aims. Not only that, he carried through a moderate colonial policy, and secured for Germany almost all the extra-European territory that she possessed before the World War. If Germany had devoted her whole attention to the development of her industry, to the employment of her people and to the production of ever higher and cheaper grades of goods, she would have been able to more than hold her own in the world, and she would have

415

been able to do so without arousing the serious antagonism of England or any other power.[1]

This argument strikes one very much as an argument *ex post facto*. It leaves out of account the peculiar mentality of the last decade of the dying century. Anyone who has immersed himself in the contemporary writing will come away with the overwhelming impression of the almost panicky feeling which seized upon the European nations at that time. The phenomenal development of industry raised problems of which the solution could not be known. Even the most eminent economists, in Germany men like Adolf Wagner, Gustav Schmoller and Max Weber, believed in the absolute necessity for securing all that was possible of the world markets. They regarded the question of expansion as nothing less than a question of life and death. In a previous chapter something has been said of the reaction of these new problems upon the British mind. Attention has been called to the growth in England of a dogged determination not to be downed, and to the rapid spread of a ruthless and bellicose attitude in questions of international relations.

Much the same development took place in Germany. If the British came to dislike the Germans as uncomfortable competitors, the Germans came to resent British power and even British efforts to maintain their position unimpaired. The first colonial crisis of 1884–1885 had called forth a symptomatic outburst of hostility to England, which, to be sure, had died out somewhat in the last years of the Bismarckian period, when German interest was absorbed by continental tension. After Bismarck's fall, however, it revived and in a remarkably short time became a much deeper and more widespread feeling than it had ever been before. It was the sacrifice of German claims in Africa in the so-called Heligoland Treaty of 1890 that led to the foundation of the *General German League,* which was in 1894 reorganized as the *Pan-German League* (Alldeutscher Verband). Composed of professors and teachers, business men, officials and professional men, this group aimed to arouse

> " patriotic self-consciousness at home and to oppose vigorously any development of the German people along unpatriotic lines; to support and aid German endeavours in all lands where members of the German people must struggle to retain their individuality, and the union of all Germans on the earth for the furtherance of these aims; to promote an energetic German policy of might in Europe and oversea; above all to carry forward the German colonial movement to tangible results." [2]

The organization was avowedly anti-English, and combined its efforts with those of the Colonial Society and later with those of the Navy League to propagate the ideas of a world policy. Its leaders talked of establishing a central Euro-

---

[1] Otto Becker: " Bismarck und die Aufgaben Deutscher Weltpolitik " (in Hans Delbrück: *Am Webstuhl der Zeit,* Berlin, 1928, pp. 103–23).

[2] Mildred Wertheimer: *The Pan-German League* (New York, 1924), p. 37.

pean customs union and possibly an even closer connexion; Holland, Belgium and Switzerland, it was hoped, would somehow or other be brought into a greater German Empire. All this was, of course, to be effected through peaceful methods, through cultural propaganda, through the strengthening of the German "idea." But it could not be expected that other nations should take a naive view of this agitation. It is certainly true that the League never had an immense membership, that it never enjoyed heavy representation in the Reichstag, that it never succeeded in deluging the world with its pamphlets and other propaganda. But even Miss Wertheimer, who is apt to take a somewhat too indulgent view of the League's activity and to underrate its importance, is bound to admit that it " was doubtless one of the most strident jingo societies in the world and its noise was quite incommensurate with its size," that it " was a ringleader in the anti-English agitation in Germany," and that its " indirect influence was probably larger than its direct importance." [3] The fact is that the theories of the League, in one form or another, very soon found their way into much of the German political writing of the years 1895 to 1914, and that they raised apprehensions abroad which are reflected in the periodical literature at an early date. When, in 1899, the Germanized Englishman, Houston Stewart Chamberlain, published his *Foundations of the Nineteenth Century,* in which he declared that the whole present-day civilization and culture was the work of the Teutons and asserted that Germany was destined to become the heart of humanity, he was simply striking the loudest chords of the theme of race superiority. The idea no doubt went back to Count Gobineau's essay on *The Inequality of the Human Races,* which was first published in 1854, but the cult of this extravagant racialism and nationalism came only in the last lustrum of the nineteenth century. In England as in Germany it was carried to absurd heights. There is nothing in all the Bismarckian period to compare with this exaggeration of national egotism, with this hot passion for expansion. Whatever may have been the influence of the Pan-German League as such, there can be no question of the popularity and widespread influence of the new Pan-Germanic religion as expounded by Chamberlain and his enthusiastic followers.[4]

While theories of race superiority were being advanced in England and Germany to prove that one or the other of these great nations was the salt of

[3] Wertheimer, op. cit., pp. 210, 213, 217. On the history of the League see also Otto Bonhard: *Geschichte des Alldeutschen Verbandes* (Leipzig, 1920), pp. 1–17, 105 ff.; Anonymous: " Pan-Germanism " (*Quarterly Review,* July, 1902, pp. 152–75).

[4] It is worth noting that the Gobineau Vereinigung was founded at Freiburg in 1894. See Ludwig Schemann: *Gobineau, eine Biographie* (Strassburg, 1913–1916); Idem: *Fünfundzwanzig Jahre Gobineau-Vereinigung, 1894–1919* (Berlin, 1919); Idem: *Die Rasse in den Geisteswissenschaften* (Munich, 1928); Ernest Seillière: *Le Comte de Gobineau et l'Aryanisme Historique* (Paris, 1903); Idem; *Houston Stewart Chamberlain, le Plus Récent Philosophe du Pangermanisme Mystique* (Paris, 1917); Idem: *Introduction à la Philosophie de l'Impérialisme* (Second edition, Paris, 1911). Among the best critical studies are Frank H. Hankins: *The Racial Basis of Civilization* (New York, 1926), especially chapters iii and iv; Friedrich Hertz: *Race and Civilization* (New York, 1928), especially chapter viii.

the earth and preordained to ultimate victory over all competitors, another current of thought had sprung up which served in every way to fortify the teachings of the imperialists. In 1890 an American naval officer, Captain Alfred Thayer Mahan, published a book on *The Influence of Sea Power upon History*. This work was followed in 1892 by the same author's *Influence of Sea Power upon the French Revolution and Empire,* and in 1897 by his *Life of Nelson.* Of the first of these books thirty-two editions have been published to date. Of the other two seventeen and seven respectively. According to the publishers' figures almost twenty-three thousand copies of the first, almost twelve thousand of the second, and more than twenty thousand of the third have been disposed of in the United States alone.[5]

Mahan's books consisted of a general discussion of the elements of sea-power, followed, in the various volumes, by an analysis of the history of naval warfare, with special reference to the struggle of England with Holland and France in the seventeenth and eighteenth centuries, and down to the battle of Trafalgar and the death of Nelson. It has been objected by some writers that Mahan was a poor historian, that he used only a few secondary works, that his general ignorance of other aspects of history led him to exaggerate the importance of sea-power, and that he never realized that ideas similar to his own had been put forward by earlier writers. Bacon and Raleigh, not to speak of Leopold von Ranke, had had a very clear conception of sea-power, it was pointed out.[6]

Much of this is true, no doubt. It is also worth noting that at the very time when Mahan's first book appeared Admiral Philip H. Colomb of the British navy was publishing in the *Illustrated Naval and Military Magazine* a series of essays which appeared in book form in 1891 under the title *Naval War, its Ruling Principles and Practice Historically Treated,* in which he set forth much the same arguments and reached much the same conclusions arrived at independently by Mahan. But Colomb's book was verbose and heavy, while Mahan's was written with unusual charm, precision and breadth of view. Colomb's book was completely overshadowed by the American volumes, which literally took England by storm in the first years of the 1890's. Hardly had his first book appeared when the leading journals published extensive reviews. The second work, on the French Revolution and the Napoleonic Era, made an even deeper impression, in as much as it was less technical and of more immediate interest. One British officer declared that no book on a naval or military subject had attracted one tenth the notice given this study, and another, writing in 1893, remarked that Mahan's " discovery " of sea-power had been so widely discussed

---

[5] Letter of Little, Brown and Company to Dr. Gordon Benedict, one of my students, who has been kind enough to show me these figures.

[6] See especially the reviews of Mahan's books by Emil Daniels (*Preussische Jahrbücher*, March, 1898, pp. 567–9), and by Gustav Roloff (*Historische Zeitschrift*, LXXXVI, 1901, pp. 309–13); the very competent criticism of Fred T. Jane: *Heresies of Sea Power* (London, 1906); Vice-Admiral Alexander Meurer: *Seekriegsgeschichte in Umrissen* (Berlin, 1925), Introduction.

that its nature could no longer be unfamiliar to many people.[7] Admiral Sir Cyprian Bridge declared that "Mahan's opinions govern the naval thought of the world." "His volumes were inevitably accepted as final, and, in the true sense, were epoch-making," wrote another naval man. "I can remember no event in my time in the Navy so epoch-making as the publication of Mahan's first books," says Admiral Sir Reginald Bacon, looking backward.[8] When Mahan visited England in 1893 and 1894 as commander of the American cruiser *Chicago,* he was overwhelmed with attention. Earl Spencer, first lord of the admiralty, gave a great dinner for him. A public banquet was given by the lord mayor of London at St. James Hall. Over a hundred admirals and captains of the British navy received him at the Royal Navy Club. The Queen, the Prince of Wales, Lords Rosebery and Salisbury entertained and honored him. Both Oxford and Cambridge conferred honorary degrees. In short, Captain Mahan was lionized. Rarely if ever has a serious historical work produced on this side of the Atlantic been received with such favor and enthusiasm on the other side of the water. It may well be doubted if any historical work of the last few generations has had so great and profound an influence on the political development of the world.[9]

What was the secret of this great success, which Mahan himself was unable to understand? The answer is that the American officer first grasped, interpreted and made understandable the concept of "sea-power," which Admiral Colomb called "command of the sea." The popularity of his books in England was due further to the fact that they constituted a "scientific inquiry into the causes which have made England great."[10] Mahan was a pronounced Anglophil. He was filled with admiration for the accomplishments of British seamen, and he was convinced that British naval power had always been a boon to the world. The British therefore felt flattered, and rightly so.

But apart from these special aspects of Mahan's influence, it must be remembered that his thesis came as a revelation. If sea-power had been appreciated by earlier writers, it certainly had played no part in the thinking of the common man. Since the days of the Crimean War interest in the navy had waned in England. Great sums were spent upon the army and upon fortifications, but

---

[7] Captain F. N. Maude: "The Influence of Sea Power" (*National Review,* March, 1894, pp. 110–17); Nauticus (Laird Clowes): "Sea Power, its Past and Future" (*Fortnightly Review,* December, 1893, pp. 849–68); see also the important reviews of the first two books by Professor John Laughton in the *Edinburgh Review,* October, 1890, pp. 420–53; April, 1893, pp. 484–518.

[8] Charles C. Taylor: *The Life of Admiral Mahan* (London, 1920), p. 40; C. S. Alden and R. Earle: *Makers of Naval Tradition* (Boston, 1925), pp. 237 ff.; John Leyland: "Recent Naval Literature" (in *Brassey's Naval Annual,* 1897, p. 210); Admiral Sir Reginald Bacon: *A Naval Scrapbook* (London, n.d.), pp. 264–5. Similar opinions in Lord Fisher: *Records* (London, 1919), p. 135; Sir F. Maurice and Sir George Arthur: *Life of Lord Wolseley* (London, 1924), p. 285, and in many other books.

[9] For Mahan's reception in England see especially Taylor: *Life of Admiral Mahan,* pp. 61 ff.

[10] Review, "The Influence of Sea-Power upon History" (*Blackwood's Magazine,* October, 1890, pp. 576–84).

there was little faith in the navy. It was only in 1895–1896 that the expenditure for the navy once more came to equal that for the army. Many people had the idea that the advent of the steamship had nullified all the laws of naval warfare as they had been evolved in the days of sail. No new strategy had been worked out and no one had shown, as Mahan and Colomb did, that the fundamental principles of naval combat, as they could be derived from history, were still valid. The rapid changes in the design of steamships and ironclads reduced the world's navies to motley assemblages of craft of all types. The leading authorities were far from agreement on anything, and in the building programs ideas of coast defense, cruiser warfare and high-seas fleets were all entangled.

Mahan cleared the ground of all this confusion and misconception. Painting on a broad canvas he stressed not only the teachings of history, but the inter-relation of geographical factors, national character, commerce and colonial ex-pansion in the determination of sea-power. From the standpoint of strategy his greatest contribution was the conclusive demonstration that commerce-destroy-ing, much in vogue among naval theorists in 1890, had never been decisive in itself:

> " Such a war cannot stand alone; it must be *supported,* to use the military phrase; unsubstantial and evanescent in itself, it cannot reach far from its base. That base must be either home ports, or else some solid outpost of the national power, on the shore or on the sea; a distant dependency or a powerful fleet. Failing such support, the cruiser can only dash out hurriedly a short distance from home, and its blows, though painful, cannot be fatal." " It is not the taking of individual ships or convoys, be they few or many, that strikes down the money power of a nation; it is the possession of that overbearing power on the sea which drives the enemy's flag from it, or allows it to appear only as a fugitive; and which, by con-trolling the great common, closes the highways by which commerce moves to and from the enemy's shores. This overbearing power can only be exercised by great navies, and by them (on the broad sea) less efficiently now than in the days when the neutral flag had not its present immunity." [11]

In other words, the ultimate, determining factor in sea-power is the possession of a strong battle-fleet, capable of overcoming the enemy and driving it from the sea.[12]

In France the theory of cruiser warfare had been most completely worked out by the writers of the so-called " Young School," of which Admiral Aube was the chief. Aube and his followers, Admirals Touchard, Jurien de la Gravière, Reveillère, and the journalists Étienne Lamy and Gabriel Charmes, argued that since the advent of the ironclad, which was independent of wind, sea battles of the old type had become impossible, for the weaker power would avoid combat and would seek to ruin its adversary by raiding and commerce destroying. The

---

[11] Mahan: *The Influence of Sea Power upon History, 1660–1783* (Boston, 1890), pp. 132, 138.
[12] The argument is well developed, along the lines of Mahan, by Spenser Wilkinson: *The Com-mand of the Sea* (Westminster, 1894).

important thing, then, was to have a large number of fast cruisers and torpedo-boats. For the price of one battleship one could build sixty torpedoboats. Besides, battleships were clumsy Goliaths, the expression of the megalomania of potentates and therefore unsuitable to a democratic republic. They were in contradiction to the principle of the division of labor. A swarm of little Davids would be much better.

This whole conception was well expressed by Aube in his many writings, one of which may be quoted:

> "To-morrow war breaks out; a torpedoboat has sighted one of these ocean steamers freighted with a cargo of greater value than that of the richest galleons of Spain; the torpedoboat will follow at a distance, keeping out of sight, and when night comes on will, unobserved, close with the steamer and send to the bottom cargo, crew and passengers, not only without remorse, but proud of the achievement. In every part of the ocean similar atrocities would be seen. Others may protest; for ourselves we accept in these new methods of destruction the developments of that law of progress in which we have a firm faith and the final result will be to put an end to war altogether."

It was an attractive theory and one which for twenty years profoundly influenced the course of French naval development. The French continued to build some battleships, of mixed types, but the emphasis until 1900 was upon cruisers and small craft of great speed.[13]

The British admiralty had never been won over to the theory of cruiser warfare to the extent of neglecting the battle-fleets. But naval authorities were much exercised by the great activity of the French in this branch of building, and they were particularly anxious when, in the late 1880's, the Russians began to devote large sums of money to naval construction. Like the French, the Russians put much emphasis on fast cruisers and devoted attention to the increase of the so-called volunteer fleet, consisting ostensibly of merchant ships plying between the Black Sea ports and the Far East, but composed in reality of convertible cruisers and commerce raiders, for which armaments were kept in readiness both at Odessa and at Vladivostok.[14] In 1887 there appeared in Russia the story of an imaginary war with England and of the exploits of a Russian cruiser which, equipped with the newest torpedo appliances and capable of developing great speed, was able to outsteam and capture British merchantmen while at the

[13] Admiral Aube, as quoted in the *Naval Annual*, 1890, p. iv. The texts of the Young School were the books of Commandant Z. and H. Montechant: *Les Guerres Navales de Demain* (Paris, 1892); and *Essai de Stratégie Navale* (Paris, 1893). Aube and his associates expounded their ideas in the *Revue des Deux Mondes*. See also Édouard Lockroy: *La Marine de Guerre* (Paris, 1897), especially pp. 30–1, 93. On the other side Admiral F. E. Tournier pleaded for a battle fleet in the sense of Mahan. See his books *La Flotte Nécessaire* (Paris, 1896) and *La Flotte de Combat* (Paris, 1899). A good general account may be found in René Jouan: *Histoire de la Marine Française* (Paris, 1932), II, pp. 260 ff.; and in Vice-Admiral Salaun: *La Marine Française* (Paris, 1934), pp. 16–40.

[14] A. Stroumillo: "The Russian Navy" (in *Brassey's Naval Annual*, 1898, chap. iv); Sir George S. Clarke: *Russia's Sea Power* (London, 1898), chaps. vii, viii; N. Monasterev and Serge Terestchenko: *Histoire de la Marine Russe* (Paris, 1932), chap. xi.

same time evading British warships. This story, which enjoyed great popularity, bore the significant title: " The ' Russia's Hope,' or Britannia no longer Rules the Waves." [15]

British alarm at the naval policy of Russia and France led in 1889 to the adoption of the principle of the two-power standard and the passage of the Naval Defence Act. The alliance of France and Russia, as symbolized in the great Toulon demonstration of October 1893, made the situation appear even more dangerous to British eyes. The Mediterranean was regarded as the chief route to the Far East, and England kept her newest and most formidable ships there. For this reason, and because of the growing naval power of Italy, the French did likewise. They had a splendid naval base at Toulon and in 1895 they built a second one at Bizerta, in Tunis. The establishment of the Russian Mediterranean squadron was so serious a threat to the British position that many experts advocated the abandonment of the Mediterranean entirely. So radical a solution met with considerable opposition, however, and in the end the situation was dealt with in other ways. It was decided to build new dockyards at Gibraltar and to modernize that base for the use of the Mediterranean fleet. The Channel, or Home fleet, was strengthened and kept off the Portuguese coast in order to be on hand to support the Mediterranean forces. At the same time a new naval program of large dimensions was introduced, after great popular pressure had been brought to bear upon the Gladstone government.[16] A number of leading naval and military authorities, Admiral Colomb, Colonel Maurice and others, collaborated in publishing one of those imaginary battle stories so dear to the British heart. In *The Great War of 189–* the avid public was treated to a thrilling account of a great European conflict in which British sea-power proved to be the decisive element. William Le Queux, popular teller of lively yarns, took the suggestion of Alfred Harmsworth (Lord Northcliffe), and outdid the naval men. In his novel *The Great War in England in 1897,* which went through edition after edition in 1894, he pictured a Franco-Russian invasion of England, the capture of Manchester and Birmingham, and the horrors of the attack on London. The preface of the book stated quite baldly: " The extraordinary preparations now going forward in France and Russia are being made in view of an attack upon England, and it is ominous that the downfall of our empire is a perpetual subject of discussion in the Paris press." Literature of this type may have no great artistic value, but it must be remembered that the man in the street read, not the long-winded, small-printed material in the *Times,* but just this sort of stuff, published in ephemeral journals like *Black and White,* or thrown on the book-stalls for a few pence.

From this time on there was little or no break in the rapid development of

---

[15] English translation, London, 1888.

[16] The naval situation in the early nineties is treated at some length in my *Franco-Russian Alliance,* pp. 336 ff., 359 ff.; since then there has appeared a solid, detailed though uninspired dissertation by Angela von Schönberg: *Um den Twopowerstandard* (Stuttgart, 1933).

the British navy. The English were irritated by the competition of France and Russia: "To all other Powers a strong navy is more or less of a luxury, useful for certain subordinate purposes, the chief of which is to act as a counterpoise to the maritime supremacy of England. To England alone it is from the very nature of the case an absolute and primordial necessity," wrote one of the leading authorities.[17] The clash of interests between Britain and France in Egypt and the Sudan, the advance of Russia in central Asia, and the developments in the Far East were all of them added arguments for greater and greater sea-power. It may easily be imagined how well the teaching of Mahan fitted into this general international tension. We have the best contemporary evidence of his influence not only on the public, but on public men. "It would be impossible to overestimate the effect which his books have had on the practical tendencies of our politics," says one writer. "Mahan's books have done the country, and the Navy for that matter too, a world of good," wrote Lord Wolseley. "He had," according to another, "a distinct influence on the views of some of our public men in the direction of strengthening their conviction of the necessity of a large ship-building programme." Eminent merchants in the city confessed that he had awakened them to a realization that London depended on trade and that trade required adequate protection. At last it was clear to all that "every power in the world holds all its transmarine possessions merely as the caretaker of the ultimate Naval Power."[18]

From this time on British governments no longer had difficulty in persuading parliament of the need of increased appropriations. There was no subject so dear to the poets of imperialism as the greatness of England on the sea. In an unbroken line from Swinburne's *The Armada* (1888) to Kipling's *A Fleet in Being* (1898) there was an outpouring of verse, good, bad, and indifferent, but all of it serving to stimulate popular pride and arouse popular interest. The *Navy League,* founded in 1894, through lectures, meetings and the dissemination of thousands of leaflets and pamphlets, kept urging the needs of the navy and kept stressing England's dependence on sea-power for her daily bread, for her raw materials, for her trade outlets, for security against invasion and for "peace with honor." The chief object of the League was to prevent the cutting of appropriations for party purposes. There was hardly much need of that. When Lord Goschen in 1896 brought in estimates much larger than any preceding ones, he was criticized by the Liberal Sir Charles Dilke, who maintained that for safety's sake England required not a two-power standard but a three-power standard. The annual estimates, which were, roughly, thirteen million pounds for the year 1888–1889, rose to over seventeen and a half million for 1894–1895 and to more than twenty-six and a half million for 1899–1900. The

[17] James R. Thursfield: "Command of the Sea" (*Quarterly Review,* October, 1893), p. 123.

[18] "Balance of Power" (*National Review,* March, 1896), p. 24; Maurice and Arthur: *Life of Lord Wolseley,* p. 285; Admiral R. Vesey Hamilton: "Our Invasion Scares and Panics" (*Nineteenth Century,* March, 1896, pp. 399–415); John Leyland (in *Brassey's Naval Annual,* 1897, pp. 213 ff.).

expenditure for new construction, which had been twenty-four and a quarter million pounds for the eleven years from 1876 to 1887, amounted to forty-nine and a half million for the eleven years from 1887 to 1898. During these last eleven years England added to her fleet twenty-nine battleships, twenty-six first-class cruisers, forty-five second-class cruisers, thirty-one third-class cruisers, twenty-nine torpedoboats and fifty-five torpedoboat destroyers. By 1898 even the most insatiable navalists were obliged to admit that the fleet was big enough and that it was equal to all eventualities.[19]

Lord Goschen, in bringing in the estimates for the great expansion of the British fleet in the years 1895-1900 spoke of them as "estimates not of provocation, but of self-defence." The British navy was at that time on the two-power standard and was intended as a means of self-defense against France, the second naval power of the world, and Russia, the fourth. Both these powers, especially Russia, were greatly increasing their naval appropriations, while Italy, after the disaster at Adua, was obliged to retrench and give up the extensive program of earlier years. But the British were arming not only against the combination of France and Russia, which had been paraded before the world at Toulon and proclaimed from the rooftops in 1895-1896. The south African crisis of January 1896 had brought another factor into the situation. Theretofore the British had always counted on the assistance or at least on the benevolent neutrality of the Triple Alliance. After the Kruger telegram episode there was no further thought of such an alignment. Austria was of little moment as a naval power, and Italy was almost paralyzed after the collapse of her Abyssinian policy. The Germans were clearly hostile. Indeed, they were evidently drawing closer and closer to the Franco-Russian combination. The intervention at Shimonoseki had demonstrated the feasibility of co-operation in extra-European problems. In the Cretan and Greek crises of 1896-1897 the continental powers once again stood together and frustrated the British program.

The speech of Sir Charles Dilke on the naval estimates on March 5, 1897, reveals the preoccupation of British statesmen with this new alignment. Few politicians were so well versed in military and naval questions. Dilke's opinions carried weight, and are therefore worth quoting:

"What had occurred in Northern China in joint pressure by the three Powers — Russia, Germany and France — in the acceptance of the Russian loan as against our proffered loan, and in the dominance of Russia in Manchuria and Korea, recently secured by treaty, pointed to great risk of common action against ourselves by three great maritime Powers, and it seemed improbable that we could ourselves break up that Concert except by giving way upon points which were vital to our interests, such as our China trade. We had been told on the Naval

---

[19] Abundant figures may be found in the volumes of *Brassey's Naval Annual*, but see also Elliot: *Life of George J. Goschen*, II, pp. 207-19, and the splendid survey account written by the great British naval designer Sir William H. White: "The Latest Reconstruction of the Navy" (*Nineteenth Century*, April, 1898), pp. 534-48. On the origins of the Navy League see Harry Spenser Wilkinson: *Thirty-Five Years* (London, 1933), pp. 187-97.

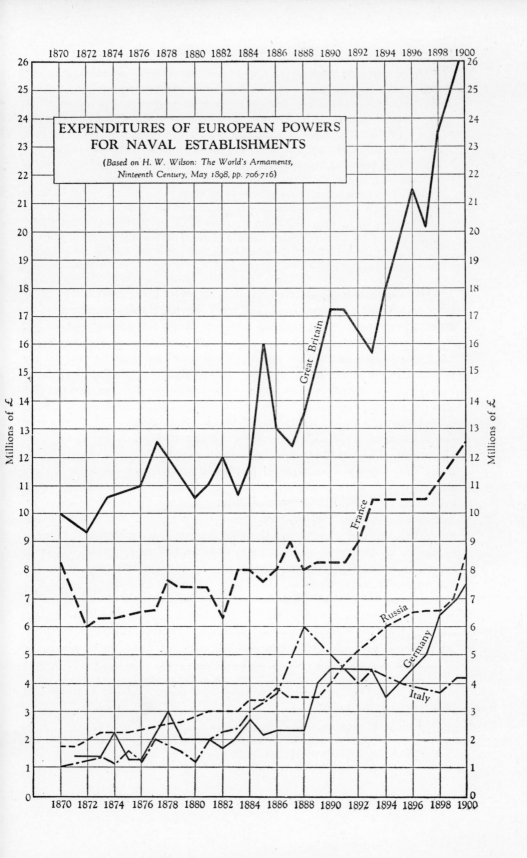

EXPENDITURES OF EUROPEAN POWERS
FOR NAVAL ESTABLISHMENTS

(Based on H. W. Wilson: The World's Armaments,
Ninteenth Century, May 1898, pp. 706-716)

Estimates last year, what was in fact obvious, that we were isolated, and he himself was all for isolation, as against a policy of alliances; for nothing could be weaker as a policy than one of sham alliances where there was no common purpose; but it must never be forgotten for a moment that isolation meant a predominant fleet. The risks were increasing. . . . The three great maritime Powers of the Northern Continent were, as their recent actions showed, able now to agree on a policy of Continental peace — joint support of the policy of Russia of expansion on the Pacific, of France in the Further East, and of Germany in Africa. This conjunction could only be faced by us being strong enough at sea to hold our own. . . . Peace was happily certain for the present, but in the long run would only be preserved if our naval strength was such as to cause a combination of three Powers, which could be formed for certain purposes, to pause before attacking us. . . . As Captain Mahan had put it, the British Navy was the best security for peace." [20]

Dilke's speech merely reflected the ideas that were being expressed by many other writers. A German officer, Baron von Lüttwitz, at this time published an article advocating a strong German fleet as a means for getting colonies and for coping with England. The essay was not very convincing nor very important, but it was at once seized upon and translated into English and was made the point of departure for many warnings of Germany's aggressive intentions.[21] H. W. Wilson, one of the most active of the British navalists, pointed out that after the Kruger telegram episode it was only logical that Germany should build a large navy. Lüttwitz' article was taken as official evidence of far-reaching designs. Germany was clearly planning a coalition directed against England. Had not the *Kreuzzeitung* said in so many words (March 9, 1897): " Germany must aspire to a naval power which will make her an important ally for the other great naval States if England should assume an attitude of selfish predominance in reckless disregard of all interest except her own." [22] George W. Steevens, another well-known writer, had declared even before this that Germany was the real enemy, and that the danger of a combination between Germany, France and Russia was a very real one. Professor Spenser Wilkinson harped on the same theme, and stressed the threat to the English position that was implied in such a coalition.[23]

It is sometimes argued that the extremely anti-German articles appearing in the British press at this time had no effect upon the conduct of British policy, and that they were simply hysterical effusions unworthy of serious attention. This view is certainly over-optimistic. We may not know much about the

---

[20] Hansard: *Parliamentary Debates*, Series IV, vol. XLVII, pp. 68–70.

[21] Baron von Lüttwitz: " German Naval Policy and Strategy " (*Journal of the Royal United Service Institution*, March, 1897).

[22] H. W. Wilson: " The Naval and Colonial Policy of Germany " (*Fortnightly Review*, June, 1897, pp. 923–935); see also the *Saturday Review*, March 13, 1897.

[23] George W. Steevens: *Naval Policy* (London, 1896), pp. 184, 190; Spenser Wilkinson: *The Nation's Awakening* (Westminster, 1897), especially pp. 125 ff.

deeper motives of British policy in these years, in as much as the documents have not been published and the memoir material is scant. But here and there may be found bits of evidence that illuminate the attitude of higher circles. Take for example a letter of Lord Salisbury to Lord Lansdowne, written in April 1897 when, for a short time, there was serious danger of renewed trouble in south Africa. Salisbury informed his colleague that he had warned Chamberlain of the inconvenience of war at that time, if only because of the unfavorable effect it would have upon relations with Holland:

> "I dread great unpopularity in the Netherlands. In the next year or two the young Queen of Holland will probably be married. If she marries anyone under the Emperor William's influence the Germans will get out of the Dutch some form of Kriegsverein which may enable them to man their fleet with Dutch sailors. His great ambition is to have a fleet, but until he gets a maritime population he cannot have a fleet. Some control over Holland is very necessary to him." [24]

These few remarks speak volumes. They show that Salisbury shared the expectation of H. W. Wilson that the Germans hoped " at no very distant date to win Holland to a voluntary union, or to annex her by force." It was an apprehension that had been widespread in the years just after 1870, an apprehension that was now growing strong once more, at a time when the writings of the Pan-Germans could only just have become known in England.[25]

It should be clear from the preceding discussion that German writers are in error when they assert that the British paid little or no attention to German naval power before 1904. It is perfectly true that the British did not fear the German navy, though they were quite aware of its high quality and general efficiency. What they did fear was that Germany might actually succeed in realizing the Emperor William's dream of a continental coalition against England, and that then a naval combination would result which Britain could not hope to combat on equal terms.

As a matter of fact there was some ground for the British uneasiness. We know of the Emperor's continuous efforts to effect a close understanding with France and Russia, and it can also be shown that the important German policy of naval construction which began with the first naval bill of 1898 hinged more or less upon this idea of a " continental combine."

William II, even before he had ascended the throne, had developed an almost abnormal interest in things maritime. When, in 1889, Queen Victoria named him admiral of the British fleet, it was her hope and Salisbury's hope that the appointment would put an end to the Russophil proclivities of the young ruler and would draw him over to the English side. This hope was entirely justified. In fact, the scheme worked only too well. William not only took a lively interest

[24] Lord Newton: *Lord Lansdowne* (London, 1928), pp. 144–5.

[25] *Die Alldeutsche Bewegung und die Niederlande,* by Fritz Bley, an active Pan-German, was published at Munich in 1897.

in the British fleet, but became more and more convinced of the necessity for a larger and more powerful German fleet. In 1894 his mother wrote to Queen Victoria in her usual extravagant fashion: "William's one idea is to have a Navy which shall be larger and stronger than the British Navy, but this is really pure madness and folly and he will see how impossible and needless it is." [26] Overdrawn though this statement was, so much was true, that the Emperor kept up a constant agitation about the fleet, referring to the matter in his speeches, bombarding the Reichstag deputies with charts and plans, and never failing to call the attention of his ministers to Germany's impotent position at sea when, as in the Far Eastern and Cretan affairs, the powers tried to reinforce their decisions by a demonstration of sea-power.

At first the country showed little interest in the naval problem. It was felt by many that Germany, which already maintained one of the largest military establishments, could not hope to pose as a first-class naval power. Besides, the fleet agitation was generally regarded as just one of the young Emperor's whims. Not even the ministers of marine had any use for far-reaching plans. Stosch had declared in a memorandum of 1883 that " naval battles alone seldom decide the destinies of States, and for immeasurable time the decision of every war will for Germany lie with her land army." [27] Stosch's successor, General von Caprivi (later chancellor) took the same military view. For him the fleet was simply a secondary factor in the operations of a future war against France and Russia. The important thing was a really adequate coast defense and if possible a fleet strong enough to prevent an effective blockade of the German coasts. Caprivi resigned in 1888 because he was unwilling to subscribe to or support the plans of the new ruler. Admirals Monts and then Hollmann, the first naval officers to hold the position of minister of marine, might have done something, but Monts died in a few months and Hollmann's efforts from 1890 to 1897 seem to have been devoted chiefly toward maintaining the good will of the Reichstag by avoiding unreasonable demands. He appears to have had no very clear conception of what was wanted, and pursued a mere hand-to-mouth policy. The result was that, while France and Russia were forging ahead, Germany sank from the position of third sea power to that of fifth in the decade from 1885 to 1895.[28]

By the middle of the 1890's this situation began to call forth anxiety in German circles that previously had not been impressed with the Emperor's attitude.

---

[26] *Letters of the Empress Frederick,* p. 447.

[27] Quoted by Archibald Hurd and Henry Castle: *German Sea-Power* (London, 1913), p. 94.

[28] Good general accounts in Ulrich von Hassell: *Tirpitz* (Stuttgart, 1920), chaps. i–iv; Admiral Hopmann: *Das Logbuch eines Deutschen Seeoffiziers* (Berlin, 1924), pp. 171–4; Hans Hallmann: *Krügerdepesche und Flottenfrage* (Stuttgart, 1927), pp. 15 ff.; Raimund Foerster: *Politische Geschichte der Preussischen und Deutschen Flotte* (Dresden, 1928), pp. 50 ff.; Eckart Kehr: *Schlachtflottenbau und Parteipolitik* (Berlin, 1930), pp. 25 ff.; and above all in the recent detailed study of Hans Hallmann: *Der Weg zum Deutschen Schlachtflottenbau* (Stuttgart, 1933), chaps. i, ii, iv.

The phenomenal development of German industry and trade was probably the decisive factor. The teachings of Mahan, directly or indirectly, began to affect the thinking of scholars and business men alike. German economic interests were forcing her into a " World Policy " whether she desired it or not. Colonies, sea-power, naval bases, all these things took on a new value. " A Navy does not make trade," wrote an English authority, " but trade either makes a navy that is strong enough to support it, or passes into the hands of more provident merchants." [29] Now the German merchant marine had increased in tonnage by almost 150% between 1873 and 1895, and the value of German maritime imports and exports had increased over 200% in the same period. Apart from the wealth thus entrusted to the sea there was the further consideration that Germany had become dependent on overseas countries for a not inconsiderable share of her food supply. Even English writers of a much later period were obliged to admit " that at this time (i.e. 1897–1898) the German fleet bore no reasonable relation to Germany's growing trade and oversea interests." [30] Germany was the second power in the world so far as foreign trade was concerned. Yet in sea-power she ranked not only behind England, France and Russia, but behind Italy.

There is something convincing, then, in the argument that dependence on food and the development of trade interests would have forced a fleet upon Germany irrespective of the efforts of individual statesmen.[31] From 1894 onward the Hamburg merchants, led by Woermann, began to agitate for more cruisers to protect German commerce. Karl Peters, the stormy petrel of German colonial policy, joined in the cry and before long carried with him the German Colonial Society with its twenty thousand members. The Pan-German League took its side by the sister society, and from the very beginning, in 1894, came out strongly for an increase in the navy. Eminent historians, like Dietrich Schäfer and Hans Delbrück, created popular interest in the German Hanse of the middle ages and argued that this great commercial league had fallen simply because it lacked sufficient naval power to compete successfully with the rising national states. For Germany, it was said, the question of an adequate fleet was a question of life and death. There was no example in history of a great commercial state that was able to maintain its position for any length of time without the support of sea-power. The teachings of biological determinism were used to buttress the same viewpoint. Gustav Schmoller, Adolf Wagner, Max Weber and other prominent economists were carried away by the problems arising from Germany's spectacular evolution. " With terrifying rapidity we are approaching the time when the provision of half-civilized Asiatic peoples will have reached its greatest expansion. Then nothing but might, nothing but

---

[29] Nauticus (Laird Clowes): " Sea-Power; its Past and Future " (*Fortnightly Review*, December, 1893, pp. 849–68); on Mahan's influence see Georg Wis(licenus): Reviews of Mahan's first two books in *Literarisches Zentralblatt,* May 29, 1897 and April 28, 1900.

[30] Hurd and Castle, op. cit., p. 118.

[31] See Hans Herzfeld: " Der Deutsche Flottenbau und die Englische Politik " (*Archiv für Politik und Geschichte,* VI, 1926, pp. 97–146), pp. 99–100.

naked force will decide the question of foreign markets," wrote Max Weber. "German sea-power," asserted Schmoller, "will moderate present-day trade hatred and hostile economic tension; it will keep open the door for a just international division of labor." Germany, it was argued on all sides, must face the situation squarely. Sir Charles Dilke had advanced the theory that in a relatively short time the world would be divided between three great empires, the British, the American and the Russian. Obviously it behooved the Germans to assure themselves of what Prince Bülow later called " a place in the sun." [32]

By 1895–1896 the members of the Reichstag had become less hostile than they had been to the appropriation of larger sums for the navy. The trouble was that they could not make out what it was that the minister of marine wanted. There seemed to be no rhyme or reason to the government's building program. It was impossible even to discover whether the object aimed at was a large fleet of cruisers to protect commerce, or the strengthening of the battle-fleet. Then, in January 1896, came the acute international tension resulting from the Jameson raid and the Kruger telegram. Emperor William was determined to make use of the popular excitement to present a supplementary program and to ask approval for a loan of one hundred million marks for this purpose. Even this program was intended to be merely the first installment of a larger plan running over a period of perhaps ten years. In order to prepare public opinion a beginning was made toward the mobilization of the newspapers and the enlistment of the aid of friendly organizations and individuals. On January 18, 1896, the twenty-fifth anniversary of the foundation of the Empire, William made his first great speech on world policy: " Colonial policy is only a branch of world policy which the German Empire must follow for the protection of its continental position. The time of Germany's philistinism is past, when she was oblivious to whatever went on in the world."

In the meanwhile, on January 8, the Emperor had been in conference with Hohenlohe, Hollmann and Admiral von Knorr, chief of the naval high command. William urged upon his advisers the need for striking while the iron was hot. So favorable an opportunity would not present itself again. The Reichstag would not dare refuse a demand for a loan for the purchase of cruisers abroad. But Hohenlohe was lukewarm and even Hollmann objected to the introduction of an extensive program at that time. Such a policy would only endanger the annual estimate, which had not yet been voted. Informally Hohenlohe consulted the party leaders. He reported them opposed to the scheme and finally the Emperor was persuaded that his plan was impracticable for the time being. In

[32] The contemporary pamphlet and periodical literature is simply immense. See the accounts of the early agitation in Foerster, op. cit., p. 80; Kehr, op. cit., pp. 40 ff., 55 ff. and pp. 390–422 (discussion of the writings and influence of the historians and economists). See also Heinrich Dietzel: " Die Theorie von den Drei Weltreichen " (Die Nation, XVII, 1899–1900, pp. 414–8, 431–5, 443–7, 456–9, 472–4), where a large number of economists are quoted. Contemporary statistical material is conveniently assembled in Die Seeinteressen des Deutschen Reiches, zusammengestellt auf Veranlassung des Reichs-Marine-Amts (Berlin, 1898).

March Baron Marschall denied in the Reichstag that the government was considering " boundless " (uferlose) plans for the navy.[33]

The Emperor now decided to replace Hollmann, and his choice fell upon Alfred von Tirpitz, chief of staff of the high command of the navy. Tirpitz was probably the ablest naval man produced by any country in modern times. In 1896 he already had behind him a long and distinguished career; during many years he had been chief of the torpedo service and had done much to perfect this new weapon of naval warfare. He had, furthermore, given much attention to strategy and tactics, and had, in contrast to the French, come to the same conclusions as Colomb and Mahan. In a memorandum of 1891 he had expressed his conviction " that the decision for our navy must be sought in open battle." As chief of the naval staff he organized the modern battle squadron and worked out battle-line tactics. Perhaps most interesting of all his writings was an important memorandum (Dienstschrift no. IX) of June 16, 1894, in which his views were expressed in concise form.

" The starting point for the development of a fleet must be the marine interests of the nation." " A state that has marine or world interests, must be able to represent them and must be able to make its power felt beyond its territorial waters. Rational world trade, world industry, to a certain extent deep-sea fishing, world communications and colonies are impossible without a fleet capable of assuming the offensive." " The natural purpose of a fleet is the strategic offensive." Or, as he says in his memoirs, " The navy never seemed to me to be an end in itself, but always a function of these maritime interests. Without sea-power Germany's position in the world resembled that of a mollusc without a shell." [34]

In this memorandum Tirpitz did not confine himself to generalities. He outlined a plan for a fleet of seventeen battleships (two squadrons of eight each and one flagship), six first-class cruisers, twelve third-class cruisers and six torpedoboat flotillas. The Emperor was much impressed with Tirpitz' views, but was evidently too uncertain in his own mind or too much under Hollmann's influence to make them wholly his own. Despite the fact that he knew Mahan's writings (he received Mahan on his yacht at Cowes in 1895), he still showed a pronounced partiality for the theories of cruiser warfare. In November 1895 the high command was urging the need of building battleships. It pointed out that by 1901 France and Russia would each have twice as many as Germany. At least twelve battleships should be constructed by 1908. The Emperor referred this document back to Tirpitz for an opinion, and the latter, on January 3, 1896,

---

[33] Hallmann: Krügerdepesche, etc., pp. 34–53; Idem: Deutscher Schlachtflottenbau, pp. 171 ff.; Kehr, op. cit., pp. 51 ff. These accounts may be supplemented by Hohenlohe: Denkwürdigkeiten der Reichskanzlerzeit, pp. 151–8, 161, 164, 240–1.

[34] See Alfred von Tirpitz: My Memoirs (New York, 1919), I, p. 77; Ulrich von Hassell: Tirpitz (Stuttgart, 1921), pp. 88 ff.; Hopmann, op. cit., pp. 181 ff.; Hallmann: Krügerdepesche, pp. 25 ff.; Hallmann: Deutscher Schlachtflottenbau, chap. iii; Bernhard Michalik: Probleme des Deutschen Flottenbaues (Breslau, 1931), pp. 20 ff.

handed in a report running to twenty-nine folio pages. Tirpitz subscribed entirely to the view of Admiral von Knorr, and suggested only a few changes in the projected long-term program. The south African crisis put a new aspect on the whole problem, for it had now become clear that British friendship could not be counted on in the future as in the past. " Even the greatest sea power," said Tirpitz in his report, " would act more accommodatingly towards us if we were able to throw into the scales of international politics, or if necessary into the scales of conflict, two or three well-schooled squadrons. With cruisers nothing of this sort could be accomplished." Tirpitz disapproved of the Kruger telegram because it made Germany, weak as she was at sea, an easy butt for British ill humor. On the other hand he realized how much the Transvaal crisis helped to awaken popular interest in German sea-power.[35]

Despite the urgent and convincing arguments of Knorr and Tirpitz, the Emperor, in the discussions of January 8, 1896, seems to have talked only of more cruisers. Why he should have decided to appoint Tirpitz minister of marine when he was not ready to accept his program remains a mystery. It is at any rate not surprising that Tirpitz accepted the appointment without enthusiasm. He was probably glad when, after the Reichstag had accepted the ordinary annual estimates, the Emperor changed his mind, retained Hollmann and named Tirpitz commander of the squadron in the Far East.[36]

The admiral remained abroad for a full year. In the meantime Hollmann met his doom. The naval estimates for the year 1897–1898 were exceedingly modest, amounting only to seventy million marks. But they were so poorly managed by the minister that the Reichstag refused to accept them. In March 1897 parliament reduced the appropriation by twelve million marks, striking two cruisers from the list of projected ships. The Emperor was infuriated by this action, partly because the Catholic Centre party was chiefly responsible for the fiasco, but even more because he was already busily at work evolving a new long-term program. As time passed he had become more and more firmly convinced that trade rivalry was at the bottom of the Anglo-German tension, and that Germany's whole commerce was at the mercy of one hundred and thirty British cruisers, to which Germany herself could oppose only four. Hohenlohe shared this opinion entirely, though he appears to have had no sympathy with a huge program of battleship construction.[37]

So far as one can detect (the matter is not at all clear) the Emperor had decided, even before the failure of the estimates in the Reichstag, to embark upon an extensive program of construction. The German fleet, he declared, must be half as strong as the combined French Atlantic and Russian Baltic fleets. The

---

[35] Tirpitz: *My Memoirs*, I, pp. 84–6; Hallmann: *Krügerdepesche*, pp. 30–8; Idem: *Deutscher Schlachtflottenbau*, chaps. iv, v; Hassell, op. cit., pp. 105–15.

[36] Tirpitz: *My Memoirs*, chap. viii; Hallmann: *Deutscher Schlachtflottenbau*, pp. 183 ff.

[37] *Die Grosse Politik*, XIII, no. 3396; Hohenlohe: *Denkwürdigkeiten*, pp. 191–2, 193, 382–3; Hallmann: *Deutscher Schlachtflottenbau*, chap. vi.

high command of the navy was ordered to prepare proposals and details. In the meanwhile the Emperor decided to accept the resignation of Hollmann and to recall Tirpitz. Marschall, the foreign minister, whom the Emperor had disliked intensely for some time, was allowed to go. In his stead William appointed to the foreign office Count von Bülow, the ambassador at Rome, who was willing to devote himself to the realization of the Emperor's naval plans.

The high command reported on May 10, 1897. Its suggestions were a curious medley of the battleship proposals of Tirpitz and the cruiser plans so dear to Hollmann and the Emperor. But William, despite the fact that he had replaced Hollmann with Tirpitz, was still unprepared to accept the battleships. He struck several of them off the plans and very considerably increased the number of projected cruisers. The whole program, he decided, should be sanctioned by legislation, in order to avoid in future the annual wrangling about estimates. By 1910 the whole new fleet was to be ready.[38]

Tirpitz returned from the Far East in the middle of June. His first move was to induce the Emperor to scrap the scheme which had been so laboriously evolved. Tirpitz says himself that his stay in the Far East had shown him more clearly than before the keen commercial rivalry between British and Germans, and had made him realize all the more keenly what a disadvantage the lack of sea-power was from the German standpoint. Cruiser warfare, he argued to the Emperor, was of little importance to Germany because of her unfavorable geographical position and because of her lack of overseas bases for coaling, re-victualling and repairs. The only decisive factor would be the battle-fleet in the North Sea. Curiously enough the Emperor made but slight objection. The admiral was surprised at the ease with which William was willing to change his mind and adopt the new views which he presented.

Having persuaded the sovereign, Tirpitz was able to apply himself to the elaboration of his own scheme. The plan was characterized throughout by moderation, precision and clarity. Nothing like it had been done before. Tirpitz knew what he wanted and why he wanted it. All the details were gone over meticulously, all the arguments *pro* and *con* were carefully weighed and considered. In August the whole matter was discussed at length by the Emperor, Bülow and Tirpitz in a series of conferences at Wilhelmshöhe. Bülow seems to have had no doubt that the plan could be gotten through the Reichstag, but he did doubt whether England would ever give Germany time to carry the program through. The political situation, he pointed out, would be easier " if, in our new building, we did not put battleships into the foreground and laid stress rather on cruisers, torpedoes and coast defences." It was the same objection that Tirpitz had had to meet so often before. But the Emperor, who had always been a cruiser advocate himself, would no longer tolerate what had come

---

[38] Hallmann: *Krügerdepesche*, pp. 57 ff.; Idem: *Deutscher Schlachtflottenbau*, pp. 239–47; Waldersee: *Denkwürdigkeiten*, II, pp. 392–5; Foerster, op. cit., pp. 98 ff.; Hohenlohe: *Denkwürdigkeiten*, pp. 295, 297, 311, 317, 319, 321, 326–7.

to sound like heresy. The Tirpitz program was accepted and put into final form
in October 1897.[39]

The basic provision of the projected naval bill was the construction of eleven
battleships, five first-class cruisers and seventeen smaller cruisers by 1905. This
was regarded as a minimum, barely enough to raise the German fleet above the
status of a *quantité négligeable*. With such a naval force Germany would be
able, in a war against France or Russia or against both, to prevent a blockade
of the German coasts and so keep open the lanes of commerce and food supply.
But Tirpitz' thought no longer moved exclusively along the traditional lines of
the war on two fronts. Since the Kruger telegram episode and since his observation of Anglo-German trade rivalry in the Far East, the problem of a possible
conflict with England never left his mind. In his memoirs he admits his conviction that if Germany had not built a fleet the British would soon have called
a halt to German economic expansion. Writing to the Emperor in 1898 he formulated his idea in a few direct sentences:

> " The imposing economic development of Germany in the last decade stands in
> direct relationship to the political power of the Empire. The essential connexion
> which exists, especially between sea-power and the development of economic in-
> terests, will in future become even more sharply delineated. In the economic
> struggle which the nations must wage in the coming century it will become ever
> more necessary to defend the maritime interests of Germany by armed force." [40]

But what prospect had Germany of protecting herself from a war of attri-
tion waged by England? Tirpitz was bound to admit that in 1897 Britain, with
her home fleet alone, could destroy the German fleet and blockade the German
harbors within a few weeks. The German merchant marine would be captured
and the colonies lost. The projected increase in the fleet would not put Germany
in a position to fight England on even terms, not by any means. But it " would
give us a maritime fighting force of such strength that it could not be overcome
without much ado even by one of the larger naval forces." The geographical
position of Germany would make the new fleet particularly dangerous for England. For safety's sake she would have to recall part of her Mediterranean and
other squadrons. To avoid this Britain, he felt certain, would be more prepared
to adjust her quarrels with Germany in an amicable way.[41]

Here is the whole " doctrine of risk " (Risiko-Gedanke) upon which the
Tirpitz naval policy was built up in the succeeding years. There was no thought
of attempting to build a fleet as large as the British. There was no need for so
large a force, for the Germans always reckoned on the fact that the English
would never be able to concentrate all their squadrons in the North Sea. What

---

[39] Tirpitz: *My Memoirs*, chap. ix; *Memoirs of Prince Bülow* (Boston, 1931), I, pp. 132 ff.;
Hallmann: *Deutscher Schlachtflottenbau*, pp. 247 ff.; Foerster, op. cit., pp. 104 ff.

[40] Hohenlohe: *Denkwürdigkeiten*, pp. 441–3. The Emperor shared these ideas even before
the Navy Law was passed (*Die Grosse Politik*, XIII, no. 3413).

[41] Tirpitz' draft for a speech to the Reichstag, March, 1896 (printed in Hallmann: *Krügerdepesche, etc.*, pp. 79 ff.).

Tirpitz aimed at, from the very beginning, was a fleet sufficiently powerful to make an attack by the British *home* fleet a risky undertaking for the aggressor. Once Germany had so strong a force he believed that the British, rather than run the risk of a collision, would be more accommodating in their relations with Germany. And this brings us to the third point: the alliance value of the fleet.

" Our policy," he complained in a letter of February 13, 1896, " does not understand that Germany's alliance-value, even from the point of view of European states, does not lie altogether in our army, but in our fleet." Or again: " German trade, the 'Open Door,' could no longer be protected by flying squadrons; we had to increase in general power all round, i.e. to qualify ourselves for an alliance with the Great Powers. But alliance-value could be achieved only by a battle-fleet." [42]

Whether Tirpitz envisaged an eventual alliance with England it is hard to say, but it seems doubtful. The point he made in his writings and speeches, especially in the years 1896–1898, deals rather with another aspect of the alliance-value of the fleet. Time and again he argued that in an age of world policy the interests of the great powers were bound to be extra-European. In such matters soldiers were of little aid. What was needed was sea-power. For example, the great antagonism of the later 1890's lay between France and Russia on the one side and Great Britain on the other. If this antagonism were to eventuate in an armed conflict, what would be the position of Germany? She would be of no value to Russia or France so long as she could furnish only soldiers. The French and the Russians had large enough armies of their own. But if she had a respectable fleet, then the combined sea-power of the three states might be of decisive value. France and Russia, as well as England, might therefore be expected to assume an entirely different attitude toward the Germans in world affairs once Germany had a fleet that was more than a *quantité négligeable*. There can be no doubt whatever that Tirpitz looked forward to closer relations with Russia and that he even hoped for an ultimate readjustment of the Franco-German problem. In other words, he shared the Emperor's enthusiasm for a continental league and believed it feasible. All this comes out clearly enough in his contemporary letters, and is borne out by his memoirs, where he says: " The object in view had to be the institution of a constellation of Powers at sea, which would remove the possibility of any injury to or attack upon our economic prosperity." " I must say that I did not myself regard the prospective battle-fleet as a panacea without an alliance with another secondary sea power." Tirpitz, says Bülow in his memoirs, lacked political sense and his lack of understanding for the finer nuances " led him to entertain occasional illusions about Russia and even about France, countries in which he sought support against England, the land he especially hated." [43]

---

[42] Tirpitz: *My Memoirs*, pp. 84, 120; Hallmann: *Deutscher Schlachtflottenbau*, pp. 248 ff.

[43] Tirpitz: *My Memoirs*, pp. 79, 121; Hopmann, op. cit., p. 242; Bülow: *Memoirs*, I, p. 127. See also Tirpitz' draft speech of March, 1896 (Hallmann: *Krügerdepesche, etc.*, pp. 79 ff.), and his

So much for Tirpitz' plans and the ideas that lay behind them. The admiral was not content, however, with a meticulous program and sound arguments. He understood that, if the scheme was to be realized, not only the Reichstag, but the nation at large would have to be convinced of its necessity and desirability. The Germans would have to be made sea-minded. So he threw into the work his extraordinary organizing abilities and set out on a campaign of propaganda such as Germany had never before seen. He himself visited many of the German princes and won their support, while the Emperor was persuaded to keep quiet in order not to give rise to the idea that the plan was a personal hobby: " You can understand that with such an advocate in prospect I naturally keep my mouth shut and use it only for eating, drinking and smoking," William wrote to Eulenburg.[44] Systematic agitation for a larger navy had already been initiated by the Pan-German League, with which Tirpitz secretly collaborated.[45] At the ministry of marine Tirpitz organized a publicity bureau, where newspaper men were cordially received and given information of which they could make good use. A great many journals were enlisted and a great many meetings arranged for. Through his assistants the admiral was able to secure the support of many scholars, historians like Schäfer and Delbrück, and especially economists, who, so Tirpitz says, showed more understanding than the historians. Hundreds of eloquent pamphlets were turned out and distributed by the thousand. Tirpitz himself arranged for the translation of Mahan's books. In order to get them before the public as quickly as possible they were issued in sections, beginning in the autumn of 1897. It will be readily seen that the American officer's arguments were exactly suited to Tirpitz' needs, and that the economists needed only to embroider upon the same themes. They showed that the expenditure on the fleet would be a productive outlay, they stressed the insecurity of Germany so long as she lacked sea-power, and they pointed out the danger that the superfluous population might become an intolerable burden instead of a source of wealth. Germany would be condemned to vegetate as a small nation unless she had the power to defend her interests and throw real might into the scales.[46]

In the fleet agitation which spread far and wide through Germany in the autumn of 1897 the theme of German maritime interests shared the honors with the theme of British trade hatred. On July 28 the English government had denounced the commercial treaty concluded with the German Zollverein in 1865. The reason for this action lay in the new tenderness for the colonies which was part of the Chamberlain program. The treaty in question contained a provision

letters to Stosch of February, 1896 (Hassell, op. cit., pp. 106–10). There is a good discussion of this whole problem in Michalik: *Probleme des Deutschen Flottenbaues*, pp. 20 ff., 31 ff.

[44] Bülow: *Memoirs*, I, pp. 158 ff.

[45] Bonhard: *Geschichte des Alldeutschen Verbandes*, pp. 105 ff.; Heinrich Class: *Wider den Strom* (Leipzig, 1932), p. 33.

[46] Tirpitz: *My Memoirs*, chap. xi; Foerster, op. cit., pp. 109 ff. By far the most detailed and best account is that of Kehr: *Schlachtflottenbau und Parteipolitik*, pp. 93 ff.

that German imports into the colonies should pay no higher tariff than imports from the United Kingdom into the colonies. Henceforth, after the expiration of the Treaty a year later, the colonies would be free to charge German goods whatever rates they chose. It is perfectly clear that this action of the English government simply served to revive in Germany the fear of a commercial war and the banging of the colonial door in the face of German merchants. The British action, wrote Emperor William, means the beginning of war to the knife against our flourishing state.[47]

Worse yet was the determined and systematic German-baiting of part of the British press, especially of the *Saturday Review*. In an article of September 11, 1897 this violently anti-German paper established a new record for extravagance of language. The text of the sermon was an apocryphal interview with Prince Bismarck which was printed in the Paris *Gaulois* on September 7 and reproduced in the London *Times* on the following day. The old chancellor was there made to say that during the visits of Emperor William and President Faure to St. Petersburg the chief topic of conversation must have been England and the prospect of forming a continental league against her. He pointed out, it was reported, that in Ferry's time he himself had gotten along even with the French, and that he had assisted them in the foundation of their new colonial empire. To this the *Saturday Review* added that Bismarck's object had also been to divert Russia to southeastern Europe:

"France busy with her Tunis and her Tonkin, Russia quietly pushed to the east and the south, and there was left for Germany the simple task of sitting peacefully on her bulging coffers, while her merchants captured the trade of England and her diplomatists guided the diplomatists of England into perpetual bickerings with other countries. Prince Bismarck has long recognised what at length the people of England are beginning to understand — that in Europe there are two great, irreconcilable, opposing forces, two great nations who would make the whole world their province, and who would levy from it the tribute of commerce. England, with her long history of successful aggression, with her marvellous conviction that in pursuing her own interests she is spreading light among nations dwelling in darkness, and Germany, bone of the same bone, blood of the same blood, with a lesser will-force, but, perhaps, with a keener intelligence, compete in every corner of the globe. In the Transvaal, at the Cape, in Central Africa, in India and the East, in the islands of the Southern Sea, and in the far North-West, wherever — and where has it not? — the flag has followed the Bible and trade has followed the flag, there the German bagman is struggling with the English pedlar. Is there a mine to exploit, a railway to build, a native to convert from breadfruit to tinned meat, from temperance to trade gin, the German and the Englishman are struggling to be first. A million petty disputes build up the greatest cause of war the world has ever seen. If Germany were extinguished to-morrow, the day after to-morrow there is not an Englishman in the world who would not be the richer. Nations have fought for years over a city or a

[47] *Die Grosse Politik*, XIII, no. 3414.

right of succession; must they not fight for two hundred and fifty million pounds of yearly commerce? " The outrageous follies of William the Witless, the German schemes in the Transvaal and other transgressions have brought home the realization of the imminent probability of war. England is the only great power that could fight Germany " without tremendous risk and without doubt of the issue." " The growth of Germany's fleet has done no more than to make the blow of England fall on her more heavily. The ships would soon be at the bottom of the sea or in convoy to English ports; Hamburg and Bremen, the Kiel Canal and the Baltic ports would lie under the guns of England, waiting, until the indemnity were settled. Our work over, we need not even be at pains to alter Bismarck's words to Ferry, and to say to France and Russia ' Seek some compensation. Take inside Germany whatever you like: you can have it.' " " Germaniam esse delendam " was the fitting close of this extraordinary effusion.

No doubt this article was not representative of British opinion generally speaking. But it would be wrong to deny it all importance. It simply expressed in unpardonably strong language what a good many Englishmen unquestionably felt. And after all, the article was not a sporadic outburst. It was part of a systematic campaign carried on by the *Saturday Review,* and the *Review* was not an obscure or unimportant organ. In any case, whatever its significance from the British angle, no one could deny that this article had disastrous effects on Anglo-German relations. It may not have been widely read in England, but it certainly went the rounds in Germany. Just as the Kruger telegram furnished the British with a plausible excuse for giving vent to their trade hatred, so this article served the purpose of many a German extremist. Anyone who will take the trouble to read the contemporary material, and particularly the literature bearing on the projected naval law, will be impressed with this fact. One writer after another called attention to this specific article, pointing out that " it would be insane and criminal levity and neglect of all the teachings of history, not to take such discussion seriously." The article might be regarded as the sound of a few overloud notes from the war hymns that were being sung in England. If Britain had her way Germany would soon meet with the fate of Holland and France. The only adequate protection lay in a strong fleet.[48] Even Bismarck was not uninfluenced by this turn of events. He too believed that Germany required a larger navy, though he was still partial to cruisers and small ships " that could swarm like hornets around the big ships." There was no danger, he thought, of a British attack upon Germany: " If they came, we should slay them with the butt ends of our rifles," he told Tirpitz. But he realized that relations between England and Germany were getting worse and worse. Writing to a friend in

---

[48] Dietrich Schäfer: *Deutschland zur See* (Jena, 1897), pp. 53 ff.; Georg Wis(licenus): *Kernpunkte der Flottenfrage* (Berlin, 1898), pp. 44 ff.; *Eine Starke Flotte eine Lebensbedingung für Deutschland, von einem Vaterlandsfreunde* (Berlin, 1897), p. 37; B. Eckhorst: *Hermannschlacht* (Leipzig, 1898), pp. 17 ff.; R. A.: " England und Deutschland " (*Die Grenzboten,* 1897, IV, pp. 393–403), pp. 400–1. On the influence of the article see also Foerster, op. cit., pp. 114 ff.; Kehr, op. cit., pp. 89 ff.

April 1898, that is just before the old statesman's death, his son-in-law remarked: "Unfortunately he (Bismarck) does not know of any adequate remedy for this state of things, since the only one he is acquainted with — that we Germans should restrict our commercial industry — is not well applicable." [49]

When the naval bill was finally presented to the Reichstag on November 30, 1897, the government quite naturally said nothing about the English aspect of the naval problem. The stress was laid upon the need for adequate coast defense and commerce protection, and upon the indispensability of a fleet if Germany was to continue as a world power pursuing a world policy. Both the Emperor William and Hohenlohe flatly rejected any idea of competing with the greatest sea powers or of embarking upon a policy of adventure. But Germany, they claimed, had to have a fleet large enough to inspire respect and to serve as a factor in international relations. Tirpitz declared that the fleet was meant only as a protective measure: "When we have a fleet as strong as the one here proposed you will have provided Germany with a naval force which even a sea power of the first class would not attack on our coast without first thinking it over three times." [50]

The bill was, on the whole, well received by the Reichstag. Its moderation and clarity were in its favor, and Tirpitz' reasonable and accommodating attitude made it easier to discuss and to compromise. The National Liberals were strong in their support, and the Conservatives, while lukewarm, were prepared to vote for it. The Progressives were dead opposed, and so were the Socialists, while the decisive Centre party was rather unfriendly and uncertain. Several of the non-German groups were opposed to the government on principle. During the winter the bill went into committee. Objections centred on the long-term provision, which in a sense deprived parliament of control of expenditure. But the leader of the Centre, Herr Lieber, was willing to make an adjustment. Tirpitz agreed to the reduction of the time limit from seven to six years, and to a number of less important changes. In the final balloting two thirds of the Centre party voted for the bill, which was passed by the Reichstag on March 28, 1898 without a formal counting of votes.

There can be little doubt that the representatives of the people expressed the general wishes of the country on this occasion. The sentiment for a larger fleet had taken firm root in the country. According to the Emperor, Tirpitz had, single-handed and in the brief space of eight months, accomplished what everyone had regarded as impossible: he had succeeded in converting fifty million obstinate, ill-informed and ill-willed Germans. [51] Even though this be somewhat overdrawn, it cannot be denied that Tirpitz had done his work and done it well.

---

[49] Sidney Whitman: *Personal Reminiscences of Prince Bismarck* (New York, 1903), p. 288; see also Tirpitz' account of his visit to Bismarck (*My Memoirs,* chap. x); and Bismarck's remarks to Maximilian Harden (*Die Zukunft,* September 4, 1897).

[50] The speeches and debates are summarized and discussed by Foerster, op. cit., pp. 127 ff., and by Kehr, op. cit., pp. 122 ff.

[51] Hohenlohe: *Denkwürdigkeiten,* p. 437.

He had given the national feeling a direction and a program. His support came, naturally enough, from the munitions makers (especially the Krupps), and from the large trading interests (led by Woermann and the Hamburg merchants), who had done much to finance his extensive propaganda. These classes were, of course, those most interested in German expansion, those most conscious of the competition, those most hostile in their sentiments toward England. The Conservatives voted for the bill not because they had any love for colonial expansion and world policy, nor because they shared the viewpoint of the capitalist and industrial classes. They disliked England as the representative of liberalism and industrialism, but the real reason for their support of the bill seems to have lain in a more or less tacit gentlemen's agreement with the National Liberals. It was understood that if the Conservatives voted a fleet for the protection of industry and trade, the National Liberals would agree to the maintenance of a tariff on foodstuffs that would protect the agrarian interests. Both of these large and important groups shared in the common fear of the rise of socialism and the proletariat. In a letter written in 1895 Tirpitz pointed out that the fleet would serve as a palliative against socialism. It would give the country a new bond of union and would divert attention from domestic problems by focussing attention on a world policy. Perhaps it was in part the recognition of this purpose that made the socialists so uncompromisingly opposed.[52]

We are not here concerned, however, with the domestic aspect of the German naval problem. It is only the international side of the great programs of the dying century that we have to consider. It will be noticed that the tremendous increase in the British appropriations coincided with the acute tension in Anglo-German relations. By the Naval Defence Act of 1889 and the Spencer program of 1894 England had been put on the two-power standard. Ships were being constructed in reasonable number to meet the growing strength of Russia and France. But with the increasing certainty of an alliance between these two nations and the appearance of a strong Russian squadron in the Mediterranean the need for yet greater protection was felt. Still, at that time England was still reckoning on the aid of Italy and the benevolent neutrality, to say the least, of Germany. It was only after the Kruger telegram had opened the eyes of the public at large to the real state of affairs as between England and Germany that the great Goschen estimates were brought in. Not that England feared Germany in a maritime way, but that the loss of German neutrality or support in a possible war with Russia and France was acutely felt. To make matters worse

---

[52] Tirpitz: *My Memoirs*, pp. 88 ff. This theme is fully developed and discussed with great learning in several articles by Eckart Kehr: "Die Deutsche Flotte in den Neunziger Jahren und der Politisch-Militärische Dualismus des Kaiserreichs" (*Archiv für Politik und Geschichte*, IX, 1927, pp. 187–202); "England-Hass und Weltpolitik" (*Zeitschrift für Politik*, XVII, 1928, pp. 500–26); "Soziale und Finanzielle Grundlagen der Tirpitzschen Flottenpropaganda" (*Die Gesellschaft*, September, 1928, pp. 211–29), and particularly in his book *Schlachtflottenbau und Parteipolitik, 1894–1901*, more especially pp. 209 ff. I am disposed to agree with the criticism of this viewpoint advanced by Hallmann: *Deutscher Schlachtflottenbau*, chap. x.

there was, since the intervention against Japan in 1895, the prospect of Germany's joining with Russia and France in an anti-British policy. Hence the talk of a three-power standard, and the warning words of Dilke. The influence of Mahan's writings had been so considerable that the government had no difficulty in securing whatever sums it desired. The criticism levelled against it was rather that it did not ask enough.

British writers have often pointed out that Mahan's theories proved to be no unmixed blessing for England, for they justified not only the British navy, but sea-power in general. " The secret of our world power stood revealed, and there began, all over the world, and especially in Germany, a race for naval power which did not indeed deprive us of our supremacy at sea, but left us no longer in a position to confront all combinations with equanimity," writes Repington.[53] Germany was certainly deeply affected. Tirpitz saw the propaganda value of Mahan's books, while the Emperor found in them more than enough proof of his own theories. " I am just now not reading but devouring Captain Mahan's book," he wrote a friend in May 1894, " and am trying to learn it by heart." [54] It would certainly be wrong, however, to accept the argument of Mahan's biographer, that his books were primarily responsible for the change in German naval policy. Tirpitz, who may surely be described as the father of the modern German fleet, had reached his conclusions before Mahan could possibly have influenced him. Indeed, he reached his conclusions very largely through experiment and direct observation. Yet even Tirpitz could not possibly have succeeded with his program unless the spectacular development of German industry and trade had created a favorable atmosphere in Germany. Tirpitz stressed, and we must stress, the fact that the fleet was simply a function of maritime interests, that it was simply one of many manifestations of the new world policy.

To be sure, the first naval bill of 1898 did not provide Germany with a fleet comparable to those of France or England. Tirpitz himself spoke of it as only " a raiding fleet," and the London *Times* wrote (March 28, 1898) that Germany, situated between Russia and France, and committed to activity in the Far East, was justified in reconsidering her naval position, even if she was acting somewhat too ambitiously and under the influence of somewhat crude ideas. Later British writers have admitted that " in the light of the vast development of Germany's colonial and commercial interests the Navy Act of 1898 was of an unambitious character." [55] The British paid little attention to it in its own right. The *Saturday Review,* to be sure, thought that the Kaiser's naval schemes would " confirm the suspicions so widely entertained in England since the day of the famous letter to Kruger, that Germany is steadily preparing to measure her

[53] Charles à Court Repington: *Vestigia* (Boston, 1919), p. 277; similarly General Sir George Aston: *Memories of a Marine* (London, 1919), p. 96.

[54] Charles C. Taylor: *Life of Admiral Mahan,* pp. 131 ff.

[55] Tirpitz: *My Memoirs,* p. 149; Hurd and Castle: *German Sea Power,* p. 115.

strength against England." But it was the alliance value of the German fleet that concerned the English more than anything else.

"Were Germany the real ally of France," wrote H. W. Wilson, "the neutrality of Holland and Belgium would not stand for a week. Germany might confidently be calculated to march her troops into Holland, where the Dutch would make little or no resistance. Belgium would as certainly fall to France. The Scheldt and the Texel might then, as in the days of the great Napoleon, harbour a flotilla, destined for the transport of an army of invasion. . . . Politically a coalition of Russia, France and Germany would be immensely strong. The allies would run little or no risk whilst they would impose the gravest risks upon us. At the best, supposing us successful, we could not effectually blockade their vast coast-line. . . . Nor should we stand favourably from the purely naval point of view. . . . The opinion of the best-instructed naval officers would not countenance the belief that in battleships we are equal to the three powers." [56]

These were the fears already expressed by Dilke a year before. As we have seen, they had a real foundation in fact. Tirpitz' writings show that he regarded co-operation with one and preferably with both of the members of the Dual Alliance as a *sine qua non*. The new German fleet would be large enough, he thought, to enhance Germany's alliance value, and strong enough to make the British hesitate before a commercial war like those of the 17th and 18th centuries. If one bears in mind the "great fear" of the 1890's and the desperate struggle for markets in a contracting world, one can easily understand the outburst of navalism which characterized the imperialism of that day; one can without difficulty explain and defend both the British and the German viewpoints. On the other hand, as we look back we cannot fail to note that this fundamental change was one of the most important factors making for the later alignment of the powers. It was one of the most dangerous of innovations. It helped tremendously to embitter Anglo-German relations, and thereby to set the stage for the ultimate conflict.

BIBLIOGRAPHICAL NOTE

MEMOIRS, AUTOBIOGRAPHIES, BIOGRAPHIES, AND LETTERS

ELLIOTT, ARTHUR D.: *Life of George J. Goschen*. Two volumes, London, 1911. The standard biography of the man who was first lord of the admiralty in the Salisbury cabinet. Not as full as it might be on the naval policy of the time.

LORD SYDENHAM OF COMBE: *My Working Life*. London, 1927. The autobiography of one of the most active naval propagandists, in the 1890's still known as Sir George S. Clarke.

[56] *Saturday Review*, December 11, 1897, p. 654; H. W. Wilson: "Our Navy against a Coalition" (*Fortnightly Review*, June, 1898, pp. 898–909), pp. 898–9.

TAYLOR, CHARLES C.: *The Life of Admiral Mahan*. London, 1920. The only full biography, based upon Mahan's papers. Leaves much to be desired.

TIRPITZ, ALFRED VON: *My Memoirs*. Two volumes. New York, 1919. Belongs with the most interesting and instructive of all memoirs of the pre-war period. Frank and outspoken, this book is indispensable to students of modern naval problems.

HASSELL, ULRICH VON: *Tirpitz, sein Leben und Wirken mit Berücksichtigung seiner Beziehungen zu Albrecht von Stosch*. Stuttgart, 1920. A very important supplement to the preceding, containing many new letters of great interest.

TROTHA, VICE ADMIRAL ADOLF VON: *Grossadmiral von Tirpitz*. Breslau, 1933. Primarily a character study and an attempt to put Tirpitz' policy in the larger national setting. Does not add much to Tirpitz' memoirs.

HOHENLOHE, FÜRST CHLODWIG ZU: *Denkwürdigkeiten der Reichskanzlerzeit*. Stuttgart, 1931. Contains a number of entries bearing on the fleet question at this time. An important contribution.

Memoirs of Prince von Bülow. Four volumes. Boston, 1931–1933. Bülow discusses the Tirpitz program, but what he adds to our knowledge is very meagre.

HOPMANN, ADMIRAL A.: *Das Logbuch eines deutschen Seeoffiziers*. Berlin, 1924. A fascinating volume of recollections covering the period of German naval expansion.

SPECIAL STUDIES

TRAMOND, JOANNÈS and REUSSNER, ANDRÉ: *Éléments d'Histoire Maritime et Coloniale Contemporaine*. Paris, 1924. One of the few attempts to survey European international relations from the colonial and naval viewpoint. Curiously enough the book is particularly weak on the period discussed in this chapter.

MEURER, VICE ADMIRAL: *Seekriegsgeschichte in Umrissen*. Berlin, 1925. This is perhaps the best brief account of modern naval policy and history.

SCHÖNBERG, ANGELA FREIIN VON: *Um den Twopowerstandard. Englische Flottenpolitik 1880–1895*. Stuttgart, 1933. One of the few systematic, scholarly studies of British naval policy.

McHARDY, C. M.: *The British Navy for 100 Years*. London, 1897. One of the publications of the Navy League. A good survey of the situation, with statistics, quotations, etc.

STEEVENS, GEORGE W.: *Naval Policy*. London, 1896. Another excellent survey of the world's fleets in 1896, with a discussion of Britain's position and needs.

CLARKE, GEORGE S. and THURSFIELD, JAMES R.: *The Navy and the Nation*. London, 1897. A collection of essays contributed to the *Times* and to leading periodicals. The work of two prominent navalists.

CLARKE, GEORGE S.: *Russia's Sea-Power*. London, 1898. The best contemporary study of Russia's naval policy and its political implications.

MONASTEREV, N. and TERESTCHENKO, SERGE: *Histoire de la Marine Russe*. Paris, 1932. A well-informed account, unfortunately very brief.

JOUAN, RENÉ: *Histoire de la Marine Française*. Paris, 1932. The best brief account of the French navy in the 19th century.

SALAUN, VICE ADMIRAL: *La Marine Française*. Paris, 1934. The only systematic account of French naval policy and history devoted entirely to the Third Republic.

LOCKROY, ÉDOUARD: *La Marine de Guerre*. Paris, 1897. The author was for a short time French minister of marine and was regarded as a leading authority. The book describes his projected reforms, but also gives a good survey of the French navy at the time.

HURD, ARCHIBALD and CASTLE, HENRY: *German Sea-Power*. London, 1913. A general account, well-informed and generally fair. Now outdated, but still worth consulting.

GALSTER, VICE ADMIRAL KARL: *England, Deutsche Flotte und Weltkrieg*. Kiel, 1925. A general discussion, with little that is new on the earlier period.

THALHEIMER, SIEGFRIED: *Das Deutsche Flottengesetz von 1898*. Düsseldorf, 1926. A doctoral dissertation, containing nothing of great importance, though based upon newspaper material and other contemporary sources.

HERZFELD, HANS: " Der Deutsche Flottenbau und die Englische Politik." (*Archiv für Politik und Geschichte*, VI, 1926, pp. 97–146). A thorough and independent piece of work. Deals chiefly with the later period.

HALLMANN, HANS: *Krügerdepesche und Flottenfrage*. Stuttgart, 1927. Based upon the German marine archives. An important and interesting contribution. The book is by no means as poor as Kehr tries to make out.

—: *Der Weg zum Deutschen Schlachtflottenbau*. Stuttgart, 1933. An expansion of the previous title. Based on the Tirpitz papers and other materials, this is the best single study of the origins of the first naval bill.

ZIEBERT, ALEXANDER: *England und der Bau der Deutschen Schlachtflotte*. Endingen, 1927. Contains almost nothing of interest on the earlier period.

FOERSTER, RAIMUND: *Politische Geschichte der Preussischen und Deutschen Flotte*. Dresden, 1928. One of the best general accounts, dealing strictly with the political aspect of the question.

KEHR, ECKART: *Schlachtflottenbau und Parteipolitik, 1894–1901*. Berlin, 1930. This is certainly the most noteworthy contribution to the history of the German naval policy. The author has been through an immense amount of contemporary material of all kinds and shows an unusual grasp. He is concerned, however, chiefly with the social factors entering into the naval policy, and these, it seems to the present writer, he somewhat over-emphasizes.

MICHALIK, BERNHARD: *Probleme des Deutschen Flottenbaues*. Breslau, 1931. Chiefly an analysis of the political and strategical views of Tirpitz. A useful survey of the material which does not alter accepted notions in any important respect.

XIV

The Far Eastern Crisis
Kiao-chow and Port Arthur

⌇

IN AUGUST 1897 EMPEROR WILLIAM AND PRESIDENT FAURE OF FRANCE
appeared in succession at St. Petersburg to pay their respects to the autocrat
of all the Russias. The German ruler arrived accompanied by his chancellor,
Prince Hohenlohe, and by the secretary for foreign affairs, Count Bülow. Between them there was no difference of opinion touching Germany's relations
with Russia. The Emperor declared that the English were behaving so dis-
gracefully toward him that it was necessary for him to cultivate good relations
with Russia all the more assiduously. Hohenlohe was determined that everything possible should be done to make amends for " the biggest piece of foolish-
ness in the whole of our last seven years' policy, namely, the termination of the
Re-insurance Treaty." Bülow himself was firmly convinced that so long as Germany maintained friendly relations with Russia, England would never attack.[1]
Cecil Spring Rice was quite correct when he reported, in the last days of July,
that German policy had veered definitely in the Muscovite direction, and that
the Russians had taken care to capitalize this German affection by borrowing
ten million pounds on the Berlin market.[2]

The visit of the German ruler and his counsellors was a complete success.
At the great banquet reference was made to the " traditional ties " that bound
the two countries. In private conversation the foreign minister, Count Muraviev,
repeatedly stated that at bottom he would have preferred an alliance with Germany to the alliance with France. This may have been a lie, for Muraviev was
not noted for his truthfulness. In any event it was too late for Russia to change,
as he himself took care to point out. But at the same time it was fairly clear that
the Russians had no intention of making the alliance with France an instrument
of aggression. Relations with Germany were, as Muraviev said, not only friendly
and cordial, but truly intimate.[3]

Hardly had the German party left the Russian capital when President Faure
and the French foreign minister, M. Hanotaux, arrived aboard the battleship

---

[1] Bülow: *Memoirs*, I, pp. 11, 19, 55.

[2] *Letters and Friendships of Sir Cecil Spring Rice*, I, p. 225.

[3] *Die Grosse Politik*, XIII, nos. 3438–44; Meyendorff: *Correspondance de M. de Staal*, II,
pp. 348–9.

Pothuau. There was another round of festivities, receptions and reviews, culminating on the last day with the famous *Pothuau* toasts in which the two nations were referred to as *amies et alliées.* It is said that the French had pressed for an announcement of the alliance and the use of the word *alliance,* to which the Russians objected. Hanotaux finally insisted that the French cabinet of M. Méline would undoubtedly fall unless some sop could be thrown to the impatient public. And so the words *amies* and *alliées* were at last agreed to, the Russians adding the further phrase " equally resolved to contribute with all their power to the maintenance of the peace of the world." This phrase was not designed to appeal to the French patriots who saw in the alliance a promise of the reconquest of Alsace and Lorraine. Clemenceau, for example, protested against the maintenance of a peace that was the Peace of Frankfurt. Under the circumstances, he declared, Nicholas and Faure might just as well have combined with the powers of the Triple Alliance.[4]

Even if the circumspection of the Russians displeased the French irreconcilables, it served the purpose of reassuring the Germans. The last thing the Russians wished at the time was to become involved in war about Alsace-Lorraine or any other European issue. They were deeply committed to the Far Eastern policy, and needed security on their western frontier. At the same time they desired the support of the Germans against the British in Asia. " The time has come for a decision as to Germany's fate," wrote one influential paper; " either open rivalry with England, with the support of continental Europe, or impotent protests against English activity." " From day to day," declared another, " it becomes clearer and clearer that the two continental alliances, acting in the same sense, are able to direct the destinies of the whole of civilised humanity, by protecting it against the consequences of the ambition, the implacable egoism, and the avidity of England." [5] The same stress on the possibility and necessity for co-operation between the two alliance groups was to be found in most of the German and Austrian papers. The continental combine was in the air. " The whole sum of the tendency here is distinctly — organise a continental alliance against England," wrote Spring Rice from Berlin.[6]

In a vague and general way the Emperor William had been advocating such a policy for some time. Even after the disillusionment occasioned by the refusal of France and Russia to co-operate in the critical days after the Kruger telegram he had clung to the idea that the continental powers should stand shoulder to shoulder in order to frustrate the " designs " of England. In the Cretan-Greek

---

    [4] Hohenlohe: *Denkwürdigkeiten der Reichskanzlerzeit,* p. 380; Bernhard Schwertfeger: *Amtliche Aktenstücke zur Geschichte der Europäischen Politik, 1885–1914* (Berlin, 1925), II, no. 1; Georges Michon: *The Franco-Russian Alliance* (London, 1929), pp. 93 ff.; *Questions Diplomatiques et Coloniales,* September 1, 1897, pp. 172 ff., September 15, 1897, pp. 233 ff., for French and European press comment.

    [5] *Petersburgskaia Viedemosti and Novoie Vremiia,* quoted in *Questions Diplomatiques et Coloniales,* September 1, 1897, p. 178; October 15, 1897, p. 366.

    [6] *Letters and Friendships of Sir Cecil Spring Rice,* p. 226.

crisis this policy had succeeded, much to William's delight. He was then already envisaging a broadening of the policy and a welding together of the continental powers for resistance against the tariff policies of the United States. During his visit to St. Petersburg he discussed the matter with General Obruchev, the chief of staff, and with Count Witte, the finance minister. These gentlemen seem to have been well impressed with the idea, though they were more interested in its anti-British than in its anti-American aspect. Tsar Nicholas asked the Emperor to send him a memorandum on the subject. William was so elated that he wrote his friend Eulenburg:

" The visit to Russia turned out far better than I expected, and in several exhaustive discussions I reached *complete agreement* with Nicky on all important political questions, so that together we have, so to say, disposed of the world. A restoration of Alsace and Lorraine to France by Russian aid is an *absolute and downright impossibility.* Thus a war between Gaul and us and Russia and us is, God willing, *no longer* to be feared. The *Continental blockade* against America, and, *it may be,* England has been *decided* upon. Russia has *pledged* herself to bring France over to the idea *bon gré mal gré.*" [7]

The Emperor's enthusiasm was distinctly premature and exaggerated. Witte was plainly unwilling to become involved in a policy of excluding American products, and it was more than doubtful whether the French could ever be won over either to the tariff scheme or to the league against England. Furthermore, it can be shown quite conclusively that the German foreign office did not share the Emperor's sanguine hopes. William was impulsive, but at bottom he was himself never prepared to go the limit of an anti-British policy. His advisers, from Hohenlohe to Holstein, were more than dubious about a continental league and were genuinely anxious not to antagonize England too much. They never went so far as to join France in challenging the British position in Egypt. All they wanted was to scare Britain into taking a more considerate attitude toward German aspirations in the field of world politics. When, in September 1897, General Obruchev suggested to Bülow the conclusion of a defensive and offensive alliance for three years between the continental powers, the Germans not only evaded, they actually empowered the ambassador at London to communicate this interesting item to Lord Salisbury! [8]

The upshot of it all was that in practice the continental " combine " was

---

[7] Bülow: *Memoirs,* I, pp. 160–1; see further *Die Grosse Politik,* XIII, nos. 3426, 3433, 3438; " Kuropatkin Diary " (*Krasnyi Arkhiv,* II, p. 10); *The Memoirs of Count Witte,* pp. 408–10; Claus Grimm: *Graf Witte und die Deutsche Politik* (Freiburg, 1930), pp. 16–7, 25. There is a good anonymous account and defense of the German policy under the title " Der Zusammenschluss der Kontinentalen Mächte " in *Die Grenzboten,* 1897 (III), pp. 577–94. See also the discerning analysis of the international situation by E. J. Dillon: " The New Political Era " (*Contemporary Review,* November, 1897, pp. 609–31). The study of Hilde Prowaseck: *Der Gedanke einer Kontinentalliga gegen England unter Wilhelm II* (Leipzig, 1928), is almost worthless.

[8] *Die Grosse Politik,* XIII, nos. 3451–2; Hohenlohe: *Denkwürdigkeiten,* pp. 261, 296–7, 393–4. The point is well discussed in Michalik: *Probleme des Deutschen Flottenbaues,* pp. 77 ff., and in Friedrich von Trotha: *Fritz von Holstein* (Berlin, 1931), pp. 177 ff.

little more than the pursuit of a common policy in the Near East and in the Far East. It had been born in the united action of Russia, Germany and France in intervening at Shimonoseki in 1895 and it continued to function best in the further development of the Chinese problem.

Since the intervention of the three powers against Japan in 1895 the policy of Germany in the Far East had been dominated by two ideas: to engage Russia in Asia and thus weaken the Franco-Russian Alliance as it touched Europe; and to secure, through Russian support, some sort of commercial and naval base in Chinese waters. Time and again in the years from 1895 to 1898 Emperor William wrote the Tsar that Germany would keep Europe quiet and guard her rear while she was busy in Manchuria. To Muraviev he said in January 1897: "Even if you had to send all your troops to the East, following political aims in accordance with your interests, I not only will not attack France, but will not allow anyone in Europe to stir; there, that is what I mean by my promise to guarantee your rear." [9] The Emperor may have been genuinely impressed by the so-called Yellow Peril. Many remarks of his would seem to testify to the fact. But at the same time he saw how useful an argument this cultural danger would be in discussion with so religious a person as the Tsar. In 1895 he had had the German artist, H. Knackfuss, draw an allegorical picture from an imperial design. The first copy of this was presented to the Tsar. In William's own words: "It shows the powers of Europe represented by their respective Genii called together by the Arch-Angel Michael, — sent from Heaven, — to *unite* in resisting the inroads of Buddhism, heathenism and barbarism for the Defence of the Cross. Stress is especially laid on the *united* resistance of *all* European Powers, which is just as necessary also against our common internal foes, anarchism, republicanism, nihilism." The picture was lurid enough to stir even the most immovable. On a high rock overlooking a rich and prosperous plain stood Michael, while the European powers in female personification (Germany, France and Russia in the lead, Austria taking reluctant England by the hand, Italy in the background) were gazing upon the distant menace. Behind them in the sky was a gleaming cross, while on the farther side of the plain, enveloped in flame and riding a dragon, was a figure of Buddha, not at all blood-curdling, but pensive and contemplative.[10]

So much for the general policy of Germany with regard to the Far Eastern situation. The special problem confronting the Berlin government was to find the necessary props for the world policy that was being initiated. Unlike England and France, Germany had no coaling stations or naval bases scattered over the world. In the years from 1895 to 1900 much of her world policy hinged upon this search for foreign establishments. The West Indies, the Brazilian coast, the

9 F. V. Kelyin: "Zagranichnoe Puteshestvie M. N. Muravieva v 1897 g." (*Krasnyi Arkhiv*, XLVII, 1931, pp. 71–89), pp. 86 ff. See also *The Kaiser's Letters to the Tsar* (London, 1920), pp. 10, 11, 13, 27.

10 *The Kaiser's Letters to the Tsar*, pp. 17 ff. The picture is reproduced and described in Arthur Diosy: *The New Far East* (London, 1898), pp. 326 ff.

Philippines and other Pacific islands, and especially the Chinese coast, were surveyed with this object in view. Here again the Emperor was the moving spirit. In the very midst of the war between China and Japan he was already urging that advantage be taken of the situation to secure what Germany needed. After all, German commerce in China was second only to the English. Yet Germany possessed no commercial base like Hongkong, no coaling station, no docking and repairing facilities, no fortified naval post. She was dependent almost entirely upon Hongkong, which meant that she was dependent on British good will.

The conclusion of peace between China and Japan and Germany's championing of the Chinese cause seemed to offer a rare opportunity for the realization of German desires. The prospect of a reward certainly had some bearing upon German policy in the spring of 1895. Unfortunately, however, the foreign office did not share the Emperor's eagerness in the matter, and — more unfortunately yet — there was no agreement as to the place to be demanded. Everyone who was consulted recommended a different locality. The arguments between the admiral on the spot, the naval high command, the ministry of marine and the foreign office were so interminable that years elapsed before a definite decision could be reached. Many years before this the German geographer, Baron von Richthofen, had recommended Kiao-chow, on the south side of the Shantung Peninsula, pointing out the value of the coal deposits in that region, the high quality of the inhabitants and the nearness of the north China market. But Kiao-chow made little appeal, since it was not on one of the main trade arteries, would require large expenditures for development, and, it was believed, was not entirely ice-free in winter. The naval authorities at first insisted on the acquisition of two bases, one in the north and one in the south. Their preference was for the Chusan Islands in the Bay of Hangchow, near the mouth of the Yangtze, and for Amoy, which lay opposite Formosa. Neither of these places, however, proved feasible, for in 1846 the Chinese government had promised the British government never to alienate Chusan, while Amoy, being a treaty port, could hardly be secured without conflict with other powers. The naval authorities kept coming back to these places, but in the meanwhile other possibilities were canvassed: the Montebello Islands, off the Korean coast; Weihaiwei on the north side of the Shantung Peninsula; Wusung at the mouth of the Yangtze; Samsah Bay, just north of Foochow; and Mirs Bay, near Hongkong. Occasionally Kiao-chow was mentioned, but no one seemed impressed with its possibilities. Despite the Emperor's constant prodding no great progress was made and the Chinese government, when the matter was first broached in the autumn of 1895, treated it evasively, pointing out that to abandon or even lease a port to the Germans would whet the appetite of the other powers and possibly result in a concerted attack upon China's territorial integrity.

In the summer of 1896 Tirpitz went to the Far East as commander of the German squadron stationed in Chinese waters. At the same time the easy-going

German minister at Peking, Schenck von Schweinsberg, was replaced by Baron von Heyking, who had made a reputation for energy as representative of his government in Cairo. These two men, it was hoped, would be able to accomplish something. But even they could not agree. Heyking continued to insist upon Amoy, though Tirpitz, after careful investigation, came to the conclusion that the easiest and most profitable acquisition, from almost every point of view, would be Kiao-chow. The Emperor was very eager to do something in the autumn of 1896, but the squadron was not in condition to act and differences of opinion paralyzed action. It was not until an expert in harbor construction, Georg Franzius, was sent out and reported favorably in the summer of 1897 that Kiao-chow Bay was definitely decided upon.[11]

In choosing a suitable location on the Chinese coast the German government had, from the start, tried to avoid collision with either British or Russian interests. Chusan, which was probably the most desirable of all the stations considered, was finally rejected because of the British interests and claims. With Kiao-chow it was long feared that the Russians had a lien on the place. Their Far Eastern squadron had wintered there in the season of 1895-1896 and in the newspaper reports of the Russian-Chinese Treaty (the so-called Cassini Convention) it was said that the Chinese had granted the Russians a lease of Kiao-chow for a period of fifteen years. It was considered necessary, therefore, to clear up this important point. On inquiry it turned out that the Chinese government refused to recognize any Russian rights to the place. Admiral Alexeiev, the commander of the Russian Far Eastern squadron, admitted to Tirpitz that the place had been considered by the admiralty, but said it had been rejected. At St. Petersburg the foreign office did not pretend that the Russians had rights in Kiao-chow, though the foreign minister, Count Muraviev, and the minister to China, Count Cassini, were evidently displeased by the prospect of a German occupation and tried to discourage the plan. Cassini, to be sure, egged on the Germans to help themselves, but he was very anxious to have them locate themselves in the south, where they would come into conflict with the English.[12]

In order to clarify the Russian attitude it was decided that Emperor William during his visit to St. Petersburg in August 1897, should take up the matter directly with the Tsar. Nicholas replied to William's query that Russia was interested merely in assuring herself access to the bay until she had obtained a more northern harbor already selected, namely Ping-yang, on the northwest coast of Korea. There was no objection whatever, he said, to German ships anchoring at Kiao-chow in case of need, after securing the consent of the Rus-

11 The main sources are *Die Grosse Politik,* XIV, chap. xc (A); Tirpitz: *Memoirs,* chap. viii; Elisabeth von Heyking: *Tagebücher aus vier Weltteilen, 1886–1904* (Fourth edition, Leipzig, 1926) chap. v; Hohenlohe: *Denkwürdigkeiten,* pp. 279 ff.; George Franzius: *Kiautschou* (Seventh edition Berlin, 1900); Gérard: *Ma Mission en Chine,* pp. 156, 207–10. All this material, together with some unpublished correspondence, is so well reviewed in Arthur J. Irmer: *Die Erwerbung von Kiautschou 1894–1898* (Cologne, 1930), chaps. i–iv, that it has seemed unnecessary to go into greater detail or to give more specific references.   12 See especially Heyking, op. cit., pp. 192, 214.

sian naval authorities. On the German side the Tsar's declaration was taken to mean approval of Germany's desire to make use of the port. Toward the end of September the Chinese government was informed of Germany's intention, Baron Heyking making special reference to the approval of the Russian government. A few weeks later the St. Petersburg foreign office was officially notified. The news seems to have made a bad impression. Count Lamsdorff, chief assistant to the foreign minister, immediately pointed out that the Germans had agreed to secure the assent of the Russian naval authorities on the spot. Why the German government had ignored this point it is hard to say: possibly because there were no Russian ships at Kiao-chow. However that may have been, they did give the Russians an opening for opposition by not keeping to the strict letter of the St. Petersburg arrangement.[13]

On the German side the plan seems to have been to send the Far Eastern squadron to winter at Kiao-chow as a first move in extorting the concession of the port from the Chinese. In the discussions with the Russians mention had been made only of the right to use the harbor. But on November 1 (not November 4 as stated by Joseph and many other writers) two German Catholic missionaries in southern Shantung were killed by a Chinese gang in the course of an attempted robbery.[14] The incident came most conveniently. The news reached Germany on November 5 and was confirmed on November 7. Between these two dates the Emperor had already determined on a course of action. Thoroughly tired of procrastinating and absolutely convinced that nothing could ever be secured from the Chinese without a show of force, he suggested that the squadron be immediately sent to Kiao-chow, that it occupy the Chinese settlement and threaten heavy reprisals unless the Chinese authorities at once agreed to a heavy indemnity and to the punishment of the offenders: " I am firmly determined to give up our over-cautious policy which is regarded as weak throughout eastern Asia, and to demonstrate through the use of sternness and if necessary of the most brutal ruthlessness toward the Chinese, that the German Emperor cannot be trifled with."

Prince Hohenlohe was not so completely carried away by the incident. He warned the Emperor that an occupation of Kiao-chow would require the consent of the Russian government, according to the agreement made in August. With a sense of humiliation the Emperor therefore wired to the Tsar: " Chinese attacked German missions Shantung, inflicting loss of life and property. I trust you approve according to our conversation Peterhof my sending German squadron to Kiautschou, as it is the only port available to operate from as a base against marauders. I am under obligations to catholic party in Germany to

[13] *Die Grosse Politik*, XIV, nos. 3679 ff.; Irmer, op. cit., chap. v. The account given by Dillon: *The Eclipse of Russia*, pp. 245 ff. and by Witte: *Memoirs*, pp. 98–9 is distinctly misleading.

[14] It is generally stated, on the basis of a report in the *North China Herald*, November 17, 1897, that the missionaries were killed by members of an anti-foreign organization. The Chinese sources do not bear this out, as I see from an unpublished dissertation by Benjamin M. Bee: *The Leasing of Kiaochow* (Cambridge, 1935), pp. 166 ff.

show that their missions are really safe under my protectorate." To which Nicholas replied promptly: "Cannot approve, nor disapprove Your sending German Squadron to Kiao-Chou, as I have lately learned that this harbour only had been temporarily ours in 1895–1896." This was enough for the Emperor. Orders were at once despatched to the admiral in command in Chinese waters, and William wrote to Bülow, who happened to be in Rome: "Thousands of German Christians will breathe easier, when they know that the German Emperor's ships are near; hundreds of German traders will revel in the knowledge that the German Empire has at last secured a firm footing in Asia; hundreds of thousands of Chinese will quiver when they feel the iron fist of Germany heavy on their necks; and the whole German nation will be delighted that its government has done a manly act." [15]

The Emperor was in a state of high elation: a sense of outraged national honor, religious sentiment and thirst for conquest all combined to call forth an almost abnormal emotional outburst. But within a day or two the Russians turned a cold douche on the Emperor's enthusiasm. On November 9 the Russian chargé d'affaires at Berlin handed in two telegrams from Count Muraviev in which the Russian foreign minister declared that Russia would do all that was possible to induce the Chinese to give satisfaction for the murder of the missionaries, but at the same time set forth a Russian claim to Kiao-chow. According to Muraviev Russia had received from China a right of first anchorage (droit de premier mouillage) which amounted to priority if ever the port were to be alienated to another power. Therefore the Russian admiral had been instructed to enter the port with his ships in the event that the Germans attempted to do so.

These telegrams came like a bombshell to the Germans. In the foreign office there was something akin to panic. The Emperor was not in Berlin; neither was the chancellor or the foreign minister. Holstein seems to have been convinced that the news from Russia put Germany before the alternatives of war or retraction. He had been opposed all along to the Emperor's Chinese policy and was deeply distrustful of the Russians. Now his feeling was that the Germans would have to withdraw and give up their plans. Both the Emperor and Hohenlohe, however, took a somewhat calmer attitude. William stood firmly by the Tsar's telegram and insisted that the admiral in the Far East should follow the instructions already sent him. Russia, he was convinced, would not start a war about Kiao-chow. Hohenlohe shared this conviction, adding that Muraviev was evidently attempting a game of intimidation and bluff. [16]

For ten days to two weeks the situation was really tense, with constant exchange of telegrams between Berlin and St. Petersburg. The Germans refused to recognize any earlier arrangements and insisted on the letter of the Tsar's

---

[15] *Die Grosse Politik*, XIV, nos. 3688–90.

[16] *Die Grosse Politik*, XIV, nos. 3693 ff.; Hohenlohe: *Denkwürdigkeiten der Reichskanzlerzeit*, pp. 409 ff.

telegram, which Muraviev attempted to explain away. At the same time they repulsed all efforts of the Russians to act as mediators in securing satisfaction for Germany. Both Hohenlohe and Bülow spoke very frankly to the Russian ambassador at Berlin, Count Osten-Sacken, pointing out that Russia should be glad to see Germany establish herself in the Far East and that the German occupation of Kiao-chow would not hinder the Russians from using the port. He encouraged the Russians to take a port of their own, meaning, presumably, Port Arthur. At the same time it was indicated to Osten-Sacken that if the Russians persisted in their stiff attitude, it might be necessary for the Germans to turn toward the west for support.[17]

The Germans did, in fact, sound out the British at the very height of the crisis. Hatzfeldt was empowered, if necessary, to offer the British compensation in the form of a free hand in south Africa and in the southern part of the Portuguese colony of Mozambique, including Delagoa Bay. He was to hint that in the event of British opposition to Germany's action it might be necessary for the Germans to get out of the scrape by paying a " high price," by which was probably meant the purchase of an alliance with Russia. On the other hand the ambassador was given permission to show Lord Salisbury the suggestions made by Obruchev for an offensive and defensive alliance between Russia, France and Germany against Britain. Whether the proposal was ever communicated to the English prime minister cannot be said. Hatzfeldt found the British statesman rather well disposed. Despite the fact that the English press was almost as rabid in its denunciations as the Russian, Salisbury appears to have thought that the German enterprise would lead to friction between Russia and Germany and that in any event the Germans at Kiao-chow would serve as a useful counterweight to the Russians in the north. At any rate he raised no objection to the German action and thus strengthened the Berlin government in its dealings with Russia.[18]

In the meanwhile the German admiral, Diederichs, had landed troops in Kiao-chow Bay on November 14. The Germans were working out their demands upon the Chinese government. They had now decided to establish themselves on the Bay in any case, and therefore aimed to make their terms so stiff that the Chinese could not accept them. At the same time arrangements were made to send more ships and troops to the Far East. But despite veiled threats it proved difficult to do much with the Chinese mandarins. Russia stood behind them and gave detailed advice. The Tsungli Yamen or foreign office therefore offered to meet all the German demands, provided the troops and ships were first withdrawn from Kiao-chow. The German minister replied that this was the one point which he was not authorized to discuss. Negotiations took a different turn when the Chinese suggested that Germany give up Kiao-chow and

[17] Hohenlohe, op. cit., p. 413; Bülow: Memoirs, I, pp. 214–5.
[18] Die Grosse Politik, XIV, nos. 3698, 3702–4, 3708–10; R. Stanley McCordock: British Far Eastern Policy, 1894–1900 (New York, 1931), pp. 196–7.

take some other port farther south (evidently another Russian suggestion designed to enhance the antagonism between Germany and England). Nothing
could be done under these conditions. But finally, toward the close of the year,
the Russians gradually withdrew their support from the Chinese and made their
peace with the Germans. Baron von Heyking, the German minister at Peking,
took a stronger and stronger tone until, early in January 1898, the Yamen was
obliged to yield. There were many details to be worked out, and it was only on
March 6 that the agreement was formally signed. Germany secured the lease of
Kiao-chow for ninety-nine years, with a neutral zone fifty kilometers wide surrounding the concession. Two railroad lines (from Kiao-chow by way of Wei-
hsien to Tsinanfu on the Yellow River, and from Kiao-chow to Ichow and
thence to Tsinanfu) were to be constructed by a Chinese-German company. In
a zone fifteen kilometers wide on either side of these lines German subjects were
to be allowed to hold and develop mining properties. German nationals were
also given priority in furnishing the Chinese government with personal assistance, capital or materials "for any purpose whatever within the Province of
Shantung." Clearly the Chinese-German agreement gave Germany not only a
naval base in China, but also a strong and promising position in the development of the whole rich Shantung province.[19]

The outstanding development of the Far Eastern crisis in the last weeks of
the year 1897 was the settlement of the German-Russian dispute and the re-
establishment of co-operation between the two governments. The resurrection
of the entente was due in part to Germany's inflexible attitude in the matter of
Kiao-chow, but chiefly to the momentous decision taken by the Russian government to salve its disappointment by occupying Port Arthur. To understand this
remarkable *volte face* one must have clearly in mind the peculiar circumstances
of Tsarist policy in the Far East. Why did Muraviev object so strenuously to the
German occupation of Kiao-chow? Evidently because the Russians sincerely
feared that the German move would result in a general scramble for Chinese
territory. They wanted China to remain intact, not from altruistic motives, but
because the whole Russian plan of campaign as worked out by Witte envisaged
a steady peaceful penetration of Russian influence, eventual undisputed control
at Peking and so something in the nature of a protectorate over all China. To
be sure, the Russians were determined to secure a port in Chinese waters themselves, for Vladivostok was frozen for four to five months in the year, and even
though American ice-breakers had successfully kept it open in the winters from
1895 to 1897, the port was too far north to meet Russian needs. Evidently Kiao-
chow had been considered in the winter of 1895–1896, but had been given up
on advice from the naval authorities and out of consideration for China.

---

[19] The final negotiations may be followed in *Die Grosse Politik,* XIV, chap. xc (B) passim, and
in Heyking, op. cit., chap. vi, which adds considerably to the documents; an important account, making full use of the Chinese sources, is to be found in the unpublished thesis of B. M. Bee, mentioned
above. There is a good summary in Irmer, op. cit., chap. vii.

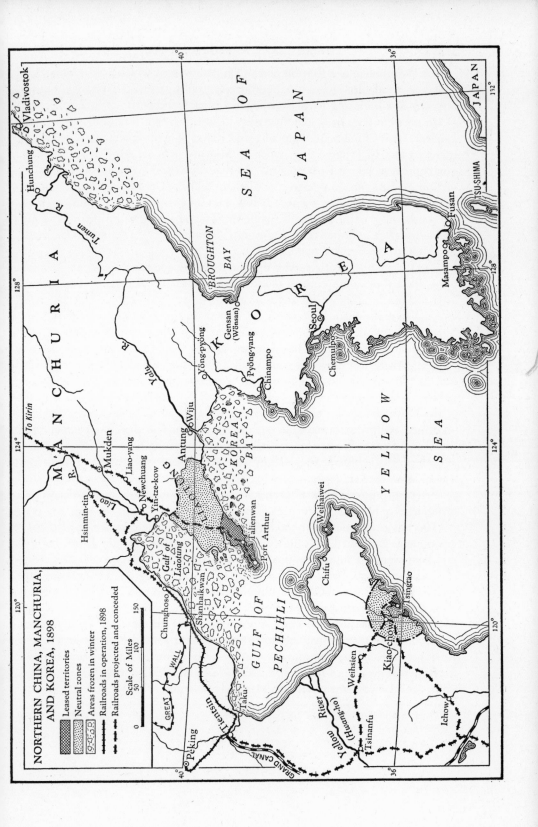

NORTHERN CHINA, MANCHURIA,
AND KOREA, 1898

■ Leased territories
░ Neutral zones
◌◌◌ Areas frozen in winter
╫╫╫ Railroads in operation, 1898
━•━•━ Railroads projected and conceded

Scale of Miles
0   50   100   150

But the problem of a Russian port in Chinese waters, which was so important from the standpoint of the naval authorities, could be easily solved without in any way compromising Russian policy in China. Good ports on the north coast of China were few. In Korea they were plentiful. Korea was supposedly independent. The Chinese government could not take umbrage at what went on there. In fact Li Hung-chang, when at Moscow in 1896, advised the Russian government to take a Korean port.[20] At that time the Tsar repudiated the suggestion. So far as one can detect, the Russians, like the Germans, had a hard time deciding what port they wanted. Naval men apparently favored Masampo, at the southern tip of the peninsula, while the Tsar, speaking to Emperor William in August 1897, indicated that Ping-yang (Phyöng-yang) on the northwest coast had all but been decided upon.[21]

The question then arises, why did the Russians not seize upon one of these ports, instead of attempting to block the action of the Germans? They were, after all, nearly all-powerful at Seoul at this time. Two factors evidently contributed to make them hesitate. In the first place the new Russian minister to Japan was convinced that a new arrangement with Japan about Korea was both possible and necessary. The Japanese armaments would be complete in 1902 or 1904, and there was always a good chance that England would support Japan and that Russia would find herself in a serious predicament. " It cannot be doubted," he reported home in September 1897, " that the immense armaments of the Japanese are directed against us and that Japan is eagerly preparing for an armed conflict with us. It is equally unquestionable that this conflict will break out over the Korean question." In his opinion the Japanese would attack as soon as Russia became involved in war in Europe or with England. Japanese statesmen desired an agreement with Russia and it would be a mistake for the St. Petersburg government to persist in its effort to establish an unofficial protectorate over Korea.[22]

This advice was not taken too seriously at first. On the contrary, the Russian government continued with the mission of officers to organize the Korean army and Witte lent his support to this policy by arranging for the establishment of the Russian-Korean Bank and by sending off his agent Kyril Alexeiev. Alexeiev arrived at Seoul early in October. On November 5 the Emperor of Korea signed with the Russian minister, M. Speyer, an agreement naming Alexeiev chief adviser to the treasury and chief superintendent of customs for an indefinite period, and specifying that in future this position should be held only by a Korean or a Russian. The move was a daring one, for the position was that of financial dictator. Since 1895 it had been held by Mr. M'Leavy Brown, formerly of the Chinese customs service, an extremely able and efficient person who had

[20] *Die Grosse Politik*, XIV, no. 3663.

[21] *Die Grosse Politik*, XIV, nos. 3663, 3695, 3697.

[22] G. Trubetzkoi: *Russland als Grossmacht* (Stuttgart, 1917), pp. 52–5; Baron Rosen: *Forty Years of Diplomacy* (New York, 1922), I, pp. 142–51.

in a few years straightened out the Korean finances and paid back a large part of the Japanese loan. Brown's term had not expired and he therefore refused to move. Alexeiev won over to his side the officials of the administration, whose salaries he doubled. But Brown could not be manoeuvred from his position. He was waiting for support from the British government. Before long this support was forthcoming. England had no great interests in Korea, but such as they were the government was not prepared to sacrifice them to Russia. Speaking in the house of commons in August 1897 Mr. Curzon said: " Our interests in Korea are commercial, and, first, to see that the independence of Korea is maintained, and that it is not territorially or administratively absorbed into the Empire of Russia; secondly, that Korean territory and Korean harbours are not made the base for schemes for territorial aggrandizement, so as to disturb the balance in the Far East and give to one Power a maritime supremacy in the Eastern seas." In pursuance of this policy the British government determined to act. We know nothing of the negotiations with Russia following Brown's dismissal. Perhaps there were none. But a strong British squadron composed of nine cruisers and accompanied by a few Japanese ships suddenly appeared late in December in the harbor of Chemulpo. The hint was enough for the Russians. After some talk Brown was reinstated, and in March 1898 Alexeiev was recalled.[23]

It must have been quite obvious to the Russian authorities that action in Korea would certainly lead to trouble. Both the British and the Japanese were opposed to the acquisition by Russia of territory in Korea. Under the circumstances Muraviev would have preferred blocking the German action at Kiao-chow. But he was unable to do so. The appeals of the Chinese for support could not be heeded for long. Orders to the Russian squadron to repair to Kiao-chow had to be countermanded. For not even Muraviev could explain away the Tsar's compromising telegram of November 7, which gave the Germans practically a free hand. Yet something had to be done, and so the Russian minister decided that the proper course of action would be to follow the example of Germany. On November 23 he presented to the Tsar a memorandum in which he pointed out that circumstances were favorable and that Russia should not allow the opportunity to slip by for occupying the Chinese port of Talien-wan at the southern tip of the Liaotung Peninsula. Russia had in years past considered Kiao-chow as a possible naval base, but it was now " inconvenient " to order the Far Eastern squadron to that port. Nicholas agreed that it was " inconvenient." On November 26 he presided over a council of ministers to discuss the Muraviev memorandum. Those present were Muraviev, Witte, Vannovsky (minister of war) and Tyrtov (minister of marine). The foreign minister repeated his argument: this was the time to secure both Talienwan and

[23] *Korean Repository,* January, 1898, pp. 35–6, September, 1897, pp. 353–4, November, 1897, pp. 434–5; Glinskii: *Prolog Russko-Iaponskoi Voiny,* pp. 64–5; F. A. McKenzie: *The Tragedy of Korea* (London, 1918), pp. 94–5; William F. Sands: *Undiplomatic Memories* (New York, 1930), p. 52.

Port Arthur, which was close by. But his proposal met with the bitterest opposition, especially from Witte. The finance minister insisted that such action would be contrary to the spirit of the Moscow Treaty of 1896. If Japan followed the example of Germany and took territory in China, Russia would be obliged to come to China's assistance. Yet now it was proposed that she should do the very thing that she had promised to prevent others from doing. The proper course of action would be not to imitate Germany, but to send the Russian squadron to Kiao-chow and do everything to force the Germans to withdraw.

To these arguments Muraviev replied that the treaty with China obliged Russia to aid only in resisting an attack upon China or Korea by Japan. As for Kiao-chow, " peculiar circumstances " made it impossible for Russia to prevent the German occupation. Witte remained unconvinced. The war minister threw the responsibility for choosing the proper naval base upon the minister of marine. Tyrtov was perfectly frank: the naval authorities had examined and considered Port Arthur and had found it not very suitable. The best thing would be to get along with Vladivostok for a few more years in the hope of ultimately getting a port in Korea.

Not a single minister supported the plan put forward by Muraviev. Witte redoubled his attack upon the scheme. Of course Russia needed a base in the Far East, he said. But that was a question of time, and could be settled by peaceful methods. Who would have believed a few years before that Russia would so easily secure the right to run the railroad through Manchuria? If Russia maintained her traditional policy and played her cards right she would get everything she needed without the use of force. These arguments evidently carried the day. For the time being the Muraviev plan was shelved.[24]

But Muraviev did not relinquish his scheme. The Tsar was with him, and the Germans were constantly assuring Russia that their presence at Kiao-chow would make it easier for them to support the Tsarist policy in the Far East. So Muraviev proceeded, carefully feeling his way. On December 14 the German government was informed that, with the consent of the Chinese government, a detachment of the Russian Far Eastern squadron would temporarily anchor at Port Arthur. The Tsar, persuaded " that Russia and Germany ought and could go hand in hand in the Far East," wished the German government to be informed of this fact. The Emperor William's delight can be better imagined than described. He summoned the Russian ambassador and assured him of Germany's support and good will: "Your enemies, whether they be called Japanese or English, now become my enemies, and every trouble maker, who-

---

24 The best and most detailed accounts in Glinskii, op. cit., pp. 43 ff. and in Romanov: *Rossiia v Manchzhurii,* pp. 186 ff.; but see also Dillon: *The Eclipse of Russia,* p. 249; Witte: *Memoirs,* pp. 99 ff.; Rosen, op. cit., I, p. 156; Alexander Iswolski: *Memoirs of an Ambassador* (New York, 1921), pp. 119 ff. The Muraviev memorandum of November 23 has now been published by A. Popov: "Pervie Shagi Russkogo Imperializma na Dal'nem Vostoke" (*Krasnyi Arkhiv,* LII, 1932, pp. 34–124), pp. 103 ff.

ever he be, who wishes to hinder your intentions by force, will meet the German squadron side by side with your warships." [25] His brother, Prince Henry, was just about to leave for the Far East with additional ships and troops. On the evening of December 16 the Emperor gave him a farewell dinner in the castle at Kiel. He there made one of his most bombastic and extravagant speeches, talking as though his brother were embarking on a mission of the greatest danger:

> " Make it clear to every European there, to the German merchant, and, above all things, to the foreigner in whose country we are or with whom we have to deal, that the German Michael has set his shield, decorated with the imperial eagle, firmly upon the ground. Whoever asks him for protection will always receive it. . . . But if any one should undertake to insult us in our rights or wish to harm us, then drive in with the mailed fist and, as God wills, bind about your young brow the laurels which no one in the entire German Empire will begrudge you."

To which Henry replied that his sole purpose was " to declare abroad the gospel of your Majesty's anointed person; to preach it to everyone who will hear it, and also to those who will not hear it."

This high-flown language was undoubtedly due in part to the changed attitude of Russia. At any rate the German congratulations upon the Tsar's decision were hardly less remarkable. The Emperor applauded the energetic measure which Nicholas had taken and hailed the re-establishment of the Russian-German entente in the Far East. " Russia and Germany at the entrance of the Yellow Sea," he wired the Tsar, " may be taken as represented by St. George and St. Michael shielding the Holy Cross in the Far East and guarding the Gates to the Continent of Asia. May you be able fully to realise the plans you often unrolled to me; my sympathy and help shall not fail in case of need." [26]

Emperor William understood well enough that the mission of Russian ships to Port Arthur was simply the prelude to the acquisition of the place. Witte must have known it too, but it was hard for him to object so long as no definite move was made in that direction. Muraviev claimed that the Russian fleet was sent to forestall action by the British, and he asserted further that the Chinese government had " invited " the measure. This was certainly not the fact. The Russian representative at Peking knew nothing about the matter until he received a telegram from the Russian admiral. He then had to convince the Chinese that the ships were being sent for China's protection.[27]

For many weeks it was not clear what was to happen at Port Arthur. The Japanese were much excited by the appearance of the Russians in the very port

---

[25] L. Teleshev: " Vil'gel'm II o Zaniatii Tsarskoi Rossiei Port-Arthura " (*Krasnyi Arkhiv*, LVIII, 1933, pp. 150-5).

[26] *Die Grosse Politik*, XIV, nos. 3733, 3734, 3739; Bülow: *Memoirs*, I, pp. 236 ff.

[27] Glinskii, op. cit., p. 48; and especially B. Romanov: " Konzessia na Yalu " (*Russkoie Proshloye*, I, 1923, pp. 87–108), p. 93.

from which they themselves had been debarred in 1895 on the plea that the presence of a foreign power there would be a menace to the independence of China. The press, already much wrought up by Germany's occupation of Kiao-chow and by recent developments in Korea, became violent in its denunciations.[28] Some diplomats, like Hayashi and Kato, the minister at London, favored an arrangement with England and co-operation against the Far Eastern Triplice, but other influential figures, like Ito, Inouye, and the foreign minister Nishi, still hoped that an agreement could be come to with Russia. In December advances for an alliance with China were made to some of the most powerful governors in the Yangtze region. Chang Chih-tung, the influential viceroy of Liang-hu, strongly recommended the alliance with Japan and England to the Peking authorities, but the Tsungli Yamen was set on a policy of non-resistance, which was based on the fear that war might lead to the loss of all important coastal towns. At Peking the distrust of England was very great, and there was, in addition, a chronic sense of fear of China's "friend," Russia.[29] Whether Muraviev learned of the Japanese soundings we do not know, but he evidently saw the need of appeasing the indignation of the Japanese. In January 1898 he suggested an accommodation. The Tokyo government thereupon proposed that Russia accept a free hand in Manchuria in return for similar freedom of action for Japan in Korea. This was more than the Russian government was prepared to concede, but negotiations were under way and finally resulted, in April 1898, in the Rosen-Nishi agreement, which will have to be discussed later.[30]

Had the English taken a stronger stand the Japanese might have been less ready to compromise with the Russians. But in British government circles, as in the Japanese, there was divided opinion. Lord Salisbury appears to have favored a waiting game, and gave no encouragement to Kato. Chamberlain, on the other hand, favored at least an understanding with Japan, and Curzon, at that time undersecretary for foreign affairs, strongly urged the need for such an agreement: "If the European Powers are grouping themselves against us in the Far East, we shall probably be driven sooner or later to act with Japan. Ten years hence she will be the greatest naval Power in those seas, and the European Powers who now ignore or flout her will be then competing for her alliance. . . . I argue for a watching attitude, but for a determination to pounce the moment anyone else pounces."[31] Other influential members of the government, like Hicks Beach, insisted on continuing the policy of the last years and striving for an arrangement with Russia. Even Chamberlain, speaking to the Russian am-

[28] See H. W. Wilson: "England and Japan" (*Fortnightly Review,* March, 1898, pp. 503–12).

[29] This is all drawn from the Chinese sources, as reported in the manuscript thesis of B. M. Bee, pp. 315 ff. and appendix A.

[30] Rosen, op. cit., I, pp. 155–8; Trubetzkoi, op. cit., pp. 59 ff.; *The Secret Memoirs of Count Tadasu Hayashi* (New York, 1915), p. 93.

[31] Garvin: *Life of Chamberlain,* III, p. 249; Curzon to Salisbury, December 29, 1897 (Earl of Ronaldshay: *The Life of Lord Curzon,* London, 1928, I, pp. 278–9). For British press opinion in favor of an· alliance with Japan see Chung-Fu Chang: *The Anglo-Japanese Alliance* (Baltimore, 1931), pp. 63 ff.

bassador, declared that in his view there was only one sane policy for England to follow: that of an entente with Russia and *par ricochet* with France.[32]

It is almost always stated by writers on the subject that British policy in the Far East at this time rested firmly upon the principle of Chinese integrity. Britain's interests were largely commercial; she wished to preserve the Chinese Empire because it was a huge market; if it were divided, large parts of it would be shut off by high tariff barriers.

The argument seems logical enough, and with certain qualifications it may be accepted. But it must be remembered that since 1895 many of the most competent writers on Chinese affairs entertained grave doubts whether the Empire could be kept intact. Henry Norman, for example, was convinced that before long it would be partitioned among the powers. Demetrius Boulger in 1895 predicted the course of Russian policy and insisted that, since dismemberment was certain, England should arrange to take over southern China. Holt Hallett declared the only solution to be a division of the spoils. England should take over the Yangtze Valley, Kuantung and Yunnan, and abandon the rest of southern China to France. Japan and Russia could settle the division of the north between them. Archibald Colquhoun agreed that China was no longer an effective buffer, and that Britain should therefore occupy the Yangtze region and southern China.[33]

So far as the British government was concerned, the evidence would seem to indicate the same doubt as to the endurance of the Celestial Kingdom or the possibility of preventing encroachment upon it by other powers. The materials on British policy are by no means adequate for a final judgment, but there are certain illuminating points. For example, in February 1896 a member of the government, Mr. Balfour, had in a public speech all but invited the Russians to secure for themselves an ice-free port, while immediately afterward Mr. Curzon had made it clear that this port should not be in Korea. It could, then, be only in China. In the same spirit England showed no great objection to the German action at Kiao-chow. It must be concluded then that the British, while desiring the integrity of China, were prepared to see this principle infringed to a certain extent by other powers in order to prevent its being discarded entirely. It seems that in the autumn of 1897 the British were ready to go even further in their anxiety to reach an agreement with Russia. The evidence may be found in the correspondence regarding the so-called Kinder incident. Mr. Kinder had for many years been in the employ of the Chinese government. He was a very able engineer who was in charge of the Chinese railways running north from Tientsin toward Manchuria. From October to December 1897 the Russian representative

---

[32] Meyendorff: *Correspondance de M. de Staal,* II, pp. 355–8. See also Victoria Hicks Beach: *Life of Sir Michael Hicks Beach* (London, 1932), II, pp. 58–9.

[33] Henry Norman: *The Peoples and Politics of the Far East* (New York, 1895), p. 593; Demetrius C. Boulger: "The New Situation in the Far East" (*Contemporary Review,* December, 1895, pp. 815–25); Holt S. Hallett: "The Partition of China" (*Nineteenth Century,* January, 1898, pp. 154–64); Archibald R. Colquhoun: *China in Transformation* (New York, 1898), p. 140.

at Peking, M. Pavlov, tried repeatedly to have him removed or transferred and to have a Russian engineer put in his place. In the course of discussion with the British minister, Sir Claude MacDonald, Pavlov said quite frankly "that the Russian Government intended that the provinces of China bordering on the Russian frontier must not come under the influence of any nation except Russia." To this pretension the British government, so far as the documents show, raised no objection, though it did insist on the retention of Kinder as it insisted on the retention of Brown in Korea.[34]

It would certainly be going too far to deduce from this that England was ready to abandon northern China to Russia. But British statesmen no longer had much confidence in their ability to uphold the principle of Chinese integrity. When it was learned that the Russian squadron had gone to Port Arthur, Chamberlain wrote to Salisbury to point out that English opinion would demand " some sensational action " on the part of the government. To this Salisbury replied with his usual amusing cynicism that he had no doubt that the public would require " some territorial or cartographic consolation in China." " It will not be useful," he added, " and it will be expensive; but as a matter of pure sentiment, we shall have to do it. I think it will be Chusan." [35] From which we may conclude that Salisbury was already more or less reconciled to a policy of grab. One gets the impression that the British government was interested above all things in the preservation not of China's territorial integrity but in the maintenance of the open door in the territories that were lost. In the Kiao-chow affair the London cabinet made its acquiescence in German action conditional on the principle of equal opportunity and no special privileges. The Germans refused to give a formal undertaking of this nature, but met the British desires in an informal way.[36]

What the fate of the territories coveted by Russia would be was still a matter of doubt. As between Russia and England the matter was fought out over the question of a loan to China and the conditions of such a loan. The Peking government required funds for the payment of the third and last installment of the indemnity to Japan. Negotiations had been opened with both British and Russian interests in June 1897, but the conditions, of which we know nothing much, appear to have been too hard and the matter was postponed. Now, on December 14, Li Hung-chang approached the Russians with renewed proposals. Witte on December 26 submitted his conditions, of which the most important were the following: only Russian subjects were to be permitted to build railroads and establish industrial enterprises in the three provinces of Manchuria and in Mongolia; China was to grant to the Chinese Eastern Railway Company a concession to construct a branch line to whatever port the company might choose

    [34] China No. I (1898), nos. 13, 14, 19, 38, 44; Kent: Railway Enterprise in China, p. 51; McCordock: British Far Eastern Policy, pp. 176 ff.; A. Popov: " Anglo-Russkoe Soglashenie o Razdele Kitaiia " (Krasnyi Arkhiv, XXV, 1927, pp. 113–34), p. 113.
    [35] Garvin: Life of Chamberlain, III, pp. 248–9.
    [36] China No. I (1898), nos. 17, 21, 24, 39, etc.; Die Grosse Politik, XIV, nos. 3747, 3750.

on the Yellow Sea east of the town of Yin-tse (mouth of the Liao-ho and port for Newchuang); China was to allow Russia to construct a port in the harbor chosen, with the exclusive right for Russian ships to enter.[37]

The object of the Chinese was evidently to play off one side against the other in the matter of the loan, for even before the Russian conditions were known, advances had been made to the British minister, Sir Claude MacDonald. At the latter's suggestion the London government too laid down conditions which can in no sense be described as modest. The Chinese were to allow the necessary control of the revenue to ensure repayment; to sanction the building of a railway from the Burmese frontier to the Yangtze Valley; to guarantee not to cede any territory in the Yangtze Valley to any other power; to make Talienwan a treaty port; to permit greater freedom of internal trade, and to free foreign goods from likin (internal customs) in the treaty ports.[38]

We need not here enter upon a discussion of the long and involved negotiations which took place during January 1898 with respect to this loan. The Chinese wanted the money to pay off the indemnity and thus secure the evacuation of Weihaiwei by the Japanese. They took the opportunity to bring Russia and England on the scene to counterbalance each other. The Russians saw their chance to put forward the demand for a port on the Yellow Sea and a railway from the Transsiberian to this port. The English on the other hand did not want to let the chance slip by for checkmating the French designs in southwest China, for safeguarding the market of the great Yangtze Valley and for blocking the known designs of the Russians by demanding that Talienwan be made a treaty port. As for the Chinese, they miscalculated very seriously, for the conditions on both sides were very hard, and they soon found themselves sailing between Scylla and Charybdis. The Russian minister at Peking declared that refusal of the Russian terms would " entail an interruption of the friendly relations " between the two governments. His British colleague warned the Tsungli Yamen that any attempt to exclude Britain from the loan would " seriously imperil " relations between China and England. A suggestion by Li Hung-chang that the loan be divided between England and Russia was not taken up. The attempt to raise the money by a domestic loan failed completely. What were the Chinese to do?

As between the conditions set by the two opponents the demands of the British, hard as they were, represented the lesser evil. The one proposition that even Li Hung-chang had steadfastly refused to consider was the Russian plan for a harbor on the Yellow Sea and a railway from there to the Transsiberian. In vain Li tried to induce them to select a harbor in Korea near the mouth of the Yalu. In vain the Russian government authorized its agents to bribe Li and his associates to the tune of a million rubles and more. Nothing could move

---

[37] Glinskii, op. cit., p. 47 ff.; Romanov: *Rossiia v Manchzhurii*, pp. 191 ff.; the terms as given in *China No. I (1898)*, no. 26 are incorrect in several respects, and the argumentation of writers like Joseph and McCordock has suffered from their reliance exclusively upon this source.

[38] *China No. I (1898)*, nos. 30, 46.

the Tsungli Yamen. The Russian demand had confirmed its worst fears. The Russians were asked for a written promise to evacuate Port Arthur. Muraviev evaded, and said that the Russian ships would leave " when circumstances permitted." There could be no further doubt of the Russian designs. The Chinese thereupon all but invited the British to send a few ships to Port Arthur, where they arrived from Korea early in January 1898.

The Peking court was gradually turning toward England. The British demands were never met in connexion with the loan, but the Chinese government finally agreed to several important concessions. It had been rumored that the Russians were insisting that the position of inspector-general of the Chinese customs, a post long held by Sir Robert Hart, should be given to a Russian when it became vacant. The Chinese agreed that the post should remain in the hands of an Englishman so long as British trade with China exceeded that of any other nation. They further engaged never to cede territory in the Yangtze Basin to any other power. Once these concessions were secured the British did not press for the other points, and the Chinese government in February 1898 signed an agreement with the Hongkong and Shanghai Bank (an English concern) for a private loan. Therewith this difficult problem was gotten out of the way.[39]

The discussions of January caused acute tension in Anglo-Russian relations. It is hard to see what the British were driving at when they demanded the opening of Talienwan as a treaty port. Most of the English ministers seem to have been favorable to an understanding with Russia, and they had, after all, invited Russia to find a commercial outlet on the Yellow Sea. Now Talienwan was the only possible port for the purpose, as all the others were frozen during part of the winter. Why did the British open the door to the Russians and then slam it in their face? The only reasonable explanation seems to be that they hoped not so much to keep Russia out of Talienwan, as to secure from her a promise that the port should be a free port. If the Chinese could be brought to recognize it as a treaty port, then England and all other nations would secure treaty rights (most-favored-nation rights) which Russia would be bound to respect. The theory that the demand regarding Talienwan was meant chiefly as a bargaining point is borne out to some extent by the utterances of British statesmen during the month of January. Balfour, speaking at Manchester on January 10, expounded the British policy in detail. British interests, he said, were not territorial but commercial. In view of the fact that British trade in China was eighty per cent of the total foreign trade of that country, England had a special claim to see that Chinese policy was not directed to the discouragement of foreign

---

[39] The important source on the British side is *China No. 1 (1898)*, passim; on the Russian side the accounts of Glinskii, op. cit., pp. 47 ff. and Romanov, op. cit., pp. 195 ff. Detailed accounts based on the British Blue Book may be found in Joseph: *Foreign Diplomacy in China*, pp. 226 ff., and in McCordock: *British Far Eastern Policy*, pp. 164 ff., neither of whom make use of Russian material. The documents on the bribing of Li Hung-chang were published in the *Krasnyi Arkhiv*, II (1924), pp. 287–93: " Perepiska o Podkupe Kitaiiskikh Sanovnikov " and are translated in George N. Steiger: *China and the Occident* (New Haven, 1927), pp. 69 ff.

trade, either by setting up regulations in favor of particular countries or by allowing other powers to dot the coast with stations through which world trade could not freely permeate. England could and would resist such action. There was no objection to Russia's seeking an outlet for her commerce below the line of winter and ice, provided always that " we are not excluded from going there too." On January 17 Sir Michael Hicks Beach, in an address at Swansea, re-iterated these principles, but went even further and attempted to set up what amounted to a Monroe doctrine for China: " We do not regard China as a place for conquest or acquisition by any European or other Power. We look upon it as the most hopeful place of the future for the commerce of our country and the commerce of the world at large, and the Government was absolutely determined, at whatever cost, even — and he wished to speak plainly — if necessary, at the cost of war, that the door should not be shut against us." [40]

These bellicose words caused something like an attack of war fever in Eng-land. The *Times* made them its own and declared that all parties stood together behind the government in support of this policy.[41] And yet it seems fairly clear that the strong language used by Balfour, Hicks Beach, and a little later in January by Chamberlain was meant to impress not the English public, but the Russian government. All these men were in favor of an agreement with Russia and anxious to secure one if possible. There was nothing especially new about this policy, which had been tried by the Rosebery cabinet in 1894–1895 and which had been taken up time and again by the Salisbury administration. In January 1898 the British government was faced with two alternatives: either to try to secure German and Japanese support against Russia, or to try to reach an adjustment with Russia. For co-operation with Japan there was a good deal of public sentiment, though there were still many people " to whom an alliance with a non-Christian power against Christians would seem something like trea-son to God." [42] But with Germany it was different. The occupation of Kiao-chow had called forth a storm of angry protest in England, where it was generally regarded as part of a French-Russian-German plot. In December opinion was so wrought up that the British military attaché at Berlin could write: " We must go for the Germans and that right soon or they will go for us later." The same apprehensions appear in Spring Rice's correspondence from Berlin:

" The whole incident has been used as a sort of peg to hang their hatred of Eng-land on — which is so plain and evident that no one who is resident in this part of the world can doubt it. . . . It would be absurd to deny that both the

---

[40] Joseph, op. cit., pp. 234 ff.; Victoria Hicks Beach: *Life of Sir Michael Hicks Beach*, II, pp. 58–9; Diplomaticus: " A Monroe Doctrine for China " (*Fortnightly Review*, February, 1898, pp. 321–33).

[41] London *Times*, January 19 and 31, 1898; see also Meyendorff: *Correspondance de M. de Staal*, II, pp. 364–6, 369; *Die Grosse Politik*, XIV, no. 3751.

[42] H. W. Wilson: " England and Japan " (*Fortnightly Review*, March, 1898, pp. 503–12); Arthur Diosy: *The New Far East* (London, 1898), pp. 361 ff.; Chang: *The Anglo-Japanese Alliance* (Baltimore, 1931), pp. 63–4.

Emperor and his people are actuated by feelings of hostility against England which are only limited by the German regard for law and by the practical fear of reprisals. . . . The reason for this is quite simple. We stand in their way everywhere — we have most to take — and we are personally objectionable." "I should say that the desire here was to organize a common course of action against us — less perhaps for the sake of Asia than for Europe; to unite in China what Europe has disunited: to establish themselves in China, to have a point d'appui so as no longer to be treated as a negligible quantity by the two allied powers: but at the same time to avoid a direct conflict with us until they are ready — which will certainly not be yet." [43]

As a matter of fact the German policy at this time was marked by very great caution. Public opinion was certainly very hostile to England, and even a man like Delbrück declared that no amount of diplomatic courtesy, no political tactics could ever bridge the fundamental trade antagonism between the two countries.[44] Emperor William, too, was completely under the spell of the continental league. He blamed Muraviev, not the Tsar, for the unpleasantness regarding Kiao-chow, and was quite prepared to continue support of Russia in the Far East. Speaking to Grierson on January 15, 1898, he said that he had tried for eight years to be friendly with Britain and to gain her alliance, but had failed. The British would never have that chance again. What, he asked, was the British policy anyway? Grierson replied that England aimed to hold aloof from both continental groups. She was strong enough against either and it was unlikely that they could combine. To which the Emperor replied warmly: "You are mistaken. They can combine and they *shall* combine. Socialism and other causes will force the Monarchs of the Continent to combine for mutual assistance and the yellow races of the East are our greatest danger." [45]

But the German foreign office was much more circumspect. Bülow was ready to go a long way to meet the needs of Russia. When the Russians, in correspondence with Berlin, set up a claim to a sphere of "exclusive action" to include all of Manchuria, the province of Chihli and Chinese Turkestan, the Germans offered no objection. They thought the demand for Chihli a "rather big bite" but were interested chiefly in reserving Shantung and the valley of the Yellow River, to its bend northward, for their own sphere.[46] At the same time Bülow refused to commit the German government in advance to the support of Russian policy. He continued his efforts to take the edge off the Anglo-German tension and his policy was ably seconded by Hatzfeldt in London. German assurances that Kiao-chow would, at least for the present, be made an open and free port, helped to calm British opinion somewhat. Lord Salisbury himself seems to have been anxious to better relations. It was probably at his

---

[43] *Letters and Friendships of Sir Cecil Spring Rice*, I, pp. 243–4; Macdiarmid: *Life of Grierson*, p. 133.

[44] Hans Delbrück: "Politische Korrespondenz" (*Preussische Jahrbücher*, October, 1897, p. 176).

[45] Macdiarmid, op. cit., pp. 134 ff.; *British Documents on the Origins of the War*, I, nos. 62–3.

[46] *Die Grosse Politik*, XIV, nos. 3743 ff.

request that the Queen asked Sir Theodore Martin to see the important editors of English newspapers and induce them to adopt a better tone towards the German Emperor and people. This démarche had an almost instantaneous effect and the improvement in the tone of the newspapers was immediately noticeable. Later on Lord Salisbury hotly refuted the idea that he had been an obstacle to an agreement with Germany. That charge he declared to be " the very reverse of the truth." [47]

It appears, however, that Salisbury, if he was really desirous of an understanding with Germany, was obliged to yield to the opposition in the cabinet, that is, to Balfour, Chamberlain and Hicks Beach, who, while stirring up British opinion against Russia, were hoping to scare Russia into an agreement. At any rate, about the middle of January, at the height of the competition for the loan to China, the British government began to make approaches to Russia. M. de Staal, the Tsar's ambassador at London, had already complained of the presence of British ships at Port Arthur, and the same point had been taken up by Muraviev with the British ambassador at St. Petersburg. The presence of these ships, he said, was so unfriendly as to have set afloat rumors of war with Great Britain. Lord Salisbury, while stressing the fact that the ships had a perfect right to be there, declared that they had gone on orders of the British admiral in the Far East, not on orders of the government. Nevertheless instructions were soon sent out to withdraw the ships, whereupon the Russians began to start rumors that the ships had left on the demand of the Russian authorities.[48]

In the meanwhile Salisbury had sent instructions to Sir Nicholas O'Conor on January 17: " If practicable ask Monsieur Witte whether it is possible that England and Russia should work together in China. Our objects are not antagonistic in any serious degree: on the other hand we can both do each other a great deal of harm if we try. It is better therefore we should come to an understanding. We would go far to further Russian commercial objects in the north, if we could regard her as willing to work with us." [49]

This is a curious document which deserves some scrutiny. It must not be taken too seriously, because, in the first place, it was an instruction to sound out Witte, not to negotiate with the Russian foreign minister; in the second place it makes the strange statement that British and Russian objects are not antagonistic in any serious degree; in the third place it expresses willingness to make concessions only " to further Russian *commercial* objects in the North." Now what actually happened was that O'Conor, instead of approaching Witte, spoke to Muraviev; instead of sticking to his instructions and discussing China, he expressed the opinion that " any understanding, to be really effective and last-

---

[47] *Letters of Queen Victoria*, III, pp. 224–5, 259; see also *Die Grosse Politik*, XIII, no. 3423; XIV, 3747–53; Karl O. Herkenberg: *The Times und das Deutsch-Englische Verhältnis im Jahre 1898* (Berlin, 1925), pp. 44 ff.

[48] See *China No. I (1898)*, nos. 48, 61, 63, 67; Meyendorff, op. cit., II, p. 370.

[49] *British Documents*, I, no. 5.

ing ought to extend to the general area of our respective interests, and not to be confined to the important questions affecting the Far East." [50]

The material on these negotiations, both from the British and the Russian sides, is pretty incomplete, but it seems fairly clear that O'Conor distorted the affair from the start and gave Muraviev a wrong impression of the points at issue. The Russian minister said he would lay his cards on the table if Salisbury would do likewise. He went even further and revealed the fact that Russia claimed a sphere " which was practically all northern China from Tientsin to Peking and from Peking to Manchuria." Apparently he thought the British were inviting a discussion of spheres. Witte, when approached a few days later, evidently gained the same impression, for he spoke of Russia's willingness to recognize the Yangtze Valley as England's sphere, at the same time drawing from his desk a map of China and saying that sooner or later Russia would probably absorb the entire provinces of Chihli, Shansi, Shensi and Kansu.

The Russian ministers must have been more than a little astonished when Salisbury's proposal was laid before them in detail. The document, dated January 25, is a remarkable one, and worth quoting at some length:

> " Our idea was this. The two Empires of China and Turkey are so weak that in all important matters they are constantly guided by the advice of Foreign Powers. In giving this advice Russia and England are constantly opposed, neutralizing each other's efforts much more frequently than the real antagonism of their interest would justify; and this condition of things is not likely to diminish, but to increase. It is to remove or lessen this evil that we have thought that an understanding with Russia might benefit both nations. We contemplate no infraction of existing rights. We would not admit the violation of any existing treaties, or impair the integrity of the present empires of either China or Turkey. These two conditions are vital. We aim at no partition of territory, but only a partition of preponderance. It is evident that both in respect to Turkey and China there are large portions which interest Russia more than England and *vice versa*. Merely as an illustration, and binding myself to nothing, I would say that the portion of Turkey which drains into the Black Sea, together with the drainage valley of the Euphrates as far as Bagdad, interest Russia much more than England: whereas Turkish Africa, Arabia and the Valley of the Euphrates below Bagdad interest England much more than Russia. A similar distinction exists in China between the Valley of the Hoango with the territory north of it and the Valley of the Yangtze. Would it be possible to arrange that where, in regard to these territories, our counsels differ, the Power least interested should give way to and assist the other? I do not disguise from myself that the difficulty would be great. Is it insuperable? I have designedly omitted to deal with large tracts in each Empire, because neither Power has shown any keen interest in them." [51]

Salisbury indicated his readiness to define " spheres of preponderance," but on the understanding that there should be no infraction of existing rights, no violation of existing treaties, no impairment of the integrity of China or Tur-

---

[50] Ibid., no. 6.   [51] *British Documents,* I, no. 9.

key, and that, furthermore, the agreement should extend to the Near as well as to the Far East. All this ran counter to the Russian conception. What was wanted in St. Petersburg was a definition of spheres in China and the right to an absolutely free hand in those spheres. The Russians were distinctly averse to a discussion of Turkey at this time. Even the Tsar, who seems to have favored an understanding, insisted on its restriction to China. The Russians were prepared to abandon the loan, but only on condition that England agree to a lease by Russia, say for twenty years, of Talienwan and Port Arthur or any other port in the north that might be considered more desirable. A railway was to be built to this port. At first, making full use of the friendly discussions with London, they felt out the ground very carefully. England, they pointed out, had recognised Russia's right to a commercial outlet. If Russia took Talienwan the port would be " open to commerce of all the world." On the strength of this assurance the British seem to have given up the demand that Talienwan be made a treaty port, as put forward in the loan discussions with China. Lord Salisbury announced the happy news in the house of lords on February 8, only to learn from Staal the next day that what the Russians meant was a treaty port (that is, open to all nations), not a free port (that is, without special tariffs). Furthermore, the Russian assurance, he said, could not be looked upon as a formal written one.[52]

Soon the Russians became more specific. Count Lamsdorff, Muraviev's aide, bluntly told the British ambassador that the Russians intended to hold these ports at any cost, though they were still open to a deal. By that was meant that the Russians would agree to a loan by the British. When it became known that the Chinese government had made arrangements for this loan with the Hongkong and Shanghai Bank, the St. Petersburg government took it as an excuse to drop the entire negotiation and press its demands for Talienwan and Port Arthur upon the Chinese government. And so ended the episode of the British advances to Russia. On the British side they seem to have been carried on without confidence or enthusiasm from the very start. O'Conor pointed out in the beginning how important it was " to take care that any understanding we may come to gives no such headway that it cannot be set aside when it may seem to Russia to have served its temporary purpose." Before the discussion had proceeded very far Salisbury wrote to the minister in China that the Russians were insincere and their language ambiguous. When the whole affair came to an end the British officials saw clearly what they had suspected all along: the Tsar had performed an " acquit de conscience " towards his English relatives by showing good will to the theoretical idea of a general understanding, but he could not run counter to his ministers' designs.

All this is not to be wondered at, for the British proposals were fairly transparent. The London government was prepared to recognise the Russian sphere

---

[52] *China No. 1 (1898)*, nos. 72, 76, 82, 83, 87; Meyendorff, op. cit., II, p. 372.

in China if it could extort a recognition of treaty rights and the Open Door in this whole vast tract, and if the arrangement could be extended to the Near East. Chamberlain made no bones about saying this afterward. In his famous speech at Birmingham on May 13, he declared:

> " The present government did try to come to an understanding with Russia. We took care to inform her that we had no jealousy, no objection to what we understood to be her commercial objects, or to the development of her trade, or to the expansion of her legitimate authority, but we sought to induce her to give up the idea of political predominance and military occupation. We failed — that was not consistent with the ambition of her Government — we failed to persuade her."

The Russians had no difficulty in seeing through the English tactics. As the Tsar wrote later to his friend William, the British proposals " were of such a new character that I must say we were quite amazed and yet their very nature seemed suspicious to us; never before had England made such offers to Russia. That showed us clearly that England needed our friendship at that time to be able to check our development in a masked way in the Far East." [53] Taken all in all, then, one can hardly describe the British advances as a serious offer of an entente or agreement. They were hardly more than a half-hearted and none too adroit move to commit the Russians to a program which they had no intention of following. The Russians never took them very seriously, but merely debated until they had secured from England something like an unofficial and informal recognition of the great sphere which they had mapped out for themselves, and until their own preparations for further action were complete. [54]

Since the middle of February (that is, long before the discussions between Russia and England came to an end) a committee of high officials had been sitting in St. Petersburg engaged in the task of working out the demands to be presented to China. The new war minister, General Kuropatkin, had come out definitely in favor of the retention of Port Arthur, and even Witte had given up his opposition. He disliked the whole idea as much as ever, but he felt that it was better, now that the decision was all but irrevocable, to join in the action and serve as a moderating influence rather than lose all control of the situation. The committee finally decided to ask for the lease of the southern tip of the Liaotung Peninsula, with Port Arthur and Talienwan, and for the right to build the Railway via Kirin and Mukden south to Port Arthur, or, if necessary, to any other point on the Liaotung Peninsula. On March 3 these demands were laid before the Tsungli Yamen, buttressed by the argument that Russia, once in occupation of the Liaotung Peninsula, could the better defend China against her enemies. The Russian minister, Pavlov, asked for acceptance within five days.

---

[53] *Die Grosse Politik*, XIV, no. 3803.

[54] The chief documents, in *British Documents on the Origins of the War*, I, nos. 5–24, should be supplemented by the Russian documents published by A. Popov: " Anglo-Russkoe Soglashenie o Razdele Kitaiia " (*Krasnyi Arkhiv*, XXV, pp. 111–34), pp. 114 ff., and the discussion in Romanov: *Rossiia v Manchzhurii*, pp. 201 ff.

As a matter of fact the negotiations dragged out for more than three weeks, because the Chinese left no stone unturned to evade these demands. They appealed to England and Japan to give assurances that they had no designs on Manchuria or Liaotung. They tried to procrastinate by sending a special negotiator to St. Petersburg. They argued that the lease to Russia would inevitably lead to demands by other powers. Eventually they attempted to bribe England with the offer of a lease of Weihaiwei, in the hope that thus they might effect an alliance between England, Japan and China directed against Russia. But all these efforts proved to be of no avail. Whatever else may be said about the Russian policy in appropriating Port Arthur and Talienwan, it must be confessed that the affair was ably handled from the diplomatic standpoint. The French evidently disliked the whole business, but there was no chance of their openly opposing it.[55] The Germans made it clear that they would do nothing to increase Russia's difficulties.[56] There remained Japan, and the danger of action from Japan, supported by England, was, of course, always in the minds of the Russian statesmen. Muraviev, however, embarked boldly upon the only sound procedure. He decided to buy off the Japanese by making concessions in Korea. Ever since the middle of February the Japanese government had been pressing for an agreement based upon the idea that Japan should accord Russia a free hand in Manchuria in return for similar freedom for Japan in Korea. This was too much for the Russians, who were unwilling to abandon Korea entirely and equally unwilling to have Japan in sole control on the flank of Manchuria. They therefore temporized, putting off the Japanese with demonstrations of good will. The Russian military instructors and the financial adviser were withdrawn, and the Russian-Korean Bank, which had been established only three months before, suspended its operations. Eventually the negotiations were brought to a close after the Port Arthur matter had been disposed of. In the Nishi-Rosen Agreement of April 25, 1898 the two governments recognized the full independence of Korea and engaged to abstain from all interference in the domestic affairs of that country. They agreed further that if Korea appealed to either of them for counsel or support, they would take no steps to appoint military instructors or financial advisers without reaching an understanding first between themselves. In Article III it was specified that in view of the large industrial and commercial enterprises of Japan in Korea and the large number of Japanese resident in the country, Russia would not in any way hinder the development of these interests. The agreement, in short, put Russia and Japan on an equal footing of abstention, with the sole exception that Japan was given a free hand economically in Korea.[57]

From the information we have it is pretty clear that the Japanese govern-

---

[55] *British Documents*, I, no. 33.   [56] *Die Grosse Politik*, XIV, no. 3756.

[57] The fullest account in Glinskii, op. cit., pp. 65 ff.; see also Romanov, op. cit., pp. 206 ff.; Rosen: *Forty Years of Diplomacy*, I, pp. 156 ff.; Trubetzkoi: *Russland als Grossmacht*, pp. 59 ff. On the Japanese side see K. Asakawa: *The Russo-Japanese Conflict* (Boston, 1904), pp. 269 ff.

ment, particularly Marquis Ito, was at the time much opposed to antagonizing Russia. The Japanese political situation was uncertain, and the national finances in bad shape. Military and naval preparations would not be complete for some years, and there was, besides, the danger that Japan, if she antagonized Russia, might have to deal with France and Germany as well. So it was deemed advisable to postpone the struggle which was already regarded as inevitable.[58]

While the Japanese were patching up their differences with Russia, the English, having tried to square the Russians and having failed, could do little but nurse their mortification. For a man like Chamberlain that was a hard course to follow, and he did not accept Salisbury's laisser faire policy without question. In the early days of February he had written to Balfour warning that the government would meet with disaster if it did not follow a stronger line in China. He proposed that the British approach the American and German governments with a suggestion that all occupied ports be made treaty ports. If the Russians refused, they should be driven out of Port Arthur.[59]

We do not know what Balfour's reply to this proposal was, but at all events Chamberlain seems to have stuck by his idea. On March 8 the British ambassador at Washington submitted to the state department an unofficial memorandum asking whether the British government " could count on the co-operation of the United States in opposing action by foreign Powers which may tend to restrict freedom of commerce of all nations in China either by imposing preferential conditions or by obtaining actual cession of Chinese coast territory." The American government returned an evasive reply, something to the effect that it saw no immediate danger.[60]

The response was discouraging, but it did not prevent Chamberlain from approaching other governments, first the Japanese and later the German. On March 17, at the most critical moment of the Port Arthur affair, he had a long talk with the Japanese minister at a dinner party. With his usual bluntness Chamberlain asked Baron Kato what Japan proposed to do. The minister replied that he did not know. England's policy, he said, seemed to be based on purely commercial considerations, but how did England expect to keep her commercial position intact if she lost her political influence in China? How far would England be prepared to go to defend China's integrity? Chamberlain agreed with Kato in principle, but hinted that England lacked the land forces necessary to oppose Russia in Manchuria. How could the Russian advance be stopped? he inquired. To which Kato replied by asking whether the guns of the British ships would not reach to the Liaotung Peninsula? Chamberlain rejoined by asserting that such action would not stop Russia. Japan, he said, must desire Chinese integrity as much as England. Why should the two countries

---

[58] Ito Masanori: *Kato Takaaki* (Tokyo, 1929), I, pp. 280 ff.
[59] Garvin: *Life of Chamberlain*, III, p. 251.
[60] Alfred L. P. Dennis: *Adventures in American Diplomacy, 1896–1906* (New York, 1928), pp. 170–1.

not act together? Why did Japan not make a proposition? Kato answered that the Tokyo government might be wondering why the British did not make a proposition, but Chamberlain deprecated the silence of the Japanese. The two countries, he thought, should open their hearts and say what they meant. England would receive Japanese overtures with great good will and would give full consideration.[61]

Kato forwarded a report of this interesting conversation to his government and followed it up on March 26 with a memorandum of ten thousand words urging the desirability and need of an alliance with England, which would give the two powers undisputed naval control in the Far East and make them all-powerful. But Ito was anxious to get out of the crisis without making larger commitments. He preferred an arrangement with Russia about Korea, and was prepared to be put off with very meagre concessions even in that matter. Kato secured no support for his plan, and thereupon resigned his position.[62]

The British were left to settle their score with the Russians alone. What was to be done? The Russian government insisted that there was no intention of infringing the sovereign rights of China: the two ports were to be leased, not taken. Furthermore, Russia was willing to promise that they should be open to the trade of all nations and that the treaty rights of other powers should be respected. The British statesmen had no undue confidence in Russian assurances. It was not Talienwan that they objected to, but the idea of Russia securing Port Arthur. Everyone knew that this port could never be made a commercial centre. It was a purely military stronghold, but as such was of tremendous importance, commanding as it did the entire Gulf of Pechili and the approaches to Peking by sea. From the time when the Russian demands on China became known the English government considered the advisability of leasing Weihaiwei if the Russians could not be brought to give up the demand for Port Arthur. The place was still occupied by the Japanese, under the terms of the Treaty of Shimonoseki, but they were to withdraw in May 1898, when the final installment of the indemnity would have been paid by China. The Tsungli Yamen was quite prepared to have the British take it over as a counterweight to Russia, but the British government hesitated to join in the scramble for territory, the more so as parliament had passed a resolution on March 1 declaring " that it is of vital importance for British commerce and influence that the independence of Chinese territory should be maintained." The government had accepted the resolution, though Curzon warned the House that he could conceive " of circumstances arising in the future, circumstances gravely affecting, and perhaps seriously imperilling our interests in China, which might tempt us to depart from that attitude of reserve."

---

[61] Such is the account given in Kato's memoirs: Ito Masanori: *Kato Takaaki* (Tokyo, 1929), I, pp. 292 ff. These advances are mentioned also in *The Secret Memoirs of Count Hayashi*, p. 89, and are vaguely referred to in *Die Grosse Politik*, XIV, nos. 3759, 3782.

[62] Masanori, op. cit., I, pp. 280 ff., 313 ff., 330 ff.; see also Atsushi Hiratsuka: *Ito Hirobumi Hiroku* (Tokyo, 1929).

Curzon himself shared the opinion of the ambassador at St. Petersburg, namely that the Russian action could not be blocked and that it would be better to secure Weihaiwei before the Russian demands had been accepted by the Chinese. But the majority of the members of the cabinet seem to have been opposed. Lord Salisbury was ill and Balfour, who had taken his place at the foreign office, had a hard time convincing his colleagues. To allow Russia to lease Port Arthur and to have England take Weihaiwei as a makeweight would mean abandoning northern China, he argued, but after all that region was bound to fall to Russia sooner or later. To require the Russians to abstain from taking Port Arthur might lead to war, but it would prevent the partition of China, would check Russian influence at Peking and would save the balance of power in the Far East. Lord Salisbury from his sick-bed seems to have decided the cabinet's choice of these alternatives. He thought it would be best to secure from China a promise not to alienate Weihaiwei and to give England the first refusal of it. As for Russia's influence at Peking, this he thought would not be affected by her occupation of Port Arthur, since this influence rested on Russia's proximity to China by land and the existence of several thousand miles of common frontier. " The only thing to be done," concluded Salisbury, " is to object to the military occupation of Port Arthur in language sufficiently measured to allow Russia to find a way out."

In the meanwhile the Russians had been bringing greater and greater pressure to bear at Peking. Li Hung-chang and Chang Yin-huan were the two negotiators on the Chinese side. They were quite amenable to reason. On March 21 the Russian chargé d'affaires, Pavlov, and the Russian financial agent, Pokotilov, carried out instructions from St. Petersburg and offered the two Chinese a bribe of five hundred thousand taels each if the matter were arranged in the next few days. Li protested, but not too much. On March 24 the British minister at Peking could report that the Chinese were going to yield. They did. On March 27 the agreement between China and Russia was signed. The Russians secured all they wanted.[63]

The British cabinet had decided on March 25 that Port Arthur was not worth a war and that the best solution would be to secure a lease of Weihaiwei. They therefore notified the Russian government of their " grave objections " to its action and reserved to themselves liberty " to take what steps they think best to protect their own interests and to diminish the evil consequences which they anticipate." [64] As for Weihaiwei, this aspect of the problem was not serious. The

---

[63] Details of the negotiations in Glinskii, op. cit., pp. 53 ff.; *China No. I (1898)*, nos. 95 ff.; *British Documents on the Origins of the War*, I, nos. 23 ff. On the attitude of the British cabinet see especially *Letters of Queen Victoria*, III, pp. 237–8; Earl of Ronaldshay: *Life of Curzon*, I, pp. 283 ff. Witte: *Memoirs*, pp. 102–3, admits the bribery of Li Hung-chang. The documents on this subject are in the *Krasnyi Arkhiv*, II, pp. 290–3.

[64] *British Documents*, I, no. 41. Balfour told Staal that the occupation of Port Arthur was regarded as a matter " of immense gravity " (Meyendorff: *Correspondance de M. de Staal*, II, pp. 375–7).

Japanese were ready to evacuate when the indemnity was paid. They expected the Chinese to take it over, but if the Chinese were too weak they preferred to see it in the hands of Britain rather than in the hands of any other power. They therefore gave their assent, on the understanding that if Japan should later find it necessary to take similar measures to " strengthen her defences or to promote her interests " they might count on the " concurrence and support " of England.[65] The Germans were squared by being given assurances that England, in establishing herself at Weihaiwei, had " no intention of injuring or contesting the rights and interests of Germany in the province of Shantung or of creating difficulties for her in that province." " It is especially understood," continued the British note, " that England will not construct any railroad communication from Weihaiwei, and the district leased therewith, into the interior of the province." [66]

In the Chinese scramble of the winter 1897–1898 the French government played a subordinate rôle. M. Hanotaux assured the British ambassador that France desired " the maintenance as long as possible of the integrity of the Chinese Empire." The " attacks " on China by Germany and Russia he considered " premature and consequently regrettable." But, despite his dislike for the principle of spheres of influence, he insisted that " France must sustain her claims to consideration in the provinces contiguous to Tongking." [67] As a matter of fact the struggle between England and France in southwest China had been going on apace. When, in June 1897, the British secured from China the opening of the West River to commerce, the French regarded this as a direct blow at their interests. They therefore obliged the Chinese to agree to the eventual extension of the railroad from Langson to Longchow in the direction of Nanning and Pe-se. Furthermore, the Chinese government was to turn first to French engineers and contractors for all mining services in the three provinces of Kuangtung, Kuangsi and Yunnan. In the meanwhile the French, like the Germans, were carefully canvassing the possibilities of establishing a coaling and naval station on the Chinese coast. In 1896 a Frenchman, Claudius Madrolle, for the first time explored the interior of the island of Hainan, and presented to the Geographical Society a glowing report of its possibilities. In January 1897 the French induced the Chinese government to promise not to alienate this island to any other power. French naval vessels were busy throughout the year 1897 taking soundings around the island and about the Leichow Peninsula. In January 1898 it was reported that French ships had seized Hainan, and a British warship was hastily sent to investigate. The report proved unfounded, but the French had gone north to the harbor of Kuangchow. In the meanwhile the French representative at Peking loyally supported the Russian demands on China, while the Russian chargé d'affaires did the same for his colleague. The French desiderata were put forward immediately after the Russian, on March 7,

[65] British Documents, I, nos. 28, 30, 39 ff.
[66] Die Grosse Politik, XIV, no. 3770. For the negotiations see ibid., nos. 3760 ff.; British Documents, I, nos. 47 ff.   [67] British Documents, I, no. 33.

1898. France asked for a Chinese promise not to alienate the three provinces of Yunnan, Kuangtung and Kuangsi; the appointment of a Frenchman to the position of director of the posts; the definitive concession for a railroad to Yunnan-fu; the right to establish a coaling station on the south coast. On April 10 these demands were conceded, and on April 22 the French flag was raised at Kuangchowwan, leased by the French for ninety-nine years. Outrages against French nationals in southern China soon gave the Paris government a pretext for further demands. On May 28 the Chinese government agreed to the construction of a railroad from Pakhoi on the coast, to some point on the West River. By this method the French hoped to draw the commerce of the southern provinces away from Canton and Hongkong and bring it down to the Gulf of Tongking.[68]

So ended the first phase of the victimization of China after her defeat by Japan in 1895. The occupation of Kiao-chow by the Germans was a very important landmark. Thus far the Russians and the French, followed by the British, had been pursuing their policy of "peaceful penetration." Had this process been allowed to continue uninterrupted, Russia would, in a relatively short time, have established control over Manchuria and even over the province of Chihli and the capital, Peking. Of that there can be little doubt. Russia was the champion of Chinese integrity, for she saw endless possibilities in a policy of friendship and restraint. The British could not have frustrated these plans. That comes out clearly enough from the British documents. The London government was quite prepared to accept the inevitable and to allow northern China to fall under Russian influence. The great aim of the British was to preserve, if at all possible, the rights laid down in the treaties, to open as many Chinese ports as possible to foreign trade and to make sure that everywhere the open door and equality of opportunity should be the rule.

Prior to 1898 the Russians had done nothing to interfere with British interests, which were, as a matter of fact, rather slight in northern China. The British raised no objection to the Russian railroad schemes or to the project for a commercial terminus on the Yellow Sea. In fact, they took rather the attitude that a Russian railroad into Manchuria would open the way for the influx of British goods. In the years before 1898, then, the British were almost entirely concerned with French activity in the south. The duel for the control and exploitation of Yunnan and Szechuan has been less written about, but it was of tremendous importance and has been neglected simply because in the following years the Russian policy drew all the fire of objection. British interests in the Yangtze Valley and in the southwest were very great, and there can be no ques-

---

[68] Documents Diplomatiques: *Chine, 1894–1898*, nos. 34 ff., 59 ff.; *China No. 1 (1899)*, passim; Claudius Madrolle: "Kouang-Tchéou, Sancian, Hainan" (*Questions Diplomatiques et Coloniales*, May 1, 1898, pp. 6–12); J. Silvestre: "La France à Kouang-Tchéou-Ouan" (*Annales des Sciences Politiques*, July 15, 1902, pp. 473–93); Alfred Bonningue: *La France à Kouang-Tchéou-Wan* (Paris, 1931), pp. 7–8.

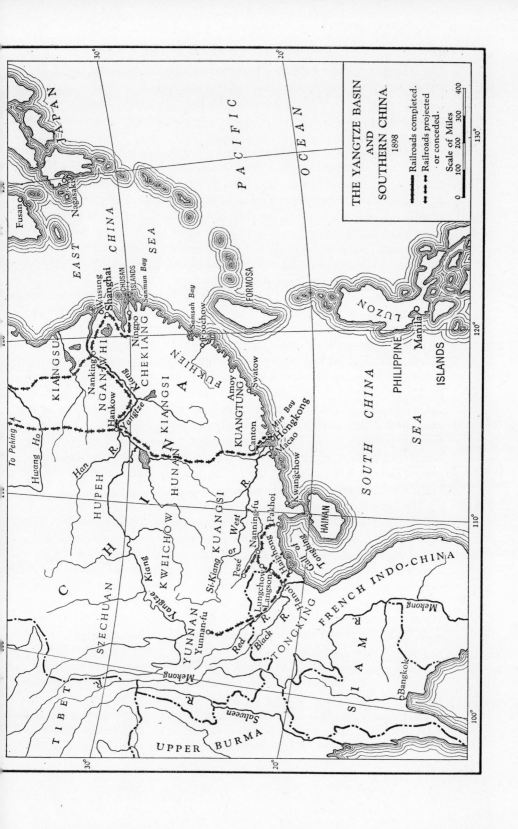

THE YANGTZE BASIN
AND
SOUTHERN CHINA.
1898

━━━━ Railroads completed.
╍╍╍ Railroads projected
 or conceded.

Scale of Miles
0   100 200 300 400

tion whatever that the English government would have opposed to the utmost any cession of territory or any system of economic privilege in these areas which might have injured the British position. This was *the* great Chinese market, the preservation of which was regarded by many Englishmen as almost a matter of life and death.

The Germans were at a great disadvantage in dealing with the Chinese situation. Their commercial interests were second only to those of Britain, but they had no territorial contact, no base from which to operate a policy of peaceful penetration. Even when they decided to build up their fleet the problem was brought no nearer a solution, for they had no Far Eastern base for this fleet. They were dependent for coal and repairs upon the docks at Hongkong. In other words, their position in the Far East was more or less at the mercy of England. So the Germans took Kiao-chow, after having scrupulously considered the merits of other ports and after having tried to secure the friendly approval of the Russians. It is certainly an exaggeration to claim, as M. Witte does in his memoirs, that the Germans started the scramble for Chinese territory. On the other hand, it will not do to minimize the significance of Germany's action, as Mr. Joseph for example does, in his *Foreign Diplomacy in China*. Russia, France and England had been pushing forward into Chinese territory with a policy of concessions. But it was a very different thing to take or lease a port on the Chinese coast. The German attack, one might say, was a frontal attack. Only the action of England in securing Hongkong many years earlier can be compared to it. At the time this was generally realized, particularly in Britain. The English public was rabid about the German action, and if the government acquiesced without much protest, it was because of larger considerations of general politics and because of the feeling that Germany might be used as a buffer against Russia.

The German occupation of Kiao-chow unquestionably precipitated the Russian action at Talienwan and Port Arthur, the special contribution of Muraviev and the Tsar to the development of the Far Eastern situation. As one looks back on this move it is hard to escape the conviction that Witte's policy was right and Muraviev's was wrong. Had Russia continued her policy of peaceful penetration, had she made even a show of helping the Chinese against the German demands, her position would have been stronger than ever. As it was Muraviev effected a clear break with the Witte policy, he wrecked the good understanding with China, he placed himself in a position where he had to make concessions to Japan in Korea, and he drew upon himself the heavy burden of British opposition. One must be fair, of course. The British policy in the matter of the Chinese loan was incredibly clumsy. Balfour had announced that the British had no objection to Russia's securing a commercial outlet, while Curzon had made it clear that Russia was not to aspire to such an outlet in Korea. What was there left? The only ice-free commercial harbor on the Yellow Sea coast of China was Talienwan. When the British demanded that this port should be made a treaty port, they were, clearly, trying to secure treaty rights there before the Russians could establish themselves. The motive was correct enough, but from the tactical standpoint it was a challenge. A port with a wide open door and with equal opportunities for all may have been a British or a German ideal, but it wasn't a French ideal, much less a Russian, for these powers simply could not compete with Britain and Germany on equal terms. The Russians therefore fought the British demands tooth and nail. The French and the Germans stood behind them. The British would not fight. In fact their squadron in the Far East was barely superior to the Russian, to say nothing of the French and German contingents.[69] In the end they had to let the Russians win. Talienwan was leased, and Port Arthur too. The latter was the " helmet and shield " of the former, to quote the phrase of William T. Stead. The commercial port was unprotected without the naval fortress. Knowing as they did that the Russians were determined to have both, the English government made an obvious mistake in lodging more protests.

But the taking of Weihaiwei was perhaps an even greater mistake. The place was of little value. Its harbor was not deep enough for large ships, it was expensive to fortify, and it was cut off from the hinterland by a range of high hills.[70] The English had to commit themselves to support Japanese aspirations in order to get Weihaiwei, and they had to give the Germans assurances that they would never do anything with the place that was worth doing. In other words they assumed a liability instead of securing an asset. Not only that, they placed themselves opposite the Russians at Port Arthur, thus taking the vanguard in opposition to the Russian policy. The Germans were delighted to have the British act as a wedge between themselves and the Russians. Germany, Bülow told the Reichstag on April 29, had no objection if Russia and England watched the play of the waves in the Gulf of Pechili from their respective windows.

What was worse yet was the abandonment of Britain's traditional policy of respecting the integrity of the Chinese Empire, a policy which had just been reaffirmed by the resolution of the house of commons on March 1. If Germany, Russia and France were following a criminal policy, Britain, having protested, now decided to join the criminals. This did her position in China no good, while it weakened her in relation to other powers. Furthermore, every new concession extorted from China made the scramble more general. France joined, and it was merely a matter of time before Japan and other nations would put forward their demands. It is a mistake to call in Beelzebub to fight Satan. It was all well and good to talk, as all the powers did, of the need for preserving the integrity of the Chinese Empire. It was all well and good to maintain that the leases taken in the spring of 1898 left Chinese sovereignty untouched. This was mere camouflage

---

[69] Brassey: *Naval Annual,* 1898, pp. 59–60; " Naval Squadrons in the Far East " (London *Times,* March 28, 1898).

[70] See, e.g., Anonymous: " Wei-hai-wei: Its Value as a Naval Station " (*Blackwood's Magazine,* June, 1899).

and the statesmen knew it. Nothing is to be gained by cynicism of this kind. The plain facts were that in 1898 China, unless she could rouse herself, was doomed. Her break-up and partition among the powers had begun. It was a calamity for the British, who could find not a single power to stand by them. So they jumped from the frying pan into the fire.

BIBLIOGRAPHICAL NOTE

(SUPPLEMENTARY TO THE BIBLIOGRAPHY OF CHAPTER VIII)

DOCUMENTARY SOURCES

Accounts and Papers. 1898, volume CV: *China No. 1 (1898).* An important and rather full collection of papers on the Kiao-chow and Port Arthur episodes.

British Documents on the Origins of the War, 1898–1914. Edited by G. P. Gooch and Harold Temperley. London, 1927—. Important chiefly for the documents bearing on Anglo-Russian negotiations. The documents on the Chinese situation do not add greatly to the material in *China No. 1.*

Die Grosse Politik der Europäischen Kabinette, 1871–1914. Volume XIV, part I. Contains a large number of documents on the background and negotiations concerning the German occupation of Kiao-chow.

TELESHEV, L.: " Vil'gel'm II o Zaniatii Tsarskoi Rossiei Port Artura." (*Krasnyi Arkhiv,* LVIII, 1933, pp. 150–5). Three reports by Osten-Sacken of conversations with William II in the winter of 1897–1898.

POPOV, A.: "Pervyie Shagi Russkogo Imperializma na Dal'nem Vostoke." (*Krasnyi Arkhiv,* LII, 1932, pp. 34–124). Contains the text of the famous Muraviev memorandum of November 23, 1897.

MEMOIRS, AUTOBIOGRAPHIES, BIOGRAPHIES, AND LETTERS

HOHENLOHE, FÜRST CHLODWIG ZU: *Denkwürdigkeiten der Reichskanzlerzeit.* Stuttgart, 1931. Contains a few notes of interest on German policy in the Far East and especially touching on Kiao-chow.

BÜLOW, PRINCE VON: *Memoirs.* Four volumes. Boston, 1931–1932. The first volume of Bülow's memoirs has some discussion of the Kiao-chow episode, but adds relatively little.

TIRPITZ, ALFRED VON: *My Memoirs.* Two volumes. New York, 1919. The admiral gives a detailed account of his command in the Far East in 1896–1897 and of the preparations for the occupation of Kiao-chow.

HEYKING, ELISABETH VON: *Tagebücher aus vier Weltteilen, 1886–1904.* Fourth edition. Leipzig, 1926. Fascinating and instructive diaries of the wife of the German minister at Peking. A valuable source.

GARVIN, J. L.: *The Life of Joseph Chamberlain.* Three volumes. London, 1933—. Not as valuable as one might expect.

RONALDSHAY, EARL OF: *The Life of Lord Curzon.* Three volumes. London, 1928. The authoritative biography of Curzon, who in 1898 was undersecretary for foreign affairs. Contains a few interesting letters and memoranda.

MEYENDORFF, ALEXANDRE: *Correspondance Diplomatique de M. de Staal, 1884–1900.* Two volumes. Paris, 1929. Very disappointing. Contains little of value.

MASANORI, ITO: *Kato Takaaki.* Two volumes. Tokyo, 1929. The biography and papers of the Japanese minister to England. Contains much on the problem of an Anglo-Japanese alliance.

HIRATSUKA, ATSUSHI: *Ito Hirobumi Hiroku.* Tokyo, 1931. Diplomatic papers of the Japanese premier. Valuable as a reflection of the views of the school of statesmen who favored an agreement with Russia.

POOLEY, A. M.: *The Secret Memoirs of Count Tadasu Hayashi.* New York, 1915. Still one of the best sources from the Japanese side, but rather slight on this period.

SCHELKING, E. DE: *Recollections of a Russian Diplomat.* New York, 1918. The author was attached to the Russian embassy in Berlin. His book is sensational and unreliable. A source to be avoided.

SPECIAL STUDIES

IRMER, ARTHUR JULIUS: *Die Erwerbung von Kiautschou, 1894–1898.* Cologne, 1930. The best monograph on the subject, digesting not only the German documents, but also some unpublished correspondence of Tirpitz.

—: *Kiautschou. Die Diplomatische Vorbereitung der Erwerbung.* Cologne, 1932. This is the same as the preceding title, with a few minor changes. The documentation is omitted and some pictures added.

ROLOFF, GUSTAV: "Die Erwerbung von Kiautschou." (*Preussische Jahrbücher,* June, 1918, pp. 348–54). Now out of date. Primarily a summary of the revelations in Hayashi and a few other books.

BECKER, WILLY: "Die Deutsch-Russische Krise bei der Erwerbung von Kiautschou." (*Zeitschrift für Politik,* XV, 1925, pp. 58–71). A careful survey, based chiefly on the German documents. Now superseded by Irmer.

POPOV, A.: "Anglo-Russkoe Soglashenie o Razdele Kitaiia, 1899 g." (*Krasnyi Arkhiv,* XXV, 1927, pp. 110–34). Based upon Russian archive material. An important supplement to the British documents.

GRIMM, CLAUS: *Graf Witte und die Deutsche Politik*. Freiburg, 1930. A doctoral dissertation, based upon Russian material, but adding little to the German documents and the Witte memoirs.

PROWASECK, HILDE: *Der Gedanke einer Kontinentalliga gegen England unter Wilhelm II*. Leipzig, 1928. A doctoral thesis of very little value. Hardly more than a summary of the material in the German documents.

ASAKAWA, K.: *The Russo-Japanese Conflict*. Boston, 1904. Still the best account of these critical years as seen from the Japanese side. A careful, moderate and helpful book.

KLEIN, ALFRED: *Der Einfluss des Grafen Witte auf die Deutsch-Russischen Beziehungen*. Münster, 1931. Makes no use of Russian materials and adds very little.

HSIA, CHING-LIN: *Studies in Chinese Diplomatic History*. Shanghai, 1924. A collection of essays on concessions, leased territories, spheres of influence, etc., with reference to the international law of the subject.

CHANG, CHUNG-FU: *The Anglo-Japanese Alliance*. Baltimore, 1931. The best book on the subject, but has little to say on this period.

RICHTHOFEN, FERDINAND, FREIHERRR VON: " Kiautschou, seine Weltstellung und Voraussichtliche Bedeutung." (*Preussische Jahrbücher,* January, 1898, pp. 167–91). Written by the most eminent authority on the geography of China, this is a compact and in every way excellent study of the importance and prospects of the German acquisition.

FRANZIUS, GEORG: *Kiautschou*. Seventh edition. Berlin, 1900. The author, who investigated the Bay of Kiao-chow for the German government in 1897, gives a detailed general survey of the territory.

MADROLLE, CLAUDIUS: " Kouang-Tchéou, Sancian, Hainan." (*Questions Diplomatiques et Coloniales,* May 1, 1898, pp. 6–12). A concise account of the French activities and the taking of Kuang-chow; written by a prominent French explorer.

SILVESTRE, J.: " La France à Kouang-Tchéou-Ouan." (*Annales des Sciences Politiques,* July 15, 1902, pp. 473–93). Perhaps the best study of the French policy that led to the occupation.

BONNINGUE, ALFRED: *La France à Kouang-Tchéou-Wan*. Paris, 1931. Not of much account. Chiefly a survey of the station and a review of the administration.

HOYNINGEN GENANNT HUENE, HEINRICH, FREIHERR VON: *Untersuchungen zur Geschichte des Deutsch-Englischen Bündnisproblems, 1898–1901*. Breslau, 1934. The first part of this book is an analysis of the Far Eastern crisis of 1898, based upon the Romanov book and upon some of the other Russian material. It is one of the best accounts available.

BEE, BENJAMIN MING-CHU: *The Leasing of Kiaochow*. Cambridge, 1935. This is an unpublished doctoral dissertation submitted at Harvard, which the author has been kind enough to let me use. It goes over the western materials thoroughly and draws upon recently published Chinese sources. Of these latter the most important seem to be:

1. *Ching-chi wai-chiao shih-liao.* Edited by Wang T'ao-fu and Wang Hsi-yin. Peiping, 1932 ff. A collection of Decrees, Instructions, Reports, etc., for the years 1875–1911.

2. Chang Chih-tung: *Chang Wên-hsiang-kung chi.* Peking, 1919–1921. The works of the viceroy of Liang-hu.

3. Hsü Ching-ch'eng: *Hsü Wên-hsü-kung i-kao.* Peking, 1918. Valuable papers of the Chinese representative at St. Petersburg and Berlin.

4. Wêng T'ung-ho: *Wêng Wên-kung-kung jih-chi.* Shanghai, 1925. Important diaries of a member of the Tsungli Yamen.

5. *Ch'ing-shih-kao.* Edited by Chao Erh-sun. Peiping, 1929. A dynastic history of considerable source value.

XV

The Anglo-German Negotiations

ᧁ

THE EVENTS OF THE WINTER OF 1897–1898 IN THE FAR EAST CAUSED something akin to panic in England, where public opinion had a keen sense of the danger of losing part of the Chinese market. Rarely was the political world so united behind the government as in January 1898 when Mr. Balfour enunciated the guiding principles of the government's Chinese policy. But two months later almost everyone was disillusioned. The Russians, so far as one could determine, had been successful all along the line, while the British government, despite its brave utterances, had yielded on all essentials and had sacrificed even the fundamental principle of maintaining the independence and integrity of the Celestial Empire. The press was almost unanimous in its criticism and condemnation of Salisbury's conduct of affairs, and when he went on vacation in March it was generally assumed that he would never again take up the dual burden of the premiership and the foreign office. Every sort of charge was brought against him — accusations of vacillation, pusillanimity and loss of nerve, together with cynical remarks about the famous policy of "amicable understanding" and "graceful concession." Even the supporters of the government, notably the Unionist element, joined in the general indignation. Salisbury received the brunt of the attack, but his associates, "Port Arthur Balfour" and "Cocksure Curzon," were not let off easily. It was the general opinion that the British handling of the situation had been "a triumph of diplomatic incompetency," and that there was not much to choose between the helplessness and weakness of the Chinese and British governments. "A sadder and sorrier attempt to steer a ship of State through the waters of which every sandbank was distinctly marked on the charts and every rocky headland clearly denoted by a lighthouse it would be hard to find even in the histories of the States which have already declined," wrote one of the ablest and sharpest of the government's critics.[1]

According to the fault-finders the government had talked big and acted little.

---

[1] Anonymous: "The Failure of our Foreign Policy" (*Contemporary Review*, April, 1898, pp. 457–80), p. 462. See also Diplomaticus: "Where Lord Salisbury has Failed" (*Fortnightly Review*, April, 1898, pp. 513–23); Idem: "The Breakdown of our Chinese Policy" (ibid., May, 1898, pp. 844–54); Anonymous: "Lord Salisbury and the Far East" (ibid., June, 1898, pp. 1029–38); A. Michie: "Our Future Policy in China" (*National Review*, July, 1898, pp. 654–70); W. T. Stead: "Russia and Mr. Chamberlain's Long Spoon" (*Contemporary Review*, June, 1898, pp. 761–77).

It had withdrawn the British ships from Port Arthur at the " demand " of the Russian government, it had abandoned the proposal that Talienwan be made a treaty port because of the Russian " threats," it had dickered with Muraviev for assurances about Talienwan and Port Arthur and had allowed itself to be put off by equivocal and variable promises, and it had crowned the whole policy of ineptitude by taking Weihaiwei (renamed Woe! Woe! Woe!), thereby scrapping the sacred principle of Chinese integrity.

Balfour had a very hard time trying to answer these objections. Twice he rose in the house of commons to defend the government's policy, on April 5 and on April 29, that is, before and after publication of the Blue Book. He admitted the " considerable anxiety " not to say " irritable anxiety " of the country and tried to explain the situation by stressing the " entirely new political phenomena " that had resulted from the " extraordinary," almost " unaccountable weakness of China." But at the same time he insisted that the British ships had not been withdrawn from Port Arthur because of Russian pressure. He denied that he had ever " invited " the Russian government to take Port Arthur, or that the British cabinet had ever intended Russia to have more than a " commercial " port. The objection to the lease of Port Arthur was simply that it would constitute a perpetual threat at the Chinese capital, as the Russians had themselves pointed out to Japan in 1895. Russia had a great and inevitable influence at Peking because of her four thousand miles of land frontier. It was intolerable, therefore, that she should control the sea approaches as well. But Port Arthur was not worth a war and so the government had decided to re-establish the balance of power in the Gulf of Pechili by occupying Weihaiwei, which, to be sure, was not as strong as Port Arthur, but which would serve the purpose. As for the rest, there was no good ground for attacking the government. Russia's railroad policy in Manchuria was one to which England need take no exception, as it would help to open up the whole area to British trade, despite any special duties that might be levied. Furthermore, no British treaty rights had been violated. The Russian government had promised that they should not be in any way infringed. Besides, there were the concessions obtained by the British government, the opening of new treaty ports, the opening of the rivers to foreign trade, the promise that the director of the customs should be an Englishman as long as British trade exceeded that of other nations, and the promise not to alienate territory in the Yangtze Basin.[2]

The speech was admittedly a good one, but it did not satisfy the opposition. Eminent speakers like Harcourt, Dilke, Grey and Beresford upheld their previous criticisms. " The measures adopted were maladroit, and the retreat consequently has been undignified. Proposals of an irritating character were advanced, and they were withdrawn under menace." The action of the government had been a " record of continual failure at every point," declared Harcourt.[3] What-

---

[2] Hansard: *Parliamentary Debates*, Series IV, vol. LVI, pp. 224 ff., 1581 ff.
[3] Hansard, LVI, pp. 1560 ff., especially pp. 1569, 1579.

ever the government might say it was clear that the ships had been recalled from Port Arthur because of Russian protests. The whole Port Arthur occupation had been precipitated by the ill-timed demand for the opening of Talienwan. Weihaiwei was of little value, and was certainly not worth the sacrifice of Britain's traditional policy. As for the assurances and concessions obtained, those of Russia were of little use, and would be thrown into the discard whenever convenient. "I would not believe in any assurances Russia might give to this country if they were twenty fathoms long," declared Beresford. The concessions granted by China were all right so far as they went. But there was always the objection that the assurance not to alienate territory in the Yangtze Basin might give the impression that England was reserving this as her sphere and was withdrawing from her rights in the rest of China. The bald fact was that Manchuria was lost to all intents and purposes. Already there had arisen the spectre of Russia training fifty to sixty thousand Manchus and using them to overrun northern and central China.[4]

Under the fire of strong criticism the British government, constantly prodded by the China Association, the London Chamber of Commerce and kindred organizations, began to take a stronger line in its dealings with China. In the months following the crisis it entered frankly upon the race for concessions. To counterbalance the French advance in south China, it secured from the Tsungli Yamen, on June 9, a ninety-nine year lease of the territory on the mainland opposite Hongkong, from Deep Bay to Mirs Bay, thus increasing about eightfold its territorial holding at the mouth of the West River. At the same time efforts were made to open up more and more towns to foreign trade (notably Nanning-fu, to which the French planned to build a railway), to regulate internal navigation, and so on. The greatest activity of the powers during the year 1898 was, however, concentrated on the matter of railroad and mining concessions. The question of communications seemed to be the key to the whole future development of the Chinese situation. This is certainly not the place to go into the details of the many and complicated negotiations carried on by the British and other governments. The Blue Book contains nearly five hundred documents bearing almost exclusively on concessions of this kind in the period from April 1898 to January 1899. Suffice it to say that the British policy aimed directly at the recognition by the Chinese and other governments of the Yangtze Valley as a British sphere, in which British interests should be given the first opportunity in the construction of railroads and the exploitation of natural resources. Recapitulating what had been done, the English minister to Peking was able to write in November 1898: "Not a single *bona fide* or approximately practical scheme which has been brought to this Legation has failed to be put through. Every single *bona fide* complaint from the Treaty ports has been looked into and settled." Specifically this meant that the British had secured nine concessions for railroads, totalling twenty-eight hundred miles. Next came the Rus-

---

[4] Hansard, LVI, pp. 284, 1669, 1674.

sians with three concessions totalling fifteen hundred miles; the Germans, with two concessions of seven hundred and twenty miles; the Belgians, with one concession of six hundred and fifty miles; the French, with three concessions of four hundred and twenty miles; the Americans with one concession of three hundred miles. Together with German interests the Hongkong and Shanghai Bank was to construct the important Tientsin-Chinkiang line, which, it was hoped, would compete successfully with the Belgian Peking-Hankow line. Furthermore, British interests were to build the Shanghai-Nanking railway, and it was hoped that an arrangement could be made with the American concessionaires to share in the Hankow-Canton line. The extension of the Burma railroad system toward the upper Yangtze was also envisaged. Mining rights had been secured by the Peking Syndicate in the provinces of Shansi, Hunan and Chekiang. Sir Claude MacDonald was speaking the plain truth when he remarked that England had not come out second best.[5]

But a more vigorous policy in dealing with the Chinese situation did not entirely meet the needs of the moment. What impressed many critics of the government's policy was the inability of the British to enlist the aid of other nations in support of the policy of the status quo in China.

"Never before in this century, at least, has the British Empire been in such serious danger as today, despite the frequent boast that our means of defence are most efficient and the absolute certainty that our Government not only disposes of an overwhelming majority in Parliament, but has a united people outside at its beck and call, ready and even anxious to lend it every conceivable assistance," wrote one of the ablest commentators. "Great Britain, the very essence of whose existence is foreign commerce, is being gradually ousted out of the neutral markets of the world; her political prestige has so completely disappeared that, whenever her Government ' puts its foot down,' foreigners laugh and tell us truly that the attitude is assumed the better to spring backwards; territory purchased with the life blood of her best men is being frittered away in ' graceful concessions ' leading to further losses, and now even the very conditions essential to commercial expansion are being deliberately and systematically destroyed by our pushing rivals . . ." " It is hardly too much to say that since the days of Charles II foreign states have never treated the rights and interests of Great Britain with less consideration and more studied disrespect." " There is not a serious politician on the Continent of Europe who believes that our present Government will risk a war, however great the provocation." [6]

As a matter of fact this aspect of the situation had occupied the government more than any outside contemporary could know. There is still but little material available to enlighten us about the discussions which took place in a series

---

[5] *China No. 1 (1899)*, nos. 295, 459. The details may be read in this voluminous collection of documents. Among the secondary accounts the reader may consult Joseph: *Foreign Diplomacy in China*, chaps. xii–xiv, passim; McCordock: *British Far Eastern Policy*, chap. iv, passim.

[6] Anonymous: "The Failure of our Foreign Policy" (*Contemporary Review*, April, 1898, pp. 457–80), especially pp. 457, 471, 477.

of important cabinet meetings during the last ten days of March. The British documents thus far published are silent on the matter, and of the authorized biographies not even Garvin's *Chamberlain* is of much help. All we can do, then, is to piece together what scraps of evidence may be gleaned from divers sources. This much we know, that various solutions were discussed. Balfour, speaking in the house of commons on April 29, lifted the curtain to a certain extent. Defending the occupation of Weihaiwei, he asked the question whether the Russians could have been prevented from taking Port Arthur. His answer was affirmative but qualified:

"It would have been, I believe, perfectly possible for us to do so," he maintained. "I believe it is extremely probable that if we had sent our Fleet to Port Arthur and occupied the port Russia would not have made it a *casus belli*. There is no certainty about it. It might have involved us and Russia, and by a not unnatural consequence the whole of the civilised world in arms, and, for my part, I would never consent to take part in a game of bluff, which may have consequences like that unless I am prepared to face those consequences. I do not think we should have been wise to engage, and I do not believe anybody in this House would have the courage to say we ought to have engaged in a European war in order to prevent the Russians from going to Port Arthur."

But, he continued, even if the Russians had not gone to war, where would England be? She would have had to hold Port Arthur with large forces and to fortify it to the hilt. Relations with Russia would have been strained to the breaking point. Russia would have employed all her efforts to get Britain involved in war elsewhere. In the meanwhile the Russian railroad would be creeping southward, and nothing would be able to stop it.[7]

This revelation of Balfour's is supported by the evidence contained in Curzon's biography and by statements which Chamberlain made to the German ambassador. We know that the suggestion to lease Weihaiwei was at first opposed by all influential members of the cabinet — Balfour, Chamberlain, Goschen, the Duke of Devonshire, Lansdowne and Hicks Beach, and that it was only after five cabinet meetings that the proposal was finally adopted. In the meanwhile the British fleet was ordered to leave Hongkong and steam north, probably with instructions to await further orders. According to Chamberlain it was discovered that there was a height near Talienwan from which Port Arthur could be completely dominated.[8]

But, in the end, the cabinet decided that Port Arthur was not worth the chance of war. Balfour went over to the Weihaiwei project and Salisbury approved the decision. Then there arose the further question, how could Russia be prevented from advancing yet further in the months or years to come? The British were convinced that before long the Russians would throw the mantle of

---

[7] Hansard, LVI, pp. 1592–4.
[8] Ronaldshay: *Life of Curzon*, I, pp. 284–5; *Letters of Queen Victoria*, III, p. 238; *Die Grosse Politik*, XIV, no. 3782.

their influence over the Peking government and gradually smother it. Anxiety on this point speaks out of all the critical writing and out of all the debates in parliament. After all, the negotiations with Russia had shown that the Tsar's government was unwilling to draw even an imaginary line to define the limits of its aspirations.

In the Near East the British had always been able to check Russian expansion by drawing upon the support of Austria and Italy. Who would perform the same service in the Far East? Chamberlain, who took the Far Eastern crisis more seriously than any of his colleagues and who had already become convinced that isolation was more dangerous than profitable, was very intent on developing a close friendship with the United States. He had harbored the phantastic notion that the great Republic might be induced to co-operate with England in the Near Eastern crisis, and it was therefore natural that he should have thought first of America in connexion with the Far East, where American interests were considerable and well recognized. It must be admitted that there was some ground for hoping that the Americans would play an active part. The occupation of Kiao-chow had called forth a storm of protest in the American press, which accused Germany of " land-grabbing propensities " and described the Kiao-chow episode as a " piratical seizure." In December 1897 the *New York Times* had gone so far as to declare: " Our interest in the cutting up of China is that the British lion shall get his share." The United States and Britain should collaborate in keeping the door open. Alfred Austin was apparently expressing a feeling widespread on both sides of the Atlantic when he published, on March 29, 1898, his poem, *A Voice from the West,* which read in part:

> " Yes, this is the voice of the bluff March gale;
> We severed have been too long;
> But now we have done with a worn-out tale —
> The tale of an ancient wrong —
> And our friendship shall last as love doth last
> And be stronger than death is strong."

To all appearances the blood-brothership of America and Britain was in the air.[9]

Chamberlain was by no means the only statesman of note who favored an Anglo-Saxon understanding. Leaders of both parties, from Salisbury and Balfour to Rosebery and the other Liberal Imperialists, were convinced protagonists of the idea. The American ambassador at London, John Hay, and his first secretary, Henry White, were hand in glove with these men. At home President McKinley, Senator Lodge, Richard Olney, Whitelaw Reid, Theodore Roosevelt, Admiral Mahan, Lyman Abbott and many other influential men expressed themselves favorably. The New York press threw its weight on the same side of the scales. On the side of Britain this unprecedented outburst of affection was

---

[9] Bertha A. Reuter: *Anglo-American Relations during the Spanish-American War* (New York, 1924), pp. 74–6, 118 ff.; Clara E. Schieber: *American Sentiment toward Germany, 1870–1914* (Boston, 1923), chap. iii, passim.

due in part to the rapidly spreading cult of race solidarity, in part to the international exigencies of the moment. On the American side the approaching war with Spain was certainly a decisive factor. Henry White was surprised to find that even the most rabid English-baiters among the senators had suddenly become converted to the new gospel. American friendliness was, if we may adopt the phrase of White's biographer, "the friendliness of a country shivering a little to find herself out in the great arena of world affairs, feeling the chill hostility of all the continental nations, and glad for once to meet John Bull halfway." [10]

But all this "billing and cooing," which the hostile *Saturday Review* (April 30, 1898) condemned as "indecent humbug," never got far beyond the domain of sentiment. There was really little prospect that the United States would give up her freedom from "entangling alliances" and join forces with Britain. Even the most enthusiastic supporters of close relations were disposed to think that an alliance was impossible. They therefore declared it unnecessary. Only Chamberlain, whatever he may have said later, cherished hopes of real collaboration. In the preceding chapter mention has been made of his approaches to the American government in the early days of March, and of the evasion which was the only reply. At bottom the United States, which had generally maintained very cordial relations with Russia, had no idea of entering the lists against the Muscovite advance. The oncoming Spanish War was, in the crucial first months of 1898, absorbing all the public attention on this side of the ocean. [11]

Next to the United States Chamberlain would have preferred an understanding if not an alliance with Japan, which, after all, had the same interest as Britain in preventing China from becoming a Russian protectorate. There was, in England, a considerable body of opinion in favor of such a combination and there is no reason to suppose that if an understanding had been consummated it would have aroused much opposition. At any rate, Chamberlain does not seem to have had any apprehensions in the matter. He boldly approached Baron Kato, as we have seen. If Kato had had his way the proposal would have been followed up. In Tokyo a number of the younger statesmen, like Count Hayashi, were very well disposed. But Count Ito and the Elder Statesmen were circumspect. They felt that Japan would have to bear the brunt of the conflict and that she was not yet sufficiently prepared. No move was made to negotiate with the English. On the contrary every effort was bent to the attainment of a settlement

---

[10] Allan Nevins: *Henry White* (New York, 1930), pp. 129–35. See further William R. Thayer: *The Life and Letters of John Hay* (Boston, 1915), II, pp. 165 ff.; Tyler Dennett: *John Hay* (New York, 1933), pp. 188–9, etc.; Garvin: *Life of Chamberlain*, III, chaps. liii and lx. Of contemporary writings see especially Sir Charles Dilke: "The Future Relations of Great Britain and the United States" (*Forum*, January, 1898, pp. 521–8); Richard Olney: "The International Isolation of the United States" (*Atlantic Monthly*, May, 1898, pp. 577–88); and the very large body of opinion collected by the English *Review of Reviews*, June, 1898, pp. 602 ff.

[11] On Russian-American relations see P. Kelyin: "Severo-Amerikanskie Soedinennie Shtati i Tsarkaia Rossiia v 90 gg. XIX v." (*Krasnyi Arkhiv*, LII, pp. 124–42).

with Russia. Apparently even the inconclusive Nishi-Rosen agreement was preferred to the prospect of an alliance with Britain.[12]

Of the remaining powers directly interested in the Far East only Germany could be considered as a possible ally. Relations between England and Germany had not been good. In fact public opinion in both countries had rarely been so wrought up as in the autumn of 1897. There was friction, too, between the governments, for the Germans were constantly pressing for a favorable settlement of disputed questions in Togoland, Samoa and elsewhere.[13] The British government showed no disposition to make concessions, but was, nevertheless, very careful not to identify itself with the popular animosity. It was a time when England had enough troubles without incurring unnecessary hostility. Steps were taken to moderate the tone of the press, and the London editors who, it was always said, could not be influenced, responded most readily to the hint from high quarters.[14] On the German side there was the same desire not to push matters too far. A breach with England was a thing that the foreign office was most anxious to avoid. England's acceptance of the German occupation of Kiaochow was a striking contrast to the desperate opposition of Muraviev. It helped to instill something like cordiality into the relations of the two countries and at the same time served to make the German Emperor realize the futility of the continental league. The Berlin government was bound to conclude that in the Far East Germany's interest and that of Britain were more nearly alike than the interests of Germany and Russia. During the winter the general tone of Anglo-German relations underwent a marked change for the better. Even the Emperor, while still complaining that all his advances had been rejected, was taking an attitude of aggrievement and regret rather than an attitude of anger and defiance.[15]

It was evidently this perceptible change in Anglo-German relations that decided the London cabinet to try for an agreement with Germany. The decision appears to have been reached in the crucial cabinet meeting on March 25, 1898, when the whole question of British action in reply to the occupation of Port Arthur was discussed. We know that on that day Balfour lunched with the German ambassador, after which he called upon Lord Salisbury, who was about to leave for the Continent the next day at eleven. The cabinet met at about three-thirty and remained in session until seven in the evening, all the leading members being present.[16]

It is quite important to bear these details in mind, for the impending negotia-

---

[12] In addition to what has been said in the preceding chapter, see Sir Ellis Ashmead Bartlett's account of his conversation with a Japanese statesman, evidently Baron Kato (Hansard, LVI, pp. 1672–3), and the statements of Chamberlain to the German ambassador (*Die Grosse Politik*, XIV, nos. 3782, 3789).   [13] Garvin: *Life of Chamberlain*, III, pp. 245–7.

[14] *Letters of Queen Victoria*, III, pp. 224–5.

[15] *British Documents*, I, no. 63; MacDiarmid: *Life of Grierson*, pp. 134–6.

[16] *Letters of Queen Victoria*, III, p. 238; *Die Grosse Politik*, XIV, no. 3781. The visit of Balfour to Salisbury is reported in the *Times*, March 26, 1898, p. 7. Salisbury was unable to leave London on account of a very severe storm. He departed for the Continent on March 28.

tions with Germany have been made the subject of an extraordinary amount of critical writing, and the question has been raised again and again whether Lord Salisbury was a party to the policy. It cannot be proved that Balfour and Salisbury discussed the projected understanding with Germany, or that the matter was taken up in the cabinet meeting of March 25, when it was decided not to go the limit in opposing the Russian action. But it would certainly be strange if the matter was not brought up. What evidence we possess would indicate that it was. When Balfour lunched with Hatzfeldt he clearly did not yet have a mandate from the cabinet, though he may have already gone over the question with Salisbury. His remarks were of a general nature. He expressed the desire for better relations between England and Germany, pointing out that the two nations had no great conflicting interests. Hatzfeldt, who had no instructions, made a cordial if evasive reply, taking the opportunity, however, to bring up once more the German grievances touching African affairs and German desires in Shantung. The whole conversation was obviously intended as a reconnaissance, and it ended with Balfour's expression of the hope that Hatzfeldt would soon look him up.[17]

Four days later the ambassador had a long, informal and very frank talk with Chamberlain, who acted as the chief British negotiator throughout the forthcoming discussions. This is in itself surprising, for Balfour, not Chamberlain, was acting foreign minister in Salisbury's absence. It has been thought by some German writers that the colonial secretary was working on his own and that his proposals were at best nothing more than personal advances. That there is no foundation for such a surmise has been conclusively shown by the recently published biography of Chamberlain. It is perfectly clear that not only Salisbury and Balfour, but other cabinet members, like the Duke of Devonshire, desired a closer connexion with Germany. They were, perhaps, less sanguine and less ready to go all the way to an alliance, but they sympathized with the effort. Chamberlain apparently carried on the conversations because he was, next to Salisbury, the most influential member of the government, because he was most impressed with the danger in the Far East and because his Unionist followers were most dissatisfied with the policy of Salisbury in the preceding few months. The Unionists had, in fact, formed a " Committee to Promote a Policy of Resistance to the Ascendency of Russia and other Foreign Powers in China," and this committee, composed of members of parliament, had passed a resolution on March 24 " that the doors through which our trade in China must pass should be kept open at the risk of war." [18] This helps to explain Chamberlain's strong line in the cabinet on March 25 and his determination to do something to prevent further gains by Russia. At the time there was much talk of a split in the cabinet. The *Saturday Review* went so far as to speak of a " fierce fight." [19] That

[17] *Die Grosse Politik*, XIV, nos. 3782, 3788.   [18] London *Times*, March 24, 25, 1898.
[19] *Saturday Review*, February 26, 1898; Gardiner: *Life of Harcourt*, II, pp. 450–1; Elliot: *Life of Goschen*, II, pp. 219 ff.

was overshooting the mark. Salisbury and Chamberlain did not see eye to eye, especially in the Far Eastern business. Weeks before the critical days of March the colonial secretary had confessed to a friend that he had had " a strong difference of opinion with Lord Salisbury." [20] But despite all this the two men were far more tolerant of each other than one would have thought possible. Hatzfeldt and other diplomats surely exaggerated the disagreement in the cabinet. We now know that Chamberlain informed Balfour and the cabinet promptly of what passed between him and Hatzfeldt, and that he laid the whole matter before Lord Salisbury immediately on the latter's return on April 29. It is senseless, then, to try to make out that Chamberlain was playing a lone hand.[21]

The colonial secretary was by nature a business man. He had no professional training as a diplomat and was apt to approach problems of international relations too directly, too bluntly, and rather with the idea that anything could be had for a price. German support was needed for a particular purpose. Bids were to be made, and if they were found satisfactory the " deal " could be closed. Unmindful of Talleyrand's famous saying that language was given men to enable them to conceal their thoughts, Chamberlain scorned circumlocutions and went straight to the point.[22]

For more than a decade after the publication of the German documents we had no other source than that for the story of the Chamberlain-Hatzfeldt conversations. Now at last we have, in Garvin's *Life*, the memoranda of the British statesman, which enable us to check more closely the aims and arguments of both sides. In the first meeting, on March 29, there was some skirmishing and some talk of the identity of British and German interests on larger issues of world affairs. Hatzfeldt reported Chamberlain as saying that the world situation had taken a turn which made it impossible for England to maintain any longer her traditional policy of isolation. According to the British account the proposition was not so bald. The ambassador had remarked that the former community of interest and feeling had been wrecked by the Jameson episode and that " there was a general impression on the Continent that the policy of the United Kingdom was to bring about a war between other powers but to take no part in it herself," which tended to produce irritation and distrust. It was this that led Chamberlain to remark: " It is possible that the policy of the United Kingdom may be changed by circumstances which are too strong for us to resist." Thereupon the conversation turned to the question of an alliance. Hatzfeldt's version was that Chamberlain suggested that if Germany would stand on the side of England, England would stand on Germany's side if she were attacked. This

---

[20] January 29, 1898 (*Journals and Letters of Reginald Viscount Esher*, [London, 1934], I, pp. 210–1).

[21] See especially Garvin: *Life of Chamberlain*, III, pp. 256 ff.

[22] There is a rather interesting anonymous estimate of this side of Chamberlain, entitled " Mr. Chamberlain as Foreign Minister " (*Fortnightly Review*, August, 1898, pp. 317–25). I need hardly say that my estimate does not agree entirely with that of Mr. Garvin, though the latter has undoubtedly done much to put matters in a clearer setting.

would be the equivalent of England's joining the Triple Alliance, and could be arranged through a formal treaty. A decision should be reached within the next days. In Chamberlain's own record of the discussion there is no mention of the Triple Alliance, and nothing to suggest the need of haste. The suggestions as they emerged from the conversation were these: " That an alliance might be established by Treaty or Agreement between Germany and Great Britain for a term of years. That it should be of a defensive character based upon a mutual understanding as to policy in China and elsewhere." [23]

These two accounts do not differ in any fundamental respect, but it is worth noting the difference of emphasis. Hatzfeldt, even though he rather disliked and distrusted Chamberlain, was undoubtedly very favorable to an agreement with England. He reported to his government as forcefully as possible, making Chamberlain appear more positive than he really was and bringing in the Triple Alliance to make the prospective arrangement more attractive. Evidently he feared that the Berlin foreign office was too pro-Russian and that the advantages of the British connexion would not be duly considered. As a matter of fact, however, the foreign office showed more than a slight interest in the English advances and promptly outlined the conditions of an agreement. First and foremost, wrote Bülow, the alliance would have to be sanctioned by parliament, so that all British governments would be bound by it. Germany, he admitted, had a great interest in the preservation of British power, for if England were ruined, Russia and France would turn on Germany unmolested. It was a mistake, he pointed out, for England to become embroiled with Russia and France at the same time. The wise course would be to settle with the Russians, so that they would no longer support the French. France, on the other hand, would always back Russia, no matter what concessions were made to her. Having squared the Russians, then, the British would have no need to fear France, for if war broke out Germany would remain neutral and Italy, too, would stand by England. French troops would be tied up on the frontiers, while the British ruled the seas.

The Bülow reflections smack strongly of the Holstein reasoning. They dealt less with the problem of an Anglo-German agreement than with the ways and means for England to get herself out of an unenviable situation. Certainly they do not betray a very ardent desire for an immediate agreement. But Hatzfeldt communicated Bülow's ideas to Chamberlain at once, in a second meeting of the two men on April 1. He made rather far-reaching assurances respecting Germany's position and policy: " As regards Germany, their interest was against any policy which would materially cripple the sea-power of England. They knew perfectly well that in such a case they would be attacked next. Therefore, in no case would they join a combination against us. Treaty or no Treaty, the worst we had to anticipate from them was that they would remain neutral." Chamberlain on his side tried to dissipate all ideas that England would not remain true to any obligations she undertook. What he wanted, he said, was a

[23] *Die Grosse Politik*, XIV, nos. 3782, 3789; Garvin: *Life of Chamberlain*, III, pp. 259–60.

treaty which would be approved by parliament and made public. Turning then to the concrete purposes of the proposed agreement he stressed the fact that there was no thought of trying to undo what Russia had done. "We object most strongly to what we think she (Russia) may and will obtain." That is, the purpose of the agreement would be to check Russian advance beyond Manchuria. " I said if we had a clear understanding with Germany and a joint policy we might adopt a much stronger attitude than if we were alone, and in this case we could lay down the bases of a settlement in China which neither France nor Russia would be likely to resist." Asked what kind of arrangement he proposed, he went on: "I said, speaking only for myself, that I thought we might say to Russia—'You have got all you say you want. We are ready to recognise your position, but you must not go further. The rest of China is under our joint protection.'" Germany, he suggested, might act as protector of Shantung and the hinterland, assume a certain financial control, and use the money to train a native army under German officers. England could do the same in the central and southern provinces. Then, " if in the future Russia attempted further aggression, she would have to confront not only a war with two great European Powers but also the defensive forces of China organised and led by European officers." [24]

Chamberlain had certainly laid his cards on the table. While Bülow had suggested that Britain and Russia reach an agreement which would have left France isolated and helpless, the colonial secretary had put forward the suggestion for an agreement, a public alliance, unqualifiedly directed against Russian policy in China. The Celestial Empire was to be divided into Russian, German and British spheres, the British being the largest and most populous, while at the same time furthest removed from the Russian. The Germans, indeed, were to serve as buffers, as shock absorbers. No wonder that Hatzfeldt avoided reporting to his government the details of Chamberlain's suggestions. He toned it all down, emphasizing the fact that the English statesman was interested, not in opposing the Russian action at Port Arthur, but merely in checking any future advance. He indicated that Chamberlain might be willing to accord Germany an extension of her sphere of influence, but said nothing of what the British would demand for themselves.

If the Berlin government had known as much of Chamberlain's remarks as we can now learn from his memorandum, it is almost a certainty that it would have taken a stronger stand against the alliance project. Even on the basis of the somewhat misleading Hatzfeldt report the foreign office showed little enthusiasm and a good deal of incredulity. It seemed hardly believable that the British parliament would approve the alliance, for, as Bülow pointed out, the Kruger telegram had shown the depth of English animosity and not even Chamberlain could honestly believe that such feelings could be transformed overnight. If the treaty were submitted to parliament and rejected, Germany

---

[24] *Die Grosse Politik*, XIV, no. 3784; Garvin, op. cit., III, pp. 263–6.

would be left at the mercy of the greatly enhanced hostility of Russia and France. It would therefore be better to wait until England was still harder pressed — until she needed the alliance even more urgently. In the meanwhile German opinion could be brought around to the idea if England were more considerate in her dealings with Germany.[25]

At this stage in the discussion came the government's explanations to parliament, on April 5. These have already been touched upon, and it is necessary to note here only the fact that Balfour on this occasion sounded out the House on the question of alliances. The German assurances regarding Kiao-chow, he said,

"indicate what I believe to be the absolute truth, which is that within China — certainly in China — I do not limit the statement to that, but certainly in China — British interests and German interests are absolutely identical. Jealousy, I suppose, there may be between individual traders, individual concessionaires, and individual producers. But fundamentally the interests of the two countries are the same and must be the same, and I certainly believe that we shall be able without difficulty to work hand in hand towards carrying out these general commercial objects, which I believe approve themselves to the sense of this House." And towards the end of his statement he referred to the possibility of a time coming "when the great Powers primarily interested in the commerce of the world" might "feel that their interests draw them together, and require them to join an alliance which no man can resist for the purpose of seeing that China shall not fall a prey to any exclusive interest." [26]

Sir William Harcourt described this idea of a general alliance as a "Utopian dream," but Sir Edward Grey came to the support of Balfour. "There is," he said,

"a group of six Powers more likely to be interested in the Far East than any other — Russia, France, Germany, United States, Japan and ourselves; but surely it is for the interests of several of these Powers, as much as our own, that there should be an open door to China and a neutral market? We have heard much in recent years of the successful commercial competition of Germany, the United States as successful all over the world, and Japan as competing in that part of the world; and it becomes more and more to the interest of these nations that the policy of the open door should be maintained. It may be a paradox to say that out of successful commercial rivalry may come political agreement; but I do not see why in future years the interests of these Powers should not, through commercial rivalry, more and more make themselves felt, to help attain this. . . . Isolation is sometimes apt to be mistaken for indifference, and in future years, when it is required, is likely to become unsuccessful. We must not look to isolation. We must find a common ground of interest with other Powers."

---

[25] *Die Grosse Politik*, XIV, no. 3785.
[26] Hansard: *Parliamentary Debates*, Series IV, vol. LVI, pp. 232, 238.

Sir Charles Beresford went even further, and declared: " I believe that the time for our ' splendid isolation ' is gone. It was very useful for Noah, but it is not suitable for the present time, and I believe if the Government of this country would try to make an alliance with Germany, that really would make for peace for a very long period." [27]

On the very day of this debate Balfour had a second talk with the German ambassador. He admitted that there was room for doubt whether an alliance could be gotten through parliament (on this point Chamberlain was confident), and agreed with Hatzfeldt that the immediate task was to prepare the ground and improve public opinion in both countries. Balfour hinted quite broadly that in his estimation Chamberlain was trying to go too fast. Hatzfeldt thought Balfour would not be sorry if the colonial secretary failed in his efforts. This was certainly an erroneous impression, the result, probably, of the ambassador's dislike of Chamberlain. Still, Hatzfeldt reported home that he was convinced of Chamberlain's sincerity and believed that the cabinet was behind the advances to Germany. Even the Liberal leaders, he thought, were well disposed (which Grey's utterances in parliament would seem to bear out).[28]

The question of whether parliament and the country would have accepted an alliance with Germany in the spring of 1898 is a really crucial one, for any judgment of the negotiations must of necessity hinge upon it. So much, at least, is clear: there was no widespread sentiment in the country for such a connexion. In parliament, apart from Grey, only those two amusing and erratic members, Beresford and Ashmead Bartlett, spoke openly in favor of an alliance with Germany. The major organs of the periodical press made no response, though Henry M. Stanley declared isolation to be a " gaudy air-bladder " and recommended that England join the Triple Alliance, which would be backed by the moral support of the United States and the material forces of Japan, if it came to a question of blocking the Russians and French in China.[29] As against this lone note of warning there sounded the strident calls of the vigorously anti-German papers, like the *Saturday Review,* which asserted roundly that Germany was the chief enemy in the Far East: " It will be well for England when our natural and inevitable hostility towards our greatest rival can have free play." " It is natural for Germany to look to us; but she is our rival, our true ' natural enemy'; and it would be better for England to fight than be ' friendly.' " [30]

It may be conceded at once that the *Saturday Review* was not typical of the press at large. But what do you find if you consult a newspaper like the *Times,* which generally supported Chamberlain and which was almost rabid in its denunciations of Russian schemes in China? Editorially the *Times* hardly men-

---

[27] Ibid., pp. 280–1, 285–6.

[28] *Die Grosse Politik,* XIV, no. 3786.

[29] Henry M. Stanley: " ' Splendid Isolation ' or What? " (*Nineteenth Century,* June, 1898, pp. 869–78).   [30] *Saturday Review,* March 26, April 16, 1898.

tioned the suggested rapprochement with Germany. When the Blue Book was published toward the end of April, the editor recognized that Germany's attitude in the Far Eastern crisis had shown anxiety not to antagonize England. Nevertheless the *Times* criticized sharply the government's assurances to Germany with respect to Weihaiwei, and the Berlin correspondent from the very outset warned his countrymen against cherishing hopes of German support. "It must be remembered," he wrote, "that it is far from likely that an understanding between Germany and England could assume other than a commercial aspect. Germany's position in the map of Europe dictates to her the necessity of maintaining her friendly relations with Russia." To which the editor of the *Times* added: "It seems difficult for Germans to comprehend that an identity of commercial interests does not imply that this country should or would make political concessions, either to Germany or her allies, in order to purchase co-operation in the sphere of trade." A month later the Berlin correspondent, summing up the discussion of the problem by the German press, wrote at some length:

> "It is a matter of elementary knowledge to those who have followed the trend of German foreign policy for even a very few years that neither 'spontaneous' declarations nor far more material concessions have the slightest prospect of succeeding in placing Germany in the position of an ally of England against Russia, either in Europe or in Asia. The only conceivable result of such amiable and well-meant endeavours would be to facilitate for Germany the development of the essentially Bismarckian policy of grasping the tongue of the balance between England and Russia and reaping a handsome commission as 'honest broker' from both sides. It is equally to the interest of England and Russia to prevent the realization of such schemes, and this interest ought undoubtedly, amid many subjects of conflict, to be one of the considerations which from time to time may smooth the path for a good understanding and for loyal co-operation between the two greatest Asiatic Powers." [31]

What shall we conclude, then, with regard to the chances of an alliance being accepted by the English parliament and by the country? My personal impression is that in this matter Balfour, and perhaps most of those in the cabinet who were sympathetic, were nearer the right track than Chamberlain. Certainly the country would have been glad of an agreement with Germany which would have assured England support against Russian aggression in China. Through such an agreement England would have had everything to gain and very little, if anything, to lose. But there was, of course, almost no chance that the Germans would gratuitously enlist in a crusade against Russia, the more so as they were glad to see Russia deeply involved in China. They had no desire to stop her. Chamberlain was keen-witted enough to see that. He therefore suggested a defensive alliance as a makeweight. The real question is whether this alliance, not

---

[31] London *Times*, April 9, May 2, 1898. I have made no use of Karl O. Herkenberg: *The Times und das Deutsch-Englische Verhältnis im Jahre 1898* (Berlin, 1925), because it is incomplete and the dates are not always accurate.

the Far Eastern agreement, would have proved acceptable. The answer depends in part on the control of Chamberlain and Salisbury over their parliamentary majority. Let us assume that there was enough discipline to get the treaty through parliament. There would have still remained the opinion of the country. The view of Balfour seems to have been that there should be careful preparation of opinion before the treaty were brought forward. I think this was the sound approach to the problem. The yawning chasm between violent popular hostility and close political alliance was still too wide to be bridged without long and arduous labor. Even if the treaty had been made and put through parliament, its existence would not have been healthy until the popular attitude had changed or been changed.

On the German side there was no more popular enthusiasm than on the English. Many influential papers, like the *Vossische Zeitung,* the *National Zeitung,* the *Kölnische Zeitung* and the *Hamburgische Correspondent* spoke appreciatively of Balfour's references to the community of British and German interests in the Far East, and expressed the desire for friendlier relations. On the other hand they one and all rejected the idea of hostility to Russia, and took the stand that England must deal with Germany as an equal — she must be willing to pay the price. " Our answer to the voice of the charmer," said the Hamburg paper on April 9, " should be dictated exclusively by our own practical political interests, and these interests point to the necessity for holding on in the course we are at present following. . . . To give up for the sake of a few fine words, which every breeze may blow away, the principles of our east Asiatic policy, to let ourselves be elbowed out of our entente with Russia and France, these are things which are, of course, quite out of the question." " Our policy," wrote the *Vossische Zeitung* on April 13, " will continue to be guided solely by the dictates of German interests, which require the cultivation of friendly relations with Russia quite as much as with England." In a long and obviously inspired review of the international situation the *Kölnische Zeitung* on May 1 flatly denied that there had been any cooling off of German-Russian relations or any change in German policy respecting England: " German policy, in a word, will never be oblivious of the fact that its most essential interests lie in Europe and that its most important task is to maintain and to establish peace with honour for Germany in Europe." [32]

These newspapers gave a fair reflection of the attitude of the German foreign office toward the suggestions of Chamberlain. In all probability the papers were inspired by the press bureau of the Wilhelmstrasse. From the German documents the reaction of the Emperor and of Bülow is quite clear. " Chamberlain," noted the Emperor, " must not forget that in East Prussia I have one Prussian army corps against three Russian armies and nine cavalry divisions located close to the frontier; that no Chinese Wall separates me from them and no British warship can keep them away from me." " The Niger and the Gulf of Pechili

---

[32] I quote from the abstracts in the London *Times,* April 7, 8, 9, 11, 14, May 2, 1898.

concern us less than Alsace-Lorraine." Colonial concessions would not out-
weigh the increased hostility of Russia and France resulting from an Anglo-
German agreement on the Far East and Africa. If the British were willing later
on to extend the entente to Europe that would be another story. In the meanwhile England should be kept warm: "Through a well-disposed England we
have one card more to play against Russia, and we have besides the prospect
of securing from England concessions in the colonial field and in tariff negotiations." To all of which Bülow agreed: "We must remain independent between the two powers (Russia and England); we must be the tongue of the
balance, not the restlessly swinging pendulum." [33]

Whatever may be said of the Emperor and Bülow, their attitude in this
question was clear and understandable. It is important to bear it in mind in
order to understand a little interlude which occurred at this stage in the negotiations. Baron von Eckardstein, secretary of the German embassy at London,
married to a wealthy English heiress and prominent in high financial and social circles, was an almost fanatical adherent of the idea of an alliance and had
had something to do with the initiation of the discussions. In mid-April, so he
tells us in his memoirs, he went off to Germany ostensibly for private purposes,
but in reality to visit the Emperor at Homburg, lay the facts before him and
thus counteract the nefarious influence of Holstein and the foreign office. His
interview with the Emperor fell in the very days (around April 10) when the
correspondence between Homburg and Berlin, mentioned above, was taking
place. Yet when Eckardstein was back in London he arranged for a conference with Chamberlain, and gave him a very different picture of the Emperor's
attitude.

"The Emperor," he said, "viewed such a possibility (of an alliance) with the
greatest favour, and was most anxious that an agreement should be come to.
He was very desirous that the matter should be dealt with immediately, as he
feared, if there was any delay, that the pourparlers would leak out and would
come to the knowledge of Russia. . . . The Emperor thought that at an early
date Italy and Austria should be made acquainted with any proposals, and was
confident that they would eagerly join in such an arrangement. The Russians
were intriguing most actively to bring about a combination against England, but
he recognised that the interests of Germany lay in the opposite direction. The principle of such an arrangement would be a guarantee by both Powers of the possessions of the other. Baron Eckardstein seemed to think that this guarantee might
be against any attack by any other Power, or, if it were desired to limit it, against
any attack by two Powers combined. In the event of such an agreement the Emperor recognised that we ought to have a free hand in Egypt and the Transvaal.
Baron Eckardstein again and again repeated that the Emperor was most anxious
that the matter should be dealt with quickly." [34]

---

[33] *Die Grosse Politik,* XIV, nos. 3788–90.
[34] Garvin: *Life of Chamberlain,* III, pp. 2712; Hermann Freiherr von Eckardstein: *Lebenserinnerungen und Politische Denkwürdigkeiten* (Leipzig, 1919), I, pp. 294 ff.

Chamberlain, in making a memorandum of this conversation, noted that he told Eckardstein that the discussions were absolutely personal and unofficial (which had been agreed to from the beginning), and that Salisbury, being away, was not yet informed of what had taken place. He evidently and naturally took everything that had been told him to be true and important. But, having the materials on both sides, we can see that one of two things was true: either the Emperor entirely misled Eckardstein, or else Eckardstein misrepresented the Emperor and misled Chamberlain. There can, I think, be little if any doubt that Eckardstein was the culprit. We have here a first glaring example of the appalling and disastrous mystification which he practiced in 1901. Knowing the German foreign office to be lukewarm, he tried to go over the heads of Bülow and Holstein and enlist the aid of the Emperor. Finding William no more enthusiastic, he simply falsified the facts and gave a glowing account to Chamberlain. The constant emphasis on the need for haste was probably meant to stampede both sides into an agreement before there was time to think too much about it. The worst part of the situation was that the ambassador, Count Hatzfeldt, was not entirely innocent of this work of deception. We have seen that, from the very outset, he had tended, in his reports, to gloss over the difficulties and to magnify Chamberlain's " offers." Now in April he knew that the Emperor was not enthusiastic, as Eckardstein pictured him, for he had instructions from Berlin which made the German view perfectly clear. Yet he apparently did nothing to prevent Eckardstein from going to Chamberlain and arousing false hopes. Of course Eckardstein may have misled Hatzfeldt as he did others, though it would have been more difficult.

On April 25 the colonial secretary lunched with Hatzfeldt at the home of Eckardstein. (Hatzfeldt reported to Berlin that the meeting had been arranged at Chamberlain's request, though in reality it was Eckardstein's suggestion). The ambassador's report of the conversation makes a very long document. He maintained that Chamberlain once again " pressed " for an alliance and stuck to his guns even after all the familiar German arguments against it had been marshalled once more. Hatzfeldt indicated the possibility of reviving the Mediterranean Agreements of 1887, with the idea that a closer connexion between England on the one hand and Austria and Italy on the other would of necessity lead to closer Anglo-German relations. Chamberlain showed little interest in this approach and reiterated that Germany and the alliance with Germany were the crucial points. England needed the agreement to check the further advance of Russia in China. If Germany rejected the British offer, England might find it necessary to make separate agreements with Russia or France.[35]

Chamberlain's memorandum of the conversation is much briefer and much more to the point. He says nothing of having pressed for an alliance, but of course discretion may have kept him from recording his eagerness. He does, however, speak of the arguments which Hatzfeldt brought forward against

---

[35] *Die Grosse Politik*, XIV, no. 3793.

an immediate agreement and of the suggestion to revive the Mediterranean Agreements. But there is no mention of any hints on Chamberlain's part that England might seek an agreement with Russia or France. The colonial secretary's report ends thus: " I said that I gathered that he thought any attempt to secure a direct defensive alliance between Germany and England was premature. He assented, but said the opportunity might come later. I reminded him of the French proverb, ' le bonheur qui passe.' " [36]

It is most difficult to reconstruct an accurate account of this conversation from the reports of the two participants, for even if there is general agreement on the facts, the tone of the two records is quite different. It is likely that, after his conversation with Eckardstein, Chamberlain was more eager and enthusiastic than would appear from his memorandum, and it may well be that, when his eyes were opened to the real state of affairs, he spoke more sharply about the possibility of an arrangement with Russia and France than he was willing to admit in writing. At any rate, so much is beyond dispute: Hatzfeldt, following his instructions, had definitely deflated the idea of an alliance and admitted to Chamberlain in so many words that the Germans thought the project premature. In reporting to his government, however, Hatzfeldt still tried to provoke favorable action. He not only stressed the eagerness of Chamberlain, but also underlined the danger of agreements between England, Russia and France. But the warnings disturbed neither the Emperor nor Holstein, both of whom made heavy annotations on the Hatzfeldt report. Bülow made the marginal notes his own and wrote cold-bloodedly to London that Germany was not menaced by Russia and therefore could not take the risk of throwing herself in Russia's way. Chamberlain, he said, was evidently trying to play off Germany against France. Let him try to reach an agreement with France. He would find that France would never abandon Russia. When the British had learned this lesson, it would be easier to talk to them of a profitable alliance.[37]

To all intents and purposes the alliance discussions were over. Eckardstein, who hurried to the colonial office to smooth things over, tried to assure Chamberlain that the Emperor was really strongly in favor of the alliance, and suggested that Prince Hohenlohe must have interfered to spoil the whole thing. To which Chamberlain gave an unanswerable reply: " I said that I did not see that there was anything to be done. Either Count Hatzfeldt's language was that of the Emperor, in which case the matter was ended; or it was not, and in this case it was for the Emperor to make the next move." [38]

Lord Salisbury returned from the Continent on April 29 and was informed at once by Chamberlain of the discussions that had been going on. The letter of the colonial secretary shows that in spite of his disappointing experience he had not changed his mind about the dangers of England's position and the desirability of the alliance with Germany:

[36] Garvin, op. cit., III, pp. 273–4. [37] *Die Grosse Politik*, XIV, no. 3794.
[38] Garvin, op. cit., III, pp. 276–7.

" Recent experience seems to show that we are powerless to resist the ultimate control of China by Russia, and that we are at a great disadvantage in negotiating with France, as long as we retain our present isolation, and I think the country would support us in a Treaty with Germany providing for reciprocal defence. I think such a Treaty would make for peace and might be negotiated at the present time. But it is for you to say whether the matter should be pressed or allowed to drop."

The prime minister, as Chamberlain's biographer says, " shared the wish but not the faith." Hatzfeldt came to see him on the afternoon of May 2 and spoke in a general way of the desirability of better relations. But he took care to add that nothing must be hurried and hinted that if England wished an alliance, it must be prepared for by amiability in other matters. " His business," wrote Salisbury to Chamberlain, " was evidently to throw cold water. . . . I quite agree with you that under the circumstances a closer relation with Germany would be very desirable; but can we get it? " There was some talk between the two men on May 3, after the cabinet, and Salisbury suggested that, if Eckardstein came again, Chamberlain might say that the Government was prepared to consider the idea favorably. It is clear from the record of these conversations that Chamberlain was still taken in by Eckardstein, and that he put considerable stock in the latter's story of the Emperor's being led astray by his advisers.[39]

Though Salisbury would have been as glad as any other Englishman to secure German support against Russia, he did not take the Far Eastern situation as seriously as Chamberlain and was not as deeply impressed with the dangers of isolation. This he revealed in the famous " Dying Nations Speech " which he delivered at the Albert Hall on May 4, and which may be taken as a classic example of the projection of Darwinian ideas into political calculations. As on previous occasions the prime minister spoke half lightly, half cynically about the international situation. The Chinese question, he thought, had perhaps received more attention than it deserved. It had been " a sort of diplomatic cracker that has produced a great many detonations, but I think the smoke of it has now floated into the distance." The government had been absolutely opposed to Russia's taking Port Arthur, and the Russians had probably made a mistake in going there. Since the British had leased Weihaiwei, however, the possession of Port Arthur could no longer enhance Russian influence at Peking. Weihaiwei could be defended from the sea, which Port Arthur could not. To be sure, similar crises might occur in the future:

" But we know that we shall maintain against all comers that which we possess, and we know, in spite of the jargon about isolation, that we are amply competent to do so."

---

[39] Garvin: *Life of Chamberlain*, III, pp. 278–80; there is no record of the Salisbury-Hatzfeldt conversation in the German sources.

But that in itself might not secure peace for the world, for there were living and dying nations, the ones growing ever stronger, the others ever weaker:

"For one reason or another — from the necessities of politics or under the pretext of philanthropy — the living nations will gradually encroach on the territory of the dying, and the seed and causes of conflict amongst civilised nations will speedily appear. Of course, it is not to be supposed that any one nation of the living nations will be allowed to have the profitable monopoly of curing or cutting up these unfortunate patients, and the controversy is as to who shall have the privilege of doing so, and in what measure he shall do it. . . . These are the dangers which, I think, threaten us in the period that is coming on. It is a period which will tax our resolution, our tenacity and imperial instincts, to the utmost. Undoubtedly we shall not allow England to be at a disadvantage in any rearrangement that may take place. On the other hand, we shall not be jealous if desolation and sterility are removed by the aggrandisement of a rival in regions to which our arms cannot extend."

This speech, coming as it did after much bitter criticism of the government, is of great interest. It shows beyond question that Salisbury took the Far Eastern situation less seriously than most people and that he was less upset by the Russian advance. It shows — and this is more important — that he felt no disposition to give up isolation. England was, he maintained, quite able to hold her own.[40] It was in this sense that the speech was read by his contemporaries. In a long letter to the *Times* a Tory member of parliament voiced his condemnation and insisted that Salisbury should give over the foreign office to Balfour. Everybody, he wrote, knows that Salisbury has handled foreign affairs by himself: "Neither the Cabinet nor the party exercise the slightest influence or control in that *mare clausum*." Therefore Salisbury alone must be held responsible for the turn events had taken. The nation was grateful that he had preserved peace, but wished he had been somewhat more solicitous to preserve honor as well. In a leading article the *Times* subscribed to these sentiments, which, it declared, were widely shared. With great bitterness it recalled Salisbury's remark of two years before to the effect that people were apt to "foreshorten distance" in dealing with the Chinese problem. It was time to put an end to the handling of vital national interests by the methods of "neatly-turned epigrams."[41]

In view of the expressed sentiments of Salisbury, it is no cause for wonder that Count Hatzfeldt found him sceptical about entering upon a discussion of the matter broached by Balfour and so frankly debated by Chamberlain. In a conversation of May 11 the prime minister recurred to the question, but only to remark irritably: "You ask too much for your friendship." Hatzfeldt urged

---

[40] This is, it seems to me, the only possible interpretation of the speech. It is incomprehensible to me how writers like Joseph: *Foreign Diplomacy in China*, p. 318, can read it as an invitation to the English people to give up isolation.

[41] London *Times*, May 5, 1898.

his government not to take this remark or, in fact, the general pessimism of Salisbury too seriously. He believed that most members of the cabinet still favored a rapprochement with Germany, though Chamberlain was said to be as disappointed as Salisbury was pessimistic.[42]

The German ambassador was a very experienced, a very well-informed and a very clever man. But he could not foresee the remarkable turn which the situation was to take in the next days. On May 13 Chamberlain addressed the Liberal Union Association in his Birmingham constituency. Even for Mr. Chamberlain the speech was an extraordinary utterance, remarkable throughout for its absolute frankness and strong language. After reviewing the history and domestic policies of Liberal Unionism he turned to a long disquisition upon foreign affairs, the importance of which he emphasized: " There is, and there has been for some time past, a combined assault by the nations of the world upon the commercial supremacy of this country, and if that assault were successful our existence would be menaced in a way in which it never has been threatened since the time . . . when the great Napoleon attempted to lay an interdict upon British trade." The situation was too serious a one to be dealt with along party lines and it was neither wise nor patriotic to do what some party leaders had done, namely to represent the foreign minister as " discredited and defeated," to " gloat over the alleged humiliation of the country," and to " say on every occasion that the Government as a whole is weak and vacillating." If such statements were believed in foreign countries those countries might make a great mistake. He personally intended to speak frankly to the people, whose judgment he would take as soon as that of the wisest diplomatist in the world.

> " Now the first point I want to impress upon you is this. It is the crux of the situation. Since the Crimean War, nearly fifty years ago, the policy of this country has been a policy of strict isolation. We have had no allies, — I am afraid we have had no friends. That is not due altogether to the envy which is undoubtedly felt at our success; it is due in part to the suspicion that we are acting in our own selfish interests, and were willing that other people should draw the chestnuts out of the fire for us; that we would take no responsibilities, whilst we were glad enough to profit by the work of others. In this way we have avoided entangling alliances, we have escaped many dangers; but we must accept the disadvantages that go with such a policy. . . . A new situation has arisen, and it is right the people of this country should have it under their consideration. All the powerful states of Europe have made alliances, and as long as we keep outside these alliances, as long as we are envied by all, and as long as we have interests which at one time or another conflict with the interests of all, we are liable to be confronted at any moment with a combination of Great Powers so powerful that not even the most extreme, the most hotheaded politician would be able to contemplate it without a certain sense of uneasiness."

---

[42] *Die Grosse Politik,* XIV, no. 3796 footnote.

What was the duty of the government in these circumstances? First of all " to draw all parts of the Empire closer together, to infuse into them a spirit of united and Imperial patriotism." This had been done. The next duty was

" to establish and to maintain bonds of permanent amity with out kinsmen across the Atlantic. They are a powerful and a generous nation. They speak our language, they are bred of our race. Their laws, their literature, their standpoint upon every question are the same as ours; their feeling, their interest in the cause of humanity and the peaceful development of the world are identical with ours. I do not know what the future has in store for us. I do not know what arrangements may be possible with us, but this I know and feel, — that the closer, the more cordial, the fuller, and the more definite those arrangements are, with the consent of both peoples, the better it will be for both and for the world. And I even go so far as to say that, terrible as war may be, even war itself would be cheaply purchased if in a great and noble cause the Stars and Stripes and the Union Jack should wave together over an Anglo-Saxon Alliance."

Turning then to the Far East, Chamberlain recognized that it was on this score that the government was most commonly attacked. Again and again he insisted that " we are only at the beginning of great events," that the campaign was not yet over, and that therefore it was too early to condemn the government. That the " absolute corruption, the crass ignorance and the gross mis-government " of the Chinese mandarins had reduced China to a state of impotence had become known when the previous government was in power, yet that government had taken no adequate measures to come to an understanding with Russia, at whose mercy China was.

" The expected happened, and Russia did go down to Port Arthur and to Talienwan. As to the way in which Russia secured that occupation, as to the representations which were made and repudiated as soon as they were made, as to the promises which were given and broken a fortnight afterwards, I had better perhaps say nothing except I have always thought that it was a very wise proverb, ' Who sups with the Devil must have a long spoon.' The present government did try to come to an understanding with Russia," but failed to persuade her, and had to fall back on the alternative policy of taking Weihaiwei. In the " preliminary skirmish " England had done pretty well, but the general situation was " far from satisfactory." An understanding with Russia had proved impossible. The only other alternative would be war. " I am one of those who think that for any country there are worse things than war; there is loss of honour; there is loss of those interests which are so vital to the security of the existence of the nation. But, in any case, I hope I am sensible enough never to give my voice for war unless I can see at the commencement of the war a fair probability that at the end of the war the objects of the war will have been obtained. Now, what does history show? It shows that unless we are allied to some great military power, as we were in the Crimean War . . . we cannot seriously injure Russia, although it may also be true that she cannot seriously injure us. If that is the case, it is a case which deserves the serious consideration of the people of this country. It is impossible to over-rate the gravity of the issue. It is not a question of a single port in China — that is a very small matter. It is not a question of a single province; it is a question of the whole fate of the Chinese Empire, and our interests in China are so great, our proportion of the trade is so enormous, and the potentialities of that trade are so gigantic that I feel that no more vital question has ever been presented for the decision of a Government and the decision of a nation, and for my part I have tried to-night to state clearly and without exaggeration the conditions of the problem that we have before us. I think you will see that it is complicated enough to preclude all hasty judgment. One thing appears to me to be certain. If the policy of isolation, which has hitherto been the policy of this country, is to be maintained in the future, then the fate of the Chinese Empire may be, probably will be, hereafter decided without reference to our wishes and in defiance of our interests. If, on the other hand, we are determined to enforce the policy of the open door, to preserve an equal opportunity for trade with all our rivals, then we must not allow jingoes to drive us into a quarrel with all the world at the same time, and we must not reject the idea of an alliance with those Powers whose interests most nearly approximate to our own."

Chamberlain's speech appeared to most readers to be a direct contradiction of Salisbury's address of May 4. The prime minister was optimistic about China and disdainful of the " jargon of isolation." The secretary for the colonies drew an alarming picture of the Far Eastern situation and seemed to indicate that England would be lost without the alliance of a strong military power. In many quarters his remarks were interpreted as a speech against Salisbury, as a " counter-manifesto," to borrow the phrase of Sir William Harcourt. While the chief of the government was administering " soothing syrup " his colleague was sounding " the tocsin of alarm." [43] When the opposition tried to draw out Lord Salisbury on the subject in the house of lords on May 17 the prime minister refused to discuss the question. But he did say: " Our general policy is not changed. We shall cultivate to the utmost of our ability the friendship of all the Powers with whom we come into contact." Which simply amounted to a reiteration of his earlier statements.[44]

What is the real explanation of the Chamberlain speech? Hatzfeldt thought that Salisbury must have known in advance about it, and that he had approved of it as a sounding out of public opinion in the matter of an alliance.[45] But from Chamberlain's later utterances and from other evidence it is plain that the prime minister at best knew only of the general tenor of his colleague's forthcoming speech. We know that he thoroughly disapproved of the strong expressions used, which he considered in bad taste.[46] But Chamberlain himself in a later debate in parliament hinted broadly that he had not written out the speech

---

[43] Hansard: *Parliamentary Debates*, Series IV, vol. LVIII, pp. 1412 ff.
[44] Hansard, op. cit., LVII, p. 1514.   [45] *Die Grosse Politik*, XIV, no. 3797.
[46] Meyendorff: *Correspondance de M. de Staal*, II, pp. 386–7; *Die Grosse Politik*, XIV, no. 3800; Elliot: *Life of Goschen*, II, pp. 219 ff.

beforehand and that therefore it could not have been approved by the cabinet. Besides, he said, the cabinet could not be held responsible for "every word, every phrase, every turn of expression" on the part of one member, but only for "every declaration of principle, every statement of important fact, every declaration of policy." If there was disagreement between the prime minister and a member of the cabinet, it was the duty of that member to resign. The fact that he himself had not resigned, had not been cast out by his colleagues, had not been rejected by the prime minister should be enough to explode all stories of a split in the cabinet.[47]

At bottom there was no fundamental difference of opinion between Salisbury and Chamberlain. Both men, so far as one can detect, would have preferred an understanding with Russia, which would have been welcomed by the country at large. But, the attempt having been made and having failed, they saw the necessity of strengthening relations with the United States, Japan and Germany. The only divergence between them was with respect to how fast and how far England should go. Salisbury and Balfour evidently thought there was no hurry, and envisaged a gradual rapprochement, for which the price would not be exorbitant. It seems more than doubtful whether they had much hope of a hard and fast alliance. Chamberlain, on the other hand, began by thinking of an immediate alliance agreement and did not shrink even at the idea of war to check the Russians. But by May 1898 he had certainly seen the futility of this idea. His language in the Birmingham speech was strong and tactless, but there is no reason to question his later explanation of it. Speaking in parliament on June 10 he declared that the object of the speech "was not to lay down a policy. . . . It was to state the facts." "We are the most powerful Empire in the world; but we are not all-powerful." He had aimed simply to point out what England could not do under the existing circumstances. "I neither spoke for nor against alliances . . . except in regard to one particular nation," by which he meant the United States. His chief point, he went on, was to stress the fact that if the country insisted on maintaining the policy of isolation, which had been the right one for a long time, it must take the consequences, it must not make impossible demands upon the government, it must not expect to exercise a controlling influence in China as it had in the past. "Nobody ever talked of a permanent alliance. All I said was that the policy of this country, hitherto well known to all nations of the world and declared again and again, was that we would not accept any alliance . . . but once it becomes known that we are willing to consider alliances, provided they are for mutual interests with reciprocal advantages, I do not think we shall find the difficulty right honourable Gentlemen suggest in getting offers well worth our consideration." To wait until war broke out, he said, might be to wait too long. Permanent alliances did not necessarily lead to trouble. The Triple Alliance was founded to keep the peace. To join such an alliance for such purposes

---

[47] Hansard, LVIII, p. 1426; Garvin: *Life of Chamberlain*, III, pp. 282 ff.

would not be a " jingo proceeding." England could defend her present possessions, but what about future interests, about " potentialities of trade and
commerce " ? As things were England would have to vote naval expenditures
sufficient to enable her to meet not two, but three powers. " It seems to me
that any assurance, I will not say of an alliance — I am not speaking of an
alliance, but of a thorough and complete understanding — a mutual arrangement for particular interests — with any one of the great Powers would be
one of the most economical things that this country could possibly undertake,
because it would save at once one, at all events, of the great Powers from entering into a combination against us, and we should then be satisfied that the
preparations we have made against all eventualities were absolutely sufficient."
He then admitted that there was no great hurry. The Transsiberian Railroad
would take three to five years to complete. Nevertheless the country should
look forward to the problems of the next ten to twenty years, and it was with
this idea that he had examined the situation.[48]

Whatever the truth may be with regard to the Salisbury-Chamberlain relationship, it is not surprising that the Birmingham speech should have come as
a shock to public opinion both in England and on the Continent. At home
some people objected to the " new " diplomacy which involved calling other
nations and rulers by unpleasant and discourteous names. Even more people
resented Chamberlain's " abject confession of weakness." " What have we
done," demanded Asquith in parliament, " what have the people of Great
Britain done or suffered, that, after bearing, as we have done for nearly fifty
years, the ever-growing weight of empire on our own unaided shoulders, without finding the burden too heavy for the courage, the enterprise, the self-
reliance of our people, what have we done or suffered that we are now to go
touting for allies in the highways and byways of Europe? " [49]

Chamberlain's key suggestion, the possibility of England's concluding alliances, found no response in the country. Take the matter of an alliance with
the United States. The American ambassador, John Hay, speaking at the Lord
Mayor's banquet on April 21, 1898 went even further than Chamberlain when
he asserted that " all who think cannot but see there is a sanction like that of
religion which binds us in partnership in the serious work of the world. . . .
We are joint ministers in the same sacred mission of freedom and progress."
Hay claimed that Chamberlain's references to America were partly due to his
(Hay's) warning that the opposition should not be allowed to have a monopoly of expressions of good will toward America. Yet despite the unusual
cordiality on both sides of the Atlantic, serious writers and politicians had no
faith in the possibility of a formal alliance: " Every man welcomes an alliance,

---

[48] Hansard, LVIII, pp. 1427–37. On Salisbury's attitude see also *Die Grosse Politik*, XIV,
no. 3801; Meyendorff, op. cit., II, p. 387; and Salisbury's letter to the Queen repudiating the idea
that he had been less friendly to Germany than Chamberlain (*Letters of Queen Victoria*, III, p. 259).
[49] Hansard, LVIII, pp. 1347 ff.; similarly Labouchere and Harcourt (ibid., pp. 1375, 1418).

if you like to call it so, of hearts between the two countries, but none of us, and few Americans, think that it would be likely to produce what may be called a war alliance," said Sir Charles Dilke. " Expressions of friendship with England are almost universal," reported the New York correspondent of the *Times,* but it is remarked that Mr. Chamberlain made, and could make, no definite proposal. The question of an alliance is for this Government and people novel. We have not advanced to that point. . . . Most members of Congress continue to decline to express other than general views. They are politicians bred in a school of distrust. Distrust of England is with many of them traditional. They distrust her no longer, but when the word ' alliance ' is pronounced, they ask for time." [50]

Much the same attitude was taken toward the suggestion of an alliance with " a strong military power." Everyone understood that this could mean only Germany, and not a single speaker in the house of commons had anything to say in favor of the idea. Sir Charles Dilke doubted whether Germany would ever be willing to make such an alliance; Asquith thought German policy in the Far East more reprehensible than the Russian, and pointed out that an alliance with Germany would cost too much; Labouchere was dubious whether Germany would be anxious to pull the chestnuts out of the Chinese fire for England. " I am no particular friend of Germany," he said, " but I am bound to say that the German people are all a great deal too intelligent to dance to the piping of the Right Honourable Gentleman the Member for West Birmingham." England would have to guarantee Germany's possessions before an alliance could be made, and that would involve a guarantee of Alsace and Lorraine, to which he objected strongly. Harcourt joined the other opposition speakers in declaring against the whole idea of permanent alliances. [51]

Let us turn now to the German side. The first reaction of the German press was one of astonishment and shock at the bluntness of the Chamberlain statement. The *National Zeitung* declared that it amounted to " a declaration of the bankruptcy, not only of past English policy, but, what is more, of the whole power of England." This impression was shared by most of the other German papers, until the London *Times,* which tried to correct the erroneous idea of British weakness, warned the continental nations that England had no thought of purchasing aid at an exorbitant price: The speech, it wrote, was " neither a cry for foreign help nor necessarily a preparation for a new departure." If a departure were made in British policy

" it will be the Foreign Secretary who will have to bring forward the subject. He will do so with the utmost regard for the conventions of European and other diplomacy, we may be sure, nor will the matter of ' concession ' be forgotten. But when that delicate topic comes to be debated in connexion with a review of the general balance of advantages to either side, we are not satisfied that they

[50] *Times,* May 17, 1898; Hansard, LVIII, pp. 1335 ff.; William R. Thayer: *Life of John Hay,* II, p. 169.   [51] Hansard, op. cit., LVIII, pp. 1337 ff., 1348 ff., 1377–8, 1420.

will have to be made by us. After all, the British Fleet, a chain of coaling stations encircling the globe, the command of the seas will be considerable assets
on our side of the account." [52]

On second thought the German press became more circumspect. The *Kölnische Zeitung,* often inspired by the government, was cordial but vague.
Chamberlain, it said, seemed to take the attitude that Providence had assigned
to other great powers the honorable mission of fighting England's battles.
What the British minister evidently desired was a "continental sword." But
in the German view alliances were concluded for peaceful purposes, not for
war and conquest. It would be better to wait until the English proposition was
made clearer. "As yet Mr. Chamberlain has only set continental politicians a
riddle." The Berlin correspondent of the *Times* thought that in secret the German statesmen would probably endorse Chamberlain's reference to the long
spoon required for supping with Russia, but they were unwilling to jeopardize
their relations with the Tsar.[53]

This was a fairly accurate estimate of the situation. In the conversations between Salisbury and Hatzfeldt in the weeks following the Chamberlain speech
it turned out that an alliance was still in the far and foggy future. The British
prime minister was distinctly unenthusiastic and complained that England
could not always be the giving party. He had little faith in alliances concluded
far in advance. Hatzfeldt came away with the impression that, while the British
statesmen all desired an agreement, they were unwilling to pay a high price.
Under the circumstances it would be best to keep them hopeful. On the German
side there was the same mixed feeling. Speaking to the English ambassador the
Emperor said that he would welcome "a thoroughly good understanding with
England . . . but it must be clearly understood that Germany did not intend to
go to war with Russia for the purpose of driving her out of China." He did not
share Chamberlain's fear of the Russian advance. It would take Russia generations to assimilate what she had already secured. Even if the Germans were
prepared to fight England's battles, they would at once be attacked by Russia
and France. What help could the British fleet give? [54]

For the Emperor the matter evidently reduced itself to a question of bargaining. On May 30, 1898 he despatched a most astonishing letter to his friend
Nicky, telling him of the whole development of the Anglo-German problem,
of Chamberlain's first approaches, of the German conditions and objections, etc.

"I thought the affair had ended. Now however the request has been renewed
for the third time in such an unmistakable manner, putting a *certain short term*
to my definite answer and accompanied by such enormous offers showing a wide

---

[52] London *Times,* May 16, 1898. For several days the *Times* published whole columns of extracts from the continental press. See also the extensive extracts from the newspaper press in *Questions
Diplomatiques et Coloniales,* June, 1898, pp. 173–81.

[53] *Kölnische Zeitung,* May 18, 1898; London *Times,* May 18, 1898.

[54] *Die Grosse Politik,* XIV, nos. 3798–801; *British Documents,* I, no. 53.

and great future opening for my country, that I think it my duty to Germany duly to reflect before I answer. Now before I do, I frankly and openly come to you, my esteemed friend and cousin, to inform you, as I feel that it is a question so to say of life and death. We two have the same opinions, we want peace, and we have sustained and upheld it till now! What the tendence of the Alliance is, you will well understand, as I am informed that the Alliance is to be with the Triple Alliance and with the addition of Japan and America, with whom pourparlers have already been opened! What the chances are for us in refusing or accepting you may calculate yourself! Now as my old and trusted friend I beg you to tell me what you can offer me and will do if I refuse. Before I take my final decision and send my answer in this difficult position, I must be able to see clearly, and clear and open without any back-thoughts must your proposal be, so that I can judge and weigh in my mind before God, as I should, what is for the good of the Peace of my Fatherland and of the world. You need not fear for your Ally in any proposal you make should she be placed in a combination wished by you." [55]

The Emperor's apologists claim that this most unedifying letter was not only suggested but actually worked out by Bülow together with William.[56] There is no proof of this, and it seems on the whole hardly plausible. The letter was too tactless and too crude to have emanated from the German foreign office, though it is always possible that the idea of asking the Tsar what he would offer if Germany refused the British proposition may have come from Bülow. The outcome, in any case, was quite amusing, for the Tsar covered the Emperor's card with a trump. In his reply he told of the "tempting proposals" made to Russia by England three months before.

" That showed us clearly that England needed our friendship at that time, to be able to check our development, in a masked way, in the Far East. Without thinking twice over it, their proposals were refused. Two weeks later Port Arthur was our's. As you know we have arrived at an understanding with Japan upon Corea and we have been since a long time on the best of terms with North America. I really do not see any reason, why the latter should suddenly turn against old friends — only for the ' beaux yeux' of England's? It is very difficult for me, if not quite impossible, to answer your question whether *it is* useful or *not* for Germany to accept these often repeated English proposals, as I have not got the slightest knowledge of their value. *You* must of course decide what is best and most necessary for your country." [57]

A neater turning of the tables could hardly be imagined. The Russians, far from making offers to the Germans, simply pricked the bubble of their pride by revealing to them the proposals of the British, the rejection of which had led to Chamberlain's approaches to Berlin. Germany was not the first love of the

[55] *The Kaiser's Letters to the Tsar*, pp. 50–5.
[56] For example Karl Friedrich Nowak: *Germany's Road to Ruin* (New York, 1932), p. 188.
[57] *Die Grosse Politik*, XIV, no. 3803.

British, but only a second choice. In communicating the Tsar's reply to Count Hatzfeldt, Bülow pointed out that the revelation of the British offers to Russia showed how unreliable the British were. To the British ambassador he recapitulated the German viewpoint: any agreement must be preceded by an assurance that the English public and parliament would accept it, by a British guarantee of reinsurance against Russia, and by a greater English generosity in colonial questions. The fundamental underlying principle must be that of *live and let live.*[58]

We need not pursue this subject farther. It has been necessary to enter into considerable detail and to enlarge upon the matter of public opinion, not only because of the intrinsic importance of the Anglo-German problem, but also because of the very extensive writing on the subject and the many aspects of the question to which attention has been called by other students. German critics are divided into two schools — those who believe that the German government was to blame for the failure of the negotiations, and those who maintain that there were, in reality, no British offers to be rejected. This much can be said with a reasonable degree of certainty: that Lord Salisbury had little use for a policy of permanent alliances and that he preferred to retain for England complete freedom of action; that, though he undoubtedly desired an improvement of Anglo-German relations and hoped for co-operation between the two powers to keep the door open in the Far East and elsewhere, his chief thought was to keep Germany from sinking entirely into the arms of Russia. Even so, he was unwilling to pay an extravagant price for German friendship and support. As he said to Hatzfeldt quite bluntly: "You ask too much for your friendship." To Queen Victoria he wrote: "The truth is that on questions of territorial cession the German Emperor and public opinion here take very opposite views. It would be impossible to do what the German Emperor desires without incurring the reproach of deserting British interests and making undue concessions."[59]

Salisbury and the foreign office never gave their unqualified *imprimatur* to the proposals and negotiations carried on by Chamberlain. The colonial secretary was no great friend of Germany, but he was infuriated by the conduct of Russia and wanted to stop her at all costs. Casting aside the traditions of diplomatic practice he threw his cards on the table and set about making a counting-house deal. But commendable though his frankness may have been in principle, it was hardly likely to make for practical success. The suggestion that the Germans throw over their friendly relations with Russia to aid the British in blocking the Muscovite advance in China was really somewhat naive. No doubt the British people would have welcomed such a combination. But it is more than doubtful whether parliament or public opinion would have countenanced a

---

[58] *Die Grosse Politik,* XIV, nos. 3804–5.

[59] *Letters of Queen Victoria,* III, p. 263; see also the illuminating letter of Hatzfeldt to Bülow, in Bülow: *Memoirs,* I, pp. 323–5.

suggestion that England join the Triple Alliance or enter upon any definite policy of permanent alliances. At all events, as the *Times* pointed out, if a departure became necessary it would have to come from the foreign minister through the regular channels. Salisbury and Balfour, as we know, had a much more modest goal in view. They did not approve of the methods of the " new diplomacy," neither did they have much faith in the policy put forward by their colleague. Salisbury made it perfectly plain to Hatzfeldt that he did not desire the discussions with Chamberlain to go on after he, the prime minister, had returned to the foreign office.[60]

Under the circumstances it is difficult to find fault with the policy of the German government, whether Bülow or Holstein was the moving spirit. Germany was not, at the time, seriously menaced by the Franco-Russian Alliance. It would have been foolhardy to break with Russia without very definite and binding agreements with England. Germany's position between the British on the one side and the French and Russians on the other side was a very strong one, which the foreign office was eager to make the most of. As Bülow said, any agreement generally or specifically eastern Asiatic would have a point against Russia, just as any agreement with Russia would have a point against England. The former would diminish the security of the German frontiers, the other would reduce the chances of gains in the colonial field. Things being what they were it would be better to retain a free hand, making special arrangements with one side or the other when that seemed desirable.[61] After all, this was the policy of Bismarck, who had never allowed himself to be made the tool of the anti-Russian policy pursued by the English in Asia. It is all well and good to maintain that the Iron Chancellor always desired close relations, not to say an alliance with England, but it must not be forgotten what a decisive rôle he assigned to Russia. It may be that the German statesmen were too much afraid that a fast agreement with England would lead to a European war on two fronts. It is probably true, as Professor Meinecke suggests, that the effect of the agreement would have been just the reverse, namely to make the Russians and the French more cautious than ever.[62] It is also likely that the Germans, especially Holstein, underestimated the possibility of an eventual agreement between England on the one hand and the Dual Alliance of Russia and France on the other. But, after all, one must not demand too much of human foresight. In 1898 an agreement between England and France was perhaps feasible, but only at the cost of great concessions by England, which the British public would hardly have agreed to make. But an understanding with Russia was practically impossible. It was tried in the first months of 1898 and

[60] Hatzfeldt to Bülow, June 27, 1898 (Bülow: *Memoirs*, I, pp. 324–5).

[61] *Die Grosse Politik*, XIV, no. 3802.

[62] Friedrich Meinecke: *Geschichte des Deutsch-Englischen Bündnisproblems, 1890–1901* (Munich, 1927), p. 92; similarly Konrad Lehmann: " Die Ablehnung des Englischen Bündnis-antrags, 1898–1901 " (*Preussische Jahrbücher*, August, 1930, pp. 162–83), p. 169.

failed completely. The British and the Russians were at daggers drawn, and it took the complete defeat of Russian policy in the Far East in 1904–1905 to bring an entente within even the range of possibility. Bismarck said somewhere that one could not predict the course of events for more than three years. Judged by the master's standard Bülow and Holstein were quite right.

And after all there was this very great obstacle to an Anglo-German Alliance, even in 1898. For Germany the greatest question, the question of life and death, was always the safety of the frontiers. For England the problem was one of her general position in the world, a problem of world empire. For Germany, of necessity a European power rather than a world power, it was important to divert the other powers to the colonial field and avoid friction on the Continent. Far from desiring to check the Russian policy in Asia, the Germans were deeply interested in seeing Russia become involved in China, where England rather than Germany and Austria would feel the impact of the northern colossus. For that very reason the British policy was to erect a bulwark against Russia in China, so as to shift the burden back to the Continent. This idea was expounded quite baldly by Lord Charles Beresford when he advocated the alliance with Germany in the house of commons on April 5, 1898: "If we have an alliance with Germany there must be 50,000 or 60,000 Russian troops kept on the frontier of Germany. At present there is not any army of Russia at all on the frontier of Germany(!), but there is a good number of troops in Manchuria, a large number in the Caucasus." [63] One could hardly blame the German government for not wanting to be used as a cat's-paw for the British. The American government, though warmly wooed, made even less of a move to follow the British suggestions. Chamberlain was not authorized to make a definite proposal. He never claimed to be speaking in anything more than an informal and unofficial way. The German government could, therefore, give nothing more than an academic answer. The terms it laid down for an eventual alliance were reasonable and necessary if the security of the country was to be safeguarded.[64]

A number of German historians have stressed the point that, in spite of the failure of Chamberlain's proposals, relations between England and Germany were not embittered; that, on the contrary, they remained on a distinctly better basis. This thesis can be accepted only with reservations. The difference was that the two governments talked more with each other than they had in the preceding two years. But the results were meagre enough. Take the case of China, for example. The Germans had refused the suggestion that they join in blocking the further advance of Russia, but they had expressed themselves as anxious for commercial co-operation. There was a good basis for such common action in

---

[63] Hansard: *Parliamentary Debates,* Series IV, vol. LVI, p. 286.

[64] I subscribe here almost unreservedly to the argumentation of Gerhard Ritter: *Die Legende von der Verschmähten Englischen Freundschaft, 1898–1901* (Freiburg, 1929), especially pp. 16–7.

the economic field, because the Hongkong and Shanghai Bank and the Deutsch-Ostasiatische Bank had joined in a loan to China soon after the war of 1894–1895 and had maintained close relations ever since. In the spring of 1898, however, a dispute arose with regard to the concession for the building of the important Shanghai-Nanking Railway. Into the very complicated details of the matter we need not go, the more so as the version of each side flatly contradicted that of the other. What interests us here is the larger aspect of the negotiation. The British government, having failed to secure in the discussions with Russia a demarcation of spheres in China, now tried to obtain from the German government a recognition of its special position in the Yangtze Valley as a set-off against the position secured by Germany in Shantung. The German foreign office, however, refused to regard these two areas as roughly equivalent and insisted that, despite its preferential position in Shantung, it still had a right to participate in railway building in the Yangtze Valley. The discussions at times took on a rather acrimonious tone and led to no satisfactory result, although in September 1898 the two banking groups made an agreement regarding the spheres of their activity.[65]

Within China the international struggle had become centred upon the definition of spheres of interest and upon the competition for railroad concessions. Outside China the great powers were engaged in the partition of the few remaining unappropriated parts of Africa and in the staking out of claims for the future in the territories of the " dying nations," as Lord Salisbury called them. The year 1898 was the year of the Spanish-American War, which thrust the United States quite suddenly into the ranks of the great imperial powers and threw open the question of the succession to Spain's colonial empire. In these questions the British and the Germans were again on opposite sides of the fence. The attention of the British was concentrated on the Far East and on Africa. There was no desire in London to secure any part of the Spanish spoils, but a very decided policy aiming to keep these territories out of the hands of other European powers, notably Germany. Lord Salisbury had, in 1897, consistently rejected German proposals for a protest against the projected American annexation of Hawaii.[66] After Dewey's naval victory over the Spanish squadron at Manila in May 1898 British statesmen and diplomats made it quite clear to the hesitant Washington government that they would like to see the United States take the Philippines. Men like Cecil Spring Rice fanned the flames of American suspicion of Germany. There was talk of England's having frustrated a German plan for a coalition against the Republic, and ever greater efforts were made during the summer of 1898 to popularize the idea of an Anglo-American alliance. An Anglo-American League was founded in London

---

[65] The documents in *Die Grosse Politik*, XIV, nos. 3771–7; *China No. 1 (1899)*, passim. They are well analyzed by Joseph: *Foreign Diplomacy in China*, chap. xiv, passim.

[66] *Die Grosse Politik*, XIII, nos. 3409 ff.

and an Anglo-American Committee in New York. There was hardly a respectable journal on either side of the Atlantic that did not do its bit in the good cause.[67]

The German attitude and policy certainly served as an effective cement for the entente between the Anglo-Saxon countries. Political circles in Berlin had been more or less swept away by the tide of navalism and imperialism, and there was a very general feeling that Germany, having entered the field of colonial activity too late, must not under any circumstances fail to make the most of what opportunities still presented themselves. The naval authorities were anxiously surveying the globe for possible coaling and naval stations and the revolution in the Philippines, followed by the destruction of the Spanish squadron, seemed to offer a rare chance. The Americans were by no means sure that they wanted the islands. The fact was well known and it was therefore quite natural that the Germans should cherish hopes of the succession, the more so as Andrew White, the American ambassador at Berlin, spoke encouragingly. Immediately after Dewey's victory the German admiral in command in the Far East was ordered to send ships to Manila, ostensibly to protect German commercial interests, which, incidentally, were impressively small.[68] Before long the Germans had a squadron at Manila as large as Dewey's, with more marines on board than there were Germans in the whole archipelago. Friction developed between the German commander, Admiral Diederichs, and his American colleague, and the American press before long was engaging in bitter attacks upon the Germans. It was felt that the German fleet, "unmannerly and provocative," was intended "not to protect existing German interests, but to find new interests to protect." By the summer of 1898 relations were so strained that John Hay, wholly under the influence of his English friends, could write to one of the most rabid of American imperialists, Senator Lodge, that the Germans were the enemy:

> "They want the Philippines, the Carolines and Samoa; they want to get into our markets and keep us out of theirs. They have been flirting and intriguing with Spain ever since the war began, and now they are trying to put the Devil into the head of Aguinaldo. I do not think they want to fight. In fact, they frankly tell us they can't. . . . But they want, by pressure, by threats, and by sulking and wheedling in turn to get something out of us and Spain. There is to the German mind something monstrous in the thought that a war should take place anywhere and they not profit by it." [69]

---

[67] See especially Thayer: *Life of John Hay*, II, chap. xxiii; Nevins: *Henry White*, chap. ix; *Letters and Friendships of Sir Cecil Spring Rice*, I, pp. 246–7, 248–53; and the excellent treatment of Bertha A. Reuter: *Anglo-American Relations during the Spanish-American War*, pp. 136, 157 ff.

[68] According to the British sources most of the "German" firms in Manila were Swiss. British interests handled 70% of the imports of the islands, and of the export of sugar, hemp and copra they controlled 80% ("Letter of the Manila Merchants," London *Times*, May 2, 1898).

[69] Alfred L. P. Dennis: *Adventures in American Diplomacy, 1896–1906* (New York, 1928), p. 98.

This letter is a flagrant example of gross exaggeration, and it is quoted merely as a reflection of feeling in high places. Anyone who reads over the documents and periodical literature of the time will be impressed by the tactlessness of German policy toward the hyper-sensitive American republic, but he will be impressed even more with the almost pathological suspicion of Germany which was prevalent in American political and diplomatic circles and with the obvious efforts of men like Spring Rice to fortify the Americans in their distrust. If dislike of Germany had anything to do with inducing the American government to retain the Philippines, then the British object was attained. British policy was successful, but the success was gained at the expense of Germany. It was a strange manifestation of the supposed rapprochement between the two countries.[70]

The German government had begun with the project of establishing a protectorate over the Philippines, and had then reduced its program to a scheme of neutralization or partition. The hostile attitude of the United States, supported by the British, had rendered these plans nugatory. In the late summer of 1898 the German government changed its policy and did everything possible to conciliate the Americans. The explanation for this change lay in the hope of the Germans to avoid American opposition to the purchase from Spain of the Caroline and other Pacific island groups. We need not pursue this matter into its minute details. Secret provisional arrangements were made with Spain on September 10 and December 10, 1898 which resulted eventually in the purchase by Germany of the Caroline, Pelew and Marianne Islands, excepting Guam. Hopes of the Germans for the Sulu Islands, the Canaries and Fernando Po had to be given up. The settlement of the Samoan question had to be left to a later date. The German acquisitions in the Pacific helped to meet the need for naval and coaling stations, the "maritime fulcra" as the Emperor called them, but from the larger viewpoint they could hardly be described as worth the hostility of the United States or the opposition of England.

In the meanwhile other possibilities opened up, possibilities of much greater promise. If Spain was defeated in war, her Iberian neighbor, Portugal, had also descended from her former high estate to the position of a " dying " nation. Since 1852 the little kingdom had been faced with a growing annual deficit which obliged the government to float no less than fourteen loans between 1856 and 1892. The public debt, which came to about twenty-eight million pounds in 1860 and to ninety-seven million in 1880, had risen to one hundred and sixty-

[70] On the whole subject of German-American relations at this time see *Die Grosse Politik*, XV, chaps. xcvii and xcviii; and the detailed treatments of Jeannette Keim: *Forty Years of German-American Relations* (Philadelphia, 1919), chap. vi; Clara E. Schieber: *American Sentiment toward Germany, 1870–1914* (Boston, 1923), pp. 110 ff.; Hermann Leusser: " Ein Jahrzehnt Deutsch-Amerikanischer Politik, 1897–1906 " (*Beiheft der Historischen Zeitschrift*, no. 13, 1928), pp. 18 ff.; Alfred L. P. Dennis: *Adventures in American Diplomacy*, chap. iii; and particularly Lester B. Shippee: " Germany and the Spanish-American War " (*American Historical Review*, July, 1925, pp. 754–77).

three million by 1898. Portuguese credit was exhausted and the government in 1893 felt obliged to resort to desperate measures. It arbitrarily reduced interest on government loans by two thirds, in gold. This measure led to strong protests from the foreign bondholders, and to the use of pretty strong language by the French and German governments, whose nationals, together with the British, held most of the government bonds. Negotiations began between the Lisbon government and the foreign investors, but these dragged on for years before they led to an even halfway satisfactory result.[71]

One of the reasons for Portugal's financial distress was the burden of her undeveloped colonies, of which Angola and Mozambique, in southwest and southeast Africa respectively, were the largest and most important. The English had been connected with Portugal by an alliance dating back to 1373 and often renewed, notably in 1703. It had been reaffirmed by Lord Granville in 1873. In the later part of the nineteenth century the development of the situation in south Africa led to close contact between the British and Portuguese colonies. Mozambique controlled the communications from the sea to the great British possessions in Rhodesia, and, what was more important, to the South African Republic. The English were anxious to secure, if possible, that part of Mozambique south of the Zambezi River, or at any rate to prevent any other power from establishing itself there. In a treaty of June 1891 Britain and Portugal had agreed that in the event of one of them proposing to part with any territories south of the Zambezi the other should be recognized as possessing a preferential right to the territories in question. The construction of the Transvaal-Delagoa Bay Railway, largely financed by German interests, made for greater and greater tension in south Africa. Between 1891 and 1897 Rhodes personally and the Cape Government officially tried on various occasions to buy the southern part of Mozambique or at least the Delagoa Bay area with Lorenzo Marques and the Portuguese part of the railway to the Transvaal. It was natural that banking interests affected by Portugal's financial collapse should try to connect the two problems by either writing off part of the debt in return for the cession of the desired territory or by offering a loan with the revenues of the colonies as security. Many efforts of this sort were made, but they were always rejected by the Portuguese government, because the Portuguese nation regarded the retention of the colonies, last remnant of former greatness, as a matter of national pride. The colonies, said the Portuguese, were their "only guarantee of national importance."[72]

---

[71] The Portuguese financial crisis is well discussed in Augusto Fuschini: *O Presente e o Futuro de Portugal* (Lisbon, 1899), chaps. v and vi. See also Angel Marvaud: *Le Portugal et ses Colonies* (Paris, 1912), pp. 80 ff.; and the excellent brief account in Herbert Feis: *Europe the World's Banker, 1870–1914* (New York, 1930), chap. xi.

[72] Marvaud, op. cit., pp. 274 ff.; Teixera de Sousa: *Para a Historia da Revolução* (Coimbra, 1912), I, pp. 239–40. The British efforts are recounted in detail in W. Basil Worsfold: *The Reconstruction of the New Colonies under Lord Milner* (London, 1913), I, pp. 114 ff.; Sir Lewis Michell: *Life and Times of Cecil John Rhodes* (New York, 1910), II, pp. 95–8; Garvin: *Life of Chamberlain*, III, p. 309.

Since the time of the Jameson raid the relations between Britain and the Transvaal had been growing steadily worse, until in April 1897 the two governments were on the verge of war. Under these circumstances the control of Delagoa Bay became of paramount importance. The British were afraid that Germans, who were acquiring land in the area, might eventually be able to establish themselves there. In any case it was of the utmost importance to England that the wide-open door to the Transvaal, through which Creusot and Krupp were shipping heavy guns for the fortification of Pretoria, should be brought under British surveillance and control. Early in May 1897 Chamberlain therefore proposed to the Portuguese representative in London that England should guarantee the African possessions of Portugal on condition that the latter open no other route from the sea to the Transvaal; Lorenzo Marques and the railway to the Transvaal frontier should be run by a Portuguese-British Company; within a specific area surrounding Lorenzo Marques the Portuguese government should grant no concessions without the consent of the British. Chamberlain also suggested that the Portuguese raise a loan in London, offering the African colonies as security. Such a loan, he thought, would justify the British guarantee suggested in the first proposal. But these proposals, which would have given Britain effective control of Delagoa Bay and the Railway, were rejected by the Lisbon government, as so many similar proposals had been rejected in the past.[73]

Rumors of impending British action in south Africa had aroused the apprehensions of the Germans in the spring of 1897. The foreign office had to make up its mind what attitude to take in the event of a British offensive against the Transvaal. Hatzfeldt, the ambassador at London, strongly urged his government not to contemplate intervention, but to try to come to an agreement with England on the basis of compensations. Seizure of Delagoa Bay by Britain would be a "serious provocation" and might be replied to by a German occupation of those parts of the Portuguese colonies adjacent to the German possessions. Salisbury, to be sure, denied any warlike intentions on the part of Her Majesty's government, but Hatzfeldt carried away the impression that the prime minister would be glad to reach an agreement with Germany regarding the Transvaal if the price were not too high. It seems to have been understood even then that an arrangement might be made with regard to the Portuguese colonies.[74]

The unwillingness of the Lisbon government to consider the British proposals and the temporary relaxation of the tension in England's relations with the Transvaal led to a postponement of the whole problem. The negotiations of 1897 are of importance only in so far as they illustrate the aims of the parties

---

[73] *British Documents,* I, no. 65; Garvin: *Life of Chamberlain,* III, p. 309; Fritz Schwarze: *Das Deutsch-Englische Abkommen über die Portugiesischen Kolonien vom 30 August 1898* (Göttingen, 1931), pp. 15-7.

[74] *Die Grosse Politik,* XIV, nos. 3403 ff.

chiefly concerned. But by May 1898 the situation was once more so acute that a solution seemed imperative. In south Africa events had taken a turn that convinced even the British high commissioner, Sir Alfred Milner, that the Transvaal government was incorrigible and that matters would have to be brought to a head.[75] At the same time affairs in Portugal had gone from bad to worse, until revolution loomed on the horizon and the fall of the dynasty seemed not unlikely. All efforts of the government to make an adjustment with its creditors had failed and there was imminent danger that far-reaching demands might be made before long by the French and German governments. The Lisbon cabinet therefore reopened negotiations with the British government in the hope of securing financial aid. The British conditions were, roughly, the same conditions laid down in 1897: a loan with the revenues of the colonies as security; Portugal to agree not to alienate in any way any part of Delagoa Bay or the approaches to the Transvaal, or to grant any concessions in that area without British consent. The Bay and Railway should be jointly managed. The British aim, wrote Chamberlain to Milner, was to secure commercial control in time of peace and right of occupation in time of war of Delagoa Bay and the Railroad.[76]

While these negotiations were going on in London, news of them leaked out and came into possession of the German and French governments. On June 14, 1898 Count Hatzfeldt interviewed Salisbury on the subject and protested against separate action by the British in the matter of the Portuguese colonies. Salisbury's attitude was not encouraging, for he took the stand that the British government had the right to lend Portugal money. Despite the ambassador's insistence that the security for a loan would necessarily involve the colonies, the prime minister continued to maintain that the question was a financial one.[77]

The German government was, from the very beginning, prepared to make far-reaching concessions in return for an agreement regarding the ultimate disposition of these colonies. Bülow had no use for the anti-British policy of his predecessor in the Transvaal question. He was ready to abandon the Boers to their fate and he was prepared to give up whatever claims or hopes the Germans might have had with regard to Delagoa Bay, if only the Germans could succeed in ear-marking for themselves a fair share of the remaining Portuguese possessions. When Salisbury refused to bargain with the Germans, the Berlin foreign office decided to bring pressure. The French were as much exercised by news of the Anglo-Portuguese negotiations as the Germans, and began to put out feelers in Berlin as to what might be done. Bülow took

---

[75] The Milner Papers, edited by Cecil Headlam (London, 1931), chap. viii, passim; Eric A. Walker: A History of South Africa (London, 1928), pp. 471 ff.

[76] Milner Papers, p. 266; Garvin, op. cit., III, p. 310 ff.

[77] The important sources are Die Grosse Politik, XIV, chap. xcii; British Documents, I, chap. ii. They are analyzed and discussed by Fritz Schwarze: Das Deutsch-Englische Abkommen über die Portugiesischen Kolonien, passim, and summarized in Raymond W. Bixler: Anglo-German Imperialism in South Africa, pp. 114 ff.

advantage of the opportunity. On June 18 he instructed the ambassador at Paris to find out what the French government was prepared to do in the way of bringing pressure on Portugal, hinting at a threat to establish an international financial control. Münster was even to suggest the possibility of practical co-operation in all special questions arising at the time.[78]

Münster discussed this matter with Hanotaux on June 19, and found the French minister much interested and impressed. Unfortunately, however, the cabinet had already fallen and Hanotaux was carrying on at the foreign office only as interim minister. He did, nevertheless, send the suggestion to the embassies, and in the meanwhile lodged a vigorous protest in Lisbon. Nothing more was done in the matter, for Hanotaux' successor, M. Delcassé, did not take the suggestion very seriously and allowed it to drop.[79]

In his later writings Hanotaux took the stand that Delcassé's indifference spoiled the chance of an understanding which might have been of very great value to France on the eve of her great conflict with England over the Sudan. This is probably something of an exaggeration. The evidence would indicate that Bülow from the beginning desired an arrangement with England. The suggested action with France was simply intended to force the British into negotiations. In any event the move was a good one. The British were evidently uneasy about French territorial designs on the African coast opposite Madagascar, and they realized that any financial agreement they might make with Portugal would be apt to arouse opposition among other powers having a financial stake in the country and being therefore unwilling to see the national income in any way impaired or endangered. As a matter of fact the negotiations with Portugal were making no satisfactory progress. The Portuguese minister in London, Marquis de Soveral, was evidently willing to go to any lengths to secure the support of England, but the Lisbon government was in constant dread of public opinion if important sacrifices had to be made.[80]

Originally, when the Germans had made known in London their objection to a separate agreement between England and Portugal, the British statesmen seem to have planned to buy off German opposition by modest concessions. Chamberlain wrote to Milner that the colonial office was willing to offer Germany Walfisch Bay in return for her services as " honest broker " to induce Portugal to give England " the predominating influence in the region of the port of Delagoa." To which Milner replied that he feared the cession of Walfisch Bay would cause an outcry at the Cape unless some further compensation were secured.[81] At the very same time the British learned of the German and French

---

[78] *Die Grosse Politik,* XIV, nos. 3812, 3813.

[79] Hanotaux: *Fachoda,* p. 132; André Mevil: *De la Paix de Francfort à la Conférence d'Algésiras* (Paris, 1909), pp. 12–8, giving the Delcassé version. Delcassé in March 1902 denied that any propositions had been made by Germany to Hanotaux concerning " the Portuguese colonies," which was mere quibbling. See *Documents Diplomatiques Français, 1871–1914,* II, no. 157.

[80] These points are well discussed by Schwarze, op. cit., pp. 19 ff.

[81] *Milner Papers,* pp. 266–7.

protests and threats to Portugal. Taken together these developments practically forced a widening of the basis of negotiation. Discussions were begun between Salisbury and Hatzfeldt early in July and continued through August. This is not the place for a day by day record of the proposals and counter-proposals. We must content ourselves with the mention of the chief points in the negotiation. From the start it should be said that there was little enthusiasm on the British side. Foreign office officials, like Francis Bertie, argued in a number of memoranda that no concessions should be made, for England could get everything she wanted without German aid, and these sacrifices would not lead to any further entente in matters like the Far Eastern. These memoranda seem to have had no important effect on the negotiations, but Lord Salisbury apparently shared the feeling expressed in them, namely that the Germans asked too much (" you want the whole of Africa," he told Hatzfeldt on one occasion), and that they were intent on securing the succession to a large part of the Portuguese colonial empire, which England would have liked to see kept intact under British influence. There was something in Hatzfeldt's remark that the British would rather make considerable concessions to other nations than to abandon any colonial territory to Germany, their chief rival.[82] Nevertheless the question had to be settled somehow. The British needed control of Delagoa Bay and the Railroad to the Transvaal. It was of key importance. "I look on possession of Delagoa Bay as the best chance we have of winning the great game between ourselves and the Transvaal for the mastery of South Africa without a war," wrote Milner. On other occasions he spoke of it as " politically invaluable," " a trump card." [83]

Realizing this, the Germans were determined to make the best of their opportunity. Their demands from the beginning were really high, and during the course of the negotiations they showed no compunction about using strong language. The English were given to understand that if they were obdurate the Germans would have to look elsewhere, that they would have to act with France and Russia, and that in African affairs they might have to seek an agreement with France that would extend even to Egypt. At other times they used the opposite tactics and dangled before the British the prospect of a larger entente, touching even the Far East, if the London government would only be reasonable.[84]

The Germans began by asking for participation in the projected loan to Portugal, security for the British part to be the revenues of Mozambique south of the Zambezi River, security for the German part to be the revenues of the northern part of Mozambique as well as of the whole of Angola. The British declared these demands to be exorbitant, but in a general way they eventually agreed to them. The arguments centered chiefly on the modalities of the loan,

---

[82] *Die Grosse Politik*, XIV, no. 3823; Garvin, op. cit., III, pp. 313 ff.

[83] *Milner Papers*, pp. 267–8.

[84] *Die Grosse Politik*, XIV, nos. 3818, 3854, 3865, etc.

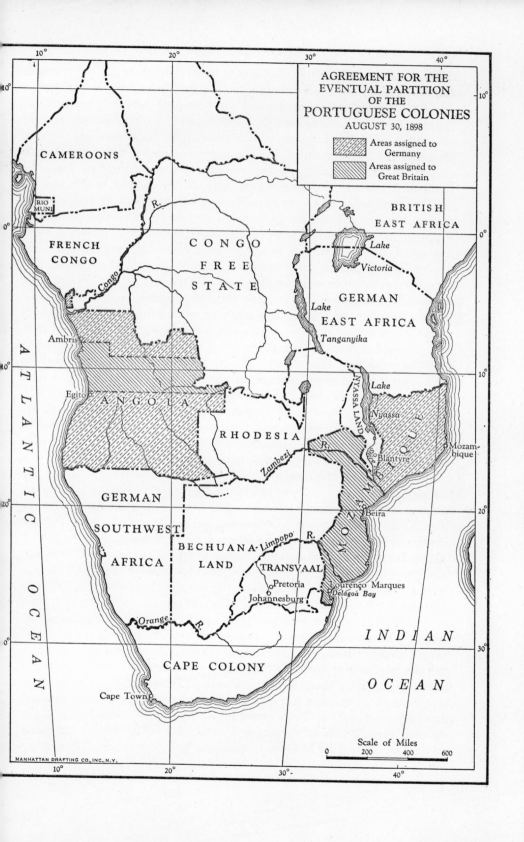

AGREEMENT FOR THE
EVENTUAL PARTITION
OF THE
PORTUGUESE COLONIES
AUGUST 30, 1898

Areas assigned to
Germany

Areas assigned to
Great Britain

CAMEROONS

RIO
MUNI

FRENCH
CONGO

BRITISH
EAST AFRICA

C O N G O

F R E E

S T A T E

Lake
Victoria

GERMAN
EAST AFRICA

Lake
Tanganyika

Ambris

Egito

A N G O L A

RHODESIA

Zambezi

R.

Lake
Nyassa

Blantyre

Mozam-
bique

NYASSALAND

MOZAMBIQUE

Beira

GERMAN

SOUTHWEST

AFRICA

BECHUANA-

LAND

Limpopo R.

TRANSVAAL

Pretoria

Johannesburg

Lourenço Marques
Delagoa Bay

Orange
R.

CAPE COLONY

Cape Town

A T L A N T I C   O C E A N

I N D I A N

O C E A N

Scale of Miles

0   200   400   600

MANHATTAN DRAFTING CO., INC., N.Y.

the time and extent of British and German control over these colonial revenues, and details of the territorial demarcation. The British from the first refused to consider the abandonment of the Blantyre district of British Nyassaland, on the Shiré River. As compensation the Germans asked for Walfisch Bay and the assignment of the Portuguese part of the island of Timor. The British, on the other hand, demanded that Germany give up her right of extraterritoriality in Zanzibar, and agree to the cession of Togo, a proposal which the Germans would not for a moment entertain. In the end the matter was adjusted by the division of Angola in such a way that the Germans were assigned the southern part and also the northern quarter, the remainder falling into the British sphere. For the rest it will suffice to summarize the agreement as it was signed on August 30, 1898. In the preamble of the convention it was stated that "in order to obviate the international complications" which might arise if Portugal required financial assistance from some foreign power or powers, and in order "to preserve her integrity and independence," it had been agreed between Germany and England that whenever either party believed it expedient to accede to a request for a loan on the security of the Portuguese colonial revenues, it should inform the other party, which should have the right to advance a portion of the loan. The part advanced by either party should be as nearly as possible proportional to the amounts of revenue respectively assigned as their security, and the loans should be on terms as favorable to Portugal as possible. Then followed the definition of the parts of Mozambique, Angola and Portuguese Timor, the revenues of which should be assigned to either Germany or England as security for their part of the loan. Delegates might be sent by either party to these areas, but they were to have no rights of administration or control unless Portugal defaulted on the interest payments, in which case the customs houses should be handed over to the contracting parties. In future neither party was to attempt to secure concessions in the areas assigned to the other. There followed a secret convention, envisaging the possibility that the integrity of the Portuguese possessions could not be maintained. In that event "Great Britain and Germany agree jointly to oppose the intervention of any third Power in the Provinces of Mozambique, Angola and in Portuguese Timor, either by way of loan to Portugal on the security of the revenues of those provinces, or by way of acquisition of territory, by grant, cession, purchase, lease, or otherwise." Henceforth both parties agreed to abstain "from advancing any claim of whatsoever kind to the possession, occupation, control, or exercise of political influence in or over those portions of the Portuguese provinces in which the Customs revenues have been assigned" to the other. Finally there was a secret note clarifying the preceding conventions. In case either party obtained from Portugal a cession of territory or the concession of special privileges not of an occasional character in its sphere before the general abandonment of the territories envisaged above, the cession or concession should not become operative until the other party had secured analogous grants in its sphere. Each party should inform the other of applications for privileges of an occasional character and should help the other get similar grants if it so desired.[85]

The course of the discussions in London was constantly disturbed by the intervention of the Emperor William. At his instigation his mother, the Empress Frederick, wrote a number of letters to Queen Victoria during the last days of July and the beginning of August, in which she seems to have stressed the eagerness of the Emperor and Bülow for an agreement with England, while hinting at the same time that Salisbury was an obstacle to a good understanding. The text of most of these letters has not been published, either in the *Letters of the Empress Frederick,* or in the *Letters of Queen Victoria.* It is clear from Salisbury's correspondence with the Queen, however, that the prime minister greatly resented the implications in the Berlin letters, that he denied having received the German proposals with " something between a joke and a snub," and that he simply felt that the German demands were so extravagant that British public opinion would never tolerate them.[86] He was probably glad when his physician ordered a vacation and he could turn over the conduct of the negotiations to Balfour.

The Emperor's conversations with the British ambassador were marked by the same querulousness. At a meeting at Friedrichshof on August 21, 1898, His Majesty spoke with great bitterness of British hesitation and close-fistedness. The English must realize, he asserted, that Germany had to have colonies and coaling stations and that she was going to get them. He much preferred to attain his object through understanding and co-operation with England, but if the London government forced him to it, he could and would succeed even against British opposition. His relations with Russia and France were excellent, and his relations with the United States government, despite British efforts to poison the American press, had also remained cordial.

Sir Frank Lascelles tried to assuage the Emperor's indignation by referring to the projected agreement between England and Germany. He understood perfectly that the Germans could not commit themselves to opposition of Russia, inasmuch as England could not help to protect the German frontier. He had told this to some of his friends during a recent visit to England. Indeed he had been at lunch with Chamberlain, Balfour, Goschen and other cabinet ministers when the whole subject was discussed. The colonial secretary had been greatly impressed with the argument that England could do nothing to defend Germany, and had finally suggested that a defensive alliance might be concluded between the two nations providing that if either were attacked by two powers, the other should come to its assistance: " One of us is strong enough to fight any *one* Power, who should attack him, but in case of *two*

---

[85] *Die Grosse Politik,* XIV, no. 3872; *British Documents,* I, nos. 90–2. By far the best digest of the negotiations is in Schwarze: *Das Deutsch-Englische Abkommen, etc.,* pp. 31–61; the summary in Bixler: *Anglo-German Imperialism in South Africa,* pp. 114–34 is dull and unenlightening.

[86] *Letters of Queen Victoria,* III, pp. 258–63; Lee: *Edward VII,* I, pp. 736–7.

Powers attacking, the issue is at least very doubtful; therefore: should Germany be assaulted by any *two Powers* at *once* England is ready to assist with every armament in her power to knock down one of her antagonists, whilst Germany is fighting the other one; the same England would wish Germany to do should the case be the reverse." The other ministers present, according to Lascelles, approved of this project. The Emperor was much taken with it and suggested that it might be a feasible basis for an agreement.[87]

So far as one can judge from the documents the Germans took Lascelles' remarks very much *au sérieux,* and immediately began to consider the advisability of a general agreement on this basis. The Emperor's remarks to Lascelles in December of the same year show that he regarded the reputed plan for a defensive alliance almost as an informal promise of assistance. German historians have, many of them, looked upon this conversation as almost crucial and have criticized the government for its hesitancy and failure to follow up the suggestion. To the present writer this all seems somewhat beside the point. Lascelles admitted later that he had had no instructions to touch upon the matter. He protested that the Emperor had made more of his remarks than had been intended. The whole scheme smacked strongly of Chamberlain's general line of thought, and there is nothing unlikely in the statement that Balfour and other members of the cabinet who desired a rapprochement with Germany approved the plan in principle. But Salisbury was not at the luncheon, and it may be doubted whether he would have approved so far-reaching a project. The whole discussion was of a purely academic character and no steps were ever taken from the British side to make the subject a matter of negotiation.

Indeed, when one looks even at the agreement respecting the Portuguese colonies it is hard to find in it any great contribution to a sound Anglo-German understanding. The two powers who concluded this agreement did not see eye to eye, they did not have the same objectives in view. England began with a burning desire to get control of Delagoa Bay and the railway to the Transvaal, or at any rate with the firm determination that no other powers should secure such control. Because of Portugal's desperate financial position, because of her financial obligations to Germany and France as well as to England, there was always the danger that the all-important Bay might be hypothecated by the Lisbon government. It was almost a certainty that any British effort to secure control of that area would meet with unyielding opposition from the continental powers. Yet the English never could shake off the feeling that they should have been allowed to make their own arrangements with Portugal without interference by other powers. Even Chamberlain had the feeling that the Germans were blackmailing the London government: " The only advantage to us," he wrote to Balfour, " is the assurance of Germany's abstention from further interference in Delagoa Bay and the Transvaal — in other words, we pay

---

[87] *Die Grosse Politik,* XIV, no. 3865; *British Documents,* I, nos. 87, 122; II, nos. 96, 97; Garvin, op. cit., III, pp. 290 ff.

Blackmail to Germany to induce her not to interfere where she has no right of interference. Well! it is worth while to pay Blackmail sometimes." [88] And so the idea of blackmail became firmly fixed in the minds of the men who conducted Britain's international affairs. The agreement did not by any means make for greater confidence or trust between the two nations, even though, as we see it now, it was of tremendous importance to England so far as the south African situation was concerned and there was every reason why the London government should have been satisfied with it. After all, it put an end not only to the pro-Boer policy of the Germans, but also shut out France from any share in the ultimate division of the south African spoils. [89]

What really lay at the bottom of British discontent was the idea that the Germans should get so large an increase in territory even prospectively. Chamberlain's thought originally was to make arrangements with Portugal and then settle with the Germans. If that plan had succeeded, we may rest assured that the Germans would have gotten very little, and *that* probably not in south Africa. For the British did not want to partition the Portuguese colonies with any other power. They wanted no other partner in south Africa and liked to think of the Portuguese colonies as a British preserve. Once the agreement with Germany was made, they did their utmost to prevent it from materializing. Within a month of the signature of the document Balfour seems to have informed the Portuguese minister, Soveral, of its general tenor, and the substance of the treaty was allowed to get into the press. The Lisbon government, possibly with English aid, managed to raise funds in Paris on the security of domestic revenues and was thus able to avoid a loan in London or Berlin with a pledge of the colonies. The satisfaction of the English, I think, still rings through the pages of Garvin's *Life of Chamberlain,* where there are gleeful references to the "imaginary repasts" which were spread before the Germans, to "imaginary reversions," to the "mirage" of which Germany was given a share, and to "the castle in the clouds" for which the Emperor William gave up his pro-Boer policy. [90]

Fortunately for Anglo-German relations and for the peace of the world, the Berlin government was not aware of British intentions. The Germans paid a high price for the agreement and they expected to realize upon it at an early date. It was to be some time before they understood that after weeks of acrimonious bargaining they had "waged and won a fight for shadows." During the autumn of 1898 they were still deluded, still hopeful. And so, for the time being, the relations between London and Berlin benefitted from the agreement.

[88] Garvin, op. cit., III, p. 315.

[89] Balfour and Milner, at least, appreciated these aspects of the agreement and therefore welcomed it. See *Milner Papers,* p. 299; *Letters of Queen Victoria,* III, p. 266.

[90] Garvin, op. cit., III, pp. 313–6; the substance of the agreement was published by Diplomaticus (probably Lucien Wolf): "The Anglo-German Agreement" (*Fortnightly Review,* October, 1898, pp. 627–34). On this whole aspect of the problem see the excellent discussion in Schwarze, op. cit., Part III, which obviates more detailed treatment here.

As we review the Anglo-German problem we can see that imperialism, as it spread to the continental nations, tended to put the British into a position where, in the opinion of some cabinet ministers at least, isolation had become dangerous and outside support indispensable. The historian, in discussing this situation, must guard against the unwarranted use of hindsight and against bootless sentimentality. Let us assume that if a close Anglo-German alliance had existed in 1914 the world cataclysm would have been impossible. Let us grant the great importance and desirability of this combination, which, as we look back, seems so logical, so sensible, so sweetly reasonable. But in 1898 affairs were such that the conclusion of such an agreement was practically impossible. In the first place there was the strong current of popular dislike on both sides. German press opinion may be discounted, since it was to a large degree inspired. But the British public saw in Germany its chief rival, the pushing parvenu whose efforts it was something of a pleasure to frustrate. It need not be assumed that this popular hostility was an insurmountable obstacle to an agreement. John Morley once spoke with some alarm of the " almost reckless vacillation of popular humour " with respect to foreign nations.[91] The government could undoubtedly have done much to change the general temper. In fact, the tone of the British press was improved as a result of the efforts of the Queen.

More important, then, than the popular hostility to Germany was the attitude of the directing statesmen. It is certain that since 1895 the British government had been trying first and foremost to effect an agreement with Russia. It was the logical policy to follow, for if successful it would have obviated many points of friction and would at the same time have undermined the Franco-Russian Alliance. This policy met with complete failure in the winter of 1897–1898. A policy of enlisting the aid of Japan and America proved illusory. The alliance with Germany was never anything more than a second or third choice. Chamberlain approached it cold-bloodedly. He really hoped to find in Germany a continental sword. Balfour appears more than any other British statesman to have seen the Anglo-German problem in its larger setting and to have worked for a gradual amelioration of the relationship between the two countries. Salisbury, however, had the deciding vote, and Salisbury had been soured by his past experiences with the Germans and especially with the Emperor. He took the Far Eastern situation more lightly and more stoically than Chamberlain, and he did not believe that the time had come to throw away the advantages of isolation, that is, the advantages of an absolutely free hand. What was more, he did not like the idea of making sacrifices to secure the support of the Germans, though he was prepared to throw half of Asia to the omnivorous Russian bear. Our material is still very inadequate, but it seems reasonably clear that Salisbury was never in favor of the Chamberlain policy and refused to assume responsibility for it. Since he was prime minister and foreign minister, it was his opinion, his policy that counted, not Chamberlain's.

---

91 Speech of March 24, 1898 (London *Times*, March 25, 1898).

In considering the German attitude one must begin with the realization that no British offers were rejected, for the simple reason that no offers were made. The British *foreign office* never went beyond the modest expression of desires for better relations and for an agreement on special points, as put forward by Balfour in March 1898. The important point on the German side was the discussion and determination of a policy to be followed if offers were eventually made. There can be little question that both the Emperor and Bülow desired improved relations. They were, however, decidedly opposed to being made the cat's-paw against Russia. If it was to Britain's interest to check the Russian expansion in the Far East, it was to Germany's interest to see her eastern neighbor deeply involved in Asia. To block the Russians in China would have meant simply to throw them back on Europe. Even if war with Russia and France had not followed the conclusion of an Anglo-German alliance (and it is unlikely that war would have resulted) the fact remains that such an alliance would have diverted to the German frontier much of the pressure that was being exerted on the Celestial Empire. The Germans were therefore sceptical, and rightly sceptical, of any far-reaching alliance with England, the more so as there was every reason to believe that further developments would make the abandonment of isolation all the more imperative for England and that eventually even the Salisbury viewpoint would have to be modified.

In the meanwhile both sides had expressed their readiness to discuss special problems. The negotiations that took place during the year indicated, however, how difficult even minor agreements were in practice. The trouble was that the proper atmosphere was lacking. Suspicion, jealousy, recrimination prevailed on both sides. The British hated the idea of making extensive concessions to the Germans, while the Germans always felt that the British, already the possessors of a large part of the globe, begrudged their late-coming cousins even the most trivial acquisitions. Of course there was more than a little hysteria in this rampant imperialism and much sleep was lost over territories of no importance. But these psychological elements must be considered. People simply became panicky as they saw the world shrinking. Nothing seemed quite so important as to get everything possible before it was too late, and to allow as little as possible to pass into the hands of competitors. It must be confessed that the Germans made something of a nuisance of themselves by interjecting themselves into every problem and by demanding compensation everywhere and at all times. But it is equally true that the British took a negative stand to begin with and showed an extraordinary tendency to look with greater equanimity upon the voracious appetite of Russia and France than upon the relatively unimpressive nibblings of the Germans. The curious thing is that the British knew that what went to Russia and France would be pretty securely locked against competing traders, while the German territories were almost as wide open as the British. The only explanation is that the Russians and the French were not serious commercial rivals of the British. One could hold one's own against them despite their exclusive policy. With the Germans the reverse was true. They were getting the better of the British even in the markets of the Empire. That was where the shoe pinched. It was that which lay at the bottom of the suspicion and the jealousy. To be sure, rivalries of this type have a way of adjusting themselves with the passage of time. The commercial antagonism between England and Germany was probably less marked in 1912 than it was in 1898. But we are concerned here with the earlier period, and when one reviews the situation as it was in the last years of the dying century one can hardly avoid the conclusion that the general setting of affairs was such that a real reconciliation between England and Germany was a high fence to ride at.

BIBLIOGRAPHICAL NOTE

DOCUMENTARY SOURCES

Accounts and Papers. 1899, volume CIX. *China No. 1 (1899)*: *Correspondence respecting the Affairs of China*. Contains the material on the occupation of Weihaiwei, on the concessions secured by the French, on various railway problems, etc.

Die Grosse Politik der Europäischen Kabinette, 1871–1914. Volume XIV, chapters xci and xcii. The most important source for the history of the Anglo-German negotiations and the agreement on the Portuguese colonies.

British Documents on the Origins of the War, 1898–1914. Volume I, chapter ii. Though the British documents contain almost nothing on the Anglo-German alliance negotiations, they are quite full on the Portuguese affair and form an admirable supplement to the German publication.

TELESHEV, L.: "Anglo-Germanskoe Sblishenie v 1898 g." (*Krasnyi Arkhiv*, LVI, 1933, pp. 65–79). A series of reports from the Russian ambassador at Berlin, revealing his uneasiness about the Anglo-German rapprochement. These documents have been translated and published in the *Berliner Monatshefte*, XI, 1933, pp. 492–510.

MEMOIRS, AUTOBIOGRAPHIES, BIOGRAPHIES, AND LETTERS

GARVIN, J. L.: *The Life of Joseph Chamberlain*. Three volumes. London, 1933—. Volume three is by far the most important English source on the Anglo-German negotiations of 1898.

The Letters of Queen Victoria. Edited by George E. Buckle. Series III, volume III. London, 1932. In view of the paucity of British source material these letters are of great interest and value.

LEE, SIR SIDNEY: *King Edward VII, a Biography*. Two volumes. New York, 1925. Contains a discussion of the Anglo-German problem, but the account is very incomplete and remarkably biassed.

The Milner Papers. South Africa, 1897–1899. Edited by Cecil Headlam. London, 1931. Apart from their value for the study of the south African question these papers contain some illuminating bits on the Portuguese colonial problem.

Memoirs of Prince von Bülow. Four volumes. Boston, 1931–1932. Volume I deals with this period but contains extraordinarily little of importance.

ECKARDSTEIN, HERMANN FREIHERR VON: *Lebenserinnerungen und Politische Denkwürdigkeiten*. Two volumes. Leipzig, 1919. The recollections of the counsellor of the German embassy in London. Full of sensational revelations, elegantly written, but thoroughly unreliable and therefore of very little use.

SPECIAL STUDIES

MEINECKE, FRIEDRICH: *Geschichte des Deutsch-Englischen Bündnisproblems, 1890–1901*. Munich, 1927. Easily the most brilliant treatment of the whole question. Written with breadth of view and fairness. Based on the German documents, this is the classic formulation of the critical view of German policy in its relation to England.

RITTER, GERHARD: *Die Legende von der Verschmähten Englischen Freundschaft, 1898–1901*. Freiburg, 1929. Another brilliant piece of synthetic work, which, in the opinion of the present writer, comes nearer the truth than Meinecke's interpretation. Ritter has used the British as well as the German documents and argues that the British offers were never concrete enough to lead to anything.

PRIBRAM, ALFRED F.: *England and the International Policy of the European Great Powers, 1871–1914*. Oxford, 1931. A series of lectures, giving in brief scope an excellent factual and interpretive account.

FISCHER, EUGEN: *Holsteins Grosses Nein*. Berlin, 1925. One of the most extensive and one of the most critical and hostile accounts of the policy of Bülow and Holstein. Now rather out of date.

SALOMON, FELIX: " Die Englisch-Deutschen Bündnisverhandlungen von 1898– 1901, im Weltpolitischen Zusammenhang." (*Die Grenzboten,* August 29, 1920, pp. 200–14). Though now out of date this essay is still worth reading.

ROLOFF, GUSTAV: " Die Bündnisverhandlungen zwischen Deutschland und England 1898–1901." (*Berliner Monatshefte,* December, 1929, pp. 1167–222). One of the best systematic accounts, based on both the British and German documents. Supersedes the author's earlier essay in the *Preussische Jahrbücher,* September, 1919, pp. 345–64. Critical of the Meinecke viewpoint.

HALLER, JOHANNES: *England und Deutschland um die Jahrhundertwende*. Leipzig, 1929. Written by one of Bülow's keenest and most merciless critics. Sticks by his condemnation of the German policy despite the British documents.

BECKER, WILLY: *Fürst Bülow und England, 1897–1909.* Greifswald, 1929. An extensive study of Bülow's English policy. Conventional and adds little. See also the same author's article " Englands Bündniswerben — eine Legende " (*Vergangenheit und Gegenwart,* XX, 1930, pp. 21–8), which is a reply to Ritter.

EHRINGHAUS, FRITZ: " Die Ergebnisse der Englischen Akten über die Deutsch-Englischen Bündnisverhandlungen 1899–1901." (*Vergangenheit und Gegenwart,* XIX, 1929, pp. 471–80). Goes even beyond Ritter in deflating the conventional German view.

ROTHFELS, HANS: " Zur Beurteilung der Englischen Vorkriegspolitik." (*Archiv für Politik und Geschichte,* 1926, no. 12, pp. 599–615). A brilliant discussion of the larger problem of general British policy.

LEHMANN, KONRAD: " Die Ablehnung des Englischen Bündnisantrags, 1898–1901." (*Preussische Jahrbücher,* August, 1930, pp. 162–83). An excellent recent presentation of the Meinecke viewpoint, with due consideration for the British documents.

KEHR, ECKART: " Das Deutsch-Englische Bündnisproblem der Jahrhundertwende." (*Die Gesellschaft,* July, 1928, pp. 24–31). Elaborates the idea tentatively put forward by Meinecke, that the fundamental reason for the failure of the negotiations was the objection of certain social classes in Germany to any connexion with England.

HOYNINGEN GENANNT HUENE, HEINRICH FREIHERR VON: *Untersuchungen zur Geschichte des Deutsch-Englischen Bündnisproblems, 1898–1901.* Breslau, 1934. Does not deal with the negotiations properly speaking, but gives a good analysis of the international background.

MECENSEFFY, GRETE: " Die Deutsch-Englischen Bündnisverhandlungen 1898–1901 im Lichte der Englischen Aktenpublikation." (*Vierteljahrschrift für Politik und Geschichte,* I, 1929, pp. 175–91). A conventional analysis of the British documents.

LÖDING, WALTER: *Die Deutsch-Englischen Bündnisverhandlungen 1898–1901.* Hamburg, 1929. A doctoral dissertation that adds very little, but gives one of the most complete factual digests of the material.

JOHNSON, EDGAR N., and BICKFORD, JOHN D.: " The Contemplated Anglo-German Alliance. 1890–1901." (*Political Science Quarterly,* March, 1927, pp. 1–57). A fairly pedestrian piece of work, of no great importance.

STAL'NYI, V.: " Popytka Anglo-Germanskogo Sblisheniia v 1898–1901 gg." (*Istorik Marksist,* X, 1928, pp. 89–120). A Marxian interpretation, based chiefly on Eckardstein and the German Documents.

GOOCH, GEORGE P.: " Baron von Holstein." In the author's *Studies in Modern History.* London, 1931. Easily the best scholarly study of the extraordinary figure who had so much to do with directing German policy in these years.

BECKER, OTTO: Review of the books by Meinecke and Ritter. (*Deutsche Literaturzeitung,* L, pp. 903–25). This extensive review of two conflicting interpretations is in itself an interesting contribution to the discussion of the problem.

PICK, FRITZ: " Das Deutsch-Englische Bündnis." (*Preussische Jahrbücher,* January, 1935, pp. 56–65). A discussion of the third volume of Garvin's *Chamberlain.*

ROSEN, FRIEDRICH: " Die Deutsch-Englischen Bündnisverhandlungen des Jahres 1898." (*Berliner Monatshefte,* March, 1935, pp. 192–207). Like the preceding, an evaluation of the new English material.

SCHWARZE, FRITZ: *Das Deutsch-Englische Abkommen über die Portugiesischen Kolonien vom 30 August 1898.* Göttingen, 1931. A doctoral dissertation that is far above the average. Combines good command of the material in the British and German documents with keen understanding of the broader issues involved.

BIXLER, RAYMOND W.: *Anglo-German Imperialism in South Africa.* Baltimore, 1932. Contains an extended digest of the British and German material on the Portuguese Treaty of 1898. Conventional, unilluminating and dull.

LOPES, ARTHUR RIBEIRO: *A Convenção Secreta entre a Alemanha e a Inglaterra sôbre a Partilha das Colónias Portuguesas.* Lisbon, 1933. Nothing more than a digest of the British Documents on the secret treaty of 1898.

XVI

The Struggle for the Nile

III. The Fashoda Conflict

⌒

IN THE SPRING OF 1898, DURING THE HEIGHT OF THE FAR EASTERN CRISIS AND at a time when the foreign policy of Lord Salisbury was being bitterly criticized, one of the under-secretaries of the foreign office is reputed to have said to a prominent journalist: " There are certain things we can do and certain things we cannot do. Believe me, we shall retrieve ourselves completely in the Soudan." [1] And, in very fact, when the great victory was won over the French in the autumn of 1898 the prime minister's reputation was completely re-established. Many people thought that his whole policy since 1895 had been pointed towards the great African crisis. Concessions had been made to both the Russians and the Germans, and the Far Eastern situation had not been brought to a climax, simply because the thought and determination of the foreign office had been concentrated upon the struggle for the Nile, a struggle that had been steadily developing for years and had entered upon the swelling act after the battle of Adua and the British advance to Dongola.[2]

The reader will recall the argument advanced in a previous chapter with respect to the motives that led to the first phase of the reconquest of the Sudan. The British decided to march upon Dongola not only in order to relieve the pressure upon the Italians, but also in order to anticipate action by the French upon the upper Nile. Dongola was occupied by the Egyptian forces in the autumn of 1896, but that settled nothing. From the beginning Lord Salisbury realized that the Egyptians, perhaps supported by British troops, would have to advance at least as far as Khartum. In June he told the house of lords: " We shall not have restored Egypt to the position in which we received her, and we shall not have placed Egypt in that position of safety in which she deserves to stand, until the Egyptian flag floats over Khartum." But there were great obstacles to the realization of this object. The Egyptian government did not have the one or two million pounds required for such an expedition, and could not borrow it. The British parliament almost certainly would have refused to finance the undertaking. Besides, Salisbury had always planned an advance from

---

[1] Diplomaticus: "Fashoda and Lord Salisbury's Vindication " (*Fortnightly Review*, December, 1898, pp. 1002–14), p. 1002.　　　　[2] See supra, chapter IX.

the south to meet the push from the north. But operations from Uganda were impossible before the Railway was completed to Lake Victoria. For troops to march from the coast to the interior would have required ninety days alone. The Railway was indispensable, but another two years were needed to bring it to the Lake.[3]

Because of these considerations the military operations were suspended for some time, excepting for the construction of a railway from Wady Halfa across the desert that fills the great bend in the Nile below Abu Hamed. The latter place was occupied by Egyptian troops in August 1897. In the meanwhile developments were taking place which were to force the British government to hasten operations and to press on to Khartum before it really felt ready. We must turn now to an account of events in the interior of Africa and in Abyssinia, events which make an extraordinary and thrilling story.

For years the French government had been trying to effect the evacuation of Egypt by the British. Having failed to attain this object it had decided to make a thrust at the upper Nile and to force an agreement on the Egyptian question by threatening to interfere with the water supply of the regions along the lower river. It had frustrated the effort of the British to block the advance from the French Congo by setting up Leopold as lessee of the upper Nile territory as far north as Fashoda. After the agreement between France and the Congo State in August 1894 the French expedition under Monteil was, indeed, recalled, but his place was taken by M. Liotard, who was instructed to establish effective occupation in the regions along the M'Bomu River and on the other side of the Congo-Nile watershed. In February 1896 the French government, warmly harangued by Monteil's associate, Captain Marchand, had decided to resume its earlier plan and send an expedition to the upper Nile. When Marchand left France in May 1896 he was placed under the general direction of Liotard, was told to avoid hostilities, especially with the dervishes, and to remember that his force was too small to make actual conquest possible. In other words, the purpose of the Marchand mission, whatever may have been said of it later, was to get a footing on the upper Nile to serve as a pawn in later negotiations with the British about Egypt. To quote General Mangin, who was one of the members of the expedition, the object was " to remove all pretext for the occupation of Egypt by the English and to put an end to the dream of our dear friends, who wish to unite Egypt with the Cape and their possessions in East Africa with those of the Royal Niger Company." Hanotaux himself told Marchand as the latter left Paris: " Go to Fashoda. France is going to fire her pistol." [4]

---

[3] *Letters of Queen Victoria*, Series III, vol. III (New York, 1932), pp. 39, 50, 72, 85; Lord Cromer: *Modern Egypt* (New York, 1908), II, p. 94.

[4] Général Mangin: " Lettres de la Mission Marchand " (*Revue des Deux Mondes*, September 15, 1931, pp. 241–83), pp. 246–7, 277. See also Jules Cocheris: *La Situation Internationale de l'Égypte* (Paris, 1903), p. 492. These utterances hardly fortify the arguments of Hanotaux and Lebon (at that time foreign minister and colonial minister respectively) that they tried to tone down the earlier in-

Into the details of the Marchand mission we cannot enter here. At the very outset the expedition was delayed by a native rising on the lower Congo, so that it did not leave Brazzaville until March 1897. But by August 1897 the French force had crossed the watershed of the Nile and Congo and had joined Liotard in establishing posts in the Bahr-el-Ghazal area. A small steamboat, the *Faidherbe,* was demounted, thousands of natives were pressed into service, and in a remarkably short time the steamer was carried and dragged over the high ground to the nearest navigable stream of the Nile system. Unfortunately the season of low water made it impossible to navigate the shallow, sluggish streams until the spring of 1898. But then activity was immediately resumed. On July 10, 1898 Marchand, accompanied by half a dozen European officers and some hundred and twenty Senegalese troops, arrived at Fashoda on the Nile and raised the French flag on the ruins of the old Egyptian fort.[5]

The Marchand mission, in its advance up the Congo and the Ubanghi, had been given all possible assistance by the officials of the Congo government. Indeed, the expedition had been transported on one of the Congo ships, the *Ville de Bruges.* This co-operation was merely the outward manifestation of what amounted to an alliance between France and the Congo State. Leopold, having tried repeatedly to induce Lord Salisbury to make over to him on lease all the Sudan south of Khartum, simply reversed his tactics when the British turned a deaf ear to his suggestions. His mind was still working along large lines. It was not enough to assure himself of the upper Nile area known as the Lado Enclave. Leopold had dreams of extending the power of the Congo State even to the east side of the Nile. After the battle of Adua, when the Italian government was seriously thinking of abandoning its Red Sea possessions, one of Leopold's agents appeared in Rome and carried on long negotiations with General Dal Verme. An agreement was drafted under the terms of which Italy should keep Massaua, but should cede the rest of Eritrea and the whole Abyssinian sphere of influence as defined in the Anglo-Italian Treaty of 1891 to a *Société Congolaise de Colonisation et d'Exploitation.* Half of the officials of this company were to be Italians and the Italian government was to receive half of the revenues. It was evidently planned to initiate the German Emperor into this scheme and to use him to secure the approval of England and France. The Italian government seems to have considered the scheme with some care. In November 1896 General Dal Verme sounded out political opinion by making some veiled references to the scheme in parliament. Objections were raised and the foreign minister, Visconti Venosta, appears to

---

structions to Marchand and to avoid friction with England (see Gabriel Hanotaux: *Fachoda,* Paris, 1909, pp. 105-9; André Lebon: *La Politique de la France en Afrique, 1896–1898,* Paris, 1901, pp. 3-6, 15 ff.; Louis Gillet: *Gabriel Hanotaux,* Paris, 1933, p. 79).

[5] The best accounts are those of the participants: Albert E. Baratier: *À travers l'Afrique* (Paris, 1910); J. Émily: *Mission Marchand, Journal de Route* (Paris, 1913); Général Mangin: "Lettres de la Mission Marchand" (*Revue des Deux Mondes,* September 15, 1931, pp. 241-83).

have opposed further consideration. At any rate, nothing more was heard of the plan.[6]

The failure of Leopold's Abyssinian hopes, however, had nothing to do with his activities along the Nile. In 1896 two great expeditions were organized in the Congo, one under Baron Dhanis, with more than a thousand native troops, and another under an officer named Chaltin. Dhanis, the chief in command, was to advance down the Nile to Lado and beyond, possibly in order to support Marchand against a dervish attack, and to protect his rear. It is said that Dhanis had secret instructions, to be opened only when he reached Fashoda! As a matter of fact he never reached even Lado. In February 1897 his Batetela force mutinied and slaughtered its officers, whereupon it began to return to Stanleyville. A very serious and widespread native rising followed, which was not entirely suppressed until 1899. In the meantime, however, Chaltin with the advance guard pushed on to the Nile, which he reached near Rejaf in February 1897. There was some fighting with dervish detachments, in which the Belgians were victorious. Chaltin gradually made his way to Lado, fortifying various places and increasing the Nile garrisons as he went till they numbered almost three thousand men. By the time when Marchand reached Fashoda the Belgians were already firmly established on the left bank of the upper Nile.[7]

The Marchand mission was only the most spectacular and best-known aspect of French activity in Africa in the years 1897–1898. At the same time efforts were apparently made to get in touch with the Khalifa at Omdurman and to secure his good will in return for support against the British advance from the north. So far as one can detect nothing came of these advances, which, when they were made known by the French press in the autumn of 1898, were characterized by an English writer as being " so infamous, so diabolical " that not only chivalrous Frenchmen, but even circumcised Hottentots might reasonably be supposed incapable of lending a hand to realize them.[8]

In Abyssinia, on the other hand, the French met with no serious obstacle. From the very beginning their idea had been to match an expedition from the west with another from the east. They had secured Menelik's friendship by supporting him against the Italians. If the King of Kings could be induced to make good his claim to the whole right bank of the upper Nile, set forth in his circular to the powers in 1891, the British would find before them not

---

[6] Théophile Simar: " Léopold II et l'Érythrée " (*Congo,* October, 1924, pp. 319–26), based on Leopold's papers; Pierre Daye: *Léopold II* (Paris, 1934), pp. 411 ff.

[7] Colonel Chaltin: " Vers le Nil " (in Louis Franck: *Le Congo Belge,* [Brussels, (?) 1928], II, pp. 103–14); A. J. Wauters: *Histoire Politique du Congo Belge* (Brussels, 1911), chaps. xx, xxiii; Fritz Masoin: *Histoire de l'État Indépendant du Congo* (Namur, 1913), II, pp. 282 ff., and chap. v; Arthur B. Keith: *The Belgian Congo and the Berlin Act* (Oxford, 1919), pp. 99–100, 112; Demetrius C. Boulger: *The Reign of Leopold II* (London, 1925), II, pp. 25 ff., 34 ff.

[8] Anonymous: " France, Russia and the Nile " (*Contemporary Review,* December, 1898, pp. 761–78), p. 765; see also Morrison B. Giffen: *Fashoda* (Chicago, 1930), pp. 17–8.

a mere handful of men, but tens of thousands of well-armed and warlike Abyssinians. Obviously the thing to do was to exploit the Abyssinian opportunity to the full. In December 1896 the French government decided to send M. Lagarde, governor of French Somaliland, on a special mission to Adis Abeba. He was to take large sums of money to be used for strengthening French influence in Abyssinia. As a special present for Menelik he was given one hundred thousand Gras rifles and two million rounds of ammunition. The mission was to be on a grand scale, and did, in fact, cost six hundred thousand francs. Lagarde was instructed to do all he could to prepare the way for two expeditions to the Nile, one under M. Clochette, who was already in Abyssinia, and the other under M. Bonvalot, which was to follow soon afterward.[9]

The French representative reached the Abyssinian capital early in March 1897. It is said that his reception was a cool one because Menelik suspected him of having had dealings with the Italians in the period before Adua. However this may have been, Lagarde seems to have scored an unqualified success before he returned to the coast. He arranged for a renewal of the French-Abyssinian treaty of friendship of 1843 and for the delimitation of the frontier of French Somaliland. Political reasons, taken together with the handsome present of guns and the willingness of the French to accept Abyssinian terms in the territorial settlement — all these factors appear to have softened Menelik's heart. He made Lagarde Duke of Entoto. Alfred Ilg, Swiss adviser of the King of Kings, was made counsellor of state, and threw the weight of his influence on the French side. M. Camille Mondon, correspondent of the Paris *Temps* in Adis Abeba, was made counsellor for public instruction and posts. Léon Chefneux, moving spirit behind the project of an Abyssinian railway, was named counsellor of railways and consul-general of Ethiopia in Europe. The doors were set open for French commerce. Everything seemed to be going swimmingly.[10]

So far as the Nile country was concerned, Lagarde found Menelik eager to follow the suggestions made by the French. He was determined to uphold his claim to the right bank of the Nile between the 5th and the 14th degrees north latitude, that is, from the vicinity of Lado to a point roughly one hundred and fifty miles upstream from Khartum. He was quite willing to give the Clochette and Bonvalot missions freedom of passage and to support them in every way.[11]

As soon as Lagarde was back at Jibuti the Clochette and Bonvalot missions

---

[9] Lebon, op. cit., pp. 30 ff.; Hanotaux, op. cit., pp. 133 ff.; Charles Michel: *Vers Fachoda, à la Rencontre de la Mission Marchand à travers l'Éthiopie* (Paris, 1901), pp. 8–9, 31.

[10] The Lagarde Treaty of March 20, 1897 was not published until 1908 (*Revue Générale de Droit International Public*, XV, 1908, Documents, p. 1). Sylvain Vigneras: *Une Mission Française en Abyssinie* (Paris, 1897) is a record of the mission by an official of the ministry for colonies, but the author carefully abstains from discussion of political activities. One of the fullest discussions of the mission is in L. J. Morié: *Histoire de l'Éthiopie* (Paris, 1904), II, pp. 443 ff.

[11] Lebon, op. cit., pp. 33–4.

started for the Abyssinian capital. A third group, led by Prince Henri d'Orleans, took the same course. The great traveller had no official standing, inasmuch as the French government could never summon enough courage to employ a member of the fallen dynasty. But he was always prepared to work for the glory of France, and played no unimportant part in the events of the next years. Unfortunately the three French missions failed to collaborate, for reasons that have never been cleared up. The members of the Bonvalot group maintained that Lagarde, instead of aiding them, put obstacles in their way and never gave proper support. The French governor was accused of having favored Clochette at the expense of the other mission. In any event Clochette went on toward the west, while Bonvalot returned to the coast to get the boats needed for navigation of the rivers that led to the Nile. He never returned, but abandoned the leadership of his group to Bonchamps. Bonchamps tried to get away from the capital, but the Abyssinian guides led him in great detours, evidently having been instructed to procrastinate as much as possible. Finally Bonchamps and Clochette met at Goré, in western Abyssinia. There they were both detained until further permits could be secured from Adis Abeba. In the meanwhile Clochette died and Bonchamps had to return to the capital to put an end to the obstruction which had so long delayed him. He found Lagarde at Adis Abeba on a second mission from the coast. The governor had failed to bring up the necessary boat. There were recriminations and sharp words, but finally Lagarde ordered the union of the Clochette and Bonchamps groups. Bonchamps was to proceed along the left bank of the Sobat River to the Nile. There he was to erect an Abyssinian fort on the right bank, and a French fort on the left.[12]

At last Bonchamps was able to set out. During the winter he and his companions proceeded in the direction laid down by Lagarde, signing treaties with the native chiefs along the way, not in the name of France, but in the name of Menelik. The going was incredibly hard. Once the highlands of Abyssinia were left behind the travellers found themselves in the great flat plain of the Nile, sparsely inhabited by humans, but well supplied with elephants and crocodiles. Food was scarce, the heat terrific, and fever all too common. Without boats it was almost impossible to cross the great swamps and the sluggish rivers that flowed through the grass. The expedition reached the junction of the Sobat and the Ajuba, late in December 1897. It had no means of crossing the great rivers, and was almost reduced to starvation. There was nothing to do but turn back, though the expedition was hardly more than one hundred miles from Fashoda! [13]

On the frontiers of Abyssinia the expedition came upon a large force of

---

12 Bonchamps openly accused Lagarde of obstruction; see Anon: " L'Abyssinie et la France après Fachoda " (*Le Correspondant*, February 25, 1899, pp. 675–87); see further Michel: *Vers Fachoda*, passim; Jules Cocheris: *Situation Internationale de l'Égypte et du Soudan* (Paris, 1903), pp. 457–8.   13 I follow the excellent account of Michel, who was a member of the party.

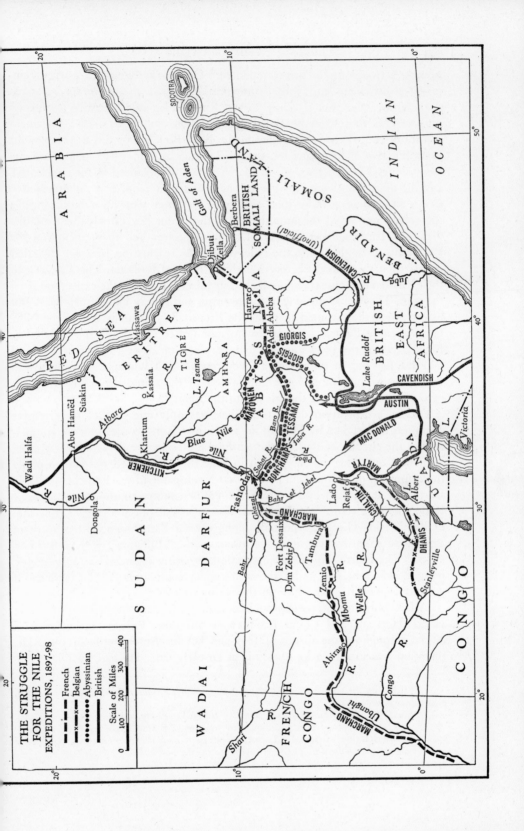

THE STRUGGLE
FOR THE NILE
EXPEDITIONS, 1897-98

French
Belgian
Abyssinian
British

Scale of Miles
0   100   200   300   400

Menelik's troops under the command of Dedjaz Tessama. This army comprised 10,000 men, and was accompanied by a Russian adventurer named
Artamanov, who was attached to the Russian legation at Adis Abeba. Its
purpose was to rescue the Bonchamps mission and to establish Abyssinian
control of the whole Sobat valley to the Nile. Bonchamps did not retrace his
steps, but two of his associates, the artist Potter and an officer named Faivre,
went along. The army set out in March 1898 and advanced as far as it could.
But the difficulties were very great. There was little food, and the Abyssinian
troops showed once more that, accustomed as they were to a high altitude,
they could not stand the humid heat of the plain. Fever took them off like
flies. Nevertheless a detachment of some eight hundred men, including the
Europeans, struggled on to the Nile, which was reached on June 22, 1898, that
is, less than three weeks before Marchand reached Fashoda. The French and
their Russian comrade therefore looked in vain for traces of the expedition from
the west. They could not stay in the swamps, and simply had to turn back. But
before going they wanted to plant the French flag on an island in the Nile.
Unfortunately Faivre could not swim and Potter was deadly ill with fever.
Finally one of the blacks agreed to take his chances with the crocodiles and
take the flag out in return for a fancy reward. But when he was already in
the water Artamanov saw the impropriety of the thing, dived into the dangerous flood and carried the tricolor to the island.[14]

Tessama's expedition down the Sobat was only one part of an extensive
operation undertaken by Menelik to secure his claims to the frontiers enumerated in the circular of 1891. In the autumn and winter of 1897–1898 three other
armies set out. The first, which left in June 1897, comprised 15,000 men under
the command of Hapta Giorgis and was accompanied by a Frenchman, Léon
Darragon. It reached and overran the entire country to the north of Lake
Rudolf. On its return another expedition was sent out under the leadership
of Ras Wedda Giorgis, who took along several Frenchmen with a force of
Senegalese sharpshooters, and a Russian, named Bulatovič, with a few cossacks.[15] The fourth Abyssinian expedition, probably regarded as the most important, was sent out under the well-known commander, Ras Makonen. It
advanced down the Blue Nile in the spring of 1898.[16]

A few words ought, perhaps, to be said of the mysterious activities of Prince
Henri d'Orleans and Count Leontiev at this time. Orleans stayed at Adis
Abeba throughout the spring of 1897 and left for Europe only in June. His
intention was to return to Abyssinia at an early date. He had " a pile of big

---

[14] Michel, op. cit., pp. 412, 431; *Bulletin du Comité de l'Afrique Française*, November, 1898,
p. 365; March, 1899, p. 95.

[15] See A. K. Bulatovič: *S Voiskami Menelika II* (St. Petersburg, 1900).

[16] The best accounts of these expeditions are those of L. J. Morié: *Histoire de l'Éthiopie*, II,
pp. 450 ff. (which is closely followed by Leonard Woolf: *Empire and Commerce in Africa*, pp. 199 ff.),
and of Conrad Keller: *Alfred Ilg* (Leipzig, 1918), pp. 163 ff.

projects " and was planning " something grand." No great secret was made of these projects. The King of Kings announced that Leontiev had been made " Governor of the Equatorial Provinces of Ethiopia " and that Prince Henri would be associated with him in the opening up of that territory. During the winter of 1897–1898 the Prince organized a syndicate, capitalized at 1,800,000 francs, for development purposes. This syndicate was a Belgian undertaking, in which King Leopold himself was heavily interested. There were very few colonial pies in which the wily King did not have a finger. This was simply another aspect of his plan to extend the Congo territory to Abyssinia and the Red Sea.

In the spring of 1898 Orleans was back at Jibuti, with a considerable force of Senegalese sharpshooters. He took, as a present to Menelik, a large shipment of rifles and ammunition. There was perfect understanding between him and the Abyssinian ruler, for it was arranged that Orleans and Leontiev should extend the frontier of Abyssinia to the Nile on the west and to Lake Victoria in the south. But in the end nothing came of the scheme. It was reported that Leontiev had been accidentally shot in both legs at Harrar, but there is also some evidence that his sharp and deceptive practices deprived him of Belgian financial support. No doubt Menelik too lost interest when the Fashoda crisis precipitated the withdrawal of the French.[17]

From the foregoing discussion it will be clear that the French, associated with the Belgians, were extremely active in Abyssinia during the years 1897–1898; that the Russians, too, were working toward the same end; and that the Franco-Russian influence was practically supreme at the court of Menelik. Unfortunately their efforts were not well co-ordinated. Lagarde's rôle is not at all clear, but there can be no doubt that he did not give the proper support to the Bonchamps mission. Bonchamps had previously been employed by King Leopold in the Congo, and seems to have gone to Abyssinia originally as an emissary of the King to enlist the help of Menelik against the dervishes. It is possible that Lagarde and the French government were suspicious of him and distrusted him. In any case, it is beyond dispute that Bonchamps got little official support. When he reached Jibuti on his way back to France, he found there the demounted boat which had been lying on the pier for some time and which might have changed the Nile expedition from failure into success. Nevertheless, it must not be forgotten that the French accomplished

[17] Prince Henri d'Orleans: *Une Visite à l'Empereur Ménélik* (Paris, 1898), passim, and the Prince's open letter to Delcassé, reprinted in the London *Times,* November 21, 1898; see also his statements to Henri Pensa in April, 1898 (*Revue Politique et Parlementaire,* XVI, May, 1898, pp. 171–5); and further Keller: *Alfred Ilg,* pp. 124–5, 207–8; Paul Bourdarie: " La Mission du Prince Henri d'Orléans en Abyssinie " (*Questions Diplomatiques et Coloniales,* August 15, 1897, pp. 68–71); G. de la Génardière: " Les Provinces Équatoriales d'Éthiopie " (ibid., May 1, 1898, pp. 12–9); Edmund D. Morel: " The Congo State and the Bahr-el-Ghazal " (*Nineteenth Century,* August, 1901, pp. 202–13); *Bulletin du Comité de l'Afrique Française,* September, 1897, p. 321; November, 1897, p. 404; August, 1898, p. 268.

at least this much: they stirred up Menelik and made him see the danger of the British advance against the dervishes. After all, they induced him to send out four sizable expeditions. Even if the nature of the territory in question was such that the Abyssinian troops could not stand it for any length of time, at least it had been made clear that the powerful King of Kings was to be reckoned with in any future settlement.

Now the important point about these French activities is that they were perfectly well known, almost without exception. Anyone who will take the trouble to look through the files of that excellent contemporary publication, the *Bulletin du Comité de l'Afrique Française,* will find abundant evidence of this fact, to say nothing of the voluminous quotations from the British, Belgian and French press indicating exactly the state of knowledge in these countries. The British papers followed the Belgian expeditions in detail, and from September 1897 onward there were periodic reports of the Marchand and Bonchamps groups. It was known that by the autumn of 1897 Marchand had reached the Bahr-el-Ghazal region. Some thought he was already at Fashoda, and it was reported that Bonchamps had joined hands with him there. Then, in December 1897, it was rumored that the mission had met with a tragic end. For two months the situation was widely discussed in the press on both sides of the Channel, and the leading English papers, like the *Times,* issued strong warnings to France as to what would be the outcome if their schemes were persisted in. All of the Abyssinian expeditions were reported, so that there was no lack of information. It is true that when Kitchener fought the battle of Omdurman on September 2, 1898 it was not certainly known in Europe whether Marchand had reached Fashoda or not; neither was it known whether the Abyssinian expedition had found its way to the Nile. But more than enough was known to cause elation in Paris and to call forth grave anxiety in London.[18]

The British government was not behind the public in close observation of the French enterprises, especially those that hinged on Abyssinia. At Menelik's court the British enjoyed no credit whatever, since their friendship with the Italians was known and it was thought that they had supported the Adua campaign with ample funds. It was therefore decided to send a mission to Adis Abeba early in 1897. Rennell Rodd, one of Lord Cromer's ablest assistants in

---

[18] See *Bulletin du Comité de l'Afrique Française,* September, 1897, pp. 316, 320; October, 1897, p. 350; December, 1897, p. 444; January, 1898, pp. 3 ff., 32–3; February, 1898, pp. 44–5, 62; August, 1898, pp. 263 ff.; September, 1898, pp. 278 ff., 286 ff.; October, 1898, pp. 325 ff. See also *Questions Diplomatiques et Coloniales,* September 15, 1897, pp. 237 ff.; October 15, 1897 (P. Vuillot: " La France dans le Haut-Nil "); January 15, 1898, pp. 99 ff., 109 ff.; February 15, 1898 (Paul Bourdarie: " Les Missions Liotard-Marchand-de Bonchamps et la Question du Nil "); October 1, 1898 (Henri Pensa: " La France au Bahr-el-Ghazal "). Further accounts in A. J. Wauters: " Autour de l'Abyssinie " (*Mouvement Géographique,* October 10, October 17 and October 31, 1897), in the *Geographical Journal,* February, 1898, pp. 169–71; and especially in Frederick A. Edwards: " The French on the Nile " (*Fortnightly Review,* March, 1898, pp. 362–77).

Egypt, was assigned to lead the mission, which was composed largely of British and Egyptian army officers who, it seems, were chosen partly for their size and physical impressiveness (*amiable giants,* Sir Charles Dilke called them). Rodd tells us in his memoirs that the British government was greatly worried by rumors of a combination between the Abyssinians and the dervishes, as well as by the reports of the projected Bonchamps mission. The object of his mission, therefore, was " to ensure if possible that there would be no co-operation with the Khalifa, and to obtain a more intimate knowledge of internal conditions." [19]

When the mission reached the end of the first stage it learned at Harrar that Lagarde and Bonvalot had a two months' start. On their arrival at Adis Abeba they found Prince Henri d'Orleans and Leontiev also upon the scene. The French made no bones about stating what their plans were. The general atmosphere was not a very friendly one. Nevertheless Rodd entered boldly upon negotiations. He seems to have convinced Menelik that the dervishes would be, in the future as in the past, dangerous adversaries of the Abyssinians as of the Egyptians. In any case the King of Kings promised not to allow shipments of arms to reach the dervishes through Abyssinia. He also agreed to certain commercial arrangements which put British goods on a par with imports from other countries. But what Menelik was most interested in was the question of territorial settlements. Rodd was willing enough to discuss the Somali frontier, and eventually an agreement was made by which the British abandoned almost 15,000 square miles of what they had claimed on that side. But so far as the all-important problem of the southern and western frontiers of Abyssinia was concerned, no progress was made. Menelik stuck by his claim to the Nile frontier and Rodd therefore decided that it would be better to let this matter go over until the British and Egyptians were at Khartum. Even after twenty-five years Rodd refused, when writing his memoirs, to reveal the course and the outcome of his discussions with Menelik on larger African problems. He was impressed with the Abyssinian ruler's quick and keen intelligence and claimed to have succeeded in establishing cordial relations by removing apprehensions. Whether or not he weakened the French position it is hard to say. Appearances are against it. After all, the treaty signed by Rodd on May 14, 1897 marked no progress toward the settlement of the frontier problem. Menelik's four expeditions, sent out after Rodd's departure, would not seem to indicate a very trustful relationship between the King of Kings and Her Majesty's government. Indeed, when Makonen returned from the Blue Nile in the spring of 1898 he brought dervish emissaries with him, who were given presents by Menelik. From this it would seem that the British had secured no guarantee even against an Abyssinian-Dervish combination. No wonder there was criticism of the Rodd Treaty in the British parliament.[20]

---

[19] Sir J. Rennell Rodd: *Social and Diplomatic Memories,* II, pp. 112–4.

[20] Rodd, op. cit., II, chaps. iv and v. A narrative of the mission by Count Albert E. W. Gleichen: *With the Mission to Menelik, 1897* (London, 1898). On Menelik's relations to the dervishes see

When Rodd returned to England in June 1897 he had a long talk with Salisbury. The prime minister made it clear that he did not care how much "light soil" in Somaliland had to be sacrificed to the Abyssinians. What he was most concerned about was the danger of the French reaching the Nile. Rodd confirmed him in his fears and urged that an expedition be pushed forward from Uganda along the Nile and to Fashoda, in the hope of anticipating Marchand. This idea was not new to Salisbury; the decision had already been made to send out a considerable force under Colonel James MacDonald, who had had much experience in Uganda. The colonel left England early in June 1897, with instructions "to explore the districts adjacent to the Italian sphere in which the River Juba is believed to rise, and to cultivate friendly relations with the tribes residing in that portion of the British sphere."[21]

MacDonald's expedition was no more fortunate than that of Baron Dhanis in the Congo. Hardly had he set out in September 1897 than his Sudanese troops mutinied. A dangerous rising followed among the Waganda in Uganda, with the result that MacDonald was obliged to spend most of the winter campaigning in country that was supposedly already under British control. By the time the expedition was ready to resume its original plans the secret of its destination had leaked out. Someone found in his instructions that the Uganda authorities were to supply MacDonald with a certain number of Dinkas and Shilluks. Now these people inhabit the Nile country about Fashoda, and it was hard to see why they should be wanted by an expedition headed for the sources of the Juba River. Sir Charles Dilke openly accused the government of having led the public astray. MacDonald's mission, he maintained, was to head off the Marchand mission. And so it was. Lord Salisbury later on admitted it in a general way (though Curzon had originally described the charge as *all imagination*). It seems that the sources of the Juba which MacDonald was to investigate were not the sources of the great Juba River which flows into the Indian Ocean, but the sources of another Juba River (also Jubba, Adjuba, etc.) which was a confluent of the Sobat and which, it was thought, would give a clear route from the vicinity of Lake Rudolf to the Nile at Fashoda. When MacDonald finally did make his journey in the summer of 1898 this was the course he took. While he did not reach the Nile, he came within one hundred miles of Lado. His subordinate, Lieutenant Austin, led another column to the northern end of Lake Rudolf. A French writer has asserted that the Abyssinians, coming from the north, met one or the other of these columns and that the British cleared out, leaving their baggage. This is probably an exaggeration. Neither MacDonald nor Austin say anything of meeting the Abyssinians, though they do say that the

Augustus B. Wylde: *Modern Abyssinia* (London, 1901), pp. 73–5. For criticism of the treaty in parliament see Hansard, Series IV, vol. LIII, pp. 489–90 (February 14, 1898), pp. 1527–8, 1579 ff. (February 24, 1898). See also *Bulletin . . . de l'Afrique Française*, July, 1897, pp. 238–9; August, 1897, pp. 276–7.
  [21] *Africa No. 2 (1898)*, appendix.

country had been so thoroughly ravaged by them that their expeditions had to turn back for want of food.[22] It is conceivable that the Abyssinians met an expedition under Mr. Cavendish, which was non-official but attracted a great deal of attention in France.[23]

The serious rising in Uganda rendered MacDonald's mission impotent during the winter of 1897–1898, and the British government therefore had to make up its mind as to what else might be done to block the French schemes on the upper Nile. Lord Wolseley, commander in chief of the British forces, argued warmly in October 1897 that Kitchener's troops should advance from Abu Hamed upon Khartum, and that he should be given two British infantry brigades to help the Egyptian forces. In this way the Khalifa's army could be certainly destroyed and Khartum and the White Nile could be occupied before the French established posts there: " As far as I can learn," he wrote to Lansdowne, " the French are now working hard to forestall us on the upper Nile, and if they do so we may have to face serious complications with them when we attempt the job in the autumn of 1898." [24] Lansdowne, however, was opposed to the action suggested by the commander in chief. It was felt that a further advance would be too hard on the troops and that the financial aspects of the problem would be hard to settle. Lord Salisbury supported Lansdowne. He seems to have stressed the consideration that Britain, faced with a rather serious war on the Indian frontier and deeply involved in other parts of the world, would do well to avoid further complications. He appreciated the fact that the French might get to the Nile before the Egyptian troops reconquered Khartum, but, he wrote to Lansdowne: " I am not greatly impressed by this danger, because we shall have to meet it anyhow." If England tried to apply the Anglo-German Treaty of 1890, which defined her sphere on the upper Nile, it would mean a row with the French whether they reached the Nile or not. " It is to be remembered," he added, " that by destroying the dervish power we are killing the defender who is holding the valley for us now." To Lord Cromer he wrote in a similar vein: " If ever we get to Fashoda, the diplomatic crisis will be something to remember and the ' What next? ' will be a very interesting question." [25]

So the decision was made to let matters take their course. The advance on

---

[22] Morié: *Histoire de l'Éthiopie*, II, p. 452; J. R. L. MacDonald and H. H. Austin: " Journeys to the North of Uganda " (*Geographical Journal*, August, 1899, pp. 129–47); Herbert H. Austin: *With MacDonald in Uganda* (London, 1903). See further the discussion of the mission in parliament, in Hansard, LIV, pp. 528, 537, 544 ff., 557; LXIX, p. 9; LXVII, pp. 703 ff., 718 ff.; LXXV, pp. 1513–4; also H. R. Fox Bourne: " The Uganda Protectorate and its Relation to the Sudan " (*Asiatic Quarterly Review*, April, 1899, pp. 322–37); J. W. Gregory: *The Foundation of British East Africa* (London, 1901), pp. 244 ff.; Sir Harry Johnston: *The Nile Quest* (New York, 1903), p. 271.

[23] H. S. H. Cavendish: " Through Somali Land to Lake Rudolf " (*Geographical Journal*, April, 1898, pp. 372–96).

[24] Sir F. Maurice and Sir George Arthur: *The Life of Lord Wolseley* (London, 1924), p. 304. Similarly Wolseley's letter to the Queen (*Letters of Queen Victoria*, III, p. 206).

[25] Lord Newton: *Lord Lansdowne* (London, 1929), pp. 147–8; Marquess of Zetland: *Lord Cromer* (London, 1932), p. 259; *Letters of Queen Victoria*, III, p. 208.

Khartum was to be resumed only at the next high Nile, that is, in September 1898. During the winter, however, relations between England and France were strained to the breaking point as a result of the dispute which arose regarding the frontier of their respective possessions on the upper Niger. The details of this complicated problem may be omitted here, interesting though they are. Suffice it to say that there were good arguments on both sides and there were questionable proceedings on both sides. British and French alike attempted to send expeditions into the disputed area and to secure actual control of as much territory as possible while the negotiations were going on. On one occasion British and French actually clashed, through a misunderstanding. In February and March 1898 war seemed not far in the offing. But in the end the matter was settled by a compromise, and an agreement was duly signed in June 1898.[26]

During this whole Niger dispute British public opinion, as expressed in the newspapers and periodicals, was astonishingly rabid. From Queen Victoria's letters and Garvin's recent biography it appears that Chamberlain was no less determined to hold fast. Salisbury complained to the Queen that the colonial secretary was " a little too warlike, and hardly sees the other side of the question." Still, Salisbury himself found it necessary to assume a very firm stand and to refuse all concessions of importance.[27] The French government, on the other hand, was obviously anxious to avoid trouble and come to some agreement. In their apologies both Hanotaux and Lebon have stressed the hopes they entertained at the time that an agreement with regard to west Africa would lead to a similar compromise agreement with respect to the valley of the Nile. They bemoan the fact that the discussions of the Niger problem were drawn out so long that the Méline cabinet fell from power (June 1898) before the other problems could be raised. They accuse Delcassé (Hanotaux' successor at the foreign office) of having failed to open negotiations immediately and of having neglected to reach some settlement before Kitchener reconquered Khartum.[28]

It is rather difficult to understand how the French statesmen could have deluded themselves in this way. They themselves raised the question of a general settlement in their discussions with the British ambassador in December 1897 and were given a most unambiguous reply. England, said Sir Edmund Monson, " must not be understood to admit that any other European power than Great

---

[26] *British Documents on the Origins of the War,* I, chap. iv, part I; Accounts and Papers, *Treaty Series No. 15, 1899,* with map; Documents Diplomatiques: *Correspondance et Documents relatifs à la Convention Franco-Anglaise du 14 juin, 1898.* The best French accounts may be found in Darcy, op. cit.; *Bulletin . . . de l'Afrique Française,* December, 1897, pp. 410 ff.; P. Vuillot: " La France et l'Angleterre sur le Niger " (*Questions Diplomatiques et Coloniales,* April 1, 1898, pp. 404–30). On the British side see especially Garvin: *Life of Chamberlain,* III, chap. lv; Frederick A. Edwards: " The French on the Niger " (*Fortnightly Review,* April, 1898, pp. 576–91); J. Westlake: " England and France in West Africa " (*Contemporary Review,* April, 1898, pp. 582–92). An excellent critical examination of the question may be found in Heinz Kossatz: *Untersuchungen über den Französisch-Englischen Weltgegensatz im Fashodajahr* (Breslau, 1934), pp. 23 ff.   [27] *Letters of Queen Victoria,* III, pp. 209–12; Garvin, op. cit., III, pp. 212 ff.
[28] Hanotaux: *Fachoda,* pp. 118 ff., 144–5; Lebon: *La Politique Française en Afrique,* pp. 43 ff.

Britain has any claim to occupy any part of the valley of the Nile." [29] It is perfectly true that M. Hanotaux immediately voiced reservations to the British claims, but it is nevertheless difficult to see how he could have deluded himself with the hope that England would be willing to negotiate on this question. As a matter of fact the British government decided almost at once to resume the advance up the Nile. It was said that the threat of a dervish attack on Berber forced this reversal of the decision made in October, but few people were taken in by this explanation.

There is not much more to be told about the Khartum campaign. Supported by several battalions of British troops, the Egyptian army pushed vigorously ahead. The dervishes under Emir Mahmud were swept aside on April 8, 1898 at the battle of the Atbara. On September 2 the decisive engagement was fought against the Khalifa himself on the plains of Kerreri, outside Omdurman and Khartum. Some twenty-two thousand Egyptian and British troops turned the Maxims on the valorous ranks of the advancing dervishes (some forty thousand in all). The slaughter might have been foreseen and probably was. While the Anglo-Egyptian forces had fifty men killed and a couple of hundred wounded, the dervishes left ten thousand dead on the field, and had another five thousand wounded. The Khalifa himself escaped from Omdurman, but his power was broken. The Egyptian and British flags were soon flying side by side from the old palace at Khartum.

Before the resumption of hostilities against the dervishes there had been an important cabinet meeting at London, at which Lord Cromer was present. It was there decided that when Khartum was reconquered, the British and Egyptian flags should fly side by side in the Sudan, and that Egypt should be expected to follow British advice with respect to the government of this region. Furthermore, it was decided to instruct Kitchener to send gunboat flotillas up the Blue Nile and to push on up the White Nile with a small force as far as Fashoda or beyond if possible. He was to acknowledge no French or Abyssinian claims to any part of the Valley, and was to avoid a collision with the troops of Menelik at all costs.[30]

Kitchener found it necessary to act upon these instructions almost at once after the defeat of the Khalifa, for on September 7 a Mahdist steamer, coming down the Nile, was stopped near Khartum. On being questioned the crew reported that the steamer had been sent up the White Nile some time before, but had been fired on by white men ("Turks") at Fashoda and had been turned back. An examination of the bullets which still lodged in the woodwork of the steamer bore out the fact that there were Europeans at Fashoda. The authorities at Khartum hardly needed to guess who they were. Three days later Kitch-

---

[29] *Egypt No. 2 (1898)*, no. 1; Documents Diplomatiques: *Affaires du Haut-Nil, 1897–1898*, no. 1.

[30] *Egypt No. 2 (1898)*, no. 3; Sir George Arthur: *Life of Lord Kitchener* (London, 1920), I, p. 246; *Letters of Queen Victoria*, III, p. 260.

ener set out with five steamers and a force of Sudanese, supplemented with a small number of British troops. As he approached Fashoda, on September 18, he sent a letter to Marchand, to which the French commander replied saying that he had occupied the territory since July 10 and that he could not leave without further instructions from his government. On the following day the two men met. Marchand refused to retire, despite the protests of Kitchener. The negotiations were carried on throughout as between gentlemen, Marchand behaving "with quiet dignity and soldierly bearing," while Kitchener and his officers, who felt a "twinge of pity and not a little admiration" for their gallant enemies, were "the pink of politeness." The matter was soon adjusted in an amicable way, for Marchand made no objection to the raising of the Egyptian flag at the southern end of the station and the establishment of a Sudanese battalion. For the rest the settlement of the affair was left to the home governments and the discussions ended with Kitchener's proposing that they both take a whiskey and soda.[31]

In England the victory at Omdurman called forth a remarkable outburst of enthusiasm. Moved far beyond their wont, says Winston Churchill, the people sat themselves down to give thanks to their God, their Government, and their General. To judge by the press, the whole country had gone mad with the lust of fighting glory.[32] Then, within a week, came rumors of the French "apparition" on the upper Nile. Despite Kitchener's efforts to keep his moves secret, his encounter with Marchand was reported home by the correspondents at Khartum, and before the end of September the incident was common property in England. Churchill, again, gives a vivid picture of the popular reaction. The Fashoda episode was a "discordant note" in the general rejoicing. The British public was "confronted with the fact that a 'friendly power' had, unprovoked, endeavoured to rob them of the fruits of their victories. They now realised that while they had been devoting themselves to great military operations, in broad daylight and the eye of the world, and prosecuting an enterprise on which they had set their hearts, other operations — covert, deceitful, behind-the-back — had been in progress in the heart of the Dark Continent, designed solely for the mischievous and spiteful object of depriving them of the produce of their labours. And they firmly set their faces against such behaviour."[33]

In almost complete unison the British press launched upon an attack against the French. Here and there a liberal paper like the *Manchester Guardian* kept its head, but many of the British journals were abusive and most of them un-

---

[31] *Egypt No. 3 (1898)*, no. 2; *British Documents on the Origins of the War*, I, no. 193; General Sir Horace Smith-Dorrien: *Memories of Forty-eight Years' Service* (London, 1925), chap. viii; *Letters of Queen Victoria*, III, pp. 285 ff.; Arthur: *Life of Kitchener*, I, pp. 247 ff.; A. B. de Guerville: *New Egypt* (London, 1905), pp. 330 ff.; Marchand's somewhat dramatized account in the *Figaro*, August 26, 1904 (reprinted in London *Times*, August 27, 1904); see also General Mangin: " Lettres de la Mission Marchand " (*Revue des Deux Mondes*, September 15, 1931, pp. 241–83), pp. 265 ff.; Morrison B. Giffen: *Fashoda* (Chicago, 1930), pp. 7–11, 35–6.

[32] Winston Churchill: *The River War* (London, 1899), II, p. 311; Wilfrid S. Blunt: *My Diaries* (London, 1919), I, p. 365.   [33] Churchill, op. cit., II, pp. 311–2.

compromising. Marchand's party was described as a band of "irregular marauders" and as the "scum of the desert." The newspapers were impatient of negotiation and wholly averse to elaborate arguments. In the British view the whole Marchand mission was a demonstration of "indubitable hostility" and of "conscious antagonism" to England. Marchand was an intruder, who would have to be ejected, even though it meant an ultimatum, mobilization and war.[34]

The unanimity of the press was matched by the unanimity of the politicians. Liberals vied with Unionists and Tories in putting themselves at the disposal of the government and in calling upon the cabinet to assume an unyielding attitude. Rosebery struck the keynote in his speech at Epsom on October 12. There followed a veritable flood of eloquence. Asquith, Grey and ultimately even Harcourt were among the Liberals who came out in support of a firm policy, while among the members of the government the hard-hitting Sir Michael Hicks Beach capped the movement in an address at North Shields on October 19, when he declared that "the country has put its foot down. If, unhappily, another view should be taken elsewhere, we, the Ministers of the Queen, know what our duty demands. It would be a great calamity. . . . But there are greater evils than war."

It may be questioned whether Lord Salisbury required all the encouragement and prodding which was given him by the press and by the politicians. Whatever may have been his own view of the merits of the case, he had long since come to see that in the question of the Nile the British public simply would not stand for a policy of "graceful concession." The French had been warned time and again that the British foreign office could not and would not consider or discuss claims to any part of the Nile Valley. After the battle of Omdurman Sir Edmund Monson, the ambassador at Paris, had been instructed to inform the French foreign office that "all territories which were subject to the Khalifa passed to the British and Egyptian Governments by right of conquest" and that this right was not open to discussion.[35] Throughout the debate which followed the news of the Marchand-Kitchener meeting Salisbury stuck to his guns. He refused to talk about French claims until Marchand should have been recalled.

We must turn now to a consideration of the situation as it presented itself in Paris. And above all we must remember that the autumn and winter of 1898–1899 was perhaps the most critical period in the whole domestic history of the Third Republic prior to the World War. The famous and dreadful Dreyfus case, which dated back to the autumn of 1894, had entered upon the crucial phase and France was already torn between Dreyfusards and Anti-Dreyfusards. It was in January 1898 that Zola published his astonishing letter: *J'Accuse*. He

---

[34] A good digest of the press in T. W. Riker: "A Survey of British Policy in the Fashoda Crisis" (*Political Science Quarterly*, March, 1929, pp. 54–78), pp. 65–6; see also the extracts in the *Bulletin . . . de l'Afrique Française*, October, 1898, pp. 334 ff., and in Jules Cocheris: *La Situation Internationale de l'Égypte*, pp. 452 ff., 461–2. [35] *British Documents*, I, no. 189.

had been tried and condemned, but before the excitement had in any way sub-
sided Colonel Henry, forger of the documents that had been used against Dreyfus, committed suicide on August 31. General Cavaignac, the minister of war,
resigned on September 3, 1898. On the same day Madame Dreyfus appealed to
the minister of justice for a revision of the trial of 1894. During the next weeks
and months the Dreyfus case reached the climactic phase and threatened to assume the character of a civil war. On both sides the forces had been marshalled.
The revisionists, still a minority but reinforced by a large group of intellectuals,
had closed their ranks. The socialist fractions joined hands. Committees of
vigilance were formed and innumerable meetings of protest were organized in
Paris and the provinces.

On the other side the Anti-Dreyfusard forces were rallying around the stand-
ards of patriotism, anti-Semitism and royalism. Déroulède came out of retirement, reopened his League of Patriots and began a campaign of heckling the
revisionists. Guérin, Buffet and others, financed by the Orleanists, came to the
assistance of the Jew-baiters, the clericals and the army. On September 13 there
began a strike in Paris which soon involved 20,000 men in the building trades.
Some 60,000 troops were concentrated in and near the capital, there was march-
ing and countermarching, bivouacking of soldiers in the squares — everything
that might be taken to indicate action by the patriots. There was talk of a great
military plot and the whole capital was on edge for days on end. Even when the
strike was settled, the tension continued. October was filled with demonstrations
and conflicts, with rumors of all kinds, and with a general revival of the " great
fear." [36]

It may well be imagined that in the midst of the furor caused by the Dreyfus case the average Frenchman, never much interested in colonial affairs, had
little thought left for Egypt and the Sudan. The active proponents of expansion
did, of course, follow the progress of events with considerable attention. These
circles evidently believed that the reconquest of Khartum, by raising the whole
problem of the Sudan, would of necessity result in the resumption of discussions
between England and France regarding Egypt.[37]

Delcassé, the foreign minister, was evidently not suffering from such illusions. Just what his ideas of foreign policy were in these first months of office
has always been a matter of dispute. Various schemes were attributed to him
at the time, but to the foreign representatives in Paris he appeared as a contradictory character, an opportunist, a garrulous and yet secretive *arriviste*.[38]

---

[36] The most detailed and on the whole the best account is still Joseph Reinach: *Histoire de
l'Affaire Dreyfus* (Paris, 1904), IV, pp. 270 ff., 296 ff., 300 ff.; but see also Alexandre Zévaès:
L'Affaire Dreyfus (Paris, 1931), pp. 135 ff.

[37] See the abstracts from the press in *Questions Diplomatiques et Coloniales,* September 15,
1898, pp. 111 ff.

[38] *Die Grosse Politik,* XIII, no. 3555; *British Documents,* I, no. 183; Constantin Dumba:
Dreibund und Entente-Politik (Zürich, 1931), p. 100; E. Malcolm Carroll: *French Public Opinion,*
p. 171; Kossatz, op. cit., pp. 40 ff.

Hanotaux and Lebon accused him later of having failed to follow up the west African settlement with England, of June 1898, with further negotiations respecting eastern Africa and the Nile. This accusation can hardly be taken seriously, however. Hanotaux knew from his own discussions with the British foreign office that while the British were prepared to recognize French claims to the east of Lake Chad in return for recognition of British claims in the Nile Valley, they would not discuss French pretensions in the Nile Valley itself. Hanotaux also knew that he himself had rejected these offers "with no excess of courtesy." [39] It is hard to see on what basis Delcassé was to negotiate when the English claims were so well known and when the unwillingness of the London government to discuss these claims had been so often demonstrated.

There is probably more point in Hanotaux' charge that Delcassé failed to follow up the advances made by Germany with regard to the Portuguese colonies in June 1898. Delcassé was a political disciple of Gambetta. In Boulangist times he had been secretary-general of Déroulède's League of Patriots, and it is said that in 1898 he was taken into the Brisson cabinet because Déroulède promised to support the new government if Delcassé were made foreign minister.[40] Whether all this be true or not, it is clear that Delcassé's political antecedents and connexions were with the patriot party, and there is no inherent improbability in the story told of him: that he took office with the idea of grouping about France the largest number of European friends, in the hope of securing their support for an eventual war with Germany. It is said that he hoped to add England to the Franco-Russian grouping and that he declared that he did not want to leave office until he had re-established a friendly understanding with England.[41]

These stories of Delcassé's desire to reach an agreement with England gain some weight from the British documents on the crisis of the autmun of 1898. It is, of course, true that Delcassé, in 1893 and 1894 when he was at the colonial office, was one of the prime movers in organizing the expedition to the Nile. But that was in the days before the Congo Treaty of 1894, in the days before the Grey declaration, in the days before the Dongola expedition and the breakdown of the negotiations which had been carried on from time to time between London and Paris. There is no evidence of any kind to show that Delcassé continued to approve and support the scheme after 1894. Within a week of the British victory at Omdurman he spoke to the British ambassador and remarked that Marchand might be met with. The explorer, he continued, was "only an emissary of civilisation." He had no power to make decisions, and it was hoped

---

[39] *British Documents,* I, no. 175.

[40] André Mévil: *De la Paix de Francfort à la Conférence d'Algésiras* (Paris, 1909), p. 140; Charles Maurras: *Kiel et Tanger* (Third edition, Paris, 1921), p. 176; Auguste Gérard: *Mémoires* (Paris, 1928), p. 316.

[41] Victor Bérard: "Politique Française" (*Revue de Paris,* July 1, 1905, pp. 208–24); Georges Reynald: *La Diplomatie Française. L'Œuvre de M. Delcassé* (Paris, 1915), p. 22; René Pinon: *France et Allemagne* (Paris, 1913), pp. 117–8.

that all differences might be " amicably arranged by the exercise of patience and conciliation." In other conversations with Monson in September the French foreign minister kept insisting that there was really no " Marchand mission " in the ordinary sense of the term. The French cabinet, he reiterated, was strongly desirous of avoiding serious difficulty with England. He personally would much prefer an understanding with England to the existing one between France and Russia.[42]

The British government does not seem to have questioned the good will of Delcassé, and there is no reason why we should. A conciliatory attitude was the only sensible one for the French government to take in 1898. The country was in the throes of a full-blown domestic crisis and was quite unprepared to wage war. Marchand's own position was most precarious. He himself and his associates always claimed that the position at Fashoda was strong. A dervish attack had been turned back and the neighboring Shilluk tribes were friendly. The expedition still had 130,000 cartridges and 18,000 kilograms of wheat. Gardens had been planted, so there was no threat of famine. Reinforcements and supplies were expected from the French Congo and from Abyssinia. According to General Mangin the French force could have given the British a great deal more trouble than had the dervishes at Omdurman, the more so as the Sudanese troops in the Sirdar's forces were disposed to side with the French. Kitchener, on the other hand, reported from the beginning that Marchand's position was " as impossible as it is absurd." Only the victory of Omdurman had saved him from annihilation by the Mahdists, and it was inconceivable that he could have held his position for long in the fever-ridden swamp area around Fashoda.[43]

Delcassé's readiness to negotiate and to reach an amicable settlement was not reciprocated in London. The British had always refused to define their own claims or discuss the claims of others. From the start Salisbury took the stand that the Sudan belonged to Great Britain and Egypt by right of conquest and that this right was not open to debate. " No offer of territorial concession on our part would be endured by public opinion here," he wrote to the Queen, who agreed.[44] It was this unwillingness of the British even to discuss the question, together with the uncompromising rabidness of the British press, that made it almost impossible for Delcassé to give in. He made it perfectly clear that Marchand could be and would be recalled if the London government would negotiate. To which Salisbury responded by a flat rejection of all debate until the French post had been evacuated.

Nothing would be drearier than to review here the detailed arguments ad-

---

[42] *British Documents,* I, nos. 188, 190, 191, 196, 198; *Letters of Queen Victoria,* III, p. 288.

[43] *British Documents,* I, no. 193; *Die Grosse Politik,* XIV, nos. 3890, 3894; General Mangin: " Lettres de la Mission Marchand " (*Revue des Deux Mondes,* September 15, 1931, pp. 241–83), p. 276; Cocheris, op. cit., p. 496; A. B. de Guerville: *New Egypt* (London, 1905), pp. 330 ff., reporting conversations with British and Egyptian officers; Bennet Burleigh: *Khartoum Campaign 1898* (London, 1899), p. 309; Giffen: *Fashoda,* pp. 45 ff.

[44] *Letters of Queen Victoria,* III, p. 290.

vanced in the following weeks to prove or disprove the French right to be at Fashoda. Since the days of the Crimean War no international dispute had been clouded with such contradictory and illogical argumentation. Wilfrid Blunt very wittily noted in his diary that, both sides being in the wrong, each saw the other's wickedness and so believed itself right. M. Cocheris, one of the ablest writers on the subject, pointedly remarked that at bottom the French and British arguments were the same. The trouble was that the same argument was never advanced by both sides at the same time. The Sudan had been evacuated by the Egyptians under protest and at the behest of the British. What was its international status after that? The opinion even of the most eminent French jurists, men like Despagnet and Bonfils, was that the Egyptian claims stood, and that the Sudan was neither *res nullius* nor *res derelicta*. On the other hand such competent people as Sir Samuel Baker and Sir Frederick Lugard took the view that the territory had been abandoned and that it would belong to the first power which could take it from the Mahdists. The British government itself had appropriated parts of the former Egyptian territory along the Red Sea and in Uganda and Unyoro. It had helped the Italians get other parts on the Red Sea and had leased sections to the King of the Belgians. In the agreement with Germany of 1890 the British had claimed a large part of the Equatorial region as a British sphere.

It was because of the freedom with which the British government took or signed away parts of the erstwhile Egyptian possessions that M. Hanotaux had, in 1894 and 1895, insisted upon rejecting the *res nullius* theory and stressing the rights of the Khedive and the Sultan. Despite this stand, Hanotaux had given his blessing to the Marchand mission, and the whole French policy in the years after 1895 was to secure part of the spoils. When the crisis arose in 1898 the positions of the two rivals were reversed. The French now claimed that the Sudan was *res nullius,* that they had as much right there as the Italians on the Red Sea, or the British in Uganda, or the Belgians in Lado. Marchand, despite his small force, had established effective occupation in the Bahr-el-Ghazal province. To which the British replied that the rights of the Khedive had never been more than dormant and that Britain was acting for Egypt, by what right was not clear. Not content with this line of argument the British struck another note: assuming that the territory was lost to Egypt and that it had belonged to the dervishes, it had now been conquered from them and belonged entirely to the Egyptian and British conquerors.[45]

It is perfectly clear now that these arguments and other subsidiary ones had

---

[45] See the correspondence in *Egypt No. 2 (1898)* and *Egypt No. 3 (1898); Affaires du Haut-Nil et du Bahr-el-Ghazal, 1897–1898; British Documents,* I, nos. 198 ff. Among the best secondary studies are Georges Blanchard: " L'Affaire de Fachoda et le Droit International " (*Revue Générale de Droit International Public,* VI, 1899, pp. 380–430); Cocheris: *Situation Internationale de l'Égypte,* etc., pp. 472 ff.; Despagnet: *La Diplomatie de la Troisième République,* pp. 744 ff.; Fernand Vatin: *La Vérité sur Fachoda* (Chaumont, 1923), pp. 52 ff.; Riker, op. cit., pp. 61–63; and the detailed review in Giffen: *Fashoda,* chap. iv.

very little if anything to do with the final disposition of the case. Briefly summarized the situation was simply this: The French, disappointed in their hopes
that the Gladstone government of 1892 would arrange for the evacuation of
Egypt, and inspired by the engineering report of M. Prompt of 1893, had sent
first Monteil and then Marchand to establish himself on the Nile at Fashoda,
where he was to be reinforced by an Abyssinian army. With the Abyssinians on
the one side and the French on the other the British Cape-to-Cairo schemes
would be wrecked. At the same time the threat to construct a barrage on the
lower Sobat and cut off the summer water supply of Egypt would force the
British to negotiate, to arrange for a reconsideration of the Egyptian problem.
All this can be proved to the hilt from what has been said in previous chapters
concerning the origins and instructions of the mission. It is equally clear from
what we know of the unpublished instructions sent to Cairo by Hanotaux on the
eve of his fall in June 1898.[46] Marchand's activities bear it out. French critics have
often accused Hanotaux of not having devoted enough men and supplies to the
mission, of having made of it " une aventure de condottiere " or an " hors d'œuvre
colonial." [47] But these criticisms are really unjustified; the conception of the Marchand mission was as grand as it was daring. The trouble was not with the plan
or with Marchand's part in it. The hitch came rather with the failure of the
Abyssinian contribution. Hardly had Marchand reached Fashoda than he sent
out his lieutenant, Baratier, to find the Abyssinians. Later Mangin was sent up
the Sobat. He actually met the Abyssinian Ras and together they began to march
back to Fashoda. But it was too late; the order to evacuate had already reached
Marchand.[48] To crown the disappointment of the French it turned out that M.
Prompt was quite in error with respect to the possibility of building a barrage
at the mouth of the Sobat. When Marchand came to Cairo early in November
1898, he had a long talk with the Belgian consul. He pointed out to him that
there was not a stone within miles of the position and that Prompt's idea was
therefore not realizable. The Nile at the mouths of the Sobat and the Bahr-el-
Ghazal ran in a number of lateral arms, all of which would have to be blocked.
And yet, he complained, it was a mistake to sacrifice the expedition. Failing the
Abyssinians, the French government could in a few weeks have put two hundred companies of Senegalese on foot and have swept the British out of western
Africa, thus relieving pressure on the Nile.[49]

The French government could not be blamed for the inability of the Abyssinians to hold out on the Nile until Marchand arrived. Neither could the government have predicted the errors in the calculations of M. Prompt. The French

[46] André Mévil: *De la Paix de Francfort à la Conférence d'Algésiras* (Paris, 1909), pp. 26–7.

[47] J. L. de Lanessan: " L'Évacuation de Fachoda " (*Questions Diplomatiques et Coloniales*,
November 15, 1898, pp. 321–9); Robert de Caix: " La Leçon de Fachoda " (*Bulletin . . . de
l'Afrique Française*, November, 1898, pp. 358 ff.).

[48] Mangin: *Regards sur la France d'Afrique* (Paris, 1924), p. 255.

[49] Report of the Belgian consul, printed in Th. Simar: " Léopold II et le Soudan " (*Congo*,
November, 1924, pp. 506–28), pp. 521–2.

schemes simply did not work out properly. But apart from this it must be remembered that when Marchand was despatched the Dongola expedition was only beginning. The British, warned by Sir Samuel Baker of the danger of another power's getting control of the upper Nile and constantly reminded by men like Lugard and Scott-Moncrieff of this menace, had had their attention called to the Prompt projects and had realized what the French were up to. This came out in the parliamentary debates at the time of the Grey declaration in 1895. Egypt depended upon the White Nile flow for her summer water, which was essential for the £10,000,000 cotton crop. By 1898 there was already a crying need for more summer water and for more storage reservoirs.[50] Sir Edward Grey enlarged upon the danger of diversion of Nile water by a hostile power in his speech at Huddersfield on October 28, 1898. In the house of commons the question was gone over in detail on February 24, 1899, when Grey said in so many words: " The possibility of danger to the interests of Egypt in the Nile Valley, rendered possible by engineering science, is such as has never existed before, and the conditions are entirely altered." [51]

It is not to be wondered at, then, that the British pushed forward the reconquest of the Sudan, even at their own financial expense, or that they decided to add British troops to the Egyptian forces. Once Kitchener had conquered the dervishes no time was lost in seeking out Marchand or in investigating the situation on the upper Nile. A gunboat was sent up the Bahr-el-Ghazal almost to the French post at Meshra-el-Rek, and another was despatched up the Bahr-el-Jebel, where it was blocked by sudd. Then the Bahr-el-Zeraf was reconnoitred and an expedition was sent up the Sobat and its confluent the Pibor (Juba). Forts were erected along the course of the Sobat River, presumably to meet any Abyssinian force which might try to reach the Nile again.[52]

A mere review of this evidence will show that the Marchand mission was not a " French picnic party that was outstaying its welcome," [53] and that the British government could not and did not regard it as such. Here was a question which involved the whole welfare of Egypt. Salisbury was determined not to yield, not to consider any concessions to the French view. That being the case, it became chiefly a problem of power. Marchand could easily have been swept aside by the forty thousand troops of Kitchener, but that would have meant a war between England and France. This was realized in London, but the government did not shrink from the prospect. Writing when the crisis was practically over, the *Times* pointed out that in 1878 the British had

---

[50] *Egypt No. 1 (1898): Reports on the Finances, Administration and Condition of Egypt,* pp. 19 ff.

[51] Hansard: *Parliamentary Debates,* Series IV, vol. LXVII, pp. 493 ff. See also the speeches of Brodrick, Durning-Lawrence and Balfour (ibid., pp. 475 ff., 487 ff., 518 ff.).

[52] *Egypt No. 3 (1899): Report on the Finances . . . of Egypt and the Soudan,* p. 7; *Egypt No. 5 (1899): Despatch . . . enclosing a Report on the Soudan by Sir William Garstin.* This was the first of the remarkable hydrographic reports of Garstin.

[53] William Stead, in the *Review of Reviews,* November 15, 1898, pp. 431 ff.

bravely sung "We've got the men, we've got the ships, we've got the money too." In 1898, said the great London journal, there was no singing. The British had no need to stimulate public confidence. It was the first time that England had faced a great crisis without a scare.[54]

This general confidence appears to have been wholly justified. The last years of ardent shipbuilding and general naval increases had put British supremacy at sea beyond discussion. There was no need of "flying squadrons" and other spectacular devices. Of battleships less than ten years old and having a speed of at least sixteen knots, England had thirty-four as against the thirteen of France and the seventeen of Russia. It was only in first-class cruisers and torpedoboats that she was inferior. So eminent an authority as Sir Thomas Brassey, writing on the eve of the crisis, thought that the British fleet was equal in battleships to the French, Russian and German fleets combined and pointed out that the British ships were assembled in much more homogeneous squadrons. A French critic expressed the opinion that, aside from ship-by-ship counts (which never mean much), the British fleet was four times as strong as the French and stronger than all the fleets of Europe put together.[55]

British naval preparations were pushed forward during the whole month of October. At Portsmouth all provisions were made to enable the less mobile part of the forces to take to sea at short notice. Of the details nothing has ever become known, as the deepest secrecy was observed. It appears, however, that the Channel squadrons cruised off the French coast, ready to blockade the French battleships at Brest. Another force watched the Straits of Gibraltar to prevent the French Mediterranean fleet from coming out. In the Mediterranean itself a large squadron was posted between Malta and Gibraltar, ready to blockade Toulon or to debark at Bizerta. Another force was despatched to Alexandria to guard the Suez Canal.[56]

The British felt that they were prepared for all eventualities. Among the French, on the other hand, there was something akin to a general panic. The French fleet was, by common consent, next to the British the strongest in the world. But the French naval staffs had been more or less paralyzed for years by the never-ending dispute between the advocates of capital ships and the proponents of cruisers and torpedoes. Politics may also have had something to do with the condition of French naval preparations. In any event there seems to be no room for doubt that the situation in 1898 was pathetic. French

---

[54] London *Times,* November 22, 1898.

[55] See especially T. A. Brassey: "Can we hold our own at Sea?" (*Fortnightly Review,* July, 1898, pp. 141–7); H. W. Wilson: "The Navies and Naval Construction Programmes of 1898" (*Engineering Magazine,* August, 1898); Lieutenant X: *La Guerre avec l'Angleterre* (Paris, 1900), pp. 22–3.

[56] J. L. de Lanessan: *Histoire de l'Entente Cordiale Franco-Anglaise* (Paris, 1916), p. 203. Lanessan was a former French minister of marine and had good sources of information. See also Sir Thomas Barclay: *Thirty Years* (Boston, 1914), p. 145. I find no evidence whatever for his story that the French Mediterranean fleet actually slipped by the British at Gibraltar with lights extinguished, and that it reached Cherbourg.

naval power, in relation to the English, was about on a par with the Spanish with respect to the American. The Channel fleet was composed of battleships built prior to 1885. The ships were of diverse design, and there was no definite plan of campaign. The naval ports, at home and in the colonies, were suffering from a serious lack of men, while the arsenals were inadequately equipped. At Brest, Cherbourg and Toulon only one third of the batteries could have been manned on the first day of mobilization.[57]

The Paris government was quite aware of the dangers of the situation. Having put the match to the Fashoda powder barrel, the French woke up astonished, frightened and impotent.[58] The tone of the British press was rightly taken as symptomatic of a bellicose spirit. There was certainly a widespread idea in England that the moment was favorable for settling accounts with France. In most circles war would have been popular. Within the cabinet itself voices were evidently raised in favor of this solution. Among several members of the cabinet, of whom Chamberlain was one, there was some apprehension lest Salisbury might yield. There is no evidence that he had any intention of doing so; in fact, he had been quite clear in his own mind for years that no "graceful concessions" could be made in this matter. But the prime minister was clearly anxious to avoid provocation as much as possible. On October 28 the cabinet decided that the fleet should be concentrated. Salisbury was worried by the decision, because, as Lord Esher noted at the time, "the others seemed to take the view that the row would have to come, and that it might as well come now as later." On the very same day Lord Rosebery told Esher that he was inclined "to think that a war with France now would simplify difficulties in the future." There can be no doubt whatever that there was considerable sentiment in governing circles for a preventive war.[59]

Reports of all this reached Paris all through October. At the ministry of marine there was general agreement that the British might provoke a war in order to dispose of the French fleet before the new German fleet had become too strong. The French officers were mostly of one mind, namely that France could not fight at sea, not even by commerce-destroying. Some thought that France's honor required her to fight even if defeat were certain, but these heroes were looked at askance. They were suspected of being in league with the general staff, which was in turn supposed to be not wholly averse to a war which would compromise only the navy, while it made way for a military dictatorship. At all events the minister of marine was convinced that a war would

---

[57] The revelations of the minister of marine, Édouard Lockroy, in the Chamber, March 17, 1899; see also Lockroy: *La Défense Navale* (Paris, 1900), pp. 4 ff.; Comm. H. Chassériaud: "Politique Navale" (*Nouvelle Revue,* January 15, 1899, pp. 216–31).

[58] Cocheris, op. cit., p. 466.

[59] *Journals and Letters of Reginald Viscount Esher* (London, 1934), I, pp. 221–2; Garvin: *Life of Chamberlain*, III, pp. 228, 231; Gardiner: *Life of Harcourt*, II, p. 468; Blunt: *My Diaries,* I, pp. 368, 372, 377 (quoting statements of George Wyndham, the undersecretary for war); *Die Grosse Politik,* XIV, nos. 3898, 3899.

be hopeless, and the prime minister, Brisson, as well as President Faure, agreed with him.[60]

Delcassé's strategy appears to have hinged on the desire to gain time enough to enable France to do two things: firstly, to make the most urgent naval preparations; secondly, to sound out Russia with regard to the chances of securing support. In the meanwhile he pleaded with the British for time until he should have received Marchand's report, and then for time to get an oral report from Captain Baratier, who was summoned to Paris. At the same time everything was done to put at least the coasts in a state of defense. Troops and ammunition were rushed to Brest and Cherbourg; the ships were hurriedly made ready for service. At Toulon the yards were working day and night, and all leave was cancelled. The whole Mediterranean squadron was revamped and put under the command of Admiral Fournier, one of the ablest sea officers. Ultimately President Faure induced the chairmen of the finance committees of the Senate and Chamber to sanction the expenditure of about one hundred million francs without the approval of parliament. An extensive naval reform program was then initiated.[61]

At the height of the crisis, in the midst of the domestic turmoil, the Russian foreign minister arrived in Paris on October 15, followed shortly by M. Witte and by General Kuropatkin, the minister of war. What transpired in the course of the conversations which extended over several days has never been revealed, though it is not hard to conjecture. Franco-Russian relations were not of the best at the time. Political groups in France, from the Right to the Left, were disappointed and disillusioned about the alliance with Russia, an alliance which appeared to be little more than an arrangement to maintain the status quo on the Continent and to draw France into the orbit of German policy. In August 1898 the Tsar had issued his famous peace rescript without consulting his allies. The French were pretty sure that they did not want to disarm, and the general reaction in political circles could be summed up in the phrase: *on nous lache.*[62]

On the Russian side the dissatisfaction was hardly less pronounced. What good was an ally who was paralyzed by so acute a disease as the Dreyfus Affair? What could one do anyway with a radical ministry like that of Brisson, which was supported by men like Clemenceau, Jaurès, Ranc and other well-known opponents of the Franco-Russian Alliance? The inspired Russian press made no secret of its dislike of the French government and of its determination to

---

[60] London *Times,* October 31, 1898 (quoting a high French official); Lockroy: *La Défense Navale,* pp. 19 ff., 187 ff.; de Lanessan: *Histoire de l'Entente Cordiale,* p. 202; Dumba: *Dreibund und Entente-Politik,* pp. 104–5; *National Review,* January, 1899, editorial; Reinach: op. cit., IV, p. 359.

[61] Lockroy, op. cit., pp. 130 ff., 298–310; *Times,* October 20, October 25, November 2, November 3, November 12, November 15, 1898; Barclay: *Thirty Years,* pp. 145–6; Charles Maurras: *Kiel et Tanger* (New edition, Paris, 1913), appendix iii; Ernest A. Vizetelly: *Republican France* (Boston, 1913), pp. 440–1.

[62] Sir Thomas Barclay: *Thirty Years,* p. 149. See also Michon: *The Franco-Russian Alliance,* pp. 99–102.

lend it no support. " When a man ceases to think his wife handsome he begins to think her dowry meagre," wrote the Paris correspondent of the *Times* on October 14, pointing out that on both sides there was nothing but discontent and recrimination.[63]

According to the newspaper reports the French government in October 1898 told M. Witte that he had better wait before trying to float another loan in Paris. This may or may not have been so; in any case it concerns us less than the outcome of the Muraviev-Delcassé conversations. So far as one can detect, the Russian foreign minister was convinced that his French colleague was loyal to the Alliance. For the rest he seems to have assured Delcassé that Russia would honor her obligations, but that her mobilization would take a long time, that her fleet would be frozen up for the winter, and that therefore it would be better for France to yield, the more so as the Fashoda swamps could not be regarded as a matter of vital interest. Later on Russia might help France to reopen the whole Egyptian question.[64]

Sir Edmund Monson, the British ambassador at Paris, was never quite certain whether, in the event of a rupture, the Russians might not give the French more than moral aid, but the government at London lost no sleep over this possibility. It is hard to understand how anyone could have been under any illusion after reading the articles in the French press. The *Soleil,* for example, wrote on November 13 as follows:

> " We sent our sailors to Kiel on the occasion of the opening of the Baltic Canal in order to please Russia; we consented after the Chino-Japanese War to pull the chestnuts out of the fire for Russia, and she thereby gained Manchuria and obtained a preponderating position in the China Seas without spending a single rouble and without risking the bones of a single Cossack; we have given Russia several milliards of francs from our savings, which might perhaps better have been employed at home. In the Fashoda Affair Russia has not lifted a finger to defend us. She doubtless considers that the services we have rendered her are sufficiently repaid by some telegrams which have flattered the vanity of M. Félix Faure and some decorations which have pleased M. Hanotaux." [65]

The situation of France, then, was one of complete helplessness. In the throes of domestic unrest she found herself militarily unprepared and without the whole-hearted support of her ally. The British were determined to go the limit if necessary. There was therefore no other solution for the French but to yield. Naturally no one, least of all Delcassé, liked to be the agent of France's disgrace. One can understand his efforts to make capital out of the downfall of

---

[63] Reports in the *Times,* October 13, 15, 19, 1898; see also the press quotations in *Questions Diplomatiques et Coloniales,* November 1, 1898, pp. 270–3.

[64] *British Documents,* I, nos. 213, 215, 218, 221; *Letters of Queen Victoria,* III, pp. 299–300; London *Times,* October 20, 1898; *Die Grosse Politik,* XIII, no. 3558; XIV, nos. 3891 ff.; Barclay, op. cit., p. 150; Witte: *Memoirs,* p. 178; Reinach, op. cit., p. 315. Giffen, op. cit., chap. ix; and Kossatz, op. cit., pp. 61 ff. give a detailed discussion.

[65] Quoted in the London *Times,* November 14, 1898.

the Brisson cabinet on October 25 by threatening not to join the new ministry if England persisted in humiliating France. But Delcassé was too fond of power to relinquish it if he could avoid doing so. It is certain that by this time he had become convinced that Fashoda had to be evacuated. The British cabinet had met on October 28 and had showed no sign of yielding. On the contrary military and naval preparations were being pushed with more vigor than ever, and on many sides there was talk of an ultimatum that was to be presented to France. So in the end Delcassé retained his portfolio in the new Dupuy cabinet, fully resigned to the necessity of advising retreat from a position thus far so staunchly maintained. The new ministry was formed on October 29, and on that very day the Paris press began to talk of the impending decision. The matter was discussed by the French cabinet on November 3. On the following day the world knew that France had decided to draw back. Fashoda was to be unconditionally evacuated.[66]

Marchand, who had come down the Nile to Cairo, evidently without authorization from Paris, was ordered back to Fashoda to arrange for the departure of his force. He was to leave the disputed post and travel by way of the Sobat to Abyssinia and thence to the French possessions on the Red Sea. It was on December 11 that the French flag was finally hauled down and the valiant adventurers departed. After further trials and tribulations they ultimately reached the Abyssinian capital, and in the spring were back in Paris. It is said that Marchand was forbidden to publish any account of his experiences, and that Delcassé generally took a hostile attitude, indicating that Marchand should have left when Kitchener put in an appearance. No doubt this would have spared Delcassé a distasteful step, and would have supplied him with a convenient scapegoat.[67]

Unfortunately the French withdrawal from Fashoda by no means marked the end of the international crisis. There still remained the problem of French claims in the Bahr-el-Ghazal and the delimitation of the French and British possessions in the Sudan-Congo area. It was to be expected that these matters would be taken up at once, but such was not the case. For weeks on end the British showed no disposition to embark upon negotiations. On the contrary they continued their military and naval preparations. Ministers, notably Chamberlain, continued to make unkind, not to say threatening remarks about the French, until finally Sir Edmund Monson, speaking to the British chamber of commerce in Paris, went the limit and accused the government to which he was accredited of having deliberately pursued a " policy of pinpricks which, while it can only procure an ephemeral gratification to a short-lived ministry, must inevitably perpetuate across the channel an irritation which a high-spirited nation must eventually feel to be intolerable."

---

[66] *British Documents*, I, nos. 221 ff.; *Letters of Queen Victoria*, III, pp. 299–308; *Die Grosse Politik*, XIV, nos. 3901–7; London *Times*, October 31, November 1, 1898; Riker, loc. cit., pp. 71 ff.
[67] On this see especially C. Castellani: *Marchand l'Africain* (Paris, 1902), pp. 337 ff.

Sir Edmund was one of the most cautious and circumspect of diplomats. His utterance, it was felt in Paris, must have rested upon definite instructions from home. In actual fact this was not so, but the French took it to be symptomatic and became more firmly than ever convinced that the British were preparing to provoke a war. The German ambassador at Paris, Count Münster, thought this apprehension quite justified, and it was widely shared in the political circles of other European capitals.[68] In all probability the British activities are to be explained in another way. It was essential for the London government to settle the matter of *Egyptian* claims to the Sudan first of all. Not until January 19, 1899 was the agreement between the British and Egyptian governments signed which decided that the Sudan should be governed by a partnership of two, with England the predominant partner. The British claim to this position rested frankly upon the right of conquest. Other powers might question this right and query the validity of the agreement in international law, but it was more than unlikely that any one of them would be prepared to contest the arrangements made.[69]

While the British remained uncommunicative and the fear of war spread in Paris and on the Continent generally, it was natural that the French, unable to count for much upon their ally, should look elsewhere for support. We have to do here with fundamental problems of foreign policy. There was the Alliance with Russia, which, despite much disappointment and criticism, most Frenchmen regarded as the sheet-anchor of security and which few would have been prepared to give up. But this Alliance had proved of no value in the Anglo-French dispute, which had wide ramifications and which was, for the moment, the most important aspect of French foreign policy. Political circles in Paris were of different opinions regarding the methods for dealing with this situation. A considerable group of staunch republicans favored the conclusion of a general agreement and an entente with England, which, it was hoped, might eventually be extended into an English-French-Russian combination. In this group were a number of business men, who remembered that Britain was France's best customer and took one and a half milliards of francs' worth of French products each year. Under the leadership of J. L. de Lanessan, eminent scientist, colonial administrator and one-time minister of marine, an Entente Cordiale Society had been founded in France in April 1897. It had some enthusiastic supporters but found an early death because the French foreign office and the politicians, so Lanessan claims, were not well disposed towards the idea.[70]

---

[68] *British Documents,* I, nos. 237, 241; Garvin, op. cit., III, pp. 231–2; *Die Grosse Politik,* XIV, nos. 3908–13, 3921–3, 3927; Dumba: *Dreibund und Entente-Politik,* pp. 104–5; Hohenlohe: *Denkwürdigkeiten der Reichskanzlerzeit,* pp. 470, 475–6; *Lettres de la Princesse Radziwill au Général de Robilant* (Bologna, 1933), II, pp. 152, 155.

[69] See Cromer: *Modern Egypt,* II, pp. 155–9, and the very keen and elaborate criticism of the agreement in Cocheris, op. cit., chap. xiii.

[70] J. L. de Lanessan: *Histoire de l'Entente Cordiale Franco-Anglaise* (Paris, 1916), pp. 229–33.

This last statement was only partially true, for there always was a group of French diplomats and statesmen, mostly Gambettists, who favored such a rapprochement. The Comte de Chaudordy was perhaps the most eminent, but D'Estournelles de Constant was also an active protagonist of the idea. M. Ribot, one of the best-known French politicians, appears to have been favorably disposed, while M. Paul Cambon, the ambassador at Constantinople, had been working all through the Armenian crisis to effect an understanding with England. That Delcassé's inclinations were in the same direction has already been emphasized in another connexion. It was obviously in the hope of coming to some general agreement and entente that Delcassé sent Cambon to London as ambassador in the midst of the Fashoda crisis, and it is worth noting that Cambon accepted the post only on condition that efforts be made in that direction.[71]

In the autumn of 1898 this question of an entente with England became closely bound up with the domestic situation in France which arose from the Dreyfus agitation. The Radicals, men like Clemenceau, Zola, Ranc and others, were at one with the Socialists in their dislike of the Russian and German monarchical systems and in their desire to defend the Republic. They were the Dreyfusards, the anti-militarists, the champions of justice and of the common man. Jean Jaurès, the rising socialist leader, attributed the whole trouble to the Anglophobia of M. Hanotaux, and insisted that only British capitalism, not British labor, was bellicose. De Lanessan, after consulting with President Faure, published two articles in the *Rappel* on October 14 and 18, 1898, in which he urged the need for an adjustment. Later on, in January 1899, D'Estournelles de Constant, Denys Cochin, Ribot and Delcassé spoke in behalf of an entente in the Chamber, the first named demanding an end of *all* misunderstandings, and *at once*.[72]

Opposed to these forces of conciliation were the advocates of an arrangement with Germany. These were mostly the patriots, the army circles, the Anti-Dreyfusards, curious though it may seem. The most violent of them, men like Maurras, Déroulède, Cassagnac, Drumont, and Rochefort, maintained that the whole Dreyfus scandal was started and financed by England to weaken France.[73] "If Germany is an object of hatred," wrote Cassagnac, "it is for a definite past which can be effaced. . . . But England's hatred against us is inextinguishable, England is the enemy of yesterday, tomorrow and for ever."[74]

---

71 Eugène Julien: "Notice sur la Vie et les Travaux de M. Paul Cambon" (*Séances et Travaux de l'Académie des Sciences Morales et Politiques*, March–April, 1929, pp. 177–217), pp. 187, 193–4; Schéfer: *D'Une Guerre à l'Autre*, p. 232; Theodor Wolff: *Das Vorspiel* (Munich, 1924), p. 140; *British Documents*, I, no. 238.

72 *Œuvres de Jean Jaurès*, edited by Max Bonnafous (Paris, 1931), I, pp. 212–5; De Lanessan: "Les Relations de la France et de l'Angleterre" (*Questions Diplomatiques et Coloniales*, March 1, 1899, pp. 259–72); De Lanessan: *Histoire de l'Entente Cordiale*, pp. 236–7; *Journal Officiel*, January 23, 1899, pp. 107 ff., 109 ff., 114 ff., 118 ff.

73 See Charles Maurras: *Au Signe de Flore* (Paris, 1931), pp. 58–9.

74 Quoted in the London *Times*, November 14, 1898.

This *volte face* on the part of the reactionaries and partisans of the general staff would have been of little consequence if the unbending attitude of England had not obliged France to drink the cup of humiliation to the dregs. During November and December there was a steady growth of feeling in the direction of an entente with Germany. Apparently the Russian government exerted itself in behalf of this policy. Colonialists, disciples of Ferry and followers of Hanotaux, maintained then and afterward that Delcassé's predecessor had always envisaged some arrangement and that the Marchand mission without the proper diplomatic preparation was an act of insanity.[75] This group blamed Delcassé for his failure to follow the line marked out by Hanotaux. The moderate republican press began to strike the same note and to favor some rapprochement with Germany. M. Lemaitre of the Academy came out openly in this sense, and the eminent jurist, Paul Fauchille, argued that the Continent should unite economically and politically to put a check on England. France should learn to accept the consequences of her defeat. A government, he claimed, that had the courage to ignore the yelping of a few chauvinists would earn the gratitude of the whole country.[76]

There can be no doubt that the feeling of *revanche* receded considerably in France under the influence of the clash with England. The older generation and the Radicals like Clemenceau stood by their guns, but many of the younger intellectuals and even the younger officers were prepared to let bygones be bygones.[77]

Delcassé's stand in this whole matter is not entirely clear. As a Gambettist it seems hardly plausible that he should have seriously considered an agreement with Germany, though he may have wanted to keep a line out for the event of an actual war with England. There is some evidence that the Russians brought pressure to bear in favor of a rapprochement. The St. Petersburg government was profoundly moved by the news of the Anglo-German understanding regarding the Portuguese colonies, and feared that there might be some more far-reaching agreement between the two countries. From Russian documents we know how anxious Muraviev was to hold the Germans on the Russian side.[78] Whether it was this pressure or other considerations that moved Delcassé,

[75] See for example the articles by Robert de Caix in the *Bulletin . . . de l'Afrique Française,* September, 1898, pp. 278 ff.; November, 1898, pp. 358 ff. The same view is taken by Cocheris, op. cit., p. 469.

[76] Press comment in Carroll: *French Public Opinion,* etc., pp. 176 ff. See further Paul Fauchille: "L'Europe Nouvelle" (*Revue Générale de Droit International Public,* January 15, 1899, pp. 5–8); Anonymous: "Le Dilemme de notre Politique Extérieure" (*Revue de Paris,* May 1, 1899, pp. 224–32).

[77] See the numerous quotations from the French and Russian press in *Questions Diplomatiques et Coloniales,* January 15, 1899, pp. 43–5, March 1, 1899, pp. 300–4, and the enquête of the *New York Herald,* summarized in the London *Times,* December 12, 1898. Similarly Theodor Wolff: *Das Vorspiel,* pp. 114 ff.; Constantin Dumba: *Dreibund und Entente-Politik,* pp. 106 ff.; *Die Grosse Politik,* XIII, no. 3556.

[78] L. Teleshev: "Anglo-Germanskoe Sblishenie v 1899 g." (*Krasnyi Arkhiv,* LVI, 1933, pp. 65–79), especially pp. 77–9.

we do not know. But it is interesting to observe that in the last number of the *Revue Générale de Droit International Public* for 1898 there appeared an article by a high French official, who was commonly believed to be one of Delcassé's adherents. The author of this article pleaded for an understanding between France and Germany on the ground that they were both ruining themselves by armament expenditures while England and the United States were forging ahead. The question of Alsace-Lorraine, he maintained, was not insoluble. France should give up all ideas of retrocession, for no victorious nation could be expected to give up territory voluntarily and the German people would never allow the government to abandon the provinces, even if the government wished to do so. In the same way it was, he said, futile to talk of neutralization. That solution had been put forward in 1871 and had been rejected as impracticable. What the author thought really feasible was a plan put about by Admiral Reveillère: Alsace and Lorraine should remain with Germany and be in the complete military control of Germany, but they should be given full autonomy — a position like that of Jersey and Guernsey in the United Kingdom. This plan would satisfy the German desire for military security and the French desire that the faithful Alsatians and Lorrainers should have free opportunity to develop as they wished. Economically too they would remain in the German system, but possibly in the future they might serve as a bridge to a Franco-German tariff union.[79]

In keeping with this general attitude was Delcassé's behavior in the course of his conversations, early in December, with Arthur von Huhn of the *Kölnische Zeitung,* who had already, in 1896, been the intermediary in discussions of the possibility of a Franco-German rapprochement. Huhn noted in his reports how bitter was the feeling toward England among the members of the French foreign office. Delcassé personally assured him that the spirit of revenge was rapidly dying out and that he regarded a rapprochement with Germany as a highly desirable development.[80] A few days later the French foreign minister dined rather ostentatiously at the German embassy.

From the beginning the Germans accepted these advances cordially but sceptically. The hint was constantly being thrown out in Paris that Germany might take some French colony in return for a part or for the whole of Alsace-Lorraine, a suggestion which historians like Vandal and de Broglie declared from the start to be impracticable. Huhn's paper, the *Kölnische Zeitung,* on December 15 made this quite clear: " The possibility of a Franco-German rapprochement can only arise when the word Alsace-Lorraine shall have disappeared from the vocabulary of French statesmen and of the French press. . . .

[79] Anonymous: " La Question d'Alsace-Lorraine est-elle Insoluble? " (*Revue Générale de Droit International Public,* V, 1898, pp. 744–9).

[80] *Die Grosse Politik,* XIII, nos. 3558, 3559. The matter is discussed by Carroll, op. cit., p. 177, and by Giffen: *Fashoda,* pp. 195–6. See also Manfred Zapp: *Deutsch-Französische Annäherungsversuche* (Weida, 1929), pp. 137 ff.

Germany will persist in declining to enter upon any interchange of views so long as she has reason to apprehend that were any conversation opened it might by so much as a hint allude to a subject which for Germany is completely settled." [81] The German ambassador at Paris, Count Münster, was also pretty sceptical about the whole matter. The French would, he thought, try to get the Germans to pull the chestnuts out of the English fire for them, and in addition would demand some concession in the matter of Alsace-Lorraine, if a really sincere entente was to be effected. In this he was quite right. Delcassé, while avoiding official steps, did approach an influential Alsatian shipowner and asked whether he thought the Emperor William would consider an exchange of Alsace-Lorraine for a French colony. The answer, of course, was negative, and before long the whole idea disappeared from political discussion. The Emperor, to be sure, still liked to toy with the idea of a continental combine, a dyke against British pretensions, a naval league against the mistress of the seas. In February 1899 he was saying to the French naval attaché that the time had come for the Continent to unite. The French ambassador at Berlin was convinced that something could be done. But the obstacles to such a settlement were too great. On both sides the governments knew it, and the whole flirtation might be said to have come to a close when on March 2, 1899 the *Temps* remarked: " France has not yet reached the point of repudiating the fundamental principles of her public law by passing off to the account of profit and loss the sacrilegious mutilation which has taken from her the flesh of her flesh and the purest of her blood." [82]

While the question of Alsace-Lorraine still formed an insurmountable barrier in the way of a Franco-German reconciliation, the British were able to pursue their policy without serious misgivings regarding the German attitude. The agreement concerning the Portuguese colonies, which had been signed on the eve of the Fashoda crisis, came just in time to put the Berlin government in a friendly frame of mind. To be sure, the excitable Emperor William took the gloomiest view of the international situation and tried to exploit the occasion to strengthen his relations with the Tsar. In the drafts of the correspondence which passed at that time there is more evidence of jealousy and dislike for the British than of friendship. The Tsar did not react to the suggestions made to him, while the English, on their part, continued to make advances. Salisbury suggested to the Queen in mid-November that it would be well to invite the Emperor to visit England in the coming year. " The attitude of France," he wrote, " makes it desirable that the world should believe in an

---

[81] Quoted by the London *Times*, December 16, 1898.

[82] Quoted by Carroll, op. cit., p. 181. See also the summary of an inquiry among German deputies, made by *La Vie Illustrée*, as given in *Questions Diplomatiques et Coloniales*, February 15, 1899, pp. 240–5. Delcassé's advances in Hohenlohe: *Denkwürdigkeiten*, p. 483; there also, p. 470, a letter from Münster. The Emperor's advances in Bourgeois and Pagès: *Les Origines . . . de la Grande Guerre*, pp. 266, 277–8.

understanding between Germany and England." Victoria followed up the suggestion in December, and before the year was out the Emperor had accepted the invitation with his usual enthusiasm. In a speech at Wakefield on December 8 Chamberlain had underlined the British desire for co-operation and for an agreement with Germany based on common defense of common interests. The address had been very well received by the German press, and the German public no doubt shared the smug feeling that there were prophets on the right and prophets on the left, while Germany was the child of the world between them. It was both comfortable and flattering to be wooed by France and England at the same time, while relations with Russia were good.[83]

This brief review of the Franco-Russian, the Franco-German and the Anglo-German relationships will make it perfectly clear that when the British, having settled accounts with the Egyptians, were at last ready to talk with the French, the Paris government found itself all alone. Paul Cambon, who had taken up his work as ambassador at London, advised from the start that the French foreign office give up all claim to territory on the Nile. When the discussions at last got under way in February 1899 the French no longer pressed even the claim to the Bahr-el-Ghazal area. Cambon suggested a delimitation which would take the Nile-Congo watershed as a basis. The proposal was, of course, wholly satisfactory to the British, and the agreement which was finally signed on March 21, 1899, ran along these lines. France was excluded from the whole Nile Basin, but was left Wadai and the whole Sudan region from Darfur in the east to Lake Chad in the west.[84]

The agreement which disposed finally of the French claims in the Nile Valley did not, however, mark the end of the Sudan problem. We know how much Kitchener feared a possible clash with the Abyssinians.[85] That they had large armies on foot was perfectly well known when the Sirdar went to meet Marchand at Fashoda. After Omdurman, forces had been sent up the Blue Nile and up the Sobat, where garrisons were established. These precautions proved to be somewhat superfluous, for at the very time of the Fashoda crisis King Menelik was obliged to devote himself to a serious revolt led by Ras Mangasha, the turbulent governor of Tigré. By the time this rising was suppressed, in February 1899, Marchand had already reached Abyssinia on his way home. The Franco-Abyssinian campaign was no longer a matter of practical politics.

French writers have thought that the British meant to proceed militarily against Menelik, whose territorial claims extended to the Nile at Khartum. They believe that the outbreak of the Boer War in the autumn of 1899 alone

---

[83] London *Times*, December 10, 12, 1898. The Emperor's correspondence with Nicky in *Die Grosse Politik*, XIV, nos. 3900, 3905, 3913-9. For British policy see especially the *Letters of Queen Victoria*, III, pp. 312, 321-5.

[84] Documents Diplomatiques: *Correspondance Concernant la Déclaration Additionnelle du 21 mars, 1899; British Documents*, I, nos. 242-5; *Die Grosse Politik*, XIV, nos. 3931-3, 3941 ff.; Cocheris, op. cit., pp. 499 ff.; Giffen, op. cit., pp. 87 ff.

[85] *Letters of Queen Victoria*, III, p. 315.

saved the King of Kings from an attack. This is probably an exaggeration. The English were not looking for trouble. But it is likely that the Boer War postponed serious efforts to come to an arrangement with Menelik. We know next to nothing of what went on in the ensuing years. Colonel Harrington, the British minister at Adis Abeba, was a very able man, who seems to have succeeded in drawing Menelik away from the French influence. It is said that Menelik never could get along with M. Lagarde, who had become the regular French representative, and that the African ruler was much put out by the high-handed activity of the Ethiopian Railway Company, which was a French concern. However this may have been, all we know for certain is that on May 15, 1902 the British and the Abyssinians concluded a treaty which defined the eastern frontier of the Sudan. Menelik gave up his earlier claims and contented himself with a boundary which, in general, followed the line of the highlands. In view of what has been said previously of the Nile problem, it is interesting to note that Article III of this treaty engaged Menelik " not to construct, or allow to be constructed, any work across the Blue Nile, Lake Tsana, or the Sobat which would arrest the flow of their waters into the Nile except in agreement with His Britannic Majesty's Government and the Government of the Soudan." [86]

More difficult to deal with was the King of the Belgians, who had already made so much trouble for the French and the British. It will be recalled that in the Treaty of May 1894 the English government had leased to Leopold for the duration of his life a considerable strip of territory on the west bank of the Nile between Lake Albert and Fashoda, to say nothing of the lease to the Congo State of the rest of the Bahr-el-Ghazal region. Because of French opposition the King had been unable to take advantage of this lease in the area north of 5° 30' north latitude. Now when the Marchand expedition reached Fashoda and the crisis between England and France ensued, Leopold came forward with his own solution. He suggested to the French that the Congo State be substituted for France in the conflict, inasmuch as the Congo had treaty rights in the area. The proposal was, however, at once rejected by the French government.[87]

By this time the Congo forces had effectively occupied the region along the upper Nile. They had posts at Rejaf, Lado, Kero, Dufilé and Wadelai. As soon as the French were ejected from Fashoda, the Congolese troops began to invade the more northern region. In May 1899 the British government protested against such action, pointing out the rights of Egypt and the rights which had accrued to England by conquest. There then followed years of argumentation between London and Brussels. Leopold insisted throughout that the treaty of

---

[86] Sir E. Hertslet: *The Map of Africa by Treaty* (Third edition, London, 1909), II, pp. 431 ff. On events in Abyssinia from 1899 to 1902 see Morié: *Histoire de l'Éthiopie*, II, pp. 461 ff.; Darcy: *France et Angleterre*, pp. 459 ff.; *Bulletin . . . de l'Afrique Française*, July, 1902, pp. 254–6; January, 1903, pp. 5–10.   [87] Auguste Gérard: *Mémoires* (Paris, 1928), p. 348.

1894 was fully valid, and quoted a despatch of Lord Salisbury to Sir Edmund Monson of October 6, 1898 in which he said in so many words that this agreement was " in existence and full force still. It has never been cancelled and never been repudiated by this country." [88] The French, said the Belgian King, had obliged him to suspend the occupation of the leased area, but now that they had been forced to evacuate there was no reason why the operations of the Congo State should not be resumed. To which the British replied by claiming that Leopold had, in 1894, handed over the exploitation of these territories to the British Tropical Africa Company and the Anglo-Belgian Africa Company without taking guarantees for their treatment of the natives; that, in actual fact, nothing had been done to occupy or administer the region, inasmuch as the Congo State had given them up in the treaty signed with France in August 1894; that, indeed, the whole British-Congo Treaty of May 1894 had fallen flat when Leopold, at Germany's behest, had given up Article III (leasing the twenty-five kilometer strip between Lakes Tanganyika and Albert Edward to England), and had thus deprived England of the one gain she was to make in return for the lease of the Bahr-el-Ghazal.

In rebuttal of these arguments the Belgian King pointed out that the French-Congo Treaty of 1894 was, so far as Britain was concerned, a *res inter alios acta* and had no bearing on the dispute. Furthermore, he stressed the point that in the agreement of May 1894 what the British wanted most was not the twenty-five kilometer strip, but the recognition, by the Congo government, of the British sphere of influence, and this they had secured.

One can hardly resist the conviction, after reading the documents, that the logic and the right was on the side of Leopold. But it had been shown over and over again in the course of the struggle for the Nile that logic and right were of secondary importance. We need not pursue this subject in all its minute details. Leopold offered to submit the matter to arbitration, but the London government rejected the proposal. Instead it made the King a compromise offer in 1902. In return for the cancellation of the leases of 1894 the British government was prepared to cede to the Congo State in full sovereignty a block of territory bounded on the east by the Yei River, on the north by parallel 6° 30′ north latitude, and on the west by the Nile-Congo watershed. In order to make this scheme comprehensible it should be pointed out that the River Yei is a confluent of the Nile on the left side. It flows roughly south to north and is, at 6° 30′ north latitude, about ninety to one hundred miles west of the Nile. In other words, the point of the British suggestion was that Leopold should agree to the Congo State's being cut off from the Nile, with a frontier removed by a hundred miles from the great river.

Leopold rejected this proposal, and matters began to drift toward a crisis. The British had begun to re-occupy the French posts in the Bahr-el-Ghazal and

---

[88] *Egypt No. 3 (1898),* no. 1.

Belgian expeditions began to push up into the disputed area. There was every prospect that another Fashoda crisis would ensue, but ultimately an agreement was come to on May 9, 1906, after the British had cut Leopold's communications by way of the Nile. Leopold gave up his claims to the Bahr-el-Ghazal lease, but was given, for the duration of his life, the so-called Lado Enclave, that is, the area along the left bank of the Nile from Mahagi on Lake Albert northward to 5° 30' and westward to the 30th meridian and the Nile-Congo watershed. In this treaty, too, one can find the inevitable water clause. Article III specifies that the government of the Congo State shall "not construct, or allow to be constructed any work on or near the Semliki or Isango River, which would diminish the volume of water entering Lake Albert, except in agreement with the Soudanese Government." [89]

With these concluding arrangements the great struggle for the Nile came to a close; the whole course of the river, from its sources in the central African lakes to the sea, was under British or Anglo-Egyptian control, and after the death of Leopold the territory of no other power extended to within a hundred miles of it. More than perhaps any other great international problem in the pre-war period this question of the control of the Nile had the quality of an epic. You have here issues of primary importance, you have grand conceptions, and you have a rivalry drawn out over more than a decade and marked at every stage by drama, daring and heroism.

Despite the immense literature on the subject and the undeniable excellence of much that has been written upon it, no study has yet treated it adequately in all its multitudinous aspects. Its complexity is simply baffling and the many contradictions on all sides only serve to enhance the confusion. Under the circumstances a brief résumé may not be taken amiss. The question as such has its beginning about the year 1889. At that time the situation was still essentially what it had been five years previously, when the British practically obliged the Egyptian government to evacuate the Sudan with the clearly expressed idea that it should be allowed to revert to the native chiefs. The Egyptians, who knew the significance of the Sudan for Egypt, never got over this move. In a memorandum of December 1888 Riaz Pasha wrote rather eloquently: "No one will deny, so clear and evident a proposition is it, that the Nile is the life of Egypt. Now the Nile means the Soudan, and nobody will doubt that the bonds and

[89] Text in Hertslet, Third edition, II, no. 165. The most important material on this dispute was published in the *Deutsches Kolonialblatt,* June 1, 1916, pp. 135–61: "Aus den Archiven des Belgischen Kolonialministeriums, III. Das Lado und Bahr-el-Ghazal-Pachtgebiet des Kongostaates," especially pp. 149–59. See also the highly interesting Belgian memorandum of 1899 published by Th. Simar: "Léopold II et le Soudan" (*Congo,* November, 1924, pp. 506–28), pp. 509–19. There is some discussion of the problem in A. J. Wauters: *Histoire Politique du Congo Belge* (Brussels, 1911), chap. xxix; in Fritz Masoin: *Histoire de l'État Indépendant du Congo* (Namur, 1913), II, pp. 285 ff.; and in Arthur B. Keith: *The Belgian Congo and the Berlin Act* (Oxford, 1919), pp. 112–3. See also Victor Collin: "La Question du Haut-Nil et le Point de Vue Belge" (*Bulletin de la Société de Géographie d'Anvers,* XXIII, 1899, pp. 149–223); and Edmund D. Morel: "The Congo State and the Bahr-el-Ghazal" (*Nineteenth Century,* August, 1901, pp. 202–13).

connections which unite Egypt to the Soudan are as inseparable as those which unite the soul to the body." [90] But the British officials had not changed their minds. Cromer stated emphatically: " There is not now and since the destruction of General Hicks' army there never has been, any serious idea of deliberately adopting a policy involving the reconquest of the Soudan by force of arms." Or again: " I have pointed out over and over again during the last five years that the true interests of Egypt are not to reconquer, but to trade with the Soudan." [91]

What, then, brought about the change? There were two distinct reasons. In the first place, the unusually low Nile of 1888 led to much talk of the possibility of interference with Nile water beyond the frontiers of Egypt. It was then that Sir Samuel Baker wrote his highly interesting letters to the *Times*. Their effect can hardly be doubted, as echoes of them can be found in most writings on the subject in the ensuing years. The growing need of summer water in Egypt raised, at the same time, the problem of further storage of water. The Aswan Dam came under discussion, but already engineers were beginning to talk of the possibility of storing water at Lake Tsana in Abyssinia or at Lake Albert or Victoria in central Africa. All this quite naturally resulted in a growing conviction that the upper Nile was of vital importance to Egypt and that, under no circumstances, could another power be permitted to secure control of these areas.

Now it was at this very time that the danger of such foreign interference in the Sudan became real. With the death of King John of Abyssinia in 1889 Menelik came to the throne. The Italians had concluded with him the Treaty of Uccialli and were preparing to establish a protectorate over a country which claimed and always had claimed territory extending to Khartum and the Nile. Everyone knew that the Mahdist power was on the down-grade and that, if it did not soon collapse, it could easily be defeated. There was no knowing, then, whether the Italians might not become a factor in the Sudan problem. But they were not the only ones. In east Africa the Germans were uncomfortably active and in this very same year, 1889, Peters was pushing inland to Lake Victoria. The hectic enterprises of the British East Africa Company and the hasty negotiations with the Germans in the spring of 1890 indicate plainly enough how seriously this aspect of the problem was viewed in London.

In the Anglo-German Treaty of 1890 and in the Anglo-Italian Treaty of 1891 the danger from Germany and Italy was removed. Neither power, henceforth, would extend its claims and activities into the Nile Basin. The British themselves then embarked on the work of establishing their own control over the upper Nile. For years the country was exercised by the Uganda problem, which in the end became the great test case of imperialism and led to the mortal split in the Liberal party and to the definitive victory of the Liberal Imperialists.

---

[90] *Egypt No. 1 (1889)*, no. 35, inclosure.
[91] Ibid., nos. 22, 35.

Uganda was retained and before long Unyoro was conquered. British officers appeared on the right bank of the upper Nile and stations were established.

In the meanwhile a serious menace had appeared on the left bank. King Leopold, sovereign of the Congo State, had really been the first to move. For the Emin Pasha Relief Expedition, sponsored by him, aimed primarily at the removal of the last Egyptian governor and the acquisition of his Equatorial Province by Leopold. Now in the years 1891–1894 Belgian forces were over-running the whole Equatorial Province, and before long the French were joining in the rush for the Nile. At Paris there had been high hopes that the Gladstone government, which came into power in 1892, would evacuate Egypt. Rosebery had blasted these hopes in no uncertain way. It was clear that not even the Liberals would fulfill the oft-repeated British promises. It was just at this moment that President Carnot became acquainted with the report of M. Prompt, who suggested that a power in command of the upper Nile could build barrages which, if opened, could drown out the whole of Egypt. It is perfectly obvious that the French had no idea of committing so monstrous an atrocity. But they did see that if they were in a position to make the threat, the British would be forced to reopen the question of evacuating Egypt. Whatever may have been said later of French objects in the Bahr-el-Ghazal, it is beyond dispute that the original plans were intended to secure for France an effective " talking point " with respect to the Egyptian question.

The British had protested against the activities of Leopold. When the French began to push into the Nile area the matter became more serious. Ultimately, in order to shut the door on the French, the British government leased the terri-tory in question to Leopold. The French protested and, probably because of the German protests regarding another clause of the British-Congo Treaty, were able to force Leopold to eschew activity in the Bahr-el-Ghazal. The British did nothing to support their lessee. In the treaty of August 1894 the Belgian King was obliged to accept the French terms.

The rest of the story we need not repeat. French plans and the collapse of the Italian-Abyssinian front induced the British to decide on the reconquest of the Sudan from the north, though Salisbury had always hoped the matter could wait until the Mombasa Railway was finished to Lake Victoria and troops could be brought up from the south. So what happened in the end was that the British pushed up the Nile from Wady-Halfa and Dongola to Khartum while the French were advancing from the Atlantic through the French Congo and the Belgian Congo and at the same time organizing a complementary movement in conjunction with the Abyssinians. After the Battle of Omdurman a crisis was inevitable and the Fashoda affair ensued.

Knowing the deep significance of the problem and realizing all its ramifica-tions, we can see now that the British could not yield. Their warnings to France had been absolutely sincere. The trouble was that the British position was legally weak. The levity with which one argument was discarded in favor of another is truly astounding. Unfortunately for the French their own policy and arguments also lacked continuity and consistency. But we can leave the debate to the jurists. From the standpoint of diplomacy so much is clear: that nothing further could be gained by argument. The time for the *ultima ratio* had come. The British were prepared to fight. Some, it seems, were rather anxious to fight, knowing full well the superiority of the British naval forces and the helplessness of France, wracked as she was by the domestic crisis of the Dreyfus affair. The outcome of the conflict was a foregone conclusion. France ended by recalling Marchand and by abandoning all claims to the whole Bahr-el-Ghazal region. After which the British proceeded to evict Leopold, who had an indubitable claim to a lease of the territory, a claim which the British themselves held up to the French in the course of the Fashoda debate. Here again the rights and wrongs did not play any rôle. Leopold was forced to give in by the stoppage of his communications on the Nile by the British. Once again it was a matter of *force majeure*. And it should not be forgotten that the British, through clever financial and military manipulation of the Sudan campaign, had established, or claimed to have established, an indubitable right to joint administration in the Sudan. So long as they remained there the Egyptian question was settled. Even in our own day the independence of Egypt is a mere illusion so long as the British continue in the Sudan.

From the angle of European international relations very little need be said about the Fashoda crisis. France was all alone, for the Russians, with their attention focussed on the Far East, had no stomach for African adventure. They felt that the French had deserted them in the Near Eastern crisis of the winter of 1896–1897 and they took their revenge. The Franco-Russian Alliance had reached its nadir. The Russians kept it up because of its financial value and because it more or less guaranteed them a well-behaved Germany. The French stood by it because for them it was the keystone of security in Europe and they could not dispense with it. But the illusions of the honeymoon period were all gone. Even in 1898 the Radicals and Socialists, who had little use for autocratic Russia, were talking of the need of a general understanding with England. The harsh tone of the British in the Fashoda crisis, and the uncompromising attitude of the British government made the *entente cordiale* for the time being a pious hope and little more. But the lines of the future were already being marked out.

The much discussed Franco-German reconciliation and the continental coalition against Britain were hardly more than extravagant fancies in 1898 and 1899. In France the whole idea was a counsel of despair. Hard-headed reactionaries and militarists, in general the Anti-Dreyfusards, championed a union with the strong military monarchies. No doubt the revenge feeling generally was gradually diminishing, but still the reconciliation between the two great nations was a long way off. Good Frenchmen would not have considered it without having been first given some satisfaction in the matter of Alsace-Lorraine. This fact in itself ruined all prospects of the scheme, for the Germans would not for a moment entertain the suggestion of returning even part of the conquered provinces. Why should they? Their position in international affairs was never better. With England they had come to some sort of *modus vivendi*. The London government much resented what was called the German policy of blackmail, but it had seen the need for accepting it. Germany had been admitted to a share in the future Portuguese colonial spoils. In other words, the Germans felt very smug, sitting in the middle, as they did, while the Anglo-Russian, Anglo-French antagonisms raged around. It was the ideal setting for the Holstein policy of having two irons in the fire, a policy which Bülow adopted in full. The foreign minister defined Germany's standpoint during the crisis as one of careful abstention. Germany would maintain friendly relations with all parties, but would pursue an independent policy, avoiding all attempts to enlist her on the one side or the other. So the Fashoda affair ended without any fundamental dislocation in the established international system. The Franco-Russian Alliance still existed, though relations had cooled. England still maintained her isolation, but the tension in Anglo-French relations had grown very great. In the succeeding years it was to be one of the prime factors in European diplomacy. The leading question came to be the question whether Germany could be brought to join the anti-British group without reservations.

BIBLIOGRAPHICAL NOTE

DOCUMENTARY SOURCES

Accounts and Papers. 1899, volume CXII. *Egypt No. 2 (1898)*; *Egypt No. 3 (1898)*. The original British Blue Books on the crisis, now largely superseded by the *British Documents on the Origins of the War.*

Documents Diplomatiques. Affaires du Haut-Nil et du Bahr-el-Ghazal, 1897–1898. Paris, 1898. *Correspondance Concernant la Déclaration Additionnelle du 21 mars 1899.* The French Yellow Books, less full than the British publications, but the most valuable material on the French side.

British Documents on the Origins of the War, 1898–1914. Edited by G. P. Gooch and Harold Temperley. London, 1927 ff. The first volume of this important series contains additional material on the Fashoda crisis.

Die Grosse Politik der Europäischen Kabinette, 1871–1914. Volume XIII, chapter lxxxix: Franco-German Relations in 1898–1899. Volume XIV, chapter xciii: The Fashoda Crisis. This last chapter contains documents of considerable importance, bearing especially upon the British side of the crisis.

"Aus den Archiven des Belgischen Kolonialministeriums. III. Das Lado und Bahr-el-Ghazal Pachtgebiet des Kongostaates." (*Deutsches Kolonialblatt,* June 1, 1916, pp. 135–61). Belgian documents, of prime importance for the Congolese aspect of the problem.

MEMOIRS, AUTOBIOGRAPHIES, BIOGRAPHIES, AND LETTERS

Letters of Queen Victoria. Third Series, volume III. New York, 1932. Easily one of the most important sources for the study of British policy.

GARVIN, J. L.: *The Life of Joseph Chamberlain.* London, 1933 ff. Contains but little material on the Fashoda crisis.

ARTHUR, SIR GEORGE: *Life of Lord Kitchener.* Three volumes. London, 1920. The official biography of the British commander.

SMITH-DORRIEN, GENERAL SIR HORACE: *Memories of Forty-Eight Years' Service.* London, 1925. Contains a detailed account of the Fashoda meeting, by one of the British officers present.

BLUNT, WILFRID S.: *My Diaries.* London, 1919. Contains some valuable side-lights on the Fashoda crisis.

BARCLAY, SIR THOMAS: *Thirty Years. Anglo-French Reminiscences.* New York, 1914. One of the best-known accounts, by an Englishman well acquainted with French affairs.

MANGIN, GENERAL: "Lettres de la Mission Marchand." (*Revue des Deux Mondes,* September 15, 1931, pp. 241–83). An interesting addition to the amount of eyewitness material. Mangin was one of Marchand's associates.

BARATIER, CAPTAIN ALBERT E.: *À travers l'Afrique.* Paris, 1910. The account of Marchand's chief aide. One of the best narratives of the expedition.

Mission Marchand. Journal de Route du Dr. J. Émily. Second edition, Paris, 1913. A detailed and beautifully illustrated narrative, but of little political importance.

MICHEL, CHARLES: *Vers Fachoda, à la Rencontre de la Mission Marchand à travers l'Éthiopie.* Paris, 1901. By far the most important account of the Abyssinian aspect of the French activity.

CASTELLANI, CHARLES: *Marchand l'Africain.* Paris, 1902. Probably the best biography of Marchand, though entirely uncritical.

WAUTERS, A. J.: *Souvenirs de Fashoda et de l'Expédition Dhanis.* Brussels, 1910. Important for the Belgian activities. This material is largely included in the author's *Histoire Politique du Congo Belge* (Brussels, 1911).

SPECIAL STUDIES

HANOTAUX, GABRIEL: *Fachoda*. Paris, 1909. The apology of Delcassé's predecessor. Deals chiefly with the period before the crisis.

LEBON, ANDRÉ: *La Politique de la France en Afrique, 1896–1898*. Paris, 1901. Written by a former minister for the colonies; also concerned chiefly with the earlier period.

DE CAIX, ROBERT: *Fachoda*. Paris, 1899. The best contemporary study. Very well informed and thoroughly critical.

COCHERIS, JULES; *La Situation Internationale de l'Égypte et du Soudan*. Paris, 1903. Even allowing for the French bias, this is still probably the best scholarly account of the whole question.

DARCY, JEAN: *France et Angleterre: Cent Années de Rivalité Colonial*. Paris, 1904. Another good book, though less scholarly and more highly colored than Cocheris'.

ANONYMOUS: "La Mission Marchand." (*Revue de Paris*, June 1, 1899, pp. 457–86). An excellent, well-informed, critical account.

DELONCLE, J. L.: "La Question de Fachoda." (*Revue Politique et Parlementaire*, November 1898, pp. 277–300). A good historical account, by a former French secretary for the colonies.

BLANCHARD, GEORGES: "L'Affaire de Fachoda." (*Revue Générale de Droit International Public*, VI, 1899, pp. 380–430). A sound, scholarly, legal study.

COLLIN, VICTOR: "La Question du Haut-Nil et le Point de Vue Belge." (*Bulletin de la Société de Géographie d'Anvers*, XXIII, pp. 149–223). A detailed historical review of the whole Sudan problem.

ANONYMOUS: "France, Russia and the Nile." (*Contemporary Review*, December, 1898, pp. 761–78). A rather sensational article, purporting to reveal the French-Mahdist conspiracy.

DIPLOMATICUS: "Fashoda and Lord Salisbury's Vindication." (*Fortnightly Review*, December, 1898, pp. 1002–14). A strong presentation of the case against France.

BOURDARIE, PAUL: *Fachoda. La Mission Marchand*. Paris, 1899. A general review of the incident.

GUÉTANT, LOUIS: *Marchand-Fashoda*. Paris, 1899. Another good popular survey of the origins and aspects of the problem.

VATIN, FERNAND: *La Vérité sur Fachoda*. Chaumont, 1923. Reviews the Egyptian problem and the Anglo-French relationship. Takes the view that England's claim in 1898 was good and that the French were in the wrong.

RIKER, T. W.: " A Survey of British Policy in the Fashoda Crisis." (*Political Science Quarterly*, March, 1929, pp. 54–78). The first study of the British and German documents on the subject. A very meaty article, valuable especially for the account it takes of the British press.

GIFFEN, MORRISON B.: *Fashoda, the Incident and its Diplomatic Setting*. Chicago, 1930. The best general treatment, based upon the newer documentary publications and containing most of the important information. There is little that is novel about the viewpoint, and the value of the monograph for the general reader is much diminished by the extraordinary arrangement of the material, which makes it impossible to get a systematic view of its historical development.

BATUT, GUY DE LA: *Fachoda, ou le Renversement des Alliances*. Fourth edition, Paris, 1932. A popular review of the Egyptian problem as an Anglo-French problem. Fairly well-informed, but in no sense a contribution.

KOSSATZ, HEINZ: *Untersuchungen über den Französisch-Englischen Weltgegensatz im Fashodajahr*. Breslau, 1934. In most respects a well-informed and well-balanced monographic study. Much broader in analysis and interpretation than most studies of the subject.

XVII

Peace Dreams and Political Realities

ᔕ

ADVOCATES OF PEACE AND PROPONENTS OF THE IDEA OF INTERNATIONAL co-operation regard the year 1899 as marking the opening of a new era in human history, for in May of that year the first peace conference opened its sessions at The Hague. This Conference, they say, was " in germ the true Parliament of Man." "The dream of the prophets and the songs of the poets here found their first partial realization in plain prose." [1]

For the historian of European diplomacy it is no easy task to put it into the proper setting. The last years of the century were marked by the great Fashoda crisis, by the Spanish-American War, by the ruthless assault of the powers upon China, and by the beginning of the Boer War. No doubt about it, the atmosphere of Europe was a warlike atmosphere in which talk of peace and disarmament was bound to sound like hypocrisy. How is one to integrate the episode of the Hague conference with the manifestations of exuberant imperialism?

Fortunately sufficient material is now available to enable us to speak with reasonable authority about the political aspects of the First Hague Peace Conference. Its origins must be sought in the growing movements for peace and disarmament which marked the last decade of the century. There had been, especially in England and America, an impressive " peace crusade " in the years of the mid-century, a movement typical of the humanitarian ideas of that period. Less was heard of peace in the stormy decades from 1870 to 1890, but the tremendous development of armies and armaments in those years made a revival of the movement almost inevitable. There was, on many sides, a feeling that, apart from the horrors of war itself, the cost of preparation for war was so enormous that sufficient funds could no longer be found for urgent social reforms. With the organization of the Interparliamentary Union in 1889 the demand for action, especially the demand for the extension of international arbitration, became a regular thing. The modern movement for peace may be said to date roughly from that time. [2]

---

[1] I quote from the preface of Andrew D. White: *The First Hague Conference* (Boston, 1912), which is a reprint of part of White's *Autobiography,* issued by the World Peace Foundation.

[2] The literature on the history of the peace movement is still pathetically inadequate. The best single treatment seems to me to be Christian L. Lange: " Histoire de la Doctrine Pacifique et de son Influence sur le Développement du Droit International " (*Académie de Droit International, Recueil*

Considering the financial strain of modern armament, it is not to be won-dered at that European statesmen turned their attention to the problem. One of the most cynical and disillusioned of them, Lord Salisbury, appears to have had the matter at heart for some time. He is said to have had a memorandum worked out in 1888, and on various occasions he warned Europe of the danger in his Guild Hall speeches, notably in November 1897. Lord Rosebery, who prided himself on the continuance of Salisbury's policies when the Liberals were in power, shared the convictions of the older statesman in this matter. In April 1894 a conference of the representatives of all the Free Churches in London drew up a memorial asking the government to take the initiative in bringing the matter before the powers. Many religious leaders and many heads of labor organizations signed the memorial, to say nothing of eighty members of par-liament. When presented to Lord Rosebery, at that time prime minister, it bore no less than 35,000 signatures.[3]

Rosebery appears to have taken the matter up without delay, for he began conversations with the Russian ambassador, M. de Staal, suggesting that Alex-ander III, as the greatest guarantor of peace in Europe, should summon an international conference to discuss the question of limitation or reduction of armaments. The English army, he pointed out, was too small to allow England to speak authoritatively. We do not know what the Russian reply to these pro-posals was, but it is clear from the marginal notes of Alexander III that, much as he desired peace, he regarded the suggestion as somewhat utopian and suspected that the advances of Rosebery were designed to drive a wedge into the newly formed Franco-Russian Alliance. "Only England," he noted, "would benefit, for her army is insignificant while her navy is powerful, and England would never consider a reduction of her fleet."[4]

The question of limitation of armaments came up again in Russian official circles in the spring of 1898. On March 13 the minister of war, General Kuro-patkin, spoke to the Tsar and wrote to the foreign minister, Count Muraviev, of the difficulties presented by the introduction of rapid-firing field artillery in the German army (the French had adopted the famous 75 mm. piece in 1896). The new German guns, Kuropatkin pointed out, could fire six shells per minute, compared with the single shell per minute fired by the Russian. This situation

---

des Cours, XIII, 1926, pp. 175–422), especially pp. 389 ff.; see also his Die Interparlamentarische Union und die Entwicklung des Völkerrechts (Kiel, 1927). Much may be learned, too, from G. Olphe-Galliard: La Morale des Nations (Paris, 1920); Alfred H. Fried: Handbuch der Friedensbewegung (Leipzig, 1911), and Hans Wehberg: Die Internationale Beschränkung der Rüstungen (Stuttgart, 1919), part A. A good general survey is Arthur C. F. Beales: The History of Peace (New York, 1931).

[3] William T. Stead, in the Review of Reviews, September 15, 1898, pp. 293–7; Frederic Whyte: The Life of William T. Stead (New York, n.d.), II, pp. 122 ff.

[4] Stead, loc. cit., discusses Rosebery's advances to Russia, and claims that the outbreak of war between China and Japan, followed by the death of Alexander, put an end to the discussion. The correspondence may now be found in A. Meyendorff: Correspondance Diplomatique de M. de Staal (Paris, 1929), II, pp. 241–9, and the Tsar's comments are given in L. Teleshev: "K Istorii Pervoi Gaagskoi Konferentsii" (Krasnyi Arkhiv, L–LI, 1932, pp. 64–96), pp. 74 ff.

led the general to point out that the race for armaments had reached an unprecedented and phantastic stage, which could end only in war or in a move for limitation. The moment seemed to him opportune for approaching the Austrian government, which was faced with the same problem and which, like the Russian, was hard up for funds. Each country saw before it the prospect of introducing a new weapon at the cost of some fifty million dollars, only to see it antiquated before many years had passed. He therefore suggested an agreement with Austria providing that for ten years neither would introduce a rapid-firing field piece.

It is said that Count Witte, the Russian finance minister, refused to assign the funds necessary for the introduction of the new weapon and that he was the driving force behind the idea of a general conference to check competitive armaments for a given period. Witte makes this claim himself and foreign diplomats at the time suspected that the real reason for the Tsar's generous gesture was to be found in the finance minister's inability to raise the money for further equipment.[5]

In any event, the foreign minister took up the idea with some enthusiasm. He thought of drawing all the continental powers together in a ten-year holiday, and contemplated with glee the resulting isolation of England. In a memorandum dated April 5 he recapitulated the arguments in favor of limitation of armaments and pointed out that Austria could not be expected to make a separate agreement without Germany. On the other hand it was fairly certain that a proposal for general international action would meet with the support of both Austria and Italy. England and France would probably be sympathetic. Muraviev therefore suggested a conference to discuss, not so much limitation of armaments, which would be difficult to control, but limitation of forces and of budgets, and furthermore an agreement to settle international disputes by arbitration rather than by war. The moment, he pointed out, was peculiarly favorable for Russia, inasmuch as she had just acquired her port in the Far East and an agreement not to increase forces would leave Russia her great preponderance.[6]

This memorandum, which appears to have been the work of M. Basily, an official of the foreign office who was genuinely interested in the cause of disarmament and peace, seems to have been approved by the Tsar, who gave instructions to draw up a suitable note for submission to the powers. But for unknown reasons there was considerable delay. It was only in July that the Tsar

[5] E. J. Dillon: *The Eclipse of Russia* (London, 1918), pp. 269 ff.; *The Memoirs of Count Witte* (New York, 1921), pp. 96–7; *Die Grosse Politik*, XV, nos. 4216, 4232, 4251; *British Documents on the Origins of the War*, I, nos. 263, 271. The whole matter is discussed in some detail in August Junk: *Die Mächte auf der Ersten Haager Friedenskonferenz* (Leipzig, 1928), pp. 2–13.

[6] Teleshev, op. cit., pp. 74 ff.; Idem: "Noviye Materialy o Gaagskoi Mirnoi Konferentsii 1899 g." (*Krasnyi Arkhiv*, LIV–V, 1932, pp. 49–79), pp. 55–6. This and other documents in the Teleshev articles have been translated into German and published in the *Berliner Monatshefte*, June, 1933, pp. 571–80; July, 1933, pp. 679–92; April, 1934, pp. 320–32.

showed Kuropatkin the draft of a note suggesting a conference, which had been worked out in the foreign office. There would seem to have been some opposition to the scheme in the foreign office itself.[7] It may be that Basily and one of his colleagues, Priklonsky, brought about a favorable decision. These two gentlemen had both been stationed at Budapest in 1896 during the meeting of the Interparliamentary Union, and the latter had at that time drawn up a memorandum which he exhumed in 1898 and which is said to have influenced Lamsdorff and Muraviev.[8] The better known story has it that the Tsar was so impressed by the great six-volume book on war by Ivan Bloch, which appeared at this time, that he took the initiative. Witte always denied quite stoutly that Bloch had anything to do with it, and I think we may assume that if he did have influence it must have been indirect and secondary. The Russian materials which we now have show conclusively that sentiment had very little to do with the formulation of the Russian policy.[9]

I should like to suggest that in the consideration of the origins of the peace manifesto of August 24, 1898 some thought should be given to the importance of the international situation at that time. Russia had become involved in a serious dispute with England regarding the control of certain Chinese railways. The whole matter will have to be discussed in greater detail later, in connexion with the development of the general Far Eastern problem, but it may be remarked here that the tension had reached such a point that on August 18 the British ambassador at St. Petersburg told Muraviev that refusal to yield might "lead to serious international complications." The Russians were distinctly frightened by the strong stand taken by the British, and obviously feared an attack in the Far East which might jeopardize all the gains made in past years. Muraviev therefore raised the question whether it would not be wiser to seek an agreement with the British, whereupon the Tsar commented: "Peace is more important than anything else, unless our honor is touched."[10]

It was probably to counteract the danger of a clash in the Far East that the Imperial communication was handed to the representatives of foreign powers

---

[7] W. T. Stead: *La Chronique de la Conférence de la Haye* (The Hague, 1899), p. 8, and the apparently trustworthy account of Komarov, one of the officials of the foreign office, as given in *Die Grosse Politik*, XV, no. 4350.

[8] M. Priklonsky: "Die Vorgeschichte der Ersten Haager Friedenskonferenz" (*Friedenswarte*, May, 1929, pp. 129 ff.); this is the explanation which Hans Wehberg says was given him by several high officials of the Russian foreign office; see his *Die Internationale Beschränkung der Rüstungen*, pp. 173 ff.; his statement in *Das Werk des Untersuchungsausschusses der Verfassunggebenden Deutschen Nationalversammlung*, Series I, vol. V (Berlin, 1929), pp. 5–6; and his most recent essay: "La Contribution des Conférences de la Paix de la Haye au Progrès du Droit International" (*Académie de Droit International, Recueil des Cours*, XXXVII, 1931, pp. 533–669), pp. 544–6.

[9] Bertha von Suttner: *Die Haager Friedenskonferenzen, Tagebuchblätter* (Leipzig, 1901), p. 19, and Alfred H. Fried: *Handbuch der Friedensbewegung*, II, pp. 134 ff., as well as Komarov (*Die Grosse Politik*, XV, no. 4350) asserted the importance of Bloch, who was said to have been received at this time by the Tsar. Witte's denial in *Die Grosse Politik*, XV, no. 4251, and in his *Memoirs*.

[10] Teleshev: "K Istorii Pervoi Gaagskoi Konferentsii" (loc. cit.), p. 67; A. Popov: "Anglo-Russkoe Soglashenie o Razdele Kitaiia, 1899 g." (*Krasnyi Arkhiv*, XXV, 1927, pp. 111–34), pp. 120–1.

at St. Petersburg on August 24, 1898. The document itself was couched in the most general terms. It reviewed the growth of the desire for peace and the military preparations that had been made to ensure it. Despite their great cost, armaments had not given the desired security:

> "Hundreds of millions are devoted to acquiring terrible engines of destruction which, though to-day regarded as the last word of science, are destined to-morrow to lose all value in consequence of some fresh discovery in the same field. . . . The economic crises, due in great part to the system of armaments à outrance, and the continual danger which lies in this massing of war material, are transforming the armed peace of our days into a crushing burden, which the peoples have more and more difficulty in bearing. It appears evident then that if this state of things were prolonged it would inevitably lead to the very cataclysm which it is desired to avert, and the horrors of which make every thinking man shudder in advance."

The Tsar therefore proposed the meeting of a conference to occupy itself with this grave problem.

Nicholas could not have devised a move better calculated to dumbfound the diplomatic and political circles of Europe. His manifesto struck his French allies like a thunderbolt. They had not been consulted in the matter and feared from the outset that a peace conference might end in a reaffirmation of the peace as fixed by the Treaty of Frankfurt. The stock of the Franco-Russian Alliance had already reached a very low point, and popular dissatisfaction was openly expressed in the newspapers. The *Temps,* generally regarded as the mouthpiece of the foreign office, wrote: "Until the injustice of 1871 has been rectified, until France has re-established the past at the risk of her very existence, until she has assured the future, the true heirs of the Revolution cannot subscribe to the principles of Count Muraviev." The *Autorité* was even more bitter: "The initiative of the Tsar leads to the saddest consequences for France and deprives her of the last hopes. We did not go to St. Petersburg to accept a policy of resignation. We do not need to go to that capital in order to lay down our arms. Berlin has for a long time desired nothing better than to do business with us on that basis." [11]

Delcassé himself made no secret of his disillusionment. He told the Russian ambassador that France would follow the Tsar's lead as soon as a definite program for the conference were submitted. France, he said, had carefully observed the Treaty of Frankfurt, despite her feelings about it. Thereby she had clearly shown her love of peace. To demand more of her would be unjust. France could not recognize anew or approve the theft of her territory, for which she still suffered. It was only after Muraviev had assured the French ambassador at St.

---

[11] Quoted by Junk, op. cit., p. 25. For the French attitude see further Nicolas Notovitch: *La Pacification de l'Europe* (Paris, 1899), especially chap. iii; Sir Thomas Barclay: *Thirty Years* (Boston, 1914), p. 149; *Die Grosse Politik,* XV, nos. 4227, 4230, 4231; *British Documents,* I, no. 262; and the Belgian reports in *Zur Europäischen Politik* (Berlin, 1919), I, pp. 35–6.

Petersburg that the Russians had no thought of disarming but only of limiting armaments, and that political questions would not be raised in any form at the conference that Delcassé declared himself satisfied.

Even then it appeared to the Russian authorities desirable to placate the Paris government. Kuropatkin and Muraviev as well as Witte visited the French capital in October, at the very height of the Fashoda crisis. The Russian war minister found military circles in Paris very dejected. After twenty-seven years of effort in armaments they saw themselves before the possibility of losing everything, even their hopes for the ultimate recovery of the lost provinces. Military men even began to doubt the permanence of the convention with Russia of 1893. It took no small effort to convince them that the French had not been consulted simply because that would have given the proposal the appearance of a Franco-Russian program, which the powers of the Triple Alliance would have rejected out of hand. Russia, insisted Kuropatkin, had no thought of jeopardizing the alliance with France, of reaffirming the Treaty of Frankfurt, or of interfering with French armaments past or present. The French were ultimately satisfied that the whole scheme was quite innocuous, but President Faure closed his conversation with the Russian war minister with the remark: "We French have our own problems and the conference will naturally not aim at disturbing us in the solution of these problems." [12]

It was perfectly clear from the outset that the Russian proposal would fall flat unless Germany, the most powerful continental state, agreed to participate in the work of the conference. The Tsar therefore appealed specially to his friend the Kaiser for support. William was quite ready to recognize the benevolent intentions of his younger colleague, but regarded the whole business as pure Utopia. For years, he noted, Russia had been piling armaments on armaments, and had been building railways for purely strategical purposes. Recently she had embarked upon a great naval construction program. And all this time the country had been suffering from crop failure, famine and disease. Now that Russia no longer found it possible to borrow money in Paris her finances were giving out and she was anxious to stop other powers from getting ahead of her in a military way.

This estimate was more accurate and more fair than perhaps even the Emperor realized. It did not, however, determine the German attitude. Both the Emperor and Bülow were eager not to estrange Russia. They did not want to serve as the shoal on which the Russian project should be wrecked, but hoped that the opposition of the English would serve that purpose. William therefore replied at once to Nicholas' appeal, complimenting the Tsar on his love of mankind, declaring that "honour will henceforth be lavished upon you by the whole world, even should the practical part fail through the difficulties of the detail,"

---

[12] The documents are printed by Teleshev: "K Istorii Pervoi Gaagskoi Konferentsii," pp. 80–9. On Muraviev's conversations there is no material beyond the account which he gave shortly afterward to the German ambassador at Vienna (*Die Grosse Politik*, XV, no. 4231).

and promising that the German government would give the matter its most serious attention.[13]

Of the official British response to the peace rescript little can be said. Balfour, who was acting as foreign minister in Salisbury's absence, gave vague assurances of sympathy, but it was not until late in October that the English government officially agreed to attend the conference. The foreign office first assured itself that no current political issues, like the Chinese or Egyptian questions, would be raised. Salisbury, indeed, made it clear to the German ambassador that he regarded the whole program as " not serious." Even if there were a limitation of armament it would be practically impossible to ensure its enforcement.[14]

English public opinion was distinctly divided. The tradition of humanitarianism and peace was strongly rooted in the country. Several churchmen, a number of prominent Liberal leaders, and the Trade Union Congress came out in favor of the peace program almost at once. William T. Stead, the well-known editor of the *Review of Reviews,* who incidentally might be described as the father of modern British naval programs because of his great agitation in 1884, at once championed the good cause. He was an almost fanatical Russophil as well as a lover of peace, and threw himself wholeheartedly into the organization of a great " peace crusade." In the autumn of 1898 he made a tour of the European capitals and was received by the Tsar at Livadia. Nothing much came of the Peace Crusade, as Stead himself had to admit that opinion on the Continent was not prepared for it. In England however a goodly number of town meetings were held. The churches and the labor organizations generally backed the movement.[15]

While Stead tried to mobilize British opinion through an elaborate campaign of agitation, a great many leaders of political thought remained aloof. There was in England a good deal of resentment and suspicion of Russia, especially over Far Eastern affairs. The Tsar's appeal was described in some of the leading journals as pure hypocrisy and as a rather thinly veiled ruse by which Russia hoped to gain time to prepare herself better. Some writers were not at all sure that armaments were ruining Europe (they pointed to the prosperity of Germany and France), and others were by no means convinced that war was necessarily or always an evil. It would be as wrong to ignore the strong militaristic streak in England as to attempt to deny the force of the pacifist current.[16]

---

[13] *Die Grosse Politik,* XV, nos. 4216–22.

[14] *Die Grosse Politik,* XV, nos. 4220, 4237.

[15] The story may be followed in the files of the *Review of Reviews* for the autumn of 1898 and the spring of 1899, but see further Whyte: *Life of Stead,* II, pp. 129–50.

[16] William E. H. Lecky, in his *Democracy and Liberty* (New edition, London, 1899) called attention to the growing popularity of conscription and the cult of the military virtues. See further the following articles: Sidney Low: " Should Europe Disarm? " (*Nineteenth Century,* October, 1898); Soldier: " The Tsar's Appeal for Peace " (*Contemporary Review,* October, 1898); Arnold White: " The Tsar's Manifesto " (*National Review,* October, 1898); Sir Henry Howorth: " Plain Words about the Tsar's New Gospel of Peace " (*Nineteenth Century,* February, 1899); Edward Markwick: " Is War an Unnecessary Evil? " (*New Century Review,* February, 1899); Diplomaticus:

Enough has been said, without going into further detail, to show that the idealism and love of mankind with which Nicholas II was credited played little if any part in the elaboration of the famous peace rescript. The document sprang from decidedly realistic and practical needs of the Russian government. It struck the world with amazement and bewilderment. There were, of course, plenty of people, including statesmen, who saw the dangers of the armed peace, but very few of them considered limitation of armaments feasible, and there was, from the very outset, widespread suspicion of Russia's motives — fear of a political ruse, dread of the raising of political issues and apprehension lest the conference might result in a general conflict rather than in the guarantee of peace.

The Russian statesmen themselves seem to have had little hope of realizing their plans. The great Fashoda crisis led to a violent outburst of bellicosity in England and to naval preparations on an unprecedented scale. It was generally assumed in Europe that war would break out before the end of the year. It was, indeed, an inauspicious moment to talk of limitation of armaments or of international action for peace. In view of this situation Muraviev all but decided to send out a circular asking whether the powers considered the time opportune for a conference, but a sympathetic reference in the German Emperor's speech from the throne in December made it seem desirable to reconsider the decision. The Russians were anxious lest the Germans go over entirely to the British side or join an English-American-Japanese coalition for Far Eastern action. Witte expatiated to the German ambassador on the folly of the continental states in arming against each other, while England was steadily enlarging her fleet, " the only important weapon for future world domination." The sensible thing to do, he argued, would be for Europe to suspend land armaments and save its money for naval construction. Muraviev therefore decided to arrange a conference of ambassadors at St. Petersburg to discuss the opportuneness of a larger meeting and the elaboration of a program. His memorandum shows how cynical was the Russian attitude in the whole matter. Muraviev expected a number of powers to refuse, and reckoned that such refusal would be of political advantage to Russia. England would be unwilling to consider limitation of naval armament, while the United States would insist on increasing its army. The exposure of this egotistic and dangerous policy of England and of America would make public opinion see where the shoe rubbed. It would, further, sharpen the feeling of solidarity among the continental powers in opposition to the naval supremacy of the Anglo-Saxons, and would create for Russia an enviable position between the two camps.[17]

" The Vanishing of Universal Peace " (*Fortnightly Review*, May, 1899); Sidney Low: " The Hypocrisies of the Peace Conference " (*Nineteenth Century*, May, 1899).

[17] Teleshev: " K Istorii Pervoi Gaagskoi Konferentsii," pp. 89–96; see also his article " Anglo-Germanskoe Sblishenie v 1898 g." (*Krasnyi Arkhiv*, LVI, 1933, pp. 65–79), pp. 77–9; Witte's conversation with Radolin in *Die Grosse Politik*, XV, no. 4232.

Muraviev's circular was presented to the representatives of the powers on January 11, 1899. It pointed out that "notwithstanding the strong current of opinion which exists in favor of the ideas of general pacification, the political horizon has recently undergone a change," and that "several powers have undertaken fresh armaments, striving to increase further their military forces." The question was asked whether the powers considered the time opportune for discussion. If so, they were invited to a preliminary exchange of views. The objects of the prospective conference were to be those of "seeking without delay means for putting a stop to the progressive increase of military and naval armaments, a question the solution of which becomes evidently more and more urgent in view of the fresh extension given to these armaments;" and of "preparing the way for the discussion of the questions relating to the possibility of preventing armed conflicts by the pacific means at the disposal of international diplomacy." There were other proposals for the humanizing of warfare, such as the prohibition of new and more deadly explosives and of the submarine, and the extension of the provisions of the Geneva Convention.

These proposals were, of course, purely tentative. The powers agreed to talk the situation over, and it was finally arranged to hold a conference at The Hague. The meeting opened on the Tsar's birthday, May 18, and remained in session until July 29. Representatives of twenty-six powers were present. They were a motley crew, composed almost exclusively of old and hardened diplomats, of decidedly realistic military and naval men, and of technical experts in international law. The head of the Russian delegation was M. de Staal, the ambassador at London, a suave and none too intelligent octogenarian who knew little of parliamentary procedure, but who was, nevertheless, named president of the meeting out of deference for the Tsar. M. de Martens, the Russian legal expert, was a man of world reputation who was undoubtedly devoted to the furtherance of international law. The Germans were represented by Count Münster, another octogenarian, who regarded the whole business with something akin to hatred and expected nothing good to come of it. The German military expert was Colonel Schwarzhoff, an able man with unbounded confidence in the strength of armies. The Germans sent also two international lawyers, of whom one, Freiherr von Stengel, had distinguished himself by publishing a pamphlet entitled *Perpetual Peace,* in which he pointed out that the Bible supported the idea that war is an integral part of the divine order, that war has immense cultural value, that armaments do not ruin a nation, and that eternal peace is impossible.[18]

Passing over the representatives of Austria and Italy, who played no prominent rôle at the Conference, a few words may be said of the delegates of France, England and the United States. The French government showed itself extremely clever in the selection of its men. At the head of the delegation was Léon Bourgeois, former prime minister and radical, who posed as a great and

---

[18] Freiherr Karl von Stengel: *Der Ewige Friede* (1898).

whole-hearted exponent of international co-operation, though later he was to
show himself as uncompromising as any Frenchman in matters of security. The
second representative was Baron d'Estournelles de Constant, brilliant young
descendant of Benjamin Constant, outstanding advocate of an entente with
England and genuinely devoted to the cause of international understanding.
England sent Sir Julian Pauncefote, the ambassador at Washington, a man
who had taken a leading part in the drafting of an arbitration treaty with the
United States and who was one of the outstanding exponents of that method
of settling international disputes. The experts were Sir John Ardagh, whose
views did not differ substantially from those of Schwarzhoff, and Sir John
Fisher, a fire-eating admiral who made no bones about declaring *urbe et
orbe* that in his view might was right, arbitration or no arbitration. The United
States was represented by Andrew D. White, ambassador at Berlin, like Sir
Julian Pauncefote a believer in arbitration and a man anxious to make the
best of the Conference. As naval expert the American government sent Captain
Mahan, world-famous author of *The Influence of Sea Power,* a man with little
if any sympathy with the aims of the Conference.[19]

It cannot be said that the meeting opened auspiciously. Some of the older
diplomats felt outraged at being sent to what they regarded as a farce and at
having to end their careers on a fruitless errand. " Probably, since the world
began, never has so large a body come together in a spirit of more hopeless
skepticism as to any good result," wrote Andrew White in his diary on May 17.
It was perfectly obvious, even to the most optimistic, that reduction or even limitation of armaments was out of the question, and that the most one could hope
for was some further regulation of the methods of warfare and perhaps some
progress towards establishing a recognized system of arbitration.

As a matter of fact no serious move was made in the armaments question
after the German military expert, Colonel Schwarzhoff, had set forth the difficulties of the subject. The other representatives joined in expressing a pious
wish that eventually something might be done and therewith the problem was
dismissed. Better results were obtained in the regulation of warfare — the
prohibition for five years of the use of projectiles thrown from balloons, prohibition of gas warfare and dum-dum bullets, extension of the Red Cross convention to naval warfare, the definition of belligerency, provisions for the better
treatment of war prisoners and of the sick and wounded, etc., etc. But ultimately
the work of the Conference centred upon the discussion of a so-called permanent court of arbitration. In this matter Sir Julian Pauncefote took a leading
part. Questions of national vital interest and honor were, by general consent, ex-

19 The delegates to the Conference and their attitudes are reflected in *Die Grosse Politik,* passim,
and in the writings of the participants, notably Andrew D. White: *The First Hague Conference*
(Boston, 1912); *Heinrich Lammasch: Seine Aufzeichnungen, sein Wirken und seine Politik* (Vienna,
1922), and in the narratives of W. T. Stead: *La Chronique de la Conférence de la Haye* (The Hague,
1901), and Bertha von Suttner: *Die Haager Friedenskonferenz* (Leipzig, 1901). See further August
Junk: *Die Mächte auf der Ersten Haager Friedenskonferenz* (Leipzig, 1928), pp. 37–43.

cluded from the application of the system, but it was proposed to make arbitration compulsory in certain disputes of minor importance. The Germans in particular opposed both compulsory arbitration and the erection of a permanent body of arbitrators. As Münster explained to White, arbitration would be injurious to Germany, for Germany was prepared as no other country could be. She could mobilize in ten days. Arbitration would simply give rival powers time to put themselves in readiness and would therefore be a great disadvantage to Germany.[20]

1899

In the end the idea of compulsory arbitration was completely abandoned, but the German government was finally persuaded by Münster himself that the permanent court must be accepted if Germany wished to avoid blame for the failure of the Conference and the resentment of the Tsar. It is unnecessary to go into all the details, which have been thoroughly analyzed in many other works. Suffice it to say that Holstein was unalterably opposed to the whole arbitration program and handed in his resignation when Bülow and the Emperor finally decided to give in for political reasons.[21]

The importance of the first Hague Peace Conference lay not so much in *what* it actually accomplished as in the fact that that it accomplished *something* and that it set a precedent for future meetings. The greater part of its achievement dealt not with peace, but with war, and no one knew whether even the new regulations for warfare would be observed in the heat of conflict. The question of limitation of armaments had made no progress whatever and the permanent court of arbitration was as innocuous as one could imagine. Earlier opinions of the work done were not very enthusiastic, and it was only later, when the second Conference met in 1907, that the realization gradually spread that in 1899 the first step had been taken in the direction of international organization.[22]

Politically the Conference was of no importance. It had no bearing on current political problems and it did not in any way affect the relations of the powers to each other. It was, in fact, distinctly a side show. Only one power may be said to have suffered from it, and that power was Germany. The strong stand taken by the German delegation in the matter of limitation of armaments and the German opposition to the perfectly harmless permanent court was heavily underlined by unfriendly journalists like Stead and later supplied useful ammunition for the campaign of defamation waged in the immediate pre-war and world-war periods. As we see it now, the German attitude in 1899 did not

---

[20] White, op. cit., p. 19.

[21] *Friedrich von Holstein's Lebensbekenntnis in Briefen an eine Frau* (Berlin, 1932), pp. 194–5; on Holstein's attitude see further *Die Grosse Politik*, XV, nos. 4312; Philipp Zorn: " Zur Geschichte der Ersten Haager Friedenskonferenz " (*Archiv für Politik und Geschichte*, October, 1924, pp. 285–306), p. 298.

[22] Early opinions are well summarized in Otfried Nippold: *Die Fortbildung des Verfahrens in Völkerrechtlichen Streitigkeiten* (Leipzig, 1907), pp. 94 ff.; see also Walther Schücking: *Der Staatenverband der Haager Konferenzen* (Munich, 1912), pp. 21 ff.

differ materially from the attitude of most of the other powers. It was tactless
of the Germans to take the lead in disposing of the armaments question, and it
was a serious political and psychological error to make a great issue of a board
of arbitration which had no real power. The German attitude was a perfectly
honorable one; the German objections were honest objections, and even though
the Germans had no faith in the Conference or anything connected with it,
they tried to play the game, if only to please the Tsar. One might almost say
that they were too honest. They said what others thought, and thereby assumed
the odium which other powers were only too eager to avoid. This is now
generally recognized by German writers themselves.[23]

So far as European alignments were concerned, the situation remained as
amorphous in 1899 as it had been in the previous years. Speaking to the German
ambassador in the spring of the year Lord Salisbury remarked that the day of
alliances was over. International relations had become a matter of agreements
between states with common or at least non-contradictory interests. Count
Hatzfeldt rejected this argumentation, but as one looks back on the situation
it is clear that the British premier was the more nearly right.[24] The old
alliances had pretty much disintegrated, and the day of business deals had
arrived.

Take the Triple Alliance, for instance. If Austria had been attacked by
Russia, there is no doubt that Germany would have supported her ally in 1899
as she would have done in 1879. Still, the Triple Alliance had been languishing
for years. It was not really to be resuscitated until the days of Aehrenthal. In
1899 it lacked an immediate *raison d'être*. Russia, deeply engaged in the Far
East, was not hostile to Austria. In fact the two powers had made an agreement in 1897 to preserve the status quo in the Balkans. Not only that: the Germans and the Austrians were by no means cordially friendly to each other, as
they had been in the days of Bismarck and Andrássy. The Hapsburg Monarchy
was racked by internal crises of the most dangerous sort. The Emperor
Francis Joseph was getting old, and his demise was expected in the none-too-
distant future. The Slavic elements in the empire had come to play an ever more
decisive rôle and the Vienna government had fallen largely under Czech in-
fluences. The Czech nationalists, however, were outspokenly hostile to Germany
and to the Triple Alliance. Kramarsch, one of the Czech leaders, declared in
so many words that the famous alliance was a " played-out piano," and uttered
the warning that if Pan-Germanism actually became a threat to Austria's national existence, it would have to be checked by other powers.[25] This article

---

[23] E.g. by Zorn, op. cit.; by most of the experts who testified before the post-war parliamentary
commission of inquiry (*Das Werk des Untersuchungsausschusses der Verfassunggebenden Deutschen
Nationalversammlung*, Series I, vol. V, Berlin, 1929, passim); by Junk, op. cit.; A Fonck: " Deutschlands Haltung zur Abrüstungsfrage auf der Friedenskonferenz im Haag 1899 " (*Berliner Monatshefte*, November, 1929, pp. 1091–5); Egon Gottschalk: " Deutschlands Haltung auf den Haager
Friedenskonferenzen " (ibid., May, 1930, pp. 447–56).   [24] *Die Grosse Politik*, XIV, no. 4044.

[25] K. Kramarsch: " L'Avenir de l'Autriche " (*Revue de Paris*, February 1, 1899).

was regarded in Berlin as nothing less than a direct provocation. There had been a good deal of friction between the two allies in December 1898 and the tension continued until the fall of Count Thun's ministry in October 1899. During this period there was good reason to doubt not only the continuance of the German-Austrian Alliance, but of the Hapsburg monarchy itself.[26]

Italy, too, was no longer to be counted upon as in the days of Crispi. The disaster at Adua had ushered in a period of acute domestic unrest, which culminated in the famous May Days of Milan in 1898. By many observers it was thought that the Savoy monarchy was approaching its last days, and that the republican factions would soon be in the ascendant. It was widely felt that Germany was responsible for the crushing burden of Italian armaments, for the extravagant policy of Crispi, and for the disastrous hostility of France. The irredentism of the republicans was stimulated by the uncertainty of Austrian affairs and by the forward policy of the Slavic elements.[27] Furthermore, Pope Leo XIII was old and ill. His secretary of state, Cardinal Rampolla, was notoriously anti-German and pro-French. It was always feared at Rome that the French government, working with the Papacy, was encouraging the republican agitation and undermining the monarchy.[28]

Since Crispi's fall the Italian government had set itself definitely to effect a rapprochement with France. The estrangement of England and Germany after the Kruger telegram episode undoubtedly had much to do with this, for it was obvious that Italy, for geographical reasons, could not afford to join in an anti-British policy. This point has been made by practically all writers of pre-war diplomacy, but it does not cover the whole situation by any means. In the last years of the century the hostility between England and France was so great that for Italy to give up Germany to join France was like jumping from the frying-pan into the fire so far as relations with England were concerned. The Italians had to seek a rapprochement with France because they could not hope to stand out against French pressure, political and commercial. Their problem was to improve relations with France without antagonizing Germany and without estranging England.

The accomplishment of this difficult task was the work of Marchese di Rudini, the prime minister, and of Visconti-Venosta, the foreign minister. Signor Luzzatti, the minister of finance, was an able and determined assistant. The policy was embarked upon at once and bore its first fruits in the French-

---

[26] See especially the documents in *Die Grosse Politik*, XIII, chap. lxxxvii; Johannes Haller: *Philip Eulenburg* (New York, 1930), II, pp. 76–80; and the monographic study of Wolfgang Rudert: *Die Stellung des Deutschen Reiches zur Inner-Oesterreichischen Lage . . . 1890–1900* (Leipzig, 1931).

[27] See especially the letter of Monts to Holstein, in *Erinnerungen und Gedanken des Botschafters Anton Graf Monts* (Berlin, 1932), pp. 387 ff.

[28] There are some highly interesting letters on conditions at the Vatican in Hohenlohe: *Denkwürdigkeiten der Reichskanzlerzeit*, pp. 182 ff., 404 ff., 491 ff. See also G. M. Fiamingo: " Die Politik Leos XIII und seine Diplomatie " (*Deutsche Revue,* June, 1898, pp. 280–90).

Italian agreement regarding Tunis, which has already been discussed. It will be recalled that in this agreement the Italians made the concessions in order to win the good will of France. The next step was to be a commercial treaty to put an end to the disastrous tariff war which had been going on since 1886, and perhaps after that a political understanding. Of course, the whole policy presupposed a willingness on the part of the French to make up with the Italians. For years they had been devoting themselves to the task of forcing the Italians out of the Triple Alliance by economic and political pressure. Crispi claimed that as late as the end of 1895 Bourgeois told an Italian politician that no commercial agreement would be possible so long as Italy remained in the Triple Alliance.[29]

Crispi's fall undoubtedly helped to ease the situation, for he was the favorite aversion of the French. But the French ambassador at Rome, M. Albert Billot, had, so he says, been arguing for some time that it was futile to continue on the old tack, and that the wise thing would be to seek a rapprochement which would create new interests in Italy more favorable to France.[30] At any rate, the Italian government began to take soundings for a tariff treaty almost immediately after the conclusion of the Tunis Convention in 1896. Official pourparlers were opened in the summer of 1897, but it turned out that the French government, which was highly protectionist, was unwilling to consider concessions in the matter of silk or wine imports. The terms offered Italy were hard ones. Negotiations dragged on, and were finally postponed till after the French elections of May 1898. The fall of the Méline cabinet in June 1898 and the downfall of Rudini in the following month probably served to delay matters further, though the new governments in both countries were anxious to conclude an arrangement. Finally in October 1898 Luzzatti came to Paris and the details were worked out satisfactorily in a very short time. On November 21, 1898 the agreement was signed. The essential point was that it established most-favored-nation treatment on both sides, with some exceptions to protect French " silk and wine interests." [31]

The French-Italian commercial settlement of 1898 has been regarded quite rightly as the beginning of that change of Italian policy which ended in the agreements of 1900 and 1902 and ultimately in Italy's neutrality in 1914. It has often been described as the first great triumph of Delcassé and the first step in the progressive isolation of Germany. This is undoubtedly an exaggeration. Delcassé and the famous French ambassador at Rome, Barrère, had nothing to

---

[29] Francesco Crispi: "L'Accordo Franco-Italiano" (*Rivista d'Italia*, February 15, 1899, pp. 197–208).

[30] Albert Billot: "Le Rapprochement Commercial entre la France et l'Italie" (*Revue des Deux Mondes*, January 1, 1899, pp. 131–145). This article is much more revealing than the memoirs of Billot, published under the title *La France et l'Italie* (Paris, 1905).

[31] The fullest accounts are those given by Billot in the article mentioned and in his *France et l'Italie*, II, Book III, chap. iv. See also Maximilian Claar: "Die Abkehr Italiens vom Dreibund" (*Europäische Gespräche*, VIII, 1930, pp. 425–39).

do with the initiation of the policy, which was the work of Hanotaux and Billot. If we may believe the latter, substantial agreement had been reached by the end of 1897 when he (Billot) retired from his post and Barrère was appointed. Delcassé, to be sure, was warmly in sympathy with the policy, but there is no evidence that he regarded it at the time as a part of a larger plan. During the debates in the French chamber he carefully avoided any reference to the political implications of the agreement and confined himself to saying that the French should congratulate themselves on now having a friendly people on their frontier.

The Italians, it seems, were much more interested than the French in the political side of the question. Visconti-Venosta was no longer at the foreign office, but he wrote his friend Luzzatti that " political friendship will result from friendly economic relations, and the return of a fatal conflict is made impossible." [32] In the Italian senate, too, he emphasized the important political reactions which the commercial rapprochement was bound to have.[33] But Visconti went much further than authoritative government officials were prepared to go. Admiral Canevaro, the foreign minister, insisted in parliament that Italy remained loyal to the Triple Alliance, and told the British ambassador that he saw no reason why Italy should not take advantage of the advances (!) made by the French. Italy, he went on, was not deceived by them: " The Italian Government was perfectly aware that the object of France, if she could only detach Italy from her allies, would be to proceed, in combination with the Vatican, to bring about troubles in Italy with a view to upsetting the Monarchy and establishing a Republican form of government, which would be more subservient to French influence than the Monarchy." Italy " would under no circumstances make any change in her policy as regarded the Triple Alliance or England." [34]

It is impossible to judge of the sincerity of these utterances. It may be that Canevaro really wanted the agreement for purely economic reasons, but it seems more likely that, in the midst of the Fashoda crisis, he found it necessary to placate the British and avoid suspicion in London. But Anglo-Italian relations were soon exposed to another trial. The Anglo-French agreement on the Sudan of March 21, 1899 was taken in Rome as involving the abandonment of the hinterland of Tripoli to the French and as a disturbance of the status quo on the shores of the Mediterranean. The Italians had long before marked out Tripoli as a future possession, and they were greatly alarmed by what had happened. They tried to get the British government to make a declaration in the Italian sense, and attempted to enlist the assistance of Germany for this purpose. Nothing came of the negotiations, inasmuch as Salisbury refused to bind himself for the future. Delcassé, on the other hand, scored a point by

---

[32] The letter is quoted in Luigi Luzzatti: *God in Freedom* (New York, 1930), pp. 428–9.

[33] Billot: *La France et l'Italie*, II, pp. 450–1.

[34] *British Documents*, I, no. 347.

giving the Italians an unwritten assurance that they had no reason to fear find-ing France in their way if, eventually, they decided to put forth claims to Tripoli.[35] The upshot of this incident was that the Italians failed to get satis-faction from England and found the aid of the Triple Alliance of little value, while Delcassé could and did embark upon the course that was to lead to the Tripoli-Morocco bargains of the next years.

We have surveyed the relations of the members of the Triple Alliance to each other, and have seen how much altered was the famous international combination of the Bismarckian period. It is important to note that much the same process of disintegration had been taking place in the Franco-Russian Alliance. It will be recalled that the Fashoda crisis and the Tsar's peace rescript had thrown a deep shadow upon the relations of the Republic and the Empire of the Tsar. The French people had become disabused of their ideas of Russian help in recovering the lost provinces. They were frankly sore, and at this time were quite unwilling to sink further funds into Russian securities.

Naturally the French government was obliged to take into account other fac-tors than the uncritical likes and dislikes of the population. The Military Con-vention with Russia had been concluded for very specific purposes, and the situation in Europe in 1898–1899 was not such that the French government felt free to dispense with the arrangement. The Triple Alliance, to be sure, was not as formidable as it had been, but there was a much sharper antagonism between France and England, and there was never any knowing whether Germany might not join England if it came to a clash. These military questions had been discussed between the French authorities and General Kuropatkin during the latter's visit to Paris in October 1898. It had been agreed on then that the Mili-tary Convention should continue as before, and that certain revisions should be made in the number of troops each ally was to contribute in the event of trouble.[36]

In the meanwhile a further problem arose from the crisis in Austria. There was, as aforesaid, general apprehension that the Dual Monarchy might fall to pieces and that, as a result, the Triple Alliance would come to an end. A conflict of nationalities would be inevitable, and it was to be feared that the Berlin gov-ernment might attempt to annex the German provinces of Austria. In that event a general European war would almost certainly ensue, since Russia would never allow a semi-Slavic area like Bohemia to pass under German rule.[37] The Aus-trian question, as it developed between 1896 and 1899 had not been envisaged at the time of the conclusion of the Franco-Russian Alliance. In fact the Military Convention, which constituted the really important part of the Alliance, had been timed to last only as long as the Triple Alliance. If Austria were to fall

---

[35] *Die Grosse Politik*, XIV, nos. 3946–57; *British Documents*, I, nos. 246 ff.; see also James L. Glanville: *Italy's Relations with England, 1896–1905* (Baltimore, 1934), chap. vi.

[36] L. Teleshev: "K Istorii Pervoi Gaagskoi Konferentsii 1899 g." (*Krasnyi Arkhiv*, L–LI, 1932, pp. 81–8).   [37] See especially *Die Grosse Politik*, XIII, no. 3539.

apart, the Triple Alliance, and therewith the Franco-Russian Military Convention, would simply disappear. And yet it would be at just that crucial moment that war would be most likely and the Convention most needed. It was to meet this situation that Delcassé paid a sudden, unannounced visit to St. Petersburg early in August 1899. We know next to nothing of the inner history of this move. Who brought Delcassé to a realization of the dangers inherent in the Austrian situation? It is unlikely that men like Chéradame and Henry, who later became active agitators of the question, had anything to do with it, and it seems hardly credible that the Kramarsch article referred to above should have exerted enough influence to bring about an important change in French policy. The explanation is probably this, that the Russians, not the French, were primarily alarmed by the Austrian crisis, and that Delcassé was dragged into the St. Petersburg negotiation. There is at least one bit of evidence which would appear to support this interpretation. Just before his visit to Paris in October 1898 General Kuropatkin had a long talk with Tsar Nicholas. In his diary he noted:

> " I developed the idea that we could not do much for the cause of peace until we had occupied the Bosporus. Then we shall have a firm position with relation to all other Slavic states and shall lay the foundation for a federation of the Slavic states between themselves and with us. Then we shall destroy the aim of William II: namely to draw Turkey into an alliance against us, to get control of our frontiers from Erzerum to Polangen, to influence Rumania and get her to join this alliance, and to influence the Slavic states — Serbia and Bulgaria — to preserve their neutrality at the least in the event of a war between the Triple Alliance and the powers of the Dual Alliance, France and Russia. Our appearance on the Bosporus would hasten the collapse of Austria. Then it would be possible to abandon the German territories to Germany and to oblige the latter to return Alsace and Lorraine to France. I explained that in my opinion Germany would not voluntarily do this. Germany's powers of defense are so strong that, even after the collapse of Austria and the formation of a league of the Slavic states which would go hand in hand with Russia and France, an attack on Germany might not be successful. In the last count everything would probably depend on the skill and genius of the commanders on both sides. The suitable moment for an attack will arrive when Germany becomes involved in war with England and America. Such a war is probable in view of the industrial over-production in Germany and the resulting necessity for her to seek new markets." [38]

These extraordinary speculations at least throw some light on what was being discussed in high circles of the Russian court. There is, in this whole period, a great blank in our knowledge. There are constant veiled references to Russian encouragement of a French entente with Germany and in the press no end of talk about the return of Alsace-Lorraine to France in exchange for the French Congo or some other colony. Were the Russians really planning some

---

[38] L. Teleshev: " Noviye Materialy o Gaagskoi Mirnoi Konferentsii 1899 g." (*Krasnyi Arkhiv*, LIV–LV, 1932, pp. 49–79).

such arrangement as that outlined by Kuropatkin for the event of Austria's collapse? Was Delcassé taken in by this mirage? It will be recalled that he actually took soundings to find out whether the Germans would consider an exchange of Alsace and Lorraine for a French colony.

We cannot answer these questions even now. At the time the diplomatic world was agog at the sudden departure of the foreign minister to the Russian capital. In Paris it was explained that he was merely making a courtesy call. Gallifet, the war minister, told the German ambassador that the whole business was the result of Delcassé's personal vanity: he desired recognition by the Tsar. Of course this kind of talk was not taken seriously. The Germans conjectured that Delcassé was intent on breathing new life into the nearly defunct Franco-Russian Alliance, and suspected that the visit might have some connection with the Dreyfus case or with the approaching crisis in south Africa. The British press, on the other hand, feared that the visit might be a step on the road to a reconciliation between France and Germany and therefore to the formation of a continental coalition.[39]

Nearly all we know for certain of Delcassé's visit has to do with the results. We know that on August 9 he and Muraviev exchanged letters reaffirming the Alliance and extending its scope. The agreement of 1891 had stated that the object of the two powers was the maintenance of peace. To this was now added the maintenance of the balance of power in Europe. At the same time the Military Convention was made coterminous in time with the general agreement, in other words, provision was made that it should be in full force when a crisis arose from the dissolution of the Austrian monarchy.[40]

Since we know nothing of the conversations which accompanied the drafting of these changes it is difficult to appraise them. Radical historians, like Albert Mathiez, felt that Delcassé herewith completed the betrayal of France. He put the forces of France at the disposal of Russia to secure for her a share in the spoils of the Hapsburg possessions, and furthermore put France in a position where she would be bound to oppose the right of self-determination of the Germans in Austria. Not only that: any dislocation of affairs in the Balkans might in future be described as a change in the balance of power in Europe and might therefore involve France in conflict.[41]

I see no reason for questioning this interpretation. Such evidence as we have would seem to show that Delcassé, despite the fact that Russia gave no support in the Fashoda crisis, was so eager to uphold the alliance with Russia that he committed France to a certain course of action in Near Eastern affairs which

[39] *Die Grosse Politik*, XIII, nos. 3577, 3578; *Questions Diplomatiques et Coloniales*, August 15, 1899, pp. 498–501, quoting at length from the British press.

[40] *Livre Jaune: L'Alliance Franco-Russe* (Paris, 1918), nos. 93–5.

[41] Mathiez, in the newspaper *L'Internationale*, August 2, 10, 26, 1921, as quoted by Georges Michon: *The Franco-Russian Alliance* (London, 1929), pp. 101–7. Michon's account is a reasonably full one, but see now also Pierre Renouvin: "Les Engagements de l'Alliance Franco-Russe" (*Revue d'Histoire de la Guerre Mondiale*, October, 1934, pp. 297–310), pp. 301 ff.

Hanotaux had always refused to adopt. It is true, of course, as M. Renouvin has pointed out, that the principle of maintaining the balance of power meant that Russia assumed obligations with respect to the Alsace-Lorraine question just as France shouldered certain responsibilities in Balkan affairs. But these obligations, so far as Russia was concerned, were inherent in the alliance from the outset and the French had already had ample opportunity to learn that the Russians did not take them very seriously. In the present state of our knowledge it is hard to see how the results of the St. Petersburg visit can be interpreted as a success for Delcassé's statesmanship. He proclaimed in the Chamber on November 24, 1899 that the alliance with Russia was complete and that " the union was never closer, that the dual alliance made possible far-reaching plans (longs desseins), and that, in order to realize them, there was need of patience, consistency and time."

All this sounded beautiful, but so far as one can see the Alliance continued to be after the visit what it had been before. The French were dissatisfied with it and disappointed. The radical régime, which came into power in France with the ministry of Waldeck-Rousseau in 1899, was not very favorably disposed towards Russia, and during the next years, as revolutionary movements began to develop in opposition to the Tsarist government, there was much agitation against the autocracy on the part of French radicals and socialists. The feeling was widespread at that time that the Alliance was an instrument which militated against the introduction of reform in France itself.[42] It is no exaggeration to say that between 1898 and the Russo-Japanese War the Franco-Russian Alliance reached its nadir. The best political minds in France at that time were already beginning to turn toward the idea of an entente with England. Not until the advent of Poincaré in 1912 was the Alliance to become once again an active and effective combination.

With both the Triple Alliance and the Franco-Russian Alliance more or less in eclipse there continued to be, during 1899, talk of the possibility of a reconciliation between France and Germany and of the ultimate combination of these two countries with Russia to form a counterweight to British naval preponderance. Witte, it will be recalled, expounded this idea at some length to the German ambassador, and used it as an argument for the reduction of expenditure on land armaments by the continental powers.[43] The Spanish government, which in February 1899 agreed to the sale of the Caroline and Mariane Islands to Germany, also tried to further the scheme.[44] There was, of course, something very intriguing about the whole idea, and in a sense all three of the great continental powers were bound together by a certain common antagonism to Great Britain. It appears from the German Emperor's comments on the report of Witte's suggestions, however, that he was no longer interested in the plan.

---

[42] See especially Michon, op. cit., chap. vi, where this argument is well worked out, and extensive quotations from the French press are given.

[43] Die Grosse Politik, XV, no. 4232.   [44] Die Grosse Politik, XV, nos. 4205–14.

" Too late, too late! " this was the general sense of his reaction. A few years before, at the time of the Kruger telegram, he had proposed this combination and had been rebuffed by both France and Russia. Since then, German relations with England had improved very decidedly and the Germans had come to appreciate the attractions of the policy of the free hand, which enabled them to play off the British against the French and the Russians. " The powers which could become dangerous for us," wrote Holstein in January 1899, " are at present so taken up by foreign or domestic troubles or with both, that a coalition such as formerly worried Bismarck and Moltke, is no longer thinkable unless one assumes great errors on Germany's part." [45]

This does not mean that the Germans failed to make the most of the friendly advances from Paris and from St. Petersburg. The Emperor was eager to win the good will of the French and was evidently more sanguine on this score than his ministers. In July he paid a visit to the French school ship at Bergen, and then sent to President Loubet a telegram couched in the warmest terms. In August he dedicated a German monument on the battlefield of St. Privat, and took the occasion to honor the valiant French dead who had fought as bravely for their country as the Germans had for theirs. All this made a good impression in France, though naturally it did not wipe out the problem of the lost provinces. As one looks back upon the situation one can easily see that a real reconciliation was impossible so long as the Germans were not prepared to make at least a compromise with regard to Alsace-Lorraine. But there was, clearly, a détente in the relations of Germany and France. These relations were more cordial than they had ever been since the war of 1870.[46]

Relations between Germany and Russia were not so satisfactory. The Germans were anxious to keep on the good side of Russia, but they were suspicious of and nettled by the Tsar's peace move, and personal friction between the Emperor and the Tsar did not help to improve matters. Although the Emperor had visited Nicholas on several occasions during his stays at Darmstadt, the Tsar had never yet paid a visit to Berlin or Potsdam. William now insisted that he would no longer go running after his Russian brother like a satrap. The Tsar was finally persuaded to come to Berlin for half a day in November 1899. The visit went off quite successfully. Nicholas spoke approvingly of the German naval plans and once again emphasized the need for continental sea-power to keep England in check. But at the same time both he and Muraviev referred to German activities in the Near East, which, they felt, were an indirect threat at Russian interests. Efforts had, in fact, been made by the St. Petersburg government to reach some agreement with Germany regarding Russian interests in the Straits. Such an agreement, however, would have identified the Germans too much with Russian policy and would have jeopardized relations with Eng-

---

[45] Monts: *Erinnerungen und Gedanken*, pp. 357–8.
[46] On Franco-German relations see *Die Grosse Politik*, XIII, nos. 3569, 3571 ff., 3581; Bourgeois and Pagès: *Les Origines . . . de la Grande Guerre*, pp. 278–9.

land. The advances of Muraviev were rejected, and the result was a marked cooling in the Russian-German relationship. But this factor must not be over-emphasized. The Russians, so long as they were at daggers drawn with England in the Far East, could not afford to estrange Germany. There was a certain amount of friction and a good deal of mutual suspicion, but on the whole the Germans were successful in their efforts to keep intact the wires to both Paris and St. Petersburg.[47]

Without a clear conception of the status of the great European alliances it would be impossible to follow intelligently the course of diplomacy as the century drew to its close. The peace rescript had been a sort of bomb thrown into an already confused situation. It had no immediate effect on the general alignment of the powers, which was itself anything but clear. It might be said that the situation, so far as the Continent was concerned, was a fluid one. Extra-European activities had completely dislocated the accepted groupings of the powers, which were based upon consideration of European problems. Under these circumstances it would be futile to seek the key to European diplomacy in the history of the alliances. The really important development in the year 1899 had to do with British affairs. The clouds of the coming conflict in south Africa were beginning to cast their shadows over the international scene. England was on the verge of becoming involved in a struggle much more serious and prolonged than anyone could suspect. Her policy had to be shaped to meet this new situation, and the main theme must therefore concern itself with the safeguarding of the British position in Europe, and with the countermoves of Britain's chief rivals, Germany, France and Russia.

BIBLIOGRAPHICAL NOTE

(Account is here taken only of the First Hague Peace Conference, since the other matters dealt with in this chapter are illuminated by the German documents — *Die Grosse Politik der Europäischen Kabinette,* volume XIII and by the *British Documents on the Origins of the War,* volume I).

DOCUMENTARY SOURCES

The Hague Peace Conferences of 1899 and 1907. Edited by James Brown Scott. Two volumes. Baltimore, 1909. The best documentary collection, containing all the debates.

Documents Relating to the Program of the First Hague Peace Conference. Oxford, 1921.

---

[47] For general German-Russian relations see *Die Grosse Politik,* XIII, nos. 3540–8. The problem of the Near East as it affected these relations will be discussed in a later chapter.

Livre Jaune. Conférence Internationale de la Paix. Paris, 1900.

Die Grosse Politik der Europäischen Kabinette, 1871–1914. Volume XV, chapter c. One of the most important documentary sources.

British Documents on the Origins of the War, 1898–1914. Volume I, chapter vi. Adds relatively little.

Das Werk des Untersuchungsausschusses der Verfassunggebenden Deutschen Nationalversammlung und des Deutschen Reichstages, 1919–1930. Series I: *Die Vorgeschichte des Weltkrieges.* Volume V, part II: " Deutschland auf den Haager Friedenskonferenzen." Berlin, 1929. This volume contains the studies and opinions of German experts, those of Wehberg, Montgelas and Thimme being the most important. The volume does not include any material of importance that is not to be found in *Die Grosse Politik.*

TELESHEV, L.: " K Istorii Pervoi Gaagskoi Konferentsii 1899 g." (*Krasnyi Arkhiv, L–LI,* 1932, pp. 64–96). " Noviye Materialy o Gaagskoi Mirnoi Konferentsii 1899 g." (ibid., LIV–LV, 1932, pp. 49–79). An absolutely fundamental collection of Russian documents, which had not appeared when Wehberg and other experts wrote their accounts. Some of this material has been translated into German and published in the *Berliner Monatshefte,* June and July, 1933, and April, 1934.

MEMOIRS, AUTOBIOGRAPHIES, BIOGRAPHIES, AND LETTERS

WITTE, SERGIUS: *Memoirs.* Translated by A. Yarmolinsky. New York, 1921. An important, though brief account, in which there is a frank avowal of the Russian policy. Much the same material is given, with somewhat more detail, in the book of Witte's confidant, E. J. Dillon: *The Eclipse of Russia* (London, 1918).

WHITE, ANDREW D.: *The First Hague Conference.* Boston, 1912. This is merely a reprint of the chapters in White's *Autobiography.* Two volumes. New York, 1904. White's account is one of the best and most reliable left by participants.

HOLLS, FREDERICK W.: *The Peace Conference at The Hague.* Boston, 1900. Holls was one of the American representatives. His work is rather a critical study than a volume of personal reminiscences. It is one of the best systematic accounts.

FISHER, LORD: *Memories.* London, 1919. Fisher was the British naval expert. His memoirs contain little of importance.

Heinrich Lammasch. Seine Aufzeichnungen, sein Wirken und seine Politik. Edited by Marga Lammasch and Hans Sperl. Vienna, 1922. Lammasch was one of the Austrian delegates. His reminiscences throw an interesting light on the personalities and activities of the Conference.

SUTTNER, BERTA VON: *Die Haager Friedenskonferenz. Tagebuchblätter.* Dresden, 1901. The recollections of the leading German pacifist. A valuable and interesting account of the Conference.

STEAD, WILLIAM T.: *La Chronique de la Conférence de la Haye*. The Hague, 1901. A valuable account, written by the well-known British journalist and pacifist.

WHYTE, FREDERIC: *The Life of William T. Stead*. Two volumes. New York, n.d. Adds little to Stead's own account, but contains a few unpublished letters.

ZORN, PHILIPP: *Deutschland und die beiden Haager Friedenskonferenzen*. Berlin, 1920. "Zur Geschichte der Ersten Haager Friedenskonferenz." (*Archiv für Politik und Geschichte,* III, 1924, pp. 285–306). Careful studies of German policy, by one of the German delegates.

MOWAT, R. B.: *The Life of Lord Pauncefote*. Boston, 1929. Adds nothing.

SPECIAL STUDIES

HULL, WILLIAM I.: *The Two Hague Conferences, and their Contributions to International Law*. Boston, 1908.

CHOATE, JOSEPH H.: *The Two Hague Conferences*. Princeton, 1913. A series of lectures, of no great importance.

LAPRADELLE, A. DE: "La Question du Désarmement." (*Revue Générale de Droit International Public,* 1899, pp. 651–846). One of the best and most heavily documented contemporary studies.

STENGEL, KARL VON: "Die Haager Friedenskonferenz und das Völkerrecht." (*Archiv für Öffentliches Recht,* 1900, II, 139–201). A careful, but not very favorable review of the Conference's work, by one of the German delegates.

FRIED, ALFRED H.: *Handbuch der Friedensbewegung*. Leipzig, 1911. One of the best German accounts.

LAMMASCH, HEINRICH: *Die Beiden Haager Friedenskonferenzen von 1899 und 1907*. Berlin, 1915. Written by one of the Austrian representatives, this is primarily a study in international law.

MÉRIGNHAC, A.: *La Conférence Internationale de la Paix*. Paris, 1900. Primarily devoted to technical analysis of the proceedings.

MEURER, CHRISTIAN: *Die Haager Friedenskonferenz*. Two volumes. Munich, 1905. A substantial study, dealing chiefly with the development of arbitration.

NIPPOLD, OTFRIED: *Die Fortbildung des Verfahrens in Völkerrechtlichen Streitigkeiten*. Leipzig, 1907. A careful, scholarly treatment of the problem of arbitration.

SCHÜCKING, WALTHER: *Der Staatenverband der Haager Konferenzen*. Munich, 1912. The work of a leading German international jurist, who attempts to set the Conference in the general development of international organization.

KRAFFT, E.: *Die Ersten Internationalen Friedenskongresse und ihre Entstehung*. Frankfurt, 1922. A dissertation.

JUNK, AUGUST: *Die Mächte auf der Ersten Haager Friedenskonferenz*. Leipzig, 1928. Far and away the best study of the political aspects of the Conference and of the policies of the powers. Now requires supplementing with the evidence presented to the German parliamentary commission, and by the Russian documents.

GOTTSCHALK, EGON: "Deutschlands Haltung auf den Haager Friedenskonferenzen." (*Berliner Monatshefte,* May, 1930, pp. 447–56). A review of German policy, with special reference to the evidence of the German parliamentary commission.

WEHBERG, HANS: *Die Internationale Beschränkung der Rüstungen*. Stuttgart, 1919. An excellent, thoroughly documented study. It really treats the whole problem of international co-operation and peace, and still remains one of the best historical accounts.

— : "La Contribution des Conférences de la Paix de la Haye au Progrès du Droit International." (*Académie de Droit International. Recueil des Cours,* XXXVII, 1931, pp. 533–669). The most recent and one of the best historical and analytical treatments of the Conference.

XVIII

Origins of the Boer War

∾

THE OUTCOME OF THE FASHODA EPISODE WAS A VERY GREAT VICTORY FOR the British and led to a veritable revolution in the popular attitude toward foreign affairs. The years of discouragement which followed upon the rise of Germany as a great commercial rival and upon the conclusion of the Franco-Russian Alliance had shaken the confidence of the country in its ability to hold its own against the demands of the great continental countries for a share of the unclaimed areas of the world. Fashoda had shown conclusively that Britain could still score a resounding success, that isolation after all did not necessarily mean impotence, and that Mahan was right — everything in matters of world policy depended upon sea-power. So long as Britain maintained her great fleets she was not only safe, but supreme. France, which had really been feared as a naval power, had proved herself helpless, and the Franco-Russian Alliance had been shown up as a fiction. In the eyes of the exuberant imperialists France no longer counted. George Wyndham, undersecretary for war, speaking to his friend Wilfrid Blunt in May 1899, expressed quite baldly what must have been the idea of many of the imperialists: " It is now simply a triangular battle between the Anglo-Saxon race, the German race, and the Russian, which shall have the hegemony of the whole world." France he considered gone as a great power, as much gone as Spain or Austria, but the Emperor William, he believed, meant to be supreme overlord. He was holding his hand for the moment till he could get an efficient navy, but as soon as that was ready there would be a coalition against England. He, Wyndham, and the young imperialists, however, were " going in for England's overlordship" and they wouldn't " stand half-measures or economy in pushing it on." [1]

The continental powers took due note of the great change that had been wrought in the international situation, and they were much more circumspect in their dealings with England. The Emperor William, as we have seen in the preceding chapter, was convinced that it was already too late to talk of a continental combine, and the Russians hastened to conclude with the British an agreement with regard to China, which we shall have to discuss at greater length later. The general outlook for England was extremely favorable when, in 1899, she became involved in a war in south Africa which tied up her forces almost before she was able to realize on the Fashoda victory.

---

[1] Wilfrid S. Blunt: *My Diaries* (New York, 1919), I, p. 397.

It is as difficult to discuss the origins of the Boer War as to analyze the causes of the Crimean War. Both conflicts were slow in coming to a head and both involved a host of factors which were hopelessly intertwined. Something has already been said in a previous chapter of the complications in south Africa which followed the discovery of gold in the Transvaal and the great influx of foreigners into Johannesburg, and also of the schemes of Rhodes and his associates which eventuated in the famous Jameson raid of December 1895. This abortive attempt to overthrow the government of Kruger must be taken as the starting point of the later clash. Its importance can hardly be overestimated. By common consent of all writers it left behind it a feeling of profound suspicion and resentment. Nothing could convince the Boers after the Raid that there was not a plot afoot to take their country from them and that the British were not seeking a pretext for a fight. This feeling was enhanced by the enthusiastic reception accorded Jameson in England, by the mild treatment meted out to the raiders, and by the conduct of the parliamentary committee, which in the spring of 1897 investigated the whole affair. It was common knowledge that no serious attempt was made to get at some of the important evidence. The world generally was shocked when, after the committee had roundly castigated Rhodes, Chamberlain got up in parliament and exonerated him of dishonorable action.[2]

The British position having been seriously compromised by Jameson's action, the government for a time seemed anxious to smooth matters over and reach some sort of adjustment of the questions at issue. Into the details we need not go. Suffice it to say that within a year the situation had again become critical. Legislation regulating immigration into the Transvaal and providing for the expulsion of undesirable foreigners created friction and caused something of a war scare in the spring of 1897.[3] This crisis passed when Chamberlain took a strong line and the Pretoria government decided it would be best to yield. The years 1897 and 1898 were on the whole fairly quiet. The British government was deeply involved in serious imperial problems in other parts of the world, while the Transvaal generally suffered from bad times and financial difficulties.

In the meanwhile Sir Alfred Milner was sent out as high commissioner. Milner was the author of the widely acclaimed book *England in Egypt,* and was generally regarded as one of the ablest of the young imperialist group. Since the time of the Boer War he has been generally held responsible for the outbreak of the conflict. The Boers regarded him as an agent of Chamberlain and Rhodes, sent out to pick a quarrel. Not a few English writers have felt and said the same thing.[4] We now have the illuminating papers of Milner himself, so

---

[2] See, among others, E. T. Cook: *Rights and Wrongs of the Transvaal War* (New edition, London, 1902), chap. viii: The "Committee of No Inquiry."

[3] The details may be read in such recent books as Eric A. Walker: *A History of South Africa* (London, 1928), pp. 463 ff.; Reginald I. Lovell: *The Struggle for South Africa* (Cambridge, 1934), pp. 387 ff.; Garvin: *Life of Chamberlain*, III, chap. lii, especially pp. 140 ff.

[4] E.g. J. A. Hobson: *The War in South Africa* (London, 1900), chap. xix; W. T. Stead: Leading article in the *Review of Reviews*, August 15, 1899, pp. 119–20; Blunt; *Diaries*, I, p. 401.

that it is possible to form an independent judgment.[5] From them it appears that after spending the first year in becoming acquainted with the questions at issue, the high commissioner came to the conclusion that the situation in the Transvaal offered little prospect of peaceful reform from within, and that there was no " way out of the political troubles of south Africa except reform in the Transvaal, or war." Kruger was re-elected president for five years in February 1898 and therewith all hope of a more liberal régime evaporated. In the " scandalous " abuses of the Transvaal administration Milner saw the root of all the trouble. Looking at the question from the purely south African viewpoint, Milner wrote to Chamberlain, he, the high commissioner, would be inclined " to work up a crisis." But naturally everything would depend on the imperial outlook as a whole.

Chamberlain's reply to these revelations was detailed and unambiguous. He reminded Milner of the bases of policy agreed upon when he was sent out. They were to maintain Britain's rights under the Convention of 1884 and to avoid public pressure in regard to less important grievances. The considerations upon which these bases rested were:

" (1) The conviction that a war with the Transvaal would certainly rouse antagonism in the Cape Colony, and leave behind it the most serious difficulties in the way of South African union. We felt that if a struggle was to come, it was most important that the Transvaal should be the aggressor, and that the Imperial Government should have the active sympathy of at all events a considerable section of the Dutch in the Colony. (2) We felt that the Raid has placed this country in a false position and has alienated the confidence of the Afrikander Party, and that it would be desirable that the irritation caused by this event should pass away before we resumed any pressure upon the Transvaal in regard to its internal policy. (3) We were of opinion that the waiting game was the best for this country as time must be on our side. The misgovernment in the Transvaal will in the long run produce opposition within its borders, and when the present rule of President Kruger comes to an end, as it must do before many years are over, we might confidently look for an improvement in the position. (4) A war with the Transvaal, unless upon the utmost and clearest provocation, would be extremely unpopular in this country. It would involve the despatch of a very large force and the expenditure of many millions." " Most of the grievances of which we have to complain are of a character which would not excite great sympathy in this country, and they would not be considered as sufficient to constitute a *casus belli*." The foreign situation was a further argument against war. " We have on hand difficulties of the most serious character with France, Russia and Germany. We are engaged in an important expedition in the Soudan, and it is uncertain as yet whether the war on the north-west frontier of India has been finally concluded. We may emerge from all these

---

Milner's policy is examined in great detail and favorably appraised by E. B. Iwan-Müller: *Lord Milner and South Africa* (London, 1902), and W. Basil Worsfold: *Lord Milner's Work in South Africa, 1897–1902* (London, 1906).

[5] Cecil Headlam: *The Milner Papers* (London, 1931).

troubles without a war, but I cannot conceal from myself that the prospect is more gloomy that it has ever been in my recollection. . . . Accordingly I wish to emphasize the fact that for the present at any rate our greatest interest in South Africa is peace, and that all our policy must be directed to this subject." [6]

This exchange of letters has been quoted at length because it touches almost every aspect of the situation. The British could not go to war to bring the Transvaal into a south African federation because of danger of estranging the Dutch population at the Cape, because of the unenviable position in which the Jameson raid had placed the British government, because the grievances of the Uitlanders were not such that they would arouse much sympathy in England. Public opinion in England was opposed to war, and the government had its hands full elsewhere. Thus warned, Milner was obliged to exercise patience. The year 1898 was generally a quiet one, as things went in south Africa.

A new chapter opened with the new year. Milner paid a visit home in November and worked hard on the politicians to convince them that England must secure genuine reforms from the Transvaal government.[7] The situation was now much more favorable, for the Germans had been bought off with the agreement regarding the Portuguese colonies, and France had received a decided setback in the Fashoda business. Kitchener had completed his work in the Sudan, and the Russians were negotiating for an agreement with respect to China. England was, for the moment, at the top of the pile and had no serious international complications to fear. But public opinion was still cool toward south Africa and the cabinet was sceptical of Milner's views. Chamberlain himself counselled caution and emphasized his desire not to hasten the crisis.[8]

Even though Milner received little or no encouragement in London, the situation after his return to south Africa played into his hands. In the last days of December a man named Edgar, an English miner at Johannesburg, had been shot and killed by a Boer policeman. The case itself need not detain us here. The important thing is that the affair led to a marked revival of Uitlander agitation against the Kruger system and to the presentation of the first petition to Queen Victoria, which General Butler, who acted as commissioner in Milner's absence, rejected because of a technicality. In the midst of the agitation some effort was made by Kruger to reach an agreement with the mine owners. His hope was evidently that many of the outstanding questions could be removed in this way and that the bottom could thereby be knocked out of the entire opposition movement. We need not enter upon the details of the pourparlers. The British looked upon them from the outset as a mere manoeuvre designed to split the ranks of the Uitlander population. When they consulted Chamberlain he discouraged them. Sir Percy Fitzpatrick has told us himself how he gave the

[6] *Milner Papers,* I, pp. 220–9, correspondence with Chamberlain of February and March, 1908; Garvin, op. cit., III, pp. 355 ff., 366 ff.

[7] *Milner Papers,* I, p. 298; Garvin, op. cit., III, pp. 377 ff.

[8] Garvin, op. cit., III, pp. 377 ff.

correspondent of the London *Times* at Pretoria the money with which to bribe a Boer official in order to get the text of Kruger's proposals. The premature publication of the offer was admittedly an important reason for the breakdown of the negotiations.[9] Whether Kruger was sincere or not it is hard to say, but it does seem that the old man had become convinced that some extension of the franchise was necessary, and that he was prepared to make concessions in this matter as fast as the opinion of his burghers would permit.

The question of the part played by the Rand capitalists in bringing about the war has always been a warmly debated one. It has been said that they were not interested in politics, and that they preferred to get along as best they could with the government rather than to start a row. Of course they were deeply involved in the conspiracy which ended in the Jameson raid, but that was an aberration. After the disaster Rhodes scrupulously kept out of the whole business. But this is certainly not the whole story. It would appear rather that the capitalists were against war so long as it was obvious that the British government would not play the game. Despite the low mining taxes in the Transvaal, they had grievances, of which the famous and obscure dynamite monopoly was the principal one, while maladministration, corruption, the liquor laws and the pass laws for laborers were others. Least talked about, however, was the most important question, that of labor supply. J. A. Hobson has shown pretty conclusively that the supply of native labor was a crucial matter on the Rand, and that in June 1899 there was a shortage of 12,000 men. He has shown further, on the basis of remarks made by the capitalists themselves, that they hoped, if they got control of the Transvaal government, to make a saving of two and a half million pounds sterling annually by securing for themselves an unrestricted labor supply and thus lowering the wage-rate.[10]

Now it is worth noting that the capitalists, who, according to Fitzpatrick, did not want to introduce the question of the franchise into the negotiations for the " Great Deal," did ask that the government assist the mines in getting labor, that it enforce the liquor laws, and that it admit to the executive council an " independent " financier like Rothschild to control future taxation. When the whole project fell flat through the unwillingness of the government to accept these terms, the financial interests began to take the lead in the great campaign of villification that followed. Rhodes may have stayed in the background, but the fact remains that he controlled the Johannesburg *Star* and the Transvaal *Leader,* the *Cape Times* and other south African newspapers, to say nothing of some of the London dailies. His friend Harmsworth's *Daily Mail* was one of the most violent enemies of the Boers; the Liberal *Daily News* was acquired by his friends and pressed into service; the London *Times* championed

---

[9] Percy Fitzpatrick: *The Transvaal from Within* (London, 1899), pp. 342–60; Idem: *South African Memories* (London, 1932), chaps. x and xi; see further *Milner Papers*, I, pp. 318 ff.; Garvin, op. cit., III, pp. 388–9; and among many secondary accounts E. T. Cook: *Rights and Wrongs of the Transvaal War*, chap. xxiv.   [10] J. A. Hobson: *The War in South Africa*, Book II, chap. iv.

the Uitlanders and demanded a forward policy, for reasons that are not clear.[11] Furthermore, in April 1899 Rhodes became president of the powerful South African League, representing the British nationalists as against the Dutch Afrikander Bond. The Outlanders' Council, founded in June 1899 at Johannesburg, was patently under the direction of the capitalists, who at this time healed the split in their own ranks which had occurred after the Jameson raid and who thenceforth pulled together.

In April 1899 the Uitlanders sent to the Queen a petition recounting their grievances. There were more than 21,000 signatures attached, which according to Milner were on the whole genuine and according to the Boers largely forged. Milner followed up the petition with the famous " helot " despatch of May 4, in which he reviewed the hardships of the Uitlanders, and declared that " the true remedy is to strike at the root of all these injuries, the political impotence of the injured. What diplomatic protests will never accomplish, a fair measure of Uitlander representation would gradually but surely bring about. . . . The case for intervention is overwhelming." Then, to drive the point home, he issued a significant warning:

> " The spectacle of thousands of British subjects kept permanently in the position of helots, constantly chafing under undoubted grievances, and calling vainly to Her Majesty's Government for redress, does steadily undermine the influence and reputation of Great Britain and the respect for the British Government within its own dominions. A certain section of the press, and not in the Transvaal only, preaches openly and constantly the doctrine of a Republic embracing all South Africa, and supports it by menacing references to the armaments of the Transvaal, its alliance with the Orange Free State, and the active sympathy which in case of war it would receive from a section of Her Majesty's subjects. I regret to say that this doctrine, supported as it is by a ceaseless stream of malignant lies about the intentions of the British Government, is producing a great effect upon a large number of our Dutch fellow-colonists. . . . I can see nothing which will put a stop to this mischievous propaganda but some striking proof of the intention, if it is the intention, of Her Majesty's Government not to be ousted from its position in South Africa." [12]

Before leaving this despatch a few words of comment will be in order. In the first place, it ought to be pointed out that there has always been much difference of opinion as to the extent of the grievances of the Uitlanders. It is impossible at this date to make any definite pronouncement, but the conscientious reader will want to consult the writings of men like Stead and Hobson before accepting in full the statements of Fitzpatrick and E. T. Cook, to say nothing of less responsible imperialists. Hobson was in the Transvaal in the summer and autumn of 1899 and declared that he could secure little concrete evidence of oppression, though the place was full of stock stories that could not

11 See especially Hobson, op. cit., Book II, chap. iii; Walker: *History of South Africa*, p. 476.
12 *Milner Papers*, I, pp. 348–53; Garvin, op. cit., III, pp. 394 ff.

be corroborated. " The notion that Englishmen or White British subjects have commonly been made the victims of oppression and terrorism is grotesquely and utterly false," he said. " So far as practical freedom of action, speech and publication are concerned, there was no place upon the continent of Europe which could for a moment compare with it (Johannesburg)." " There are liars and credulous folk in every land; but for a minute detailed mendacity and the wanton acceptance of the same, South Africa stands pre-eminent." There was, of course, corruption and maladministration, but corruption had been more or less fostered by the financial interests themselves, and if it had been as bad as it was made out to be, it might have been reasonably urged that the capitalists " would have found it cheaper and safer to buy the Boer Government than to enter a troublesome political campaign for its reformation or its overthrow." [13]

Hobson was convinced that reform would have come in the course of time and through the pressure of circumstances, and Professor Walker, in his *History of South Africa,* has shown that there was more than a merely negligible measure of reform between 1896 and 1899. Furthermore, by Milner's own admission only a percentage of the foreigners in Johannesburg desired the franchise. Most of them were transients, who had no desire to give up their citizenship, but were interested chiefly in making their pile and then clearing out. Finally, a word about the much-discussed Dutch conspiracy to oust the British from south Africa. Talk of this plot became prevalent in south African circles after the victory of the Afrikander Bond in the Cape elections of the autumn of 1898. In actual fact there was little justification for the imputation of disloyalty so far as the Cape Dutch were concerned. The Bond and its leader, Hofmeyr, had always been for the connexion with Britain and in 1899 did their utmost to effect a peaceful settlement. They had no use for Krugerism and certainly had no desire to spread that system to the whole of south Africa. That there were some hot-headed young bloods in the Transvaal there can be no doubt, but there is little evidence to support the idea of a general policy aimed at ejecting the British. In fact the idea is rather preposterous. " Of all the disreputable, contemptible and discreditable proceedings by which a nation has ever been jockeyed into war," wrote W. T. Stead, " this fighting for the paramountcy is about the worst." His opinion was echoed by an anonymous writer in the *Edinburgh Review,* who declared that " the notion that there is a formidable Dutch conspiracy ' to oust British influence . . . from South Africa ' is the strangest nightmare that ever afflicted the most nervous of ' Imperialist ' minds." [14]

The simple truth of the matter is that the franchise demand and the spectre of the Dutch conspiracy cannot be examined on their merits. Milner had come

---

[13] Hobson, op. cit., Book I, chaps. viii, x.

[14] W. T. Stead: Leading article, *Review of Reviews,* October 15, 1899, p. 333; Anonymous: " Great Britain and South Africa " (*Edinburgh Review,* October, 1899, pp. 530–52). The most is made of the argument by Cook, op. cit., chap. xxx; on the other side see Hobson, op. cit., Book I, chap. xiv. Garvin is circumspect in dealing with this question.

to the conclusion that the franchise would do better as a lever than a host of lesser questions which concerned the capitalists rather than the Uitlanders as a whole. The conspiracy alarm, too, was probably meant chiefly as an incentive to British public opinion. Milner was working for a crisis, though it should be carefully noted that this is not saying that he wanted war. He was ready for armed conflict if it proved unavoidable, but he undoubtedly hoped to get what he wanted by mere pressure. Rhodes told a British cabinet minister in the spring of 1899 that Kruger was " only bluffing." " If you were to employ your troops you could undoubtedly bring him to subjection." To his friend Beit he wrote: " Nothing will make Kruger fire a shot." [15] These same ideas recur in the Milner correspondence. Here are a few excerpts from his letters at the time: May 17, 1899: " I don't want war, but I admit I begin to think it may be the only way out." " Absolute downright determination plus a large temporary increase of force will assure a climb down. It is 20 to 1." May 24, 1899: " My view has been and still is, in spite of all these alarms and excursions, that if we are perfectly determined we shall win without a fight or with a mere apology for one." [16]

The great obstacle to the realization of Milner's policy was the négative attitude of British opinion and the resulting unwillingness of the cabinet to embark upon a policy that might lead to war. Milner's helot despatch was written with the idea that it should be published and that it would serve as an effective irritant. But for the time being it had to be held back and Milner was obliged to accept the mediation of President Steyn of the Orange Free State, who arranged a meeting with Kruger at Bloemfontein. There discussions took place between May 30 and June 5. From the outset they were doomed to failure. Milner had been instructed by Chamberlain to show a conciliatory spirit, but instead of doing so " he bombarded the president with dialectical artillery, bowling over in summary fashion his arguments, making debating scores off him, and eventually driving the old man to an attitude of obstinate despair." [17] It was certainly a mistake to try to deal with the old Vortrekker as though he were a polished European diplomat, but it was positively fatal to the Conference to do what Milner did, namely to demand a straight five-year retrospective franchise in place of the existing fourteen-year franchise, and to refuse to discuss other matters until this demand was accepted. Kruger seems to have come with the idea that all the " nasty questions " were to be discussed. Naturally he was not prepared to accept a measure which, he felt, would deliver his country into the hands of the Uitlanders, without some sort of guarantee of a *quid pro quo*. Even then it was Milner who broke off the conference, too hastily, as he himself acknowledged later.[18]

---

[15] Sir Lewis Michell: *The Life of Cecil John Rhodes* (London, 1910), II, p. 253.

[16] *Milner Papers*, I, pp. 384–5, 400–1.   [17] Hobson, op. cit., pp. 165–6.

[18] *Milner Papers*, I, pp. 404 ff.; Garvin, op. cit., III, pp. 392 ff., 400 ff.; *Correspondence relating to the Bloemfontein Conference*, 1899 (Command no. 9404).

Chamberlain was alarmed by Milner's uncompromising attitude and was not at all certain that Kruger had said his last word. It was essential, he wired Milner, that the Pretoria government be put clearly in the wrong. But the mistake had been made and in the succeeding weeks the colonial secretary gradually turned up the road marked out by Milner. He published the famous helot despatch and his own reply adopting the case of the Uitlanders. The despatch, says Walker, " clanged like a trumpet-call presaging war." Perhaps for this very reason it did not go over with the public nearly as well as had been hoped. Chamberlain attempted to secure the support of the Liberals for a forward policy. He told Campbell-Bannerman that he was, and always had been, striving for a peaceful settlement, " but he was afraid that a demonstration . . . would be necessary. It would, however, be a game of bluff, and it was impossible to play that game if the Opposition did not support the Government." But the Liberals were unwilling to support an " open military demonstration." Furthermore, the cabinet, convinced that a war would be very unpopular, refused to commit itself to anything beyond firm language and protests.[19]

While the British government was marking time, all sorts of pressure was being brought to bear on Kruger by the Dutch leaders at the Cape. The Dutch and German governments too sent strong advice to yield.[20] Such a course was not easy, for the burghers were filled with distrust. They hated that *verdomde Kimberlain,* who, they felt convinced, had been bought by Rhodes with a generous block of Consolidated Goldfields stock. Even reputed progressives, like Joubert, were opposed to concessions, and it was widely believed that the British were merely bluffing — that they would not fight.[21] Nevertheless, Kruger had offered a seven-year franchise during the Bloemfontein discussions, and on July 18 he got the Volksraad to accept such a scheme. Chamberlain was elated by this turn of events. He inspired a statement in the *Times* saying that the crisis was at an end, and he wired to Milner: " If . . . President South African Republic has really given seven years retroactive franchise and five seats (in the Volksraad to the Rand), I congratulate you on great victory. No one would dream of fighting over two years in qualification period and President South African Republic will have been driven by successive steps to almost exact position taken by you. We ought to make most of this and accept it as basis of settlement." [22]

Milner was horrified. The *Times* article, he telegraphed Chamberlain, had " created consternation among British party " in south Africa. The Transvaal offer, he declared, was far from satisfactory. At the same time the south African press and the Uitlanders raised a howl and reiterated their demand for the five-

---

[19] *Milner Papers,* I, pp. 444 ff.; Garvin, op. cit., III, pp. 411–5; J. A. Spender: *The Life of Sir Henry Campbell-Bannerman* (London, 1923), II, p. 234; *Letters of Queen Victoria,* III, pp. 382–4.
[20] *Die Grosse Politik,* XV, nos. 4357–4360, 4367, 4368.
[21] Hobson, op. cit., pp. 43–5.
[22] *Milner Papers,* I, p. 468; Garvin, op. cit., III, pp. 418 ff.

year franchise as a minimum. All this fuss made Chamberlain waver. He had, so his biographer points out, intended from the beginning to secure guarantees for the satisfactory working of the proposed franchise scheme, and secured cabinet approval for his next step. On July 27 he proposed a joint inquiry into the working of the new law. This idea was particularly distasteful to the Boers, who regarded it as interference in their domestic affairs. They therefore accepted the suggestion of President Steyn and, after consultation with the British agent at Pretoria, put forward (August 19) a five-year-franchise plan with the assignment of at least a quarter of the seats in the Raad to the mining areas, but all this on condition that the Imperial government drop the claim to suzerainty, interfere no more in the internal affairs of the Republic, and agree to refer minor points in dispute to arbitration.

No doubt something might have been done with this offer, if the British negotiators had been willing to make the most of it. The press of south Africa, controlled by the capitalists, was demanding nothing less than the whole hog, and Milner was constantly insisting that all that was needed was firmness: " There is at bottom a very great indisposition to fight on the part of the Boers, not only in the Colony and Orange Free State, but even in the Transvaal itself. . . . The larger our force, the smaller is likely to be theirs, and I think one good slap in the face may dissipate them " (August 2, 1899); " They will collapse if we don't weaken, or rather if we go on steadily turning the screw " (August 16, 1899).[23] With such assurances dinning in his ears Chamberlain was bound to take a cynical attitude toward the Boer offers. In a resounding speech at Highbury on August 26 he declared: " Mr. Kruger dribbles out reforms like water from a squeezed sponge, and he either accompanies his offers with conditions which he knows to be impossible, or he refuses to allow us to make a satisfactory investigation of the nature of these reforms. . . . The sands are running down in the glass. . . . The knot must be loosened . . . or else we shall have to find other ways of untying it."

A few days later the colonial secretary sent a despatch accepting the Boer proposals without the provisos, on the plea that the British government could not abandon its rights under the conventions or give up the substance of suzerainty. Chamberlain later maintained that this despatch was one of " qualified acceptance " and that he had agreed to nine tenths of the Boer proposals. This is absurd. The Chamberlain reply was what the Boers thought it was — a rejection of the terms offered.[24] They therefore withdrew the offer of the five-year franchise and fell back on the earlier British suggestion of a joint inquiry into the working of the seven-year franchise. It had been explicitly stated that the proposal of a five-year franchise did not involve a rejection of the joint inquiry on the part of the Boers, but Chamberlain now refused to entertain his

---

[23] *Milner Papers*, I, pp. 515–6.

[24] Garvin, op. cit., III, pp. 433 ff., discusses the negotiations without referring to the " qualified acceptance." For a good analysis of the problem see Lovell: *The Struggle for South Africa*, pp. 419 ff.

own earlier suggestion. He had evidently fixed on a line of action and had no intention of swerving. In a letter to Milner (September 2) he stated that he had asked for a cabinet to consider the terms of an ultimatum. The situation, he pointed out, was a difficult one, for " the technical *casus belli* is a very weak one and, thanks to past concessions and weaknesses, our hands are tied in regard to many matters which might otherwise be put forward to justify extreme action." Neither the Uitlanders nor the British at the Cape, he continued, were wholly without reproach, for the former were

" unfortunately identified with money-making — with the Raid — and are not supposed to be capable of much self-sacrifice even for a holy cause — and the latter are quite too ready to take all the profits of a war in the shape of Imperial expenditure while doing nothing themselves but shouting on every occasion that they will cut the painter if the Imperial Government does not do everything they want and do it as quickly as they consider possible and desirable."

There were other obstacles to a forward policy. Chamberlain confessed himself surprised that so much progress had been made:

" It is a great thing to say that the majority of the people have, as I believe, recognised that there is a greater issue than the franchise or the grievances of the Uitlanders at stake, and that our supremacy in South Africa and our existence as a great Power in the world are involved in the result of our present controversy. Three months ago we could not — that is, we should not have been allowed to — go to war on this issue. Now — although still most unwillingly and with a large minority against us, we shall be sufficiently supported." But " we must play out this game *selon les règles* and it seems to me to-day that we ought to exhaust the franchise proposals and get a clear refusal before . . . we ask for more. If and when we ask for more it means war, and therefore, before we do this, we must have a sufficient force in South Africa to defend ourselves during the time that will be required to get a full fighting force into the country. . . ." [25]

This letter would seem to indicate that by the beginning of September negotiation was simply a blind so far as Chamberlain was concerned. He had convinced himself that British opinion was sufficiently persuaded to make it possible to go on, but the whole situation was such that more time was needed to get troops to the scene. In order to gain time the franchise issue was to be wrung dry, but Kruger was not to escape even if he gave in, for in that event the British, like the French in 1870, would bring forward more demands, knowing full well that when they asked for more it would mean war. With this program Chamberlain went before the cabinet and carried his colleagues with him. It was decided to send 10,000 more men to south Africa and in the meanwhile to string out the discussions with Pretoria. In a despatch of the same date Chamberlain insisted on the five-year franchise without conditions and, failing that, reserved to the British government the right " to consider the situation *de novo,* and to formulate their own proposals for a final settlement."

<hr />

[25] Garvin, op. cit., III, pp. 457–9.

There was, by this time, no turning back, for the government was committed. Salisbury, Balfour and other members of the cabinet gave in to the colonial secretary, but only reluctantly and with misgivings. The prime minister wrote to Lansdowne on August 30 that Milner's view was "too heated, if you consider the intrinsic significance and importance of the things which are in controversy." But, he went on, "it recks little to think of that now. What he has done cannot be effaced. We have to act upon a moral field prepared for us by him and his jingo supporters. And therefore I see before us the necessity for considerable military effort — and all for people whom we despise and for territory which will bring no profit and no power to England." [26] Almost to the very end Salisbury seems to have hoped that Milner would prove right in his contention that the Boers would back down before a show of force. [27]

But there was absolutely no chance of that. In south Africa the exodus of the Uitlanders from Johannesburg had already begun. The local press was full of atrocity stories which were assiduously copied in the English press. Popular excitement was rising high and matters had already been pushed to the very verge of war. Kruger rejected Chamberlain's proposal on September 17 and the cabinet had to decide on the next step. Salisbury favored a temporizing policy until the time when reinforcements should have reached the scene, but Chamberlain carried the cabinet with his suggestion for secret mobilization. On September 22 he wired triumphantly to Milner: "Cabinet unanimous and resolves to see matter through." [28] Another despatch was to be sent by steamer so as to gain another four weeks for preparation.

By this time even Salisbury seems to have become convinced, or, shall we say, seems to have convinced himself that more than Uitlander grievances were at issue and that there was a Dutch conspiracy to drive the British out of south Africa. It may be that the publication of Fitzpatrick's *The Transvaal from Within* had something to do with his conversion. Fitzpatrick was one of the capitalist group who had taken an active part in the revolutionary movement which eventuated in the Jameson raid. He had, in general, served as liaison officer between the mining interests and the Uitlander agitators. His book, while still in manuscript, had been read by Milner late in 1898, and is said to have confirmed him in the policy which led to war. It is said that the book made a deep impression also upon Salisbury when it was published in England in September 1899. [29] At any rate the prime minister seems to have swallowed the plot-story whole. He wrote to the Queen on September 23: "It is impossible to avoid believing that the Boers really aim at setting up a South African Republic, consisting of the Transvaal, the Orange Free State and Your

---

[26] Lord Newton: *Lord Lansdowne* (London, 1929), p. 157.

[27] *Letters of Queen Victoria*, III, p. 395; *Die Grosse Politik*, XV, nos. 4374, 4379, 4380.

[28] *Milner Papers*, I, p. 545; Garvin, op. cit., III, pp. 461–2.

[29] Sir Percy Fitzpatrick: *South African Memories*, chap. xii, and especially p. 188; W. T. Stead in the *Review of Reviews*, November 15, 1899, pp. 521 ff.

Majesty's Colony. It is impossible to account in any other manner for their rejection of our most moderate proposals." And on October 5 he declared in a letter to Lord Courtney that while he could not convict Kruger of conspiracy in a court of law, he had become convinced, from watching the course of negotiations "that Kruger was using the oppression of the Outlanders as a lever to exact from England a renunciation of suzerainty; and the conduct of President Steyn and Mr. Schreiner (prime minister at the Cape), of the Africanders generally and of their sympathisers in Europe, has brought home to me the belief that there is an understanding among the leaders of Dutch opinion, and their aspiration is the restoration of South Africa to the Dutch race." [30]

The British were now rushing troops to south Africa and were merely sparring for time in the hope of getting 70,000 men to the scene before the storm broke. Recognizing the futility of further discussion the Transvaal government, after asking for the British terms and being put off, drew up an ultimatum demanding that the troops be withdrawn from the frontiers, that all reinforcements sent out since June 1 be recalled within a reasonable period, and that the forces then on the sea should not be landed at any south African port. This ultimatum was presented on October 9, and simply forestalled a British one. The British government simply declared these "peremptory demands" impossible of discussion and therewith the war began.

It is hardly necessary to say much by way of recapitulation. No one would deny that the south African situation had for years been a most difficult one, complicated as it was by the peculiar race problem and by the troubles that were bound to arise from the establishment of great mining interests and the influx of thousands of foreigners into an essentially backward agrarian state. Things had really come to a head with the Jameson raid, which had set all these antagonisms in a lurid light and had left an atmosphere of distrust in which it was nearly impossible to negotiate in any cordial way. Both the capitalists and the workers in the Transvaal had undoubted grievances, though they were probably not as serious as Fitzpatrick, for example, made them out to be.[31] It seems unlikely that the Transvaal government could have maintained its exclusive policy for very much longer in the face of changing conditions. At any rate it was not given the chance. Rhodes and the other capitalists were set upon a federation of south Africa and that implied control of the Transvaal government. Having failed to get what they wanted from Kruger they made use of the Uitlander grievances, mobilized the press which they controlled and raised the hue and cry of the Dutch conspiracy. Milner's views suited them perfectly and those views were that England must intervene in the domestic affairs of the Transvaal, which she was hardly justified in doing,

---

[30] Letters of Queen Victoria, III, p. 400; G. P. Gooch: Life of Lord Courtney (London, 1920), pp. 377–8.

[31] This was also the opinion of an expert observer like James Bryce: "Historical Causes of the War" (North American Review, December, 1899, pp. 737–59).

no matter what opinion one may hold of the unhappy suzerainty issue. Milner finally convinced Chamberlain, who was at first hopeful and circumspect but came round after the Fashoda crisis. He wrote to the Queen retrospectively that he had "long felt that the differences between this country and the Transvaal could only be settled by force." [32]

Affairs might well have been brought to a head in the spring of 1898 excepting for the fact that British public opinion was so little interested in Uitlander grievances and the government was so deeply involved in serious questions of international politics that it was absolutely unwilling to follow Milner and Chamberlain. It was not until Germany had been squared by the agreement on the Portuguese colonies and France had been taken care of in the Fashoda crisis that the field became clear. Even then it required a long campaign of propaganda to bring the British public into line, and to convert Lord Salisbury, who disliked both capitalists and jingoes. In the meanwhile negotiations dragged on, marked throughout by a certain insincerity. The British consistently refused to submit their final terms and thereby gave the Transvaalers good reason to suppose that every concession would be followed by further demands and that the root of the whole business was the desire of the British to get control of the Transvaal and its great wealth. Whether Milner actually believed that the Boers would not fight it is hard to say. In any event his policy of bluff was a dangerous one, which, as he himself recognized, might lead to war. But he did not fear war. In his opinion only "an apology for a fight" would be necessary. A "slap in the face" would do the business. Had he appreciated the seriousness of the struggle on which England was embarked so light-heartedly, he would undoubtedly have made greater efforts to find another way out. Chamberlain showed himself throughout to be much better informed and statesmanlike and came only gradually to the conclusion that force was the only method that would bring a solution. Salisbury and other cabinet ministers, as we have seen, were even more sceptical and reluctant. They allowed Milner to push them into a crisis from which there was no decent escape except through war.

That Salisbury did not commit himself to a policy of war without carefully considering the international situation goes without saying. Writing to the Queen on August 12 he admitted that England's position was exceptionally strong, but that there was always uncertainty and anxiety regarding France and Germany, whose colonial aspirations crossed England's more frequently than before. But two weeks later he said to the German ambassador that he did not think France or Russia would attempt to take action. France was still submerged in the chaos of the Dreyfus affair and Russia was afflicted with famine and financial distress.[33]

As a matter of fact, the problem for England narrowed down pretty much

---

[32] *Letters of Queen Victoria*, III, pp. 406–7, letter of October 12, 1899.
[33] *Letters of Queen Victoria*, III, p. 392; *Die Grosse Politik*, XV, no. 4374.

to the problem of her relationship with Germany, for the French and Russians could hardly afford to become involved in a conflict with England if Germany stood on the other side. This aspect of the situation was of course recognized in London, and for that reason Chamberlain had worked eagerly for the agreement on the Portuguese colonies, which bought off the Germans so far as south Africa was concerned. Bülow admitted quite frankly that the convention " removed from discussion the question of Delagoa Bay, which threatened to embitter the relations between the two countries and to cause an estrangement which might take thirty or forty years to overcome." [34] From the English angle the agreement worked perfectly, for the Germans thenceforth showed no interest in the Boers. In fact, they repeatedly warned the Pretoria government to yield. Dr. Leyds, the Boer agent, who has often been accused of having encouraged Kruger by assurances of foreign aid, on the contrary warned his government repeatedly that no assistance was to be expected, least of all from Berlin.[35]

But the Germans, recognizing their importance to England, were determined to make the most of the situation. They were disappointed with the Portuguese agreement, for it soon became clear that the British had concluded it with reluctance and that they had no desire to hasten the partition of the Portuguese possessions.[36] Consequently the Germans were ever ready to cast about for further concessions which might be demanded of England. It was the policy later described so bitterly by Sir Eyre Crowe as that of the " professional blackmailer," which forced Britain into a " systematic policy of gratuitous concessions." [37]

A rare opportunity to capitalize the general situation presented itself in the winter of 1898–1899, when troubles once more broke out in the Samoan Islands. It might be said by way of preface that this little island group caused more international friction than it was worth. After prolonged troubles in the 1880's the situation had been settled in 1889 by the Berlin Act, which provided that the islands, though independent, should be under the collective supervision of the British, Germans and Americans. The United States had certain rights to the island of Tutuila and the excellent harbor of Pago-Pago under the terms of a treaty concluded in 1878, but the work of converting and educating the natives had been done almost entirely by British missionaries. In fact, British nationals outnumbered the Germans and Americans together in 1899. But the Germans had long taken an active interest in the group. The great Hamburg commercial

---

[34] British Documents, I, no. 127.

[35] W. J. Leyds: Eenige Correspondentie uit 1899 (The Hague, 1919), especially nos. 47, 93, 95, 97, 101, 182, 183. See also Johannes A. Wüd: Die Rolle der Burenrepubliken in der Auswärtigen und Kolonialen Politik des Deutschen Reiches in den Jahren 1883–1900 (Nürnberg, 1927), pp. 130 ff.

[36] Die Grosse Politik, XIV, nos. 3873 ff.; British Documents, I, nos. 94 ff.; Raymond W. Bixler: Anglo-German Imperialism in South Africa, 1880–1900 (Baltimore, 1932), pp. 135 ff.; Fritz Schwarze: Das Deutsch-Englische Abkommen über die Portugiesischen Kolonien (Göttingen, 1931), part iii.

[37] British Documents, III, appendix A, pp. 416, 419.

firm of Goddefroy had organized the Deutsche Handels und Plantagengesell-schaft der Süd-See Inseln zu Hamburg (The Long Handle Company, for short) and had established several large cocoanut plantations on the island of Apia. In all the Germans held some 75,000 acres of land, valued at well over $1,000,000. They controlled the export trade in copra, though four fifths of the imports were British.[38]

The history of Samoa under the Berlin Act was by no means a happy one. The natives were constantly at war with each other and the European consuls seem to have suffered from an aggravated form of what Bismarck described as the *furor consularis*.[39] In August 1898 the Samoan king, Malietoa, died. His traditional rival, Mataafa, returned to Apia in the middle of September and was recognized by the great majority of the chiefs, as well as by the consuls. But in December the chief justice, an American named Chambers, with whom the decision rested in the event of a disputed succession, declared for Malietoa's son, Malietoa Tanu. Civil war ensued, Mataafa easily defeated his opponents, and the vanquished faction, including Chambers, took refuge on a British warship. Early in January 1899 the consuls set up a provisional government under Mataafa, pending instructions from their governments. Chambers refused to recognize it, whereupon the German head of the municipality of Apia declared the supreme court closed on account of the flight of the chief justice. But the British ship, with the consent of the American consul, landed marines and reopened the court despite the protests of the Germans.

These events caused a storm in Europe and America. For a short time relations between Berlin and Washington were extremely tense. The German government, however, hoped to make good use of the whole business to secure a long-desired partition of the islands between the interested powers: The Americans should have Tutuila and Manua, the Germans should receive the two large islands of Upolu and Savaii (the latter of no value), while the British should receive the Tonga Islands by way of compensation. This suggestion had been made in London as early as August 31, 1898, but it had met with no encouragement whatever from the British statesmen, who urged the objections of the New Zealand and Australian governments. Far from playing the German game the British seem to have been intent on building up a strong Anglo-American combination to frustrate the policy of Berlin. The recent biographer of the American secretary of state, John Hay, tells us that the British ambassador at Washington " repeatedly approached the State Department with suggestions which would have involved more aggressive measures than Hay was prepared to approve." A high official of the British foreign office later

---

[38] J. F. Rose-Soley: " German and English Interests in Samoa " (*Westminster Review,* September, 1896, pp. 277–95).

[39] See especially the excellent account of the American chief justice, Henry C. Ide: " The Imbroglio in Samoa " (*North American Review,* June 1899, pp. 679–93); and Robert M. Watson: *History of Samoa* (Wellington, 1918), chap. vii.

stated that his impression was that Lord Salisbury "did his best to rouse the opposition of the United States," to the German proposals.[40]

The American government, despite these efforts, showed itself not averse to a bargain.[41] But early in March 1899 the American cruiser *Philadelphia* arrived at Apia. The commander, Admiral Kautz, finding things in general confusion, declared both the provisional government and Mataafa deposed. The German consul protested and supported Mataafa. Factional strife broke out, and on March 15 British and American ships bombarded Apia, damaging the German consulate. For a month there was civil war in the islands, the Anglo-American forces occasionally taking part on the side of Malietoa Tanu, who was proclaimed King March 23.

During this critical period the German government renewed its efforts to draw the British into an agreement, but quite without success. Hatzfeldt was obliged to report from London that Salisbury would do nothing and that he was not disposed to make any sacrifices for German good will.[42] At this juncture a curious interlude took place in the relations of the two powers. Cecil Rhodes entered upon the scene. He had come to London in the interest of the Cape-to-Cairo telegraph and railway scheme, to which he was the more closely wedded since Kitchener had wired him from Khartum: "I have founded a post to the south of Fashoda. When are you coming up?"[43] Rhodes was trying to raise a loan of £2,000,000 to extend his railway from Bulawayo to Lake Tanganyika, and attempted, though in vain, to get a government guarantee, so that the money could be got at 3% rather than at 5%. At the same time he was confronted with the problem of running the telegraph and railway from the northern end of Lake Tanganyika to Uganda and the Sudan. This section would have to pass either through the Belgian Congo or through German East Africa. To make the necessary arrangements Rhodes went to Brussels. But Leopold was unwilling to make a deal, excepting on condition that the Bahr-el-Ghazal should be left to him as arranged in the Congo Treaty of 1894.[44]

In the meanwhile the German colonial office had been considering the possibility of enlisting the aid of Rhodes to settle the Samoan business. It was believed that he would be able to influence Chamberlain, who was as obdurate about Samoa as was Salisbury. Rhodes was invited to Berlin, where he was received by the Emperor on March 10. The audience was quite informal, and

[40] Tyler Dennett: *John Hay* (New York, 1933), p. 281; *British Documents,* III, p. 423, opinion of Lord Sanderson. The documents on the subject are in *Die Grosse Politik,* XIV, nos. 4028 ff., and the *British Documents,* I, nos. 127 ff.

[41] *Die Grosse Politik,* XIV, nos. 4041, 4042; Hermann Leusser: "Ein Jahrzehnt Deutsch-Amerikanischer Politik, 1897–1906 " (*Beiheft 13 der Historischen Zeitschrift,* Munich, 1928), p. 35.

[42] *Die Grosse Politik,* XIV, no. 4044.

[43] W. T. Stead, in the *Review of Reviews,* October 15, 1898, p. 332. Stead had the story from Rhodes himself.

[44] W. T. Stead, in the *Review of Reviews,* April 15, 1899, p. 312; November 15, 1899, p. 442; Basil Williams: *Cecil Rhodes* (London, 1921), p. 310; *Letters of Queen Victoria,* III, pp. 349–51.

the two men made a most favorable impression upon each other. Within three days an agreement was reached to run the telegraph line through German East Africa. Negotiations for the railway transit were to be undertaken when the time came. Almost overnight Rhodes became an enthusiastic supporter of the Emperor and a warm advocate of Anglo-German co-operation. When told about the Samoan friction he was beside himself and promised to do his utmost to bring his government to reason.[45]

Apparently Rhodes was unable to accomplish much in London. The Germans were quite wrong in thinking that he could influence either Salisbury or Chamberlain. The colonial secretary distrusted him and had no intention of listening to him on matters touching south Africa or any other question.[46] During the second half of March and the first half of April relations between Germany and England were badly strained. At Berlin it was felt that the British were trying to use the Americans to help them get rid of the Germans in the Samoan business. An effort was therefore made to settle with the Americans. The United States government, as before, made no objection. It let fall a suggestion for a tripartite investigating commission and at once accepted the proposal when the German government put it forward. Salisbury, however, would agree to the proposal only on the understanding that decisions might be made by the commission by majority vote, which was contrary to the unanimity rule provided for in the Berlin Act. Acrimonious discussion followed. Bülow finally told the British ambassador that the whole affair threatened " to very seriously impair the good relations," between the two countries. The Germans had determined to break off diplomatic relations if the British remained obdurate. Some inkling of this was undoubtedly allowed to reach high circles in London, and finally Salisbury yielded. The commission was appointed and arrived at Apia on May 13.[47]

In the course of the negotiations the German ambassador reported that Salisbury no longer had any use for the Germans and that England was so cocksure since the Fashoda victory that she did not even fear a coalition organized against her.[48] On both sides there were recriminations. Queen Victoria wrote to her grandson complaining of the virulence of the German press, to which the Emperor replied by bitter accusations of inconsiderate treatment by Lord Salisbury. " He knew," he said to the British ambassador, " that England was powerful and Germany weak at sea, and therefore the former could

---

[45] See first of all Rhodes' account of the meeting in Vindex: *Cecil Rhodes* (London, 1900), pp. 707 ff.; also Michell: *Life of Rhodes*, II, p. 256; *Die Grosse Politik*, XIV, nos. 4045–7; Wilhelm II: *Ereignisse und Gestalten* (Leipzig, 1922), pp. 72–4; Bülow: *Memoirs*, I, pp. 338–9, 409; Hermann Freiherr von Eckardstein: *Lebenserinnerungen und Politische Denkwürdigkeiten* (Leipzig, 1919), I, pp. 314–6; Karl F. Nowak: *Germany's Road to Ruin* (New York, 1932), pp. 205 ff.

[46] Garvin, op. cit., III, pp. 329 ff.

[47] *Die Grosse Politik*, XIV, nos. 4049 ff.; *British Documents*, I, nos. 133 ff.; Eckardstein, op. cit., II, p. 15.

[48] *Die Grosse Politik*, XIV, nos. 4067, 4071.

act with impunity, but the time would come when even England would have to consider the German fleet as an important factor, and he only hoped that it would not then be too late, and that Germany would not by that time have formed other combinations which would certainly not be agreeable to England, but which she would have brought upon herself by the constant disregard and contempt with which she treated German interests." These veiled threats were not calculated to appease Salisbury. The Queen sent a reply in which she pointed out that no government had ever spoken to another as had the German to the British; she enclosed a memorandum in which the prime minister refuted the charges brought against him. By June 1899 Anglo-German relations were at low ebb. The Emperor's plan of coming to the races at Cowes was given up and the atmosphere was frigid.[49]

But forces were working on both sides to save the situation. Bülow was genuinely anxious to avoid hostility, while Balfour and Chamberlain also were eager to maintain good relations.[50] In mid-July the report of the Samoan commission was published, recommending, among other things, that the islands be placed under the direct rule of a single power. It was understood that Tutuila and Manua should go to the United States. The real question was how the other two islands, Upolu and Savaii (the latter being quite worthless) should be divided between England and Germany. The crisis in south Africa was now rapidly coming to a head, and it was to the interest of the British to cultivate the Germans as much as possible. The Emperor William was therefore invited to pay a visit to England in November, and discussions regarding Samoa were resumed. The Germans at first suggested that the possession of Upolu be decided by an impartial arbitrator, but it was impossible to agree on the terms of reference. Then a scheme was worked out by which the Germans should leave Upolu to Britain, taking in return for their rights either British New Guinea or the Solomon Islands, or Savaii, the Savage Islands and the Tongas. Salisbury kept temporizing and complaining that too much was being asked and in the end the plan failed because of Tirpitz' insistence that the Germans keep Upolu and the harbor of Apia.

It is hardly necessary to go into the details of these dreary negotiations or to examine the innumerable deals that were suggested now by one side, now by the other. The Germans throughout insisted that the negotiations be brought to a satisfactory conclusion before the Emperor visited England. Ultimately Salisbury withdrew entirely from the discussions, which were carried on by Chamberlain and Baron Eckardstein, who acted for the German ambassador. With the application of considerable pressure the matter was finally wound up on November 1, 1899. Under the terms of the agreement Germany was assigned Upolu and Savaii, while the British received the Tonga Islands, Savage

---

[49] *Die Grosse Politik*, XIV, nos. 4074, 4076; Sir Sidney Lee: *Edward VII*, I, pp. 743 ff.; *Letters of Queen Victoria*, III, pp. 357–9, 375 ff.; *British Documents*, I, no. 141.

[50] *Die Grosse Politik*, XIV, nos. 4072, 4075, 4079.

Islands, some of the lesser islands in the Solomon group and a disputed area in Togoland.[51]

" The whole of Samoa," said a high official of the German foreign office on one occasion, " was not worth the money spent upon telegrams to and from Apia." [52] It was most unfortunate that this relatively insignificant matter should have arisen to disturb the relations of two great European powers, the more so as there were particular difficulties inherent in it. The Germans had a sentimental attachment to the place, for it was one of the very first fields of German colonial enterprise and they had a real investment in the islands. On the British side there was the perpetual problem of dominion interest. The Australians and particularly the New Zealanders had long had their eyes on the archipelago and were dead opposed to Britain's abandoning it. But beyond these factors were others which embittered the whole transaction. The Germans, having entered late upon the colonial scene, were eager to get something almost anywhere. They had distinctly the feeling that Britain ought to recognize their strong position and ought to buy them off from any continental coalition. The British, on the other hand, were filled with self-assurance after their Fashoda victory. They resented the policy of blackmail and saw no reason for making concessions to Germany, especially as Germany was less dangerous as a sea power than France and Russia. " The policy of the German Empire since Bismarck," wrote Chamberlain to Salisbury in September, " has been always one of undisguised blackmail." [53] He had used the same word a year before in connexion with the Portuguese negotiations. It was now becoming a fixed idea in the foreign office. On the German side, at the same time, there grew up the idea of English malevolence. There was at least a grain of truth in the Emperor William's bitter remark to the British military attaché: " You make any concessions asked for by France and Russia, you cede half continents to them, but when Germany asks for an island, two-thirds of which has been planted over by her subjects, she is met by a refusal." [54] Add to all this the personal ill will and pique of Lord Salisbury and the situation was as unsatisfactory as it well could be. Had the Boer War not broken out in October 1899 the Samoan affair might have taken on an even more sinister aspect. As it was, Germany's friendship had suddenly become of first-rate importance, and even Salisbury felt obliged to accept a settlement against which he had fought for months.

Possibly Lord Salisbury found some inner satisfaction in concluding at this time another agreement which was a severe blow at German hopes, though at the time the Germans did not know it. This agreement was the so-called Windsor Treaty of October 14, 1899, between England and Portugal. The

---

[51] The negotiations may be followed in *Die Grosse Politik,* XIV, nos. 4081 ff.; *British Documents,* I, nos. 146 ff.; Eckardstein, op. cit., II, chaps. i and ii; Garvin, op. cit., III, pp. 334 ff.

[52] *British Documents,* I, no. 128.

[53] Garvin, op. cit., III, p. 334.   [54] *British Documents,* I, no. 154.

British had bought off German interests in Delagoa Bay by the agreement of August 1898, but this did not give them immediate control of the famous harbor. In fact, the Transvaal was importing large stocks of arms and munitions by way of Lorenzo Marques, and the Portuguese government replied to British protests in July 1899 that the Transvaal was entitled to do so under the terms of a convention signed in 1875. The truth was that the Portuguese were by no means well disposed toward the British. The fact of the Anglo-German agreement had been allowed to leak out in the press and it caused all sorts of apprehensions. It is fairly certain that the Portuguese minister in London, Marquis de Soveral, who was a close personal friend of the Prince of Wales, knew a good deal about the terms of the Treaty, if not all the details.[55] It was therefore to the interest of the Portuguese to avert the danger to their empire as best they might.

On September 13 Soveral suggested to Salisbury a close alliance for the event of war with the Transvaal. This, he pointed out, would enable Britain to use Delagoa Bay for her own purposes. The British prime minister agreed almost at once to an offensive and defensive alliance against the Transvaal, even on the understanding that Portugal should not actually declare war. There was some discussion as to the form of the agreement, but finally Salisbury's suggestion, that the words of earlier treaties be used, was adopted. The Anglo-Portuguese Secret Declaration (there is no justification for the name *Windsor Treaty*) was signed on October 14. It renewed the treaties of 1642 and 1661, which involved a mutual guarantee of territory, and included a Portuguese promise not to let arms pass through Lorenzo Marques to the Transvaal, or to declare neutrality, which would have made it impossible for British warships to coal in the port.[56]

Sir Arthur Nicolson once described the Portuguese policy of the British government in 1898 and 1899 as " the most cynical business that I have come across in my whole experience of diplomacy." He could not see how England could agree in 1898 to partition with Germany the possessions of a power which, under the terms of former treaties, Britain was obliged to defend and maintain intact.[57] This was one side of the story, which dealt with the agreement of 1898. Hardly less reprehensible was the British policy in 1899, for, having concluded the partition treaty with Germany, Salisbury then turned back to the old treaties of guarantee and subscribed to a new declaration which completely nullified the agreement of August 1898. The partition treaty was not in keeping with Britain's obligations to Portugal, and the declaration of 1899 was incompatible with *it*.[58] Of course it may be argued that Britain did not want to

---

[55] The evidence for this statement is well examined in Fritz Schwarze: *Das Deutsch-Englische Abkommen über die Portugiesischen Kolonien* (Göttingen, 1931), pp. 75–7.

[56] For the negotiations see *British Documents*, I, nos. 111–8; Schwarze, op. cit., pp. 77 ff.

[57] Harold Nicolson: *Portrait of a Diplomatist* (New York, 1930), p. 393.

[58] On this point see especially the keen analysis by Schwarze, op. cit., pp. 84 ff. Grey admitted in 1913 that there was a " crying contradiction " between them.

partition the Portuguese colonies, and that she was more or less forced into the agreement with Germany by the insistence of the Germans themselves. This is the line taken by Mr. Garvin in his recent biography of Chamberlain. It may also be argued that the declaration of 1899 was necessitated by the situation in south Africa. Delagoa Bay, according to Milner, had become " absolutely the decisive point." [59] But even these considerations do not exonerate the British foreign office of the charge that on two occasions it played a questionable game, first with Portugal, then with Germany. If the Germans made too much of their chance in the Samoan business, the British evened the account by emasculating an agreement on which the Germans had placed the highest hopes.

BIBLIOGRAPHICAL NOTE

DOCUMENTARY SOURCES

Die Grosse Politik der Europäischen Kabinette, 1871–1914. Volume XIV, chapter xcvi: The Samoan Question. Volume XV, chapter ci: The Origins of the Boer War.

British Documents on the Origins of the War, 1898–1914. Volume I, chapter ii: Great Britain, Germany and Portugal, 1898–1899; chapter iii: Great Britain, Germany and Samoa; chapter vii: The South African War.

Accounts and Papers. There is a large series of papers relating to south Africa, of which the chief ones, with the command numbers, are the following: 1898, vol. LX: C. 8721, *Further Correspondence relating to Affairs in the South Africa Republic.* 1899, vol. LXIV: C. 9317, *Correspondence relating to the Explosives Monopoly in the South African Republic;* C. 9345, *Papers relating to the Complaints of British Subjects in the South African Republic;* C. 9404, *Correspondence relating to the Bloemfontein Conference;* C. 9415, *Further Correspondence relating to Proposed Political Reforms in the South African Republic;* C. 9507, *Correspondence relating to the Status of the South African Republic;* C. 9518, *Further Correspondence relating to the Proposed Political Reforms in the South African Republic;* C. 9521, *Further Correspondence relating to Political Affairs in the South African Republic;* C. 9530, *Further Correspondence relating to Political Affairs in the South African Republic.* 1900, vol. LVI: C. 18, *Correspondence relating to the Despatch of Colonial Military Contingents to South Africa.*

MEMOIRS, AUTOBIOGRAPHIES, BIOGRAPHIES, AND LETTERS

The Milner Papers. South Africa, 1897–1899. Edited by Cecil Headlam. London, 1931. A most important collection of correspondence, containing many letters exchanged by Milner and Chamberlain.

---

[59] *Milner Papers,* II, p. 32.

GARVIN, J. L.: *The Life of Joseph Chamberlain*. London, 1933—. The third volume contains a long and eloquent defense of Chamberlain's policy, but adds relatively little of a factual nature. Not as important as the *Milner Papers*.

Letters of Queen Victoria. Edited by George E. Buckle. Series III, volume III. London, 1932. Valuable, especially for the light they throw on proceedings in the British cabinet.

KRUGER, PAUL: *The Memoirs of Paul Kruger*. New York, 1902. Gives the Boer side, without adding much of importance.

FITZPATRICK, SIR J. PERCY: *South African Memories*. London, 1932. The recollections of the famous author of *The Transvaal from Within,* who was one of the outstanding representatives of the Uitlanders.

BUTLER, SIR W.: *Autobiography of Sir William Butler*. London, 1911. The author was commander of the forces in south Africa during the years 1898 and 1899. He is very critical of the Uitlander agitation and has much to say for the Boer viewpoint.

COOK, E. T.: *Edmund Garrett, a Memoir*. London, 1909. An illuminating study of the editor of the *Cape Times,* with many sidelights on the development of the situation.

HOFMEYR, J. H.: *The Life of Jan Hendrik Hofmeyr*. Capetown, 1913. A valuable biography of the leader of the Afrikander Bond, and an outstanding contribution to the history of south African politics.

LEYDS, W. J.: *Eenige Correspondentie uit 1899*. The Hague, 1919. The reports of Leyds from Europe. Important for the international side of the crisis.

WALKER, ERIC A.: *Lord de Villiers and his Times*. London, 1925. Another important contribution, containing many letters by the chief actors in the south African drama.

VAN DER MERWE, N. J.: *Marthinus Theunis Steyn*. Two volumes. Capetown, 1921. The biography of the president of the Orange Free State, who played an important part as mediator.

ECKARDSTEIN, HERMANN FREIHERR VON: *Lebenserinnerungen und Politische Denkwürdigkeiten*. Two volumes. Leipzig, 1919–1920. The sensational memoirs of a German diplomat, to be used with great caution, but containing much material, especially on the Samoan negotiations.

SPECIAL STUDIES: THE AFRICAN SITUATION

COOK, E. T.: *Rights and Wrongs of the Transvaal War*. New edition, London, 1902. One of the best analyses from a viewpoint favorable to the government.

HOBSON, J. A.: *The War in South Africa*. London, 1900. Perhaps the ablest critique of the British policy, with special reference to the capitalists.

FITZPATRICK, J. PERCY: *The Transvaal from Within*. London, 1899. The best-known contemporary account of the Uitlander problem.

BRYCE, JAMES: *Impressions of South Africa*. London, 1899. A vivid and searching contemporary analysis.

BOTHA, P. R.: *Die Staatkundige Ontwikkeling van die Suid-Afrikaanse Republiek onder Krüger en Leyds*. Capetown, 1926. The best scholarly study from the Boer side.

WALKER, ERIC A.: *A History of South Africa*. London, 1928. A sound, well-balanced and scholarly book, but rather unreadable.

WÜD, JOHANNES A.: *Die Rolle der Burenrepubliken in der Auswärtigen und Kolonialen Politik des Deutschen Reiches in den Jahren 1883–1900*. Nürnberg, 1927. A dissertation which brings together most of the material on German policy.

LOVELL, REGINALD I.: *The Struggle for South Africa, 1875–1899*. New York, 1934. The most recent and on the whole the best critical scholarly account of the development of the crisis.

SCHWARZE, FRITZ: *Das Deutsch-Englische Abkommen über die Portugiesischen Kolonien vom 30 August 1898*. Göttingen, 1931. An unusually able and keenly analytical study of the Portuguese problem.

SPECIAL STUDIES: THE SAMOAN QUESTION

HENDERSON, JOHN B.: *American Diplomatic Questions*. New York, 1901. Contains a detailed discussion of the problem as seen from the American angle.

MARQUARDT, CARL: *Zur Lösung der Samoafrage*. Berlin, 1899. The account of one of the German officials in the islands.

LEUSSER, HERMANN: "Ein Jahrzehnt Deutsch-Amerikanischer Politik, 1897–1906." (*Beiheft no. 13 der Historischen Zeitschrift*). Munich, 1928. Contains a succinct account of the problem, with reference to the German-American relationship.

DENNIS, ALFRED L. P.: *Adventures in American Diplomacy, 1896–1906*. New York, 1928. Contains a brief discussion of the problem and makes use of some unpublished American material.

XIX

The Bagdad Railway Project

✍

WHILE THE BRITISH WERE GIRDING THEMSELVES FOR THE CONFLICT IN south Africa, an important though little noticed event took place in the Near East. On November 25, 1899 the Sultan signed a preliminary concession granting a German company the right to construct a railway to Bagdad and Basra. This concession was the consummation of a policy that went back a full decade and that introduced an entirely new factor into European international relations. The development of German interests in the Ottoman Empire was to become a crucial issue of European politics; it was to influence profoundly the relations between Germany on the one hand and England and Russia on the other. It is therefore essential that some account of its earlier stages be given here, the more so as its implications were already recognized by the powers when the preliminary concession was awarded.

The story of the Bagdad Railway scheme may be said to go back to the time just before the Crimean War. The British, ever deeply interested in the problem of communications with India, had in the 1830's sent out a very capable officer, Colonel Chesney, to explore the Euphrates River and report on its navigability. His report was extremely favorable, and one of his party, Captain Lynch, opened up steamship traffic as far as Bagdad in the succeeding decade. It was the heyday of European railway building, and it is therefore not to be wondered at that phantastic schemes cropped up for opening up the whole east to British commerce. In 1842 Mr. William Pare, of the Seville Ironworks in Dublin, put forward a plan for a railway to run from Calais to Constantinople, and thence to Calcutta and Peking! The very next year Mr. Alexander Campbell proposed to the British East India Company a railway to run from Ostend by way of Vienna and Belgrade to Constantinople and thence across Asia Minor to Aleppo, along the Euphrates and the coast of Persia to Kurrachee and Calcutta. A similar scheme was put forward in 1851 by James B. Thomson, who spent many years collecting data and ultimately secured the favorable consideration of the Porte as well as the support of Lord Stratford de Redcliffe.[1]

---

[1] F. R. Chesney: *Narrative of the Euphrates Expedition* (London, 1868); William P. Andrew: *Memoir on the Euphrates Valley Route to India* (London, 1857), p. 6. Many of the early projects are catalogued and discussed in Noel Verney and George Dambmann: *Les Puissances Étrangères dans le Levant* (Paris, 1900), pp. 293 ff.; but by far the best critical account is that of Halford L. Hoskins: *British Routes to India* (Philadelphia, 1928), especially pp. 148 ff., 327 ff.

On the close of the Crimean War the project was taken up by William P. Andrew, chairman of the Sindh Railroad, who, together with Chesney, put forward a more modest plan for a railway from Suedia (Seleucia) on the Gulf of Alexandretta to Jaber Castle on the upper Euphrates, a distance of some eighty miles. This line was intended to connect with steamer service on the Euphrates, though it was planned to extend the road ultimately to Bagdad and Basra (Bussorah), where ocean-going ships could call. A Euphrates Valley Railway Company was formed, and Lord Stratford helped it secure a 6% guarantee from the Turkish government, which at that time was still enthusiastically encouraging foreign enterprise and capital investment. An active campaign was carried on in England, Andrew stressing the value to Turkey of developing the formerly rich territories of Mesopotamia, and the commercial and strategic value to England of a short route to India. Andrew's book is colored throughout by suspicion of Russian designs in Armenia and Persia and the need for frustrating them.[2] But the plan fell through because Lord Palmerston, probably out of consideration for Napoleon III, could not be brought to consent to a British government guarantee, which was regarded as indispensable.[3]

Nothing further was done with regard to Asiatic railways until after the Franco-Prussian War, though in 1856 and in 1863 British interests were granted concessions for lines from Smyrna to Aidin and Cassaba respectively. The whole idea of a railway from the Syrian coast was dealt a severe blow by the studies of the eminent Austrian engineer, Wilhelm von Pressel, who made careful surveys for the Sultan in the years 1872–1874. Pressel finally recommended a network of railways totalling 6000 kilometers. The trunk line was to run from Haidar Pasha (opposite Constantinople) through Angora, Diarbekr and Mosul to Bagdad and Basra, with branches to Eskishehr, Kutahia, Konia and other places. Pressel's opinion was that a line from Syria running through the desert and through the barren area along the middle Euphrates could never be made a paying proposition. A more northerly route through Anatolia would tap richer provinces, which should be colonized. He suggested the settlement of some two million Germans along the line in order to hasten the development of the country.[4]

We may assume from the attitude of the Sultan later that he was not much taken with the idea of a large-scale immigration, but for the rest the report of

---

[2] Andrew, op. cit., especially pp. 2, 18, 124; Hoskins, op. cit., pp. 330 ff.

[3] The address of the deputation to Palmerston is given in W. P. Andrew: *Euphrates Valley Route to India* (London, 1882), pp. 64 ff. In addition to the excellent account of Hoskins, op. cit., pp. 330 ff., some discussion of these projects may be found in the anonymously published article of Alwyn Parker: "The Bagdad Railway Negotiations" (*Quarterly Review*, October, 1917, pp. 487–528), p. 489, and in Edward M. Earle: *Turkey, the Great Powers and the Bagdad Railway* (New York, 1924), pp. 176 ff.

[4] Wilhelm von Pressel: *Les Chemins de Fer en Turquie d'Asie* (Zürich, 1902), passim. See also the excellent analytical account of A. von Schweiger-Lerchenfeld: "Die Euphrat-Thal Bahn und kein Ende" (*Oesterreichische Monatsschrift für den Orient*, IX, March 15, 1883, pp. 45–51), who analyzes the report of von Pressel.

von Pressel became the general guide of the Turkish government. Work was at once begun on the first section of the line, from Haidar Pasha to Ismid, and this section, when completed, was turned over to a British company for exploitation. Just before Pressel made his investigations, the English government had indicated a renewed interest in the problem of land communication with India. The Suez Canal was finished, but that was a French undertaking and many Englishmen felt that there ought to be some alternative route under British control. A select committee of the house of commons was therefore appointed to " examine and report upon the whole subject of railway communication between the Mediterranean, the Black Sea and the Persian Gulf." It heard much evidence and many suggestions and finally recommended a line from Alexandretta or Suedia to Bagdad, Basra and Kuwait. It was pointed out that the Euphrates route would secure speedier transportation of mail and would provide a second and safer route for the conveyance of troops to India. The line would serve further to block any Russian advance towards the Persian Gulf, to say nothing of the great commercial advantages it would confer on England and India. The Committee pointed out, however, that sufficient traffic could not be expected soon, and that a government guarantee would be necessary. This guarantee the government refused to give in 1872 as in 1857.[5]

The matter came once more to an active stage in the years following the Russian-Turkish War and the Treaty of Berlin. Abdul Hamid had seen for himself the tremendous value of railways for the transport of troops, and the need for better communications if the Empire was to be held together. There can be no doubt whatever that throughout the succeeding years his railroad policy was based almost entirely upon military and political considerations. The British government, too, was interested in maintaining the Ottoman Empire as a bulwark against Russia. The Cyprus Convention and the whole program of reform in Asia Minor were designed with this idea in mind. Disraeli seems to have chosen Cyprus with the thought that it would serve to protect a railroad terminus on the Gulf of Alexandretta. He is said to have told Bismarck as much during the Berlin Congress, and to have had a high military officer trace a possible route.[6] In any event the subject was much debated in England, and an influential association, the so-called Stafford House Committee, began to elaborate schemes for a line from Constantinople to Alexandretta and thence to the Persian Gulf. The Sultan was anxious for action, but the plan died a lingering death, for reasons that are not wholly clear. The British occupation of Egypt in 1882 led to a distinct cooling in English relations with the Porte, and this fact may have had something to do with the disappearance of the scheme.[7]

---

[5] The report of the Select Committee is given in Andrew: *Euphrates Valley Route,* pp. 75 ff. See further Parker, op. cit., p. 490; David Fraser: *The Short Cut to India* (London, 1909), pp. 32 ff.; and especially Hoskins, op. cit., pp. 428 ff.

[6] Andrew: *Euphrates Valley Route,* p. 45; Hoskins, op. cit., pp. 439 ff.; and the interesting observations of Parker, op. cit., p. 490.

[7] See especially Andrew, op. cit., passim; D. G. Hogarth: " The Bagdad Railway " (*National*

In the meanwhile the Germans were showing increasing interest in Turkey, more particularly in its possibilities as a field for economic penetration. In the days of Chesney's explorations von Moltke, who was then in Turkish service, had called attention to these possibilities, and his views had been echoed by later mid-century writers, like Rodbertus and Roscher. In the 1880's there was a considerable body of German writing calling attention to Anatolia as a suitable territory for German colonization.[8] Bismarck, however, was not prepared to favor any activity that might estrange Russia and he therefore never went beyond giving consent for the mission of von der Goltz as instructor for the Turkish army.[9]

In 1888 the European trunk line was completed to Constantinople and the first train from Vienna entered the Turkish capital. The Sultan was more eager than ever to develop the Anatolian network, and to knit up the outlying provinces of Mesopotamia and Syria with the rest of the Empire. He had tried, through Pressel, to interest German financiers in 1885, but without success. In 1886 he approached the British company which ran the Haidar Pasha-Ismid Railway with a proposal that it extend the line to Angora and ultimately to Bagdad. For unknown reasons nothing came of these advances.[10] Nevertheless concessions were granted in 1888 for the extension of the Smyrna-Aidin and Smyrna-Cassaba lines, and the question of a railroad to Bagdad was very much to the fore. The British showed little interest; political relations were bad and London bankers had no confidence in Turkish finances. Furthermore, they looked upon the project primarily from the business angle and saw but little chance of an Anatolian line paying a reasonable return. The best policy, they held, would be to extend gradually the existing lines as conditions warranted.[11] The French, on the other hand, were very much interested. They had an enormous investment in Turkey already, and they controlled the Ottoman Bank, on which the Turkish government had to rely for financial aid. So strong, indeed, was their financial position that it had become irksome to the Sultan. He was determined not only not to grant them further concessions, but if possible to

---

Review, May, 1902, pp. 462–73); Hoskins, op. cit., pp. 441 ff. All previous accounts of this phase of the problem are now superseded by the thorough and illuminating study of Dwight E. Lee: *Great Britain and the Cyprus Convention Policy of 1878* (Cambridge, 1934), pp. 66 ff., 76 ff., and especially pp. 125 ff.

8 Paul Dehn: *Deutschland und die Orientbahnen* (Munich, 1883); K. A. Sprenger: *Babylonien, das Reichste Land in der Vorzeit und das Lohnendste Kolonisationsfeld für die Gegenwart* (Heidelberg, 1886); Loehnis: *Beiträge zur Kenntniss der Levante* (Leipzig, 1882); Karl Kaerger: *Kleinasien, ein Deutsches Kolonisationsfeld* (Berlin, 1892); Edmund Naumann: *Vom Goldenen Horn zu den Quellen des Euphrates* (Munich, 1893). See further André Chéradame: *Le Chemin de Fer de Bagdad* (Paris, 1903), pp. 2–5; Georges Gaulis: *La Ruine d'un Empire* (Paris, 1913), p. 127; Earle, op. cit., p. 123.

9 His attitude is discussed at length by Hajo Holborn: *Deutschland und die Türkei, 1878–1890* (Berlin, 1926), pp. 83 ff.

10 Earle, op. cit., p. 31; Karl von Helfferich: *Georg von Siemens* (Berlin, 1923), III, pp. 28 ff.

11 *Turkey No. 4 (1896), Report by Major Law on Railways in Asiatic Turkey*, passim; Parker, op. cit., p. 493.

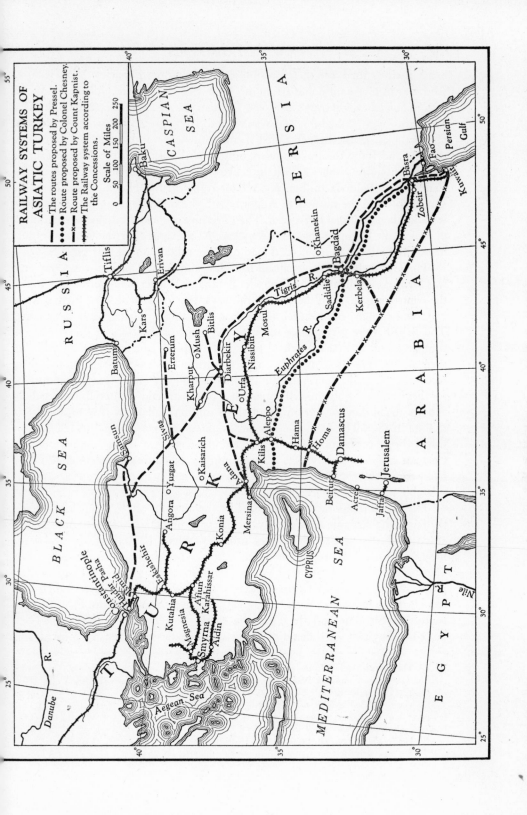

RAILWAY SYSTEMS OF
ASIATIC TURKEY

- - - The routes proposed by Pressel.
••••• Route proposed by Colonel Chesney.
×××× Route proposed by Count Kapnist.
——— The Railway system according to
the Concessions.

Scale of Miles
0   50 100 150 200 250

CASPIAN SEA

PERSIA

RUSSIA

Baku
Tiflis
Erivan
Kars
Batum
Erzerum
Mush
Bitlis
Kharput
Diarbekir
Nissibin
oUrfa
Mosul
oKhanekin
Bagdad
Sadidie
Kerbela
Zobeir
Basra
Fao
Persian Gulf
Kuwait

T U R K E Y

Samsun
Sivas
Angora
Yuzgat
oKaisarich
Adana
Kilis
Aleppo
Hama
Homs
Damascus
Beirut
Acre
Jaffa
Jerusalem

Tigris R.
Euphrates R.

A R A B I A

BLACK SEA

Constantinople
Ismid Pasha
Eskischir
Kutahia
Magnesia
Smyrna
Aidin
Afiun Karahissar
Konia
Mersina

MEDITERRANEAN SEA

CYPRUS

E G Y P T

Nile R.

Danube R.

Aegean Sea

break their control. He therefore interested a German financier, Herr Kaulla, who was in Constantinople arranging for a large sale of munitions. Kaulla in turn managed to win over Georg von Siemens, head of the Deutsche Bank. The concession was applied for, and was vigorously supported by the "conspirators of Therapia," as the French called them, namely the ambassadors of England, Austria and Italy, the three powers united at that time in the Mediterranean Agreements. On October 4, 1888 the concession went to Kaulla and the Deutsche Bank, which paid six million pounds for rights in the Haidar Pasha line and agreed to build the railway to Angora, with the understanding that ultimately it should be continued to Bagdad. The government gave a kilometric guarantee to protect the Company against heavy loss. At the same time the German group made the Sultan a much-needed loan of some million and a half pounds.[12]

The Germans now went ahead full blast. An Anatolian Railway Company was formed, and in 1889 the Deutsche Bank and Wiener Bankverein purchased the controlling share in the Balkan railways. In 1890 a Bank for Oriental Railways was established at Zurich to serve as a holding company for both systems. The British were given three seats on the board of directors of the Anatolian company, and at first subscribed part of the capital. But in 1890 they sold out their shares. The Italians took no part, fearing French reprisals upon Italian securities.[13] For the Germans the Anatolian Railway was a good proposition, for they were now able to sell a good deal of construction material. In fact their exports to Turkey rose from about three million dollars in 1888 to about ten million in 1893. The Deutsche Levante Linie, which was opened in 1889, established direct communication by water and became an important part of the German commercial advance. A large number of German traders engaged in lively competition with the British and French, and before long captured a considerable part of the market.[14]

The line to Angora was completed by the autumn of 1892. But long before that time the struggle between rival concessionaires had been resumed. In the autumn of 1891 a French-Belgian group, probably backed by the Russians, brought forward a project for a line across Anatolia north and south, from Samsun on the Black Sea to Aleppo. The Sultan was greatly alarmed by this proposal and invited the German interests to apply for an extension of their line from Angora by way of Sivas to Bagdad. Engineers were sent out to survey the route, but Siemens and the Deutsche Bank showed little enthusiasm. They lacked money and the difficulties of the terrain indicated expensive construction

---

12 The French interest in the scheme is reflected in such writings as Jean Blomdus: "La Lutte pour les Communications avec l'Asie" (*Journal des Sciences Militaires*, Series IX, vol. XVIII, 1885, pp. 65–93); Alexander Bérard: *La Route de l'Inde par la Vallée du Tigre et de l'Euphrate* (Lyon, 1887). The concession may be found in George Young: *Corps de Droit Ottoman* (Oxford, 1906), IV, pp. 120 ff. On the negotiations see Helfferich, op. cit., III, pp. 26 ff.; Earle, op. cit., pp. 31 ff.; Holborn: *Deutschland und die Türkei*, pp. 83 ff.

13 Helfferich, op. cit., III, pp. 40–1, 51; Holborn, op. cit., p. 105.

14 See especially Georges Gaulis: *La Ruine d'un Empire*, pp. 135 ff.

work. At best they were willing to consider a somewhat more southerly route, from Angora to Bagdad by way of Kaisarieh and Kharput, but they preferred building a long branch from the Angora line through Afiun Karahissar to the rich area around Konia.[15]

The matter dragged on. Abdul Hamid appealed to the Emperor William to support his scheme. William had paid an historic visit to the Sultan in 1889, and, unlike Bismarck, was profoundly interested in the Near East and its possibilities.[16] But even his approval failed to move the German bankers, who looked upon the whole affair from the business standpoint and saw little profit in a line which, after all, was designed for strategic rather than for economic purposes.

Negotiations took a new turn when, in the last months of 1892, the French-Belgian interests, who were arranging the purchase of the Smyrna-Cassaba line from the British, applied for an extension of this line to Konia. The Germans, in alarm, now pressed their own project for a line to Konia, and expressed readiness to build the Angora-Sivas-Bagdad route also. Abdul Hamid was much pleased and the bargain would undoubtedly have been closed at once, excepting for the fact that the British ambassador, Sir Clare Ford, quite unexpectedly registered a vigorous protest. The German Konia line, he argued, would injure the British Smyrna-Aidin line, which was the natural outlet for the products of the Konia region. This British opposition created quite a flurry for a time. The German government intervened and used strong language in London. Ultimately it even threatened to withdraw its support of British policy in Egypt. The moment was a critical one in Egypt and Lord Cromer used all his influence to induce the government to give in. Rosebery disclaimed any knowledge of the affair or any desire to antagonize the Germans. " Her Majesty's government," he wrote, " have no desire to take any step inimical to German influence or interest at Constantinople." Ford was obliged to desist from his protests, and on February 15, 1893 the Germans secured their concession.[17]

The concession of February 1893 provided for the construction of two lines: one from Eskishehr to Konia, which was to be built at once, and another from Angora to Kaisarieh. This second line was to be extended from Kaisarieh to Sivas as soon as the Haidar Pasha-Angora line showed receipts of 15,000 francs per kilometer for three consecutive years. It was to continue to Diarbekr and Bagdad as soon as the other German lines showed receipts large enough to enable them to dispense with the government guarantee. But the Turkish government reserved the right to demand at any time the prolongation of the line from Kaisarieh to Bagdad, making the necessary arrangements for guarantee.[18]

[15] *Die Grosse Politik*, XIV, nos. 3939 ff.; Helfferich, op. cit., III, pp. 58 ff.

[16] See especially Josef Maria von Radowitz: *Aufzeichnungen und Erinnerungen* (Berlin, 1925), II, pp. 249, 287, 288, 300–7.

[17] Helfferich, op. cit., III, pp. 62–9; *The Memoirs of Ismail Kemal Bey* (London, 1920), pp. 239 ff.; *Die Grosse Politik*, VIII, nos. 1816 ff.; XIV, nos. 3963 ff.; Parker, op. cit., pp. 499–500.

[18] Young: *Corps de Droit Ottoman*, IV, p. 147.

For some reason, however, only the Eskishehr-Konia line was built. The Sultan was chiefly interested in the Angora-Sivas-Bagdad scheme, but the terrain was difficult and the Germans did not promise themselves much profit from it. It has been said by many writers that this northern route was abandoned because of Russian protests, but there is no evidence of this. That the Russians were unfavorable to German enterprise in Anatolia even in 1893 is borne out by the German documents, but their opposition seems to have been to the general strengthening of Turkey by the development of communications, rather than to any particular line. It is perfectly obvious, of course, that they could not approve of a line which would have facilitated Turkish mobilization in the Erzerum area, but no material at present available shows any actual protest in 1893, and it seems more likely that the Kaisarieh-Sivas-Bagdad route was not constructed because the Germans were not interested in it.[19]

The railroad from Eskishehr to Konia was completed in 1896, but in the years from 1894 to 1898 little interest was shown in Europe in any scheme of Turkish development. It was the time of the great Armenian massacres. Abdul Hamid was generally hated and the European public, far from wishing to strengthen his position, hoped for his deposition and expected the collapse of his empire. Furthermore, these were years of poor crops in Anatolia. The existing railroads were not paying and with money tight in London, Paris and Berlin there was no prospect of further construction. The Sultan kept urging his Angora-Bagdad project upon the German bankers, but they lacked both interest and money. With British co-operation they might have been able to do something, but apart from political considerations the British looked upon the Bagdad railway scheme as a thing of the past. Lord Curzon wrote in 1892 that the idea, which had been so popular during the 1870's, had become " almost extinct." " It does not, for the present at least, lie within the domain of practical politics." British interests would be best served by keeping a firm hold on Egypt and a safe watch on the Suez Canal, and in cheapening and quickening the maritime service between England and India.[20] Even Major Law, the British financial expert, who made a survey of the Anatolian railroads in 1895, considered that there was no immediate prospect of the construction of a Euphrates line. As a route to India it would be 200 miles shorter than the Suez route, but would require two transshipments. He doubted if forty-eight hours could be saved by the overland route, and thought the whole matter had become less urgent since steamships had made travel by sea better and faster.[21]

---

[19] There is nothing in the elaborate and plausible argumentation of Hermann Schmidt: *Das Eisenbahnwesen in der Asiatischen Türkei* (Berlin, 1914), p. 7. On the Russian attitude in 1893 see *Die Grosse Politik*, XIV, no. 3970, and Helfferich, op. cit., III, pp. 69, 81. Helfferich does not repeat the statement he made in his earlier book, *Deutsche Türkenpolitik* (Berlin, 1921), p. 17, that Russian objections in 1893 led to the abandonment of the Angora-Bagdad route.

[20] George N. Curzon: *Persia and the Persian Question* (London, 1892), I, pp. 631 ff., especially pp. 633, 635.

[21] *Turkey No. 4 (1896), Report by Major Law on Railways in Asiatic Turkey;* Theodore

After the victory of the Turks over the Greeks in 1897 had shown once again the value of railways and had demonstrated the vitality of the empire, there was renewed interest in Anatolia as a field for economic enterprise. The Pan-German League put out a pamphlet expounding extravagant hopes for the future, and a number of other German books emphasized the importance of the question.[22] The new German ambassador at Constantinople, Baron von Marschall, was enthusiastically in favor of pushing German influence almost from the moment of his arrival in 1897. But the German bankers held back, partly because the Sultan and the military men were still insisting on the Angora-Kaisarieh route. Finally, however, the German group was goaded into action by the projects of rival interests. M. Cotard, representing the Smyrna-Cassaba line, applied for a concession for a line from Konia to Bagdad, while a Russian and an English promoter both put forward plans for a line from the Syrian coast to Bagdad. Siemens and his friends regarded it as essential that competitors should be kept out. They considered an understanding with British financial interests, but this was frowned upon by the German ambassador at Constantinople. They then applied to the Berlin government for a guarantee, but this was refused after some delay. By the autumn of 1898 matters stood where they were before.[23]

In the interval the Emperor William embarked upon a second visit to the Near East. Apparently he had for some time been determined to make a pilgrimage to the Holy Land, largely from a genuine religious sentiment. But the plan undoubtedly had political implications, too. For many years the French had claimed a rather hazy right of protectorate over the Roman Catholics in both the Near and the Far East. The claim was naturally distasteful to national feeling in both Italy and Germany, and had led to an ever more insistent counter-claim on the part of the Italian and German governments not to a general protectorate over Catholics, but to a protectorate over their own Catholic subjects abroad.[24] These counter-claims found some support in the fact that France, since the conclusion of the Franco-Russian Alliance, did little or nothing to counteract the advance of Russian influence in Palestine and Syria. The influential Russian Imperial Palestine Society was doing its utmost to replace the Greek Orthodox clergy with Arab members of the Orthodox Church. It was organizing Russian pilgrimages on a large scale, opening training schools for missionaries, and generally spreading its influence in all directions. French writers themselves complained bitterly that their government was doing nothing to make good its claims to a protectorate, that it was giving the Russians a free

Monson and George T. Hutchinson: *The Life of Edward Fitzgerald Law* (London, 1911), pp. 149 ff. I do not see that the excellent report of Major Law has been used by other writers.

22 Pan-German League: *Deutschlands Ansprüche an das Türkische Erbe* (Munich, 1896); Karl Kannenberg: *Kleinasiens Naturschätze* (Berlin, 1897); Ernst Friedrich: *Handels- und Produktenkarte von Kleinasien* (Halle, 1898).

23 Helfferich, op. cit., III, pp. 85–7; *Die Grosse Politik*, XIV, nos. 3975–77; Earle, op. cit., p. 58.

24 Theodore Aube: *Italie et Levant* (Paris, 1884); Anonymous: " La Politique Allemande et le Protectorat des Missions Catholiques " (*Revue des Deux Mondes*, September 1, 1898, pp. 5–41); Étienne Lamy: *La France du Levant* (Paris, 1900), pp. 217 ff.

hand, that the Alliance was undermining the French position in the Levant, and that the Russians were earmarking Syria as their base on the Mediterranean.[25]

The Germans decided to capitalize this situation, to undermine the French position in the east and to strengthen their own standing both with the Sultan, who disliked the French pretensions, and with the German Catholics, whose political support was always needed. In the spring of 1898 the German government encouraged the Sultan and the Pope to establish direct diplomatic relations. At the Vatican there was undoubtedly an active German party, of which Cardinals Hohenlohe, Galimberti and Ledochowski were the leaders. But ultimately the French minister, Lefevre de Béhaine, backed by the Papal secretary of state, Cardinal Rampolla, frustrated the scheme.[26]

The French regarded the Emperor's forthcoming visit with the most profound distrust. It was said, quite rightly, that German religious activity was a new thing and did not amount to much. Some claimed that the real object of the pilgrimage was to enlist the missionaries as agents for German influence and trade. Others noised it about that the Germans were planning to colonize in Palestine and Syria, and that they were out to get some harbor like Haifa, St. Jean d'Acre or even Rhodes.[27] Even in the midst of the Fashoda crisis the Paris press did not lose sight of the Levant. *Le Rire* published a special number on November 26, 1898 entitled *Tournée Guillaume II — Quinze Jours en Turquie, Palestine, Jérusalem et les Lieux Saints,* which was filled with unbelievably scandalous cartoons, one showing the Emperor off on an Armenian hunt with his friend the Bloody Sultan.[28]

As a matter of fact the whole business need not have been taken so seriously. Before the Emperor set out, in October 1898, the French had secured from the Pope a reaffirmation of their claims to the protectorate, and the trip itself was more amusing than important. *Simplicissimus* struck the right note with a cartoon for which the editor was condemned to a prison term. It showed Godfrey of Bouillon saying to Barbarossa: " Don't laugh so hard, Barbarossa, — our crusades, too, were really pointless."

²⁵ P. Pisani: " Les Russes en Syrie " (*Le Correspondant*, March 10, 1898, pp. 879–902); " La Propagande Russe en Palestine " (*Échos d'Orient, Chronique, février,* 1898, pp. 153–4); Lamy, op. cit., chap. iii; Alphonse d'Alonzo: *La Russie en Palestine* (Paris, 1901), passim. A detailed survey of Russian activities at this time may be found in Noel Verney and George Dambmann: *Les Puissances Étrangères dans le Levant, en Syrie et en Palestine* (Paris, 1900), pp. 131 ff.; Gaulis, op. cit., pp. 223 ff.

²⁶ *Die Grosse Politik,* XII, nos. 3351 ff., especially nos. 3357, 3358, 3359, 3361–5; Anonymous: " La Politique Allemande et le Protectorat des Missions Catholiques " (*Revue des Deux Mondes,* September 1, 1898, pp. 5–41); G. M. Fiamingo: " Die Politik Leos XIII und seine Diplomatie " (*Deutsche Revue,* June, 1898, pp. 280–90).

²⁷ " La Politique Allemande," loc. cit.; Pisani: " Les Allemands en Palestine " (*Le Correspondant,* September 10, 1898, pp. 895–920), p. 899; Étienne Lamy, op. cit., pp. 185 ff. The same fears were expressed in an English journal: Anonymous: " The German Emperor and Palestine " (*Fortnightly Review,* October, 1898), where it was said that the Germans were planning to settle ten to fourteen million colonists in Syria and Palestine!

²⁸ This was republished in translation in 1917: *The All-Highest Goes to Jerusalem* (New York, 1917).

The Emperor and Empress started out with a grand entourage. They visited the Sultan at Constantinople from October 18–22, and then went on to Palestine. The Turks had undertaken a grand housecleaning before the arrival of Their Majesties, and the Sultan had hurriedly bought from the Arab owner a holy place at Jerusalem, the *Dormition de la Vièrge,* which was only a cabbage patch worth a few hundred francs, but for which the Germans paid 120,000 francs in order that the Emperor might present it to the German Catholics. The pilgrimage was hot and uncomfortable, but it gave William a rare opportunity to indulge his love for theatricals and grandiloquence.[29]

The Imperial journey ended with a visit to Damascus, where William made his most resounding speech, proclaiming the fact that the three hundred million Mohammedans in the world could count upon him as a friend. This unfortunate utterance, which Bülow says he tried to excise before publication, pleased Abdul Hamid immensely, but did the Emperor no end of harm. It was quoted against him and against the Germans almost *ad nauseam* in the years before and during the World War, as evidence of German efforts to raise the Islamic world against England and France and Russia. As a matter of fact it created little stir at the time. The British, in the midst of the Fashoda crisis, took a rather benevolent view of the Emperor's motives, and indeed of the whole question of German influence in Turkey.[30]

The Emperor's pilgrimage had no direct bearing on the Bagdad Railway scheme. Siemens was at Constantinople at the time of William's visit to Abdul Hamid, and he was received by the Sultan in audience. But the Turks were still determined to have the road from Angora to Diarbekr and the German bankers had no heart for it. Siemens had little confidence in the future of Turkey so long as Abdul Hamid ruled, and his general attitude was to do nothing unless driven to it by pressure from competitors.[31] So for the time being the Germans concentrated their efforts on securing a concession for the construction of harbor works at Haidar Pasha, which was the terminus for the Anatolian line. In the last days of January 1899 they secured what they wanted and at once began work on the new development.

This Haidar Pasha concession proved to be a crucial step in the evolution of the Bagdad Railway policy. The French interests, which had a monopoly of harbor works at Constantinople, claimed that their rights extended to the Asiatic side and raised a grand protest against the German concession. Legally their protest appears to have had little basis, and nothing came of it, in fact. But it drove the French bankers to face squarely the whole problem of German

---

[29] One of the best accounts of the trip is in Gaulis: *La Ruine d'un Empire,* pp. 156–242, but see also the amusing account of Prince von Bülow, in his *Memoirs,* I, pp. 281 ff.

[30] London *Times,* October 28, 1898; *Morning Post,* October 12, 1898; see further *Die Grosse Politik,* XII, nos. 3345–7, 3366–83.

[31] See his conversation with Spring Rice (Sir Cecil Spring Rice: *Letters and Friendships,* I, p. 264), and Helfferich, op. cit., III, pp. 87 ff.; *Die Grosse Politik,* XIV, no. 3992.

enterprise. The new French ambassador, M. Constans, was anxious to restore French influence at the Porte. Where his predecessor, M. Cambon, had put himself in the front line of protesters at the time of the Armenian massacres, Constans tried to win back the confidence of the Sultan. At the same time he recognized that the Franco-Russian Alliance was not likely to inspire the Turks with friendly feelings and that the best course to pursue would be that of an entente with Germany. Delcassé seems to have approved this policy and the German government gave it its blessing. In April discussions were opened in Berlin which resulted in an agreement between the German and French bankers. The rivalry between the Anatolian and Smyrna-Cassaba lines was to be given up and each company was to appoint a number of directors to the board of the other. The French were to abandon their Bagdad Railway scheme and co-operate with the Germans in return for a 40% interest in the new line.[32]

Even more serious than the French protests were the objections of the Russian government. Whether these were at first inspired from Paris it is hard to say, but the Russians no doubt felt directly interested in the new turn of events at Constantinople. Count Osten-Sacken, the ambassador at Berlin, expressed to Bülow the uneasiness of his government. Constantinople, he said, was for Russia a *noli me tangere*. German economic interests in Turkey might easily develop into political hegemony and ultimately into a conflict of interests between Germany and Russia. Bülow stoutly denied this construction. Germany, he said, needed markets. Her aims were purely commercial and she had no idea of opposing Russian political aims. Russia, after all, could not claim the whole of Turkey as her own preserve.

These arguments did not satisfy the Russians. Osten soon returned to the charge. The Russians, he maintained, did not desire the collapse of the Ottoman Empire, but this collapse was bound to come before very long. Russia then could not tolerate the presence of another power at Constantinople. She would have to be sure of securing the Straits. If Germany could give her assurance on this point, then Russia might leave Germany a free hand for the furtherance of her projects in Anatolia.[33]

The Russian proposals were much more far-reaching than might at first appear. What Osten-Sacken was asking for was roughly what the Russians had secured from Bismarck under the terms of the famous Reinsurance Treaty. Consequently the Germans had to consider, as they had considered in 1890, whether they were prepared to orientate their policy towards the east and identify themselves with the Franco-Russian group. They argued the question in their inner councils and decided as they had decided nine years before, namely

---

[32] Helfferich, op. cit., III, pp. 92–7; Earle, op. cit., pp. 59–60; *Die Grosse Politik*, XII, no. 3349, XIV, nos. 3983–6; Louis Rambert: *Notes et Impressions de Turquie* (Paris, n.d.), pp. 62 ff. Delcassé later denied that French diplomacy had had a hand in the business, but the truth was well known. See the detailed discussion in André Chéradame: *Le Chemin de Fer de Bagdad* (Paris, 1903), pp. 266–75.

[33] These negotiations took place in April 1899 (*Die Grosse Politik*, XIV, nos. 3982, 4015–8).

that such an agreement would undermine and ruin the Triple Alliance and would mean turning their backs upon England. In return for such far-reaching sacrifices Russia was offering only commercial concessions. The game would not be worth the candle unless France could be gotten to join on the basis of a tripartite guarantee of territory, or at least unless Russia could be brought to promise friendly neutrality in the event of a Franco-German conflict. This proposal was made to Osten, but found little response. The ambassador maintained that Russia favored a combination with Germany and France to oppose England, but France could not officially abandon her claims to Alsace and Lorraine. To which Bülow replied that until France was willing to give up the idea of revenge Germany could not afford to turn her back on England. As long as Russia refrained from encouraging the French hopes, Germany would not antagonize Russia.

Although the Germans had quite definitely rejected the Russian advances, Count Muraviev came back to the question in the last days of June, using rather strong language and threatening quite clearly that if the Germans persisted in their refusal he would seek an agreement with England. But the Germans, who were on reasonably good terms with the French, stood by their earlier decision. The Emperor, in fact, was more than a little irritated by the high tone of the Russian foreign minister.[34]

Some German historians have made much of these discussions, and have interpreted them as something of a turning point in German policy. This is certainly a mistaken line. The Russians offered very little in return for the extensive concessions they demanded of the Germans, and it was impossible in 1899 to revive the situation as it had existed prior to the conclusion of the Russian alliance with France. The Germans, on the other hand, did not seriously consider the abandonment of the policy of the two irons. They were doing very well in playing off the Russians against the English, and they looked forward confidently to the time when both parties would be in even greater need of German support and would be prepared to pay an even higher price. As a matter of fact they had already made their peace with French financial interests, so that Russian displeasure did not seem very formidable.[35]

The immediate result of the rejection of the Russian advances was the systematic opposition of St. Petersburg to any further concessions being granted to the Germans. The Russian press was full of recriminations, claiming that the German scheme would hurt the Transsiberian Railway (!) and that it would make Anatolia and Mesopotamia a great granary competing with Russian agriculture. Furthermore, it would be a blow to Russian political preponderance in central Asia. Russia, said the *Novoie Vremia,* must tell the Germans to keep

---

[34] *Die Grosse Politik,* XIV, nos. 4019–25.

[35] Even Friedrich Meinecke: *Geschichte des Deutsch-Englischen Bündnisproblems, 1890–1901* (Munich, 1927), who discusses the matter at great length on pp. 118 ff., admits that there were almost insuperable obstacles to a German agreement with Russia.

hands off: " Our dear neighbors must know that Russia will never tolerate any infringement of the status quo in Asia Minor or Mesopotamia." [36]

The Germans were not greatly moved by Russian opposition, because, in 1899, they had the support not only of the French, but of the British. Feelings in London were rather mixed so far as the Bagdad Railway scheme was concerned. Or perhaps it would be more correct to say that the British cared little about a railway that would end at Bagdad or even Basra. " We may safely disregard croakings concerning the strategic danger offered to India by a railway which will set troops down at a point over 500 miles up a river navigated with difficulty by small sternwheelers and unfortified," wrote an English expert on the Near East in 1902.[37] From the very outset the British were interested in the control of the Persian Gulf, which they had policed for over a hundred years and where they claimed and maintained a special position.

In the autumn of 1898 Lord Curzon had been appointed viceroy of India. He went out filled with suspicion of Russian activity in Persia and central Asia, and determined to uphold the British position at all costs. In his book on Persia he had written years before: " I should regard the concession of a port upon the Persian Gulf to Russia by any power as a deliberate insult to Great Britain, as a wanton rupture of the status quo, and as an intentional provocation to war." [38] Curzon was very suspicious of Russian designs. He recognized the fact that any Bagdad railway scheme, to be successful, would have to envisage a terminus on the Gulf, and he saw that Kuwait (Grane), a wonderful harbor on the northwest end of the Gulf, would in all probability be the terminus chosen. In most of the earlier Euphrates Valley projects Kuwait had been regarded as the obvious terminal. The scheme for a railway from Syria to Kuwait, put forward by the Russian, Count Kapnist, in 1898, only served to confirm Curzon's fears. Kuwait formed part of the Turkish vilayet of Basra and paid tribute to the Turks, but its sheikh was little interfered with in the management of local affairs. He was very well disposed to the British and evidently hoped to secure from them support against eventual encroachments by the Turks. Curzon therefore arranged with him an agreement which was signed on January 23, 1899 by which the sheikh promised to cede no territory and to receive no agent of a foreign power without the sanction of the British government.[39]

The secret Kuwait agreement was directed squarely at Russian plans, though as a matter of fact it was to become much more important in the history of Anglo-German relations. At the very time of the conclusion of the agreement the Germans were turning over in their minds the possibility of acquiring a

---

[36] Quoted in *Questions Diplomatiques et Coloniales*, July 1, 1899, p. 313. On the Russian attitude see also Earle, op. cit., pp. 147–9.

[37] D. G. Hogarth: " The Bagdad Railway " (*National Review*, May, 1902, pp. 462–73), p. 473.

[38] G. N. Curzon: *Persia and the Persian Question* (London, 1892), II, p. 465.

[39] Curzon: *Persia and the Persian Question*, II, pp. 462 ff., 597 ff.; Earl of Ronaldshay: *Life of Lord Curzon* (London, 1928), II, p. 50; *Peace Handbooks*, no. 76, pp. 51 ff.; Sir Arnold T. Wilson: *The Persian Gulf* (Oxford, 1928), pp. 251–3; *British Documents*, I, p. 333.

footing at Muscat or Kuwait, but they were scared off by the harsh treatment meted out by the British to the French, when the latter secured the lease of a coal depot from the Sultan of Oman in February 1899. The British had a secret agreement with the Sultan, made in March 1891, by which he promised never to cede, sell, mortgage or otherwise give for occupation, save to the British government, the dominions of Muscat and Oman. This treaty was not wholly in consonance with earlier agreements by which England and France had engaged to respect the independence of Oman, but in 1899 the British consul at once assembled all available naval forces, went to Muscat and submitted an ultimatum. Under threat of bombardment he forced the Sultan to cancel the concession. Salisbury was greatly irritated by the affront offered to France at the very moment when the agreement about the upper Nile was being negotiated, but Curzon took a strong stand and the action was over before anything could be done to stop it. In any event, the French scheme was frustrated, and the Germans were too wise to repeat the experiment.[40]

From even this sketchy reference to the question of the Persian Gulf it should become clear that the British were intent on blocking any designs of the Russians and the French. The Germans as yet had not entered upon the scene. So long as they brought forward no plans to bring a railway to the Gulf they had no need to fear British opposition. British interests were represented on the board of directors of the Anatolian Railway Company, and they supported the idea of buying out the British-owned Smyrna-Aidin line as well as the idea of co-operation in the project of a line from Constantinople to Bagdad or even the Gulf.[41] Anonymous writers in the British press pointed out that it would be better to have the Germans in Anatolia and Mesopotamia than to have the Russians secure a footing there and then bang the door in the face of British commerce. German investment would give Germany an interest in bolstering up and reforming Turkey: " Germany thus becomes a sentinel, watchful against attack from without and an organiser of internal improvements." [42] Even the British ambassador to the Porte, Sir Nicholas O'Conor, favored support of the Germans on the basis of British participation.[43]

It was in general keeping with this attitude that Rhodes, during his visit to

---

[40] On German aspirations see *Die Grosse Politik,* XIV, nos. 3996–4006. The Muscat affair is dealt with in *British Documents,* I, nos. 255–60; see also *Die Grosse Politik,* XIV, nos. 3934 ff.; Ronaldshay, op. cit., II, pp. 45 ff.; Wilson, op. cit., pp. 239–40. There is a good account of French enterprise in the Gulf at this time in R. Vadala: *Le Golfe Persique* (Paris, 1920), pp. 26 ff. and a full discussion of the French case in the anonymous articles " L'Incident de Mascate " and " La Question de Mascate " (*Questions Diplomatiques et Coloniales,* March 1, 1899, pp. 281–6; March 15, 1899, pp. 367–9). See also Brunet-Millon: *Les Boutriers de la Mer des Indes* (Paris, 1910), pp. 209 ff., and Firouz Kajare: *Le Sultanat d'Oman* (Paris, 1914), pp. 196 ff.

[41] Monson and Hutchinson: *Life of Sir Edward Fitzgerald Law,* pp. 234 ff.

[42] Anonymous: " Asia Minor " (*Edinburgh Review,* April, 1899, pp. 515–42), pp. 530, 542; Anonymous: " Germany's Influence at Constantinople " (*Blackwood's Magazine,* May, 1899, pp. 921–4).

[43] *British Documents,* II, no. 202.

Berlin in March 1899, encouraged the Germans to proceed with their scheme. It was Germany's mission, he said, to open up Asia Minor and irrigate Mesopotamia, just as it was England's mission to develop Africa.[44] Bülow thereupon encouraged Siemens to embark upon the project. Siemens was not sanguine, but finally, in May 1899, he applied for a concession to extend the line from Konia to Bagdad. This route was chosen because the more northern Angora-Diarbekr-Bagdad line was longer and more difficult to construct. It may well be that the northern variant, which the Sultan had had so much at heart and which he abandoned only with great regret, was given up also out of consideration for Russia. So it has been claimed by many writers, though there is no direct evidence of Russian protest against any specific route.[45]

The negotiations with the Porte ran the usual course of intrigue and counter-intrigue. "To complicate simple affairs," wrote the German ambassador when it was all over, " is regarded here as service to the state." There was no serious danger of the project falling through, though in the summer there was something of a flurry when an Englishman named Rechnitzer came forward with an offer to build a line from Alexandretta to the Persian Gulf without a government guarantee. The proposal was supported by the Ottoman ministry of public works, perhaps chiefly in the hope of being bought off by the German group. As a matter of fact the Rechnitzer project lacked adequate financial backing, and it is more than unlikely that the Sultan would ever have accepted a scheme for a railway from Syria to the Gulf, especially when no secret was made of the fact that the line was intended to strengthen the British position. Even O'Conor regarded it as counterfeit and wrote home that no one would undertake the work without a solid guarantee of some sort. Nevertheless, the Germans feared for a time that the project was being officially backed by the British embassy, and were uneasy about their own prospects. It was only after more disheartening intrigue that the Rechnitzer proposal was put aside. On November 27, 1899 the Sultan issued an *iradé* announcing the award of a preliminary concession to the Anatolian Railway Company. All the details were left to future decision, but in general the company undertook to build a line within eight years from Konia to Bagdad and Basra. The crucial step had been taken and the great Bagdad Railway project, so much discussed and so long hoped for, was definitely launched on the road to fulfilment.[46]

The story of the Bagdad Railway belongs to this narrative only in so far as it fits into the general picture of international relations in 1899 and in so far as it touches on the relations between Germany on the one hand and England,

---

[44] Wilhelm II: *Ereignisse und Gestalten*, pp. 73–4; Karl F. Nowak: *Germany's Road to Ruin* (New York, 1932), pp. 205 ff.; Bülow: *Memoirs*, I, pp. 338–9, 409.

[45] *Die Grosse Politik*, XIV, nos. 3980, 3987; Helfferich, op. cit., III, p. 98; Parker, op. cit., p. 503; Earle, op. cit., p. 34.

[46] For the last discussions see Helfferich, op. cit., III, pp. 99 ff.; Earle, op. cit., pp. 60–2; *Die Grosse Politik*, XIV, no. 3992; and *British Documents*, II, no. 202.

Russia and France on the other. Its great significance in the history of European diplomacy began several years later, when, after endless negotiations, the German bankers failed to interest British finance and when, after the transformation of the preliminary concession into a definitive concession in 1903, the Germans proceeded to build the line themselves in the teeth of opposition from England and Russia. Nevertheless it is quite legitimate and quite important to say a few words about the implications of the scheme and its larger bearings.

In the first place it should be noted that German enterprise was at first of a purely economic nature. Siemens, in fact, stuck to this view until his death. He was anxious not to antagonize other groups and always envisaged co-operation with the British. When the German plans collided with the powerful interests of the French, he was quite ready to strike a bargain and to give a fair share of the spoils to those who were willing to come into the scheme. This attitude resulted quite naturally from the magnitude of the project and the tremendous amount of capital it required. It must be remembered further that Siemens and the Deutsche Bank did not care much for the Bagdad scheme in itself. They wanted to open up the economically promising parts of Anatolia and cared nothing about the Sultan's strategic needs. In the end they undertook the construction of the line primarily in order to prevent other interests from cutting them out. But their activities underwent a profound change of character during the 1890's from the very force of circumstances. The mounting investment of German capital just naturally created a certain political interest in the strengthening and preservation of the Ottoman Empire, and the German government took a growing interest in this new field of endeavor. It was not to be wondered at, then, that the vision of a great German route from Berlin by way of Vienna and Belgrade to Constantinople and from Haidar Pasha to Konia, Bagdad, Basra and possibly the Gulf should seize upon the German imagination and conjure up hopes of a great economic dependency in the east.

But the emergence of a political interest in Turkey was bound to make the Bagdad Railway plan an important factor in the relations of Germany with the other European powers interested in the Near East. The French were most reasonable. They fought the growth of German influence tooth and nail until they saw that it was impossible to stop it. Then they consoled themselves with the reaffirmation of their protectorate claims in religious matters, with minor concessions for railway lines in Syria and Palestine and with participation in the German project. After all, for the French the matter was relatively simple. Their financial investment in the Ottoman Empire far exceeded that of any other European country. In government bonds and in economic enterprises they had sunk about two and a half billion francs. It followed, then, that they too had a tremendous interest in the maintenance of the Empire and the safeguarding of their investment. Failing to run the show themselves, the sensible thing for them to do was to join the Germans, whose interest at bottom was the same. In this matter the French stood more closely related to the Germans than to the Russians.[47]

The government of the Tsar was notoriously interested in preventing the strengthening of the Ottoman Empire, and for that reason it objected to any enterprise likely to benefit the Porte. But, as Bülow said, the Russians could not expect to put a fence around the Turkish Empire and let it gradually die. They were therefore obliged to restrict themselves to general protests against the political implications of the German enterprise. They tried, as we have seen, to safeguard their political position at Constantinople and to reserve the Straits for themselves. In this they failed, whereupon they fell back upon the policy of protesting against the construction of railways in the area adjacent to the Russian frontier. In April 1900 they extracted from the Sultan an agreement that no railways should be built in the Black Sea areas of Anatolia excepting by Russian interests. This agreement, of which but few of the details are known, secured the immediate needs of the Russians, though it left the larger problem of the growing German activity in Turkey unsolved.[48]

In the later period the German policy in the Near East was confronted with the joint opposition of the Russians and the English. The English attitude was the most important factor, for Russian objections might have been met or ignored had it not been for the fact that the British took the lead. It is therefore worth remembering that English policy was originally not hostile to the progress of German influence. The British had, to be sure, a great interest in all questions touching the communications with India, but they also had an interest in bolstering up the Ottoman Empire to serve as a bulwark against Russia and in preventing the Porte from becoming wholly dependent upon Russia's ally, France, in a financial way. For that reason Sir William White had encouraged the Germans and had helped them in 1888. Leaving aside the peculiar interlude of Sir Clare Ford's opposition in 1893 (and this seems really to have had no larger implications) the British attitude remained generally favorable throughout the rest of the century and there was every reason to suppose that the British would collaborate in the financing of the German scheme, as many English representatives advocated. It has been pointed out in the course of this chapter that they had pretty much lost interest in the Euphrates Valley route to the Gulf and India because the improvement of steam shipping through Suez and the avoidance of transshipments by that route had made it the more attractive as it was the cheaper. They no longer cared for the Bagdad route and it meant nothing to them so long as it did not reach the Gulf. All they needed do, therefore, was to safeguard their position in the Gulf, which they did by blocking French plans to establish a coaling station near Muscat and by concluding a

---

[47] Figures on the French investment about 1900 may be found in Chéradame, op. cit., pp. 261 ff., and in Herbert Feis: Europe, the World's Banker (New York, 1930), pp. 51, 320 ff.

[48] On these negotiations see especially Die Grosse Politik, XVII, nos. 5211, footnote, 5217, 5218, 5221.

non-alienation agreement with the Sheikh of Kuwait. The Agreement was secret, but in 1900 it became generally known when the British first warned the Germans of their special position at Kuwait and then openly deterred the Sultan from sending an expedition to reassert his authority over the dominions of the Sheikh.[49] There was no reason, then, for British opposition to the German enterprise, and it is greatly to be regretted, from the standpoint of general European politics, that British financiers did not at once take an active part in the construction and control of the line. It is fairly clear that the Germans were ready to strike a reasonable bargain which would have secured British interests in the Gulf.

Discussion of these factors is necessary because the charge has often been brought against German policy in the east that it was a great mistake because it involved the hostility of England and Russia and helped to bring these two antagonists together in common opposition to Germany.[50] The point need not be entered upon in detail here because, in the first place, it is ridiculous to argue that a state should abstain from all activity which may involve friction with another state. Under such conditions almost no activity abroad would be possible. It is the business of diplomacy to smoothe out such friction as inevitably arises. No one can deny that in the economic sense the German expansion in Anatolia was the most natural thing in the world. The growth of political interest flowed just as naturally from the economic. The Germans were willing from the start to avoid treading on the toes of others and it was hardly their fault if the British did not choose to follow the example of the French. At the same time it should be noted that the Bagdad Railway itself was never an insuperable obstacle in the way of good German-Russian or German-English relations. A multitude of other factors entered in, and ultimately the Bagdad difficulty was overcome by the Potsdam agreements with Russia of 1910 and 1911, and by the understanding with England which was concluded on the very eve of the Great War.

BIBLIOGRAPHICAL NOTE

DOCUMENTARY SOURCES

Die Grosse Politik der Europäischen Kabinette. Volume XII, chapter lxxxiii: The Question of the Protectorate of German Catholics and the Emperor's Journey to the East. Volume XIV, chapter xciv: The Bagdad Railway; chapter xcv; Russian Proposals for an Agreement regarding the Straits and Anatolia.

---

[49] Helfferich, op. cit., III, pp. 109 ff.; *Die Grosse Politik,* XVII, nos. 5278–86; Earle, op. cit., pp. 197–8.

[50] The question is discussed at great length in such books as Friedrich Meinecke: *Geschichte des Deutsch-Englischen Bündnisproblems* (Munich, 1927), pp. 122 ff.; Rudolf Ibbeken: *Das Aussenpolitische Problem Staat und Wirtschaft in der Deutschen Reichspolitik, 1880–1914* (Schleswig, 1928), chap. iv; Willy Becker: *Fürst Bülow und England* (Greifswald, 1929), pp. 50 ff.

British Documents on the Origins of the War. For some reason the Bagdad Railway negotiations were omitted from this collection. There is merely a short précis of documents in Volume II, no. 202.

Accounts and Papers. 1896, volume XCVI: *Turkey No. 4 (1896), Report by Major Law on Railways in Asiatic Turkey.* This is an excellent review of the history and general problem of Anatolian railways, which seems to have been little used by writers on the Bagdad Railway.

Young, George: *Corps de Droit Ottoman.* Seven volumes. Oxford, 1906. Volume IV contains many of the texts of concessions for railway construction.

MEMOIRS, AUTOBIOGRAPHIES, BIOGRAPHIES, AND LETTERS

Helfferich, Karl: *Georg von Siemens.* Three volumes. Berlin, 1923. This is the authorized biography of the great German banker. Volume III contains what is probably the best single account of the Bagdad Railway project in the first phase.

Bülow, Prince von: *Memoirs.* Four volumes. Boston, 1931. Volume I contains an entertaining but not very informative account of the Emperor's journey to the east.

Ronaldshay, Earl of: *Life of Lord Curzon.* Three volumes. London, 1928. Important for Curzon's views and for his action with regard to the Persian Gulf.

Rambert, Louis: *Notes et Impressions de Turquie.* Paris, n.d. Gives an interesting view of the political alignment at Constantinople in these years, with some sidelights on the activity of French finance.

Monson, Theodore, and Hutchinson, George T.: *The Life of Sir Edward Fitzgerald Law.* London, 1911. Law was president of the Ottoman Public Debt Administration in 1899 and was a director of the Anatolian Railway Company.

SPECIAL STUDIES

Earle, Edward M.: *Turkey, the Great Powers and the Bagdad Railway.* New York, 1924. This is still the best general study of the diplomacy of the Bagdad Railway scheme, though its arrangement is such that one does not get a clear picture of the development of the problem. The book is based upon a considerable amount of new material, but now requires revision in the light of the German documents and other sources.

Hoskins, Halford L.: *British Routes to India.* Philadelphia, 1928. An indispensable historical study of the communications problem. By far the best account of early railway schemes.

Ibbeken, Rudolf: *Das Aussenpolitische Problem Staat und Wirtschaft in der Deutschen Reichspolitik, 1880–1914* (Schleswig, 1928). Contains a detailed discussion of the political aspects of the enterprise, without adding much.

BECKER, WILLY: *Fürst Bülow und England*. Greifswald, 1929. A careful study of Bülow's general policy, with a detailed treatment of the Bagdad Railway. Based upon the obvious sources.

CHÉRADAME, ANDRÉ: *Le Chemin de Fer de Bagdad*. Paris, 1903. The work of a well-known propagandist. Contains much interesting contemporary material, and should not be neglected.

JASTROW, MORRIS: *The War and the Bagdad Railway*. Philadelphia, 1917. Of no value.

FRASER, DAVID: *The Short Cut to India*. London, 1909. Primarily a book of travel along the route, but contains a fair account of the early schemes for railway connexion.

HOLBORN, HAJO: *Deutschland und die Türkei, 1878–1890*. Berlin, 1926. A most important essay, based in large measure on unpublished German archive material. The best account of German policy prior to 1890.

SCHMIDT, HERMANN: *Das Eisenbahnwesen in der Asiatischen Türkei*. Berlin, 1914. Deals almost exclusively with the later period.

GÉRAUD, ANDRÉ: "The Story of the Bagdad Railway." (*Nineteenth Century*, May, 1914, pp. 958–72). A good general account, which, however, adds little.

(PARKER, ALWYN): "The Bagdad Railway Negotiations." (*Quarterly Review*, October, 1917, pp. 487–528). This is an inspired British account and is probably the best single treatment of British policy.

SCHÄFER, CARL A.: *Deutsch-Türkische Freundschaft*. Berlin, 1914. Deals chiefly with general German interest in Turkey and contains some good statistical material.

MORAWITZ, CHARLES: *Die Türkei im Spiegel ihrer Finanzen*. Berlin, 1903. A study of the Turkish financial system, with a good history of Turkish railway problems.

DU VELAY, A.: *Essai sur l'Histoire Financière de la Turquie*. Paris, 1903. Like the preceding title. Contains one of the best accounts of Turkish railway history in its financial aspects.

BENNETT, T. J.: "The Past and Present Connection of England with the Persian Gulf." (*Journal of the Society of Arts*, June 13, 1902). A good systematic review, now superseded by more detailed studies.

VADALA, R.: *Le Golfe Persique*. Paris, 1920. The work of a former French consul at Bushire. The book is devoted largely to trade problems, but contains much of interest on French activities and interests.

WILSON, SIR ARNOLD T.: *The Persian Gulf*. Oxford, 1928. A standard account, by a man who served for many years as a British official in the Gulf and in Mesopotamia.

VERNEY, NOËL, and DAMBMANN, GEORGE: *Les Puissances Étrangères dans le Levant*. Paris, 1900. An encyclopedic work based on very extensive research into contemporary material. Contains detailed statistics on foreign interests in Turkey as well as on Turkish railways and their history.

GAULIS, GEORGES: *La Ruine d'un Empire*. Paris, 1913. A collection of articles written in 1898 and later years. One of the best accounts of the Emperor's trip to Palestine and of the growth of German influence in Turkey.

LAMY, ÉTIENNE: *La France du Levant*. Paris, 1900. Another collection of periodical articles. Particularly valuable for the discussion of the protectorate issue.

REY, F.: *La Protection Diplomatique et Consulaire dans les Échelles du Levant et de Barbarie*. Paris, 1899. A sound systematic study of the protectorate problem.

LINDOW, ERICH: *Freiherr Marschall von Bieberstein als Botschafter in Konstantinopel, 1897–1912*. Danzig, 1934. This is a conscientious review of Marschall's ambassadorship. It is based on the more obvious sources and adds relatively little, though it brings much material together in convenient form.

BUTTERFIELD, PAUL K.: *The Diplomacy of the Bagdad Railway, 1890–1914*. Göttingen, 1932. A German dissertation, based on a narrow range of material. Of no value as a contribution to the subject.

XX

Europe and the Boer War

∽

W HEN BRITAIN EMBARKED UPON WAR WITH THE TWO BOER REPUB-
lics, both the statesmen and the soldiers were convinced that what
was before them was just another "sporting war," as Bismarck
called England's colonial conflicts. All that was necessary was a "slap in the
face" for Kruger and the thing would be over. Yet the most serious disillusionment was in store for them. It soon turned out that they had miscalculated on almost every count. They underestimated the forces of the Boers,
who could put about 50,000 burghers in the field, and they greatly underrated
the number of troops required to overcome their opponents. The Boers showed
little knowledge of strategy, but they were experienced fighters, they had a
better rifle than the English and they completely baffled the enemy by their
open fighting. At the outset the British had only about 25,000 men available.
The rest had to be sent from England, 6000 miles away, or from India and the
dominions. Before the end of the war in 1902 the British had no less than
300,000 men in south Africa.

Under these circumstances it was almost inevitable that the struggle should
start with a series of setbacks for the British. General Sir Redvers Buller, who
was in command, showed himself quite incompetent. Abandoning his original
plan of keeping his forces together and pressing on to Bloemfontein and Pretoria, he divided his army into three parts, hoping thereby to block the Boers
at Kimberley in the west, at Colesberg in the centre and at Ladysmith in the
east. But his hopes were everywhere disappointed. The Boers defeated the British in three important engagements during the famous Black Week (December 9–15, 1899) and shut up their forces in Kimberley and Ladysmith. The
situation continued black for several months, despite the hurrying out of reinforcements and the mission of Lords Roberts and Kitchener to command the
operations. It was not until the second half of February 1900 that Kimberley and
Ladysmith were finally relieved and Roberts was able to proceed slowly to the
invasion of the Republics. The first, regular phase of the war closed with the
annexation of the Transvaal in September 1900, but there followed almost two
more years of desultory guerrilla warfare before the resistance of the Boers
was finally broken.

The seriousness of Britain's problem and the magnitude of the army she was obliged to send to Africa naturally placed her in a most delicate international situation. In a hundred years she had never been so entirely without friends. Continental opinion was violently hostile and roundly declared the whole business a predatory enterprise plain and simple. The great, greedy British Empire was making no bones about attacking two valiant little republics simply in order to seize their gold mines. It was high time, said the press in more than one continental country, to put an end to British aggression and to deal the empire a telling blow. Everywhere there was talk of a continental coalition, of a union between Russia, France and Germany which would prove irresistible.

Few points in recent diplomatic history have been made the subject of so much recrimination as the question of intervention against England in the winter of 1899–1900. The French have accused the Germans of having made suggestions to this end, while the Germans have pointed to the Russian foreign minister, Count Muraviev, as the real culprit. It is therefore essential to review the evidence and to make some attempt to determine the true course of events.

Even before the outbreak of the war the British ambassador at Paris reported home on the hostility of the French press and noted that the favorite subject of discussion was the prospect of a combination of the continental powers against England.[1] The British newspapers were decidedly uneasy about the possibility of such action, the more so as Muraviev was at this very time paying a visit to the Spanish foreign minister at San Sebastian and to Delcassé at Paris. Almost nothing is known of the discussions that took place during these visits. The English ambassador at Paris, Sir Edmund Monson, learned that Muraviev had told the Spanish foreign minister that " the time had arrived when it became necessary for the Powers of Europe to take common action against the ever-increasing aggressions and expansion of England," and that he had dangled before the Spaniards prospects of acquisitions in Morocco. Monson learned further that the Russian minister had tried to bring Delcassé to adopt a hostile policy, but that the French statesman had resisted. Evidently the French attitude put an end to the scheme, if there was one, for nothing was said to the Germans by Muraviev when he and the Tsar visited Berlin in the first week of November. In any event there is no evidence to substantiate the later claim of French writers that Muraviev's proposal had been inspired by the German government.[2]

The French, including Delcassé, have always maintained that at the very time of Muraviev's démarche advances were made by the German Emperor

---

[1] *British Documents*, I, no. 285. It should be noted that the better French papers doubted the possibility of action. See the summaries of the press in *Questions Diplomatiques et Coloniales*, November 1, 1899, p. 301 and November 15, 1899, pp. 366–7.

[2] *British Documents*, I, nos. 286, 287, 294; VI, no. 129. The story was told in detail by Diplomaticus: " Count Muraviev's ' Indiscretion ' " (*Fortnightly Review*, December, 1899, pp. 1036–45) and is recounted by Delcassé's apologist André Mévil: " Delcassé and the Entente Cordiale " (*National Review*, July, 1908, pp. 712–9), and in his book *De la Paix de Francfort à la Conférence d'Algésiras* (Paris, 1909), p. 55. See also E. J. Dillon: *The Eclipse of Russia* (London, 1918), p. 318. Dillon drew his information from Witte.

to the French ambassador. In 1905 Delcassé told a British diplomat that the Emperor called on Noailles and spoke violently about England. The war, he is reputed to have said, offered " a unique opportunity which would not recur in a century for putting an end to the arrogance and aggression of England." A few days later Bülow is reported to have shown Noailles a map, from which he tried to prove that French and German interests clashed nowhere while Britain stood in the path of both. All they needed do was to combine their efforts.[3] Now there is nothing in the German archives bearing on this conversation. The French have published Noailles' despatch (October 18, 1899) but from the text it would appear that the talk was much more innocent than Delcassé made it out to be. The Emperor merely spoke of the community of French and German interests, especially in Africa. Ten days later he had another talk with the ambassador, the record of which has been published by the Germans but not by the French. From the Emperor's version it seems that Noailles began by expressing his uneasiness about the south African situation and by asking whether those powers interested should not eventually do something to check British expansion. To which the Emperor claims to have replied that it was already too late for such action. England would throw those who interfered into the sea. In 1896 she was still unprepared and surprised. If at that time other powers had joined Germany something might have been done. But now Germany had no fleet. In twenty years she would talk differently, but for the present she would have to remain neutral.[4]

What is one to make of this episode? So much, I think, is clear, that at this particular time, in the second half of October, the Emperor was exceedingly wrought up about the Samoan affair and the apparent unwillingness of Salisbury to make concessions. He may very well have spoken indiscreetly to Noailles about the possibility of co-operation with France in colonial matters. But even so the German suggestions were very vague. Delcassé seems to have been willing to follow up the lead. He wrote Noailles that the German proposition was worth considering in concert with Russia, and the ambassador did try to get Bülow to make a concrete suggestion. But the foreign minister evaded, and nothing came of the feelers, which were clearly not very seriously intended from the German side.[5] As for any combination against England, it is now obvious from the German documents that no proposition of that nature would have been entertained in Berlin. In mid-October Holstein wrote to Eckardstein that so long as German foreign policy remained in the same hands a rapprochement with France and Russia would hardly take place.[6]

In the autumn of 1899 German military men were generally of the opinion

[3] British Documents, III, pp. 432–3.

[4] Émile Bourgeois and Georges Pagès: Les Origines . . . de la Grande Guerre (Paris, 1921), pp. 281 ff.; Die Grosse Politik, XV, no. 4394.

[5] Bourgeois and Pagès, op. cit., pp. 281–2.

[6] H. Freiherr von Eckardstein: Lebenserinnerungen und Politische Denkwürdigkeiten (Leipzig, 1919), II, p. 61.

that the British army would be beaten in south Africa.[7] Bülow claims that he did not share this belief, and neither did the Emperor. William, whatever his opinion of the British army, was immensely impressed with the British fleet, which he took at the English valuation and which, he was certain, would give short shrift to any power that interfered.[8] For that very reason he had long since grown into a feeling of helplessness with regard to England, and had made himself the champion of a large German navy. The Samoan business in particular proved once more that a continental state had to expect cavalier treatment from Britain if it had no fleet to inspire respect.

When the first naval law was passed in the spring of 1898 it was thought of by the Emperor and Tirpitz as only a first step in the right direction. It was designed to give Germany battleship power, but the size of the battle-fleet was such that it could hardly be classed as more than a mobile coast-defense. Its offensive possibilities were small and Tirpitz intended to ask for much more when the first program was completed in 1904. By the summer of 1899 he had convinced himself that a new program must be brought in at least a couple of years sooner. The Spanish-American War, the Fashoda crisis, the Philippine and Samoan episodes had, he felt, created a new world situation which made an increase of the fleet much more urgent.[9]

But Tirpitz meant to proceed carefully and methodically and not to shock the German public and Reichstag into opposition. His hand was forced by the Emperor, who on October 18, 1899 made a speech at Hamburg at the launching of the steamer *Karl der Grosse* in which he declared: "Bitter need have we of a strong German fleet." The speech called forth downright consternation in the ministry of marine. Tirpitz as well as Hohenlohe hesitated long whether to follow up the Emperor's precipitate lead. Finally it was decided to take advantage of the Boer War to bring in a second naval bill. Bülow made a great speech in the Reichstag on December 11, 1899, in which he first enunciated officially the idea of a risk-fleet, that is, the idea that Germany must have a fleet so powerful that even the strongest naval power could not attack it without serious risk.

The government had a much easier time than it had anticipated. Since 1898 German opinion had been educated to the idea of naval power. The Colonial Society had carried on a large-scale agitation, but even this was overshadowed by the work of the Navy League. This organization had been founded in April 1898 and was heavily financed by the Krupps and other steel interests, which were deeply interested in the guns and armor required for the ships. The League had 100,000 members in the middle of 1899 and the figure grew rapidly to 250,000. Its publication, *Die Flotte,* had a circulation of 250,000, while its

---

[7] *Die Grosse Politik,* XV, no. 4408, footnote; Prince von Bülow: *Memoirs* (Boston, 1931), pp. 341–2.   [8] His marginal note in *Die Grosse Politik,* XVIII, no. 5861.

[9] Alfred von Tirpitz: *Erinnerungen* (Leipzig, 1919), pp. 103 ff.: Bernhard Michalik: *Probleme des Deutschen Flottenbaues* (Breslau, 1931), pp. 68 ff.

lecturers made no less than three thousand speeches in the winter of 1899–1900.[10] There was undoubtedly great popular interest in the fleet and in world policy. German writers have pointed out that in the voluminous literature of the time it is impossible to find any consensus of opinion as to the purpose of the projected fleet. There was less talk of its value for the protection of commerce and colonies and more talk of its political value as an instrument of world policy, but generally speaking the conception of the problem was nebulous. By some writers this is taken as proof that the naval bill was not the result of an urgent foreign situation, but rather the result of a bargain between industrial and agrarian interests: the former were to have their fleet and world policy, the latter protection for agriculture and a continuance of their social predominance.[11] No doubt there is more than a grain of truth in this interpretation, though it seems to me to lay too little stress on the imponderables. The new generation in Germany did not, like its fathers, feel saturated. It felt cramped within the continental horizon and yearned for a world policy. The fleet was for it an aspiration, a symbol of added power, and for that reason the government project found such wide support.[12]

We need not enter upon the detailed history of the Second Naval Bill. It provided for a German fleet comprising thirty-eight battleships, to be completed in twenty years. It went through the successive readings in the Reichstag in the spring of 1900 and was passed on June 12 with a vote of 201–103. Only the Socialists, a small part of the Centre and a part of the Progressives voted against it. The rest of the deputies accepted the government explanations, that if Germany were stronger at sea the other powers would respect her more highly, and that for German purposes nothing less than a fleet strong enough to impress even the strongest naval power would be sufficient. Parliament voted the government program without tying financial strings to it. The fleet was to be built whatever the cost.

As we look back on the passage of the great German naval law, which was, in a short space, to lift Germany from the position of fifth sea power to that of second, we cannot help but feel that the Emperor, Bülow and Tirpitz were laying the foundations of serious conflict with England. It seems fairly clear that they did not realize how far the question of sea-power would lead. The accusation may be justly brought against them that they worked on the subconscious assumption that things would remain as they were in 1900. Of course they did not envisage a fleet as strong as the British. What they aimed at was simply this: a fleet large enough to proceed offensively against the British Home fleet (at that time about thirty-two ships) and at the same time a fleet

---

[10] Eckart Kehr: *Schlachtflottenbau und Parteipolitik, 1894–1901* (Berlin, 1930), pp. 98 ff., 169 ff.; Archibald Hurd and Henry Castle: *German Sea-Power* (London, 1913), pp. 208 ff., 321; Tirpitz, op. cit., pp. 95–6.

[11] This is the general burden of Kehr's very interesting book.

[12] The point is well argued in Michalik, op. cit., pp. 103 ff.

that would give Germany an alliance value, a fleet so strong that England would respect it and ultimately seek an agreement with Germany, or, failing that, a fleet so strong that Germany would become an attractive ally for France and Russia. What they did not foresee was that the British would put their own interpretation on German policy and that they would reply by building an ever more powerful navy. What they did not foresee was further this, that the English, instead of seeking an agreement with Germany, would ultimately find it cheaper to strike a bargain with Germany's potential allies at sea, France and Russia.

All this is clear as we look back, but it will not do to make too much use of hindsight. The European world in 1900 was obsessed with the ideas of imperialism and world policy and the idea of sea-power was an integral part of the larger imperial idea. Even sane people were victims of the obsession. Prince Hohenlohe, the octogenarian German chancellor, who was deeply rooted in the ideas of the Bismarckian age, wanted the naval bill passed. "We must not," he wrote, "expose ourselves to the danger of suffering the fate from England that Spain suffered from the United States. That the English are merely waiting for a chance to fall upon us is clear." Count Münster, the ambassador at Paris, who was also a left-over of an earlier period, shared the desire for sea-power, though his train of thought was more nearly that of Bülow and Tirpitz: If Germany had a strong fleet England would have to cultivate German friendship in order to prevent a naval coalition being formed against her: "The civilization of the world depends upon a naval agreement between England and ourselves, and therefore England must regard us not as an enemy, but as an equal; this she will do only if we are strong enough, even on the sea." [13]

But the introduction of the bill for a greatly increased navy in no sense reflected hostility to Britain at the time. In fact Anglo-German relations were distinctly good in the critical first months of the Boer War. Once the Samoan business had been disposed of in a way satisfactory to the Germans the Emperor was ready to start off on his long-discussed visit to England, the first he was to pay since the ill-fated visit to Cowes in 1895. The German public was as violently hateful of England and as favorable to the Boers as the public of any European country, so the Emperor's journey to England at a time when it appeared like an endorsement of British policy called forth no end of criticism. For that reason the private nature of the visit had to be underlined and William from first to last resisted all attempts that were made to have him visit London. He visited his grandmother at Windsor and spent some days with the Prince of Wales at Sandringham; in all he spent less than ten days in England (November 20–28).

Bülow accompanied the Emperor during the visit, and arrangements had been made for conferences between the German statesmen on the one hand and Salisbury, Chamberlain and Balfour on the other. As it happened, Lady Salisbury died just as the Imperial party arrived and the prime minister there-

---

[13] Hohenlohe: *Denkwürdigkeiten der Reichskanzlerzeit*, pp. 554, 575.

fore excused himself. In all probability he was not anxious to be drawn into the conversations. After the Emperor's attacks upon him in the summer he had less use than ever for the German connexion. It is quite clear that if Chamberlain had not taken the Samoan negotiations out of his hands a settlement would not have been reached in time. The Germans were under no illusions about Salisbury's feelings. Hatzfeldt had written home discussing the peculiar relationship between the prime minister and Chamberlain and pointing out that German hopes could be realized only through the latter. But Chamberlain would require careful and discreet handling.[14] Bülow, indeed, claims that after his arrival in England he received, through Sir Frank Lascelles, a letter from Salisbury warning him that Chamberlain would be speaking only for himself, not for the cabinet.[15] There is no trace of the letter in the German documentary publication and Bülow merely summarizes it in his memoirs. Its authenticity seems very doubtful, for it is rather hard to believe that one British statesman should write such a letter about another. Certainly it would have been contrary to all the accepted etiquette of English politics.

We may assume, I think, that the conversations at Windsor were frank and aboveboard. Chamberlain told both the Emperor and Bülow that what he wanted was an understanding between England, Germany and the United States. Britain, he said, was uneasy about Russian progress in China and needed Germany and America to help check it. He admitted that Salisbury was opposed to a formal alliance because he disliked being definitely bound in any direction. But an understanding would be possible, in Chamberlain's opinion. Britain, he said, would rather see the Germans than the Russians in Anatolia and he therefore favored English co-operation with Germany in the Bagdad Railway enterprise. He hinted further that England and Germany might work together in Morocco, England marking off for herself Tangiers and leaving to Germany part of the Atlantic coast area. To all of which the Emperor and Bülow replied by stressing England's aversion to binding alliances and pointing out that German relations with Russia and even with France were good and that Germany could not afford to compromise her relations with Russia. The Germans favored separate agreements on special points, but displayed no great interest in more extensive commitments.

The conversations between the visitors and Balfour were of a more general nature. Balfour, too, favored an agreement between England, Germany and the United States, though he was not as insistent as Chamberlain. He spoke at some length of the Anglo-German trade rivalry, which he attempted to minimize. There was no jealousy on the British side, he asserted, for both nations were pursuing much the same policy of the open door and both were making progress. On the other hand he complained bitterly of the violence of the German press. Bülow countered with complaints of Mr. Saunders, the *Times* correspondent in Berlin, who, he said, collected the worst utterances from obscure

---

[14] Bülow: *Memoirs*, I, pp. 362–3. [15] Ibid., p. 367.

papers and sent them on to London. Parenthetically it might be said that Bülow returned from his visit much impressed with England and convinced that the British were much less hostile to Germany than the Germans were toward the British. For that reason, he noted, men like Saunders and Chirol, who really knew German opinion, were a menace to good relations.[16]

The Windsor visit was undoubtedly a great success, having been marred by no personal or other friction. It was welcomed by the British government and by the public as a mark of good will in a very dark hour and it demonstrated to the world that Germany could not be counted on for any hostile action. This was the interpretation current at the time. The Emperor, wrote the French ambassador at Berlin on November 26, was ill-disposed toward any long-term combination: " He does not want to bind himself definitely on any side, intends not to become involved with anyone, but to be on good terms with everybody, to keep abreast of opportunities, perhaps he even seeks to create them, and in any event profits by them." [17] This is a succinct and correct estimate of the German position. The Windsor conversations went no further than those that had taken place in 1898. The Germans were on their guard from the outset. They wanted to keep Chamberlain friendly, because they thought that through him alone they would be able to secure concessions in special questions. The colonial secretary, as usual, laid his cards on the table. He admitted that Salisbury was opposed to a formal alliance, yet advocated a triple grouping to block the Russian advance in the east. If Germany co-operated she would be rewarded with British support in Anatolia and Morocco.

German emphasis upon the necessity of maintaining good relations with Russia should have showed Chamberlain that his scheme had little prospect of success, for the very crux of the business was common action against Russia. He claimed later that Bülow had expressed the wish that he say something publicly of the mutual interests which bound the United States to an understanding with Germany and England.[18] But even if that was the case, the suggestion certainly could not have been reasonably interpreted as an invitation to say what Chamberlain said in his famous Leicester speech, delivered on November 30, just after the imperial party had left. He prefaced his remarks with a warning to the French press that if its attacks upon Her Majesty did not stop there might be " serious consequences." He then went on to pay a tribute to the friendly attitude of the United States, and finally came to the question of relations with Germany:

> " There is something more which I think any far-seeing English statesman must
> have long desired, and that is that we should not remain permanently isolated
> on the Continent of Europe; and I think that the moment that aspiration is

---

[16] On the Windsor visit see *Die Grosse Politik*, XV, nos. 4396 ff.; Bülow: *Memoirs*, I, pp. 369 ff.; Eckardstein: *Lebenserinnerungen*, II, chaps. iii and iv; Garvin: *Life of Chamberlain*, III, pp. 496 ff.; Sir Sidney Lee: *Edward VII* (New York, 1925), I, pp. 745 ff.

[17] Bourgeois and Pagès, op. cit., pp. 283–4.   [18] Eckardstein, op. cit., II, p. 107.

formed it must have appeared evident to everybody that the natural alliance is between ourselves and the great German Empire. We have had our differences, our quarrels, misunderstandings, but at the root of things there has always been a force which has necessarily brought us together. What interest have we which is contrary to the interest of Germany? I can foresee many things which must be a cause of anxiety to the statesmen of Europe, but in which our interests are clearly the same, and in which that understanding of which I have spoken in the case of America might, if extended to Germany, do more perhaps than any combination of arms to preserve the peace of the world. At bottom the character of the Teutonic race differs very slightly indeed from the character of the Anglo-Saxon race. If the union between England and America is a powerful factor in the cause of peace, a new Triple Alliance between the Teutonic race and the two great branches of the Anglo-Saxon race will be a still more potent influence in the future of the world. I have used the word alliance, but it matters little whether you have an alliance which is committed to paper or whether you have an understanding which exists in the minds of the statesmen of the respective countries. An understanding is perhaps better than an alliance."

This remarkable speech created something of a furor even in England, where it found very little favor. The *Times* declared that relations with Germany could never be as close as those with the United States, and Stead wrote in the *Review of Reviews* that England wanted no alliance and was thoroughly sick of concessions, the newest of which were Samoa and Anatolia. As a matter of fact Stead and others were already suspicious of the German naval program, which was regarded as "a direct challenge addressed to Great Britain, intimating that Germany is going into training to snatch from us that sea-power upon the maintenance of which our Empire depends." In the same tone the *National Review* denounced the idea of friendship with Germany because the Emperor was obviously making use of German Anglophobia to build up a fleet with the hardly concealed object of threatening British naval supremacy.[19]

The Americans showed no more interest in the projected alliance. Public opinion beyond the Atlantic was cooling off in its affection for Britain since the Spanish War was at an end, and the Irish and German elements were loud in their attacks upon British policy in south Africa.[20] But what was more important was the violently negative attitude of German opinion, which was nothing less than brutal in its denunciations. Chamberlain was accused of exploiting the Emperor's visit in order to compromise German relations with other powers. Bülow could not resist this hostile pressure. On December 11 he

---

[19] *Review of Reviews,* November 15, 1899, p. 435; December 15, 1899, pp. 547 ff.; *National Review,* December, 1899, pp. 481–3. There is a good review of British opinion on the Leicester speech in the *Economist,* December 10, 1899, and in *Questions Diplomatiques et Coloniales,* December 15, 1899, pp. 504 ff. Garvin, op. cit., III, pp. 506 ff., recognizes that the Leicester speech was a *faux pas.*

[20] A. M. Low: "American Affairs" (*National Review,* April, 1900, pp. 276–88); Alfred L. P. Dennis: *Adventures in American Diplomacy* (New York, 1928), pp. 127 ff.; Tyler Dennett: *John Hay* (New York, 1933), chap. xx.

delivered a great speech in the Reichstag in which he reviewed Germany's relations with all the powers. He pointed out that Germany had always been able to work in harmony with France in colonial questions, and that he had always found Russia friendly and reasonable in such matters. Relations with the United States were good, and the same was true of relations even with Japan.

"As for England, we are quite ready to live in peace and harmony with her on the basis of full reciprocity and mutual consideration. But just because our foreign position is now a favorable one, we must use it in order to secure ourselves for the future. I wish, we all wish, that this future may be a peaceful one. Whether it will be a peaceful one, no one can tell. We must be secured against surprises not only on land, but on the sea. We must build a fleet strong enough to prevent an attack — I underline the word *attack*, for with the absolutely pacific nature of our policy there can be no talk of anything but defense — from any power."

To which he added veiled references to past disputes with England which had shown conclusively the urgent need of a German fleet.

Chamberlain's Leicester speech was surely a *gaucherie*, as Bülow claimed, but the German foreign minister's reply, too, was inexcusable. Not only did he definitely reject all ideas of more than bargainings between the two powers, but he seized the opportunity to inject the naval question and to put forward officially the thought of building a fleet strong enough to resist English attack. It was no wonder that Chamberlain felt that, after being invited to say something friendly, he had been given a smart slap in the face.[21]

But the friction engendered by the "new" diplomacy had no effect on the actual policies of the two countries. The British simply could not afford to estrange Germany at so critical a moment and the Germans had no intention of giving up their policy of the free hand or their hopes for reward for good behavior. Bülow gave assurances that Germany would abstain from any continental grouping or collective action against Britain and told the English ambassador that "any diminution of the authority and prestige of Great Britain would be little short of a calamity for Germany."[22] On the other hand, when General Buller urged a blockade of Delagoa Bay in order to prevent supplies going up to the Boers, the Germans made no secret of the fact that British action would necessitate some sort of compensation to Germany, and that Walfisch Bay would not be sufficient. Nothing less than Zanzibar would do. In the end the British government gave up the idea for fear of complications with Germany and France.[23]

---

[21] On Bülow's reply see Eckardstein, op. cit., II, pp. 123 ff.; Garvin, op. cit., III, pp. 511 ff.; Willy Becker: *Fürst Bülow und England* (Greifswald, 1929), pp. 141 ff.; *Die Grosse Politik*, XV, nos. 4401, 4456.

[22] Eckardstein, op. cit., II, pp. 126–7; *British Documents*, I, no. 302.

[23] *Die Grosse Politik*, XV, nos. 4404–11; Eckardstein, op. cit., II, pp. 128 ff.; *Letters of Queen Victoria*, III, pp. 428, 431; *British Documents*, I, no. 301; Garvin, op. cit., III, pp. 492 ff.

Yet the importation of arms and goods by way of Delagoa Bay was a matter of prime importance for the British. Efforts had to be made to stop it and Salisbury hoped to obtain the effects of a blockade " by carefully searching every vessel that comes in for contraband of war." [24] The immediate application of this decision was the stopping of the German mail steamer *Bundesrath* during the last days of December. Other German ships were stopped on suspicion soon afterward. It was believed later that the Boer representative in Europe had indirectly spread rumors that the German ships were carrying volunteers and armaments. However that may have been, the German ships were stopped on the basis of very inadequate evidence and they were taken into port for examination despite the protests of the Berlin government. During the first weeks of January the incident threatened to reach the proportions of a first-rate crisis, for German opinion was violently outraged and freely attacked the government for its weak policy toward England. The British, it was said, were making up for their reverses in the war by striking a blow at German commerce. Bülow pressed for the release of the steamer, but got little satisfaction. Finally he felt obliged to go so far as to suggest that if this was the reward for neutrality Germany would be obliged to seek some other combination. In London it was thought, evidently quite erroneously, that a German admiral was to be sent over to demand satisfaction and to break off relations if satisfaction were refused.[25] On January 16, 1900 the British government backed down. It admitted that no contraband had been found and promised that the *Bundesrath* should be released at once. It agreed further to pay an indemnity, not to stop other ships at a great distance from the scene of action and not to detain mail-steamers on mere suspicion.

The disposal of the matter came just in the nick of time so far as Bülow was concerned, for he had postponed as long as he could interpellations in the Reichstag. On January 19 he spoke on the subject in parliament and in order to appease German opinion underlined the fact that England had given in on every point to the strong representations of the German government. This speech in turn called forth so much dissatisfaction and criticism in England that the government felt constrained to publish a Blue Book in which the strong German notes were reproduced.[26] The English statesmen, to be sure, had at first thanked Bülow for his considerate handling of the matter, but after the Reichstag speech Chamberlain complained bitterly of the sharp telegrams from Berlin and declared that so long as such a tone were struck, better relations would be impossible.[27]

---

[24] *Letters of Queen Victoria*, III, p. 431.

[25] *Die Grosse Politik*, XV, nos. 4425, 4429; Eckardstein, op. cit., II, pp. 144 ff.

[26] *Africa No. 1 (1900), Correspondence respecting the Action of H. M.'s Naval Authorities with regard to Certain Foreign Vessels.*

[27] *Die Grosse Politik*, XV, no. 4456. The whole matter is dealt with in great detail in *Die Grosse Politik*, XV, chap. cii, but see also the Blue Book mentioned above and *British Documents*, I, nos. 304, 306; Eckardstein, op. cit., II, pp. 144 ff. and the analysis of the documents in Ray-

The *Bundesrath* affair was a most unfortunate interlude. Salisbury admitted in a letter to the Queen that the ship had been stopped " on very inadequate evidence " and that the mistake might prove a costly one.[28] A costly one it certainly was, for it not only interjected a further element of irritation into Anglo-German relations, but greatly facilitated the German government's task of passing the naval bill. When Tirpitz heard of the incident he is reported to have been delighted and to have exclaimed: " Now we have the wind we need to bring our ship into the harbor; the naval law will pass." [29]

In a sense it may be said that the stopping of the German ships revived also the question of possible international action against Britain. Since Chamberlain's Leicester speech the Paris press had been more rabid than ever. The whole country, wrote the British ambassador, " appears to have gone mad with jealousy, spite and resentment." [30] Everywhere the demand for intervention cropped out. Delcassé and the government were undoubtedly opposed to any policy of adventure, but the government was weak and the nationalist tide was strong. The German ambassador reported in January 1900 that French hatred of the English was almost deeper than it ever had been against Germany. The French public counted on the good will of the Germans.[31] On some sides it was felt that this was the moment to take revenge for Fashoda, and that if France failed to act England would ultimately make good her losses in south Africa by an attack on France or by the seizure of French colonies. France therefore needed a navy strong enough not only to defend herself but to make possible an eventual descent upon England. This was the burden of countless articles and books that appeared during the winter.[32]

In the hour of trial the British government relied upon the firm support of public opinion and upon the power of the fleet. " I am not in the least anxious about foreign complications," wrote Chamberlain on October 11. " It is a pleasant habit of our friends on the Continent to show their teeth when we are engaged with another dog. But in certain tempers of the British public these demonstrations are dangerous, and if I were ' a Frenchman or a Roosian or a Proosian ' I should be inclined not to twist the lion's tail at this precise juncture." [33] Nevertheless precautions were taken. It was reported to London at the very beginning of the war that the French were moving a large fleet into the Mediterranean. Thereupon Salisbury had a flying squadron organized at Port-

---

mond W. Bixler: *Anglo-German Imperialism in South Africa, 1880–1900* (Baltimore, 1932), pp. 152 ff.

[28] *Letters of Queen Victoria*, III, p. 462.

[29] Wilhelm II: *Ereignisse und Gestalten*, p. 197. See also Hurd and Castle, op. cit., p. 119 on the Bundesrath blunder and its effect on the German naval program.

[32] E.g. J. Legrand: *La Leçon de Fachoda* (Paris, 1899); Général de la Rocque: " Esquisse

[30] *British Documents*, I, no. 300.   [31] *Die Grosse Politik*, XVIII, nos. 5860, 5862.

d'un Programme Naval " (*Revue des Deux Mondes*, February 15, 1900, pp. 758–92); Anonymous: " Considérations sur une Guerre entre la France et l'Angleterre " (*Questions Diplomatiques et Coloniales*, March 15, 1900, pp. 352–7); Lieutenant X: *La Guerre avec l'Angleterre* (Paris, 1900).

[33] *Journals and Letters of Reginald Viscount Esher* (London, 1934), I, p. 240.

land and ordered the Channel fleet to Gibraltar and the Mediterranean, a very unusual step. For weeks the French movements were watched with eagle eye; when the fleet went through the Suez Canal to proceed to Madagascar, Lord Curzon telegraphed from India that he feared some intrigue on the Persian Gulf and that he thought the French should be shadowed. Salisbury refused to act provocatively, but he did warn the French that on account of the war they must not expect to find coaling and other facilities in south Africa.[34]

The government thus showed itself to be constantly on the alert. It was generally felt in England that the navy was strong enough to deter France and Russia, and that so long as Germany remained favorably neutral there was no real danger.[35] But the British public was distinctly worried. William T. Stead in the *Review of Reviews* organized a veritable invasion scare. Nothing, he maintained, could prevent the French from seizing the opportunity while the Channel fleet was at Gibraltar to transport 50,000 troops to England, destroy the only British arsenal at Woolwich and attack London. " The Empire, stripped of its armour, has its hands tied behind its back and its bare throat exposed to the keen knife of its bitterest enemies." " No fleet in the world can guarantee our shores against a sudden descent." Responsible people might not want war, but " the men in the street both in France and in England at this moment are rolling drunk with the heady wine of Nationalism and Jingoism. They regard each other with intense suspicion and deep-rooted dislike. Both are armed to the teeth. In their promenade up and down the international thoroughfare no one can say how soon or how violently they may reel up against each other in some narrow alley where one or the other must back down and out. And there is only one opinion everywhere: that if that should occur France will fight. Never again will she submit to a Fashoda humiliation." Since there were practically no troops left in England there was imminent danger of a raid.[36]

This scare must not be taken as a mere extravaganza or as a mere product of the journalistic imagination. Lord Rosebery on February 15 warned the house of lords of the danger and urged the introduction of conscription, and Lord Salisbury himself, in a speech delivered to the Primrose League on May 9, dilated upon the hostility of other countries and the consequent danger to England. London itself, he confessed, was in peril, and, he reminded his hearers, maritime powers had always perished by a blow struck at their heart.

The key to the whole situation lay in Berlin. It was more than unlikely that France would dare move unless she were secured on her eastern frontier.

---

[34] *Journals and Letters of Viscount Esher,* I, pp. 240–1; *Letters of Queen Victoria,* III, p. 475; Meyendorff: *Correspondance Diplomatique de M. de Staal,* II, pp. 424–7.

[35] Letter of Hatzfeldt, December 26, 1899 (Bülow: *Memoirs,* I, pp. 485 ff.).

[36] *Review of Reviews,* January 15, pp. 3, 32 ff.; February 15, pp. 123 ff.; April 15, p. 315. Similarly the *National Review,* January, 1900, p. 646; March, 1900, pp. 3–4, and W. S. Lilly: " The Parlous Position of England " (*Nineteenth Century,* April, 1900, pp. 580–93); H. W. Wilson: " Are we Misled about the Fleet " (*Nineteenth Century,* April, 1900, pp. 568–80); Edmund Robertson: " The Question of the Submarine Boats " (ibid., May, 1900, pp. 713–23).

For that reason the *Bundesrath* crisis of January was so fraught with danger. It will be recalled that at the height of that crisis Bülow had suggested the possibility of Germany's joining a combination hostile to England. In those very days some rather interesting conversations took place between Bülow, the Emperor, and the Russian ambassador at Berlin, Count Osten-Sacken. On January 13 the Russian representative spoke to the Emperor about the general situation and hazarded the opinion that the British fleet was probably not what it was supposed to be. Three smaller fleets, he thought, could probably handle it. The Emperor suggested whimsically that the Greek, Portuguese and Danish fleets might do for the purpose. Osten then touched upon the British violation of sea-law in stopping neutral ships, but the Emperor evaded by suggesting that the Tsar call a conference to settle the matter. The Emperor claimed, in his report of the conversation, that he rejected the idea of joining a coalition unless actually driven to it by the inconsiderateness of the English, but he renewed his former assurances that he would never attack Russia if she engaged in any enterprise in Asia.[37]

Now we have Osten's report of this same conversation. The ambassador said nothing of his own remarks concerning the naval situation and British violations of international law, but recounted the Emperor's assurances about not attacking Russia: " He would stand guard on our frontiers," William was reported as saying. Osten then wrote: " If my impressions do not deceive me . . . the Emperor is still somewhat irritated with the English and, circumstances being favorable, he might be brought to make common cause with England's enemies, always on the sole condition that we be a party to it." Osten hinted that he, personally, thought the time was ripe.[38]

If one compares these two accounts it becomes clear that the ambassador, anxious to start the ball rolling, reported only the half of the conversation which suited his purposes. Here again the Emperor may have been indiscreet, but judging from what we know of his general policy toward England at this time, there is every likelihood that his rejection of the coalition against England was actually made. Yet Osten felt, from what the Emperor said and from what Bülow had remarked some days before regarding the possibility of joint action to block any British action at Delagoa Bay, that there was some prospect of Germany's entering a coalition if the opportunity offered. There was some room for misunderstanding, for the German attitude was veiled in uncertainty.

What we have to consider now is the effect of the report of this conversation upon the Russian foreign office. Russian public opinion, which, according to the

---

[37] *Die Grosse Politik*, XV, no. 4465.

[38] Meyendorff: *Correspondance de M. de Staal*, II, pp. 447 ff. Sir Sidney Lee (*Edward VII*, I, pp. 762–3) saw the copy of this despatch in the Russian embassy archives in London. By using the old style date, January 1, he antedates the document and completely distorts the situation. His account should be left entirely aside, as it is extremely partial and hopelessly biassed. There is an account of this conversation, given to Spring Rice by a high Russian official in 1905, in *British Documents*, VI, no. 129.

German ambassador, had become a much more potent force than it had ever been before, was as hostile to England as the French or the German.[39] From the very beginning of the war there had been a pronounced demand for action against England and against British interests in Asia. But the London government relied upon the friendly disposition of Tsar Nicholas. He was supposed to be much attached to his English relatives and to be deeply moved by the ideas of international peace. He did, in fact, write to Queen Victoria that " nothing was further from his thoughts than to take advantage of our difficulties or to countenance any step likely to increase them " (December 17). A month later the English ambassador at St. Petersburg reported that the Tsar had " forbidden anything being done to embarrass us in our present difficulties." [40] But a recently published letter shows that these assurances were pure cant. Writing to his sister at the very beginning of the war (October 21) Nicholas revealed his real sentiments:

" You know, my dear, that I am not proud, but it is, nevertheless, pleasant to think that it is entirely up to me to decide the ultimate course of the war in South Africa. The reason is very simple: all I need do is to telegraph orders to all the troops in Turkestan to mobilize and advance to the border. That is all! No fleet in the world, however strong, can prevent us from striking at England at her most vulnerable point. But the time for this is not yet ripe: we are not yet sufficiently prepared for serious action, chiefly because Turkestan is not yet connected with the interior of Russia by an unbroken railway line. I have let myself go, but you will understand that there are times when one's innermost yearnings thrust themselves into the light of day and when one cannot resist putting them into words." [41]

This letter is significant not only because it reveals a side of the Tsar's character to which the English, for the most part, always remained blind, but because it supplies the key to the understanding of Russian policy. Muraviev, it will be remembered, made suggestions for action in October. They may have been sincerely intended, and they may have been meant simply to show up the Germans or to frighten the English. By January 1900, at any rate, even Muraviev had come to the conclusion that intervention was not practicable, even for Russian policy. We have a long memorandum of his, dated January 25 / February 7, in which the whole question of policy was gone over in great detail and examined from every angle. In this document Muraviev pointed out the demands of Russian opinion that some advantage be taken of England's temporary impotence. The idea of joining a coalition he put aside at the outset, for the following reasons: 1) the United States could not be induced

[39] *Die Grosse Politik,* XV, no. 4395.

[40] *Letters of Queen Victoria,* III, pp. 439, 461.

[41] " Nikolai Romanov ob Anglo-Burskoi Voine " (*Krasnyi Arkhiv,* LXIII, 1934, pp. 124–6). This letter has been published in German translation in the *Berliner Monatshefte,* December, 1934, pp. 1005–8.

to join; 2) the French government was too much involved in domestic diffi-culties and too much taken up with the coming world exposition at Paris; 3) the Italian government seemed to have some agreement with England; 4) Aus-tria was completely immersed in a serious constitutional crisis; 5) the German Emperor had demonstrated his intention of maintaining neutrality and was obviously aiming at an agreement with England. He had already secured Samoa and the Bagdad Railway concession as a price of his good will.

A coalition being out of the question, there remained the possibility of Russia's scoring a few peaceful victories at England's expense. People talked of taking Ceuta, or Burgas, or some points in the Mediterranean, the Black Sea or the Persian Gulf. The answer to this demand, said Muraviev, was that all naval bases, however valuable, were expensive to fortify and difficult to hold in war. Then there was the question of Russia's seizing the Bosporus. The foreign minister admitted that such a step was necessary and inevitable sooner or later, and that Russia must be prepared to anticipate all competitors. For the moment, however, such action would precipitate war. Russia should, for the time being, content herself with an agreement with Turkey by which the Sultan should promise not to let other interests than Russian build railways in northern Anatolia and by which he should agree further not to fortify the Bosporus. As for Persia, Russia had neither the money nor the political need for building railways in the northern part. If she made such a demand, England would reply by securing concessions for railways in southern Persia. Russia had therefore induced the Shah to renew for ten years his promise of 1890 not to build railways without consulting the Russian government. There was, said Muraviev, no point in Russia's trying to conclude with England a treaty partitioning Persia into spheres of influence, for the Russian position in northern Persia was already unassailable and she could not hope to get more by an agree-ment with England. Afghanistan was another point of great importance. People talked of the seizure of Herat, but such a move would only call forth the hostility of the Amir and weaken Russia's reputation in central Asia.

This memorandum was submitted to the ministries of finance, war and navy, and we have the replies of the various ministers, which were handed in between February 23 and February 29. Witte in his comments made much of Russia's financial troubles and generally took a stand adverse to any further advance or expensive project. Operations in central Asia would require a great many troops and would call forth further armaments by Britain, so that the costly competition would become greater than ever. As for the Bosporus it would be difficult to make plans in advance. It was unlikely that Russia would ever get possession of it except through a general war or through making far-reaching concessions elsewhere. The minister of marine, on the other hand, regretted that Russia was to get nothing from the favorable situation that ex-isted at the time. He stressed the urgent need of a port in southern Korea, and agreed that all possible preparations should be made for action against the

Bosporus. It was this last point that interested the war minister, General Kuropatkin, more than any other. The occupation of the Bosporus he declared to be Russia's most important problem. He too favored all possible preparations and an agreement with Germany to this end.

Taking this series of documents together it is significant to note that the Russian foreign ministry excluded the possibility of a coalition against England. All the ministries consulted saw, too, the hopelessness of any expensive military or naval action. Whatever was to be gained would have to be gained by diplomacy. For the rest they agreed that the occupation of the Bosporus was more important than any other question.[42]

Muraviev, in his summary of the discussion, pointed out that Russia had already made a number of peaceful gains, and that was the fact. The British, in their usual businesslike way, had foreseen the possibilities and had made up their minds to some sacrifices. While Chamberlain, for example, was apprehensive of French designs in Morocco and talked to the Germans about an eventual agreement to frustrate these designs, Salisbury had made up his mind from the start that England would take Tangiers if trouble arose, and that there would be no point in opposing the French advance from Algiers. Nothing was done to stop the French encroachment on the important oasis of Tuat and the Germans suspected, probably with justice, that Salisbury would be ready for a bargain with France if the matter came to a head.[43]

The same attitude was taken in London with respect to Russian designs. When the war broke out Salisbury told the German ambassador that England would do nothing if Russia attempted to open the Straits for her warships, but in actual fact the powerful Mediterranean fleet was at once concentrated at Saloniki as a warning. The Germans were probably right in their conjecture that England would oppose Russia in the Near East if Austria and other powers joined, and that an understanding with Russia would be made only if England got no support from Germany. After all, Russia would hardly dare move unless she were certain of not being attacked on her German and Austrian frontiers. It would be more sensible on the part of the Muscovites, thought the Germans, to advance in areas where other powers were not interested. The Russians thought so, too. In fact they realized that common sense dictated action in regions where the British fleet would be of no avail.[44]

One such area was Persia. The story of Anglo-Russian rivalry is a long and important one, but the question became a burning one only in a later period and we shall have to content ourselves here with only casual references.

---

[42] M. Pokrovski: "Tsarskaia Diplomatiia o Zadachaiakh Rossii na Vostoke v 1900 g." (*Krasnyi Arkhiv*, XVIII, 1926, pp. 3–29). These documents have been translated into German and published in full under the title "Die Zaristische Diplomatie über Russlands Aufgaben im Orient im Jahre 1900" (*Berliner Monatshefte*, July, 1928, pp. 638–69).

[43] *Die Grosse Politik*, XVII, nos. 5152–68; *British Documents*, II, nos. 304, 307; Augustin Bernard: "Touat et Maroc" (*Questions Diplomatiques et Coloniales*, June 1, 1900, pp. 653–64).

[44] *Die Grosse Politik*, XVIII, nos. 5640–4.

By the end of the nineteenth century the Russian influence had made very great strides. It had, in fact, become the dominant influence at the Persian court, so there was a real prospect of the whole country's falling within the Russian sphere. Muraviev, as we have seen, pointed out in his memorandum that the Russian position in northern Persia was unshakeable, but that there was not much hope of advancing in the center and south excepting at the expense of large troop concentrations and possible conflict with England. This estimate, we now know, was substantially correct. No serious Englishman had any idea of being able to stem the Russian tide in northern Persia. Even the central areas were regarded as practically lost. Lord Curzon, as viceroy of India, contemplated the situation with more than a little apprehension. It was on September 21, 1899 that he wrote his great memorandum on the Persian question, indicating the urgent need of a well-defined British policy. England, he thought, should openly oppose the Russian advance or else seek an understanding with Russia. In any event it was imperative that Russia should be kept from reaching the Persian Gulf. It was only in July 1900 that he received a reply, and an evasive one at that, to his communication. Salisbury was above all things anxious not to force the issue, and almost nothing was done to prevent the Russians from arranging with Persia the great loan of January 1900, which was secured by the revenues of all Persia excepting the southern areas. The London government was determined not to stand on anything but the question of southern Persia and the Gulf. Encroachment there, to be sure, " would be a very serious matter indeed," but the danger of Russian aggression did not seem a pressing one for the moment. In other words, Salisbury was prepared to let the Russians spread themselves in northern and central Persia just as he was willing to see the French help themselves to a large part of Morocco. In both places there was a limit for which England would fight, but France and Russia both had a long way to go before that limit was reached.[45]

Finally there was the Afghan question, so often a bone of contention between England and Russia. In January 1900 the Russians sent a force of men from the Caucasus to the Afghan frontier opposite Herat. It was reported that 30,000 men were being concentrated there and that an attack upon the key position, Herat, was imminent.[46] The Russians announced that the expedition was simply a trial mobilization and Kuropatkin told the German ambassador that only about 2500 men had been sent. Russia, he said, had no designs on Herat. All she wanted was a couple of forts at the entrance of the Bosporus, and

---

[45] The unpublished parts of the Curzon memorandum and the reply may now be found in the *British Documents*, IV, nos. 319–20. See also *Die Grosse Politik*, XVII, nos. 5212, 5335, 5336; General Sir Thomas Gordon: " The Problem of the Middle East " (*Nineteenth Century*, March, 1900, pp. 413–25). Details on Russian policy and the developments in Persia may be found in General Krahmer: *Die Beziehungen Russlands zu Persien* (Leipzig, 1903) and in Sir Percy Sykes: *A History of Persia* (Second edition, London, 1921), II, chap. lxxx.

[46] *Questions Diplomatiques et Coloniales*, January 15, 1900, p. 116; March 1, 1900, p. 307; *Review of Reviews*, February 15, 1900, p. 107; Demetrius C. Boulger: " Cabul and Herat " (*Contemporary Review*, January, 1900, pp. 40–50).

these she would get sooner or later. Salisbury himself put little stock in the rumors of an attack on Afghanistan, but he must have been very disagreeably surprised when, on February 6, 1900, the Russians handed in a memorandum pointing out that, while observing earlier declarations that Afghanistan lay outside the sphere of Russian influence, trade relations had made it necessary for them to establish direct relations with Cabul in order to settle frontier matters. It was well recognized in London that this was simply the opening wedge to the establishment of political relations between Russia and Afghanistan. The British did not like the move at all, but they abstained from making an issue of it at the time.[47]

After this long digression we must return to the European scene. The second half of February marked the turning of the tide in a military sense, for with the relief of Kimberley and Ladysmith and the surrender of General Cronje at Paardeberg the British could look forward to the ultimate conquest of the two republics. This situation induced Muraviev to make a suggestion that came nearer than any other to being a proposal for intervention against England. On February 28 he suggested to Delcassé that the German government might be brought to take sides as between England and the Franco-Russian Alliance by an invitation that she join in a démarche to bring about peace. Delcassé, it is said, was dubious about the proposal, but agreed to take part in order not to estrange Russia. France, he said, would join if Russia carried on the negotiations with Berlin and if Germany would agree to take the initiative.[48]

The Russian proposition was laid before the German government on March 3. The three powers were to join in " amicable pressure " to prevent the complete crushing of the Boers. Bülow's reply was definite: Such a step would be a long-term affair and Germany could not think of joining in it unless the three powers first agreed to a mutual guarantee of their territory for a certain number of years. To which Muraviev replied that all Russia wanted was to act in the interests of humanity. The negotiation of such a guarantee agreement would take a long time. Furthermore it would nullify the chief purpose for the action, namely the early termination of the war. The Germans were asking too much. No cabinet could stand for twenty-four hours in France if it proposed what amounted to a recognition of the Treaty of Frankfort. So the whole business fell flat. Shortly afterward the Boers themselves appealed to the powers for mediation on the basis of the independence of the republics, whereupon Salisbury declared publicly that Britain would not accept mediation on that basis. This firm stand put an end to suggestions for intervention, for it was then perfectly obvious that England would fight first.[49]

---

[47] *Die Grosse Politik,* XVII, nos. 5212, 5334, 5336; *British Documents,* I, nos. 376, 377.

[48] Mévil: *De la Paix de Francfort, etc.,* p. 57; Bourgeois and Pagès, op. cit., pp. 286 ff.

[49] The fundamental documents and accounts of the Muraviev démarche are in *Die Grosse Politik,* XV, nos. 4472 ff. and in Bourgeois and Pagès, op. cit., pp. 286 ff. See further the misleading account given by Delcassé to Mallet in 1905 (*British Documents,* III, pp. 432–3); the inspired ac-

There has been no end of speculation as to the origin and purpose of the Muraviev proposal. It seems the more mysterious since we know of the February memorandum in which he excluded a combination against England as not feasible. Later on he tried to make out that he had been led to take the step by the hints made by Bülow and the Emperor in January! The obvious explanation is probably the correct one. Muraviev told Delcassé that his démarche would oblige the Germans to show their colors. He must have known that the Germans would reject the proposal. Certainly everything possible was done to misrepresent their position. The English were informed indirectly that the Germans had made suggestions for action against England, and when the Prince of Wales visited his relatives in Denmark in April he was given a long Russian memorandum recounting the sins of the Berlin government. Russia was to be rewarded in Asia, and France in Africa, if they would join Germany in common action against England.[50]

This was, of course, a complete reversal of the facts. There was never any possibility of Germany's joining with Russia and France in any project for intervention, and there is no reason to doubt the sincerity of Bülow's argument that the guarantee formula was intended only to show up France and to crawl out of an embarrassing situation with some grace.[51] This is perfectly clear from the contemporary documents. The Emperor William, in conversation with the British ambassador on February 6, had shown himself very friendly, even though he complained of the "kicks in the shins" which the British occasionally gave him. At the same time he sent his grandmother further "aphorisms" on the conduct of the war, which, whatever else may be said of them, appear to have been well-intentioned. When the Emperor learned of the advances of Muraviev he noted: "If the Russians are itching for intervention, let Muraviev do it himself, or with France." [52] Throughout the remainder of the war the German attitude continued to be perfectly correct. Neither the Boer delegation nor Kruger himself was received in Berlin.

The Germans were quick, however, in making capital of Muraviev's *faux pas.* William at once informed Queen Victoria and the Prince of Wales. The Queen thought Muraviev's conduct "really too monstrous" and noted: "William, I am sure, wishes to be our true friend, and he indeed deserves our thanks and confidence." Lord Salisbury, too, found the Russian minister's action "very inexplicable," while the Prince of Wales wrote to his nephew: "What you tell me about Mouraviev's conduct does not surprise me, as I believe there is nothing he would not do in conjunction with France to annoy us in every possible

count of André Mévil: "Delcassé and the Entente Cordiale" (*National Review,* July, 1908, pp. 712–9); the inspired anonymous account written by Fritz Heilbron: "Deutsche Intrigen gegen England im Burenkriege, von einem Wissenden" (*Deutsche Revue,* September, 1908, pp. 257–63); and the strongly biassed account of Sir Sidney Lee: *Edward VII,* I, pp. 765 ff.

[50] *Die Grosse Politik,* XV, no. 4493; Eckardstein: *Lebenserinnerungen,* II, pp. 167 ff.
[51] *Die Grosse Politik,* XV, no. 4496.
[52] *Die Grosse Politik,* XV, nos. 4479, 4507; *British Documents,* I, no. 311.

way. . . . You have no idea, my dear William, how all of us in England appreciate the loyal friendship which you manifest towards us on every possible occasion." To which William replied in a letter to the Queen: " I am most thankful to Providence that I was granted such an opportunity of saving your country from a most dangerous situation in warding off a combination aiming a blow at England in a moment which was vital to her." [53]

The history of European diplomacy during the Boer War is a chronicle of distrust, intrigue and innuendo. Few chapters in the history of modern Europe are more disgusting. It was indeed a long call from the diplomacy on the grand scale of the days of Bismarck. The gist of the whole problem was, of course, that the advent of colonial expansion and imperialism had created a new and serious set of antagonisms which was superimposed upon the old continental rivalries. England, having the lion's share of empire and the instrument *par excellence* for the carrying out of a policy of colonial expansion, was of necessity looked upon askance by all the others, and was soon put down as the dog in the manger who had all he needed, who wanted more and who snarled at everyone who looked for a few scraps. There can be no doubt that the " new diplomacy " of Chamberlain had a good deal to do with exciting public opinion in other countries. Speeches like the " Long Spoon Speech " and the Leicester Speech were not soon forgotten, and the whole diplomacy that led to the Boer War looked suspiciously like a flagrant attack upon two small states which were wanted for their mineral wealth.

With hatred of England rife on all sides, it was inevitable that the moment of her trial and tribulation should tempt other powers. No subject was more discussed in the winter of 1899–1900 than the possibility of a coalition against England. The scheme was bound to fail, for the Germans had definitely made up their minds that France and Russia, however well-disposed, were not safe company. It would be better for Germany to stand by England and put in her claims for reward afterward. So long as the Germans took this attitude (and there is no satisfactory evidence that they thought seriously of departing from it) action by France or Russia was out of the question. The mistake of German policy was that Bülow and the Emperor were clumsy in their manipulation of it. They kept on harping upon their good will, but at the same time kept stressing the need for payment. Not only that, they kept toying with the idea of co-operation with France or Russia in colonial matters in the event of the British not showing due recognition. In this way they laid themselves open to compromising interpretations in London.

As for the French, their stand is by no means clear. The public, to be sure, was ready for almost anything and was literally thirsting for revenge for Fashoda. But the government does not appear to have shared this enthusiasm. The great world exposition, for which long preparations had been made, was

---

[53] *Letters of Queen Victoria,* III, pp. 499–500, 503, 507–8, 519; *Die Grosse Politik,* XV, nos. 4480, 4484, 4485; Eckardstein, op. cit., II, pp. 167 ff.

about to open in April 1900, and its success depended on peace and quiet. Delcassé gave the British ambassador the distinct impression that the government was opposed to any action against England. On the other hand he was willing to make what he could out of the situation. There was the French advance on the frontier of Morocco, for example. Further yet, he seems to have been quite ready to listen to German hints for common action in colonial affairs, and the Russian ambassador reported him deeply disappointed that the German advances in October 1899 had not been followed up by concrete proposals.[54] From all of which one is led to believe that Delcassé would not have hung back if Russia had actually succeeded in drawing the Germans into a common action. He was certainly more discreet and circumspect than were the Germans or the Russians.

Both the Tsar and Muraviev, it may be taken for granted, would have been glad to deal England a telling blow. The latter certainly made advances in October and again in March, but these were chiefly manoeuvrings. The Russians wanted to act, but they weren't ready. They had no money, and so they had to eschew all policies that would entail heavy expenditure. They made some gains at Britain's expense, but the gains were nothing compared to what the public and Muraviev would have liked. The only chance of getting more was through action with other powers, and that chance faded completely after the German rejection of Russian advances.

So far as England was concerned there is only this to be remarked: That the British government fully understood the value of German neutrality and good will. Chamberlain, Balfour and others were, in fact, ready to go beyond mere co-operation and were prepared to pay a price for a close understanding, a price which would probably have taken the shape of a Moroccan agreement. Salisbury, on the other hand, had become by this time opposed to buying the support of the Germans. He disliked them intensely and resented their constant demands for the pound of flesh. He had held out to the end on the Samoan affair and he showed no readiness whatever to discuss questions like the Moroccan. His policy was rather to take what he could and leave what he must. If France could be kept quiet by the abandonment of part of Morocco, well and good. If the Russians really made a move to seize the Bosporus, either England could join with Austria and Italy in opposing her, or England could strike a bargain and get adequate compensation. An advance in Persia was permissible so long as the Russians stayed away from the south and from the Persian Gulf. Northern Persia was already theirs so far as Salisbury was concerned. In fact he stomached a rather serious setback in Afghanistan rather than provoke a conflict. In all this one sees already the broad outlines of the future ententes with France and Russia. The dawn of the new century was already casting over Europe the rays of future developments.

---

[54] Meyendorff: *Correspondance de M. de Staal*, II, p. 453.

BIBLIOGRAPHICAL NOTE

DOCUMENTARY SOURCES

Die Grosse Politik der Europäischen Kabinette, 1871–1914. Volume XV, chapter cii: The seizure of German ships; chapter ciii: The question of intervention during the Boer War. Volume XVII, chapter cxiii: The Moroccan Question. Volume XVIII, chapter cxix: The Dardanelles Question; chapter ccxxvi: German-French relations.

British Documents on the Origins of the War, 1898–1914. Volume I, chapter vii: The Boer War. Volume II, chapter xiv: France, Spain and Morocco.

Accounts and Papers. 1900, volume LVI. *Africa No. 1 (1900), Correspondence respecting the action of H. Mj's Naval Authorities with regard to certain Foreign Vessels.*

" Tsarskaia Diplomatiia o Zadachaiakh Rossii na Vostoke v 1900 g." (*Krasnyi Arkhiv,* XVIII, 1926, pp. 3–29). Edited by M. Pokrovski. The important Muraviev memorandum of February 1900. These documents have been translated and published in full under the title: " Die Zaristische Diplomatie über Russlands Aufgaben im Orient im Jahre 1900 " (*Berliner Monatshefte,* July, 1928, pp. 638–69).

" Nikolai Romanov ob Anglo-Burskoi Voine " (*Krasnyi Arkhiv,* LXIII, 1934, pp. 124–6). A most illuminating letter of the Tsar to his sister. A German translation has been published in the *Berliner Monatshefte,* December, 1934, pp. 1005–8.

MEMOIRS, AUTOBIOGRAPHIES, BIOGRAPHIES, AND LETTERS

LEE, SIR SIDNEY: *King Edward VII, a Biography.* Two volumes. New York, 1925. Discusses in detail the Emperor's visit to England and the question of intervention during the war. Contains a number of interesting documents, but for the rest is biassed and misleading.

GARVIN, J. L.: *The Life of Joseph Chamberlain.* Three volumes. London, 1933—. Contains very little on European diplomacy during the war, and that chiefly from the German Documents.

BÜLOW, PRINCE VON: *Memoirs.* Four volumes. Boston, 1931. Discusses in detail the Anglo-German relationship, but adds very little to what may be learned from the documents.

ECKARDSTEIN, HERMANN FREIHERR VON: *Lebenserinnerungen und Politische Denkwürdigkeiten.* Two volumes. Leipzig, 1919. Interesting but not always reliable. The period dealt with in this chapter forms the most instructive part of Eckardstein's book.

MEYENDORFF, BARON A.: *Correspondance de M. de Staal.* Two volumes. Paris, 1929. Valuable chiefly because it gives the text of important reports from Berlin in January 1900.

Letters of Queen Victoria. Edited by George E. Buckle. Third series, volume III. London, 1932. Of interest chiefly for the correspondence of the English and German ruling families.

TIRPITZ, ALFRED VON: *Erinnerungen.* Leipzig, 1919. One of the chief sources for the history of the German naval policy.

HOHENLOHE, PRINCE CHLODWIG ZU: *Denkwürdigkeiten der Reichskanzlerzeit.* Stuttgart, 1931. Contains some interesting notes on the evolution of the second German naval bill.

SPECIAL STUDIES

BOURGEOIS, ÉMILE, and PAGÈS, GEORGES: *Les Origines et les Responsabilités de la Grande Guerre.* Paris, 1921. Contains the French documents bearing on the question of intervention. Incomplete, but of considerable importance.

DIPLOMATICUS (?LUCIEN WOLF): " Count Muravieff's ' Indiscretion.' " (*Fortnightly Review,* December, 1899, pp. 1036–45). A remarkable article, revealing pretty accurately the démarches of Muraviev in October 1899.

MÉVIL, ANDRÉ: " Delcassé and the Entente Cordiale." (*National Review,* July, 1908, pp. 712–9). An inspired article, giving Delcassé's version of the intervention projects.

—: *De la Paix de Francfort à la Conférence d'Algésiras.* Paris, 1909. Practically repeats what is said in Mévil's article.

ANONYMOUS (FRITZ HEILBRON): " Deutsche Intrigen gegen England während des Burenkrieges." (*Deutsche Revue,* September, 1908, pp. 257–63). A reply to Mévil's article. This article was written from the German documents and published anonymously by the foreign office. It says substantially what the Emperor said at the same time in his famous *Daily Telegraph* interview on October 28, 1908.

TREUE, WILHELM: " Presse und Politik in Deutschland und England während des Burenkrieges." (*Berliner Monatshefte,* August, 1933, pp. 786–803). A quite inadequate article, dealing chiefly with the unsuccessful efforts made during the war to influence the press. Based almost entirely upon the German and British documents and the obvious memoir material.

HURD, ARCHIBALD, and CASTLE, HENRY: *German Sea-Power.* London, 1913. Still one of the best general accounts of the German naval policy. Contains the essential documents.

KEHR, ECKART: *Schlachtflottenbau und Parteipolitik, 1894–1901.* Berlin, 1930. The most detailed study of the German naval policy, extremely useful despite the fact that it deals very largely with the domestic aspects.

MICHALIK, BERNHARD: *Probleme des Deutschen Flottenbaues.* Breslau, 1931. A good antidote to Kehr's book, and an interesting discussion of the international aspects of the German naval policy.

BECKER, WILLY: *Fürst Bülow und England.* Greifswald, 1929. One of the most detailed studies of German policy with respect to England. Not particularly instructive.

MEINECKE, FRIEDRICH: *Geschichte des Deutsch-Englischen Bündnisproblems, 1890–1901.* Munich, 1927. Another detailed analysis of the period, with conclusions which seem to me frequently unsound.

LÖDING, WALTHER: *Die Deutsch-Englischen Bündnisverhandlungen 1898 bis 1901.* Hamburg, 1929. One of the best factual accounts of Anglo-German negotiations during this period.

XXI

The Boxer Rising

∽

O F ALL THE ISSUES WHICH CONFRONTED THE EUROPEAN GOVERNMENTS in the period between Bismarck's fall and the conclusion of the Anglo-French Entente in 1904 the Far Eastern question was the most serious and the most complex. To be sure, it lacked the high drama and color of the African problems. There was no Menelik, no Mahdi, no Marchand and there was no Paul Kruger, no Cecil Rhodes, in fact no spectacular clash of personalities whatever. If you except Li Hung-chang and the old Empress Dowager, of whose innermost thoughts we know little or nothing, there were no great figures to captivate the imagination. But the conflict of interests was of infinitely greater importance. In the Far East the powers were dealing with the fate of an empire of upward of three hundred million souls and no less than five major states were disputing the spoils.

We left the Far Eastern situation as it was in the spring of 1898, after the spectacular occupation of Kiao-chow, Port Arthur, Weihaiwei and Kuang-chow and after the great scramble for concessions. Needless to say, these thrilling events made an even deeper impression upon the Chinese than upon the Europeans. The utter helplessness of the Empire was patent to all, the days of the state were obviously numbered and the partition of China was discussed among high and low. Even the Emperor, Kuang-hsü, could no longer shut his eyes to the imminence of collapse. Kang Yu-wei, the great Chinese reformer, had appealed to him in a great memorial of December 1895, urging the need of a thoroughgoing reorganization of the Empire on western lines if the situation was to be saved. No attention was paid to the prophets of disaster at that time, and Kang's Reform Club was reduced to impotence. But now that the catastrophe had happened and the hated foreigner sat in the most desirable ports along the coast, Kang renewed his efforts with more success. In a memorial to the Emperor in the spring of 1898 he warned in no vague terms: " If Your Majesty will not decide, or will prefer to remain in the old grooves of the Conservatives, then your territories will be swallowed up, your limbs will be bound, your viscera will be cut up, and Your Majesty will scarcely manage to retain your throne or to rule over more than a fragment of your ancient Empire."

This time the Emperor listened. He saw his country, says Kang, " about to sink in the earth, about to be buried in ruins, about to burst like an egg, about

677

to be divided up, about to mortify, about to be torn in shreds, about to become like India or Annam, or Burmah — a dependent of another Power! . . . If one had but the lightest knowledge of this, at every thought of it one would get so anxious as to burst into perspiration, and be so angry as to make one's hair stand on end, one's eyes stare out of their sockets, and not be able to endure it for a single day." [1] He therefore called Kang to Peking, and in the summer of 1898 embarked upon the remarkable Hundred Days of Reform. Day after day during this short period decrees were issued aiming at the modernization of the educational system, the administration, the finances, the army and navy and the economic life of the country. There was hardly a phase of government activity that was not touched. If the policy had been carried through it would undoubtedly have transformed and greatly strengthened China. But authoritative writers are generally agreed that the reform policy, however well-intentioned, never had much chance of success. Kang was immensely impressed with the story of Peter the Great and would have wished the Emperor to play the part of the ruthless Russian iconoclast. But Kuang-hsü was anything but a Peter. He meant well, but he lacked understanding and he lacked force of character. Kang himself failed to appreciate the difficulties of the problem. He had only a general knowledge of European affairs and thought China could follow the path of Japan much more easily than was the case. He tried to do too much in too short a time and took far too little account of the forces of opposition. The Chinese Emperor was far from all-powerful; reforms meant nothing unless they were carried through by the provincial authorities. And then there was the canny old Empress Dowager and her following of Manchu conservatives to be taken into account. The opposition of the local authorities to any attempt at greater centralization and the dislike of the conservatives for any radical westernization sealed the fate of the reform experiment. When, in September, Kang and his associates planned to remove the old Empress from the scene, the plot was revealed to her by Jung-lu, the military chief. On September 21 the old lady, with her usual decision, turned the tables upon the Emperor, carried through a coup d'état and brought the work of the reformers to an abrupt close. [2]

The reform movement in China in 1898 remained an interlude, interesting as a reflection of the Chinese reaction to the aggression of the European powers but devoid of any direct bearing upon international relations. It has been aptly

[1] Kang Yu-wei: "The Reform of China" (*Contemporary Review,* August, 1899, pp. 180–98).

[2] There are many good accounts of the reform interlude, among which may be mentioned Kang Yu-wei's "The Reform of China," loc. cit.; George S. Owen: "The Reform Policy of the Chinese Emperor" (*National Review,* September, 1899, pp. 119–32); Charles Johnston: "The Struggle for Reform in China" (in *The Crisis in China,* New York, 1900); J. O. P. Bland and E. Backhouse: *China under the Empress Dowager* (Philadelphia, 1910), pp. 178–200; Hosea B. Morse: *The International Relations of the Chinese Empire* (New York, 1918), III, chap. vi; George N. Steiger: *China and the Occident* (New Haven, 1927), pp. 81 ff.; Borton Butcher: "The Emperor's Attempt to Reform the Chinese Government in the Summer of 1898" (*Political Science Quarterly,* XLIII, 1928, pp. 544–66); and, most recently, Meribeth E. Cameron: *The Reform Movement in China, 1898–1912* (Stanford, 1931), chap. ii.

pointed out that the efforts of the Emperor met with no support from European governments, that, in fact, the battle for concessions reached its apogee during the summer of 1898.[3] It was this complete misunderstanding of the Chinese mentality that was to cost the European powers dearly in the not far distant future, but for the moment we must neglect Chinese domestic affairs and return to the problems of European policy.

The Far Eastern crisis of the winter of 1897–1898 had left the two chief rivals, England and Russia, at daggers drawn. Both powers had joined in the scramble for leases and concessions, but no compromise had been reached between them and the British had been unable to find allies to assist them in blocking the Russian advance. It was not enough that the Russians had planted themselves firmly in Manchuria, to the horror of British business interests at Tientsin and Newchuang.[4] They were also invading central China, using Belgian and French interests as spearpoints. On June 27, 1898 the Franco-Belgian syndicate, backed by the Russo-Chinese Bank, secured the definitive concession for the all-important Peking-Hankow line, which, when completed, would bring Russian influence and interests to the banks of the Yangtze Kiang. The British protested vigorously against the award of the concession, pointing out that " a concession of this nature is no longer a commercial or industrial enterprise, and becomes a political movement against British interests in the region of the Yangtze." But despite these protests the Chinese government, insisting that the Russians had nothing to do with it, granted the application of the syndicate and ratified it in August 1898.[5]

The advance of Russia and her friends led to continued criticism of British policy by the press. In a strongly-worded article published on July 30, 1898, the *Times* declared:

" While we are lulled to sleep for months by parliamentary statements of a more or less disingenuous character, other nations are acting with indefatigable energy. While we go talking about a policy of open doors, other nations are consolidating and extending their spheres of exclusive influence at such a rate that there will soon be no door to open. . . . Are we to go on forever, trying to keep out the ocean with a mop or are we going to take the world as we find it, and to secure at least some area of Chinese territory where British enterprise may have a chance? " [6]

The British government was, as a matter of fact, doing its best. It gave the utmost support to a project advanced by the Hongkong and Shanghai Bank which would serve as an effective reply to the Russian invasion of central China.

---

[3] Steiger, op. cit., pp. 81 ff.

[4] Cf. Lord Charles Beresford's observations, recorded in his *The Break-up of China* (New York, 1899), pp. 14 ff., 32 ff.

[5] Jean de Marcillac: " Les Chemins de Fer en Chine " (*Questions Diplomatiques et Coloniales*, July 1, 1899, pp. 265–74); Percy H. Kent: *Railway Enterprise in China* (London, 1907), pp. 93–101; Philip Joseph: *Foreign Diplomacy in China* (London, 1928), p. 337.

[6] Quoted by Chung-fu Chang: *The Anglo-Japanese Alliance* (Baltimore, 1931), p. 59.

Since before the war with Japan the Peking government had planned to build a railroad from Tientsin along the coast of the Gulf of Pechili to Shanhaikwan and thence into Manchuria. Part of the road had already been built by the English engineer, Mr. Kinder, and in 1898 the line was open to beyond the great wall, to the little town of Chunghuso. Now, on June 7, 1898, the Peking authorities concluded a preliminary agreement with the Hongkong and Shanghai Bank by which the latter was to furnish a loan of sixteen million taels for the extension of the line from Chunghuso to Sinminting (some fifty miles to the northwest of Mukden), with a branch line to Ying-k'ou and Newchuang, the busiest port on the Manchurian coast. The permanent way, the rolling stock, the earnings of the entire line from Peking to Tientsin and thence to Sinminting, and various coal and iron mining rights were to serve as security for this loan. In other words, the all-important railway from Peking and Tientsin into Manchuria was to be built by the Chinese, but it was to be mortgaged to the British.

The Russian minister protested at once against this arrangement. He claimed that the Chinese government had promised Russia on December 8, 1897 that only Russians should be allowed to participate in the construction of railways to the north of Shanhaikwan, and recalled warnings he had made against the award of the loan to British interests in the early months of 1898.[7] As usual, the Chinese authorities were between the devil and the deep sea. Pavlov threatened while Sir Claude MacDonald insisted. The British government was determined not to back down, but to make an issue of the question. " You may inform Yamen that Her Majesty's Government will support them against any Power which commits an act of aggression on China because China has granted to a British subject permission to make or support any railway or similar public work," Lord Salisbury wired to the British minister on July 22, 1898.[8] But even this offer of support did not lessen the fright of the Chinese. On July 31 Pavlov extracted from the Yamen a promise not to use the projected railway beyond the great wall (that is, Shanhaikwan) as security for a loan and not to allow foreign control of the operation of the line.[9]

But the Russian government was by no means prepared to force a crisis in its relations with England. Lessar, the chargé d'affaires at London, was instructed to approach the British foreign office in a spirit of conciliation. On this same July 31 he had an excited talk with Balfour, in the course of which Lessar suggested the possibility of an agreement. Balfour, in turn, proposed a general discussion between all interested powers regarding their spheres of influence in China, a proposal to which Muraviev was unwilling to give any support.[10] In the end the British government accepted the Russian suggestion

[7] B. B. Glinskii: *Prolog Russko-Iaponskoi Voiny* (Petrograd, 1916), pp. 78 ff.

[8] *British Documents,* I, no. 55.

[9] Glinskii, op. cit., pp. 81–2; A. Popov: " Anglo-Russkoe Soglashenie o Razdele Kitaiia " (*Krasnyi Arkhiv,* XXV, 1927, pp. 111–34), p. 119.

[10] Popov, op. cit., pp. 119–20.

for negotiations à deux. From the great speech delivered by Balfour in the house of commons on August 10 it is clear that English hopes of maintaining the Open Door were rapidly vanishing. " A concession must be given to someone," he remarked, " and when the someone has got it, other people must be excluded. . . . That is not inequality of treatment." In other words, the British were practically giving up the Open Door policy so far as concessions were concerned. Their aim henceforth was to use the Manchurian railway project as a bargaining point, and to secure in return for the recognition of Manchuria as a Russian sphere a similar recognition by Russia of the Yangtze Valley as a British sphere. The award of the Peking-Hankow line to the Franco-Belgian syndicate was ratified in mid-August and served to bring matters to a head. In a sharp note of August 17 Balfour informed the Russian government that England could not " acquiesce in an arrangement which while excluding England from her share in the railway enterprises of Manchuria leaves all China open to the railway enterprise of Russia. Such a pretension, if persisted in, must inevitably produce the most serious international difficulties." [11]

But even this strong stand did not help much. The Chinese refused to ratify the preliminary arrangement with the Hongkong and Shanghai Bank, though they were forced by British threats and by the concentration of British naval forces to grant new concessions to counterbalance the award of the Peking-Hankow line. In rapid succession English interests, associated to some extent with German and Italian interests, secured concessions for railroads from Kowloon to Canton, from Soochow to Hangchow, from Pukow to Sinyang and from Chinkiang to Tientsin, most of them lines designed to consolidate the British position in the Yangtze Valley.[12] At the same time the London government suggested to Russia an arrangement regarding the Manchurian line: the Hongkong and Shanghai Bank should be allowed to make the loan to China, but as security it was to accept the Peking-Tientsin-Shanhaikwan line and only the profits of the line beyond Shanhaikwan. This solution the Russians were glad to accept, since they regarded the line as far as the great wall as already under British control. The British, however, wanted to tie up this arrangement with a larger agreement regarding spheres of influence, their object being always to secure, if possible, the recognition of the Yangtze Valley as the British sphere, and also a guarantee of the Open Door for trade in the spheres of Russia and other powers. Chamberlain declared quite frankly in a speech delivered on November 16, 1898 that it was not to England's interest " to give anything like a guarantee of the integrity and independence of an empire which appeared to be decaying." Neither was it her business, he continued, to impede the ambitions of others or to appear as the champion of China, providing only that the others observed the principle " that no acquisition of territory by any foreign power should alter the existing state

---

[11] British Documents, I, no. 57.
[12] The best discussion may be found in Joseph, op. cit., pp. 345–63.

of things in this respect, that the markets of China should be open to fair and even competition to all through the open door." This Open Door, he admitted, did not apply to concessions. In other words, Britain would not defend the independence and integrity of China or oppose the establishment of spheres of exclusive influence so far as concessions were concerned. But she would insist on a fair field and no favor in the matter of trade, even within the spheres of the other powers.[13]

In another speech, on December 8, 1898, Chamberlain pleaded for an agreement with Russia, which was, he said, necessary if very serious complications were to be avoided. It was quite possible, he maintained, " to conciliate what we may call the reasonable ambition of Russia with the fixed and settled policy of this country to maintain equal opportunities in trade for all nations." But the Russians were not much interested in British attempts to secure promises of equal trade opportunities in the Russian sphere and they were not much impressed with the suggestion that they recognize the Yangtze Valley as a British sphere in return for recognition of Russia's special position in Manchuria. Witte, in particular, objected to an agreement along such lines. The British proposals, he pointed out, would give Russia no rights in Manchuria which she did not already possess. Furthermore, Manchuria had an area only half that of the Yangtze Basin as defined by the British (the provinces adjacent to the Yangtze River and in addition the provinces of Hunan and Chekiang), and Manchuria was much less populous. Besides, the British proposal would restrict the field of activity of the Russo-Chinese Bank, which had the right to undertake affairs anywhere in China. The French, who had put up most of the money for the bank, would resent any such arrangement. In the large, said Witte, the British suggestions were " impossible and disastrous." [14]

The Russian foreign minister and the minister of war, however, felt the urgent need of some agreement with England, and deprecated the necessity of defending Russian enterprises as far south as the Yangtze River. After months of wrangling between the Russian ministries it was finally decided to return to the original proposal of an agreement on spheres of influence for railroad concessions, leaving aside all reference to the Open Door for trade. Negotiations with England were initiated in February 1899 and finally led to the exchange of notes of April 28, 1899. By the terms of these notes Russia engaged " not to seek for her own account or for Russian subjects any railway concessions in the basin of the Yangtze, nor to obstruct, directly or indirectly, in that region any applications for railway concessions supported by the British Government." England undertook similar obligations with regard to the area " north of the great wall." The agreement included further the arrangements made with regard to the Shanhaikwan-Sinminting Railway, but contained the further

---

[13] Quoted by Joseph, op. cit., pp. 378–9.

[14] Glinskii, op. cit., pp. 84 ff.; B. A. Romanov: *Rossiia v Manchzhurii* (Leningrad, 1928), pp. 212–2; Popov, op. cit., pp. 122–5.

clause stating that it did not "interfere in any way with the right of the Russian government, if it think fit, to support applications of Russian subjects or establishments for concessions for railways which, starting from the main Manchurian line in a south-western direction, would traverse the region in which the Chinese line, terminating at Sinminting and Newchwang, is to be constructed." [15]

This agreement was much less extensive than the British had hoped for. To be sure, it secured Russian recognition of the Yangtze Basin as a British railroad sphere, but no other power had officially recognized it as such, and the Russian acceptance was therefore of qualified value. In return the British had recognized as a Russian railroad sphere not only Manchuria, but all China north of the great wall. No guarantee whatever had been secured for equal trade opportunities in the Russian sphere, and in return for recognition of British interests in the Peking-Tientsin-Sinminting railway line the English government had been obliged to admit the Russian right to a concession for a line to Peking itself, which, if built, would have been a serious competitor of the Chinese-British line and would have constituted the all-important link between Peking and Europe. The Russo-Chinese Bank, to the surprise of the British, applied at once for the concession, but the Chinese government, which had announced in December 1898 that it would not grant further railway concessions for the present, resisted the demand and was supported by the British. The Russians, who had enough to do already in Manchuria, therefore contented themselves with a promise that if foreigners should ever be asked to build the line, the Russians would be given the preference (June 1899). [16]

The Chinese government had definitely set its face against further demands from the foreigners, as the Italians learned to their disappointment in March 1899, when they put forward a request for the lease of San Mun Bay and the recognition of the larger part of Chekiang as a sphere of influence. The demand was supported by the British, but was flatly rejected by the Yamen. There was talk of an ultimatum, but in the end the Italian minister was recalled on the plea that he had exceeded his instructions. Although the demand was pressed again on various occasions during the spring and summer of 1899, it was clear that nothing would come of it, and finally even the Italian government dropped it. [17]

The rejection of the Italian demands did not impress the European powers as deeply as it should have done. To be sure, there were no further attempts to

---

[15] *British Documents,* I, no. 61. The negotiations are well summarized in Kent, op. cit., p. 55; Mongton Chih Hsu: *Railway Problems in China* (New York, 1915), pp. 48 ff., 65 ff.; Popov, op. cit., pp. 125–8; Joseph, op. cit., chap. xvii; R. S. McCordock: *British Far Eastern Policy, 1894–1900* (New York, 1931), pp. 277–88.

[16] Glinskii, op. cit., pp. 88 ff.; Popov, op. cit., pp. 128–9; Joseph, op. cit., pp. 391 ff.

[17] Guido Cora: "La Baia di San Mun" (*Nuova Antologia,* March 16, 1899, pp. 341–53); Anonymous: "L'Italia in Cina" (ibid., April 16, 1899, pp. 746–58); A. A. Fauvel: "L'Italie au Tché-kiang" (*Le Correspondant,* August 10, 1899, pp. 505–26).

secure concessions during the year 1899 and the first half of 1900, but the situation remained ominous and there was a latent feeling that the definitive partition of China was just round the corner. As between the powers, the antagonism between England and Russia was still the dominant factor. " Nine out of ten persons in the United Kingdom believe that Russia wants to take possession of the whole of China, or at least of Peking and all North China," wrote one observer.[18] Lord Charles Beresford, who made an extensive tour of China in the autumn of 1898 as the representative of the Associated Chambers of Commerce, came back to England through the United States in the spring of 1899. He was immensely impressed with the dominant position of Russia in the Far East and reported the conviction of the Chinese that England was afraid of Russia. British business interests, he found, were entirely demoralized by the Russian advance and by the uncertainty and weakness of British policy. There was no hope, he believed, of saving the situation unless England, Germany, the United States and Japan could arrange to undertake the reform of China, especially the reform of the Chinese army. As an alternative to this policy, England's only hope would be the setting aside of a sphere for herself in the Yangtze Valley.[19]

The same feeling of dissatisfaction and hopelessness with regard to British policy was frequently voiced in the English press and parliament. Sir Charles Dilke accused the government of having tried to ride two horses: " The muddle between the policy of the ' open door ' and that of the Yangtze sphere has led to confusion which seems to have caused failure." Beresford shared the same feeling: " From what I can gather from Her Majesty's Government," he said in parliament, " they have been bellowing for the open door, but they have been working all the time for the spheres of influence." He was sick, he said, of the " pipe down " policy.[20]

The government's reply was not very promising. England was still for the Open Door and was still reluctant about staking off a sphere. " We cannot make the Yangtze Valley a province like Shantung or Manchuria, first, because it is infinitely larger, and secondly, we are not prepared to undertake the immense responsibility of governing what is practically a third of China." [21] Which was another way of saying that the government was determined to continue the attempt to ride two horses, despite the fact that it was impossible to preserve the Open Door (which the British government had itself given up so far as con-

---

[18] Gilbert Reid: " The Powers and the Partition of China " (reprinted from the *North American Review* in *The Crisis in China*, New York, 1900).

[19] Charles Beresford: *The Break-up of China* (New York, 1899) and similarly his article " China and the Powers " (in *The Crisis in China*).

[20] Debates of June 9, 1899 (Hansard, Series IV, vol. LXXII, pp. 778 ff., 785 ff.). Much the same stand was taken by writers in the periodical press, for example Senex: " The White Man's Burden in China " (*Contemporary Review,* September, 1899, pp. 318–32); R. S. Gundry: " The Yangtse Region " (*Fortnightly Review,* September, 1899, pp. 448–64).

[21] Statement by Mr. Brodrick, June 9, 1899 (Hansard, LXXII, pp. 803 ff.).

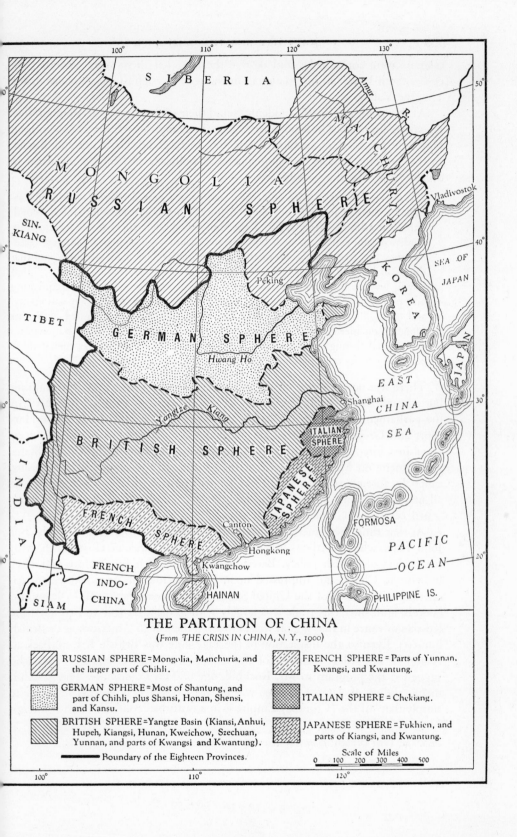

THE PARTITION OF CHINA
(From THE CRISIS IN CHINA, N. Y., 1900)

RUSSIAN SPHERE = Mongolia, Manchuria, and the larger part of Chihli.

GERMAN SPHERE = Most of Shantung, and part of Chihli, plus Shansi, Honan, Shensi, and Kansu.

BRITISH SPHERE = Yangtze Basin (Kiansi, Anhui, Hupeh, Kiangsi, Hunan, Kweichow, Szechuan, Yunnan, and parts of Kwangsi and Kwantung).

Boundary of the Eighteen Provinces.

FRENCH SPHERE = Parts of Yunnan, Kwangsi, and Kwantung.

ITALIAN SPHERE = Chekiang.

JAPANESE SPHERE = Fukhien, and parts of Kiangsi, and Kwantung.

Scale of Miles
0   100   200   300   400   500

cessions were concerned), and despite the fact that there were obvious difficulties, both local and international, in the way of establishing a sphere in the
Yangtze Valley.

At this point the British suddenly found their efforts supported from a rather
unexpected quarter. On September 6, 1899 the American secretary of state, John
Hay, sent out his famous Open Door note to England, Germany and Russia.
In this note the powers claiming spheres of influence in China were asked to
declare: first, that they would

> " in no wise interfere with any treaty port or any vested interest within any so-
> called ' sphere of interest ' or leased territory " they might have in China; second,
> " that the Chinese treaty tariff of the time being shall apply to all merchandise
> landed or shipped to all such ports as are within said ' sphere of interest ' (un-
> less they be ' free ports '), no matter to what nationality it may belong, and that
> duties so leviable shall be collected by the Chinese Government "; third, " that
> it will levy no higher harbor dues on vessels of another nationality frequenting
> any port in such ' sphere ' than shall be levied on vessels of its own nationality,
> and no higher railroad charges over lines built, controlled, or operated within its
> ' sphere ' on merchandise belonging to citizens or subjects of other nationalities
> transported through such ' sphere ' than shall be levied on similar merchandise
> belonging to its own nationals transported over equal distances."

There was nothing new or original about these proposals; they were nothing
but a re-edition of the British policy as it had been put forward for years. In
the parliamentary debates of March and April 1898 Liberal leaders like Harcourt and Grey had suggested an international agreement to secure the Open
Door in China, and the government itself had proposed to the United States
government on March 8, 1898 that the two powers co-operate " in opposing
action by foreign powers which may tend to restrict freedom of commerce of
all nations in China either by imposing preferential conditions or by obtaining
actual cession of Chinese coast territory." [22]

At that time the American government had returned an evasive reply, but
John Hay, who was then ambassador to London, was in close touch with
the leaders of British policy. Beresford consulted with him before and after
his visit to China, and impressed upon him the idea of Anglo-American co-
operation. The trade of the United States in China was increasing by leaps and
bounds, and, since this trade was largely with Manchuria (oil and cotton), the
Russian advance in that region was as much a menace to American as to British
interests. Even so, the inspiration of the Hay note was British. It went back to
Alfred E. Hippisley, formerly of the Chinese maritime customs service, who
suggested the program to Mr. Rockhill, one of Hay's assistants. The Rockhill
memorandum of August 28, 1899 was the basis of the Hay note. It stated quite
simply that " if the (Chinese) Empire is in a disturbed condition, and if foreign

---

[22] Alfred L. P. Dennis: *Adventures in American Diplomacy, 1896–1906* (New York, 1928),
chap. viii; Tyler Dennett: *John Hay* (New York, 1933), pp. 284–5.

interests suffer thereby, this is entirely due to the unseemly haste of some of the treaty powers in their scramble for commercial advantages and acquisition of territory." But, Rockhill went on to say, the spheres of influence " have now been recognized by Great Britain as well as by France, Germany and Russia, and *they must be accepted as existing facts*." " We should insist on absolute equality of treatment in the various zones, for equality of opportunity with the citizens of the favored powers we can not hope to have." [23]

In other words, the American position was exactly that of Britain. The spheres were there, and there was no hope of preventing preferential treatment in the spheres so far as concessions were concerned. All that could be hoped for was respect for treaty rights and equal trade opportunities within the spheres. The Hay note was decidedly not an attempt to proclaim the principles of Chinese independence and integrity. The question was whether even the limited program of the Open Door for trade could be carried through. The British and German governments accepted it, and so did the Italian, French and Japanese governments when it was presented to them somewhat later. But the crux of the whole problem lay in the Russian policy.

It will be recalled that the assurances asked by Hay had been demanded by England in her negotiations with Russia in the winter of 1898–1899, and that they had been rejected. The Russians had agreed to a restricted railway sphere arrangement rather than bind themselves not to levy preferential rates and differential tariffs in their sphere. It was unlikely that they would change their attitude to please Hay. As a matter of fact we know that Muraviev was enraged by the American démarche and that at first the Russians were determined to make no reply whatever. Then they made their policy dependent on that of France, their conviction being that France would not give a favorable reply. When the French deserted them and went their own way, the Russians were obliged to crawl out as best they could. Their reply was a masterpiece of equivocation: " In so far as the territory leased by China to Russia is concerned, the Imperial Government has already demonstrated its firm intention to follow the policy of the ' open door ' by creating Dalny (Talienwan) a free port; and if at some future time that port, although remaining free itself, should be separated by a customs limit from other portions of the territory in question, the customs duties would be levied, in the zone subject to the tariff, upon all foreign merchandise without distinction as to nationality." No mention was made of Russia's sphere of influence in Manchuria, and no mention was made of navigation dues or preferential railway rates. Russia rejected the proposals of Hay as she had rejected those of Lord Salisbury, and since all the powers had made their acceptance of the Open Door policy conditional on the acceptance of the other governments, the whole program really fell to the ground.

Hay understood this perfectly well, but for practical purposes he chose to regard the Russian reply as an acceptance and notified the powers that the

---

[23] Dennis, op. cit., pp. 208 ff.

United States considered the assent of the various powers to be final and definitive. The whole move greatly enhanced Hay's reputation in his own country, though, as his most recent biographer remarks, " it would have taken more than a lawyer to define what new rights had been recognized, or acquired, or even what had actually been said." [24]

The efforts of Hay, then, had no practical bearing on the situation as it was at the turn of the century. The powers were all busy consolidating their past gains, the Russians in particular pushing forward their construction program, developing the new commercial port of Dalny, refortifying Port Arthur and building the southern branch of the Manchurian Railway. The only immediate international danger lay in a possible clash between Russia and Japan.

Since the seizure of Port Arthur Japanese influence had, to a large extent, replaced that of Russia at Peking. The Chinese reformers looked to Japan as a model and an inspiration. They planned to send students to Tokyo and even talked of calling in Count Ito to direct the work of reorganization. This same policy was pursued by the Empress Dowager after the coup d'état of September 1898. Ito urged upon the Peking government the need for reform if China was to be saved from the Europeans. He paid a visit to Peking himself, and was reported to have offered China an alliance. In the autumn of 1899 a Chinese mission was sent to Tokyo asking for support, and soon afterward some forty Japanese officers were sent to China. The Japanese League of Culture and Education aimed directly at the spread of Japanese influence and the development of Chinese-Japanese solidarity against Europe. It opened schools in China and in general unfolded an extensive program of propaganda.[25]

For this development the Russians had only themselves to blame, though there was nothing they could do about it. But with Korea the situation was somewhat different. Since the Rosen-Nissi Agreement of April 1898 the Japanese had been spreading themselves in Korea, establishing commercial settlements and securing concessions. The Korean Independence Club, which worked for reform along western lines, was well known to be under Japanese influence. Here, as in China, the Japanese were intent on building up resistance to the encroachments of the Europeans.[26] The question was whether the Russians were

[24] Dennett: *John Hay,* p. 295. The most important account is that of Dennis, op. cit., chap. viii, which is based on unpublished American documents, but see also Paul S. Reinsch: *World Politics* (New York, 1900), pp. 176 ff.; Shutaro Tomimas: *The Open Door Policy and the Territorial Integrity of China* (New York, 1919), chap. iii and iv; M. J. Bau: *The Open Door Doctrine* (New York, 1923), chap. i; Joseph: *Foreign Diplomacy in China,* chap. xviii; R. S. McCordock: *British Far Eastern Policy, 1894–1900* (New York, 1931), pp. 291 ff.; Paul H. Clyde: " The Open Door Policy of John Hay " (*Historical Outlook,* May, 1931, pp. 210–14).

[25] Glinskii: *Prolog Russko-Iaponskoi Voiny,* pp. 90–103; Charles Johnston: " The Struggle for Reform in China " (in *The Crisis in China,* New York, 1900); O. Franke: " Japans Asiatische Bestrebungen " (*Deutsche Rundschau,* August, 1903, pp. 256–74); C. E. Maitre, in *Bulletin de l'École Française d'Extrême Orient,* IV, 1904, pp. 499–522.

[26] Arthur D. Brown: *The Mastery of the Far East* (New York, 1919), pp. 150 ff.; André Chéradame: *Le Monde et la Guerre Russo-Japonaise* (Paris, 1906), pp. 104 ff.

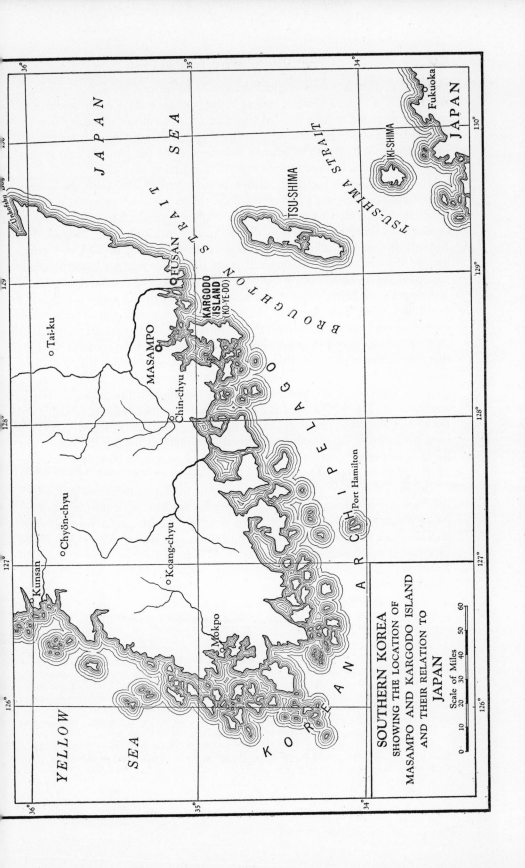

SOUTHERN KOREA

SHOWING THE LOCATION OF
MASAMPO AND KARGODO ISLAND
AND THEIR RELATION TO
JAPAN

Scale of Miles
0   10   20   30   40   50   60

prepared to abandon their original designs in Korea and leave the Japanese a free field. The foreign office, as well as Witte, appears to have made up its mind to that policy, and to have decided once and for all to throw all energy into the consolidation of the position in Manchuria and northern China. This appears quite clearly from the government's attitude toward the famous Yalu concession, which was to become so important in the ensuing period.

In 1896 a Russian merchant named Brinner had secured from the Korean ruler a concession for the exploitation of the timber preserves along the northern boundary of Korea. In view of Russian commitments he had been unable to develop this concession, which in 1897 he turned over to a group composed of Russian diplomats, bankers and developers. In the spring of 1898 this group succeeded in interesting the imperial court in the scheme. An Eastern Asiatic Company was to be formed, which should serve as a cloak for the absorption of northern Korea. Some 20,000 troops were to be smuggled in under the guise of woodsmen. The Tsar approved the scheme and supplied the 250,000 rubles needed to send out an expedition of reconnaissance. The party set out in June 1898 and made extensive surveys as well as a description of the country. Not only that, the leader of the expedition, who was disappointed with the lumbering possibilities of the Yalu area, secured from the Korean King a concession for the exploitation of all the mines in Korea on condition that he arrange a much-needed loan. The whole story is an exceedingly complicated one, which need not be recounted here in all its details. Suffice it to say that Witte, who had not been informed of the expedition, refused absolutely to furnish the money for the loan, or to have anything to do with the Yalu project. In November 1899 the affair had to be dropped for the time being.[27]

But even though Witte was able to frustrate the Korean schemes with which the Tsar himself sympathized, it was harder for him to counteract another policy which was dangerous to his own designs. The Russian naval authorities had for years set their hearts on the acquisition of a base in Korea. Since 1895 they had concentrated their attention on Masampo and the near-by island of Kargodo (Ko-ye-do) at the southeastern tip of Korea, just opposite the Japanese island of Tsushima and commanding the all-important straits between Korea and Japan. The Tsar had been completely converted to the idea that Russia must secure such a port.[28] Masampo was certainly a most desirable place. By

---

[27] The main account of the project was published by one of its leading spirits (V. M. Vonliarliarski): " Why Russia Went to War with Japan, the Story of the Yalu Concession " (*Fortnightly Review*, May and June, 1910, pp. 817–31, 1031–44). Since then there have appeared two important studies based on Russian archive material: B. A. Romanov: " Kontzessia na Yalu " (*Russkoe Proshloye*, I, 1923, pp. 87–108) and Friedrich von Steinmann: *Russlands Politik im Fernen Osten und der Staatssekretär Bezobrazov* (Leipzig, 1931). Curiously enough neither of these writers seems to be aware of Vonliarliarski's published account. See further W. L. Langer: " Der Russisch-Japanische Krieg " (*Europäische Gespräche*, June, 1926, pp. 279–322), pp. 290–3.

[28] A. Popov: " Pervie Shagi Russkogo Imperializma na Dal'nem Vostoke " (*Krasnyi Arkiv*, LII, 1932, pp. 34–124), pp. 67 ff., 76–7, 103 ff.; Baron Rosen: *Forty Years of Diplomacy* (New York, 1922), II, p. 141.

many writers it was considered the best harbor in the whole Far East. The French had surveyed it carefully in 1895 and had hopes all along of securing it at some favorable opportunity.[29]

During 1899 the Russian ministry of marine made several attempts to obtain a concession of land at Masampo, but in every case they seem to have been anticipated by Japan. The Russians threatened reprisals at Seoul, but the Koreans were supported by the Japanese representative. By the autumn of 1899 war between the two powers seemed not at all unlikely, and English writers were already calling for an alliance between England and Japan to block the Russian advance.[30] But Japan was not ready for a conflict at that time, and the Russians too were anxious to postpone the clash which they regarded as inevitable until the Transsiberian Railway should have been finished.[31] The whole question was gone over in the great memorandum drawn up by Muraviev in January 1900. He there pointed out that Japan would oppose Russian action even if England did not. Only when the railroad to Port Arthur was completed could Russia proceed with the scheme.[32]

This argumentation, however, did not satisfy the naval authorities. In reply to Muraviev's memorandum Admiral Tyrtov pointed out that Russia's position in the Far East could not be regarded as secure until she had a base in southern Korea. Port Arthur would be of no use against Japan. In fact, if Japan seized the Korean harbors she could cut off all communication between Port Arthur and Vladivostok. On the other hand, if Russia could get control of Masampo and Kargodo she would have in hand an effective weapon with which to threaten Japan. This would force the latter power to consider carefully before challenging Russia in the Far East.[33]

The argument was reinforced by renewed efforts on the part of the naval authorities to secure an establishment at Masampo. On March 16, 1900 a Russian squadron anchored at Chemulpo. The admiral went up to Seoul, where, together with Pavlov, the Russian minister, he was received in audience by the King. Two days later the Russians secured a lease of land at Masampo for a coal depot and naval hospital, as well as a promise of the non-alienation of Kargodo. News of this success caused great excitement in Japan and England. "This establishment, unimportant in the beginning, might later on assume a more formidable character constituting a permanent menace to Japan," re-

---

[29] This interesting fact is revealed in the anonymous article "L'Occupation de Cargodo par la Russie" (*Questions Diplomatiques et Coloniales,* November 1, 1899, pp. 276-9).

[30] Holt S. Hallett: "The War Cloud in the Far East" (*Nineteenth Century,* December, 1899, pp. 988-95); Ignotus: "The Coming Storm in the Far East" (*National Review,* December, 1899, pp. 494-505). By far the best account of the whole matter is that of K. Asakawa: *The Russo-Japanese Conflict* (Boston, 1904), pp. 274-8, based on Japanese sources. But see also Rosen, op. cit., II, p. 161; Brown, op. cit., pp. 142 ff.

[31] *Die Grosse Politik,* XVII, no. 5336; Hatzfeldt to Bülow, November, 19, 1899 (Bülow: *Memoirs,* I, p. 363).

[32] "Tsarskaia Diplomatiia o Zadachaiakh Rossii na Vostoke" (*Krasnyi Arkhiv,* XVIII, 1926, pp. 3-29).   [33] Ibid.

ported the British minister at Tokyo. For a short time the situation was very tense. Practically the whole Japanese navy was mobilized and part of the army was put in a state of readiness. The details are not known, but it seems that the Japanese accepted the situation only when they learned late in April that the Russians had been obliged, in return for the lease, to bind themselves never to apply for their own use or for the use of Russian subjects for any land on the island of Kargodo or on the opposite mainland or on any of the surrounding islands.[34]

With the atmosphere of Far Eastern affairs heavily charged, the storm broke in May 1900 in what is commonly called the Boxer Rebellion. There has always been a good deal of uncertainty and not a little misunderstanding with respect to the anti-foreign outbreaks in China in 1900, but recent researches have helped considerably to clarify the problem. Hatred of the " foreign devils " was nothing new in China, but it came to a head chiefly after the crisis of 1897-1898. The Emperor Kuang-hsü had tried to meet the emergency by a program of strengthening the Empire through reform along western lines. The effort was frustrated by the Empress Dowager, supported by the conservative Manchu party at court. But it would be a mistake to suppose that the Empress did not share the apprehensions of the reform party. She too was alarmed by the encroachments of the foreigners and she too was determined to offer resistance. Not all the reforms of the Hundred Days were cancelled, but the policy of the government after September 1898 became concentrated more and more upon the problem of military reorganization. Decrees of November and December 1898 ordered the increase and strengthening and drilling of local militia companies, which were the traditional organization used against bandits. The Chinese name of this militia was the I-ho T'uan, which, translated, means The Righteous and Harmonious Band. The fact that the young men who enrolled for this service engaged in elaborate gymnastic exercises and mystic rites gave rise to misinterpretation on the part of missionaries and diplomats, who believed the organization to be part of one of the great secret societies. The name was translated as The Society of Harmonious Fists, hence the popular name Boxers. References to them have been found in missionary correspondence as early as January 1899.[35]

The Boxer groups were unquestionably intended for purposes of defense against foreigners, and their organization was decreed first in the provinces of Chi-li, Shantung, Shansi and Fengtien (Manchuria), which were the provinces at the same time most loyal to the dynasty and most exposed to European encroachments. There were some outbreaks and demonstrations against foreigners in the autumn of 1898, when extra guards were brought up to Peking to pro-

---

[34] *British Documents,* II, nos. 39, 40; Hansard: *Parliamentary Debates,* Series IV, vol. LCCCIII, pp. 730–1, 1503–4; Ignotus: " Britain's Debt to Japan " (*National Review,* May, 1900, pp. 378–88), pp. 382–3; Asakawa, op. cit., p. 276.

[35] I follow here the interesting argumentation of George N. Steiger: *China and the Occident* (New Haven, 1927), chaps. vii and viii, which is sound so far as I can tell.

tect the legations. But serious trouble began in Shantung in the autumn of 1899, when popular feeling against the "foreign devils" assumed alarming proportions. European commerce in China had almost doubled since 1891 and everywhere telegraphs and railroads were penetrating the countryside. Considering the popular opposition to the first railways in Europe it is not surprising that the Chinese disliked the innovation, the more so as the railroads often interfered with the sacred burial places and threw out of work large numbers of porters, boatmen and other transport workers. Add to this the fact that northern China was suffering from two successive years of drought and bad crops, to say nothing of a disastrous flood of the Yellow River, and it is not hard to understand that a superstitious people should have held the outsiders responsible for all their woes. Hatred of the European became widespread and violent and, quite naturally, took the form of attacks upon Chinese converts to Christianity and their protectors, the missionaries, who were generally put down as the agents of foreign business.[36]

From November 1899 the European ministers at Peking began to protest against the activities of the Boxers and to demand their abolition as an illegal organization. They got little satisfaction from the government, partly because the organization was not illegal and could not be proceeded against without outraging Chinese opinion, partly because the Empress sympathized with its aims and felt the need of its support. This is clear from the secret edict of November 21, 1899 sent to all the viceroys. In this paper it is said:

> "The various powers cast upon us looks of tiger-like voracity, hustling each other in their endeavors to be the first to seize upon our innermost territories. They think that China, having neither money nor troops, would never venture to go to war with them. They fail to understand, however, that there are certain things which this Empire can never consent to, and that, if hardly pressed upon, we have no alternative but to rely upon the justice of our cause, the knowledge of which in our breasts strengthens our resolves and steels us to present a united front against our aggressors." The viceroys were urged "to fight for the preservation of their homes and native soil from the encroaching footsteps of the foreign aggressor."[37]

Although this document became known to the foreign ministers in January 1900 they persisted in regarding the Boxer movement as a rebellion and continued to press restrictive measures upon the government. Some concessions were made and orders were issued prohibiting violence, but yielding on the

---

[36] Steiger, loc. cit. Among other accounts of the rise of the movement see the very fair study of George B. Smyth: "Causes of Anti-Foreign Feeling in China" (in *The Crisis in China*, New York, 1900); A. de Pourvoirville: "À Propos des Boxers" (*Nouvelle Revue*, July 1, 1900, pp. 115–27); Arthur H. Smith: *China in Convulsion* (New York, 1901), chaps. x, xi; Bland and Backhouse: *China under the Empress Dowager*, chap. xvi; Henri Cordier: *Histoire des Relations de la Chine avec les Puissances Occidentales* (Paris, 1902), III, chap. xxiv; Paul H. Clements: *The Boxer Rebellion* (New York, 1915), pp. 70 ff.

[37] *United States Foreign Relations 1900*, pp. 85–6, quoted by Clements, op. cit., pp. 105–6.

part of the government was accompanied by rising indignation on the part of the population. By the end of May the situation was getting out of hand. On May 28 an attack was made on the foreigners working on the Peking-Hankow railway, and therewith the critical phase of the Boxer rising may be said to have begun.

The story of the Chinese crisis of 1900 and the siege of the legations has been so often told that no good purpose could be served in recounting it here. The ministers at Peking at once called up additional guards, but these amounted to only a few hundred men. When disorders began to break out along the Tientsin-Peking railway there was obvious danger that the foreigners in the capital would be cut off. General panic seized the Europeans. On June 10 Admiral Seymour, with a small force of 2,000 men from the ships at Taku, set out from Tientsin. He met with serious opposition and was obliged to turn back after a week of fighting without having reached the capital. Prince Tuan, patron of the Boxers and leader of the anti-foreign faction at court, was made head of the Yamen on June 10 and from that time on the government openly identified itself with the movement. The Boxers appeared in Peking on June 13. Two days later telegraphic communication with the outside world was cut off. Thereupon the admirals demanded the surrender of the forts at Taku. The demand remaining unanswered they bombarded and took the forts on June 17. Technically the powers were at war with China, and so the Chinese evidently regarded the situation. Imperial troops began to take part in the fighting along with the Boxers. On June 19 the German minister, von Ketteler, was assassinated on the streets of Peking and the attacks on the legations began. Most of the foreigners took refuge in the British legation, which was valiantly defended until a relief force reached Peking on August 14. In the interval the rising spread to Shansi and Manchuria. Considerable numbers of Chinese converts and European missionaries were killed, and it was reported that the ministers at Peking themselves had been murdered. During June and July 1900 Europe had little thought for anything but the catastrophe in the Far East.

In the early stages of the crisis the European powers had been obliged to act together from force of circumstances. There was little discussion about the Seymour expedition. But this did not imply that the European governments had in any way overcome their earlier rivalries and traditional suspicions. In order to prevent the spread of the movement to central and southern China they adopted the fiction that there was no war, that the Boxer rising was a " rebellion," and that their purpose was simply to relieve the legations and secure guarantees for the future. Beyond that they continued to regard themselves with the deepest distrust. The British government, sadly incapacitated by the South African War, was unable to take as active a part as it might otherwise have done. It did send a considerable force from India, but for the rest devoted itself to the conclusion of arrangements with the viceroys of the Yangtze region to prevent disturbances in what the British regarded as their sphere. Determined efforts were made to induce the Japanese to send a strong force to relieve the legations and to secure for the Japanese something akin to a European mandate. Suggestions of this sort were, however, rejected by the German and Russian governments, for fear that the Japanese and their English friends might be planning to feather their own nests.[38]

England, then, was obliged to fall back on her own resources and to rely upon the benevolent support of Japan and the United States, while trying throughout to maintain contact with Germany and prevent that power from following the lead of Russia. " Russia, not China, seems to me the greatest danger at the moment," wrote Lord Salisbury on June 10.[39] Everywhere in England it was feared that Russia stood behind the Empress and that the outcome of the whole business would be the establishment of Russia in Chi-li and at Peking. The press during July and August called for revenge for the supposed murder of the ministers, pointed out that the conquest or partition of China was inevitable and demanded that England secure her share.[40]

The Russian policy, however, was not as single-minded as the British supposed. Ever since 1895 there had been different opinions in official Russian circles with respect to the policy to be pursued in China. Witte had been opposed to the seizure of Port Arthur and had always favored the policy of an alliance with China, which would serve as a cloak for Russian penetration and ultimate control of a large part of the Empire. The military and naval men, and to some extent the foreign office, had taken the opposite view and had advocated taking whatever could be taken whenever the opportunity presented itself. This same divergence of view cropped up at once when the Boxer disturbances began, with this important difference, that the foreign office now sided with Witte. Muraviev had died suddenly in the last days of June and was succeeded by the much more conservative and circumspect Lamsdorff. On the other hand, Witte's influence upon the Tsar was not what it had been. Kuropatkin, the war minister, was now Nicholas' favorite, and it was therefore a very debatable question whether Witte and Lamsdorff would be able to counteract the demands of the forward party.

Witte tells us in his *Memoirs* that when news of the Boxer rising reached St. Petersburg Kuropatkin exclaimed: " I am very glad. This will give us an excuse for seizing Manchuria. . . . We will turn Manchuria into a second

---

[38] *Die Grosse Politik*, XVI, nos. 4527 ff. These questions have been so thoroughly gone over by various writers that I eschew specific references to the voluminous contemporary and later documentary sources, except when definite references seem desirable. On this point see especially McCordock: *British Far Eastern Policy*, pp. 336 ff.

[39] *Letters of Queen Victoria*, III, p. 561.

[40] Demetrius Boulger: "The Scramble for China " (*Contemporary Review*, July, 1900, pp. 1–10); Idem: " Peking — and After " (*Fortnightly Review*, August, 1900, pp. 198–208); Anonymous: "Distracted China " (*Blackwood's Magazine*, August, 1900, part II, pp. 287–94); Diplomaticus: " Have We a Policy in China? " (*Fortnightly Review*, August, 1900, pp. 327–37); Emerson Bainbridge: " China and the Powers " (*Contemporary Review*, August, 1900, pp. 172–82), etc.

Bokhara." [41] This is in keeping with what we know generally of the war minister's attitude. In a memorandum of March 1900 he had expressed the opinion that Manchuria should, preferably, remain a part of China, but that Russia should secure " absolute commercial control " and generally consolidate her position.[42] During June and July he made it perfectly clear in conversations with German diplomats that Russia was much more interested in Manchuria than in the Peking legations, and that Russia demanded for herself a free hand in Manchuria.[43]

Witte, too, favored leaving Manchuria in the hands of the Chinese and confining Russian activity to a policy of peaceful penetration. But he objected to Kuropatkin's idea of seizing the opportunity for establishing control of the Manchurian provinces. He was very anxious to avoid attacks on the Railway and tried to arrange with Li Hung-chang for protection of the Russian enterprise.[44] Nothing came of these efforts, for in the middle of July Chinese bands began to attack the Railway. The Russians had only about 6000 men in Manchuria and were unable to hold their own. They were obliged to evacuate Mukden, Kirin and Tsitsihar, while the Chinese besieged their forces in Harbin and at Blagovestchensk. There was nothing for it but to send in considerable numbers of troops. A regular campaign was undertaken from the north, south and east, and by mid-October the Russians were in complete military control of the three Manchurian provinces.[45]

In the meanwhile the question of an international expedition to relieve the legations had become a burning one. Witte and Lamsdorff were flatly opposed to Russian participation, on the plea that China's friendship could be regained by a tolerant attitude. Kuropatkin, however, saw in the expedition a chance to extend Russian influence over Chi-li. He convinced the Tsar and in the end Russia contributed 4000 men to the relief forces. The Russian commander was ordered, however, not to advance beyond Yang-tsun. The fact that he entered Peking in the van of the other troops on August 14 was due entirely to accident — the order did not reach him until it was too late to obey it.[46] But hardly had the legations been relieved when the Russian foreign office surprised the world by an invitation to withdraw the ministers and forces to Tientsin, since it was clear that the Empress and the court, which had fled to Sian-fu, would not return and negotiate so long as the capital was occupied by the foreigners. In a circular to the powers on August 25 the Russian government declared that its

---

[41] *The Memoirs of Count Witte* (New York, 1921), p. 107.

[42] Kuropatkin: *The Russian Army and the Japanese War* (New York, 1909), p. 70.

[43] *Die Grosse Politik*, XVI, nos. 4537, 4548, 4552.

[44] Glinskii: *Prolog*, etc., pp. 106 ff.; Romanov: *Rossiia v Manchzhurii*, pp. 250 ff.

[45] The German translation of the official Russian account: *Die Kämpfe der Russischen Truppen in der Mandschurei im Jahre 1900* (Leipzig, 1901); Glinskii, op. cit., pp. 118 ff.; Clive Bigham: *A Year in China* (London, 1901), chap. xiv.

[46] Glinskii, op. cit., pp. 116–8; Witte: *Memoirs*, p. 108; *Die Grosse Politik*, XVI, nos. 4558, 4573.

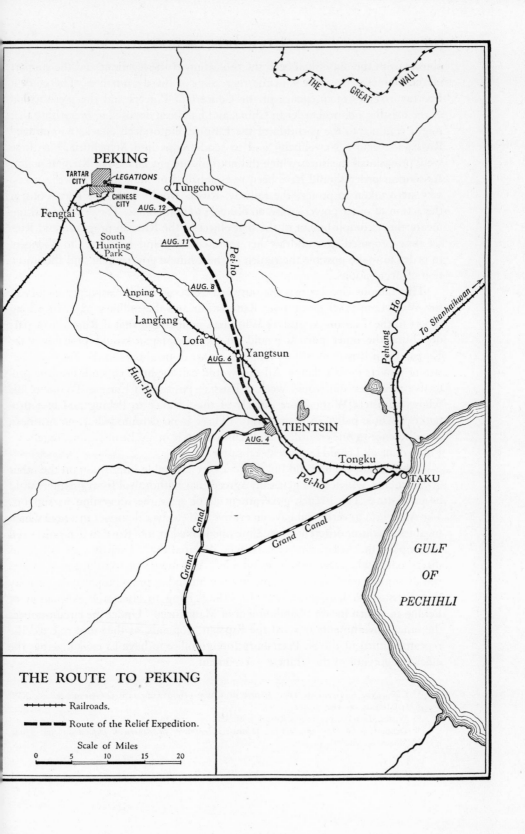

THE ROUTE TO PEKING

objects from the outset had been the protection of the legations and the support of the Chinese government in the repression of the disturbances. Therefore it had favored the maintenance of the Concert of Powers and the preservation of the existing political order in China, and had been opposed to everything that might conduce to the partition of the Empire. Unforeseen attacks had obliged Russia to occupy Newchuang and to send troops into Manchuria, but these were provisional measures which did not indicate any change in Russian policy. As soon as order should have been re-established in Manchuria and the necessary steps taken to protect the railway, Russia would withdraw her troops, if the action of other powers were no obstacle to that course. The relief of Peking meant the accomplishment of the first object of the Russian program, and Russia now proposed to withdraw her representative and her forces to Tientsin, in order to make possible the return of the Chinese government and the initiation of negotiations.[47]

This famous circular was the outward expression of a temporary victory of the Witte-Lamsdorff group over Kuropatkin and the military men. In a long report to the Tsar on August 24 Witte had pointed out that if Russia took part of China, the other powers would do likewise. Japan would probably seize Korea. Then Russia would no longer have weak neighbors in the Far East, but strong powers on her flanks. All this would call for huge expenditures for protective measures and would weaken Russia's position in Europe. To one of his fellow ministers Witte wrote bitterly of the advance to Peking and of Kuropatkin's whole policy in Manchuria: " There is no definite policy, no firmness, no adherence to one's word, — and Kuropatkin is in a state of chronic rage. . . . I have done all I could to prevent a disaster." [48]

The Russian circular did not make a very favorable impression on the other governments, which were generally agreed that withdrawal from Peking would be premature. The French government alone gave the suggestion its support. The American government gave an evasive and equivocal answer in a note which meant something different every time one looked at it.[49] Russian assurances did not impress the American secretary, who declared that " her vows are as false as dicers' oaths when treachery is profitable." As a matter of fact the Far East was full of rumors of Russian designs, and the Shanghai press propagated the story that Russia had bargained with Li Hung-chang to effect the evacuation of Peking in return for the abandonment of Manchuria.[50] Under the circumstances the other governments rejected the Russian proposals, as they also rejected the repeated efforts of the St. Petersburg foreign office to have Li recognized as the official negotiator of the Chinese government.

---

[47] *China No. 1 (1901)*, p. 113; *Affaires de Chine (1900)*, no. 258; *Die Grosse Politik*, XVI, no. 4621; Glinskii, op. cit., p. 121.

[48] Witte: *Memoirs*, pp. 113–4; Glinskii, op. cit., pp. 119–20.

[49] Dennett: *John Hay*, pp. 311 ff.; Dennis: *Adventures in American Diplomacy*, pp. 230 ff.

[50] Morse, op. cit., III, p. 305.

The German cabinet felt itself more directly touched than any other by what was regarded as Russian perfidy. From the very outset the Emperor William, who suffered severely from the Yellow Peril idea, had taken a vigorous and bold initiative in the move against the Boxers. He had sent out troops on his own responsibility and had bidden them farewell in that most unfortunate of all his utterances, the speech of July 27, in which he instructed his men to give no quarter and take no prisoners: " Let all who fall into your hands be at your mercy. Just as the Huns a thousand years ago, under the leadership of Attila, gained a reputation by virtue of which they still live in historical tradition, so may the name of Germany become known in such a manner in China, that no Chinese will ever again even dare to look askance at a German." This hysterical attitude was no doubt due in a measure to the murder of the German minister, which, in a sense, gave the Germans some claim to leadership in the crusade of Europe. William therefore had much at heart the appointment of a German general as commander in chief of the associated forces. He tried in vain to get the British to put forward the suggestion, and then induced the Tsar to agree to the appointment of Field Marshal von Waldersee. The Tsar's assent was then communicated to the French as a Russian proposal, and before the middle of August Bülow had the more or less grudging approval of all the European powers.[51]

Waldersee was made the object of prolonged and somewhat ridiculous ovations in Germany before his departure for the Far East on August 22. The German imperialists were greatly flattered by the idea of leadership and celebrated Waldersee's victories in advance. At the time it was generally agreed that no expedition could start for Peking before the middle of September, and it was therefore taken for granted that the Germans would play a very prominent part. Great, therefore, was the Emperor's disappointment to learn of the sudden and successful relief of the legations, in which the Russian general, Linevich, took the leading part and German troops were wholly absent.[52] Coming so close upon the expedition to Peking the Russian proposal to withdraw seemed to William a direct slap in the face for himself. The whole business would be over before the much-fêted Waldersee could appear. And to think that the Russian object was simply to win the friendship of the Chinese in order to secure Manchuria as a present. In bitter marginal notes on the diplomatic correspondence the Emperor castigated the whole Russian policy, from its initial indifference to the fate of the legations to its willingness to bargain with the arch-rascal Li and even the chief of the murderers, Prince Tuan.[53]

Fortunately for the Emperor's pride the other powers were not ready to fol-

---

[51] Die Grosse Politik, XVI, nos. 4598 ff.; Bourgeois and Pagès: Les Origines de la Grande Guerre, p. 289; Letters of Queen Victoria, III, p. 573. The whole matter is discussed at length in Willy Becker: Fürst Bülow und England (Greifswald, 1929), pp. 166 ff. and in many other older books.

[52] Die Grosse Politik, XVI, no. 4614.   [53] Die Grosse Politik, XVI, no. 4614.

low the Russian lead. But the whole Russian policy was so suspect that the Berlin government began to sound out the British with a view to co-operation. On August 22 the Emperor met the Prince of Wales at Wilhelmshöhe and discussed the Chinese situation. It was generally agreed that negotiations with Li Hung-chang should not yet be initiated. In fact, the Emperor was determined to do all he could to obstruct Russian attempts to conclude a " rotten " peace. The conversation then turned to the Yangtze problem, William pointing out that " German commercial interests were second and not far inferior to those of England in the valley of the Yangtze, and if Her Majesty's Government could see their way to give assurances that they would maintain the policy of the open door, they would find the German Government on their side." [54]

As usual Lord Salisbury did not react favorably to the idea of an agreement with Germany. Indeed there was little popular sentiment in England for such a policy. Since the passage of the second German naval law there had grown up a distinct feeling that the Berlin government harbored dangerous designs. From that time may be dated the beginning of a regular anti-German campaign in the English periodical press, a campaign in which the *National Review* was to play a prominent part. The point is worth noting, because Mr. Maxse, the editor of the review, was known to be a friend of Lord Salisbury. But other writers also took an alarmist tone. William Stead declared that the doubling of the German fleet was " a menace to the very foundation of our Empire a thousand times more alarming than all the armaments of the Boers," and an anonymous writer in the *Quarterly Review* asserted that in view of German naval ambitions it was now necessary " for this country to be prepared to meet and crush the allied navies of the three strongest and richest Powers in the Continent of Europe." [55] In the *National Review* Mr. Maxse revealed how, in the autumn of 1899, Bülow had invited Chamberlain to speak for an agreement and had then disavowed him. He accused Germany openly of the determination to smash England: " The German fleet is admittedly not yet strong enough for this task, therefore other European fleets must be requisitioned for the service of the Kaiser. That is the true meaning of his constant grovelling to Russia. Through Russia he hopes to get control of French policy and French ships. We shall certainly court a naval Sedan unless we pull ourselves together." [56] The same theme was developed by other contributors to the *Review,* who accused Germany of ulterior and sinister motives in the Far East. " It is certain that in the case of the disruption of China, Germany would claim the whole region from the Yellow River up to the north bank of the Yangtze. She supports the open door as long as possible, but when partition comes she will join France and Russia against England." It would be a mistake for England to rely on Germany to help her get control of

[54] *British Documents,* II, no. 8; *Die Grosse Politik,* XVI, nos. 4617, 4712.

[55] W. T. Stead: editorial in *Review of Reviews,* April 15, 1900, p. 314; Anonymous: " Domestic Parties and Imperial Government " (*Quarterly Review,* July, 1900, pp. 241–69).

[56] Review of current events, *National Review,* September, 1900, pp. 1–6.

the Yangtze basin or to oppose Russia.[57] " At present the greatest external danger to England arises from Germany. . . . The Kaiser is a reincarnation of Napoleon. In Europe he represents a Continental coalition against what is still the greatest maritime power of the world. He intends to displace us, with or without a struggle, and for that end is rapidly forging the means. . . . If, for any reason, Germany should decide to precipitate the contest, and should succeed in forming a coalition with Russia and France, nothing could now arrest our fall." [58]

These citations are significant, because we learn from the British documents that the fears they expressed were shared at least in part by the foreign office. In a memorandum drawn up in connexion with the German suggestion regarding the Yangtze, Mr. Bertie pointed out that the German stand was that they had a special position in Shantung, but that they also had equal rights with Britain in the Yangtze basin:

" What Germany will claim as her special field will probably be Shantung and the valley of the Yellow River. . . . Germany will further claim that between the Yellow River Valley and the north bank of the Yangtzse River the division of good things between British and Germans must be absolutely equal, viz., that every concession granted to an Englishman must be counterpoised by one to a German. On these conditions the German Government may be willing to recognise to Great Britain the same rights in the Yangtzse region *south* of that river as Germany claims in Shantung and the Yellow River Valley. We should then have to fight out with the French and other Governments, who have not recognised our Yangtzse sphere of interest, any claims which we desire to support in the special sphere conceded to us by Germany. As to making use of Germany to come between the Russians and ourselves in China, we are not likely to have much success." [59]

Despite these suspicions Salisbury finally yielded to the prodding of the German ambassador. It was agreed that the two powers should draw up an arrangement the object of which should be to keep China open to the trade of all nations, to renounce for themselves all attempts to take advantage of the crisis for purposes of further acquisitions, and to oppose other powers in making any similar attempt. The Germans tried to restrict the application of the agreement to the Yangtze Valley, but the point was finally compromised and the maintenance of the Open Door was made to apply to " the ports of the rivers and littoral of China." Thereupon Hatzfeldt made it clear that Germany would not agree to anything that might appear directed against Russia. He suggested that the ports of the Amur River and Port Arthur be specifically excluded.

---

[57] X.: " The German Danger in the Far East " (*National Review,* October, 1900, pp. 178–96). See also the very unfriendly article of Sir Rowland Blennerhassett: " The Foreign Policy of the German Empire " (ibid., September, 1900, pp. 37–52).

[58] An Englishman: " Reconstruction or Catastrophe? " (*National Review,* November, 1900, pp. 330–41).

[59] *British Documents,* II, no. 12.

There was talk on the English side of confining the Open Door agreement to the region south of 38° N.L., which would have left out not only Manchuria but Chi-li. In the end a vague wording was chosen: the principle of the Open Door should be upheld in all Chinese territory " so far as they (England and Germany) could exercise influence."

Salisbury was not much pleased with the course of the discussion. To the German ambassador he wrote frankly: " I confess that since you have altered it to make it agreeable to Russia I am not much in love with this agreement. It is liable to so much misunderstanding." [60] This feeling was undoubtedly strengthened by the German refusal to accept the phrase " will oppose " with respect to efforts of other powers to take advantage of the situation to make acquisitions at China's expense. This part, too, was finally toned down to read that the two powers should " direct their policy towards maintaining undiminished the territorial condition of the Chinese Empire."

It is fairly clear that the British government consented to the agreement only because of the growing threat of Russian action in northern China, a matter to which we shall have to recur later. In any event the document that was signed on October 16, 1900 was diluted and innocuous enough. The essential three clauses read:

1) It is a matter of joint and permanent international interest that the ports on the rivers and littoral of China should remain free and open to trade and to every other legitimate form of economic activity for the nationals of all countries without distinction; and the two governments agree on their part to uphold the same for all Chinese territory as far as they can exercise influence.

2) The Imperial German Government and Her Britannic Majesty's Government will not, on their part, make use of the present complication to obtain for themselves any territorial advantages in Chinese dominions, and will direct their policy towards maintaining undiminished the territorial condition of the Chinese Empire.

3) In case of another Power making use of the complications in China in order to obtain under any form whatever such territorial advantages, the two contracting Parties reserve to themselves to come to a preliminary understanding as to the eventual steps to be taken for the protection of their own interests in China.

Clause 4 simply provided for the communication of this agreement to the other powers and for an invitation to them to accept the principles recorded in it.

When the agreement was made public, John Hay wrote to one of his close friends: " My heart is heavy about John Bull. Do you twig his attitude to Germany? When the Anglo-German pact came out, I took a day or two to find out what it meant. I soon learned from Berlin that it meant a horrible practical joke on England. From London I found out what I had suspected, but what it astounded me after all to be assured of — *That they did not know!* When

---

[60] *Die Grosse Politik*, XVI, no. 4732; *British Documents*, II, no. 38.

Japan joined the pact, I asked them why. They said, 'We don't know, only if there is any fun going on, we want to be in.'" [61]

Even though Hay's jocularity need not be taken too seriously, there was much truth in what he said. The agreement was so vague that it was bound to cause misunderstanding later. Taking it at face value one can hardly refrain from asking: If the two powers meant what they said, what was the use of saying it? The English ministers were almost unanimous in their dissatisfaction with the agreement. It would not, they felt, prevent Russia from doing what she wished in China, and by no means assured England that Germany would take a firm attitude against Russia. The Duke of Devonshire, one of Germany's best friends, declared that he could not understand how Salisbury could have consented to the exclusion of Manchuria: "In view of this restriction the whole treaty becomes a document which is not worth the paper it is written on." [62] Whatever gains there may have been were undoubtedly on Germany's side. She had succeeded in forestalling any attempt by the British to establish themselves in the Yangtze and had secured British assurances of the continuance of the Open Door in that important area, all without in any way committing herself to opposition to the Russian designs. [63]

British fears that the agreement would prove ineffectual in stopping Russia were only too well founded. The reply from St. Petersburg was a cleverly worded evasion: "The first point of this Agreement, stipulating 'that the ports on the rivers and littoral of China, wherever the two Governments exercise their influence, should *remain* free and open to commerce,' can be favourably entertained by Russia, this stipulation not prejudicing in any way the *status quo* established in China by existing treaties." This was tantamount to restricting the principle of the Open Door to those areas where England and Germany had special interests. Salisbury protested against this wilful distortion of Article I and pointed out that the intention was to extend the principle " to the whole of the Chinese Empire so far as the two Powers can exercise influence." Apparently the Russians refused to enter upon further debate of the matter, which was certainly open to a variety of interpretations. [64]

In the interval the powers had come to an understanding with regard to negotiations with China. The basis for discussion was a note sent out on October 4 by Delcassé, which provided for punishment of guilty officials, reparation for losses suffered, and guarantees for the future. There was more than enough wrangling before the details were settled, for the Germans, more or less supported by the British, favored the stiffest possible terms, while the Russians, and to a certain extent the Americans and the Japanese, advocated gentler treatment, for reasons of their own. It is quite unnecessary to follow the dreary course of

[61] William R. Thayer: *Life and Letters of John Hay* (Boston, 1915), II, p. 248; Dennett: *John Hay*, p. 320.

[62] Eckardstein: *Lebenserinnerungen*, II, p. 202; *Die Grosse Politik*, XVI, no. 4745.

[63] *Die Grosse Politik*, XVI, no. 4766.

[64] *British Documents*, II, nos. 20, 21; *Die Grosse Politik*, XVI, no. 4747.

the negotiations here, the more so as they have been well summarized by many writers on Far Eastern diplomacy.[65] Suffice it to say that a joint note was presented to the Chinese plenipotentiaries, Li Hung-chang and Prince Ching, on December 24, 1900. Discussion of details was then begun. The negotiations, which dragged on through the winter and spring, became at times very heated, and it was only in September 1901 that the final agreements were signed.

European diplomats as a whole had no ground for priding themselves on the handling of the Boxer movement and its aftermath. Europe's treatment of China in the whole period from 1895 to 1900 had been devoid of all consideration and of all understanding. The Celestial Empire to them was simply a great market to be exploited to the full, a rich territory to be carved up like a sirloin steak. Hardly anywhere in the diplomatic correspondence does one find any appreciation for the feelings of the Oriental or any sympathy for the crude efforts made at reform. The dominant note was always that force is the father of peace and that the only method of treating successfully with China is the method of the mailed fist. The Boxers were considered to be simply so many ruffians, who deserved no better treatment than that ordinarily meted out to common criminals. When the trouble began legation guards were rushed to Peking, where they evidently took the initiative by shooting at Chinese troops. The American minister thought these " exhibitions of skill and courage " would serve as " good object lessons." [66] In their negotiations with the Yamen the foreign ministers rarely bothered with the facts. Indeed, a careful student of the problem has put on record his opinion that " each of the decisive steps taken by the diplomats at Peking, or by their naval commanders at Taku, was taken on the strength of rumors which have never been substantiated; each has been justified only by appealing to subsequent events as evidence of the wisdom and necessity of the act." [67] It is well known that the Chinese government tried to prevent an assault on the foreigners and that it spared the legations, which could easily have been taken. Against this you have to place the merciless looting of Peking by the associated forces after the relief of the legations. It was a chapter of European activity which the Oriental cannot be expected to forget for a long time to come.

So far as the relationship of the powers to each other was concerned there was little occasion for compliments. The governments worked together in the heat of the crisis, but there was no real heart for a European concert. From the outset each power regarded every other with distrust and suspicion. Russia's willingness to sacrifice the legations in order to win the friendship of the Chinese government only served to confirm British and German suspicions of ulterior motives. In the last count the Russian military men were determined to seize not only Man-

---

[65] E.g. Morse: *International Relations of the Chinese Empire*, III, chap. xii; Clements: *The Boxer Rebellion*, part iii; Steiger: *China and the Occident*, chap. xii; recent material may be found in *Die Grosse Politik*, XVI, chap. civ, and in Alfred Graf von Waldersee: *Denkwürdigkeiten* (Stuttgart, 1923), III, chap. xii.

[66] Steiger: *China and the Occident*, pp. 221–2.

[67] Ibid., pp. 232 ff.

churia, but Chi-li as part of the spoils. Britain, still paralyzed by the South African War, was unable to do much and found it advisable to quiet German fears of British designs in the Yangtze Basin by concluding the ill-fated Agreement of October 16, 1900. Salisbury regarded the thing as "unnecessary but innocuous," [68] and must have realized that it left matters just where they were. But he accepted it — accepted the German wording, chiefly in order to keep Germany from joining Russia in a general scramble when England was not in a position to get her full share.

In a sense the German policy was decisive throughout the crisis, not so much because of her leadership in the operations in China and her constant advocacy of the stiffest possible demands upon the Chinese government, but because of her careful navigation between the rocks of British and Russian policy. This delicate balancing of German policy was more or less a reflection of the division of opinion in the government with respect to Far Eastern affairs. The Emperor was positively outraged by the Russian policy and was, no doubt, extremely jealous of the gains he expected his cousin Nicky to make. His general feeling was for co-operation with England. Bülow, on the other hand, was intent on preserving close relations with Russia. He yielded to the Emperor only so far as he had to, in order to maintain his own position (he became chancellor in October 1900). The result was that while the Germans were encouraging the British to hope for support in upholding the integrity of China, they were telling the Russians that they might do what they liked in Manchuria without fear of German opposition. It was not to be expected, under these conditions, that either side would be satisfied in the long run. The time would come — the time had to come — when the Germans would be forced into the open. Friction of one kind or the other was inevitable.

BIBLIOGRAPHICAL NOTE

DOCUMENTARY SOURCES

Accounts and Papers. There is a long list of Blue Books on the affairs of China, which have been thoroughly exploited by other writers. It seems unnecessary to do more than list them here: 1899, volume CIX. *China No. 1 (1899), Correspondence respecting the Affairs of China. China No. 2 (1899), Correspondence between Her Majesty's Government and the Russian Government with regard to their respective Railway Interests in China.* 1900, volume CV. *China No. 1 (1900), Further Correspondence respecting the Affairs of China. China No. 2 (1900), Correspondence with the United States' Government respecting Foreign Trade in China. China No. 3 (1900), Correspondence respecting the Insurrectionary Move-*

---

[68] Sanderson Memorandum, 1907 (*British Documents* II, no. 1).

ment in China. China No. 4 (1900), Reports from Her Majesty's Minister in China respecting Events at Peking. China No. 5 (1900), Correspondence respecting the Anglo-German Agreement of October 16, 1900, relating to China. 1901, volume XCI. China No. 1 (1901), Correspondence respecting the Disturbances in China. China No. 2 (1901), Despatch from His Majesty's Ambassador at St. Petersburgh respecting the Russo-Chinese Agreement as to Manchuria. China No. 3 (1901), Further Correspondence respecting Events at Peking. China No. 4 (1901), Plans referred to in China No. 3. China No. 5 (1901), Further Correspondence respecting the Disturbances in China. China No. 6 (1901), same. China No. 7 (1901), Correspondence respecting the Imperial Railway of North China. 1902, volume CXXX. China No. 1 (1902), Correspondence respecting the Affairs of China.

British Documents on the Origins of the War, 1898–1914. Volume II, chapter ix contains some material to supplement the Blue Books.

United States Foreign Relations. The volumes for the years 1899–1901 contain much important documentary material on the Chinese situation, and are unusually full.

Documents Diplomatiques. Chine, 1898–1899 (Paris, 1900). *Chine, 1899–1900* (Paris, 1900). These French Yellow Books are less valuable than the Blue Books but are important for the study of French policy.

Die Grosse Politik der Europäischen Kabinette, 1871–1914. Volume XVI of this great publication is devoted entirely to Far Eastern affairs in 1900 and 1901 and is of prime importance for the study not only of German policy, but of general European diplomacy.

Popov, A., editor: "Bokserskoe Vosstanie." (*Krasnyi Arkhiv,* XIV, 1926, pp. 1–48). A collection of important Russian documents on the Boxer affair. I have not quoted these specifically, because the material they contain has been incorporated in the work of Romanov.

MEMOIRS, AUTOBIOGRAPHIES, BIOGRAPHIES, AND LETTERS

The Memoirs of Count Witte. Edited by Abraham Yarmolinsky. New York, 1921. Contains some things of interest, but is now overshadowed by later Russian studies.

DENNETT, TYLER: *John Hay.* New York, 1933. The most recent and most understanding biography of the American secretary of state, based in part on unpublished material.

WALDERSEE, ALFRED GRAF VON: *Denkwürdigkeiten.* Edited by Heinrich O. Meisner. Volume III. Stuttgart, 1923. The diary of the German commander in chief in China. A most important source.

SPECIAL STUDIES

The Anglo-Russian Railway Problem:

KENT, PERCY H.: *Railway Enterprise in China.* London, 1907. In general this is still the best single account of the railway problem.

MARCILLAC, JEAN DE: " Les Chemins de Fer en Chine." (*Questions Diplomatiques et Coloniales,* July 1, 1899, pp. 265–74; July 15, 1899, pp. 321–31). An unusually well-informed contemporary analysis.

HSU, MONGTON CHIH: *Railway Problems in China.* New York, 1915. A straight-forward conventional account which, for the period here treated, does not go beyond Kent.

POPOV, A.: " Anglo-Russkoe Soglashenie o Razdele Kitaiia, 1899 g." (*Krasnyi Arkhiv,* XXV, pp. 111–34, 1927). A most important publication, consisting primarily of the Russian documents on the agreement of 1899. An abstract of this article has been published in German translation by I. Lewin: " Neue Russische Dokumente zum Russisch-Englischen Chinavertrag 1899 " (*Zeitschrift für Politik,* XIX, September, 1929, pp. 339–48).

FAUVEL, A. A.: " Le Transsinien et les Chemins de Fer Chinois." (*Revue Politique et Parlementaire,* September, 1899, pp. 453–92). Another reliable and careful contemporary study of the railway problem.

General treatments:

CORDIER, HENRI: *Histoire des Relations de la Chine avec les Puissances Occidentales.* Three volumes. Paris, 1902. Though based entirely upon contemporary material this is still one of the most illuminating accounts, because of the author's unrivalled knowledge of Chinese affairs.

MORSE, HOSEA B.: *The International Relations of the Chinese Empire.* Three volumes. New York, 1918. Based very largely upon published British and American documents, but useful also for its references to the European press in China.

FRANKE, OTTO: *Die Grossmächte in Ostasien von 1894 bis 1914.* Hamburg, 1923. The work of an eminent sinologue, based in part on German archive material. Distinctly anti-English bias.

ZÜHLKE, HERBERT: *Die Rolle des Fernen Ostens in den Politischen Beziehungen der Mächte, 1895–1905.* Berlin, 1929. A substantial though rather conventional account, based chiefly on the British and German documents. Suffers from inadequate knowledge of Russian materials.

JOSEPH, PHILIP: *Foreign Diplomacy in China, 1894–1900.* London, 1928. Comparable to the preceding. A careful, conscientious study, but decidedly weak on the Russian side.

McCORDOCK, R. STANLEY: *British Far Eastern Policy, 1894–1900.* New York, 1931. A minute re-examination of the more obvious sources. Adds relatively little.

GLINSKII, B. B.: *Prolog Russko-Iaponskoi Voiny. Materialy iz Arkhiva Grafa S. I. Witte*. Petrograd, 1916. A fundamental Russian treatment, based chiefly on the Witte papers.

MARC, PIERRE: *Quelques Années de Politique Internationale. Antécédents de la Guerre Russo-Japonaise*. Leipzig, 1914. This is a translation of the preceding, the name *Marc* being a pseudonym.

ROMANOV, B. A.: *Rossiia v Manchzhurii, 1892–1906*. Leningrad, 1928. By far the most important Russian treatment, based on extensive archive material and counteracting the account of Glinskii.

STEINMANN, FRIEDRICH VON: *Russlands Politik im Fernen Osten und der Staatssekretär Bezobrazov*. Leipzig, 1931. A most valuable account of the Russian Korean policy. Based almost entirely on Russian archive material.

ASAKAWA, K.: *The Russo-Japanese Conflict*. Boston, 1904. An old book that can be highly recommended as a careful piece of work. Especially valuable because of its use of Japanese newspaper and other material.

DENNIS, ALFRED L. P.: *Adventures in American Diplomacy, 1896–1906*. New York, 1928. Based in large part on unpublished material, this is about the best account of American policy in this period.

The Boxer Rising:

CLEMENTS, PAUL H.: *The Boxer Rebellion*. New York, 1915. An orthodox treatment of the diplomatic side. Based almost entirely on British and American documents.

STEIGER, GEORGE N.: *China and the Occident*. New Haven, 1927. This is by far the best critical study of the Boxer movement as a domestic and international problem. Thoroughly well informed, it is distinguished from many other books by the originality of its interpretation.

CAMERON, MERIBETH E.: *The Reform Movement in China, 1898–1912*. Stanford, 1931. The most recent monographic treatment, employing most of the older material.

BLAND, J. O. P., and BACKHOUSE, E.: *China under the Empress Dowager*. London, 1910. An interesting and well-informed though somewhat colored narrative of modern China.

SERGEANT, P. W.: *The Great Empress Dowager of China*. London, 1910. A rather more scholarly and broad-minded volume on the same period.

SMITH, ARTHUR H.: *China in Convulsion*. Two volumes. New York, 1901. The best general contemporary account of the rising, and particularly of its origins.

ANTHOUARD, BARON D': *La Chine contre l'Étranger*. Paris, 1902, A narrative written by a French diplomat in China.

ALLEN, ROLAND: *The Siege of the Peking Legations*. London, 1901. Still one of the best accounts of what took place at Peking.

BIGHAM, CLIVE: *A Year in China*. London, 1901. A travel book by an English journalist. Contains an interesting account of the Seymour expedition and of conditions in Manchuria and Korea.

MARTIN, W. A. P.: *The Siege in Peking*. London, 1900. A narrative marked by violent hatred of the Empress Dowager.

PUTNAM WEALE, B. L.: *Indiscreet Letters from Peking*. London, 1907. A well-known and highly dramatized pseudonymous account of the siege.

THOMSON, H. C.: *China and the Powers*. London, 1902. A reprint of articles from the *Monthly Review,* by a very able observer. Distinctly favorable to China.

HART, SIR ROBERT: *These from the Land of Sinim*. London, 1901. A reprint of articles originally published in the *Fortnightly Review* by the famous head of the Chinese maritime customs service.

The Crisis in China. New York, 1900. A collection of interesting articles on various aspects of the crisis, originally published in the *North American Review* in 1899 and 1900.

DUYVENDAK, J. J. L.: *The Diary of His Excellency Ching-shan*. Leiden, 1924. The most important Chinese source. Evidently requires to be used with some caution.

XXII

The Anglo-German Negotiations

D URING THE AUTUMN AND WINTER OF 1900–1901 INTEREST IN FAR EAST-
ern affairs became more and more focussed upon the activities of the
Russians. It was generally suspected that the military men had made up
their minds to establish Russian power not only in Manchuria, but in Chi-li.[1]
They had some fifty thousand troops in Manchuria, they had occupied Newchuang and taken over the customs house, they had pushed their forces to the
westward as far as the line of the projected railway to Sinminting, and they had
seized the all-important line from Peking to Tientsin and from there to the
north. Early in November it was announced that the Russians had obtained from
the Chinese government a concession of land at Tientsin, on the left bank of the
Peiho, where the railway station was located. The news led to an immediate
scramble for similar concessions on the part of the French, Germans, Belgians,
Austrians and Japanese. For all one could tell, the partition of China was about
to begin in earnest.[2]

Russian activity created such serious international tension in November that
eventually the government was obliged to draw back. The Peking-Tientsin Railway was handed over to the control of the powers and the concession at Tientsin
was explained away as having nothing whatever to do with sovereignty. But
there remained the crucial line from Tientsin to Shanhaikwan, in which British
capital was invested and which the British had so long defended against Muscovite encroachments. The English hoped, at first, to secure German support
against Russia, under the terms of the October Agreement. But Bülow declared
openly in the Reichstag: " we shall take good care not to do other people's business in China. We have no thought of serving as a lightning rod for any other
power." [3] This unaccommodating attitude was very disappointing to the British,
but the question was too nearly a decisive one to permit of half measures. The
English government therefore took a firm stand, and ultimately the Russian
military authorities decided that it would be better to restrict their ambitions to
the region north of the great wall. Still, it was only in February 1901 that the
Tientsin-Shanhaikwan line finally came into the hands of the British.[4]

---

[1] Die Grosse Politik, XVI, no. 4735; Waldersee: Denkwürdigkeiten, III, pp. 25–6.
[2] Morse, op. cit., III, pp. 321 ff.; Asakawa, op. cit., pp. 147 ff., 156 ff.; and many others.
[3] Die Grosse Politik, XVI, nos. 4755 ff., 4781 ff.
[4] Morse, op. cit., III, p. 323; Waldersee, op. cit., III, passim, where all the details of the dispute
may be followed.

It remained for the Russians to regularize their position in Manchuria. Ever since September 1900 secret negotiations had been carried on between Li Hung-chang and Prince Ukhtomskii, the special agent of Count Witte. They had led to nothing because of Witte's unwillingness to pay a huge bribe until it was clear that Li would be able and willing to do something worth-while.[5] In the interval the commanders on the spot made their own arrangements with the Tartar General at Mukden, Tseng-chi. The so-called Alexeiev-Tseng Agreement, signed on November 9, provided that the civil administration of Manchuria should be restored to the Chinese, but that Russian troops should be stationed at Mukden and other points along the railroad. All Chinese troops were to be disarmed and disbanded. All weapons, arsenals and military supplies were to be handed over to the Russian authorities, and the local Chinese officials were to organize only police guards.[6]

This separate agreement met with the disapproval of both Li Hung-chang and Witte, of the former probably because he wanted to do the negotiating himself and receive an adequate bribe, of the latter because he was as firmly as ever opposed to the permanent occupation of Manchuria. Russia had given assurances, he argued, that the country would be evacuated as soon as possible. She should live up to these promises in order to retain the confidence of both China and the European powers. After all, why should troops be kept in Manchuria, at great expense? There was no real danger, now that the Boxer disturbances had been put down. If further trouble arose, Russia could always send in the necessary troops by the Railway.

This viewpoint was generally shared by the foreign office, but it did not appeal to the military men, many of whom favored the outright annexation of northern Manchuria. Long discussions ensued between the ministries of foreign affairs, finance and war, the victory resting, ultimately, with Kuropatkin. Witte, having failed to get his way, determined to get satisfaction (or perhaps to ruin the agreement) by having written into the Russian terms a goodly number of economic concessions. Further arguments followed, and in the end only a few of Witte's demands were incorporated in the draft agreement which was submitted to the Chinese minister at St. Petersburg on February 8, 1901.[7]

The further development of the Far Eastern question depended so much

---

[5] Romanov: *Rossiia v Manchzhurii*, pp. 263 ff.

[6] Romanov, op. cit., p. 267; Glinskii, op. cit., pp. 137 ff.; Witte: *La Guerre avec le Japon*, pp. 42–5; this agreement was reported by Dr. Morrison, the London *Times* correspondent at Peking, and published in the *Times* on January 3, 1901. The terms there given, reprinted in a number of English books, are not accurate.

[7] It is curious that early in February, before the draft was handed to the Chinese, Witte himself passed on to the Japanese minister at St. Petersburg the text of certain articles which, far from being the actual agreement or any part of it, appear to have been rather those clauses which Witte wanted inserted and which his colleagues threw out. Is it possible that the finance minister, enraged by the failure of his own schemes, determined to wreck the convention by putting about a draft much more extreme than that actually submitted to the Chinese? The clauses in question may be found in *Die Grosse Politik*, XVI, no. 4809.

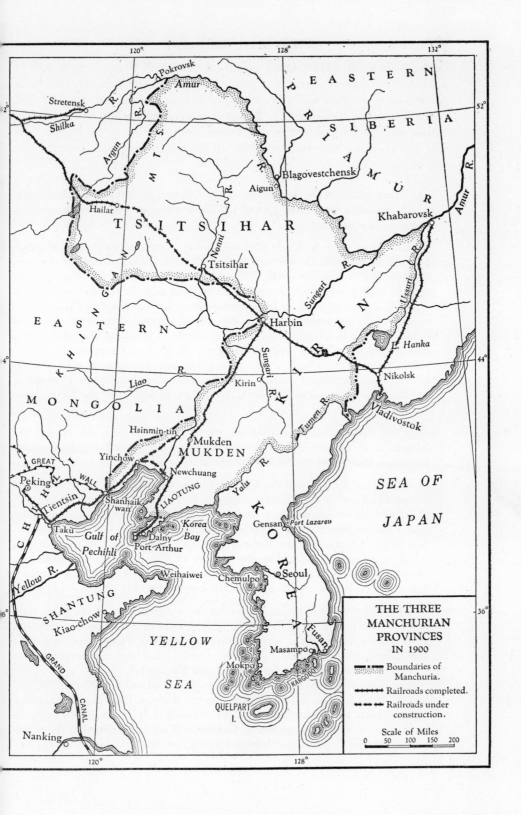

THE THREE
MANCHURIAN
PROVINCES
IN 1900

▬▬▬ Boundaries of
　　　 Manchuria.
+++++ Railroads completed.
+ ╌ + Railroads under
　　　 construction.

Scale of Miles
0　50　100　150　200

on the projected Russian-Chinese agreement that it will be necessary to give in substance the document that was handed to the Chinese minister, adding in parentheses those parts which Witte desired to have inserted and which he had communicated to the Japanese. In Europe it was generally believed that these demands were an integral part of the Russian draft. In view of the fact that the real text has never been made available in English, the sacrifice of some space will be justified.

1). Russia agrees to the restoration of the Chinese government in Manchuria, which remains a constituent part of the Chinese Empire on the same administrative basis as of old.

2). In accordance with Article 6 of the contract concluded on August 27, 1896 between the Chinese Government and the Russian-Chinese Bank for the construction and exploitation of the Chinese Eastern Railway, the Company has the right of independent administration of the lands set aside for the above-mentioned railroad, and consequently of maintaining guards for that purpose. (Taking into consideration, however, that under the present unrestored order of things in Manchuria, the above-mentioned guard is unable to guarantee the further construction of the Chinese Eastern Railway) the Russian Government (temporarily) leaves in Manchuria a part of its troops until the establishment of calm (in the above mentioned district and the execution by the Chinese Emperor of the decisions contained in Articles 9, 10, 11, 12, 13 and 14 of the present convention).

3). (The Russian troops, during the entire period of their stay within the boundaries of Manchuria, will furnish, in case of need, full assistance to the Chinese authorities in the work of maintaining order and calm in the district).

4). In view of the fact that the Chinese troops, distributed in Manchuria, took a most active part in hostile actions against Russia, the Government of the Chinese Emperor, wishing to give a guarantee for the preservation of peace in Manchuria for the future, promises not to maintain troops there (until the construction of the Chinese Eastern Railway and the establishment on it of regular service is completed. After that, the number of Chinese troops maintained in Manchuria will be determined by agreement with the Russian Government). The importation of weapons and military supplies into Manchuria is forbidden.

5). (For the purpose of maintaining calm and a correct order of things in Manchuria, which is adjacent to Russia, the Chinese Government promises to remove, at the representation of the Russian Government, those Tsian-Tsiuns and other high administrative officials . . . whose activity shall not correspond to the friendly relations established between the two Empires).

For police service and the maintenance of internal order in Manchuria, outside the lands set aside for the Chinese Eastern Railway, there is to be formed a foot and horse police guard, the numbers of which shall be determined by agreement with the Russian Government. Cannon will not be permitted in the equipment of the police guard, and foreign subjects may not serve in it.

6). (In accordance with the solemn promises given by it more than once, the Chinese Government promises not to admit foreign instructors either into the ranks of the army or of the fleet of Northern China).

7). (For the purpose of guaranteeing firmer order and calm in the neutral zone, established by Article 5 of the Convention of March 15, 1898, both contracting powers allow their local authorities to come to an agreement on this question. For the same reason the right of autonomous administration granted . . . to the city of Tsing-chow is abolished).

8). The Chinese Government will not grant on all the area of the districts adjacent to Russia, namely Manchuria and Mongolia, Tarbagatai, Ili, Kashgar, Yarkand, Khotan and Keri, any concessions for the construction of railroads, working of mineral deposits, or any industrial enterprises whatsoever to foreign powers or to their subjects without the consent of the Russian Government. On all the territory of the above-mentioned districts the Chinese Government will not build railways and will not grant parcels of land for the use of foreigners without the consent of the Russian Government, except in the free port of Newchuang.

9). The Government of the Chinese Empire will compensate the Russian Government for expenditures made in consequence of the disturbances in China, to an amount relative to the actual expenditure of the Russian Government and the compensation given to other powers. The amount of this compensation as well as the terms of payment may be determined by joint discussion with the other powers interested.

10). The Chinese Government will enter into agreement with the administration of the Chinese Eastern Railway regarding compensation for damages caused by the destruction of a considerable part of the railway, the plundering of the property of the company and its officials and the delay in the construction of the road.

11). The compensation mentioned in the preceding article may, by agreement between the Chinese Government and the Company, be paid in whole or in part by granting to the Company certain privileges, by changing the existing concession (or by granting new concessions).

12). The Chinese Government promises to grant to the Chinese Eastern Railway Company a concession for the construction and exploitation of a railway line from one of the points of the Chinese Eastern Railway or its South Manchurian branch to the Chinese Wall, in the direction of Peking, on conditions similar to those granted the Chinese Eastern Railway itself. The agreement in principle to this demand was given by the Chinese Government in 1899.

13). The Chinese Government will enter into agreement with the Russian-Chinese Bank concerning indemnification for the losses of the Bank, caused by the destruction of its property and the stoppage of its operations.

14). The claims of Russian subjects and Russian private institutions and enterprises for compensation for damages caused by the disturbances in China, the

Chinese Government promises to pay as soon as they are reviewed by the Russian mission in Peking and transmitted to the Chinese Government.[8]

The Russian government depended on Li Hung-chang to get this draft accepted. At this very time it refused to join the other foreign representatives in the demand for the punishment of guilty Chinese officials. But even the promise of a million rubles could not prevent the canny old Chinaman from playing a double game. While he put up a show of advocating the signature of the Convention, he also appealed to the powers to save his country. He suggested to the British representative that the European governments demand the communication of the Russian terms and added that " China would be delighted to communicate them and place itself in the hands of the powers for protection against Russia, whose demands it could not deny and whose constant threats terrified it." [9]

Ever since the publication of the Alexeiev-Tseng Agreement in the London *Times* on January 3, 1901 the Russian dealings with China had called forth excitement in Europe, as in Japan and in America. The Tokyo government felt more alarmed than any other, possibly because of the apprehension caused by Russian proposals that the two powers should agree on the neutralization of Korea under a guarantee of the powers.[10] The cabinet of Prince Ito (September 1900 to June 1901) was not at all ill-disposed towards an arrangement with Russia, but the foreign minister, Baron Kato, who had resigned his position as minister to London in 1898 because of the government's unwillingness to follow up his suggestions for an agreement with England against Russia, was as uncompromisingly opposed to a yielding policy as ever. His view was that " a peaceful agreement with Russia will mean a defeat for Japan. A firm attitude on our part, even a resort to arms if necessary, is the only policy left to us." On January 17 he rejected the Russian suggestion regarding Korea in rather sharp terms. Indeed, he went further and kept pressing the Russians on the matter of the evacuation of Manchuria. He realized that the proposals touching Korea were meant merely as a blind to divert the attention of the Tokyo government from Manchuria. As his biographer says, " he focussed his eyes on Manchuria; instead of being attracted by a kite in the sky, he looked for the man on the ground who was holding it." [11]

Before the middle of January 1901, that is, long before the Russian terms were actually submitted to the Chinese, the Japanese cabinet, following in this the lead of Kato, attempted to enlist the support of the British for an inquiry at St.

---

[8] Text in Romanov, op. cit., pp. 297 ff. The text hitherto known is in *China No. 2 (1904)*, no. 42. On the negotiations see Romanov, pp. 278 ff.; Glinskii, op. cit., pp. 142 ff.

[9] Rockhill to Hay, January 29, 1901 (published by Dennis: *Adventures in American Diplomacy,* p. 242); on Li's attitude and action see further Romanov, op. cit., pp. 300–4.

[10] *British Documents*, II, no. 42.

[11] *Kato Takaaki* (Tokyo, 1929), I, pp. 402 ff. The correspondence between St. Petersburg and Tokyo has now been published under the title " Nakanunie Russko-Iaponskoi Voiny " (*Krasnyi Arkhiv*, LXIII, 1934, pp. 3–54); see especially pp. 8–9.

Petersburg. Evidently the English government did not follow up the suggestion, for the Japanese seem to have approached the Russians alone. They were told by Lamsdorff on January 29 that the reputed Manchurian agreement was fictitious, but that reply did not, of course, satisfy them. There were some heated discussions between Kato and the Russian minister, Alexander Izvolski, of later fame. The result of these first exchanges was that the relations between Russia and Japan were exceedingly strained by the beginning of February.[12]

On February 5 the Japanese minister at London, Count Hayashi, again approached the British foreign office. The Japanese, he said, were going to warn China against concluding an agreement with Russia about Manchuria and would like to have the British join in this warning. The suggestion raised a serious problem, for no one could predict what might follow. The British government, however, felt that if the Japanese advances were rejected the Tokyo government might be driven into the arms of Russia. Once Russia and Japan had joined hands in the Far East, there would be little hope for British interests. But in order to fortify its own position the English cabinet decided to try to associate Germany in the action.

The official relations between England and Germany were at this time more cordial than they had been for some time. Since the Agreement of October 16, 1900 the two powers were supposedly pursuing the same policy in China. Lord Lansdowne, the new British foreign minister, was ready to make every effort to strengthen the friendly relations between the two countries,[13] a policy which enjoyed the cordial support of other cabinet members, like Chamberlain and the Duke of Devonshire. Indeed, if we may believe Baron Eckardstein, the first secretary of the German embassy at London, Chamberlain told him quite frankly that he favored strongly an alliance with Germany and the Triple Alliance. The days of splendid isolation were over, and the basis for the new order could be laid by an agreement concerning Morocco. But if this failed, England would have to reach an understanding with France and Russia, even at the cost of far-reaching concessions. There were already some voices being raised in the cabinet and in the press in favor of such a policy.[14]

It is remarkable that Chamberlain should have talked so freely to Eckardstein, though there is no reason to question his outlook as revealed in this conversation. At any rate, the German foreign office took Eckardstein's report at face value and, in characteristically German fashion, embarked upon a course of elaborate speculation regarding the Anglo-German problem. It was generally agreed by those who controlled German policy (and of these Baron von Holstein was the most authoritative) that the threat of an agreement between England and Russia or France was "pure humbug." England would never be able to

---

[12] *Kato Takaaki*, pp. 421 ff.; "Nakanunie Russko-Iaponskoi Voiny," pp. 9–12; *China No. 2 (1904)*, no. 6; *British Documents*, II, no. 42; *Documents Diplomatiques Français*, I, no. 63.

[13] Lord Newton: *Lord Lansdowne* (London, 1929), pp. 196–7.

[14] Eckardstein: *Lebenserinnerungen*, II, p. 238; *Die Grosse Politik*, XVII, no. 4979.

afford the price these powers would ask, and concessions on her part would only accentuate the appetite of her antagonists. The British were beginning to realize the absolute need of German friendship and support. Time was on the side of the Germans and ultimately the London government would be prepared to pay a high price. Only the Germans must know how to wait. Separate agreements, like the Agreement of 1898 in regard to the Portuguese Colonies, were not very profitable and nothing could be realized from them for some time. What Germany must get was a general alliance, the British paying for it at the high price of concessions in Asia and Africa and at the same time giving Germany every needed security against Russia. For the time being, however, it was essential to stand off and wait until the British had softened. In the interval they must not be discouraged by Germany but, at the same time, Germany must avoid becoming estranged from Russia.[15]

It was just at this point that the mortal illness of Queen Victoria became known. The Emperor William thereupon hurried to her bedside. He was with her when she died and stayed in England for a full two weeks afterward. This demonstration of filial piety made a deep and favorable impression upon British court circles and upon the public. Never before or after was the Emperor so popular. Even the new King, Edward VII, who had more difficulty than almost any one else in getting on with William, was apparently converted to the idea of close Anglo-German co-operation. The Emperor had a long discussion with Lord Lansdowne, which seems to have come to something like an imperial lecture. The foreign minister was warned of the danger of staking too much upon the friendship of the United States, a power which would, in the end, follow its own selfish interests. Indeed, according to the Emperor the American Republic was already flirting with Russia in the Far East. Ultimately they would divide the political and commercial hegemony between them. It was urgently necessary that England and Germany and the rest of Europe should stand together against the common danger. France, which had paid dearly in loans to Russia for the revenge which she had not secured, must be brought back into the European family. The French spirit was as necessary for Europe as the pepper on the beefsteak.

It was in keeping with this attitude that the Emperor showed his best side to the French ambassador. He even assured him that he desired a strong France, and that he would help France when she was in trouble.[16] We need not pursue this particular idea of the Emperor any further. The important thing is that William's visit to England created an atmosphere of friendliness such as had not existed since the days preceding the Kruger telegram.

---

[15] This is the burden of many letters and memoranda written between January 18 and 21, 1901 (*Die Grosse Politik*, XVII, nos. 4979–85; Eckardstein, op. cit., II, pp. 239, 260 ff.).

[16] *Documents Diplomatiques Français*, I, nos. 54, 60, 67, 69, 114; on the Emperor's visit see further *Die Grosse Politik*, XVII, nos. 4986 ff.; Bülow: *Memoirs*, I, pp. 578 ff.; Eckardstein, op. cit., II, pp. 252 ff.; Newton: *Lord Lansdowne*, pp. 197–9.

There was every reason, then, for the British government to hope for German support in backing the Japanese on the Manchurian question. These hopes were not disappointed. The matter was considered with great care at Berlin, where the officials of the foreign office viewed it against the background of the general Anglo-German problem. They saw clearly enough that support of England would arouse unfavorable criticism in the press and parliament, and they had their own compunctions about coming out definitely against Russia in the Manchurian question, which itself was of little interest to Germany. On the other hand, they thought it important not to drive either Japan or England into an agreement with Russia, and they weighed the whole question with reference to the larger prospect of an alliance with England. Now, they thought, the English are beginning to feel the pinch. They will have to appeal to Germany more and more frequently. As yet it is too early to come forward with a full catalogue of demands and conditions. But England must not be scared off. When she has been baited a little longer, Germany will be in a better position to get her own terms accepted. Germany does not need England, and therefore she can ask in return for her alliance full guarantees against complications with Russia and very extensive concessions in Africa as well as in Asia. And so the Germans formulated a very cautious program. They agreed to warn the Chinese government against concluding an agreement with any one power while the obligations of the Peking government to the other powers had not yet been definitely fixed. They hinted, furthermore, that in a war between Russia and Japan or Russia and England their neutrality could be counted upon. It was made clear to the Japanese minister at London that there was no agreement between Russia and Germany with reference to the Far East.[17]

The British foreign office was much gratified with the readiness of the Germans to join in the action at Peking. To be sure, the German note was milder than the Japanese or the British, but that was intentional, and Lord Lansdowne reckoned quite correctly that something was better than nothing. The Japanese and British representatives warned the Peking government in the middle of February that the reputed Manchurian agreement would be " a source of danger to the Chinese government and that no arrangement affecting territorial rights in the Chinese Empire ought to be concluded between the Chinese government and any one of the Powers." At the same time the German government issued its own warning.[18]

So far as one can deduce from the documents the warnings of the powers in Peking were of little avail. The Russian government consistently took the stand that the matter did not concern other governments, and that it was simply trying to arrange with the Chinese for the evacuation of Manchuria, of course with adequate guarantees for the protection of Russian interests. In the last days of

---

[17] *Die Grosse Politik*, XVI, nos. 4810–7; XVII, nos. 4988–91. It is most unfortunate that these documents, so closely related, should have been placed in separate volumes, so that the connexion is not obvious. [18] *China No. 2 (1904)*, no. 12; *Die Grosse Politik*, XVI, nos. 4815–6.

February it was reported from the Chinese capital that the Russians were renewing their pressure to force the Yamen to sign. On March 1 the Peking government again appealed to the powers for " mediation." At the same time it communicated a text in twelve articles, which seems to have been a rather seriously garbled version of the Russian draft.[19]

This further development called forth a terrific storm of indignation in Japan. From the reports of the Russian and French ministers at Tokyo we learn that Japanese naval circles in particular were eager to take up the cudgels against Russia. So serious was the situation that Izvolski advised his government to double the troops along the frontier of Manchuria. The Russian minister firmly believed that war was inevitable and he therefore prepared to leave the Japanese capital at short notice.[20] Fortunately for the peace of the Far East the Japanese premier, Prince Ito, was determined not to overreach himself. It is clear that the great statesman, mindful of what had happened to Japan in 1895, was ready to strike a bargain with Russia if possible, and, failing that, to go to war only if assured that the international alignment was favorable.[21]

Before resorting to the arbitrament of war it was essential for Japan to know exactly what the odds were. She was certain of her ability to defeat the Russians on land, and fairly certain of being able to take care of them also by sea. The question was whether France would join her ally, and whether Japan could count on the support of the British fleet to restore the balance at sea. If England could be brought to do something to hold the French in check, then nothing more would be necessary, for Japan had been assured that the Germans had no agreements with Russia, and the French would presumably not dare enter the conflict if England stood behind Japan.

And so there ensued, during the first half of March 1901, long and crucial discussions in London. The Japanese minister, Baron Hayashi, long one of the most vigorous proponents of an alliance with England, left no doubt of the fact that the Japanese were in dead earnest. He asked directly whether England would agree to hold France in check. Japan, he pointed out, would fight for Korea single-handed and under any conditions, but she would not go the limit with respect to Manchuria unless she had some assurances that she would not have to face both Russia and France. The whole problem placed the British foreign office in a serious dilemma. Cabinet meetings followed each other in rapid succession, frequently lasting for hours at a time. It was understood in London that the Japanese were rather anxious to fight, even on the Manchurian issue, because it was obvious that Russia, once she had control of Manchuria, would begin operations in Korea. From the Japanese standpoint it would be better to fight

---

[19] China No. 2 (1904), nos. 11, 14, 17, 18, 25; British Documents, II, no. 47; Die Grosse Politik, XVI, nos. 4819–23, passim.

[20] "Nakanunie Russko-Iaponskoi Voiny," pp. 13 ff.; Documents Diplomatiques Français, I, nos. 133, 181, 202.

[21] Kato Takaaki, I, pp. 421–47; Documents Diplomatiques Français, I, nos. 133, 181; Die Grosse Politik, XVI, no. 4825.

the inevitable duel before the Transsiberian Railway was complete. In other words, there was every possibility that England might become involved in a large-scale conflict. On the other hand, if no support were given Japan she would probably turn about and make some sort of agreement with Russia, to the serious detriment of British interests in China. Possibly such a development could be checked by England's trying herself to strike a bargain with the Muscovite. The Germans strongly suspected that Lord Salisbury was the great obstacle to a definite arrangement between the British and the Japanese, and that he favored direct agreement with Russia. Whether this was the fact or not (it seems likely that it was), the British government seemed unable to come to a decision.

The Berlin government was most disgusted by the "knuckling-down" policy. No one who reads the documents can escape the feeling that the German statesmen were eager to have the British take a strong stand, support Japan to the limit and, if necessary, stop Russia by force of arms. The reason for this attitude was not to be sought so much in the desire to see Russia checked or humiliated as in the hope that Britain, in the moment of crisis, would be brought to the point of really wanting an alliance with Germany and being willing to pay a high price for it. From the very outset the German ambassador at London made it clear that in the event of a conflict his government would remain benevolently neutral. Despatches from Berlin argued that Russia, already in financial difficulties, would surely not fight; that this was the grand opportunity for England to settle the score; that with Japan in the vanguard, victory would be certain, and that, if England backed down again, she would get nothing but the briefest respite from Russian encroachment. Similar encouragement was given the Japanese. Once again the German foreign office made it clear that there was no agreement between Germany and Russia, that Germany would remain benevolently neutral, and that this neutrality would have the effect of preventing France from taking any active part in operations.

Finding it most difficult to reach a decision, the British government followed an evasive policy. Inquiries were made in St. Petersburg, followed by efforts to induce the Russians to communicate their terms, a course which Lamsdorff indignantly refused to consider. At the same time the ambassador at Paris was instructed to find out whether France was under obligations to Russia to take part in a Far Eastern conflict. Sir Edmund Monson was unable to learn anything of value, but he reported that there was in France very little interest in the Far East and that "enthusiasm for the Russian Alliance has so cooled down in France that it appears to flame up only when the occasion serves to accentuate the animosity against England." [22] In the meanwhile Lord Lansdowne, after repeated encouragements from the German embassy, asked the Berlin government whether, in a crisis, it would be willing to join England in a declaration to France that the two powers wished the localization of the conflict in the Far East and would themselves maintain strict neutrality.

---

[22] *British Documents*, II, no. 56.

Bülow at once rejected this suggestion. Germany, he argued, had assured England and Japan of her neutrality, but she could not make a declaration of this sort at Paris, at least not until the first shot had been fired. As a matter of fact, France would not dare move as long as Germany remained neutral. It might be interjected here that the Germans had no thought of estranging France at this time. In fact, they, especially the Emperor, were hoping to draw France away from Russia and bring her back to the " European " family of nations.[23]

Of course the German reply could not satisfy Lansdowne. It was obvious that the Germans were intent on keeping their hands free, and that they wished, if possible, not to become embroiled with Russia. The Russian ambassador had already made it clear that Germany's warning to the Chinese had not been much appreciated in St. Petersburg. At any rate the Berlin foreign office refused to go further than the promise of benevolent neutrality, which, at the request of the British ambassador, it defined as " correct and strict neutrality." This chapter of the story may be said to have come to an end when Bülow got up in the Reichstag on March 15 to explain Germany's obligations under the terms of the agreement with England of October 1900. He referred to this agreement as the *Yangtze Agreement,* thus making it clear that for the Germans its purpose was primarily to secure a share in the Yangtze Basin. The Agreement, he went on to explain, " was in no sense concerned with Manchuria; it contained no secret clauses, but had been communicated to the public *in extenso.* There were no German interests of importance in Manchuria, and the fate of that province was a matter of absolute indifference to Germany. On the other hand, it was of importance to her that at the present moment, while China's obligations towards the Powers were as yet unsettled, her estate should not be unduly reduced, and that she should not dispose of her assets *in fraudem creditorum* while the claims of the latter remained unsatisfied."

Bülow's explanations caused something akin to consternation in England. There were some confused statements made in parliament, and some discussion between London and Berlin. Eventually the British government was obliged to admit that the Germans had, in connexion with the negotiation of the Agreement, made it clear that they excepted Manchuria from the application of the Open Door policy, but the English continuel to insist that Article II, dealing with the maintenance of the integrity of China, applied to the whole of the Empire, of which, they maintained, Manchuria was an integral part. There the matter rested, each side holding its own view, with the result that the Agreement was completely emasculated and valueless. The incident served at the time to break down the negotiations with regard to the future action of the two powers in the Far East, and it left a permanent scar on Anglo-German relations. Years later we find Sir Eyre Crowe making cutting remarks about it, and even Lord San-

---

[23] See the Emperor's talk with the Duc de Noailles, March 1, 1901 (*Documents Diplomatiques Français,* I, no. 114).

derson, who was much more favorably disposed towards Germany, speaking of the proceeding as " no doubt shifty and not over creditable." [24]

While the English and the Germans were wrangling about the interpretation of the Yangtze Agreement, the Japanese government, too, was wrestling with the larger problems of policy. Baron Kato was more insistent than ever on taking a strong line with Russia. On March 12 he handed a memorandum running to thousands of words to Prince Ito, and thereby precipitated a heated argument that lasted for weeks. Ito and the rest of the cabinet still favored some sort of compromise, but Kato stood by his guns and finally secured permission to send a protest to St. Petersburg (March 24). The note, though couched in courteous terms, was unequivocal. Kato suggested that the Russian-Chinese agreement be referred to the conference of diplomats at Peking which was engaged in settling the Boxer indemnity and kindred questions. The Russian reply, which came promptly, was purely negative. Lamsdorff refused to diverge from the position that the whole question was one between Russia and China, and that there was no excuse for outside interference.

The attitude of Russia left the Japanese cabinet exactly where it was to begin with. Kato favored even stronger action. There were long conferences between him and Ito on March 30 and 31, in which the foreign minister advocated sending a note expressing " general dissatisfaction " with the Russian reply. After several days of crisis Kato was finally persuaded to tone down this phrase, but the cabinet agreed to a note which was sent on April 6 and which read: " The Imperial (Japanese) Government is unable to accept the answer of Count Lamsdorff of March 25, and reserves its opinion under the present circumstances." [25]

The soundness of Kato's policy was proved by the results. The Russians, despite their brave declarations, recognized the seriousness of the situation and began to back down. After the first protests they scaled down their demands on China: the Peking government was to be permitted to keep some troops in Manchuria and to arrange for indemnities in accordance with the general methods applied in negotiation with the other powers. Russian demands for concessions were restricted to Manchuria.[26] But the Chinese refused to sign even on these terms. Li Hung-chang may have been willing to do so, and he was expected to do so by the representatives of the other powers, who looked upon him as nothing less than a paid agent of Russia. But the powerful Yangtze viceroys, vigorously backed by England, offered such sturdy opposition that not even Li

---

[24] British Documents, II, nos. 32–5; III, pp. 412–3, 426 ff.; Hansard: Parliamentary Debates, Series IV, vol. XCVIII, debates of July 26, 1901. All the material on the March crisis may be found in China No. 2 (1904), nos. 14 ff.; British Documents, II, nos. 33, 45, 47, 50–6; Die Grosse Politik, XVI, nos. 4819–32. Individual references have seemed unnecessary.

[25] Kato Takaaki, I, pp. 421–47; the correspondence may be found in the recent publication " Nakanunie Russko-Iaponskoi Voiny " (loc. cit., pp. 21 ff.).

[26] The details in Glinskii, op. cit., pp. 158 ff.

could act in the face of it. The Yamen therefore appealed to the powers for aid. The English joined Japan in a new warning to Peking, but the Germans refused to have anything more to do with the matter.

The language of the Japanese warning to China appears to have been pretty strong: the Yamen was told that the acceptance of the Russian terms would mean the partition of China and that Japan intended to ask for extensive concessions if the Russian demands were granted. There the matter stood when Kato sent his note of April 6 to Russia. The St. Petersburg authorities evidently thought the game was up. They announced that the draft convention with China had been withdrawn. Since the Chinese government was unwilling to make an arrangement and since the foreign powers did not appreciate Russia's efforts to evacuate Manchuria, things should remain as they were. The whole thing, explained Lamsdorff, was intended merely as a provisional arrangement, which in no way involved any infringement of Chinese sovereignty or integrity. The reports of the Agreement had been completely garbled. There had never been a draft in twelve articles, but only a program, used by various departments of the government in the course of the negotiations. Needless to say, these explanations severely taxed the credulity of the other powers; they were regarded with pronounced scepticism in all the European chancelleries. " Really the Russians are occasionally, to use their own term, colossal," wrote Lord Sanderson to the British minister at Peking.[27]

The German Emperor found it absolutely impossible to conceal his disappointment with the course of British policy in the Far East. " Was it likely," he asked the English ambassador, " that so favorable an opportunity for resisting the encroachments of Russia would occur again? " In a letter to King Edward he went even further, and called the English ministers " unmitigated noodles " for their policy in China.[28] The members of the foreign office did not much appreciate this language, but they were too level-headed to be much moved by it. They saw through the German game easily enough. " The German Emperor," wrote Lord Sanderson, " is apparently furious with us for not having got into a quarrel with Russia over the business, and obviously that would have suited the Germans very well." [29]

It was perfectly true that the Germans were consumed with the hope of seeing Britain ever more deeply embarrassed, not from any feeling of spite, but simply in order to force her to seek Germany's alliance and accept it on German terms. As viewed from Berlin the situation of England was such that only one little jog would be needed. The war in south Africa kept dragging on. With 250,000 men in the field the British seemed unable to force a decision. The policy of de-

---

[27] *British Documents*, II, no. 73. See further ibid., nos. 60, 61, 65; *China No. 2 (1904)*, nos. 36–9; *Documents Diplomatiques Français*, I, nos. 154, 162, 174; *Die Grosse Politik*, XVI, nos. 4833 ff.

[28] *British Documents*, II, nos. 72, 73; Eckardstein, op. cit., II, pp. 297–9; Lee: *Edward VII*, II, p. 119.   [29] *British Documents*, II, p. 58, footnote.

vastating the Boer farms and of concentrating Boer women and children in unhealthy concentration camps was causing a storm of indignation throughout Europe. Never in modern times was England so intensely hated and never, one might add, was she so generally underrated. The army was looked upon as an ineffectual and yet ruthless band of mercenaries, led by officers wholly unfitted for their jobs. As a military power England was regarded on the Continent as a veritable farce. Surely, with Russia threatening in Asia and France becoming stronger and more active in the Mediterranean, England would, before long, have to come touting for the alliance of the Germans. If only she could have been induced to come out strongly in support of Japan against Russia, the trick would have been turned.

It was probably for that very reason that the British pursued so circumspect a policy, even at the risk of estranging Japan. They scented the German aims and had no intention of being roped in. As a matter of fact the English were not nearly as dejected as the Germans thought they ought to be. They knew that they would carry the South African War to a successful conclusion, and they relied on their fleet to continue to stave off any hostile demonstration. So far as China was concerned they hoped to muddle along. From what few indications one can glean from the documents it is clear that Salisbury was opposed to making an issue of the Manchurian question. If anything, he, and probably a considerable part of the cabinet, desired an agreement with Russia. " We shall certainly not reject an overture, if one is made to us," wrote Lansdowne to the ambassador at St. Petersburg on April 23; " You cannot do wrong in repeating that we wish to be friends, and that we recognise the special interests which Russia possesses in Manchuria." [30]

It is true, of course, that British opinion was, on the whole, suspicious of Russia and hostile to any Russian advance. But at this very time there began a systematic campaign of education in favor of an understanding. The *Spectator,* commenting on this aspect of the problem, wrote:

" Why assume that public opinion is a great, immoveable fact? Examine it, and realize that it is a hap-hazard creation which can be modified if it is only dealt with in a proper spirit. If Lord Salisbury even now were to take the trouble to instruct and guide public opinion in regard to our relations with Russia, he would very soon have behind him a public opinion that would correspond to the true and reasonable view, and not a public opinion which, as he imagines, he must partly obey and partly get round by oblique methods." [31]

Other writers came out vigorously for an entente with the Tsarist government. So influential a journalist as E. J. Dillon criticized the British policy in Manchuria and stressed the fact that nothing was to be gained from opposition

---

[30] Newton: *Lord Lansdowne,* pp. 215 ff.; similarly Sanderson to Satow, April 12 (*British Documents,* II, no. 73): an understanding with Russia " would be much the best plan if it could be managed." On Salisbury's attitude see further his letter to Canon MacColl, in Russell: *Malcolm MacColl,* p. 282.　　　　[31] *Spectator,* April 6, 1901, p. 487.

to Russia. Sir Rowland Blennerhassett, who was to become one of the most un-
relenting German-baiters, began a long series of articles in favor of an agreement
with Russia.[32] Anonymous writers were, naturally, even more outspoken.
Calchas sounded the notes of the German peril, and declared: " To settle
with Russia . . . would relieve to an extraordinary extent the sense of diplomatic pressure under which the nation and the Foreign Office live now. It would
advance Russia's economic development by several generations, and it would
make a Continental coalition against us impossible, and it ought to be the grand
aim of British policy." " The interests of Germany clash with ours everywhere,"
said *Ignotus;* " those of Russia hardly anywhere beyond the reach of a friendly
understanding." [33]

Now as a matter of fact there is some evidence that certain Russian statesmen,
notably Witte, were ready to consider some sort of adjustment. Russia was in
dire financial straits, and the finance minister apparently hoped and tried to
secure a loan in London. The details are not known, but it is probably safe to
assume that not only the hostility of British bankers (notably Rothschild), but
also the opposition of Russian court and military circles made a rapprochement
difficult at the time.[34]

It is important to note that while, in the spring of 1901, not a few voices were
being raised in England on behalf of a settlement with Russia, hardly anything
was said in favor of Germany or of an agreement with Germany. Apropos of
the article by *Ignotus,* mentioned above, William T. Stead, who had advocated
an agreement with Russia for twenty years, wrote in the *Review of Reviews:*
" It is a very unfortunate habit of the English people that they never seem to
be happy unless in international politics they have fashioned a devil after their
own heart. The working devil of the English cosmogony for years past has been
Russia; but now those who have been most active in propagating the theory of
the diabolism of Russia are displaying an inclination to transfer this evil rôle
from Russia to Germany." [35] And yet Stead was one of those who first and most
insistently called attention to the German naval menace, and it was on this theme
that all the anti-German, pro-Russian writers most particularly harped. " The
broad issue for the twentieth century," according to *Calchas,* " is whether Great
Britain or the German Empire at the end of the next two or three generations
will possess the relative ascendancy in trade and its inseparable attribute of sea-
power." England, he went on, required a three-power naval standard, in view of
Germany's determination to fight, not alone, but at the head of a coalition. And

---

[32] E. J. Dillon: " Micawberism in Manchuria " (*Contemporary Review*, May 1901, pp. 649–
63); Sir Rowland Blennerhassett: " England and Russia " (*National Review*, March 1901, pp.
21–33).

[33] Calchas: " Will England Last the Century? " (*Fortnightly Review*, January, 1901, pp.
20–34), p. 31; Calchas: " Will Germany Fail? " (ibid., April, 1901, pp. 575–90); Ignotus: " Germany and England " (*Fortnightly Review*, April, 1901, pp. 663–74), pp. 672–4.

[34] Eckardstein, op. cit., II, pp. 277–8, tells of the Russian advances in mid-March.

[35] *Review of Reviews*, April 15, 1901, p. 372.

Ignotus, after a most hostile and distorted review of German policy since 1870, appealed to the country thus: " Let it be clearly understood that Germany is the one country in Europe with which it is quite impossible for England to arrive at a working understanding beneficial to each; and this, not from national antipathy, but from economic necessity." Germany had a growing population, which made necessary a constant expansion of trade and colonial dominion. " But Great Britain crosses her path in every direction as a formidable commercial and colonial rival, and it has been the dream of the German Foreign Office ever since Bismarck began to shape its policy, to destroy our commercial and naval supremacy."

Events in the Far East had done little to foster the idea of Anglo-German co-operation. On the contrary, the German policy, with its constant trimming between England and Russia, had caused real bitterness. Bülow's stand with regard to the so-called Yangtze Agreement had put the finishing touch on the disillusionment of the London government and of the English people. But — this must be reiterated and re-emphasized — the German government was quite blind to most of this. The reason for the misapprehension that prevailed in Berlin was two-fold. In part it was due to plain, ordinary, political miscalculation — underrating of England's position and overrating of her need for support, too great optimism with respect to Germany's alliance value, and a naive incredulity with regard to the possibility of an Anglo-Russian or Anglo-French settlement. It must be confessed that the German ambassador at London, Count Hatzfeldt, was in part responsible for this viewpoint. He was a really eminent diplomat, but in the period since 1898 he too had become convinced that England would come to Germany and be glad of the German alliance, even though the price were high. As it happened, Hatzfeldt was a very sick man in 1901. It was only rarely that he was able to leave his bed. For the Germans this was a great misfortune, for the old ambassador knew how to maintain proper relations with a foreign government, and he had been trained under Bismarck to report and report correctly.

During Hatzfeldt's illness the affairs of the embassy were conducted by the first secretary, Freiherr von Eckardstein, who, after some years of residence in the United States and England, had married the heiress of the millionaire furniture manufacturer, Sir Blundell Maple, and had then retired from the diplomatic service. In view of his excellent social connexions with the Rothschilds, the Duke of Devonshire, Joseph Chamberlain and other statesmen and financiers, he was a valuable aid to the embassy, so that in November 1899 Bülow appointed him first secretary. Bülow admits in his memoirs that he had been warned about Eckardstein. Count Metternich, Hatzfeldt's successor at the embassy in London, had pointed out that the Baron's utterances were to be taken " not *cum grano sed cum copia salis.*" The appointment, Bülow confesses, " was not a fortunate stroke." [36]

---

[36] Bülow: *Memoirs,* I, pp. 400–1.

Eckardstein was moved by the wholly commendable desire to promote the understanding between England and Germany, but it is perfectly obvious that personal vanity and the ambitious hope that he might be the instrument chosen to effect an epoch-making alliance played a leading rôle in his conduct. The famous memoirs which he published just after the war were designed to show that only the utter stupidity of the German foreign office was responsible for the frustration of his efforts. Germany, he claimed, rejected the British offer of an alliance in 1901, and therewith sealed her own fate.

These ideas dominated the minds of German historians for a decade after the war, despite the fact that the publication of the German documents showed that Eckardstein did not hesitate to alter words or phrases when printing diplomatic correspondence, if that was necessary to support his argument. Only since the publication of the British documents on this subject in 1927 has the truth finally emerged. German and English historians are now fairly well agreed as to what took place. Since it has become evident that the Anglo-German alliance project was not nearly so serious in 1901 as was formerly supposed, it will not be necessary to enter into minute detail; a general review of the main lines will suffice.[37]

On March 18, while the tension over the Manchurian question was still at its height, Eckardstein reported a conversation with Lansdowne, who raised the question whether there was still any prospect of Germany's acting to hold France in check in the event of a Russian-Japanese War. According to his own account, Eckardstein replied that there was no chance of this so long as Germany had no assurances of support from England. Thereupon, he claims, Lansdowne raised the question of a general defensive agreement, which, so he is reputed to have said, was favored by some of the most influential members of the cabinet. Naturally no official advances could be made until it was known in London that the German government would be favorably disposed towards such a proposition.[38]

Now we have Lansdowne's own account of this interview, as he reported it to Sir Frank Lascelles, the ambassador at Berlin. From this it appears that the English minister said he thought there was no prospect of England and Germany combining to " keep the ring " for Russia and Japan, since it had been made clear that the Germans would remain strictly neutral and since Bülow had repudiated

---

[37] On the English side perhaps the best account is now G. P. Gooch: "Baron von Holstein" (in *Studies in Modern History*, London, 1931); of the very extensive German literature on the subject I should mention as among the best recent studies Gerhard Ritter: *Die Legende von der Verschmähten Englischen Freundschaft* (Freiburg, 1929); the keen and critical account of Gustav Roloff: "Die Bündnisverhandlungen zwischen Deutschland und England, 1898–1901" (*Berliner Monatshefte*, December, 1929, pp. 1167–222); Heinrich Walther: "Die Deutsch-Englischen Bündnisverhandlungen von 1901 und ihre Ergebnisse" (*Historische Vierteljahrschrift*, XXV, 1931, pp. 602–35); Johannes Dreyer: *Deutschland und England in ihrer Politik und Presse im Jahre 1901* (Berlin, 1934); Heinrich Freiherr von Hoyningen genannt Huene: *Untersuchungen zur Geschichte des Deutsch-Englischen Bündnisproblems, 1898–1901* (Breslau, 1934).

[38] *Die Grosse Politik*, XVII, no. 4994. Eckardstein indicates that there were two conversations, but this is certainly not the fact.

all responsibility for what happened in Manchuria. It was Eckardstein who then raised the question of a defensive agreement directed solely against France and Russia. This would require the two allies to come to each other's aid only in the event of either one of them being attacked by those two powers. Lansdowne at once raised objections. Such an arrangement seemed to entail the adoption of an identic foreign policy by the two powers in *all* their external relations. There was the further difficulty of defining *defensive* action. In any case the matter would have to be carefully considered by his colleagues.[39]

These two accounts of the same conversation are wholly divergent. Which is to be accepted? Obviously Lansdowne's, for his narrative fits much more accurately into the general setting of the situation and reflects the attitude which we know to have been that of the British foreign office. Not only that: it would be hard to find any reason why the foreign minister should have wanted to mislead the ambassador at Berlin. Time and again, in later documents, Lansdowne referred to the initiative which Eckardstein had taken in this matter. Even German scholars are now practically agreed that only the Lansdowne account is worthy of credence.

Then Eckardstein's story is little short of a fabrication. Unbelievable as it may seem, this appears to be a shocking instance of a diplomat knowingly leading his government astray. The Baron knew perfectly well that his government hoped for an alliance with England, but wanted to wait until the British needed the Germans badly enough to be willing to pay their price. He had been instructed not to take the initiative on any account. On March 17 Holstein had written him " not to breathe a syllable about an alliance." Whether this letter had reached London by the time of the Eckardstein-Lansdowne conversation cannot be determined, but previous instructions, which Eckardstein must have had, were of the same tenor.[40] Furthermore, Eckardstein gives himself away in his own memoirs when he confesses that, contrary to instructions, he had, on March 16, given Lansdowne a very broad hint that he ought to make an alliance offer.[41] From another source we know that he was very busy at this time prodding the Japanese minister, Count Hayashi, to take the initiative in proposing an Anglo-German-Japanese alliance. Lansdowne, Balfour, Chamberlain and Devonshire, he asserted, favored the scheme, and Salisbury had accepted the suggestion.[42]

To cover up the violation of his instructions Eckardstein therefore attributed the first move in the alliance negotiations to Lansdowne. The Berlin government was led to believe that the British had at last come to the point where they felt the urgent need of German support, and that they would, in the near future, come forward with concrete proposals. Although Holstein continued to be sceptical of Salisbury's approval of an agreement with Germany, instructions were at once

---

[39] *British Documents*, II, no. 77.
[40] Eckardstein: *Lebenserinnerungen*, II, p. 314, 316.
[41] Eckardstein, op. cit., II, p. 280.
[42] A. M. Pooley: *The Secret Memoirs of Count Tadasu Hayashi* (New York, 1915), pp. 119 ff.

sent to Eckardstein. From these it is clear that the Berlin foreign office considered the moment decisive: both England and Germany were at the parting of the ways. The Germans were favorable to a defensive alliance and thought that possibly Japan might be brought into it. Not only that, they felt that the other powers of the Triple Alliance should be associated, and wished the British to open discussions with Vienna. In view of the none-too-cordial relations between the German and Austrian capitals it was felt that this would be a striking demonstration of Germany's confidence in her ally.[43]

Hardly had these instructions reached London when Eckardstein sat down to report on another conversation he had had with Lansdowne on March 22. The foreign minister, so the German diplomat claimed, had worked out a memorandum on the question and had submitted it to some of his colleagues. Even Salisbury had declared in favor of a strictly defensive pact, though he wanted all possible eventualities to be carefully weighed. Lansdowne, wrote Eckardstein, then asked a number of questions touching on the probable obligations of the contracting powers, the problem of a public as against a secret treaty, the advisability of including Japan, etc. Eckardstein, on his part, took care not to raise the question of drawing Austria and Italy into the arrangement. The time, he wrote home, had not come for this.[44]

There is no direct English report of this conversation, but there can be little doubt that Eckardstein's account of it, like his earlier report, was badly distorted. It has been pointed out by German critics that much of what he attributed to Lansdowne on this occasion had already been said on March 18, and it is, of course, clear from later documents that Lansdowne could not have said what he is reported by Eckardstein to have said. His attitude, as we see it in the despatch to Lascelles mentioned above, is not at all what Eckardstein attributed to him. Furthermore, it is absolutely certain that Salisbury was never as favorably disposed as Eckardstein reported Lansdowne as saying that he was, and it is therefore more than unlikely that the foreign minister would have misrepresented the views of his chief.[45]

It is not necessary to follow the further course of the discussions in minute detail. Eckardstein averred that he had another talk with Lansdowne on March 25 and that they practically reached an agreement at that time on the essential points. It is morally certain, however, that this conversation never took place. There is no mention of it either in the British or in the German documents. Neither is there the slightest trace of any agreement.[46] All we know is that in the last days of March the German government sent a special emissary to Lon-

---

[43] *Die Grosse Politik*, XVII, nos. 4996, 5001, 5003.

[44] *Die Grosse Politik*, XVII, no. 4997.

[45] There is a good critique of this report in Walter Löding: *Die Deutsch-Englischen Bündnisverhandlungen 1898–1901* (Hamburg, 1929), pp. 83 ff.; Roloff, loc. cit., pp. 1185 ff. seems to me to confuse this conversation with a later one.

[46] Eckardstein, op. cit., II, pp. 286 ff. On this point see Ritter, op. cit., p. 34; Löding, op. cit., pp. 86–7; Dreyer, op. cit., pp. 70–1.

don to try to bring the English to give up their opposition to German policy in the matter of the Boxer indemnity negotiations and the increase of the Chinese customs. Thinking that the British were anxious for an alliance, the Germans clearly expected to realize on the situation. As a matter of fact the English, having been approached through Eckardstein, saw the situation in a very different light. The special negotiator had no success whatever. On the contrary, his mission caused some friction. On March 29 Lansdowne told Eckardstein that Salisbury's illness made it impossible to go on with the discussions for the time being. The premier, he said, took a cautious attitude towards the proposal, and the other ministers, while they desired a good and well-assured understanding with Germany, " regarded with a certain amount of apprehension the idea of an international arrangement of the somewhat indefinite but very far-reaching character " which had been suggested. Thereupon, according to Lansdowne, Eckardstein said that he did not think the moment propitious for pursuing the subject further. There was a certain amount of anti-British feeling in Berlin at the moment, and it might be better to let the thing rest for the time being. Eckardstein on his part reported home that the British minister had suddenly shown himself reticent about the whole business. The implication was that the injection of the Chinese indemnity problem had spoiled the Baron's efforts. The reality probably was that Eckardstein, seeing that he had gone too far, was trying to get out of a tight place. Indeed, he went so far as to offer his resignation, which was not accepted.[47]

Lord Salisbury left for the Riviera early in April and did not return to London until May 10. In the interval Eckardstein continued his game. He tried to reopen the question on April 9, but found Lansdowne unwilling to do anything in Salisbury's absence. This did not prevent the Baron from encouraging his own government. On April 13 he reported that Lansdowne was considering the matter with Devonshire and Chamberlain, both of whom favored the scheme. The foreign minister, he went on, had no doubt that even Salisbury would be brought to agree to it. In actual fact we learn from Lansdowne's reports to Lascelles that he had some doubt about Eckardstein's communications and was trying to find out whether the Berlin government stood behind him. Furthermore, Lansdowne had grave questions about the feasibility of the whole plan: " I doubt whether much will come of the project. In principle the idea is good enough. But when each side comes, if it ever does, to formulate its terms, we shall break down; and I know Lord Salisbury regards the scheme with, to say the least, suspicion." [48]

While awaiting the return of the prime minister, Eckardstein bestirred himself on another tack. He attempted to get the Japanese minister to press upon Lansdowne the advantages of an English-German-Japanese combination. Hayashi, so far as we know, did open discussions, but only with regard to a possible Anglo-Japanese agreement. When the German government learned by way of

[47] *British Documents,* II, no. 79; Eckardstein, op. cit., II, p. 326.
[48] *British Documents,* II, no. 81; Eckardstein, op. cit., II, pp. 334 ff.

Tokyo of Eckardstein's talks with Hayashi, it demanded some explanation. The Baron evaded responsibility for his unauthorized action by maintaining that it was Hayashi who had made the suggestion. By this time everything was thoroughly mixed up. Lansdowne had not only refused to discuss an alliance with Germany until the prime minister's return, but had also evaded the advances of Hayashi. On April 23 he wrote to the ambassador at St. Petersburg saying that England would not reject overtures from Russia, and that she was ready to recognize Russia's special interest in Manchuria.[49]

It must be remembered that the German government was completely in the dark with regard to the real situation. Early in May, in expectation of Salisbury's return, long instructions were sent to London reiterating the views of the Berlin foreign office. What was desired was an agreement between England, the Triple Alliance and Japan. This would be sufficient to block any Russian-French action in China. To which Eckardstein replied on May 15 that Lansdowne had re-opened the discussion, and had restated his conviction that Salisbury could be brought round. But, the foreign minister is said to have argued, there were certain difficulties connected with an alliance between England and the whole Triple Alliance. The English did not object so much to a union with a vigorous and on the whole liberal and progressive state like Germany, but they had some doubts about a relationship with a moribund state like Austria-Hungary and a Latin state like Italy. Still, Lansdowne hoped to overcome these obstacles, and thought the time had now come to sit down and try to set terms on paper, so that some agreement could be come to.[50]

With regard to this report of Eckardstein it may be said that it appears that he now for the first time raised the question of England's making an agreement with the whole Triple Alliance. There is no reliable evidence that he had broached the problem before, though he knew that his government regarded this as a *conditio sine qua non*. Of course, after Salisbury's return there was no longer any possibility of dodging the issue. As for Lansdowne's proposal that they sit down and try to work out the lines of an agreement on paper, there is every reason to believe that this suggestion came from Eckardstein, who was anxious to get along with the project. In any event, it appears from the British documents that Eckardstein promised Lansdowne a memorandum setting forth the German view. All this was contrary to instructions from Berlin and the question of the memorandum was to cause a good deal of embarrassment in the sequel.

The comedy of errors was now approaching the dénouement. Count Hatzfeldt, the sick ambassador, had returned to London in mid-April. Now that the discussions were coming to a head, he asked Lansdowne to come to the embassy to talk the situation over. The crucial conversation took place on May 23. We

---

[49] Newton: *Lord Lansdowne*, pp. 215 ff.; for the rest see Hayashi: *Secret Memoirs*, pp. 121 ff.; Eckardstein, op. cit., II, pp. 339 ff.; *British Documents*, II, no. 99.

[50] *Die Grosse Politik*, XVII, nos. 5003 ff.; Eckardstein, op. cit., II, pp. 344 ff.

have the reports of both Hatzfeldt and Lansdowne, and in this case there is no divergence worth mentioning. In the two reports there is some difference of emphasis on minor points, but they agree in laying the main stress on the discussion of an alliance between England on the one hand and the Triple Alliance on the other. Lansdowne pointed out what difficulties this arrangement would cause, while Hatzfeldt insisted that Germany could not enter a pact on any other terms. After all, he remarked, there never had been an alliance with only advantages and no risks. Could England really afford to continue her isolation? She might, of course, try an agreement with Russia, but that would cost her dearly. An alliance with Germany, Austria and Italy would be of immense benefit and would protect the British Empire against attack by any two opponents. Lansdowne did little of the talking, but promised to think the matter over and discuss it again in a week or so.[51]

In the course of his conversation with Hatzfeldt the foreign minister made it clear that he would like to get down to concrete terms, even though the discussions, like the entire negotiation thus far, should be regarded as unofficial and academic. Hatzfeldt, on the other hand, shared the view of the Berlin foreign office, that details could be discussed only after there were agreement on the general principle of an alliance between England and the Triple Alliance. Still, Eckardstein had promised Lansdowne a written memorandum, and during the days following Lansdowne tried hard to get it. The ambassador had the very greatest difficulty in explaining away the rash promise of his subordinate. Eckardstein himself found it advisable to leave town for some days.[52]

That Lansdowne was prepared to take the matter up in serious fashion is indicated by the fact that he asked one of the undersecretaries, Lord Sanderson, to outline the possible terms of the projected alliance. The Sanderson draft envisaged an alliance only between England and Germany, but tried to take into account the obligations of Germany to Austria. For the rest it is interesting more particularly for Sanderson's own opinion of the project. Qualifications, he remarked, would be necessary, in order to prevent either party from being dragged into a quarrel of which it disapproved and for which it would not have popular support. At the same time these qualifications would be likely to cause serious dispute between the contracting parties, " and the Germans will be much less scrupulous in making use of them to throw us over than we can be in leaving them in the lurch. Our public opinion would not allow it — theirs would." And further: " However the Convention may be worded, it seems to me that it will practically amount to a guarantee to Germany of the provinces conquered from France, and that is the way in which the French will look at it. I do not see exactly what Germany will guarantee us." [53]

---

51 *Die Grosse Politik*, XVII, no. 5010; *British Documents*, II, no. 82.
52 *Die Grosse Politik*, XVII, nos. 5011–7; *British Documents*, II, no. 87. There is a good discussion of this point in Walther, op. cit., pp. 614 ff.
53 *British Documents*, II, no. 85.

The remarks of Sanderson are interesting as the reflection of the viewpoint of an intelligent and by no means ill-willed official. Far more important, however, was the memorandum on the subject drawn up by Salisbury himself on May 29. In it he questioned the advantages of an agreement for England: "The liability of having to defend the German and Austrian frontiers against Russia is heavier than that of *having to defend the British Isles against France*. Even, therefore, in its most naked aspect the bargain would be a bad one for this country. Count Hatzfeldt speaks of our '*isolation*' as constituting a serious danger for us. *Have we ever felt that danger practically?* " In the wars against Napoleon England had many allies, but they could not have saved her if Napoleon had been able to command the Channel. Excepting during that period England had not been in danger and it was therefore impossible to judge whether or not isolation involved any peril. "It would hardly be wise to incur novel and most onerous obligations, in order to guard against *a danger in whose existence we have no historical reason for believing*." But there were even weightier objections to the projected agreement: "The fatal circumstance is that *neither we nor the Germans are competent to make the suggested promises*." The British government could make war only if the country approved. If it did not approve, then any promises that had been given would be repudiated and the cabinet turned out. "I do not see how, in common honesty, we could invite other nations to rely upon our aid in a struggle, which must be formidable and probably supreme, when we have no means of knowing what may be the humour of our people in circumstances which cannot be foreseen." The problem might be solved by laying the agreement with the Triple Alliance before parliament, but there were "very grave objections" to such a course. The whole argument about public opinion applied, though in less measure, to the German side. "*A promise of defensive alliance with England would excite bitter murmurs in every rank of German society*." [54]

This is one of the few documents we have which throws light on Salisbury's general ideas on foreign policy during his later years. It bears out completely the indications that may be found here and there in the sources. The old statesman was still wedded to the idea of splendid isolation. Presumably the fact that no serious attempt had been made to intervene against England during the Boer War had fortified him in the feeling that the much-discussed continental coalition was a chimaera and that England was safe so long as she commanded the Channel. For the rest it is worth noting how highly Salisbury appraised the force of public opinion. The old aristocrat had never liked the appeal to the man in the street. He did not understand, as did Chamberlain and other politicians, the technique of influencing the masses. He simply felt the dead weight of popular opinion; he feared and distrusted it; he did not know how malleable it is, for he had rarely tried to mold it. It is the indisputable fact, however, that in 1901 the project of an alliance was, in Lansdowne's words, "a very stiff fence

---

[54] *British Documents*, II, no. 86.

to ride at." German opinion was violently, rabidly prejudiced against England. The press could find no words to express its scorn and its delight at Britain's discomfiture. From the quotations given earlier in this chapter from the British press it is quite obvious that much the same feeling was being developed in England. Under such circumstances the alliance project was, in a sense, something of the nature of a pipe dream. Much would yet have had to be done to educate public opinion on both sides before the agreement could have been made a reality.

The Salisbury memorandum, together with Lansdowne's failure to get the promised German draft, rang the death knell of the proposed alliance. Eckardstein, who, incidentally, had reported to his government three days before Salisbury drew up his memorandum that Lansdowne, Devonshire and Chamberlain were firmly determined to see the alliance through and that even the prime minister now saw that England could not continue isolated but would have to do something, saw himself before a complete debacle.[55] Whether or not he went to Berlin in these days it is impossible to say. But it is fairly certain that he got himself out of the scrape by blacking the eye of Hatzfeldt and convincing the Berlin foreign office that the ambassador had bungled the affair by going too fast! In the same way he told Lansdowne that Hatzfeldt had represented his conversation with the foreign minister " as indicating much more alacrity on our part than we have actually exhibited." [56] The result was that the ambassador was recalled almost at once. He died in November of the same year, the last of the really great diplomats of the Bismarckian school.[57]

Despite Lansdowne's promise to the ambassador, he did not come back to the subject. Apparently he felt that the next move, now that nothing had come of the Eckardstein memorandum, was up to the Germans. In the same way the Berlin foreign office continued to expect further advances from London. Naturally nothing was known there of Eckardstein's misrepresentations. Though Holstein in particular had his doubts from the beginning about Salisbury's readiness to make an alliance and questioned whether England was yet ready to realize her need, the foreign office continued to labor under the misapprehension that the English had raised the question and that, sooner or later, probably after Salisbury's retirement, the project would mature. Memoranda drawn up by Count Metternich and by Holstein himself in the first half of June show that the Germans were still hoping for an alliance and were only too ready to receive English proposals. The English, on the other hand, were waiting for the Germans to move, though they were evidently quite content to let the whole question rest for the time being.[58]

The problem of a defensive agreement between the two countries never

---

[55] Eckardstein, op. cit., II, pp. 351–2.   [56] *British Documents,* II, no. 89.

[57] The whole matter of Eckardstein's intrigue against Hatzfeldt is admirably treated by von Hoyningen, op. cit., pp. 128 ff., footnote.

[58] *Die Grosse Politik,* XVII, nos. 5018, 5019; *British Documents,* II, no. 89.

came to the stage of serious official discussion, but there was an interesting post-
lude, which demands some attention. The English foreign minister was plainly
interested, and for obvious reasons, in keeping the Germans friendly and in
co-operating with them so far as possible. He was quite ready to make agreements with them on special points. Indeed, it should be remembered that the
whole discussion in the spring of 1901 arose from the Far Eastern crisis and the
efforts of the English and Japanese to draw the Germans into common action
against the Russian advance in Manchuria. Nothing had come of this project,
but there was another matter of crucial importance to Britain on which an
understanding might have been reached, and that was the question of Morocco.

The Moroccan problem turned out later to be as complicated and dangerous
a question as any which confronted European diplomacy in the pre-war period.
Because of its complexity, and because of the fact that only its beginnings fall
within the scope of this volume, there would be no point in making it the subject of a minute review. That work has, in fact, been excellently done by other
writers. We need here recall merely a few of the essential features of the problem. The French occupation of the Tuat oasis in the spring of 1900 has already
been mentioned in a preceding chapter. It was quite clear at that time that
Morocco would, in the near future, become a focal point of European politics,
for the dominions of the Sultan were most attractive, the government was weak
and ineffectual and the state generally was in European eyes one of the " decaying nations " of which Salisbury spoke in a famous address.[59]

The interests of the French in this region were too obvious to require much
analysis. Their African possessions practically surrounded Morocco and unrest
in the territory of their neighbor was bound to react upon Algeria. Apart from
these political, strategic considerations there were larger interests in the balance
of power in the Mediterranean, and to some extent economic interests, though
it must be confessed that the French rarely made the most of the development
of their colonies. It is rather surprising that the French did not do more to take
advantage of Britain's preoccupation with south Africa to strengthen their position in Morocco. Possibly the explanation lies in fear of a repetition of Fashoda,
possibly in the realization that Italy and Spain, to say nothing of Germany,
would have to be squared first. At all events, Delcassé seems to have decided
upon a very circumspect policy. He scored a first great success when, with the
aid of the ambassador at Rome, M. Barrère, he induced the Italians to sign the
Agreement of December 14, 1900, which gave France a free hand in Morocco
in return for a free hand in Tripoli. The Italians, who looked with great alarm
upon the French advance in north Africa, had appealed to both Germany and
England for support. They had found encouragement on neither side, and had

[59] Conditions in Morocco at this time are interestingly depicted in such books as Walter B.
Harris: *Morocco that Was* (London, 1921) and Eugène Aubin: *Morocco of To-day* (London, 1906);
René Pinon's *L'Empire de la Méditerranée* (Paris, 1904) is still a useful discussion of the problem
as it presented itself early in the century.

therefore taken a further step along the road to the entente with France. The way was now clear for the crowning effort of Barrère. It took him eighteen months to effect the Morocco-Tripoli agreement and it was to take him just about as long again to secure from the Italians the famous statements of 1902 which rendered Italy's membership in the Triple Alliance quite innocuous.[60]

The French had much less success in their attempts to strike a bargain with the Spaniards, though their position in Spain was at the time stronger than it had been for years past. Weakened by the war with the United States, the Spanish apparently did not feel equal to taking an active part in the Moroccan question at that time. Their interest was to maintain the status quo for some years at least, and for that reason they rather attempted to obstruct than to aid the French plans. They made repeated efforts to effect a French-German understanding which would include Spain and safeguard Spanish interests in Morocco, but these efforts proved futile and ultimately the Madrid government was obliged to reopen negotiations directly with Paris.[61]

Important though Italy and Spain were for any solution of the Moroccan problem, the chief rivals of the French were the British, with their tremendous interest in the control of the Straits of Gibraltar and in the balance of power in the Mediterranean. It has been pointed out in a previous chapter that Lord Salisbury was prepared, if it came to a crisis, to strike a bargain with the French, reserving for England Tangiers and some of the other port towns and leaving the remainder for the others. Count Hatzfeldt at the time warned his government of this possibility, and Bülow agreed that it would be a departure of positively crucial importance for Germany. Whereas, a few years before, the Germans had shown very little interest in the problem and had viewed it chiefly as one element in European international relations — as a question in which Italy was concerned — they now took a very real interest in the matter. Hatzfeldt, who seems to have foreseen its future significance, made it clear to the British in 1899 that in any eventual partition the Germans would require a share on the Atlantic coast.[62]

The German demand for consideration seems to have displeased Salisbury, who thereafter showed no readiness to discuss the question with the ambassador. But Chamberlain, at that time still the exponent of the idea of the German alliance, appears to have envisaged a Moroccan agreement as the first stage in the evolution of the future alliance. The matter was discussed at various times

---

[60] The Morocco-Tripoli agreement was really signed on January 4, 1901, though it was antedated to December 15, 1900 (*Documents Diplomatiques Français*, I, nos. 1, 17, 59, 88; Abel Combarieu: *Sept Ans à l'Élysée*, Paris, 1932, pp. 106–7). This whole problem is most admirably dealt with in Pinon, op. cit., introduction, and in the well-documented books of Eugene N. Anderson: *The First Moroccan Crisis* (Chicago, 1930), chap. ii; Herbert E. Brenning: *Die Grossen Mächte und Marokko, 1898–1904* (Berlin, 1934), chap. iv; James L. Glanville: *Italy's Relations with England, 1896–1905* (Baltimore, 1934), pp. 80 ff.

[61] See Anderson, op. cit., chap. iii, and the literature there cited.

[62] *Die Grosse Politik*, XVII, nos. 5152 ff.; Anderson, op. cit., pp. 63 ff.; Brenning, op. cit., pp. 44 ff.

between him and Eckardstein, but the Samoan dispute reacted unfavorably upon general relations and caused some postponement, rather to the disappointment of the Germans, who in 1899 and 1900 were quite anxious to strike bargains on special questions, though unwilling to consider a definite alliance that would involve hostility to Russia.

The Moroccan problem hung fire, therefore, while the British were busy in south Africa. Appeals from the Sultan Abdel Aziz for support against the encroachments of the French were allowed to go unheeded. The object of the British was, if possible, to avoid complications.[63] But by the summer of 1901 it was becoming almost impossible to stay by this policy. Friction had developed very rapidly between France and Morocco in the spring. Tribal raids along the Algerian frontier resulted in a great French naval demonstration in May and a widespread fear that the Paris government would at last resort to extreme measures. The Sultan once again called upon the British for help, and in June sent his minister of war, El Menebhi, on a mission to London and Berlin, evidently in the hope that an English-German combination, backed by Spain and Italy, could be brought about to check the threat from France. Apparently the mission to London caused a good deal of uneasiness in Paris, although the Sultan had at the same time despatched his foreign minister, Abdel Krim, to Paris to negotiate a demarcation of the Algerian frontier. We need not enter upon all the details. The essential point is that on both sides, British and French, a cautious policy was pursued. The war minister got little beyond kind words in London, while Delcassé confined himself to warnings. On both sides of the Channel it was stated that nothing was to be done to raise the dangerous Moroccan issue at that time.[64]

The reason why neither the French nor the British government was ready to press the matter in the summer of 1901 was probably the uncertainty as to Germany's attitude. The two chief rivals both knew that the Germans expected to be consulted, and they both knew that, with German support, their chances of success would be greatly enhanced. They therefore both made efforts to draw the Berlin government to their side. Early in June the French foreign minister approached the German ambassador through his friend Leon y Castillo, the Spanish representative in Paris. He suggested that if the German government would take the initiative, he would be glad to discuss various matters with a view to reaching an entente. He admitted that no French minister could agree to the abandonment of claims to Alsace and Lorraine, but he suggested that a rapprochement could be sought along other lines. At the same time the inspired French press pointed out that now the opportunity had come for Germany to

[63] See especially Harold Nicolson: *Portrait of a Diplomatist* (Boston, 1930), chap. v.

[64] Nicolson, loc. cit.; G. Saint-René Taillandier: *Les Origines du Maroc Français* (Paris, 1930), chap. i; Anderson, op. cit., pp. 12 ff.; Brenning, op. cit., pp. 70 ff., who has used not only the German and British documents, but also the recently published French documents. There is an excellent review of French policy from January 1900 to August 1901 in *Documents Diplomatiques Français*, I, no. 372.

show in the Moroccan question that her good will went beyond words. But nothing came of these advances. The German government replied that it could not enter upon an agreement with France which would incur the hostility of another power unless the French were prepared to accept a mutual guarantee of territory. As on previous occasions the conquered provinces proved an insurmountable obstacle to understanding.[65]

At the time the German government was certainly much more interested in bargaining with the British. The foreign office would have been glad to make an agreement with respect to Morocco, but only as part of a larger defensive alliance. In other words, the German attitude had changed completely since 1899–1900. At that time what was wanted was a series of special agreements of the Samoa or Yangtze type, without the obligations of a broader alliance. Now no special arrangements would be considered excepting in the framework of a general agreement. The reason for this reversal was simply the disappointment of the Germans with the Agreement of 1898 regarding the Portuguese colonies. In December 1900 the whole British Channel squadron paid a visit to Lisbon, where the admiral, Sir Harry Rawson, was fêted and welcomed. In a speech made on this occasion King Carlos celebrated the alliance of Portugal and Britain in such a way that there could be no doubt in the minds of the Germans that all was not right with the Treaty of 1898. Prince Bülow says in his memoirs that he learned, at about this time, the story of the so-called Windsor Treaty of 1899. It is not entirely unlikely that some indications of the truth reached Berlin from Paris, since the British government seems at this time to have warned the importunate French creditors of Portugal not to go too far in their schemes for bringing pressure.[66] In any case it is clear from the German documents that the German statesmen were most unfavorably impressed with the Lisbon demonstrations, despite the assurances that were given them in London.[67] To this disappointment must be added the feeling that had grown up in Berlin that special agreements, whether they applied to Morocco or to Asia, would involve the same risk as a larger agreement while they would net a much smaller return, and also the fear that a special agreement with England would diminish the desire of the British for a general alliance. Taken all together these factors explain quite fully the attitude of the Berlin government in the summer of 1901.[68]

Eckardstein claims in his memoirs that early in July he was approached by Sir Arthur Nicolson, the British minister at Tangiers, who was in London

---

[65] *Die Grosse Politik*, XVIII, nos. 5868 ff.; Anderson, op. cit., pp. 13–4; Brenning, op. cit., pp. 73–4.

[66] Texeira de Sousa: *Responsibilidades Historicas* (Coimbra, 1917), II, pp. 49–53; Geoffrey Rawson: *Life of Admiral Sir Harry Rawson* (London, 1914), pp. 201–3. On Bülow's knowledge of the Windsor Treaty see his *Memoirs*, I, p. 321; Maximilian von Hagen: "Hat Fürst Bülow den Windsorvertrag Gekannt?" (*Berliner Monatshefte*, February 1931, pp. 183–6).

[67] *Die Grosse Politik*, XVII, no. 4981; Eckardstein, op. cit., II, pp. 207 ff.

[68] *Die Grosse Politik*, XVII, nos. 4993, 5174; Eckardstein, op. cit., II, pp. 314–5.

with the mission of El Menebhi. Nicolson, he says, told him that Lansdowne desired to co-operate with Germany in maintaining the status quo in Morocco, and Nicolson further suggested the possibility of collaboration for the economic exploitation of the country. Eckardstein asserts that he immediately sent a long telegram to Berlin supporting the suggestion, but never received a reply. Nothing of all this appears in either the German or the British documents, while Nicolson's biographer has shown that the English diplomat, though he favored co-operation with Germany, was probably not authorized to make such advances and in all likelihood did not make them. No doubt we have here simply another instance of Eckardstein's untrustworthiness.[69]

The British seem to have made no concrete proposals to the Germans for common action in opposition to France in the Moroccan question, even when, on his return home, El Menebhi fell into disfavor and both the London and Berlin governments used their influence to save him. Evidently the English foreign office realized that the prospects of German support were too slight to make advances worthwhile. On the German side the documents indicate that it was hoped that the English would become more deeply involved with the French and that, as a consequence, the London government would be more ready to reopen the alliance question. Eckardstein encouraged his government in this idea, and the foreign office therefore made no secret of the fact that it would not regard an attack upon Morocco as being in itself a sufficient cause for war against France. " In this matter we must for the time being maintain complete reserve and act the part of the sphinx," wrote Bülow. In a memorandum which was shown the British in August 1901 it was stated unequivocally: " The Morocco Question by itself is not sufficiently important for us to justify a policy by which Germany might incur the risk of serious international complications." [70]

With the German evasion of all advances regarding Morocco the famous negotiations for an alliance may be said to have come to a close. The problem was touched upon again later in the year and we shall therefore have to refer to it again in another connexion. But by July 1901 the important phase was over — the British had put aside the suggestion made and discussed unofficially by Eckardstein, and the Germans had made it clear that they were not interested in anything but a general defensive alliance.

Many, many books and articles have been written on these negotiations and there has been no end of wrangling over the question whether or no this was the crucial point in the whole history of pre-war diplomacy. Considerable space has been devoted to the problem here — more space really than the subject warrants. For, since the publication of the British documents, there is relatively little ground left for divergent opinions. We can now see (and the most

---

[69] Eckardstein, op. cit., II, pp. 357–8; Nicolson: *Portrait of a Diplomatist,* pp. 103–4.

[70] *Die Grosse Politik,* XVII, no. 5177 and pp. 119 ff. For details see Anderson, op. cit., pp. 73–4; Brenning, op. cit., pp. 81–5; Hoyningen, op. cit., pp. 136 ff.

recent writers are generally agreed on this point) that the Germans were never in the position to reject an alliance offer because none was ever made to them. It is now beyond dispute that the German foreign office was at the time only too ready to consider an alliance with England, even though it had rather distorted ideas regarding the need and desire of England for an alliance and regarding the price that could be gotten for German friendship. The complete misapprehension of the German foreign office was, of course, due very largely to the reporting of Baron von Eckardstein. Without the documentary evidence it would be almost impossible to believe that in a diplomatic service so rigorously trained in the Bismarckian tradition anything like the misrepresentations of Eckardstein could have been possible. Certainly his whole action, though undoubtedly well-intentioned, was in flagrant contradiction to everything that good diplomacy stands for. It is unthinkable that anything worthwhile could be accomplished by the methods he employed.

Eckardstein systematically misled his government into thinking that the British were making advances for an alliance and that even Lord Salisbury was favorable to the idea. Now we know that Salisbury himself was as much an isolationist as ever. If pressed to the limit he would have made an agreement with Russia or even with France in preference to one with the Germans, whom he distrusted and had come to dislike. It is certainly true that Lord Salisbury, now an old and infirm man, was not the only influential person in the British government. Chamberlain was hardly less powerful in the cabinet than the prime minister himself, and Chamberlain had always been the chief exponent of an agreement with Germany. It should be noted, however, that Chamberlain's idea from 1898 onward had been to draft the support of the Germans to oppose the Russians in the Far East. This policy was tried again in February and March 1901, and it failed then as it had failed before. Even he who ran could read that the Germans would not allow themselves to become involved in war with Russia, and consequently with France, either for the sake of the British or for the sake of anything the Far Eastern situation could offer. It is interesting to note that after March 1901 there is relatively little reference even in Eckardstein's correspondence to the views of Chamberlain. In all likelihood he had definitely given up the idea of enlisting the Germans. For him the alliance idea died as soon as he saw that he could not get what he wanted.

There remained Lord Lansdowne, the influential foreign minister. Obviously Lansdowne was not wedded to the idea of isolation as was Salisbury. Indeed, like Chamberlain he saw the dangers of Britain's position, at least the dangers to her interests in Asia and Africa at a time when she was too deeply involved in the South African War to play her rôle fully. But it seems probable that he, like the colonial secretary, despaired of the German connexion when it became clear that Germany would not compromise her relations with Russia. It would be most interesting to know how much there was behind the suggestion of an agreement with Russia which we find in Lansdowne's letter of April

1901. The present writer is convinced that the British statesmen generally would have preferred an arrangement with Russia to any other settlement. Failing to interest the St. Petersburg government, they were driven back upon some other solution. Lansdowne may have — probably did — contemplate a special agreement with Germany on the Moroccan question, though he was not given the opportunity to make concrete advances.

In the view of some recent writers this Moroccan aspect of the negotiations was the really crucial aspect. There is some force in this argument, for while one can understand the unwillingness of the Germans to risk a war with Russia, which would have meant a war with France, this same risk would not have existed in a Moroccan agreement with England. The Russians, we may assume, would not have backed France to the extent of war in the Moroccan affair any more than they did in the Fashoda affair. Of course, if the Moroccan question led to war between France and Germany, it would have been to the interest of Russia not to allow France to be defeated again by her neighbor. But it would still have been doubtful whether, if Germany were backed by England, the Russians would have been willing to face both. Surely one cannot escape the feeling that in the Moroccan problem, from the very outset, the Germans failed to understand the ultimate implications. They lost the loyalty of the Italians largely through their unwillingness to take the matter seriously enough. They failed to capitalize the opportunity for an agreement with England on the subject in 1901 and thereby contributed indirectly at least to the formation of the Entente between England and France. By 1904–1905 the German claims could receive a hearing only at the expense of a great international crisis. It is hard to avoid the feeling that an agreement between Germany and England on Morocco in 1901 might have led to a closer connexion later, just as the Anglo-French Entente evolved into something more than a mere colonial settlement.

But all this brings us back again to the misrepresentations of Eckardstein. It was not good will but understanding that was lacking in Berlin, and Eckardstein's distortion of the facts meant simply that the discussions came to an end leaving both sides distrustful and suspicious. The Berlin government believed that the British had made the first overtures and had then dropped them unceremoniously. It felt justified in thinking that England, having been obliged to take the first step, would soon be impelled to take the second. In London, on the other hand, it was thought that the Germans wanted the alliance and had offered it, only to follow up the offer with what seemed like impossible conditions. The result was naturally that the conviction became fixed that the Germans were playing a slippery game. From 1901 onward one notes among the members of the foreign office a steady growth of the dislike which had already become fixed in the popular mind. For psychological reasons, if for no other, an alliance was rapidly becoming impossible.

BIBLIOGRAPHICAL NOTE

DOCUMENTARY SOURCES

Die Grosse Politik der Europäischen Kabinette, 1871–1914. Volume XVI, chapter cvi: The Manchurian Agreement. Volume XVII, chapter cix: The Anglo-German Alliance Discussions; chapter cxiii: The Moroccan Question. Volume XVIII, chapter cxxv: Italy and the Triple Alliance.

British Documents on the Origins of the War. Volume II, chapter ix: The Far East, 1900–1901; chapter x: The Anglo-German Negotiations; chapter xiv: France and Morocco.

Documents Diplomatiques Français, 1871–1914. Published by the Commission de Publication des Documents Relatifs aux Origines de la Guerre de 1914. Series II, volume I, January 2–December 31, 1901. Paris, 1930. Part of the important French publication. This volume is rich particularly in documents on French relations with Italy and on the Moroccan question.

Accounts and Papers. 1904, volume CX. *China No. 2 (1904), Correspondence respecting the Russian Occupation of Manchuria and Newchwang.* A useful collection, which should be read in connexion with the *British Documents*.

Documents Diplomatiques. Affaires du Maroc, 1901–1905. Paris, 1905. This collection must now be supplemented with the material in the collection mentioned above.

Documents Diplomatiques. Les Accords Franco-Italiens de 1900–1902. Paris, 1920. Important.

" Nakanunie Russko-Iaponskoi Voiny." (*Krasnyi Arkhiv*, LXIII, 1934, pp. 3–54). A most important collection of correspondence, chiefly between St. Petersburg and Tokyo, covering the year 1901. Much of this material has, to be sure, been used by Romanov.

MEMOIRS, AUTOBIOGRAPHIES, BIOGRAPHIES, AND LETTERS

Kato Takaaki. Two volumes. Tokyo, 1929. The papers of the foreign minister in the Ito cabinet and a most important source for the study of Japanese policy.

Eckardstein, Hermann Freiherr von: *Lebenserinnerungen und Politische Denkwürdigkeiten.* Two volumes. Leipzig, 1920. These memoirs must, of course, be used with much caution, but they are important because they contain a number of private telegrams and letters that cannot be found in the German documentary collection.

Newton, Lord: *Lord Lansdowne.* London, 1929. A good but rather brief biography. It contains some letters and information not to be found elsewhere.

LEE, SIR SIDNEY: *Edward VII, a Biography.* Two volumes. New York, 1925–1927. Volume II contains some material on the relations between Edward and the Emperor William in 1901.

NICOLSON, HAROLD: *Portrait of a Diplomatist.* Boston, 1930. A most interesting biography of Sir Arthur Nicolson (Lord Carnock). Valuable for the discussion of affairs in Morocco between 1895 and 1904.

BÜLOW, PRINCE: *Memoirs.* Four volumes. Boston, 1931–1932. Contains almost nothing of importance on the Anglo-German negotiations.

SAINT-RENÉ TAILLANDIER, G.: *Les Origines du Maroc Français.* Paris, 1930. The French minister's account of his mission to Morocco, 1901–1906. An important source.

SPECIAL STUDIES

MEINECKE, FRIEDRICH: *Geschichte des Deutsch-Englischen Bündnisproblems, 1890–1901.* Munich, 1927. The best-known study, being the work of an eminent German historian. Published before the appearance of the British documents, it is no longer reliable on the factual side, though still stimulating.

RITTER, GERHARD: *Die Legende von der Verschmähten Englischen Freundschaft.* Freiburg, 1929. One of the keenest and most discerning discussions of the problem as it emerged after the publication of the *British Documents*.

ROLOFF, GUSTAV: " Die Bündnisverhandlungen zwischen Deutschland und England, 1898–1901." (*Berliner Monatshefte,* December, 1929, pp. 1167–1222). A detailed, careful criticism of the texts; constitutes perhaps the most effective indictment of Eckardstein.

WALTHER, HEINRICH: " Die Deutsch-Englischen Bündnisverhandlungen von 1901 und ihre Ergebnisse." (*Historische Vierteljahrschrift,* XXV, 1931, pp. 602–35). A study along the lines of Roloff's, with some additional points.

MECENSEFFY, GRETE: " Die Deutsch-Englischen Bündnisverhandlungen 1898–1901, im Lichte der Englischen Aktenpublikation." (*Vierteljahrschrift für Politik und Geschichte,* 1929, pp. 175–91). A perfectly conventional analysis of the British materials.

LÖDING, WALTER: *Die Deutsch-Englischen Bündnisverhandlungen 1898–1901. Ihr Verlauf auf Grund der Deutschen und Englischen Akten.* Hamburg, 1929. One of the best narratives of the negotiations, though unimportant from the critical standpoint.

DREYER, JOHANNES: *Deutschland und England in ihrer Politik und Presse im Jahre 1901.* Berlin, 1934. One of the few studies that takes account of public opinion. It is thorough and reliable. One of the best works on the Anglo-German problem in 1901.

HOYNINGEN GENANNT HUENE, HEINRICH FREIHERR VON: *Untersuchungen zur Geschichte des Deutsch-Englischen Bündnisproblems, 1898–1901.* Breslau, 1934. Another careful and generally excellent study. Noteworthy chiefly for the emphasis placed upon the Moroccan aspect of the problem.

BECKER, WILLY: *Fürst Bülow und England, 1897–1909.* Greifswald, 1929. Very critical of the German policy, but not entirely abreast of the recent material and critical writing.

FISCHER, EUGEN: *Holsteins Grosses Nein. Berlin, 1925.* An able and keen critique of German policy, following largely along the lines of Eckardstein's memoirs. No longer of much use.

HALLER, JOHANNES: *England und Deutschland um die Jahrhundertwende.* Leipzig, 1929. The work of one of Bülow's most consistent critics. The author stands by his condemnation of the German policy despite the evidence of the *British Documents.*

EHRINGHAUS, FRITZ: " Die Ergebnisse der Englischen Akten über die Deutsch-Englischen Bündnisverhandlungen 1899–1901." (*Vergangenheit und Gegenwart,* XIX, 1929, pp. 471–80). A brief analysis of the *British Documents,* the author going even beyond Ritter in his revisionary tendencies.

LEHMANN, KONRAD: " Die Ablehnung des Englischen Bündnisantrags, 1898–1901." (*Preussische Jahrbücher,* August, 1930, pp. 162–83). Perhaps the best recent presentation of the Meinecke viewpoint.

JOHNSON, EDGAR N., and BICKFORD, JOHN D.: " The Contemplated Anglo-German Alliance, 1890–1901." (*Political Science Quarterly,* March, 1927, pp. 1–57). A solid but conventional review of Anglo-German relations.

MOWAT, R. B.: " Great Britain and Germany in the Early Twentieth Century." (*English Historical Review,* XLVI, July, 1931, pp. 423–41). A general survey of the whole period 1898–1914. Adds nothing.

GOOCH, GEORGE P.: " Baron von Holstein." In his *Studies in Modern History.* London, 1931. An admirable and exceptionally well-informed study of Holstein, containing perhaps the best account in English of the Anglo-German negotiations.

BECKER, OTTO: Review of the books of Meinecke and Ritter. (*Deutsche Literaturzeitung,* L, pp. 903–25). A penetrating and illuminating discussion of the two conflicting views with regard to the alliance negotiations.

STALNIJ, V.: " Popitka Anglo-Germanskogo Sblisheniia v 1898–1901 gg." (*Istorik Marksist,* X, 1928, pp. 89–120). An interesting Marxian interpretation, covering only the period from 1898–1900. Adds nothing in the way of factual material, since it is based almost exclusively on the Eckardstein memoirs and the German documents.

OSTWALD, PAUL: " Das Deutsch-Englische Abkommen über China vom 16 Oktober, 1900." (*Berliner Monatshefte,* December, 1933, pp. 1192–1204). A keen and thorough analysis of the German and British documents on the Yangtze Agreement.

THE EARLY PHASES OF THE MOROCCAN QUESTION

HARRIS, WALTER B.: *Morocco that Was*. London, 1921. Few people knew Morocco more intimately than Harris. This is a vivid picture of conditions in the period around 1900.

AUBIN, EUGÈNE: *Morocco of To-day*. London, 1906. Another excellent discussion of conditions before the storm.

PINON, RENÉ: *L'Empire de la Méditerranée*. Paris, 1904. One of the best contemporary discussions of the political problems of the Mediterranean and north Africa.

PEYRONNET, RAYMOND: *Le Problème Nord-Africain*. Paris, 1924. The first volume of a thorough and valuable French history.

ANDERSON, EUGENE N.: *The First Moroccan Crisis, 1904–1906*. Chicago, 1930. One of the best studies of the Moroccan question, full use being made of both the German and British documents. The book contains an extended discussion of the background and developments from 1900–1904.

BRENNING, HERBERT E.: *Die Grossen Mächte und Marokko, 1898–1904*. Berlin, 1934. Another thorough, systematic study, particularly valuable because based in part upon the recently published *Documents Diplomatiques Français*.

XXIII

The Anglo-Japanese Alliance

✍

T HE MOROCCAN QUESTION MIGHT CONCEIVABLY HAVE SERVED THE PUR- pose of bridging the widening chasm between England and Germany. But the problem was not, in 1901, entirely ripe. It was not yet the crucial issue in international relations which it became a few years later. On the contrary, the dominant questions of European diplomacy still lay in Asia. It is to Far Eastern affairs that we must return in order to trace the epochal change in British policy that resulted in the conclusion of the alliance with Japan.

Russia's withdrawal of the draft agreement with China concerning Manchuria settled nothing, for the Russians remained in occupation and the European powers were still confronted with the problem of inducing them to evacuate. It will be recalled that during the crisis of February and March there had been some talk of a possible English-German-Japanese Alliance to regulate the Far Eastern situation. Whether or not this idea sprang from the fertile brain of Baron von Eckardstein is a matter of slight consequence. The important thing is that it received the warm support of Count Hayashi, the Japanese minister at London, who was one of the earliest and most persistent advocates of an alliance between Britain and Japan. Hayashi had been authorized by his government in mid-April to discuss the project with Lansdowne in an unofficial way. There had been some conversation about it in May, but Lansdowne, while he showed himself sympathetic, indicated that there would be difficulties when it came to the discussion of details. He stressed the fact that the agreement, if it were ever come to, would not need to be restricted to two powers, from which we may conclude that he envisaged the association of Germany. Very little is known of these pourparlers, which should probably be viewed as part of the Anglo-German conversations. Lansdowne was presumably holding back until he had some idea of what the Germans were prepared to do.[1]

The situation continued to be unsatisfactory. In June the Japanese cabinet of Marquis Ito was replaced by a ministry headed by Count Katsura. In Russian circles this change was regarded as a change for the worse, for Ito was looked upon as a man of compromise and peace, while Katsura was thought to be the

---

[1] The only important source is A. M. Pooley: *The Secret Memoirs of Count Tadasu Hayashi* (New York, 1915), pp. 119–25; but see also Eckardstein: *Lebenserinnerungen*, II, pp. 339, 342; *Die Grosse Politik*, XVII, nos. 5037, 5038.

leader of the war party. Waldersee, who visited Tokyo in June on his return to Europe, found the capital much excited and noted the prevalence of a feeling that Japan was on the threshold of a great decision. The Japanese were convinced that once the Transsiberian Railway was completed it would be too late to stop Russia. They were confident that they could deal with Russia single-handed, but they were worried by Delcassé's visit to St. Petersburg in April and feared that France would stand by Russia in a Far Eastern conflict. In any event, they were determined to reply with a declaration of war to any Russian attempt to acquire a footing in southern Korea.[2]

The Japanese were certainly mistaken when they feared that the Russian government was contemplating a forward move in the summer of 1901. It is perfectly true that the military men, fed by disparaging reports on the Japanese army, lost no sleep over the Japanese threat. The military attaché at Tokyo reported that it would take many years, perhaps hundreds of years, before the army could acquire the moral basis on which the organization of European armies was built up, and before it could stand on an equal footing with even the weakest European force. A strong cavalry regiment supplied with artillery, he thought, could win a decisive victory over this army if it acted reasonably promptly and energetically. An army of sucklings, was the verdict of General Ivanov after watching the Japanese forces. Not to be compared with any major European army, least of all with the Russian, reported General Jilinski.[3]

Kuropatkin, who was sick of exaggerated accounts of Japanese prowess, accepted these reports at face value. In the summer of 1901 he was still pressing for the retention of northern Manchuria as far as the line of the Transmanchurian Railway.[4] But the diplomats did not share the optimism of the war office. Izvolski appreciated the danger from Japan to the full, and both Lamsdorff and Witte understood the necessity for the early evacuation of Manchuria. The occupation, wrote Witte in June and again in July, would amount to the creation, on Russia's frontier, of a new province which would bring in nothing but would entail enormous expenditures, thus increasing the burden which already rested on the Russian people. The great task for Russia was to avoid war with Japan.[5] He therefore urged the resumption of negotiations for the withdrawal of the Russian forces. At the same time he approached the Japanese minister at St. Petersburg and suggested, unofficially, an arrangement regarding

    [2] *Die Grosse Politik*, XVII, no. 5039; Waldersee: *Denkwürdigkeiten*, III, pp. 153 ff.; see also Izvolski's report of April 5, 1901, in the collection "Nakanunie Russko-Iaponskoi Voiny" (*Krasnyi Arkhiv*, LXIII, 1934, pp. 3–54), pp. 24–7; *Documents Diplomatiques Français*, I, no. 310.

    [3] *Der Russisch-Japanische Krieg. Amtliche Darstellung des Russischen Generalstabs*. Deutsche Übersetzung von Freiherr von Tettau (Berlin, 1911–1912), I, pp. 163–6. The reports here quoted were all made in 1901.

    [4] Kuropatkin: *The Russian Army*, etc., I, p. 163; Witte: *La Guerre avec le Japon*, pp. 47–9; Romanov: *Rossiia v Manchzhurii*, p. 315; "Nakanunie Russko-Iaponskoi Voiny" (loc. cit.), pp. 28–9, 32–5.

    [5] Glinskii: *Prolog Russko-Iaponskoi Voiny*, p. 174; Romanov, op. cit., pp. 312 ff.; "Nakanunie Russko-Iaponskoi Voiny" (loc. cit.), pp. 29–35.

the crucial Korean problem. Russia, he said, would agree to a settlement making Korea a neutral area, but giving Japan the right to supply the Korean government with administrative and financial advisers as well as with a chief of police. In return Japan should officially recognize Russia's preponderance in Manchuria.[6]

Almost nothing is known of these Russian approaches to Japan. Neither can we say whether information of these moves reached the British government. All we do know is that about the middle of July rumors were put about in the British press that Russia and France were going to supply Japan with a much-needed loan. Eckardstein admits having worried the British government with warnings of a possible Russian-Japanese agreement and having inserted alarmist notices in the British press.[7] On the other hand Hayashi confesses that at this time he advised his government to hint to the British the possibility of an arrangement respecting Korea.[8] We are probably safe in assuming that these two gentlemen, both of them enthusiasts for an Anglo-Japanese alliance, made the most of the situation, for on July 15 Sir Claude MacDonald, the British minister to Japan, who was home on leave, told Hayashi that King Edward felt that an alliance was necessary and that Salisbury shared the feeling. The prime minister, he went on, realized that the matter would take time, and he rather feared that in the interval Japan and Russia might make up their differences. To this Hayashi replied: " As you know, the feelings of Japan are not friendly to Russia, but are friendly to England. Of course sentiment should be subordinated to considerations of actual profit, and without doubt if Russia should see her way to make substantial concessions to Japan, then certainly our feelings of enmity to that country would disappear." [9]

The ruse must have been completely successful, for on July 31 Lansdowne himself broached the subject in conversation with Hayashi. We have both Lansdowne's and Hayashi's account of what transpired. According to Lansdowne, Hayashi said that Japan had " a strong sentimental dislike " to the retention of Manchuria by Russia, seeing that they themselves had once been expelled from it. " But Japan's real concern was Corea. Corea could not possibly stand alone, its people were far too unintelligent, and sooner or later it would have to be decided whether the Country was to fall to Russia or not. The Japanese Government could not possibly accept the former of these alternatives. They would certainly fight in order to prevent it, and it must be the object of their diplomacy to isolate Russia, with which Power, if it stood alone, they were prepared to deal." To which Lansdowne replied that Korea was further from England than from Japan, but that, considering its geographical position, England could no more than Japan regard its fate with indifference. There was obviously much similarity between the Japanese and British policy; both de-

---

[6] *Die Grosse Politik,* XVII, no. 5041, Eckardstein's report of a conversation with Hayashi July 26, 1901.   [7] Eckardstein, op. cit., II, p. 370; *Die Grosse Politik,* XVII, no. 5040.   [8] Hayashi: *Memoirs,* p. 128.   [9] Hayashi: *Memoirs,* pp. 126–9.

sired the status quo. He, Lansdowne, would be ready to discuss the possibility of an understanding if Japan so desired.[10]

Hayashi's report is much fuller. In his memoirs he states that Lansdowne declared: " We think that the time has come to discuss seriously the question of making a permanent treaty with Japan." This remark does not, however, appear in the original despatch to Tokyo, which reported only Lansdowne's hope for the continuance of consideration of measures that might be taken to protect the interests of the two countries. It is clear, though, that Hayashi explained that Japan wanted to keep Russia out of Manchuria because " if Russia should one day occupy a part of Manchuria and extend her influence in those parts, then she would be able to absorb Korea, against which Japan would be obliged to protest. What Japan wants is to prevent Russia from coming into Manchuria, and if to do this she should be involved in war with Russia she wants to prevent a third party coming to the help of Russia." [11]

The Japanese minister relates in his memoirs that the Tokyo government approved entirely of his statements to Lansdowne and asked him to get further details. From the official correspondence it appears, however, that the government was somewhat doubtful of British intentions, and noted that MacDonald had spoken more enthusiastically than Lansdowne. Hayashi was told to continue his discussions with MacDonald, stressing the fact that Japanese policy aimed to block the expansion of any other power in Korea. If Russia went beyond existing treaties regarding Manchuria, the Japanese government would regard that as a threat to the independence of Korea. But at all events Hayashi was to continue to speak unofficially.[12]

Lansdowne spoke once more to the Japanese minister before leaving for a protracted vacation in Ireland. Hayashi told him that he felt no doubt that his government would be glad to come to an understanding, and asked for the British terms. But the foreign secretary, who in this matter as in the case of the Anglo-German discussions was not as forward as he was reported to be, pointed out that the issue concerned Japan more than England and that it was therefore up to the Tokyo government to state its requirements. He suggested further that Hayashi secure definite instructions. The Japanese minister had to explain to his government that MacDonald would not return to London before sailing for Japan, and that Lansdowne, though his language was restrained, had actually used the word *alliance* and had shown that he was really in accord with MacDonald. What party spoke first, he argued, was a matter of small import. In fact, he who took the initiative would probably have a certain advantage.[13]

10 *British Documents*, II, no. 102.

11 Hayashi, op. cit., pp. 129–31. Hayashi's original report of August 1, 1901 has now been published by Atsushi Hiratsuka: *Ito Hirobumi Hiroku* (*Personal Documents on and of Hirobumi Ito*, Tokyo, 1929), appendix, pp. 9–10 (in Japanese).

12 Hayashi: *Memoirs*, p. 132; Hiratsuka, op. cit., appendix, pp. 10–1.

13 *British Documents*, II, no. 103; Hayashi: *Memoirs*, p. 132; Hiratsuka, op. cit., appendix, pp. 11–2.

Despite this auspicious beginning, nothing further was done for almost two months. We have no documents from either side which would explain the reasons for this delay, and we are therefore obliged to fall back upon pure speculation. So far as Chinese affairs were concerned the outstanding development of these two months was the resumption of negotiations between Russia and China. Discussion was opened at the request of Li Hung-chang, who evidently feared that the longer the Russians remained in Manchuria, the more expensive it would be to get them out. The Russians on their side accepted the invitation with pleasure, for they dreaded lest the other powers might bring greater pressure to bear as soon as the Boxer settlement had been arrived at. The St. Petersburg government, indeed, proceeded with the greatest circumspection. The draft submitted to Li provided that Manchuria should be turned over to China, and that the Russian troops should be withdrawn, mostly in 1902. The Chinese Eastern Railway was to be restored to its Chinese owners and China was to be allowed to keep troops in Manchuria.

These terms were so mild and attractive that an agreement was practically reached by the end of October. But then the Russians showed their hand. Li was told that in addition to the convention for the evacuation of Manchuria China should sign a " private " agreement with the Russo-Chinese Bank, promising not to award railway or other concessions in Manchuria to foreigners other than Russians. This agreement was to be signed before the Russians would accept the Manchurian evacuation arrangements. Li was offered 300,000 rubles if he would go through with it. He objected vigorously, but ultimately intimated that he would sign the two agreements together. Then, at the crucial moment, on November 4, the aged Chinese statesman died and the whole negotiation had to be postponed.[14]

The question now arises: how much did the other powers, especially England and Japan, know of these negotiations, and did the Russian policy react in any way upon the discussion of the Anglo-Japanese alliance project? The question is a hard one to answer. All we can conclude from the British material is that the London cabinet knew that the negotiations were going on and that it did what had been done in February and March — it enlisted the aid of the powerful Yangtze viceroys to block any unfavorable settlement.[15] All this was perfectly natural. What we should like to know is whether any conversations took place between London and St. Petersburg on this subject. If so, that fact would do much to explain the suspension of Anglo-Japanese negotiations during this period.

From the contemporary material we may conclude with some assurance that the British government would have been glad at this time to come to an agreement with Russia. Quite apart from the Far Eastern situation there was much

[14] Glinskii, op. cit., pp. 177 ff.; *Der Russisch-Japanische Krieg. Amtliche Darstellung*, I, pp. 14–5; Romanov, op. cit., pp. 317 ff.; *China No. 2 (1904)*, nos. 40, 41, 42.
[15] *China No. 2 (1904)*, no. 41; *British Documents*, II, nos. 75, 76.

uneasiness in London, and especially in Calcutta, occasioned by the striking growth of Russian influence in Persia. Sir Mortimer Durand had for years been pressing upon the foreign office the danger of a policy of laisser faire and the urgent need of fixing upon a definite course of action to prevent Muscovite influence from controlling the whole country.[16] Lord Curzon, when he went out to India as viceroy, took up the cry and developed the ideas of Durand in a classic despatch reviewing the entire situation and recommending that an effort be made to come to an agreement with Russia based on the principle of the partition of Persia into a northern (Russian) and a southern (British) sphere. Curzon himself saw the objections to such an arrangement and was by no means optimistic about its possibility. The London government, while it saw the advantages, feared that proposals made to Russia might be used at Teheran to discredit the English, and that therefore it would be better, for the time being, to do nothing.[17]

In the meanwhile Russian activity was steadily increasing and Russian pretensions growing. In the years from 1899 to 1901 there were endless rumors of Russian plans to secure from the Persian government a lease of the town of Bunder Abbas and the near-by islands. Russian writers talked freely of building a railway from the Russian-Persian frontier to Teheran and thence to Bunder Abbas. In the spring of 1901 the St. Petersburg government established consulates at Bagdad, and at Bushire and Bunder Abbas on the Persian Gulf. A heavily subsidized merchant line was opened from Odessa to the Gulf Ports, while every now and then a splendid Russian cruiser would appear, give the natives an impressive display of searchlights and completely put to shame the couple of obsolete gunboats which represented the predominance of Britain. Needless to say, these developments caused no little excitement in England. By some it was thought that the French efforts to establish themselves in Muscat in 1899 were directly connected with Russian aspirations. When, in the spring of 1901, the Turks attempted to send a force to re-establish their authority over the Sheikh of Kuwait, it was suspected that the Russians had put them up to it in order to undermine the British position at that crucial point. The London government took a strong line, going so far as to threaten the Turks with bombardment if they refused to withdraw.[18]

---

16 There is nothing of all this in Sir Percy Sykes: *Sir Mortimer Durand* (London, 1926), chaps. xvii and xviii, a book which is of no political value whatever.

17 The famous Curzon despatch of September 21, 1899 seems to have been based on an unpublished despatch of Durand of February 12, 1899. It was printed in part in *Persia No. 1 (1908)*, where many of the essential passages are given. The text in *British Documents*, IV, no. 319 does not add much, but no. 320 gives the reply of Lord George Hamilton, dated July 6, 1900. No. 321 is a memorandum of October 31, 1905 which gives a succinct review of the whole problem.

18 *Die Grosse Politik*, XVII, nos. 5292–7, 5304 ff., 5339 ff.; on Russian activities and aspirations there is an extensive literature; see, among others, *Documents Diplomatiques Français*, I, nos. 225, 396; the excellent special article in the London *Times*, December 21, 1901; the anonymous article " Persia and the Persian Gulf " (*Quarterly Review*, January, 1902, pp. 245–73); Paul Rohrbach's review of Hermann Brunnhofer's *Russlands Hand über Asien* (*Preussische Jahrbücher*, June, 1899, pp.

The British representatives at Teheran felt quite helpless and useless in the face of the Russian advance. One declared that he felt like a jellyfish in a whirlpool and another wrote home that he could do nothing but give virtuous advice to dissipated Persians.[19] Curzon appealed once more, this time to Lansdowne, who had himself been viceroy in India. In a long letter of April 5, 1901 he declared that the situation had changed decidedly for the worse since 1899 and that British prestige and influence stood lower than they had in the previous twenty-five years. The Shah and the grand vizir were both disgusted with the British:

"The Russian Bank at Teheran is rapidly cutting out the Imperial Bank. Russian Consulates are being established in all parts of the country. The Persian Cossacks under Russian officers have been greatly raised in numbers. Their advanced guard is already at Ispahan, and we shall presently see detachments at Shiraz, Mohammerah, and Bushire. We affect to have prohibited Persia from making railways in Southern Persia without our consent, but bodies of Russian engineers perambulate the entire country and push their surveys unhindered. We have large claims for damage done to British persons and interests in the South, but we are unable to obtain compensation. Meanwhile, subsidized Russian steamers are making their way into the Persian Gulf, and the artificial creation of trade will assuredly be followed by the still more artificial generation of political rights and claims."

Curzon urged that the government make up its mind as to how far Russian encroachment to the south should be permitted, and then resist any effort to go beyond that. "We are at present drifting merrily towards another Port Arthur and a second Manchurian Convention," he concluded.[20]

In the preceding chapter some attention was paid to the violently anti-German articles which began to appear in the English press in 1901. It will be recalled that the authors of these articles all recommended that England seek an agreement with Russia. As the months slipped by this campaign increased in intensity. "Maintenance of an unfriendly attitude to Russia," wrote one critic in June, "is simply to play into the hands of Germany, a country which hates England with a fanatical hatred, and which is longing for the hour when she can strike at her with comparative safety."[21] Russophobism, declared *Calchas,* is "a game in which England consistently paid forfeits and German diplomacy drew the stakes." "Democracy would never fight to keep Russia out of Con-

---

531–7); H. Vambéry: "Russland am Persischen Meerbusen" (*Deutsche Revue,* December, 1901, pp. 316–29); Donald Stuart: *The Struggle for Persia* (London, 1902), chaps. xviii–xx; General Krahmer: *Die Beziehungen Russlands zu Persien* (Leipzig, 1903), especially pp. 79 ff., 101 ff.; M. Grulew: *Das Ringen Russlands und Englands in Mittel-Asien* (Berlin, 1909), pp. 97–108. There is nothing of importance in Sir Arthur Hardinge's *A Diplomatist in the East* (London, 1929), chap. ix.

[19] Newton: *Lord Lansdowne,* p. 232; *Letters and Friendships of Sir Cecil Spring Rice,* I, p. 327.

[20] Newton: *Lord Lansdowne,* pp. 230–2. This letter is not in the *British Documents,* as Lord Newton suggests in his footnote.

[21] An Old Parliamentary Hand: "The Causes of Unionist Discontent" (*National Review,* June, 1901, pp. 512–24).

stantinople, were all controversies between the two Empires adjusted." Of these, he continued, Persia was the crucial one. The Russian press had made it clear that while there was no desire on Russia's part to threaten India, the Russians simply had to get down to the Persian Gulf. Well and good, said *Calchas,* let them. Let them have Bunder Abbas. The whole idea of a Russian invasion of India is a ridiculous bogey. Opposition to Russia's establishing herself on the Gulf is out of date, now that the Germans have appeared as rivals of England in the Near East. "Politically, once the second great outlet had been secured, all the dangerous energies of Russia would turn once more to the Near East." India would thereby be relieved and England would no longer have to fear that Russia might join Germany and France in a naval coalition.[22]

Did the British government in any way share the views of this group, or did it make any effort to follow up the suggestions advanced by it? There is some pretty conclusive evidence to show that it did, though we know next to nothing as to the details. It has already been pointed out in the preceding chapter that in April 1901 Lansdowne was ready to consider an agreement with Russia. On July 26, 1901 Sir Edward Grey, speaking for the opposition, declared in the house of commons that an understanding with Russia was "really vital to any satisfactory condition of affairs."[23] From this we may assume that there was agreement between the government and the opposition with respect to the desirability of an understanding with Russia. Another question is whether advances were actually made. After the conclusion of the Anglo-Japanese Alliance, M. Cambon discussed the situation with Lansdowne and remarked that it was a pity that there was so much distrust between England and Russia. " I replied," wrote the foreign minister to the ambassador at Paris, " that I quite agreed as to this, and that I had always desired to see the establishment of more cordial relations between the two governments. I had, indeed, myself made overtures with this object, and endeavoured to bring about a better understanding as to our interests both in China and in Persia, but had not been successful." According to Cambon's report, Lansdowne said of the agreement with Japan: " We would have been very glad to make other arrangements, but we always found the Russian door closed."[24]

This conversation leaves no doubt that Russia was actually approached. When the advances were made, however, it is hard to say. In November 1901 the Russian ambassador at London, M. de Staal, told his French colleague that Lansdowne had several times hinted at the possibility of an agreement respecting China. I suspect that the discussions must have taken place in August or thereabouts, for a letter written by Lord Salisbury on September 6 already re-

---

[22] Calchas: " Russia and her Problem " (*Fortnightly Review,* June, 1901, pp. 1031–44; July, 1901, pp. 124–58), pp. 1031, 131, 135–8.

[23] Newton: *Lord Lansdowne,* pp. 215 ff.; Hansard: *Parliamentary Debates,* Series IV, vol. XCVIII, pp. 286 ff.; other members spoke in the same vein.

[24] *British Documents,* II, no. 131; *Documents Diplomatiques Français,* I, no. 493; II, no. 81.

flects the disappointment of the London cabinet. This letter is worth quoting at some length, for it is very revealing:

" I agree, and have long agreed, in the expediency of a closer friendship with Russia. . . . But the possibility of improving our relations is constantly growing more questionable. Other statesmen are acutely watching the Chess-Board of Europe: and they perfectly know that a real sympathy between Russia and England would place the other Great Powers in a very inferior position. Therefore they will lose no opportunity of hindering such a consummation: and unfortunately they have too many opportunities of doing so, for they can offer enlargement of Russian territory on the Chinese, the Persian, and the Turkish frontier, and we cannot do so. Another insuperable difficulty lies in the attitude of what is called public opinion here. The diplomacy of nations is now conducted quite as much in the letters of special correspondents as in the despatches of the Foreign Office. The result is that there is a raw state of irritation between the upper classes in the two countries, which makes any advance on the part of either government quite impracticable. If a letter could be made to give room for further reasons, my catalogue is far from being exhausted. I wish it were otherwise: but wishing is no good." [25]

Though we know nothing specific about Anglo-Russian discussions in the autumn of 1901, we can easily see why an understanding was not effected. Although the discussion will take us beyond the resumption of Anglo-Japanese negotiations in mid-October, it will be well to dispose of the subject, the more so as it will serve as a useful background for what has to be said later.

In November 1901 the *National Review,* chief exponent of the anti-German policy, published an important article on " British Foreign Policy," by A.B.C. The editor pointed out that it was written by a number of persons and represented a consensus of opinion. It was hoped that it would find a large audience on the Continent, its chief purpose being to disabuse Englishmen about Germany: " Germany may be regarded as our most formidable political rival, and eventually, enemy." [26] The article itself began with a long review of the naval situation and the need for a three-power standard. German naval policy would require England to have a strong North Sea fleet. But the German menace necessitated also an entire revision of British foreign policy. Germany had achieved greatness " by trampling on her neighbours." Her object now was " to deprive us of our position on the ocean." It would therefore be best for England and Russia to get together and put an end to German exploitation of their rivalry. Furthermore, England should stand by Japan and use her influence to effect a Russian-Japanese understanding on Manchuria and Korea. But the most important thing would be the Anglo-Russian entente, which might be based on the idea of a free hand in the Balkans in return for a free hand in Egypt; a commercial outlet on the Persian Gulf in return for a promise to observe the status

[25] George W. E. Russell: *Malcolm MacColl* (London, 1914), pp. 282–3.
[26] *National Review:* " Episodes of the Month," November, 1901, pp. 317 ff.

quo in that area; a Far Eastern settlement which would give Korea to Japan, Manchuria and Mongolia to Russia, and the Yangtze Basin to England. Germany could then be given to understand that if she tried to disturb the peace her sea-borne food-supply would be cut off.[27]

This article immediately caused a sensation. The *Times,* which received advanced copy, commented at length upon it and expressed general agreement, though it thought the authors were offering Russia too much for too little. The idea of an English-Russian-Japanese agreement struck it as splendid.[28] The *Spectator,* also, was warm in its approval, but went even further than A.B.C. Russia, it declared, should have as free a hand in Persia as England in Egypt. " For a half-hearted agreement with Russia we feel no enthusiasm. . . . If we are to have an understanding, it must be on the boldest possible lines. . . . An understanding with Russia should approach very nearly, as far as we and Russia are concerned, a partition of Asia into ' spheres of influence.' " [29]

On the other hand the response from the Continent was not very encouraging. Some of the French papers expressed their warm approval of an Anglo-Russian rapprochement, while the German press showed itself pretty sceptical. The main thing, of course, was the reaction in Russia, and that was disappointing. The St. Petersburg newspapers replied in cool language, which provoked a reversal of feeling in London. The *Times* on November 16 published a letter from a correspondent protesting against concessions to Russia in the Persian Gulf. Such concessions would be a menace to India, in the opinion of the leading experts. Thereupon the *Times* remarked editorially that there was no evidence that Russia wanted an agreement on any terms which England could accept. Furthermore, no agreement could be made without the approval of the Indian government and there was no reason to suppose that Lord Curzon would consent to any diminution of British influence in south Persia or the Gulf. On November 22 the *Novoie Vremia* asserted that the agreement was neither desirable nor valuable for Russia. Britain was no longer the great power she once had been, and her approaches to Russia were merely a demonstration of weakness.[30]

The German ambassador watched the development of this debate with the utmost care. He learned that the A.B.C. article had been written by Mr. Maxse, the editor of the *National Review,* by Sir Rowland Blennerhassett and by M. Tatistchev, a Russian financial agent in London. It had been shown to the Russian ambassador, and also to Count Lamsdorff and Count Witte. Witte, it was said, favored an agreement with England, if only in the hope of raising a much-needed loan in London, but for the rest no enthusiasm was shown. Staal, the Russian ambassador at London, told his Austrian colleague that Russia did not need England and would attain her objectives without an arrange-

---

[27] A.B.C.: " British Foreign Policy " (*National Review,* November, 1901, pp. 343-58).
[28] *Times,* October 29, 1901.
[29] *Spectator,* November 2, 1901.
[30] *Times,* November 1, 4, 16, 21, 23, 1901.

ment with the English. The price Russia would ask for an alliance would be greater than England would be willing to pay.[31]

The sum total of this first offensive, then, was that the Russians showed themselves cool and that in England itself objections were raised to a policy which would allow Russia to advance to the Persian Gulf. But this did not discourage the *National Review*. In the December number the editor returned to the attack: "Great Britain has too long been the political satellite of Germany, who has treated her accordingly. This unnatural relationship has enabled the Berlin Government, on the one hand, to exploit Europe at the expense of England, and on the other England at the expense of Europe, by threatening each in turn with the hostility of the other." Russia and France should see the wisdom of cultivating English friendship: "If the Dual Alliance will only stand aside, the present *furor Teutonicus* will cause a complete revision of British foreign policy." If they join in Anglophobia, they will simply drive England back into the arms of Germany. "For although our public men are accused of pursuing Machiavellian policies abroad, they have ever since the days of Bismarck shown themselves to be simple as little children in dealing with their German confrères, who in every transaction between the two countries succeed in taking something either without giving anything in return or else something which is not theirs to give." [32]

The same number carried a second article by A.B.C., in which the writers claimed that their proposal had the support of some of the wisest Englishmen. They repeated, in general, the argument as at first advanced, stressing the fact that an Anglo-Russian agreement need not in any way conflict either with the Franco-Russian Alliance or with Anglo-Japanese friendship. "What we demand of Russian and British statesmen is that they shall dismiss the honest broker in Berlin and have direct dealings with one another. Let not friendly relations be compromised by unfriendly intrigues; let not any unavoidable difficulties bear the additional burden of a heavy German commission." [33]

This time *Calchas* came to the rescue. In a strong article in the *Fortnightly Review* he recalled all his past efforts for an agreement with Russia and then complained that the trouble with A.B.C. was that they did not go far enough. A mere commercial port on the Persian Gulf would do Russia little good. She would not want a port she could not fortify. She ought to be given a free hand without reservation in Persia and on the Gulf.[34] The *Spectator* in turn approved entirely the stand taken by *Calchas*. It was perfectly clear, said this weekly, that England could not block both Russia and Germany in the Persian Gulf. The Germans certainly would not help to stop the Russians. They might, in fact,

---

[31] *Die Grosse Politik*, XVII, nos. 5343, 5345.

[32] *National Review*: "Episodes of the Month," December, 1901, pp. 478–87.

[33] A.B.C.: "Some Consequences of an Anglo-Russian Understanding" (*National Review*, December, 1901, pp. 513–25).

[34] Calchas: "The Crisis with Germany — and its Results" (*Fortnightly Review*, December, 1901, pp. 934–48).

join the Russians against the English. It would therefore be much better to give the Russians their port, which would not be a menace to England as long as she retained the command of the sea.[35]

These suggestions were debated on and off throughout December and January by the Russian press, which showed itself not over-enthusiastic and came to the general conclusion that in any event Russia must have a port on the Gulf. This was a *sine qua non* for an understanding.[36] But it was exactly this concession that even British opinion balked at. In the *National Review* itself an anonymous writer, who was described by the editor as a " distinguished contributor " with wide experience of foreign affairs, while expatiating on the fact that the German nation was " saturated with hatred " for England, and while urging an entente with Russia, nevertheless questioned the advisability of letting Russia have a port which might become another Port Arthur.[37] So well-known a writer as A. R. Colquhoun took the same line,[38] while the *Quarterly Review*, in an excellent survey of the whole problem, also warned against the repetition of the Kiao-chow or Port Arthur policy in the Persian Gulf: " Possibly enlightened Russian statesmen and generals have no design of invading India; but deep down in the sub-conscious aspirations of the Russian people lies the Tartar impulse of rolling down upon the prizes of Asia." Let England by all means seek an agreement with Russia, but not by merely asking what Russia wants. Let England say what she intends to keep. She must remain supreme not only in the Gulf, but in the whole zone of mountains which lie between the sea and the salt desert.[39]

It seems likely that some tentative advances were made to Russia in December by Sir Arthur Hardinge, the British minister at Teheran, who was strongly in favor of the policy put forward by the *National Review*. The offers were probably very modest, and if made, were rejected.[40] At all events the British government had made up its mind to a policy by January 6, when instructions were sent to Hardinge: England had no designs on the independence and integrity of Persia; she recognized the superior interest of Russia in northern Persia; she had no objection to a Russian commercial outlet on the Gulf, but she " could not consent to the acquisition by Russia of a military or naval station in the Persian Gulf, for the reason that such a station must be regarded as a challenge to Great Britain and a menace to her Indian Empire "; nor could she agree to Russia's having any preferential political or commercial privileges in southern

---

[35] *Spectator*, December 7, 1901, pp. 888–9.

[36] London *Times*, December 25, 1901, January 4, 17, 1902; A Russian Diplomatist: " Russia and England " (*National Review*, January, 1902, pp. 677–90); *National Review*: " Episodes," February, 1902, p. 820; *Die Grosse Politik*, XVII, no. 5350.

[37] A Free Lance: " A Plea for the Isolation of Germany " (*National Review*, January, 1902, pp. 703–15).

[38] A. R. Colquhoun: " Our German Ally " (*Monthly Review*, January, 1902, pp. 73–87).

[39] Anonymous: " Persia and the Persian Gulf " (*Quarterly Review*, January, 1902, pp. 245–73), especially pp. 258 ff.

[40] *Die Grosse Politik*, XVII, nos. 5348, 5349; Newton: *Lord Lansdowne*, pp. 234–5.

or southeastern Persia; if necessary she would take " such measures as might appear . . . best calculated to protect the interest so endangered, even though in the adoption of such measures it might no longer be possible to make the integrity and independence of Persia their first object as hitherto." [41]

Much the same statement of policy was made publicly in the House on January 22. At that time Joseph Walton, Sir Henry Norman and Sir Edward Grey all spoke warmly in favor of a far-reaching agreement with Russia extending over all Asia. Lord Cranborne, the undersecretary for foreign affairs, thereupon replied that the government desired friendly relations, but that " these friendly relations are not to be sought at the cost of any of the rights which by treaty we possess. Whether to Russia or to any other country, it does not become us and it is not our interest to go cap in hand for an understanding." England, he concluded, could not abandon her rights in Persia and on the Gulf. [42]

While the question of an Anglo-Russian accord was a live subject of discussion in England, the members of the Japanese government were also wrestling with the problem of policy. Before the Hayashi-Lansdowne conversations were approved in August, there appears to have been a conference held at the villa of Count Katsura, the prime minister. At this meeting were present Prince Ito, Marquis Yamagata, Count Inouye and Count Matsukata. Those present, including Prince Ito, agreed in principle to an alliance with England, and therefore approved Hayashi's conversations with Lansdowne. But even then Ito, the most authoritative of Japanese statesmen, seems to have had little hope that the alliance would be concluded. It was so contrary to Britain's policy of isolation that it seemed unlikely that much would come of it. At the suggestion of his friend, Count Inouye, he therefore proposed that an effort be made to reach an agreement with Russia regarding Korea. The two countries, he argued, could not go on looking at each other with " cross eyes." If an agreement were too long postponed, war would result inevitably. Katsura and the others apparently assented to this viewpoint in a general way. [43]

Ito, who was out of office at the time, was planning to take a trip to America to recover his health. Inouye and Yamagata urged him to take this opportunity of going on to Europe, visiting St. Petersburg and attempting to come to some arrangement with Russia. There seems to have been another conference on September 11, at which Katsura also requested that the eminent statesman go on to Russia. Later on the friends of Ito claimed that Katsura was set on an alliance with England and that he spoke as he did only for politeness' sake. Kurino, who was to go to St. Petersburg as the new minister, and who was to assist in work-

---

[41] British Documents, IV, no. 321 a.

[42] Hansard: Parliamentary Debates, CI, pp. 574 ff., 599 ff., 609 ff., and especially 615 ff.

[43] Hayashi: Memoirs, pp. 142 ff. (Ito's own account to Hayashi); pp. 207 ff. (revelations made later in Count Okuma's paper). Hayashi never could convince himself that Ito had approved the idea of an alliance with England, but Ito's statements are completely borne out by other Japanese sources, e.g. the memorandum of Viscount Kurino (Hiratsuka: Ito Hirobumi Hiroku, pp. 349–54), and The Memoirs of Kikujiro Ishii on Diplomatic Affairs (Tokyo, 1930), pp. 52–60 (in Japanese).

ing out an agreement, complained later that Katsura regarded Ito as something of an eyesore, because of his great influence with the Emperor. He urged him to take a long trip in order to get rid of him for the time being.[44]

At any rate the Japanese government was preparing a hard bed for itself. Hardly had Ito left for America than Count Komura was appointed foreign minister and negotiations with England were resumed on the initiative of the Japanese. On October 8 Hayashi was given authorization to discuss the matter with Lansdowne. The two statesmen opened the subject on October 16, Hayashi going once more over the familiar ground. He stated that his government was above all interested in Korea and that it was a matter of life and death for Japan to keep Russia out of Korea. Manchuria was of importance chiefly because of the fact that it might become a base for encroachments on Korea. In China, Japan stood for the principles of integrity and independence, as well as of the Open Door. The alliance desired would assure either Japan or England of the support of her ally in the event of having to go to war with more than one power in defense of her interests in the Far East.

So far the reports of Hayashi and Lansdowne agree. But there are some rather significant discrepancies, which almost suggest that Hayashi, like his friend Eckardstein, did not always report with complete accuracy. Lord Lansdowne stated in his report that Hayashi suggested that the understanding " should be made to extend even to the action of the two Powers in regard to Siam." This idea was to cause some trouble later. Hayashi says nothing of the suggestion in his report to his government. Even more serious is another discrepancy. Hayashi had, since the spring of 1901, favored the idea of including Germany in the agreement. Lansdowne noted that at the very outset of the conversation of October 16 the Japanese minister asked whether Germany should be made a party to the understanding, which, he thought, would " look much more formidable " if Germany were included. Hayashi reported that he brought up this matter not at the outset, but just before his departure. He explains in his memoirs that he asked about Germany because he was uncertain about the relationship between England and Germany and desired, as instructed by his government, " to find out whether or not there was a definite arrangement between England and Germany that the latter country would have to be invited to join in the treaty." Lansdowne's account seems more trustworthy, because it fits in better with what went before. In any case the reports on both sides agree with respect to his reply. He said that Anglo-German relations were friendly and intimate, but that Germany's interests in the Far East were smaller than the British and Japanese and that it would be better to come to an agreement à deux before considering whether Germany should be invited to join.

There is one more point of difference, which is of some importance in connexion with what followed. Hayashi says nothing of the remark of Lansdowne

<hr/>

[44] Hayashi, op. cit., pp. 140–6; the accounts of Kurino (Hiratsuka, op. cit., pp. 349–54) and of Ishii (op. cit., pp. 52–60) support Ito's own account to Hayashi.

that he presumed " that the two Powers would, in the event of such an understanding being arrived at, agree that neither should, without consulting the
other, make separate arrangements, or come to separate understandings with
another Power as to Chinese or Corean affairs." Hayashi should certainly have
reported this to the home government, the more so as he must have known from
personal experience that there was an influential group in Tokyo that for years
had favored an agreement with Russia.[45]

Matters now moved more quickly. The Japanese government approved of
Hayashi's formulation of the case, and Komura showed real anxiety to get along
with the business. On November 6 Lansdowne handed the Japanese minister a
draft treaty based upon their previous conversations. He pointed out that this
had been submitted to the cabinet, and that the only point that had been raised
in connexion with it was the extent of the projected treaty. Some members felt
that " what after all was of importance to both Great Britain and Japan was that
neither of them should be overwhelmed by a combination of foreign powers.
The disappearance of Great Britain as a sea Power in the Far East would be a
calamity to Japan, and it would make no matter to her whether such a calamity
were to be brought about by a quarrel originating in the Far East or by complications in some other part of the World." Hayashi recognized the force of the
argument and recommended to his government that the agreement be extended
to include India. At the same time he tried hard to get the first clause of the draft
re-written. In Lansdowne's draft this clause spoke of the two powers being
interested " in preventing the absorption of Corea by any Foreign Power."
Hayashi therefore urged the need for some statement by which Britain should
recognize Japan's paramount interests in Korea, and should give an assurance
that Great Britain would not interfere with Japan in any action she might feel
called upon to take to protect her interests in the peninsula.[46]

Before any decision was come to by either side with respect to these details,
Hayashi received a telegram on November 13 instructing him to wait for final
instructions: " You are now advised to go immediately to Paris, or wherever
Prince Ito may be staying, to show him all the cablegrams pertaining to the
present question, and to make an effort to obtain his endorsement of the essentials of the British draft." [47]

Before the eminent Japanese statesman arrived in Paris, careful preparation
was made. Delcassé had for some time been watching the Far Eastern situation
with some uneasiness, and was evidently more than a little worried by the evi-
dences of English-German-Japanese collaboration in the spring of 1901. In April
he paid another visit to St. Petersburg. We know nothing of the conversations

---

[45] The conversation is reported by Lansdowne in *British Documents,* II, no. 105; by Hayashi to
Komura, October 16 (Hiratsuka, op. cit., appendix, pp. 12–3); see also Hayashi: *Memoirs,* pp. 133–6.

[46] *British Documents,* II, nos. 107–10; Hayashi: *Memoirs,* pp. 137–9; Newton: *Lord Lansdowne,* p. 222; Hiratsuka, op. cit., appendix, pp. 13–4 (Komura to Hayashi, October 19; Hayashi to
Komura, November 6; Hayashi to Komura, November 7, 1901).

[47] Hiratsuka, op. cit., appendix, pp. 14–5; Hayashi: *Memoirs,* p. 139.

that went on there, but there are some indications that the main subject of discussion was the course of action to be followed in the event of war with England or with England supported by the Triple Alliance. The French general staff had worked out certain arrangements for such an eventuality and these dispositions were approved by the Tsar and by the French foreign office in May 1901. It appears, from these plans, that the French decided to concentrate their main naval strength in the Mediterranean, leaving in the Channel only second-class ships and coast-guard craft. The threat of an invasion of England was to be kept alive in order to force the British to keep part of their fleet in the north. The Russian plans evidently called for a defensive in the Baltic. Eight battleships were to be kept ready in the Black Sea and three more in the Mediterranean. The plan of holding an army corps in readiness to proceed to the Bosporus was maintained. But the Russians hoped to build up their Far Eastern force till it numbered sixteen battleships. The idea was that Russia should relieve France of the need of keeping a large squadron in the Far East and should be prepared to aid France in the Mediterranean by sending the Black Sea fleet through the Dardanelles to help the French against the British.[48]

These arrangements throw a bright light on the tension between England on the one hand and France and Russia on the other. Delcassé evidently felt the need of further Russian promises. In return for them he did his best to aid the Russians in the Far East and to prevent the outbreak of hostilities between Russia and Japan. " We must apply ourselves to the job of avoiding a clash between Russia and Japan as long as possible," he wrote in July; " we must prevent England from finding in Japan the soldier she needs in the Far East." [49] What he hoped for was an agreement between Russia, Japan and France.[50] It was known in Paris that Ito was favorable to an understanding, and it was hoped that the Japanese need of money would pave the way to an agreement through a loan. Russia, reported the chargé d'affaires at St. Petersburg, would probably never give up Korea entirely, but she needed a few more years for preparation and hoped that Ito would come to arrange a compromise. Delcassé undertook to open the discussions with Ito. The Russian foreign office gave him a memorandum stating that Russia did not envisage the annexation of Korea or any exceptional position for herself. The Russian government recognized the commercial and industrial expansion of Japan in Korea as natural, but could not admit that Korea should be made a strategic centre to the detriment of Russian interests. Russia would not annex Manchuria, but would evacuate the country as soon as she had adequate guarantees.[51]

Ito had several interviews with Delcassé during his stay in Paris. Both sides

---

48 *Documents Diplomatiques Français*, III, annexes, pp. 601 ff., nos. I, II.
49 *Documents Diplomatiques Français*, I, no. 310.
50 Combarieu: *Sept Ans à l'Élysée*, pp. 144 ff., reporting a statement by Loubet.
51 *Documents Diplomatiques Français*, I, nos. 399, 435, 447, 500; " Nakanunie Russko-Iaponskoi Voiny " (*Krasnyi Arkhiv*, LXIII, 1934, pp. 3–54), pp. 41–3.

agreed that there was no question of conflict of interests between them, and that between Russia and Japan the only crucial issue was Korea. Ito expressed the hope that an arrangement would be made and promised to appeal to French mediation if necessary.[52] The great difficulty was that Ito said nothing about a loan, so that the French foreign minister more or less lost the wind he needed for his sails.

On November 14 Hayashi reached Paris from London, bringing with him the Lansdowne draft. Ito was completely surprised to find that the negotiations with England had progressed so far. He told Hayashi how he had been asked to visit Russia and seek an agreement. He was entirely at a loss as to what to do, and apparently thought for a moment of returning to Japan. In the end he decided that it would be best to go on to Russia, where he was expected. In the meanwhile he cabled to Katsura that he had no objection to the general idea of the alliance with England, though he thought the question of inviting Germany ought to be settled before it was too late, that the government ought to decide whether the agreement should be limited to China proper or extended to the whole of the Chinese Empire, and that the clause relating to Korea should be broadened in Japan's interest. He urged the government to postpone action on the British draft until he could see what was to be done with the Russians. He and Hayashi agreed to keep each other informed. Hayashi was to temporize in London until he heard the outcome of Ito's Russian mission. Ito on the other hand was to confine his conversation in the Russian capital to " harmless gossiping." [53]

Passing through Berlin on his way to Russia, Ito received cables from his government pointing out that the negotiations with England were so far advanced that Japan could not step back without impugning her honor. Ito was urged to go to St. Petersburg as quickly as possible, but to restrict himself to " harmless gossiping " as suggested by Hayashi.[54] In the meanwhile Hayashi returned to London on November 19. Lansdowne and Bertie, who harbored strong suspicions about Ito's peregrinations, used pretty plain language in speaking to Hayashi about the delay, and all the minister could do was to make excuses. The British government was assured that Ito's visit to Russia was unofficial and that he had no power to negotiate. But the British government was obviously unimpressed with the excuses. Hayashi was warned against the danger of an agreement with Russia.[55]

Under the circumstances the Japanese government simply could not wait. On November 30 Hayashi was able to submit the proposed amendments to the

---

[52] Hiratsuka, op. cit., appendix, pp. 3–9 (Katsura to Ito, November 11; November 12; Ito's notes on conversations with Delcassé and Loubet on November 13, 14, 1901); Documents Diplomatiques Français, I, no. 527; " Nakanunie Russko-Iaponskoi Voiny " (loc. cit.), pp. 53–4.

[53] Hiratsuka, op. cit., appendix, pp. 15–6 (Ito to Katsura, November 15; Ito to Hayashi, November 24; Katsura to Ito, November 22; Ito to Katsura, November 26; Katsura to Ito, November 27, 1901); Hayashi: Memoirs, pp. 142 ff., which appear to be absolutely reliable.

[54] See preceding footnote.

[55] Hayashi: Memoirs, pp. 149–50; British Documents, II, nos. 112–3; Hiratsuka, op. cit., appendix, pp. 15–6 (Hayashi to Komura, November 23, 1901).

draft which the British had had ready on November 6. But the minister at London was at the same time instructed to send a special messenger to St. Petersburg to submit these amendments to Ito for approval. Why the amendments could not have been sent directly from Tokyo to St. Petersburg is not clear. It seems that the Japanese government was still trying to gain time.[56]

M. Matsui, who was sent from London, did not arrive at St. Petersburg until December 3, not long before Ito was to depart. Much had happened in the interval. The Japanese statesman had arrived on November 25 and had been given a splendid reception. The Tsar decorated him with a very high Russian order, and Count Lamsdorff gave a dinner in his honor at which Witte, Kuropatkin, Pobiedonostsev and other high officials were present.[57] Yet Ito was in St. Petersburg for a full week before he began his conversations with Lamsdorff and Witte. During this time several cables passed between him and his friend Count Inouye in Tokyo. Inouye wrote that he could not understand England's intentions, in view of her traditional attachment to the principle of isolation. Was she not trying to use Japan for selfish ends? It was clear that Germany would not join the alliance. Would not the conclusion of the treaty with England induce Russia, France and Germany to re-form the Triplice of 1895? Inouye thought it would be wise to sound out the Russian government with regard to Korea before going on with the negotiations at London.

To this cable Ito replied approvingly. Contrary to original plans he had been instructed not to touch on the question of an agreement with Russia, but it seemed to him that Russia desired an agreement and in his opinion it would be wise to find out how far she would go. He asked that the matter be referred to the premier and that a reply be sent to him at once. Apparently no direct reply was ever received.[58]

Ito evidently decided to proceed on his own responsibility. The Russian press spoke very warmly in favor of an accord, not to say an alliance.[59] We know further that both Lamsdorff and Witte were eager to reach some sort of understanding. They had been warned by Izvolski from Tokyo that it would be their last chance and they understood quite well that a breakdown in the negotiations might have grave consequences. Relations with Japan must be cleared up, wrote Witte on November 28. A war might be successful, but it would be very expensive and might prove disastrous for the government. " It may be advisable to give up Korea altogether. . . . Between the two evils, an armed conflict with Japan and the complete cession of Korea, I would unhesitatingly choose the

---

[56] Hayashi: *Memoirs,* pp. 153–6; Hiratsuka, op. cit., appendix, pp. 28–9 (Katsura to Ito, by way of London; Komura to Hayashi, November 30, 1901).

[57] London *Times,* November 26, 30, 1901.

[58] Hiratsuka, op. cit., appendix, pp. 18–9 (Inouye to Ito, received November 28; Ito to Inouye, November 28; Ito to Inouye, November 30).

[59] London *Times,* December 3 (St. Petersburg, December 1); December 5 (St. Petersburg, December 2).

second." [60] Witte does not quote in his memoirs the rest of the letter, in which he argued that Japan would be much enfeebled by the expenditures she would make in Korea and that she would be much more susceptible to Russian pressure, especially when the Transsiberian Railroad should have been completed. All of which would make it easier for Russia to take possession of Korea later, if circumstances required.[61]

In other words, Witte was simply searching for a *modus vivendi* until Russian preparations were complete.[62] But Lamsdorff was not willing to go so far as that. He would give Japan a free hand in Korea in the economic sense, but he refused to renounce *all* Russian interest in the peninsula. All this came out when the foreign minister had his first extended talk with Ito on December 2. The Japanese statesman pointed out that he had no official mission and was therefore ready to speak frankly. Korea, he said, was a matter of life and death for Japan. The country was still undeveloped and the government unable to maintain order or protect foreign rights. It was therefore necessary that Korea have advice and assistance. But if both Russia and Japan gave this advice and assistance, the result would probably be a clash between them. To which Lamsdorff replied that an agreement between Russia and Japan in advance would obviate any conflict. Just what did Ito mean by "assistance"? The Japanese statesman admitted that he had in mind military assistance to quell disorders.

The admission led Lamsdorff to say that Russia had no designs on Korea, but that she could not allow the country to be used by any other power for military purposes. How could Japan guarantee that troops sent to restore order would not be used for other purposes? Ito suggested a promise, but this seemed inadequate. Lamsdorff proposed instead that Russia be given a small section on the southern coast of Korea, leaving the rest to Japan. Ito objected that the southern part of the country was the most important for Japan, but the Russian minister argued that the apprehension which would be felt in Japan at the presence of the Russians in a small part of southern Korea would be as nothing compared to the apprehension of the Russians in having the Japanese control the whole of Korea. Ito refused to accept this viewpoint and suggested that if Russia were willing to give the Japanese people a sense of security by leaving them Korea, Russia might do as she liked in China without needing to fear Japanese intervention. The conversation ended with Lamsdorff's request that Ito put on paper what his ideas were with regard to Korea.[63]

On the following day Ito had an even franker discussion with Witte. The

---

[60] Witte: *Memoirs*, p. 117; *Documents Diplomatiques Français*, I, no. 545; see also the accurate account in Prince G. Trubetzkoi: *Russland als Grossmacht* (Stuttgart, 1913), p. 69.

[61] The letter in full as printed by Glinskii, op. cit., pp. 187 ff.; Romanov, op. cit., p. 338.

[62] The same thing comes out in the remarks of the Tsar to Prince Henry of Prussia early in November (*Die Grosse Politik*, XVIII, no. 5399).

[63] Hiratsuka, op. cit., appendix, pp. 19–23 (Ito's own memorandum). The Russian accounts tally exactly with Ito's (Trubetzkoi, op. cit., pp. 68–9; Glinskii, op. cit., pp. 187–9; Romanov, op. cit., pp. 333 ff.; *Documents Diplomatiques Français*, I, no. 548).

finance minister admitted that it was Japan, not Russia, that had a vital interest in Korea, but he insisted that Russia had to think of the protection of her railway interests in the Far East, which represented an investment of three hundred million rubles. Ito then went over his arguments as he had expounded them to Lamsdorff: Japan would be willing to agree to a guarantee of Korean independence and a guarantee that she would construct no fortifications on the coasts that might menace Russian communications by sea between Port Arthur and Vladivostok. Witte declared himself completely satisfied: " If you can guarantee these things, you can do what you like in Korea." [64]

On December 4 Ito had a second discussion with Lamsdorff, which was to be the last. He brought with him an itemized plan setting forth the Japanese desire for a free hand in Korea commercially, industrially, politically and militarily, and offering a guarantee that the country should not be used for military purposes against Russia. But Lamsdorff thought this too one-sided. What concession would Japan make to Russia? Would she give Russia a free hand in China? This, again, was too much for Ito, who maintained that all he had suggested was that if Russia squared Japan with regard to Korea, she would be able to take a decided stand in Chinese affairs without having to reckon with Japanese hostility. Lamsdorff then suggested a free hand in northern China, by which he said he meant the sections adjoining the Russian frontier. This Ito was willing to accept, at least tentatively. It was agreed that the Russians should set down their ideas, and that negotiations should be continued with Ito in Berlin or Paris, or directly with Tokyo, provided there was a reasonable basis for agreement.[65]

The Prince left St. Petersburg the same night, evidently very well satisfied. M. Matsui, the emissary from London, came just before he departed, bringing the news that the Japanese government felt committed to the negotiation with England, and bringing also the modified Japanese draft for the alliance. Matsui followed the Prince to Berlin, and there heard from Ito his objections, general and special, to the projected alliance.

" In both the British draft, and also in the Japanese amendments to it, there are words to the effect that the absorption of Korea by a foreign country shall be prevented. But in Korea only Japan and Russia have interests of any importance. England has no interests there. In regard to Korea the proper thing to do is to make a convention with Russia, and settle the problem of that country. Even if we make an alliance with England it is not certain that we shall reap much benefit from it. Besides this, according to the draft, England will attain the same position in Korea as Japan has already. It really means giving to England a position in that country which she has not now got. From this point of view I consider that

---

[64] Hiratsuka, op. cit., appendix, pp. 23–7. There appears to be no Russian record of this conversation.

[65] Hiratsuka, op. cit., appendix, pp. 28–31, giving the full text of Ito's draft; this is given also in Lamsdorff's report to Nicholas II, December 5, 1901, in " Nakanunie Russko-Iaponskoi Voiny " (loc. cit.), pp. 44–6.

the proposal is unreasonable. Again, even if we have another country joining in the alliance, as Germany, we shall only be giving to that country the same as we are giving to England. That country also will obtain a new position in Korea which she had not got before. Consequently the proposed instrument would be doubly bad. The Japanese Government certainly ought to make some proper amendments with regard to all that touches Korea. . . . We ought also to study carefully the whole question of the international relations between the European nations. Count Inouye's telegram shows that whilst all the members of the Cabinet have agreed, he himself has not hastily thrown himself on the side of the proposed alliance. According to his opinion, it is difficult to understand why England has broken her record in foreign politics and has decided to enter into an alliance with us; secondly, the mere fact that England has adopted this attitude shows that she is in dire need, and she therefore wants to use us in order to make us bear some of her burdens; thirdly, Germany in Count Inouye's view may not enter the alliance. It is for these reasons that the Count has telegraphed me to reconsider the relations between the European Powers and only then to form my opinions. . . .

" Now what we ought to pay special attention to in connexion with this problem is, in my opinion, the attitude of Russia. I think that all negotiations for an Anglo-Japanese Alliance ought to be suspended until we are quite sure that it is hopeless to attempt to conclude a convention with Russia. I am convinced from what I have seen and heard in the Russian capital that the attitude of that country is at least rather conciliatory towards Japan, and it appears to me that she is sincerely desirous of co-operating with us to settle the Korean question. . . . As the result of my informal negotiations in St. Petersburg we are in a position to commence formal negotiations with the Russian Government through the Japanese Minister at St. Petersburg, and this we can now do at any time. That is the situation in regard to Russia at this moment, and in my opinion the prospects of our being able to make a satisfactory convention with Russia are very favourable." [66]

At the same time Ito telegraphed to Katsura reporting his success and advising strongly that the effort be made to come to an agreement. A convention with Russia would not be possible after the conclusion of the alliance with England. The Japanese draft of the alliance with England was open to various objections, which Ito communicated to his government. But before his comments could reach Japan, the Elder Statesmen, in a council before the throne, had decided unanimously on December 7 to go on with the alliance and to drop all further negotiations with Russia. Count Inouye seems to have held out against this course until the Emperor had documents brought out to show that Ito, while still premier, favored an alliance with England. Inouye explained in a telegram to Ito that the discovery that Japan had made the first advances to England had induced him to vote with the others. [67]

[66] Hayashi: *Memoirs*, pp. 157–62.

[67] Hayashi: *Memoirs*, p. 165; Hiratsuka, op. cit., appendix, pp. 34–6 (Inouye to Ito, received December 5; Ito to Katsura, December 6; Ito to Inouye, December 6; Hayashi to Ito, December 8; Inouye to Ito, n.d.); also the account in the *Memoirs of Kikujiro Ishii*, pp. 52–60.

The die was cast. The Japanese cabinet did not even allow itself to be influenced by Ito's objections to the draft. It simply felt that further delay would lose Japan the sympathies of England as well as of Russia. On December 10 Hayashi was instructed to go on with the negotiations.[68] But before turning to this subject a few words must be said about the end of the discussions with Russia. On December 17 Ito received, through the Russian embassy in Berlin, Lamsdorff's draft of an agreement. The foreign minister had set down his objections to the Ito draft on the very day following his last talk with his Japanese guest. But Kuropatkin had insisted on some stiffening of the Russian terms. He demanded that Japan alone assume the obligation not to make any preparations in Korea for operations against Russia or any other dispositions which might interfere with the freedom of the Korean Straits. Lamsdorff refused to accept these emendations and was evidently supported by the Tsar, but Kuropatkin succeeded in having a provision written into the Russian proposals permitting Japan to introduce her troops into Korea only after previous agreement with Russia. Just as Lamsdorff was about to despatch the Russian draft to Ito, the minister of marine came forward with a blanket condemnation of the whole thing, but Lamsdorff managed to have the objections of the naval authorities overruled. The Russian proposals went off pretty much in the form worked out by Lamsdorff, with the one significant modification by Kuropatkin, mentioned above.[69]

To clarify the situation it will be well to put the Russian proposals in juxtaposition to the draft submitted by Ito.

Japanese Draft	*Russian Draft*
1. Mutual guarantee of the independence of Korea.	1. Same.
2. Mutual obligation not to make use of any part of Korean territory for strategic purposes.	2. Mutual obligation (or Japan promises) . . .
3. Mutual obligation not to make, on Korean coasts, any military preparations menacing the free passage of the Korean Straits.	3. Mutual obligation (or Japan promises) . . .
4. Recognition by Russia of Japan's freedom of action in Korea in political, industrial and commercial respects, as well as exclusive right of Japan to come	4. Recognition by Russia of Japan's freedom of action in Korea in industrial and commercial respects, as well as preferential right of Japan to come,

---

[68] Hayashi: *Memoirs*, pp. 165–7; Hiratsuka, op. cit., appendix, pp. 36–9 (Ito to Inouye, December 10; Hayashi to Ito, December 12; Ito to Katsura, December 12; Katsura to Ito, December 13).

[69] "Nakanunie Russko-Iaponskoi Voiny" (loc. cit.), pp. 48–53 (Lamsdorff to Nicholas II, December 13; Kuropatkin to Lamsdorff, December 10; Lamsdorff to Nicholas II, December 14, 1901).

Japanese Draft	*Russian Draft*
to Korea's assistance with advice and action directed to helping her fulfill the obligations incurred by every well-ordered government, including military assistance in so far as necessary for suppressing revolts and every kind of disorder likely to endanger the peaceful relations between Japan and Korea.	in agreement with Russia, but alone, to Korea's assistance with advice directed to helping her fulfill the obligations incurred by every well-ordered government, including military assistance in so far as it may prove necessary for suppressing revolts and every kind of disorder likely to endanger the peaceful relations between Japan and Korea.
5.	5. In the case provided for in the preceding article, Japan promises to send to Korea only the number of troops absolutely necessary, and to recall her troops as soon as their purpose has been fulfilled. It is agreed, at the same time, that Japanese troops shall never cross the boundary of a district to be defined exactly in the future and situated along and close to the Russian border.
6.	6. On her part Japan recognizes Russia's preferential rights in the districts of the Chinese Empire adjacent to the Russian border, and promises in no way to hinder Russia's liberty of action in these districts.
7. The present agreement replaces all the previous agreements.	7. The present agreement replaces previous agreements.[70]

It will be seen at a glance that the Russians accepted the Japanese demands with respect to Korea with only minor qualifications: Japan was to send troops to Korea only after consultation with Russia, and to withdraw them as soon as possible. In return Russia was to be left a free hand in Manchuria and the other regions bordering on the Siberian frontier. Ito was evidently very favorably impressed with the draft. He was still urging his government not to drop the negotiation. He was not opposed to the alliance with England, he wired to Katsura, and did not suggest an alliance with Russia. All he envisaged was an agreement with Russia on Korea. It was therefore urgently necessary to reserve freedom of action in this matter.[71] Now that he had the Russian terms he renewed his plea. In my opinion, he cabled, we can succeed in concluding

---

[70] " Nakanunie Russko-Iaponskoi Voiny " (loc. cit.), pp. 51–2; Romanov, op. cit., pp. 335–6; Hiratsuka, op. cit., appendix, pp. 42–4 (text); *Documents Diplomatiques Français,* II, no. 4; *Der Russisch-Japanische Krieg. Amtliche Darstellung,* I, p. 16.

[71] Hiratsuka, op. cit., appendix, pp. 39–40 (Ito to Katsura, December 13).

an agreement with Russia, if we start the negotiation at once. Article IV will
have to be modified and Article VI clarified, but this will probably be possible.
It is a question of " Now, or never." But Katsura refused to accept this argumentation. He did not show Ito's telegram to the cabinet or to the Elder Statesmen, but replied saying that the whole proposal was not in keeping with Japan's
dignity. Japan had declared time and again that she favored the territorial integrity of China and equal opportunity for all nations. If she now conceded
Russian freedom of action in Manchuria, she would lose the confidence of
other powers.[72]

Ito wired an immediate reply to Tokyo, pointing out that the Korean business was of prime importance. If Russia were to accept Japan's views on this
question, Japan should be ready to leave Russia a free hand in Manchuria. What
he intended to do was to concede Russia as much freedom there as she had had
before the occupation of the country in 1900, and such privileges as were beyond
the power of Japan to control. Once again he reiterated his conviction that an
agreement with Russia was possible, while he pointed out that an agreement
with England regarding Korea would be worthless unless Russia was also won
over.[73]

On the day after sending this telegram Ito replied to Lamsdorff stating that
the question would have to be considered further, but at the same time expressing doubt regarding the feasibility of a permanent agreement. He criticized
the Russian draft for its vagueness in Article VI, and objected that in Article
IV the Russian demand that she be consulted before troops were sent to Korea
was the very negation of the freedom of action which Japan had asked for. At
any rate, he asked for more time to think the matter over.[74]

The Russians did not take this to mean a rupture of negotiations. On the
contrary, they wanted the agreement and they still hoped it would materialize.
Ito, too, cherished the hope that something might still be done. The curious
thing is that at the last minute he convinced Katsura. On December 28 and 29
the prime minister cabled to Ito (who was at that time in London) saying that
he now realized that the proposal to make concessions to Russia in Manchuria
did not go so far as to compromise Japan, and that he hoped Ito could persuade
the Russians of his standpoint. He made objection to some of the details of the
Russian draft, but expressed readiness to enter upon official negotiations if Russia accepted the Japanese standpoint in the essentials. In any event, however,
he hoped to conclude the alliance with England before opening official discussions with St. Petersburg.[75]

---

[72] Hiratsuka, op. cit., appendix, pp. 44–7 (Ito to Katsura, December 17; Katsura to Ito, December 21).

[73] Hiratsuka, op. cit., appendix, p. 47 (Ito to Katsura, December 22, 1901).

[74] Hiratsuka, op. cit., appendix, pp. 47–9 (Ito to Lamsdorff, December 23); Romanov, op. cit.,
pp. 338–9.

[75] Hiratsuka, op. cit., appendix, pp. 49–51 (Katsura to Ito, December 28 and 29, 1901); see
also Hayashi, op. cit., p. 167 on Ito's hope of still coming to an agreement.

It was too late for Ito to continue negotiations before his return to Japan. But early in January he stopped at Paris on his way to Rome and the east. There he found his ardent supporter, Viscount Kurino, newly appointed minister to St. Petersburg. Kurino was very anxious for a pact between Russia, France and Japan, and had accepted the post only on condition that he be allowed to do something toward its consummation. He was horrified to learn from Ito that the Anglo-Japanese Alliance negotiations were already so far advanced, and decided not to go on to St. Petersburg. Ito finally induced him not to give up the ship, and indeed he received a cablegram from home on January 20, 1902 saying that the government favored an agreement with Russia and desired him to discuss the matter with the Russian foreign office. In other words, there can be no shadow of doubt that the Japanese government planned and hoped to make an agreement with Russia right down to the time of the signature of the alliance with England, and that the Russian government had the same expectation.[76]

How the Japanese government could have come to think that the British cabinet would accept an agreement between Japan and Russia collaterally with the Anglo-Japanese Alliance is a mystery hard to solve. From the very outset Lansdowne had made it clear that neither side should make separate agreements regarding China or Korea without consulting the other, and the British draft of November 6 had specifically provided against such agreements.[77] When Ito visited Lord Lansdowne in England early in January he tried to sound him out on this question. Lansdowne then restated the British view. It would depend on what kind of agreement Japan contemplated: " It would obviously be improper that Japan should enter into a bargain with us affecting our common interests in the Far East, and should then enter into another bargain of a conflicting character with a third power." Ito of course repudiated any idea of a " double-handed arrangement," but it is difficult to see how the Korean agreement, as it emerged from the discussions of Ito and Lamsdorff, could possibly have been made to conform with the Anglo-Japanese Alliance. Russia would certainly not have made concessions in Korea excepting in return for concessions in Manchuria, and that would have been in contradiction with the aims of England, as Katsura had pointed out in his correspondence with Ito.[78]

The British had been obliged to wait from November 6 until December 12 for a reply to the draft which was handed to Hayashi on the former date. We know that during these weeks there was much uneasiness in London on account of Ito's peregrinations. But whether the delay in the negotiations with Japan had anything to do with the final phase of the Anglo-German discussions it is impossible to say. All we know is that on November 9 one of the under-

---

[76] Kurino's memorandum on the alliance with England (Hiratsuka, op. cit., p. 58; also Kurino to Ito, January 20, 1902 [ibid., appendix, p. 58]); Hayashi: Memoirs, pp. 200 ff. On the Russian expectation see especially Documents Diplomatiques Français, II, no. 4.

[77] British Documents, II, nos. 105, 125.

[78] Ito's conversation with Lansdowne in British Documents, II, no. 120.

secretaries, Mr. Bertie, wrote a long memorandum reviewing the whole Anglo-German problem. Bertie, like Salisbury earlier, discounted the dangers of isolation and noted the fact that Germany in Bismarck's time had made a treaty with Russia behind the back of Austria, so that Germany could not be entirely trusted. The whole memorandum was a reflection of dislike and hostility. Bertie accused the Germans of coveting the seaboard of Holland and also the Belgian Congo. The Germans, he thought, wanted an alliance with England chiefly in order to protect themselves against the danger of an agreement between England on the one hand and France and Russia on the other. The events of the spring had shown that Germany was not to be counted upon for support against Russia in the Far East. At best it might be possible to reach an agreement defining the interests that England and Germany would defend in Europe and the Mediterranean:

> "If once we bind ourselves by a formal defensive alliance and practically join the Triplice we shall never be on decent terms with France, our neighbour in Europe, or with Russia, whose frontiers are coterminous with ours or nearly so over a large portion of Asia. In our present position we hold the balance of power between the Triple and Dual Alliances. There is but little chance of a combination between them against us. . . . Treaty or no Treaty if ever there were danger of our destruction or even defeat by Russia and France Germany would be bound in order to avoid a like fate for herself to come to our assistance. She might ask a high price for such aid, but could it be higher than what we should lose by the sacrifice of our liberty to pursue a British world policy, which would be the result of a formal defensive alliance with the German Empire." [79]

Lansdowne himself made a survey of the negotiations of the spring, emphasizing the fact that the time had come when some sort of answer would have to be given the Germans. He thought that perhaps too much could be made of the safety of isolation: "I think that we may push too far the argument that, because we have in the past survived in spite of our isolation, we need have no misgivings as to the effect of that isolation in the future. In approaching the Japanese we have, indeed, virtually admitted that we do not wish to continue to stand alone." But Lansdowne, too, felt that there were great difficulties in the way of a full-blown defensive alliance, and that these were, at the moment, "virtually insuperable." He enumerated these obstacles, with which we are already familiar from the discussions of the spring. Therefore he, too, rejected the idea of an alliance, though he favored an understanding of a limited nature with regard to certain interests common to both countries. This might be applied to the Mediterranean and possibly the Persian Gulf, and might take a form like that of the Mediterranean Agreements of 1887. In a further memorandum the foreign secretary, at the request of Lord Salisbury, specified the details of such an agreement, which would aim at the maintenance of the status quo in the Mediterranean, Adriatic, Aegean and Black Seas and

---

[79] *British Documents*, II, no. 91.

prevent territorial acquisitions on the shores of the Persian Gulf. It would amount "to little more than a declaration of common policy and of a desire to maintain close diplomatic relations," though it would be to England's advantage to have the status quo upheld and also "to exclude Russia and Germany from establishing themselves strategically on the shores of the Persian Gulf." Lansdowne thought the German government would probably want more and that it would refuse such an overture, but "should they do so, no great harm will have been done, and we shall have put it out of their power to accuse us of having 'dropped' them." [80]

Salisbury seems to have been dubious about the advisability of this course, but probably gave his consent, for on December 19 Lansdowne had a decisive interview with Count Metternich, the new German ambassador. He once again recapitulated the history of the negotiations. The British government, he said, had thought the alliance proposal over carefully and saw its advantages. But it seemed doubtful whether the government could go before parliament with such a scheme. Metternich remarked that an agreement would probably have ensured peace for half a century and expressed his surprise that England did not "jump at" the opportunity. Her isolation, he thought, was becoming ever more dangerous. To which Lansdowne replied by reiterating his desire for good and close relations, and by suggesting the possibility of special agreements. "His Excellency unhesitatingly replied that no such minor proposal was likely to find favour with the German Government. It was a case of 'the whole or none.'" [81]

Therewith ended the discussion of an Anglo-German Alliance. There was, throughout this final phase, a certain amount of unofficial side play. In the last days of October 1901 Sir Valentine Chirol, foreign editor of the *Times*, paid a visit to Berlin and had a long talk with his former friend, Baron von Holstein. The history of the Anglo-German relationship since 1895 was gone over and the German standpoint set out in detail. Bülow, too, received Chirol, and, so it appears, suggested the possibility of an agreement to uphold the status quo in Europe, Africa, America and the Pacific, leaving Asia to be provided for by the Anglo-Japanese Alliance. It may well be that this was what led to the reopening of the whole subject in the bosom of the British government and what induced Lansdowne to put forward the idea of such an agreement. We know that a report of the Bülow-Chirol conversation was presented to the foreign office. But at all events nothing came of the suggestion and nothing was gained by the later correspondence of Holstein with Chirol. It is of interest chiefly as a reflection of the misapprehension caused by Eckardstein's reports and of the distrust and soreness that remained when the whole matter was finally closed.[82]

[80] *British Documents*, II, nos. 92, 93.

[81] *British Documents*, II, no. 94; *Die Grosse Politik*, XVII, no. 5030.

[82] Valentine Chirol: *Fifty Years in a Changing World* (London, 1927), pp. 288–97; Friedrich Rosen: *Oriental Memories of a German Diplomatist* (London, 1930), pp. 179–80, contradicts some points in Chirol's narrative. See further the Holstein-Chirol correspondence and the comments of the foreign office in *British Documents*, II, nos. 96–8.

By this time public opinion on both sides of the North Sea had risen almost to the boiling point, so that the project of an alliance strikes one as something of an incongruity. It was on October 25 that Chamberlain made his famous Edinburgh speech replying to criticisms of British warfare in south Africa. He pointed out that if necessary the English would have to resort to even stiffer measures to make the Boers give in, but that even if they did, they would still be within the precedents set by other nations in war. Among these other nations he mentioned the Germans in the war of 1870. It has been suggested by some writers that Chamberlain's purpose was to notify the Germans that he was through with them, and that he must have known that his remarks would cause offense. This seems more than unlikely, because the colonial secretary included France and other nations in his list and his language, if rightly read, was not insulting, even if it was indiscreet. However that may be, the speech raised a perfect storm in Germany and brought pretty strong complaints from the Berlin government.[83] Immense crowds of students and war veterans heard speakers tell of the " robber raids " in south Africa, the purpose of which was to steal the gold of the Transvaal. Six hundred and eighty German pastors signed a document recounting the legend that the British troops in south Africa fired at the enemy while standing behind Boer women. Reputable newspapers like the *Berliner Neueste Nachrichten* declared that any comparison between the British army, " recruited from the scum of the street," and the German nation in arms was an " insult " to the latter. Here and there efforts were made to stem the tide, notably by the *Frankfurter Zeitung,* the *Kölnische Zeitung* and the Berlin *Post,* but on the other hand eminent writers and artists lent themselves to the agitation. The wave of Anglophobia, which had been steadily rising since the beginning of the Boer War, now reached its crest.[84]

The violent protests and denunciations of the German press were the counterpart of the campaign being waged in England against Germany and in favor of an agreement with Russia. The *Times* defended Chamberlain to the limit, and took care to stress the significance of German hatred:

> " It denotes the rancour pent up for years, which has been gradually growing throughout the country, which has become intensified by the war, and which has at last found an outlet in the spontaneous national demonstrations aimed at Mr. Chamberlain directly, but indirectly against the British nation and the policy of Great Britain. No greater mistake could be made than to regard these demonstrations as artificial or to think they are not genuine. They reflect the feeling of the Germans towards the British, a feeling growing in power and capable of becoming one day a serious menace to peace between the two peoples." Or again:
> " The storm of vituperation . . . represents no passing emotion, but a deep-

---

[83] *British Documents,* I, nos. 324 ff.; *Die Grosse Politik,* XVII, nos. 5073 ff.; Bülow: *Memoirs,* I, pp. 635 ff.

[84] *Times,* November 5, 22, 23, 26, 1901; there is some discussion of this press campaign in Johannes Dreyer: *Deutschland und England in ihrer Politik und Presse im Jahre 1901* (Berlin, 1934), chap. ii.

seated and apparently incurable popular disease of animosity towards the British Empire." [85]

We need not pursue this disheartening and unedifying subject much further. Perhaps the worst part of it was the fact that the governments did not keep clear. The British foreign office quite rightly rejected the idea of giving any explanation or apology. Chamberlain himself became understandably sore. In a speech at Birmingham on January 6 he practically bade adieu to any idea of co-operation with Germany. England, he said, must count on herself alone: " I say alone, yes, in a splendid isolation, surrounded and supported by our kinsfolk." Two days later Bülow declared in the Reichstag that German excitement was quite comprehensible and suggested that ministers would do well, in defending their own domestic policies, to leave foreign nations alone. Not even this was enough for the extremists. On January 10 a rabid Pan-German deputy in the Reichstag called Chamberlain " the most accursed scoundrel on God's earth " (den verruchtetsten Buben den Gottes Erdboden trägt) and characterized the British army as " a pack of thieves and brigands " (Diebe und Raubgesindel). Bülow protested, but not too much. " Seldom, if ever," wrote the *Times,* " has a friendly nation been so grossly insulted in a foreign Parliament, and never within our memory has the insult met with such a mild rebuke." The influential London paper thereupon published two long articles on *The Literature of German Anglophobia,* in which once again the German desire for sea-power and the hope of whipping England were duly underlined. The whole episode may be said to have been closed by a new speech delivered by Chamberlain at Birmingham on January 11, in which he declared: " What I have said, I have said. I withdraw nothing, I qualify nothing, I defend nothing. . . . I do not want to give lessons to a foreign Minister, and I will not accept any at his hands. I am responsible only to my own Sovereign and to my own Countrymen." [86]

The Chamberlain-Bülow debate and the mutual recriminations of the British and German press make a most peculiar setting for the discussion of an Anglo-German alliance. Whether or not the German press campaign was inspired, as Sir Valentine Chirol thought, by the German foreign office in revenge for the refusal of the London government to conclude an alliance, it is unthinkable that a coalition between the two nations, even if worked out and approved by the governments, could have found any real response in the hearts of the peoples. German opinion was undoubtedly a more artificial thing than British opinion, and the alliance project would certainly have met with more effective opposition in the house of commons than in the Reichstag. Lansdowne knew what he was saying when he spoke of the parliamentary handling of the problem as " a stiff fence to ride at." Indeed, we may say that by the end of 1901 British opinion was

[85] *Times,* November 23, 26, 1901.
[86] *Times, January* 7, 9, 11, 13; Bülow: *Memoirs,* I, pp. 636–7; Lee: *Edward VII,* II, pp. 137–9, etc.

an insurmountable obstacle to the realization of the project. After the Chamberlain episode the government capitulated entirely and became as suspicious and unfriendly as the press. Cecil Spring Rice, visiting London in April 1902, was astounded at the change of official attitude toward Germany: "Everyone in the (foreign) office and out talks as if we had but one enemy in the world, and that Germany. . . . The change in Chamberlain's mind is most remarkable." [87]

This has been perhaps too long a digression, but it seems justified in view of the great significance of the Anglo-German problem and because of the fact that the position of Germany was an important aspect of the Anglo-Japanese Alliance negotiation. To this we must now return. It will be recalled that Hayashi handed the Japanese draft to Lansdowne on December 12. The main point in the Japanese amendments involved the rejection of the proposal for a general defensive alliance. The Tokyo government felt that the agreement, if extended to India, the Straits Settlements and Siam, would involve a liability which the Japanese could not assume. England was asked further to accept a secret article to this effect: "Great Britain recognises that Japan may take such suitable measures as she deems necessary to safeguard and promote the preponderating interests which she actually possesses in Corea." Further secret articles were to provide that the naval forces of the two powers should act in concert so far as possible, and that either might use the docks and coaling stations of the other; that each of the contracting powers should endeavor to maintain in the Far East at all times naval forces superior in efficacy to the naval strength of any other power which had the largest naval forces in the Far East.[88]

Lansdowne at once pointed out the difficulties inherent in the Korean question. What Japan wanted was virtually a free hand there, and that would mean friction with Russia and possibly war between all the powers. At the same time he objected to any arrangement which would bind England to maintain a certain naval force in any one part of the world. We need not follow the negotiations of December and January in detail, the more so as they have been well analyzed by other writers. Suffice it to say that the naval question was ultimately dealt with separately and in general terms in a diplomatic note. The turning point in the whole negotiation came on December 19, when the British cabinet discussed the alliance question and Lansdowne afterward went over the Japanese draft with Hayashi. Salisbury evidently was not at all enthusiastic about the projected alliance, and Chamberlain thought it was too narrow.[89] The foreign minister was therefore obliged to be firm with respect to the scope of the agreement: "It seemed . . . scarcely reasonable that, while we were to face the possibility of war with two great European Powers in consequence of a dispute between Japan and Russia in regard to Corea, we were not to have any assistance from Japan should we find ourselves involved with the same two Powers

---

[87] *Letters and Friendships of Sir Cecil Spring Rice* (London, 1929), I, p. 350.
[88] *British Documents*, II, no. 115.
[89] Newton: *Lord Lansdowne*, p. 228; Hayashi *Memoirs*, pp. 186 ff.

in regard to a dispute as to India." But Hayashi was adamant on this point, asserting that Japan was doing enough in supporting Britain's interests in the Yangtze Valley. In the end the British accomplished nothing in this direction. The treaty remained restricted to what the Japanese called the " Extreme East."

The crucial point in the whole discussion dealt with Korea. The English objected to any separate or secret article on the subject and wanted it embodied in the Treaty itself. Furthermore (and this was the decisive consideration) they did not want to give Japan a free hand in Korea, for fear that she would make use of such freedom to provoke a conflict with Russia. Hayashi, of course, gave assurances that Japan would not lightly engage in war. But he rejected the idea that Japan and Britain should consult first before resorting to action. This would cause delay and frustrate effective operations. And so the debate continued between Lansdowne on the one hand and Hayashi and Ito on the other. The Japanese would accept nothing but recognition of their freedom of action in Korea, but they showed little inclination to entertain a proposal for strengthening the clauses regarding Chinese independence and integrity. Amendment followed amendment and proposal succeeded proposal over a period of weeks, until a wording could be found which gave Japan what she wanted, while at the same time making the concession so unnoticeable that it would not rouse strong opposition in the English parliament. The Treaty as finally signed on January 30, 1902 stated in the preamble that the two governments were actuated solely by a desire to maintain the status quo and general peace in the extreme east and were interested especially in maintaining the independence and integrity of the Empire of China and the Empire of Korea, and in securing equal opportunities in those countries for the commerce and industry of all nations. The all-important Article I was a masterpiece of careful wording. It read as follows:

" The High Contracting Parties, having mutually recognised the independence of China and Corea, declare themselves to be entirely uninfluenced by any aggressive tendencies in either country. Having in view, however, their special interests, of which those of Great Britain relate principally to China, while Japan, in addition to the interests which she possesses in China, is interested in a peculiar degree politically as well as commercially and industrially in Corea, the High Contracting Parties recognise that it will be admissible for either of them to safeguard those interests if threatened either by the aggressive action of any other Power, or by disturbance arising in China or Corea, and necessitating the intervention of either of the High Contracting Parties for the protection of the lives and property of its subjects."

Article II provided that if either party, in defense of its interests as above defined, should become involved in war with a third power, the other party should remain strictly neutral. But if (Article III) any other power or powers should join in hostilities against the ally, the other contracting party should make war in common and make peace in mutual agreement with its ally. The fourth Article provided that neither would, without consulting the other, enter into separate arrangements with another power to the prejudice of the interests above described. Article V stated that if either party thought the above-mentioned interests to be in jeopardy, the two governments should communicate with each other fully and frankly. The final article fixed the term of the Alliance at five years, or longer unless denounced one year in advance by either party. If, at the time of expiration, either party should be involved in war, the Alliance was to continue automatically until peace had been concluded.[90]

The treaty was sent to the British minister at Tokyo with a covering letter which was published with the actual text. This letter reviewed the genesis of the Alliance and its terms, but contained also an explanatory paragraph of some significance:

"His Majesty's Government have been largely influenced in their decision to enter into this important contract by the conviction that it contains no provisions which can be regarded as an indication of aggressive or self-seeking tendencies in the regions to which it applies. It has been concluded purely as a measure of precaution, to be invoked, should occasion arise, in the defence of important British interests. It in no way threatens the present position or the legitimate interests of other Powers. On the contrary, that part of it which renders either of the High Contracting Parties liable to be called upon by the other for assistance can operate only when one of the allies has found himself obliged to go to war in defence of interests which are common to both, when the circumstances in which he has taken this step are such as to establish that the quarrel has not been of his own seeking, and when, being engaged in his own defence, he finds himself threatened, not by a single Power, but by a hostile coalition." [91]

Throughout the course of the negotiations both powers had kept in mind the question of Germany's relationship to the projected pact. The Japanese were clearly anxious to have the Germans associated. They were never able to free themselves from the spectre of a new Russian-German-French combination, and it is very possible that the ostentatious visits of the Tsar to the Emperor William at Danzig and to France in September 1901 helped to revive sad memories of the coalition of 1895. But the Japanese from the outset deferred to the British in this matter, and Lansdowne took the stand that it would be wiser to settle first and consider Germany afterward. By December, that is after the violent press campaign between England and Germany was well under way, there was no further talk of inviting Germany to join, but simply of taking the Berlin government into confidence when the time came. Lansdowne had no hope that the Germans would accede, and probably no longer desired any such thing. He had constantly in mind the problem of bringing the Alliance with Japan through parliament and certainly did not want to complicate

---

[90] *British Documents*, II, no. 125; details of the negotiations may be followed in the *British Documents*, II, nos. 115 ff. and in Hayashi: *Memoirs*, pp. 168–95, where the various amendments are discussed at great length.   [91] *British Documents*, II, no. 124.

matters by adding an unpopular agreement with Germany. Furthermore, he felt certain that the Berlin government would approve an alliance which it had itself recommended. Under the circumstances there was no need for more than advance notice. This was the course agreed upon and carried through. The Germans were notified of the terms of the Alliance a full week before the Treaty was published.[92]

The text of the Alliance was laid before parliament on February 11 and was made known in Tokyo on the following day. The news took the British public by surprise and caused no little bewilderment. There had been no audible demand in the press for an agreement with Japan. In fact, the possibility of such a combination was much less discussed in 1901 than in 1898. The British public had come to look with some favor upon the idea of an agreement with Russia, yet here was an alliance which was clearly directed against Russia. It is interesting to note that the *Times,* in a leading article on February 12, while welcoming the agreement as a benefit to China, tried to make out that it was no obstacle to an arrangement with Russia. In the house of lords Lansdowne attempted to anticipate criticism of Britain's abandonment of isolation just after Chamberlain had declared that England must rely upon herself and her colonies in " splendid isolation." The foreign minister insisted that the government could not be deterred by a mere tradition. The old arguments would no longer hold good. The nations were now joined in groups and were heavily armed. War might break out very suddenly, and England therefore had to be prepared. He hoped that the House would not allow itself to be swayed " by any musty formulas or old-fashioned superstitions." Fortunately the government had the support of Lord Rosebery, who declared at once that his first impressions were favorable.[93]

Things were not quite so easy in the house of commons, where Sir Henry Norman, famous expert on Far Eastern affairs, spoke very thoughtfully of the new departure. The Treaty, he pointed out, might bring England into war with Russia and France at Japan's choosing. And for what? " Our only interest in Korea is that it is of very great importance to Japan, whose welfare is always a matter of consideration to us." But Korea was a " worthless country," and it would be horrible to become involved in war on account of it. He had always, said Sir Henry, been in favor of an agreement with Japan, but the question was whether British interests were sufficiently safeguarded in this treaty. It was quite useless to deny that it was aimed at Russia. And yet the most serious political writers and thinkers, from Lord Salisbury down, had come to favor better relations with Russia. Russia had, after all, behaved well towards England during the Boer War. Had the government tried to come to an agreement with her about Manchuria?

---

[92] *Die Grosse Politik,* XVII, no. 5043 (February 3, 1902); *British Documents,* II, nos. 118, 120, 126, 127; Hayashi: *Memoirs,* pp. 190–5.

[93] Hansard: *Parliamentary Debates,* Series IV, vol. CII, pp. 1174 ff.

To this Lord Cranborne, the undersecretary for foreign affairs, rejoined that " the real origin of this treaty was our anxiety to maintain the status quo in China. . . . This agreement merely follows on principles which have already been accepted by almost every other Power." Thereupon the question was raised by Sir Henry Campbell-Bannerman why, if most powers had agreed to the principle, the alliance was necessary? Balfour defended it by saying that it would make for peace. He agreed that England should have friendly and cordial relations with Russia: " There is no wish dearer to the heart of His Majesty's Government." [94]

The press generally took the Alliance in good grace. In fact, one may take this as a striking instance of the political instinct that leads the British people to recognize their deeper interests. While there had been no agitation for an alliance, there had been a growing feeling of community of interest, a feeling that could have been overcome only by a much more attractive arrangement with Russia. There was, of course, some criticism. William T. Stead thought the text entirely too vague, and pointed out that the statements of ministers in parliament did not agree entirely with the exact wording of the text.[95] Others complained that Lansdowne had exchanged splendid isolation for splendid complication and that he was simply driving Russia and France into the arms of Germany. Russia would take her revenge in Persia, Afghanistan and India, while Japan would play a dazzling game with limited liability. Even if Russia were defeated by Japan, others would suffer by a new explosion on the Bosporus, while Japan would make herself mistress of China and the Far East.[96]

In Japan the Treaty was given a rousing reception. Opinion was practically unanimous in approving it, and for some time there were entertainments and demonstrations to celebrate the new connexion.[97] The German government, too, was quite content: " The noodles seem to have had a lucid interval," remarked the Emperor to Sir Frank Lascelles in expressing his surprise that the British government had not made the agreement earlier.[98]

All this was to be expected. The real question was what the reaction to the agreement would be in Russia and France. The Paris government, which was certainly cherishing hopes of some kind of understanding with England with respect to Morocco, was most disagreeably surprised. Cambon spoke pretty frankly to Lansdowne about the danger of England's being dragged into war with Russia by Japan. The foreign minister tried to soothe him, and pointed

---

[94] Hansard, op. cit., pp. 1273 ff., 1281 ff., 1288 ff., 1295 ff.

[95] William T. Stead: " The Anglo-Japanese Treaty " (Review of Reviews, March 15, 1902, pp. 253–5).

[96] Zeta: " The Anglo-Japanese Alliance — and After " (Fortnightly Review, March, 1902, pp. 365–80); China Station: " A Russo-Japanese War " (Contemporary Review, March, 1902, pp. 424–36); Sir Wemyss Reid: " Last Month " (Nineteenth Century, March, 1902, pp. 506 ff.); Stafford Ransome: " Japan's Imperial Policy " (Fortnightly Review, April, 1902, pp. 565–74).

[97] Times, February 14, 15, 1901; Alfred Stead: " The Anglo-Japanese Alliance from the Japanese Point of View " (Contemporary Review, March, 1902, pp. 437–45).

[98] British Documents, II, no. 128; Newton: Lord Lansdowne, p. 247.

out that England had tried to reach an understanding with Russia but had always found the door closed. In the end Cambon consoled himself with the idea that the British government had concluded this " useless " convention simply to show the public that it had not gone to sleep about Far Eastern affairs.[99]

Most disagreeably surprised was the Russian foreign minister, Count Lamsdorff, who was still hoping for an agreement with Japan. He simply could not understand an alliance which envisaged war at a time when no one was thinking of it, and concluded that the British must have aimed chiefly at the prevention of an understanding between Russia and Japan. His first reaction was to propose a counterblast, and he approached both Germany and France with the the suggestion that they join in a declaration. The Germans declined and the French evidently attempted to evade. It was only in mid-March that the two allies, after prolonged negotiations, agreed to the note of March 20, 1902, in which they declared that they too favored the principles enunciated in the preamble of the Anglo-Japanese Alliance, and then went on to say that, being obliged to consider the possibility of aggressive action by third powers or renewed troubles in China which might jeopardize the integrity and free development of the country, they reserved to themselves the right to take counsel as to the means to be used to safeguard their interests.[100]

This declaration is sometimes spoken of as an extension of the Franco-Russian Alliance to the Far East. This is almost certainly an exaggeration. The document was probably meant only as a demonstration. At any rate, the Russians were not as calm as they pretended to be. Since November they had been negotiating once more with the Chinese and towards the end of January they had come to some sort of compromise regarding the evacuation of Manchuria. In return the Chinese were to sign a separate agreement with the Russo-Chinese Bank which would secure for Russia the concessions she wanted. But in the first days of February the United States government lodged a protest which so stiffened the back of the Chinese that on February 11 they rejected the idea of an agreement with the Bank. There matters stood when the Anglo-Japanese Alliance was published. In the debate in the house of commons on February 13 the British government spokesman stated unequivocally that " Manchuria is no more excluded from the scope of the agreement than any other province of the Chinese Empire." [101] In other words, the Manchurian affair might well lead to a clash between Russia and the new allies. Witte and Lamsdorff therefore decided not to press matters too far. In the face of opposition from Kuropatkin

---

[99] *Documents Diplomatiques Français*, II, no. 81; Combarieu: *Sept Ans à l'Élysée*, p. 178; *British Documents*, II, no. 131.

[100] *British Documents*, II, no. 145, enclosure; *Documents Diplomatiques Français*, II, nos. 97, 103, 110, 117, 129, 138, 145. On the Russian attitude see further London *Times*, February 15, 17, 1902; *British Documents*, II, nos. 130, 140, 141, 147; *Die Grosse Politik*, XVII, nos. 5047, 5049, 5050, 5051 ff.

[101] Hansard, op. cit., CII, p. 1247.

they gave up the projected bank agreement, and on April 8 signed an evacuation arrangement which was to take the Russians out of Manchuria within eighteen months. It was the first fruit of the Anglo-Japanese Alliance.[102]

The Far Eastern theme was not, of course, brought to a close by the Alliance of England and Japan. It continued unbroken to February 1904, to the outbreak of war between Russia and Japan over Korea.[103] It would be a mistake, however, to base a judgment of the Anglo-Japanese Alliance upon the later course of events. It is not entirely true that England, finding herself unable to check the advance of Russia in China by an agreement with Germany, thereupon turned to the avowed enemy of Russia, Japan, and sacrificed her highly-prized isolation in order to use the Japanese army to drive out the Muscovite. In the first place one has to face the problem presented by Manchuria. The British had practically recognized the special position of Russia in the three provinces in the agreement of April 1899, and, whatever may have been said later, they acquiesced in the exclusion of Manchuria from the Anglo-German Convention of October 1900 when that instrument was in process of negotiation. In the course of the discussions which led to the Alliance with Japan Count Hayashi said in so many words that Japan was not sufficiently interested in Manchuria to go to war about it, while Lansdowne admitted to Ito that England had never concealed from herself that Russia had special interests there. Though England objected to the terms of the agreement Russia was trying to make for the evacuation of the country, he did not think it probable that these terms would be so objectionable as to force England into war with Russia.[104] In other words, Manchuria really had nothing to do with the Alliance. Neither Japan nor England would fight to keep the Russians out of those provinces. The statements in parliament to the effect that the Alliance extended to Manchuria were probably made chiefly to nip opposition to the agreement.

Why then did the British make the Treaty? Surely it could not have been on account of Korea, where England had very small interests and where Japan could be counted upon in any event to oppose the Russians. Indeed, the great preoccupation of the British in making the Alliance was the chance that the Japanese might utilize it to force the pace in the Korean question and so bring on a war in which England might become involved. A careful study of the documents brings one almost of necessity to the conclusion that the Alliance, which turned out to be a great landmark in British policy, was in itself less impressive in 1901 than it seems to us today. Briefly stated there was a real clash of interests between England and Russia, but not so much in Manchuria as

---

[102] The details are given in Glinskii, op. cit., pp. 178–83; Romanov, op. cit., pp. 340–5; Asakawa: *The Russo-Japanese Conflict*, pp. 190 ff.; *British Documents*, II, nos. 135, 136, 143, 144; *Documents Diplomatiques Français*, II, nos. 115, 137.

[103] The later stage I have dealt with in some detail in an article " Der Russisch-Japanische Krieg " (*Europäische Gespräche*, 1926, no. vi, pp. 279–322).

[104] *British Documents*, II, nos. 117, 120.

in China generally, in Tibet, in Persia, in Turkey. Salisbury had for years tried to overcome this antagonism by striking a bargain and there is every indication that in the autumn of 1901 further advances were made to Russia by Lansdowne, who was more convinced than Salisbury that the days of profitable isolation were past. The Russians then as before turned a cold shoulder, for the simple reason that they thought they could get all they wanted without England — that there was little to gain and much to lose. They might well have proved themselves right. They were not far from an agreement with Ito with respect to the main bone of contention — Korea, but the negotiations with Ito were frustrated by the willingness of England to consider an alliance with Japan, an arrangement which struck most Japanese statesmen as more reliable and less costly than a bargain with Russia. What it comes to, then, is that the English made the agreement with Japan in order to prevent an understanding between Russia and Japan, which would have rendered the British position in the Far East almost hopeless. If one looks at the Alliance from this viewpoint there will be less difficulty in seeing why the British gave the Japanese the free hand in Korea and avoided pressing too far their demand for an extension of the Alliance to India. The important thing for England was not what was in *the* Alliance, but the fact that there was *an* Alliance.

Throughout the discussions a distinct note of distrust could be heard. The Japanese were not certain how much England could be depended upon to do, and the British on their side were more than a little suspicious of the use Japan might make of the treaty once she had got it. As a matter of fact there was no ground for this suspicion on either side. War was not nearly as close as many people thought. Russia could not afford it and was anxious to avoid it. France was even more eager to prevent friction, and would have been only too glad to see England brought into an agreement with Russia, or, failing that, to have the Russians and the Japanese make up their differences. But even the Japanese and the British were still hoping to make arrangements with Russia that would obviate the need of war. The Anglo-Japanese Alliance forbade either member making separate arrangements with another power to the prejudice of the interests mentioned in the pact, without consulting its ally. But we have seen that in parliament Balfour spoke of the desirability of better relations with Russia. The English ambassador at St. Petersburg, Sir Charles Scott, explained to Lamsdorff that the Alliance did not diminish the hope of the English government for a frank and friendly understanding with Russia.[105] The leaders of the famous campaign for an agreement with Russia also took this interpretation.[106] All of which forces us to the conclusion that the British did not mean to mobilize Japan against Russia, but still cherished hope that Russia would make an arrangement. And, after all, the efforts of the English to approach the St. Petersburg government did not end in February 1902. They went on and they became

---

[105] *British Documents*, II, no. 140.
[106] A.B.C.: " The Japanese Alliance " (*National Review*, March, 1902).

accentuated in the next years, and they were taken up again just as soon as the Russian-Japanese War drew to its end.[107]

Exactly the same thing was true of Japan. Like the English, the statesmen at Tokyo interpreted Article IV of the Alliance to mean that a separate agreement was permissible provided only that it did not prejudice the interests of the other party. In February Ito at least still expected to come to an agreement with Russia and Lamsdorff still hoped that the discussions opened in St. Petersburg would bear fruit. The plain truth is that in the years 1902–1903 the Japanese did make efforts to reach an understanding with Russia. With the material we have at our disposal now no other conclusion is possible than this: that the Tokyo government went as far as it could to settle the Korean question pacifically. The Russians had only themselves to blame for the war of 1904–1905, and when we say the Russians we need not include either Witte, who fell from power in 1903, or Lamsdorff, who favored conciliation from the outset. We refer simply to the military and naval cliques and the Korean adventurers who captured the imagination of Nicholas II and light-heartedly took up the struggle with Japan. No statesmanship can reckon with the ignorance and blindness of groups like these, and certainly the negotiators of the Anglo-Japanese Alliance did not do so. Taken in the large, then, it is really necessary to reduce the Alliance to its proper proportions and to see it in the perspective of its own time.

BIBLIOGRAPHICAL NOTE

DOCUMENTARY SOURCES

British Documents on the Origins of the War, 1898–1914. London, 1927. Volume II, chapter ix: The Far East, 1900–1901; chapter x: The Anglo-German Negotiations of 1901; chapter xi: The Anglo-Japanese Alliance. One of the most important sources for the history of the Anglo-Japanese Alliance, but not as informing as might have been expected.

Accounts and Papers. 1904, volume CX. *China No. 2 (1904), Correspondence respecting the Russian Occupation of Manchuria and Newchwang.* Contains most of the material on the British side dealing with the Manchurian situation.

Documents Diplomatiques Français, 1871–1914. Series II, volumes I and II. Paris, 1930—. These first two volumes of the great official French publication cover the years 1901 and 1902. They contain some interesting material, though little of prime importance.

---

[107] See my article " Russia, the Straits Question, and the European Powers, 1904–1908 " (*English Historical Review,* January, 1929, pp. 59–85).

Die Grosse Politik der Europäischen Kabinette, 1871–1914. Volume XVI, chapter cvi: The Russian-Chinese Agreement of 1901. Volume XVII, chapter cix: The Anglo-German negotiations; chapter cx: The Anglo-Japanese Alliance; chapter cxi: German opinion during the Boer War; chapter cxiv: Near Eastern Questions, including Persia and the Persian Gulf Problems.

ATSUSHI HIRATSUKA: *Ito Hirobumi Hiroku.* Tokyo, 1929. (In Japanese). A source of absolutely first-rate importance, containing over seventy cablegrams that passed between Ito and the government during the crucial months of the Alliance negotiations.

" Nakanunie Russko-Iaponskoi Voiny." (*Krasnyi Arkhiv,* LXIII, 1934, pp. 3–54). Important correspondence between St. Petersburg and Tokyo, together with some of the vital documents relative to the Ito negotiations.

MEMOIRS, AUTOBIOGRAPHIES, BIOGRAPHIES, AND LETTERS

The Secret Memoirs of Count Tadasu Hayashi. Edited by A. M. Pooley. New York, 1915. The material in the Ito documents shows that this remarkable volume of memoirs is entirely reliable. It remains the most important single source in English on the making of the Anglo-Japanese Alliance.

NEWTON, LORD: *Lord Lansdowne.* London, 1929. Useful as a supplement to the *British Documents.*

LEE, SIR SIDNEY: *Edward VII, a Biography.* Two volumes, New York, 1925–1927. Of importance chiefly for the study of the personal factor in the Anglo-German problem.

CHIROL, VALENTINE: *Fifty Years in a Changing World.* London, 1927. Contains some account of the discussions with Holstein and Bülow in the autumn of 1901.

GOOCH, G. P.: " Baron von Holstein." (In his *Studies in Modern History,* New York, 1931). Easily the best study of Holstein in English, and at the same time a compact and reliable review of the Anglo-German problem.

SPECIAL STUDIES: THE ANGLO–JAPANESE ALLIANCE

DENNIS, ALFRED L. P.: *The Anglo-Japanese Alliance.* Berkeley, 1923. A succinct and competent monograph, though now out of date.

ROMANOV, B. A.: *Rossiia v Manchzhurii, 1892–1906.* Leningrad, 1928. For this, as for the earlier period, Romanov is the best Russian account.

GLINSKII, B. B.: *Prolog Russko-Iaponskoi Voiny.* Petrograd, 1916. Based on material from the Witte archives, and reflecting the standpoint of the ministry of finance.

TRUBETZKOI, GREGORY: *Russland als Grossmacht.* Stuttgart, 1913. Written by an official of the Russian foreign office, this book contains much that is of interest, among other things an accurate account of the negotiations with Ito.

CHANG, CHANG-FU: *The Anglo-Japanese Alliance*. Baltimore, 1931. A good book, but remarkably slight and conventional on the making of the Alliance.

OSTWALD, PAUL: " Das Englisch-Japanische Bündnis." (*Berliner Monatshefte,* November, 1931, pp. 1081–98). A thorough analytical study, making use of the British Documents.

LANGER, WILLIAM L.: " Der Russisch-Japanische Krieg." (*Europäische Gespräche,* 1926, pp. 279–322). A detailed study of the background of the war.

MINRATH, PAUL: *Das Englisch-Japanische Bündnis von 1902.* Stuttgart, 1933. The most recent and most detailed treatment, giving a reliable account of the negotiations but indulging in somewhat too much geopolitical speculation. The author, like other writers, has made no use of Japanese materials.

XXIV

Reflections

∾

The conclusion of the Anglo-Japanese Alliance and the abandonment of British isolation have generally been taken as marking a turning point in the history of pre-war diplomacy. There is something to be said for this traditional interpretation, though it must not be carried too far. At the time of the negotiation of the treaty neither side regarded it as crucial, for both parties still hoped to make some sort of arrangement with Russia. The great problem upon which the new combination hinged was by no means settled, neither was there any way of knowing how, ultimately, it would be settled. In 1902 the war between Russia and Japan was not at all a foregone conclusion. The Russians could have made their peace with Japan on attractive terms. They probably would have done so, had the foreign office not been overridden by the military and naval authorities. To arrive at an accurate estimate of the importance of the alliance between Britain and Japan, it would be necessary to carry the story to its logical conclusion, the defeat of Russia in 1905. But to trace the course of European diplomacy to that year would have obvious disadvantages: it would require full treatment of such entirely new problems and international alignments as the Moroccan question and the Anglo-French Entente of 1904. The temporary settlement of the Far Eastern question overlaps these new developments in a way that admits no logical dividing point. I have, therefore, followed tradition and broken the narrative at the change of British policy.

There is even further justification for this division. The year 1902 marks the end of a generally recognizable period. The Victorian age had drawn to its close and the great tide of imperialism had begun to break on the resistance of the Boers. Imperial problems continued to agitate the international relations of Europe, but disillusionment was setting in and a few years later, after Russia's reverses in the Far East, interest definitely shifted to the old familiar channels of continental politics. It will not be entirely out of place, then, to review the decade following the dismissal of Bismarck and attempt some general estimate of its importance in the history of European diplomacy.

The most striking thing about international relations in this period is the extraordinary complexity. There is not, as in the Bismarckian era, any straightforward development or any understandable system. Everything and everybody seems to be at odds, and the historian finds himself confronted at every turn

787

by almost insuperable problems of presentation. This complexity was the direct result of two factors: one was the breach made in the Bismarckian system by the abandonment of the Reinsurance Treaty, which brought in its wake the Franco-Russian Alliance and the division of the Continent between two alliance systems; the other was the tremendous expansion of the field of possible conflict. Diplomacy had to deal not only with the accepted problems of European politics but with a multitude of world problems. The old questions continue to be of great importance, as a study of the Near Eastern crisis of 1894–1897 will show. But they come to be regarded almost as irritating distractions. The interests of the governments and to some extent of the peoples are focussed upon the ends of the world, upon the Nile, upon the jungles of central Africa, upon the mines of south Africa, upon Mesopotamia, Persia and the whole Far East. The great problems of the period, therefore, were not only the readjustment of international relations necessitated by the break-up of the Bismarckian system and the emergence of a new alignment, not only the continued unrest in southeastern Europe, but also the surge of imperialism, the criss-crossing of colonial aspirations, the development of new and dangerous antagonisms which reacted upon Europe and conditioned the policies of the powers in questions which themselves had nothing to do with extra-European expansion.

Three of the most eminent German historians, Meinecke, Brandenburg and Oncken, together with many other competent scholars, have studied in whole or in part the development of German policy during this period. But German policy was no longer crucial in the nineties. Germany was at the head of a group of allied powers, but the coalition of the central powers was counterbalanced by a new combination. The interplay of these competing systems was important as it was interesting, but the outstanding characteristic of the alliances in these years was their failure to function properly. The Triple Alliance was in process of disintegration and the Franco-Russian Alliance was more or less paralyzed by Russia's unwillingness to act in the matter of Alsace and Lorraine, and by the refusal of France to underwrite the aspirations of her ally in the Near East. In continental problems the powers were deadlocked. There was as much or more occasion and danger of a clash in the Near East in 1894–1897 as in 1875–1878, but there was no general war because the various powers and groups of powers checkmated each other, leaving Abdul Hamid to settle the question in his own way, through massacre and war.

To understand the diplomacy of these years I think attention must be concentrated upon British policy, for two reasons: firstly, because neither the Triple Alliance nor the Franco-Russian Alliance could upset the balance of power on the Continent in its own favor without the accession and support of England; secondly, because the European nations when they turned to world affairs were confronted with a situation in which England easily played the most prominent rôle. She had the empire which the others coveted. They met her at every turn and found her everywhere blocking the road. Even more im-

portant was England's command of the seas. Imperialism and sea-power —
these concepts were inseparable. So long as Britain had her fleets and could
challenge any other power to build beyond her, the continental powers had
their choice between backing down or pooling their forces. In the last years of
the century the British Empire really formed a third grouping in European
international relations. Whether her great power could be drafted in the interests of either of the other two combinations or whether they could coalesce
to overwhelm Britain, was still a question.

It has been the traditional policy of England, according to most historians,
to stand aloof from European affairs, so that in a crisis she might throw herself on the weaker side and prevent the hegemony of any one power or group of
powers. This is the famous theory of the balance of power, a theory which I
think should be discarded with reference to recent history, for the story of
European diplomacy in the past fifty years or more completely contradicts it.
During the Bismarckian period England was associated with the Triple Alliance, a combination which, under German leadership, dominated the Continent as it had rarely been dominated before. France was then the helpless, isolated power and England aided and abetted that isolation. Obviously England
was, in the last half of the nineteenth century, interested less in the balance of
power than in the maintenance of peace. In the heyday of her economic prosperity she had nothing to gain by war and had a good deal to lose even from
war between other powers. England, too, was satiated; in fact, the phrase which
Bismarck applied to Germany was much more appropriate for describing England.

By the balance of power theory England should have welcomed the conclusion of the Franco-Russian Alliance, which divided the continental nations
into two groups of roughly equal strength and theoretically left Britain at the
fulcrum of the balance. Of course we know that such was not the case. The
Alliance was on paper directed against Germany and her allies, but actually
England felt its first and most powerful impact. All historians may not realize
or appreciate this fact, but the British statesmen did. From the very moment
of the Toulon demonstrations and the conclusion of the alliance Downing
Street saw that a crucial decision would have to be made. England could not
hold the balance between the two continental groups because they would not
allow her to do so. With the shift of interest to world affairs there was, from
the very outset, danger of collaboration between the two alliance groups against
their common rival, England. The idea of a continental league was somewhat
nebulous and, as it proved, there were insurmountable obstacles in the way of
its realization. But that does not mean that it did not on occasion function informally or that England did not sense the threat. Co-operation between the
continental powers always implied the possibility of a pooling of naval forces,
which would have created for England a danger of the first magnitude.

Rosebery met this situation in 1894 by an attempt to revive the old connexion with the Triple Alliance. Having failed in that he tried for an agreement with Russia. Salisbury, when he came into power in 1895, followed exactly the same course: he approached Germany with his scheme for the partition of the Ottoman Empire and, having met with a rebuff, set himself to reach an arrangement with the members of the other group. Repeated efforts were made to settle outstanding disputes with France, efforts which invariably failed because of England's unwillingness to compromise on the Egyptian question. In much the same way attempts were made to reach a *modus vivendi* with Russia. These have been dealt with in detail in the preceding chapters, but it is worth emphasizing the fact, which has been very imperfectly understood, that in the entire period from 1894 to 1902 the greatest desire of the British government was to come to an agreement with Russia. The most attractive terms were offered, but they were regularly refused, partly because the Russians, with their favorable geographical position, had little reason to fear the British fleet, partly because their field of expansion was not overseas and they were consequently less exposed to the pressure of sea-power, and partly because the Russians had the feeling that they could get what they wanted without paying England a price. It took the defeat at the hands of Japan in 1904–1905 to bring the Russians to the point of bargaining with England. During the last decade of the century all the European powers still found it more profitable to shelve their own particular antagonisms and work against England, and for that reason the position of England was the key to the whole problem. England did not go down simply because the continental league never developed to the point where it could strike at her in any matter of vital interest, but especially because she managed to maintain her predominance on the sea. If there was no intervention during the Boer War, it was because the fleet stood between the continental nations and the island empire.

One of the remarkable things about the history of modern England is the singleness of purpose of all parties in the conduct of foreign affairs. There was a veritable cult of the principle of continuity, and it is consequently useless to look for fundamental divergences on matters of major importance. It is true that in 1893–1894 Gladstone and Harcourt were still opposing a policy of expansion and naval increases, but they were overruled by the younger men in their own party. Rosebery and Grey saw eye to eye with their political opponents in questions of foreign policy and national defense. One might even say that Rosebery plotted the policy which was followed by the Conservative-Unionist government after 1895. Rosebery was, in fact, a remarkably able man, with a keen feeling for the movement of interest and opinion. But he was hampered from the start by the drag of mid-century liberal thought and by the tremendous prestige and authority of Gladstone. Furthermore, he lacked the absorbing personal interest in politics which is the mark of the great statesman. Even as a young man he was world-weary, unhappy, and apathetic. He never came up to the expectations of his followers, and never gave them the sure and consistent lead they had a right to hope for from a man of his natural endowment.

The dominant figure in British foreign policy during this period was, of course, Lord Salisbury, who was at the helm during all but three years of it. In many respects Salisbury was the commanding figure of the nineties, as Bismarck was of the eighties. He alone of all European diplomats had the experience, the understanding and the poise of a really great statesman. And yet, Salisbury's accomplishment is bound to strike one as disappointing. The great, bold conceptions were there (consider the Turkish partition scheme, the suggestions to Russia in January 1898, etc.), but the driving energy was absent. We need to know much more of Salisbury's inner thoughts, but even now we can see, from what few personal letters we have, that he was half a generation behind his times. He felt himself out of place, for he realized that international relations were no longer a question merely of political and military power, but were coming more and more to be decided by economic pressures. Furthermore, he was so much the great aristocrat that he never managed to adjust himself to the new democratic conditions. The untutored, emotional crowd was for him a disturbing factor, which he did not know how to handle. It made him feel helpless and embittered, and he resented it. In his later years he tended to drift, to put off vital problems with good epigrams. To the very end he stood firm by the ideas with which he had grown up, and remained proud of British sea-power, sceptical of the dangers of isolation, confident of England's ability to take care of herself, even against heavy odds. He had a keen understanding of the continental peoples, but he did not like them. In the years of tension which closed his career he became cynical and irritable, until purely personal rancor clouded his outlook. He always disliked the German Emperor, whom he considered an ill-bred young whelp and a dangerous man because of his instability. He ended with a strong antipathy toward the whole German people, because of their dislike of England and because of their naval ambitions, the importance of which he was one of the first to recognize. Nevertheless, there was something immensely impressive in the great calm of Lord Salisbury, as there was something sad, almost tragic in his inability to keep up with the times.

Salisbury worked in harness with Joseph Chamberlain, which was remarkable in view of the difference in talent and temperament of the two men. Chamberlain was the true representative of the bourgeois capitalist class that rose to power on the tide of the industrial revolution and liberalism. He was a successful business man who had a keen appreciation of the new world forces and an incomparable understanding of the democratic psychology. Leaving aside his idealism — his social programs, his imperialism, his cult of race solidarity — his views on international relations, I think, were fundamentally sound. Being unhampered by the prejudices and traditions of the foreign office, he could see diplomatic problems in perspective against economic conflict and popular feeling and could approach them without prejudice. For him diplomacy was a business, not an art. At an early date he became convinced that under the new world conditions England could not afford isolation. He sought salvation in the German connexion until trade competition and German interference in south Africa made it seem hopeless. In the years from 1896–1898 he was as much in favor of an agreement with Russia as was Salisbury. He would, indeed, have made any arrangement with anyone so long as England profited. When the Russians turned him down he approached the Japanese, and when they turned a cold shoulder he reverted to the idea of an agreement with Germany. He made them a business proposition which they rejected. He warned them of possible consequences, but they did not heed him. It was a mistake on their part, for Chamberlain found no difficulty in reversing himself once more. After 1901 he set out to reach an agreement with France as the stepping stone to an agreement with Russia. The price was high, but it was paid. With all Chamberlain's keenness, however, with all his directness and energy, he lacked the moderation and finesse which is indispensable for success in diplomacy. His speeches carried the country, but almost invariably estranged foreign powers. With one hand he destroyed what he built up with the other until his name was anathema to the Continent. Rightly or wrongly he came to represent in continental eyes all that was least attractive in the British temperament and policy.

One will look in vain among the European nations for the singleness of policy so characteristic of the British. To be sure, the bases of the foreign policy of all nations rest upon certain conditions and traditions, but within the larger framework remains wide scope for different policies. German policy, for example, was more than anything else a function of her geographic position. The military problem of the war on two fronts dominated German diplomacy after 1870. With almost superhuman astuteness Bismarck managed to build up a central European bloc to meet possible assaults from either east or west. He succeeded, moreover, in maintaining some connexion with Russia and thereby staved off an alliance between that country and France. His management of this situation without estranging England was probably the greatest diplomatic accomplishment of modern times.

In contrast, the "new course" started out by jilting Russia and courting England. At that time the British saw no advantage in a closer relationship with Germany and stood off, while the Russians felt obliged (one can hardly describe it otherwise) to conclude a distasteful alliance with France. This Alliance was directed against Germany and undoubtedly held the threat of a joint attack on two fronts. With the Hapsburg Empire sinking into the morass of domestic discord and the Italians reeling after the Adua disaster, Germany might have found herself in acute danger. As a matter of fact, the Germans were in no serious peril in the ten or twelve years after Bismarck's fall. On the contrary, they actually came to hold the balance of power in Europe, because the Russians had no desire to fight them for France's lost provinces, but even more because both France and Russia were deeply involved in colonial affairs and were so nearly at daggers drawn with England that the line of demarcation in European international relations was not between the Triple Alliance and the Franco-Russian Alliance, but between England and this latter combination. For a time at least Germany could afford the weakening of her allies, and could pursue a free-hand policy, a policy of having two irons in the fire. She could team with France and Russia, or with England, whichever seemed profitable.

Actually, the Germans flirted with the Russians and French, but tried to collaborate with the English. The intervention of Shimonoseki taught them what to expect from the Russians. The English, who were in a tight place, should and probably would offer more, and their good will was of greater importance and value in the field of overseas expansion. Besides, the whole cast of mind of the German statesmen made them incline toward England. The Emperor's impulse in 1890 was to dish the Russians and ally with the English, an impulse so deeply rooted that it was bound to crop out again and again. He was often furious with the English, but the feeling was one of envy and jealousy rather than of dislike or hatred. Neither Caprivi nor Marschall had enough experience to formulate a policy and Baron von Holstein, the soul of the foreign office, was distinctly a man of the English orientation. Whatever else may be said of Holstein, he had nothing to do with either the Kruger telegram or the German naval policy. His political ideas were substantially sound. His chief weakness was that he, like Salisbury, was unable to keep pace with the times. He continued to think in terms of purely continental policy long after other factors had transformed the basis of international relations. There is no indication that he ever really grasped the import of economic changes or that he understood the strong current of imperialism. Besides, Holstein had too much of what Chamberlain lacked — the exaggerated calculation and the too great finesse. His deep-rooted suspiciousness, his rancor, his proclivities for intrigue helped to confuse matters that were already complicated and ended by clouding many issues.

But even if Holstein had not been Holstein, the German foreign office would still have had to reckon with the personality of the Emperor who, if he was brilliant and energetic, was also erratic and unaccountable. Hohenlohe, as we know from his memoirs, regarded it as his chief duty to guide the Emperor and save him from himself. Bülow followed another line. He humored and flattered him and accentuated his worst traits. Bülow's reputation as a statesman has been pretty thoroughly exploded by the publication of his own memoirs. His was a charming, adroit and elusive personality, but he had no deeper seriousness, in fact no depth at all. So far as one can detect he shared the general predilection for the English connexion, but he did nothing to check the naval policy of Tirpitz and offered no resistance to the rising force of popular hatred toward England. Bülow never did anything that was unpleasant or that might injure his own position.

Quite apart from personalities, however, we can see that the connexion between Germany and England was a difficult one to maintain or develop, simply because of the forces already referred to so often. If there was any *one* revolutionary change in Europe in this period it was the spectacular rise of Germany as a great industrial power and as a formidable competitor in the field of foreign trade. Under the circumstances it is hard to see how Germany could have avoided colliding with England. The shock might have been eased here and there, but the collision of economic interests was inevitable. Germany was virtually driven into colonial expansion and consequently into a big navy policy. Commercial pressure and naval rivalry quite naturally disturbed the English and gave rise to a popular dislike of Germany which is hard to measure but not to be underestimated. The French and the Russians were also competitors of the British in the colonial field, but they were not serious trade rivals, so it was easier for the British government to get popular support for concessions to Russia or France than for concessions to Germany. On the other hand, the niggardliness of the English enraged the Germans, who with some justice felt that John Bull, already bloated with colonial spoils, wanted the whole world for his private preserve. He would, if he had to, give up substantial chunks to the Russians or French, but he begrudged the German every trivial bit. It would be hopeless to try to understand the Anglo-German problem in these years without taking due account of this clash of economic forces and of the resulting embitterment on both sides of the Channel.

The Emperor William cherished the illusion that he could influence and guide his cousin, Tsar Nicholas. Looking back on their correspondence we are apt to remember the danger of condescension in personal relationships. Nicholas certainly disliked and distrusted William for his patronizing ways. But the Tsar's likes and dislikes played a relatively unimportant part in the formulation of Russian policy, for Nicholas had such a pathetically weak character that he was little more than the puppet of his ministers. His father was stolid, obtuse and bigotted, but he was firm, even to the point of stuffing the Franco-Russian Alliance down the throat of his objecting foreign office. The foreign minister, Giers, was a decent bureaucrat who believed in a moderate, peaceful policy and in the connexion with Germany. When Berlin refused to renew the Reinsurance Treaty in 1890 it cut off Giers completely. There was no alternative to the French alliance and in the end the Russians felt obliged to capitulate. Giers died in 1895 and was succeeded by Lobanov — grand seigneur, diplomat by profession and man of ideas. His chief idea was to deal England a telling blow, for he hated England and would have liked to see the Continent united against her. It was a stroke of luck for Britain that he died after a year of office, for Lobanov saw things enough in the large to make substantial sacrifices to get what he wanted. His successor, Muraviev, was something of a fool or at any rate a bull in a china-shop. It was he who got Russia so deeply involved in the Far East by the lease of Port Arthur. His strength lay in tickling the vanity of Nicholas. The Tsar, like many weaklings, was constantly dreaming of great achievements. Apparently he always supported suggestions for expansion and conquest. That accounts for the fact that from 1897 onward the influence of Witte began to decline steadily, while the military and naval authorities, notably Kuropatkin, came nearer and nearer to complete dominance. When Lamsdorff, the former assistant of Giers, came into control of the foreign office in 1900, it was already too late to check the forward party. Even when Lamsdorff and Witte stood together they accomplished little. Russian policy was being made by the soldiers who had won over the Tsar and who were, before long, to march him straight into the disastrous conflict with Japan.

Russia was, in these years, the main element of uncertainty. That the Russians did not put the Near East so completely on ice as many have supposed, has been shown in the body of this work. But there was no knowing when or where the Russians would turn. The threat of their advance stretched from the Balkans to Korea and kept Europe generally on tenterhooks. This Far Eastern policy was in most respects indefensible, and was marked throughout by a certain grandiose indifference to the rights and interests of others, by an appalling amount of wrangling within the Russian government and by a reckless levity that could end only in disaster.

We cannot discuss in detail the policy of Austria or Italy. The Austrians were obliged, in this period, to pursue a strictly defensive course. Goluchowski, who was foreign minister after 1895, lacked repose. His policy estranged the Germans and amused the English. It culminated in the status quo agreement with Russia of the spring of 1897, the arrangement which appealed to him least. In Italy there was, naturally, a sharp dividing line between the policy of Crispi and that of his successors. Crispi was the great champion of colonial expansion, for which he tried, rather unsuccessfully, to enlist the support of his allies and of England. This policy, pursued with a kind of cranky excitability, brought Italy into conflict with France, just as the expansion of Germany created friction with England. It all ended at Adua, and for that catastrophe Crispi must be held chiefly responsible. Rudini and Visconti-Venosta, the leading figures after Crispi's fall, were obliged to retrench. They withdrew so far as they could from the extravagant colonial program of their predecessor and tried to make their peace with France. It has often been argued that the estrangement of Germany and England made it necessary for the Italians to loosen the ties of the Triple Alliance. But that is a misleading interpretation of the rapprochement with France, for at that time Anglo-French relations were more tense than the Anglo-German, and the Italians consequently would have been jumping from the frying-pan into the fire. Italy bargained with France not because she wished to, but because she had to. The Anglo-French Entente of 1904 saved her from a difficult situation and enabled her to revive the friendship with England which she had had to sacrifice in the years following Adua. If England and France had not come together the Italians would hardly have thrown in their lot entirely with that of France.

We know less about the inner springs of French policy than of almost any other. We cannot even say why French statesmen like Freycinet and Ribot should have been so anxious to conclude the alliance with Russia. There was, at the time, no danger — real or apparent — of attack by Germany, yet the French leaders were prepared to buy the alliance with milliards of francs of the savings of the parsimonious French peasantry and at the price of tying themselves to the apron-strings of the reckless Russian autocracy. No doubt the Parisian populace dreamed of reconquering the lost provinces with Russian help. But it is inconceivable that French statesmen should have deluded themselves with such expectations. At any rate, the honeymoon of the alliance was short enough. The French got little beyond the satisfaction of irritating England and a few gains in the Far East. In Africa they were left to their own devices. The Russians had no stomach for African adventure.

In matters of foreign policy two men stand out from the endless ranks of French politicians; one is Hanotaux, the other Delcassé. Too little is known of either to form anything like a final estimate. Hanotaux, historian and student of Richelieu, was undoubtedly the more significant. He dominated French policy from 1894 to 1898. A disciple of Jules Ferry, he was immensely impressed with the need for empire. Since under existing circumstances he had to reckon with the hostility of England, he tried to use the Franco-Russian Alliance for imperial purposes. Indeed, he went further and attempted to ease the tension between France and Germany sufficiently to make co-operation in colonial affairs possible. There was a time, in 1896 after the Kruger telegram episode, when Hanotaux and Lobanov might very well have built up something like an effective continental combination against England. Lobanov's death put an end to that possibility, but Hanotaux, right down to his fall, attempted to maintain respectable relations with Germany and to develop collaboration between the two countries. These were the days of the decline in the revenge feeling in France. Personally I think that an agreement between Germany and France was impossible so long as the Alsace-Lorraine question could not be satisfactorily disposed of, but it is not inconceivable that a better feeling might have been established.

Delcassé, who directed French policy after 1898, put an end to all this. From his antecedents we may conclude that he had no use for co-operation with Germany. He should have had but little sympathy for autocratic Russia. His preference probably was, from the very outset, for England and for a revival of the *entente cordiale* of earlier days. But he came into office on the eve of the Fashoda crisis. His preferences could play no part. The English made him drink the cup to the bitter dregs and he was therefore obliged to pursue a protective policy during the next couple of years. His approaches to Germany were hardly meant very seriously, but were intended to forestall German hostility. The Russians had deserted the French in their hour of tribulation, and Delcassé repaid them by throwing himself into their arms. In the years after 1899 the Russians had the French completely in tow. Delcassé could not stop them from rushing into disaster in the Far East. He was lucky to be able to buy off the English in the entente of 1904, even at the price of French claims in Egypt.

We have spoken much in these last pages about personalities. That there was no Bismarck among them is clear. It would be too much to expect a Bismarck in every generation. But in this period a statesman of the highest calibre was needed perhaps more than ever, for it must not be forgotten that international relations were developing to a state of chronic tension. The European territorial settlement was by no means complete. Nationalism was still advancing in southeastern Europe and was threatening the Ottoman Empire with disruption; it was already undermining central Europe and foreshadowing the disintegration of the Hapsburg Monarchy. But for a time many of these currents ran underground. Most impressive was the rising economic pressure on the Continent, the breaking over of European energies into Africa and Asia. I have tried to show, in a separate chapter, how closely this imperialism was bound up with the spread of popular education and the wider application of the principles of democracy. I have tried to show, too, how important a part was played by current sociological interpretations of international relations and by the cramping of human energy by the industrial system. One cannot study this period without marvelling at the exuberance and optimism which went hand in hand with recklessness and confidence in the conduct of foreign affairs. It was taken for granted that the world was marked out by Providence for exploitation by the European white man and that the principle of every man for himself and the devil take the hindmost was natural law. In the writings of the statesmen and in the writings of journalists there is very little trace of deeper understanding. The rise of Japan, the Adua disaster, the Boxer rising, none of these epoch-making events really opened the eyes of Europe. Even Lord Salisbury could see in the world nothing but a few virile nations and a large number of dying nations. The basic problem of international relations was who should cut up the victims. In our own day we have learned otherwise and all this now seems long ago.

Index

i

A
NOTE
ON THE
TYPE IN
WHICH THIS
BOOK IS SET

*This book is set
on the Linotype in
Granjon, a type which is
neither a copy of a classic face
nor an original creation. George
W. Jones drew the basic design for
this type from classic sources, but deviated
from his model wherever four centuries of
type-cutting experience indicated an improvement or where modern methods of punch-cutting
made possible a refinement that was beyond the skill of
the sixteenth-century originator. This new creation is based
primarily upon the type used by Claude Garamont
(1510–1561) in his beautiful French books and
more closely resembles the work of the founder
of the Old Style letter than do any of the various modern-day types that bear his name.*

COMPOSED, PRINTED AND BOUND
BY THE PLIMPTON PRESS, NOR-
WOOD, MASSACHUSETTS. PAPER
MANUFACTURED BY S. D.
WARREN CO., BOSTON. THE
BINDING IS AFTER DE-
SIGNS BY PERCY SMITH